SELECTED SECURITIES

AND

BUSINESS PLANNING
STATUTES, RULES AND FORMS

1987 EDITION

Securities Materials Edited by

DAVID L. RATNER

Dean and Professor of Law
University of San Francisco

Corporation Materials Edited by

WILLIAM H. PAINTER

Theodore Rinehart Professor of Law
George Washington University

WEST PUBLISHING CO.

ST. PAUL, MINN., 1987

50 West Kellogg Boulevard
P.O. Box 64526
St. Paul, Minnesota 55164–0526

ISBN 0–314–60645–9

Sel.Sec. & Bus.Plan. '87 Ed.

PREFACE

This statutory supplement is specifically designed to be used with both Painter's *Problems and Materials in Business Planning* and Ratner's *Materials on Securities Regulation.* In addition, it can be used as a statutory supplement to any other casebook on Securities Regulation or Business Planning.

This supplement will be updated regularly to reflect new and amended statutes.

THE PUBLISHER

St. Paul, Minnesota
April, 1987

*

TABLE OF CONTENTS

*

SELECTED SECURITIES
AND
BUSINESS PLANNING
STATUTES, RULES AND FORMS
1987 EDITION

*

FEDERAL SECURITIES LAW

A. STATUTES

1. SECURITIES ACT OF 1933

15 U.S.C.A. §§ 77a et seq.

Schedule of Information Required in Registration Statement

TITLE I

Short Title

Section 1. This act may be cited as the Securities Act of 1933.

Definitions

Section 2. When used in this title, unless the context otherwise requires—

(1) the term "security" means any note, stock, treasury stock, bond, debenture, evidence of indebtedness, certificate of interest or participation in any profit-sharing agreement, collateral-trust certificate, preorganization certificate or subscription, transferable share, investment contract, voting-trust certificate, certificate of deposit for a security, fractional undivided interest in oil, gas, or other mineral rights, or, in general, any interest or instrument commonly known as a "security," or any certificate of interest or participation in, temporary or interim certificate for, receipt for, guarantee of, or warrant or right to subscribe to or purchase, any of the foregoing.

(2) The term "person" means an individual, a corporation, a partnership, an association, a joint-stock company, a trust, any unincorporated organization, or a government or political subdivision thereof. As used in this paragraph the term "trust" shall include only a trust where the interest or interests of the beneficiary or beneficiaries are evidenced by a security.

(3) The term "sale" or "sell" shall include every contract of sale or disposition of a security or interest in a security, for value. The term "offer to sell", "offer for sale", or "offer" shall include every attempt or offer to dispose of, or solicitation of an offer to buy, a security or interest in a security, for value. The terms defined in this paragraph and the term "offer to buy" as used in subsection (c) of section 5 shall not include preliminary negotiations or agreements between an issuer (or any person directly or indirectly controlling or controlled by an issuer, or under direct or indirect common control with an issuer) and any underwriter or among underwriters who are or are to be in privity of contract with an issuer (or any person directly or indirectly controlling or controlled by an issuer, or under direct or indirect common control with an issuer). Any security given or delivered with, or as a bonus on account of, any purchase of securities or any other thing, shall be conclusively presumed to constitute a part of the subject of such purchase and to have been offered and sold for value. The issue or transfer of a right or privilege, when originally issued or transferred with a security, giving the holder of such security the right to convert such security into another security of the same issuer or of another person, or giving a right to subscribe to another security of the same issuer or of another person, which right cannot be exercised until some future date, shall not be deemed to be an offer or sale of such other security; but the issue or transfer of such other security upon the exercise of such right of conversion or subscription shall be deemed a sale of such other security.

(4) The term "issuer" means every person who issues or proposes to issue any security; except that with respect to certificates of deposit, voting-trust certificates, or collateral-trust certificates, or with respect to certificates of interest or shares in an unincorporated investment trust not having a board of directors (or persons performing similar functions) or of the fixed, restricted management, or unit type, the term "issuer" means the person or persons performing the acts and assuming the duties of depositor or manager pursuant to the provisions of the trust or other agreement or instrument under which such securities are issued; except that in the case of an unincorporated association which provides by its articles for limited liability of any or all of its members, or in the case of a trust, committee, or other legal entity, the trustees or members thereof shall not be individually liable as issuers of any security issued by the association, trust, committee, or other legal entity; except that with respect to equipment-trust certificates or like securities, the term "issuer" means the person by whom the equipment or property is or is to be used; and except that with respect to fractional undivided interests in oil, gas, or other mineral rights, the term "issuer" means the owner of any such right or of any interest in such right (whether whole or fractional) who creates fractional interests therein for the purpose of public offering.

(5) The term "Commission" means the Federal Trade Commission.

(6) The term "Territory" means Puerto Rico, Canal Zone, the Virgin Islands, and the insular possessions of the United States.

(7) The term "interstate commerce" means trade or commerce in securities or any transportation or communication relating thereto among the several States or between the District of Columbia or any Territory of the United States and any State or other Territory, or between any foreign country and any State, Territory, or the District of Columbia, or within the District of Columbia.

(8) The term "registration statement" means the statement provided for in section 6, and includes any amendment thereto and any report, document, or memorandum filed as part of such statement or incorporated therein by reference.

(9) The term "write" or "written" shall include printed, lithographed, or any means of graphic communication.

(10) The term "prospectus" means any prospectus, notice, circular, advertisement, letter, or communication, written or by radio or television, which offers any security for sale or confirms the sale of any security; except that (a) a communication sent or given after the effective date of the registration statement (other than a prospectus permitted under subsection (b) of section 10) shall not be deemed a prospectus if it is proved that prior to or at the same time with such communication a written prospectus meeting the requirements of subsection (a) of section 10 at the time of such communication was sent or given to the person to whom the communication was made, and (b) a notice, circular, advertisement, letter, or communication in respect of a security shall not be deemed to be a prospectus if it states from whom a written prospectus meeting the requirements of section 10 may be obtained and, in addition, does no more than identify the security, state the price thereof, state by whom orders will be executed, and contain such other information as the Commission, by rules or regulations deemed necessary or appropriate in the public interest and for the protection of investors, and subject to such terms and conditions as may be prescribed therein, may permit.

(11) The term "underwriter" means any person who has purchased from an issuer with a view to, or offers or sells for an issuer in connection with, the distribution of any security, or participates or has a direct or indirect participation in any such undertaking, or participates or has a participation in the direct or indirect underwriting of any such undertaking; but such term shall not include a person whose interest is limited to a commission from an underwriter or dealer not in excess of the usual and customary distributors' or sellers' commission. As used in this paragraph the term "issuer" shall include, in addition to an issuer, any person directly or indirectly controlling or controlled by the issuer, or any person under direct or indirect common control with the issuer.

(12) The term "dealer" means any person who engages either for all or part of his time, directly or indirectly, as agent, broker, or principal, in the business of offering, buying, selling, or otherwise dealing or trading in securities issued by another person.

(13) The term "insurance company" means a company which is organized as an insurance company, whose primary and predominant business activity is the writing of insurance or the reinsuring of risks underwritten by insurance companies, and which is subject to supervision by the insurance commissioner, or a similar official or agency of a State or territory or the District of Columbia; or any receiver or similar official or any liquidating agent for such company, in his capacity as such.

(14) The term "separate account" means an account established and maintained by an insurance company pursuant to the laws of any State or territory of the United States, the District of Columbia, or of Canada or any province thereof, under which income, gains and losses, whether or not realized, from assets allocated to such account, are, in accordance with the applicable contract, credited to or charged against such account without regard to other income, gains or losses of the insurance company.

(15) The term "accredited investor" shall mean—

(i) a bank as defined in section 3(a)(2) of the Act whether acting in its individual or fiduciary capacity; an insurance company as defined in section 2(13) of the Act; an investment company registered under the Investment Company Act of 1940 or a business development company as defined in section 2(a)(48) of that Act; a Small Business Investment Company licensed by the Small Business Administration; or an employee benefit plan, including an individual retirement account, which is subject to the provisions of the Employee Retirement Income Security Act of 1974, if the investment decision is made by a plan fiduciary, as defined in section 3(21) of such Act, which is either a bank, insurance company, or registered investment adviser; or

(ii) any person who, on the basis of such factors as financial sophistication, net worth, knowledge, and experience in financial matters, or amount of assets under management qualifies as an accredited investor under rules and regulations which the Commission shall prescribe.

Exempted Securities

Section 3. (a) Except as hereinafter expressly provided, the provisions of this title shall not apply to any of the following classes of securities:

(1) Any security which, prior to or within sixty days after the enactment of this title, has been sold or disposed of by the issuer or bona fide offered to the public, but this exemption shall not apply to any new offering of any such security by an issuer or underwriter subsequent to such sixty days;

(2) Any security issued or guaranteed by the United States or any territory thereof, or by the District of Columbia, or by any State of the United States, or by any political subdivision of a State or Territory, or by any public instrumentality of one or more States or Territories, or by any person controlled or supervised by and acting as an instrumentality of the Government of the United States pursuant to authority granted by the Congress of the United States; or any certificate of deposit for any of the foregoing; or any security issued or guaranteed by any bank; or any security issued by or representing an interest in or a direct obligation of a Federal Reserve bank; or any interest or participation in any common trust fund or similar fund maintained by a bank exclusively for the collective investment and reinvestment of assets contributed thereto by such bank in its capacity as trustee, executor, administrator, or guardian; or any security which is an industrial development bond (as defined in section 103(c)(2) of the Internal Revenue Code of 1954) the interest on which is excludable from gross income under section 103(a)(1) of such Code if, by reason of the application of paragraph (4) or (6) of section 103(c) of such Code (determined as if paragraphs (4)(A), (5), and (7) were not included in such section 103(c)), paragraph (1) of such section 103(c) does not apply to such security; or any interest or participation in a single trust fund, or in a collective trust fund maintained by a bank, or any security arising out of a contract issued by an insurance company, which interest, participation, or security is issued in connection with (A) a stock bonus, pension, or profit-sharing plan which meets the requirements for qualification under section 401 of the Internal Revenue Code of 1954, (B) an annuity plan which meets the requirements for the deduction of the employer's contributions under section 404(a)(2) of such Code, or (C) a governmental plan as defined in section 414(d) of such Code which has been established by an employer for the exclusive benefit of its employees or their beneficiaries for the purpose of distributing to such employees or their beneficiaries the corpus and income of the funds accumulated under such plan, if under such plan it is impossible, prior to the satisfaction of all liabilities with respect to such employees and their beneficiaries, for any part of the corpus or income to be used for, or diverted to, purposes other than the exclusive benefit of such employees or their beneficiaries, other than any plan described in clause (A), (B), or (C) of this paragraph, (i) the contributions under which are held in a single trust fund or in a separate account maintained by an insurance company for a single employer and under which an amount in excess of the employer's contribution is allocated to the purchase of securities (other than interests or participations in the trust or separate account itself) issued by the employer or any company directly or indirectly controlling, controlled by, or under common control with the employer, (ii) which covers employees some or all of whom are employees within the meaning of section 401(c)(1) of such Code, or (iii) which is a plan funded by an annuity contract described in section 403(b) of such Code. The Commission, by rules and regulations or order, shall exempt from the provisions of section 5 of this title any interest or participation issued in connection with a stock bonus, pension, profit-sharing, or annuity plan which covers employees some or all of whom are employees within the meaning of section 401(c)(1) of the Internal Revenue Code of 1954, if and to the extent that the Commission determines this to be necessary or appropriate in the public interest and consistent with the protection of investors and the purposes fairly intended by the policy and provisions of this title. For the

purposes of this paragraph, a security issued or guaranteed by a bank shall not include any interest or participation in any collective trust fund maintained by a bank; and the term "bank" means any national bank, or any banking institution organized under the laws of any State, territory, or the District of Columbia, the business of which is substantially confined to banking and is supervised by the State or territorial banking commission or similar official; except that in the case of a common trust fund or similar fund, or a collective trust fund, the term "bank" has the same meaning as in the Investment Company Act of 1940.

(3) Any note, draft, bill of exchange, or bankers' acceptance which arises out of a current transaction or the proceeds of which have been or are to be used for current transactions, and which has a maturity at the time of issuance of not exceeding nine months, exclusive of days of grace, or any renewal thereof the maturity of which is likewise limited;

(4) Any security issued by a person organized and operated exclusively for religious, educational, benevolent, fraternal, charitable, or reformatory purposes and not for pecuniary profit, and no part of the net earnings of which inures to the benefit of any person, private stockholder, or individual;

(5) Any security issued (A) by a savings and loan association, building and loan association, cooperative bank, homestead association, or similar institution, which is supervised and examined by State or Federal authority having supervision over any such institution, except that the foregoing exemption shall not apply with respect to any such security where the issuer takes from the total amount paid or deposited by the purchaser, by way of any fee, cash value or other device whatsoever, either upon termination of the investment at maturity or before maturity, an aggregate amount in excess of 3 per centum of the face value of such security; or (B) by (i) a farmer's cooperative organization exempt from tax under section 521 of the Internal Revenue Code of 1954, (ii) a corporation described in section 501(c)(16) of such Code and exempt from tax under section 501(a) of such Code, or (iii) a corporation described in section 501(c)(2) of such Code which is exempt from tax under section 501(a) of such Code and is organized for the exclusive purpose of holding title to property, collecting income therefrom, and turning over the entire amount thereof, less expenses, to an organization or corporation described in clause (i) or (ii);

(6) Any interest in a railroad equipment trust. For purposes of this paragraph "interest in a railroad equipment trust" means any interest in an equipment trust, lease, conditional sales contract or other similar arrangement entered into, issued, assumed, guaranteed by, or for the benefit of, a common carrier to finance the acquisition of rolling stock, including motive power.

(7) Certificates issued by a receiver or by a trustee or debtor in possession in a case under title 11 of the United States Code, with the approval of the court;

(8) Any insurance or endowment policy or annuity contract or optional annuity contract, issued by a corporation subject to the supervision of the insurance commissioner, bank commissioner, or any agency or officer performing like functions, of any State or Territory of the United States or the District of Columbia;

(9) Except with respect to a security exchanged in a case under title 11 of the United States Code, any security exchanged by the issuer with its existing security holders exclusively where no commission or other remuneration is paid or given directly or indirectly for soliciting such exchange;

(10) Except with respect to a security exchanged in a case under title 11 of the United States Code, any security which is issued in exchange for one or more bona fide outstanding securities, claims or property interests, or partly in such exchange and partly for cash, where the terms and conditions of such issuance and exchange are approved, after a hearing upon the fairness of such terms and conditions at which all persons to whom it is proposed to issue securities in such exchange shall have the right to appear, by any court, or by any official or agency of the United States, or by any State or Territorial banking or insurance commission or other governmental authority expressly authorized by law to grant such approval;

(11) Any security which is a part of an issue offered and sold only to persons resident within a single State or Territory, where the issuer of such security is a person resident and doing business within, or, if a corporation, incorporated by and doing business within, such State or Territory.

(b) The Commission may from time to time by its rules and regulations, and subject to such terms and conditions as may be prescribed therein, add any class of securities to the securities exempted as provided in this section, if it finds that the enforcement of this title with respect to such securities is not necessary in the public interest and for the protection of investors by reason of the small amount involved or the limited character of the public offering; but no issue of securities shall be exempted under this subsection where the aggregate amount at which such issue is offered to the public exceeds $5,000,000.

(c) The Commission may from time to time by its rules and regulations and subject to such terms and conditions as may be prescribed therein, add to the securities exempted as provided in this section any class of securities issued by a small business investment company under the Small Business Investment Act of 1958 if it finds, having regard to the purposes of that Act, that the enforcement of this Act with respect to such securities is not necessary in the public interest and for the protection of investors.

Exempted Transactions

Section 4. The provisions of section 5 shall not apply to—

(1) transactions by any person other than an issuer, underwriter, or dealer.

(2) transactions by an issuer not involving any public offering.

(3) transactions by a dealer (including an underwriter no longer acting as an underwriter in respect of the security involved in such transaction), except—

(A) transactions taking place prior to the expiration of forty days after the first date upon which the security was bona fide offered to the public by the issuer or by or through an underwriter,

(B) transactions in a security as to which a registration statement has been filed taking place prior to the expiration of forty days after the effective date of such registration statement or prior to the expiration of forty days after the first date upon which the security was bona fide offered to the public by the issuer or by or through an underwriter after such effective date, whichever is later (excluding in the computation of such forty days any time during which a stop order issued under section 8 is in effect as to the security), or such shorter period as the Commission may specify by rules and regulations or order, and

(C) transactions as to securities constituting the whole or a part of an unsold allotment to or subscription by such dealer as a participant in the distribution of such securities by the issuer or by or through an underwriter.

With respect to transactions referred to in clause (B), if securities of the issuer have not previously been sold pursuant to an earlier effective registration statement the applicable period, instead of forty days, shall be ninety days, or such shorter period as the Commission may specify by rules and regulations or order.

(4) brokers' transactions executed upon customers' orders on any exchange or in the over-the-counter market but not the solicitation of such orders.

(5)(A) Transactions involving offers or sales of one or more promissory notes directly secured by a first lien on a single parcel of real estate upon which is located a dwelling or other residential or commercial structure, and participation interests in such notes—

(i) where such securities are originated by a savings and loan association, savings bank, commercial bank, or similar banking institution which is supervised and examined by a Federal or State authority, and are offered and sold subject to the following conditions:

(a) the minimum aggregate sales price per purchaser shall not be less than $250,000;

(b) the purchaser shall pay cash either at the time of the sale or within sixty days thereof; and

(c) each purchaser shall buy for his own account only; or

(ii) where such securities are originated by a mortgagee approved by the Secretary of Housing and Urban Development pursuant to sections 203 and 211 of the National Housing Act, and are offered or sold subject to the three conditions specified in subparagraph (A)(i) to any institution described in such subparagraph or to any insurance company subject to the supervision of the insurance commissioner, or any agency or officer performing like function, of any State or Territory of the United States or the District of Columbia, or the Federal Home Loan Mortgage Corporation, the Federal National Mortgage Association, or the Government National Mortgage Association.

(B) Transactions between any of the entities described in subparagraph (A)(i) or (A)(ii) hereof involving non-assignable contracts to buy or sell the foregoing securities which are to be completed within two years, where the seller of the foregoing securities pursuant to any such contract is one of the parties described in subparagraph (A)(i) or (A)(ii) who may originate such securities and the purchaser of such securities pursuant to any such contract is any institution described in subparagraph (A)(i) or any insurance company described in subparagraph (A)(ii), the Federal Home Loan Mortgage Corporation, Federal National Mortgage Association, or the Government National Mortgage Association and where the foregoing securities are subject to the three conditions for sale set forth in subparagraphs (A)(i)(a) through (c).

(C) The exemption provided by subparagraphs (A) and (B) hereof shall not apply to resales of the securities acquired pursuant thereto, unless each of the conditions for sale contained in subparagraphs (A)(i)(a) through (c) are satisfied.

(6) transactions involving offers or sales by an issuer solely to one or more accredited investors, if the aggregate offering price of an issue of securities offered in reliance on this paragraph does not exceed the amount allowed under section 3(b) of this title, if there is no advertising or public solicitation in connection with the transaction by the issuer or anyone acting on the issuer's behalf, and if the issuer files such notice with the Commission as the Commission shall prescribe.

Prohibitions Relating to Interstate Commerce and the Mails

Section 5. (a) Unless a registration statement is in effect as to a security, it shall be unlawful for any person, directly or indirectly—

(1) to make use of any means or instruments of transportation or communication in interstate commerce or of the mails to sell such security through the use or medium of any prospectus or otherwise; or

(2) to carry or cause to be carried through the mails or in interstate commerce, by any means or instruments of transportation, any such security for the purpose of sale or for delivery after sale.

(b) It shall be unlawful for any person, directly or indirectly—

(1) to make use of any means or instruments of transportation or communication in interstate commerce or of the mails to carry or transmit any prospectus relating to any security with respect to which a registration statement has been filed under this title, unless such prospectus meets the requirements of section 10; or

(2) to carry or cause to be carried through the mails or in interstate commerce any such security for the purpose of sale or for delivery after sale, unless accompanied or preceded by a prospectus that meets the requirements of subsection (a) of section 10.

(c) It shall be unlawful for any person, directly or indirectly, to make use of any means or instruments of transportation or communication in interstate commerce or of the mails to offer to sell or offer to buy through the use or medium of any prospectus or otherwise any security, unless a registration statement has been filed as to such security, or while the registration statement is the subject of a refusal order or stop order or (prior to the effective date of the registration statement) any public proceeding or examination under section 8.

Registration of Securities and Signing of Registration Statement

Section 6. (a) Any security may be registered with the Commission under the terms and conditions hereinafter provided, by filing a registration statement in triplicate, at least one of which shall be signed by each issuer, its principal executive officer or officers, its principal financial officer, its comptroller or principal accounting officer, and the majority of its board of directors or persons performing similar functions (or, if there is no board of directors or persons performing similar functions, by the majority of the persons or board having the power of management of the issuer), and in case the issuer is a foreign or Territorial person by its duly authorized representative in the United States; except that when such registration statement relates to a security issued by a foreign government, or political subdivision thereof, it need be signed only by the underwriter of such security. Signatures of all such persons when written on the said registration statements shall be presumed to have been so written by authority of the person whose signature is so affixed and the burden of proof, in the event such authority shall be denied, shall be upon the party denying the same. The affixing of any signature without the authority of the purported signer shall constitute a violation of this title. A registration statement shall be deemed effective only as to the securities specified therein as proposed to be offered.

(b) At the time of filing a registration statement the applicant shall pay to the Commission a fee of one-fiftieth of 1 per centum of the maximum aggregate price at which such securities are proposed to be offered, but in no case shall such fee be less than $100.

(c) The filing with the Commission of a registration statement, or of an amendment to a registration statement, shall be deemed to have taken place upon the receipt thereof, but the filing of a registration statement shall not be deemed to have taken place unless it is accompanied by a United States postal money order or a certified bank check or cash for the amount of the fee required under subsection (b).

(d) The information contained in or filed with any registration statement shall be made available to the public under such regulations as the Commission may prescribe, and copies thereof, photostatic or otherwise, shall be furnished to every applicant at such reasonable charge as the Commission may prescribe.

(e) No registration statement may be filed within the first forty days following the enactment of this Act.

Information Required in Registration Statement

Section 7. The registration statement, when relating to a security other than a security issued by a foreign government, or political subdivision thereof, shall contain the information, and be accompanied by the documents specified in Schedule A, and when relating to a security issued by a foreign government, or political subdivision thereof, shall contain the information, and be accompanied by the documents, specified in Schedule B; except that the Commission may by rules or regulations provide that any such information or document need not be included in respect of any class of issuers or securities if it finds that the requirement of such information or document is inapplicable to such class and that disclosure fully adequate for the protection of investors is otherwise required to be included within the registration statement. If any accountant, engineer, or appraiser, or any person whose profession gives authority to a statement made by him, is named as having prepared or certified any part of the registration statement, or is named as having prepared or certified a report or valuation for use in connection with the registration statement, the written consent of such person shall be filed with the registration statement. If any such person is named as having prepared or certified a report or valuation (other than a public official document or statement) which is used in connection with the registration statement, but is not named as having prepared or certified such report or valuation for use in connection with the registration statement, the written consent of such person shall be filed with the registration statement unless the Commission dispenses with such filing as impracticable or as involving undue hardship on the person filing the registration statement. Any such registration statement shall contain such other information, and be accompanied by such other documents, as the Commission may by rules or regulations require as being necessary or appropriate in the public interest or for the protection of investors.

Taking Effect of Registration Statements and Amendments Thereto

Section 8. (a) Except as hereinafter provided, the effective date of a registration statement shall be the twentieth day after the filing thereof or such earlier date as the Commission may determine, having due regard to the adequacy of the information respecting the issuer theretofore available to the public, to the facility with which the nature of the securities to be registered, their relationship to the capital structure of the issuer and the rights of holders thereof can be understood, and to the public interest and the protection of investors. If any amendment to any such statement is filed prior to the effective date of such statement, the registration statement shall be deemed to have been filed when such amendment was filed; except that an amendment filed with the consent of the Commission, prior to the effective date of the registration statement, or filed pursuant to an order of the Commission, shall be treated as a part of the registration statement.

(b) If it appears to the Commission that a registration statement is on its face incomplete or inaccurate in any material respect, the Commission may, after notice by personal service or the sending of confirmed telegraphic notice not later than ten days after the filing of the registration statement, and opportunity for hearing (at a time fixed by the Commission) within ten days after such notice by personal service or the sending of such telegraphic notice, issue an order prior to the effective date of registration refusing to permit such statement to become effective until it has been amended in accordance with such order. When such statement has been amended in accordance with such order the Commission shall so declare and the registration shall become effective at the time provided in subsection (a) or upon the date of such declaration, whichever date is the later.

(c) An amendment filed after the effective date of the registration statement, if such amendment, upon its face, appears to the Commission not to be incomplete or inaccurate in any material respect, shall become effective on such date as the Commission may determine, having due regard to the public interest and the protection of investors.

(d) If it appears to the Commission at any time that the registration statement includes any untrue statement of a material fact or omits to state any material fact required to be stated therein or necessary to make the statements therein not misleading, the Commission may, after notice by personal service or the sending of confirmed telegraphic notice, and after opportunity for hearing (at a time fixed by the Commission) within fifteen days after such notice by personal service or the sending of such telegraphic notice, issue a stop order suspending the effectiveness of the registration statement. When such statement has been amended in accordance with such stop order the Commission shall so declare and thereupon the stop order shall cease to be effective.

(e) The Commission is hereby empowered to make an examination in any case in order to determine whether a stop order should issue under subsection (d). In making such examination the Commission or any officer or officers designated by it shall have access to and may demand the production of any books and papers of, and may administer oaths and affirmations to and examine, the issuer, underwriter, or any other person, in respect of any matter relevant to the examination, and may, in its discretion, require the production of a balance sheet exhibiting the assets and liabilities of the issuer, or its income statement, or both, to be certified to by a public or certified accountant approved by the Commission. If the issuer or underwriter shall fail to cooperate, or shall obstruct or refuse to permit the making of an examination, such conduct shall be proper ground for the issuance of a stop order.

(f) Any notice required under this section shall be sent to or served on the issuer, or, in case of a foreign government or political subdivision thereof, to or on the underwriter, or, in the case of a foreign or Territorial person, to or on its duly authorized representative in the United States named in the registration statement, properly directed in each case of telegraphic notice to the address given in such statement.

Court Review of Orders

Section 9. (a) Any person aggrieved by an order of the Commission may obtain a review of such order in the Court of Appeals of the United States, within any circuit wherein such person resides or has his principal place of business, or in the United States Court of Appeals for the District of Columbia, by filing in such court, within sixty days after the entry of such order, a written petition praying that the order of the Commission be modified or be set aside in whole or in part. A copy of such petition shall be forthwith transmitted by the clerk of the court to the Commission, and thereupon the Commission shall file in the court the record upon which the order complained of was entered, as provided in section 2112 of title 28, United States Code. No objection to the order of the Commission shall be considered by the court unless such objection shall have been urged before the Commission. The finding of the Commission as to the facts, if supported by evidence, shall be conclusive. If either party shall apply to the court for leave to adduce additional evidence, and show show to the satisfaction of the court that such additional evidence is material and that there were reasonable grounds for failure to adduce such evidence in the hearing before the Commission, the court may order such additional evidence to be taken before the Commission and to be adduced upon the hearing in such manner and upon such terms and conditions as to the court may seem proper. The Commission may modify its findings as to the facts by reason of the additional evidence so taken, and it shall file such modified or new findings, which, if supported by evidence, shall be conclusive, and its recommendation, if any, for the modification or setting aside of the original order. The jurisdiction of the court shall be exclusive and its judgment and decree, affirming, modifying, or setting aside, in whole or in part, any order of the Commission, shall be final, subject to review by the Supreme Court of the United States upon certiorari or certification as provided in sections 239 and 240 of the Judicial Code, as amended (U.S.C., title 28, secs. 346 and 347).

(b) The commencement of proceedings under subsection (a) shall not, unless specifically ordered by the court, operate as a stay of the Commission's order.

Information Required in Prospectus

Section 10. (a) Except to the extent otherwise permitted or required pursuant to this subsection or subsections (c), (d), or (e)—

(1) a prospectus relating to a security other than a security issued by a foreign government or political subdivision thereof, shall contain the information contained in the registration statement, but it need not include the documents referred to in paragraphs (28) to (32), inclusive, of Schedule A;

(2) a prospectus relating to a security issued by a foreign government or political subdivision thereof shall contain the information contained in the registration statement, but it need not include the documents referred to in paragraphs (13) and (14) of Schedule B;

(3) notwithstanding the provisions of paragraphs (1) and (2) of this subsection (a) when a prospectus is used more than nine months after the effective date of the registration statement, the information contained therein shall be as of a date not more than sixteen months prior to such use, so far as such information is known to the user of such prospectus or can be furnished by such user without unreasonable effort or expense;

(4) there may be omitted from any prospectus any of the information required under this subsection (a) which the Commission may by rules or regulations designate as not being necessary or appropriate in the public interest or for the protection of investors.

(b) In addition to the prospectus permitted or required in subsection (a), the Commission shall by rules or regulations deemed necessary or appropriate in the public interest or for the protection of investors permit the use of a prospectus for the purposes of subsection (b)(1) of section 5 which omits in part or summarizes information in the prospectus specified in subsection (a). A prospectus permitted under this subsection shall, except to the extent the Commission by rules or regulations deemed necessary or appropriate in the public interest or for the protection of investors otherwise provides, be filed as part of the registration statement but shall not be deemed a part of such registration statement for the purposes of section 11. The Commission may at any time issue an order preventing or suspending the use of a prospectus permitted under this subsection (b), if it has reason to believe that such prospectus has not been filed (if required to be filed as part of the registration statement) or includes any untrue statement of a material fact or omits to state any material fact required to be stated therein or necessary to make the statements therein, in the light of the circumstances under which such prospectus is or is to be used, not misleading. Upon issuance of an order under this subsection, the Commission shall give notice of the issuance of such order and opportunity for hearing by personal service or the sending of confirmed telegraphic notice. The Commission shall vacate or modify the order at any time for good cause or if such prospectus has been filed or amended in accordance with such order.

(c) Any prospectus shall contain such other information as the Commission may by rules or regulations require as being necessary or appropriate in the public interest or for the protection of investors.

(d) In the exercise of its powers under subsections (a), (b), or (c), the Commission shall have authority to classify prospectuses according to the nature and circumstances of their use or the nature of the security, issue, issuer, or otherwise, and, by rules and regulations and subject to such terms and conditions as it shall specify therein, to prescribe as to each class the form and contents which it may find appropriate and consistent with the public interest and the protection of investors.

(e) The statements or information required to be included in a prospectus by or under authority of subsections (a), (b), (c), or (d), when written, shall be placed in a conspicuous part of the prospectus and, except as otherwise permitted by rules or regulations, in type as large as that used generally in the body of the prospectus.

(f) In any case where a prospectus consists of a radio or television broadcast, copies thereof shall be filed with the Commission under such rules and regulations as it shall prescribe. The Commission may by rules and regulations require the filing with it of forms and prospectuses used in connection with the offer or sale of securities registered under this title.

Civil Liabilities on Account of False Registration Statement

Section 11. (a) In case any part of the registration statement, when such part became effective, contained an untrue statement of a material fact or omitted to state a material fact required to be stated therein or necessary to make the statements therein not misleading, any person acquiring such security (unless it is proved that at the time of such acquisition he knew of such untruth or omission) may, either at law or in equity, in any court of competent jurisdiction, sue—

(1) every person who signed the registration statement;

(2) every person who was a director of (or person performing similar functions) or partner in, the issuer at the time of the filing of the part of the registration statement with respect to which his liability is asserted;

(3) every person who, with his consent, is named in the registration statement as being or about to become a director, person performing similar functions, or partner;

(4) every accountant, engineer, or appraiser, or any person whose profession gives authority to a statement made by him, who has with his consent been named as having prepared or certified any part of the registration statement, or as having prepared or certified any report or valuation which is used in connection with the registration statement, with respect to the statement in such registration statement, report, or valuation, which purports to have been prepared or certified by him;

(5) every underwriter with respect to such security.

If such person acquired the security after the issuer has made generally available to its security holders an earning statement covering a period of at least twelve months beginning after the effective date of the registration statement, then the right of recovery under this subsection shall be conditioned on proof that such person acquired the security relying upon such untrue statement in the registration statement or relying upon the registration statement and not knowing of such omission, but such reliance may be established without proof of the reading of the registration statement by such person.

(b) Notwithstanding the provisions of subsection (a) no person, other than the issuer, shall be liable as provided therein who shall sustain the burden of proof—

(1) that before the effective date of the part of the registration statement with respect to which his liability is asserted (A) he had resigned from or had taken such steps as are permitted by law to resign from, or ceased or refused to act in, every office, capacity, or relationship in which he was described in the registration statement as acting or agreeing to act, and (B) he had advised the Commission and the issuer in writing that he had taken such action and that he would not be responsible for such part of the registration statement; or

(2) that if such part of the registration statement became effective without his knowledge, upon becoming aware of such fact he forthwith acted and advised the Commission, in accordance with paragraph (1), and, in addition, gave reasonable public notice that such part of the registra-

tion statement had become effective without his knowledge; or

(3) that (A) as regards any part of the registration statement not purporting to be made on the authority of an expert, and not purporting to be a copy of or extract from a report or valuation of an expert, and not purporting to be made on the authority of a public official document or statement, he had, after reasonable investigation, reasonable ground to believe and did believe, at the time such part of the registration statement became effective, that the statements therein were true and that there was no omission to state a material fact required to be stated therein or necessary to make the statements therein not misleading; and (B) as regards any part of the registration statement purporting to be made upon his authority as an expert or purporting to be a copy of or extract from a report or valuation of himself as an expert, (i) he had, after reasonable investigation, reasonable ground to believe and did believe, at the time such part of the registration statement became effective, that the statements therein were true and that there was no omission to state a material fact required to be stated therein or necessary to make the statements therein not misleading, or (ii) such part of the registration statement did not fairly represent his statement as an expert or was not a fair copy of or extract from his report or valuation as an expert; and (C) as regards any part of the registration statement purporting to be made on the authority of an expert (other than himself) or purporting to be a copy of or extract from a report or valuation of an expert (other than himself), he had no reasonable ground to believe and did not believe, at the time such part of the registration statement became effective, that the statements therein were untrue or that there was an omission to state a material fact required to be stated therein or necessary to make the statements therein not misleading, or that such part of the registration statement did not fairly represent the statement of the expert or was not a fair copy of or extract from the report or valuation of the expert; and (D) as regards any part of the registration statement purporting to be a statement made by an official person or purporting to be a copy of or extract from a public official document, he had no reasonable ground to believe and did not believe, at the time such part of the registration statement became effective, that the statements therein were untrue, or that there was an omission to state a material fact required to be stated therein or necessary to make the statements therein not misleading, or that such part of the registration statement did not fairly represent the statement made by the official person or was not a fair copy of or extract from the public official document.

(c) In determining, for the purpose of paragraph (3) of subsection (b) of this section, what constitutes reasonable investigation and reasonable ground for belief, the standard of reasonableness shall be that required of a prudent man in the management of his own property.

(d) If any person becomes an underwriter with respect to the security after the part of the registration statement with respect to which his liability is asserted has become effective, then for the purposes of paragraph (3) of subsection (b) of this section such part of the registration statement shall be considered as having become effective with respect to such person as of the time when he became an underwriter.

(e) The suit authorized under subsection (a) may be to recover such damages as shall represent the difference between the amount paid for the security (not exceeding the price at which the security was offered to the public) and (1) the value thereof as of the time such suit was brought, or (2) the price at which such security shall have been disposed of in the market before suit, or (3) the price at which such security shall have been disposed of after suit but before judgment if such damages shall be less than the damages representing the difference between the amount paid for the security (not exceeding the price at which the security was offered to the public) and the value thereof as of the time such suit was brought: Provided, that if the defendant proves that any portion or all of such damages represents other than the depreciation in value of such security resulting from such part of the registration statement, with respect to which his liability is asserted, not being true or omitting to state a material fact required to be stated therein or necessary to make the statements therein not misleading, such portion of or all such damages shall not be recoverable. In no event shall any underwriter (unless such underwriter shall have knowingly received from the issuer for acting as an underwriter some benefit, directly or indirectly, in which all other underwriters similarly situated did not share in proportion to their respective interests in the underwriting) be liable in any suit or as a consequence of suits authorized under subsection (a) for damages in excess of the total price at which the securities underwritten by him and distributed to the public were offered to the public. In any suit under this or any other section of this title the court may, in its discretion, require an undertaking for the payment of the costs of such suit, including reasonable attorney's fees, and if judgment shall be rendered against a party litigant, upon the motion of the other party litigant, such costs may be assessed in favor of such party litigant (whether or not such undertaking has been required) if the court believes the suit or the defense to have been without merit, in an amount sufficient to reimburse him for the reasonable expenses incurred by him, in connection with such suit, such costs to be taxed in the manner usually provided for taxing of costs in the court in which the suit was heard.

(f) All or any one or more of the persons specified in subsection (a) shall be jointly and severally liable, and every person who becomes liable to make any payment under this section may recover contribution as in cases of contract from any person who, if sued separately, would have been liable to make the same payment, unless the person who has become liable was, and the other was not, guilty of fraudulent misrepresentation.

(g) In no case shall the amount recoverable under this section exceed the price at which the security was offered to the public.

Civil Liabilities Arising in Connection With Prospectuses and Communications

Section 12. Any person who—

(1) offers or sells a security in violation of section 5, or

(2) offers or sells a security (whether or not exempted by the provisions of section 3, other than paragraph (2) of subsection (a) thereof), by the use of any means or instruments of transportation or communication in interstate commerce or of the mails, by means of a prospectus or oral communication, which includes an untrue statement of a material fact or omits to state a material fact necessary in order to make the statements, in the light of the circumstances under which they were made, not misleading (the purchaser not knowing of such untruth or omission), and who shall not sustain the burden of proof that he did not know, and in the exercise of reasonable care could not have known, of such untruth or omission,

shall be liable to the person purchasing such security from him, who may sue either at law or in equity in any court of competent jurisdiction, to recover the consideration paid for such security with interest thereon, less the amount of any income received thereon, upon the tender of such security, or for damages if he no longer owns the security.

Limitation of Actions

Section 13. No action shall be maintained to enforce any liability created under section 11 or section 12(2) unless brought within one year after the discovery of the untrue statement or the omission, or after such discovery should have been made by the exercise of reasonable diligence, or, if the action is to enforce a liability created under section 12(1), unless brought within one year after the violation upon which it is based. In no event shall any such action be brought to enforce a liability created under section 11 or section 12(1) more than three years after the security was bona fide offered to the public, or under section 12(2) more than three years after the sale.

Contrary Stipulations Void

Section 14. Any condition, stipulation, or provision binding any person acquiring any security to waive compliance with any provision of this title or of the rules and regulations of the Commission shall be void.

Liability of Controlling Persons

Section 15. Every person who, by or through stock ownership, agency, or otherwise, or who, pursuant to or in connection with an agreement or understanding with one or more other persons by or through stock ownership, agency, or otherwise, controls any person liable under section 11 or 12, shall also be liable jointly and severally with and to the same extent as such controlled person to any person to whom such controlled person is liable, unless the controlling person had no knowledge of or reasonable grounds to believe in the existence of the facts by reason of which the liability of the controlled person is alleged to exist.

Additional Remedies

Section 16. The rights and remedies provided by this title shall be in addition to any and all other rights and remedies that may exist at law or in equity.

Fraudulent Interstate Transactions

Section 17. (a) It shall be unlawful for any person in the offer or sale of any securities by the use of any means or instruments of transportation or communication in interstate commerce or by the use of the mails, directly or indirectly—

(1) to employ any device, scheme, or artifice to defraud, or

(2) to obtain money or property by means of any untrue statement of a material fact or any omission to state a material fact necessary in order to make the statements made, in the light of the circumstances under which they were made, not misleading, or

(3) to engage in any transaction, practice, or course of business which operates or would operate as a fraud or deceit upon the purchaser.

(b) It shall be unlawful for any person, by the use of any means or instruments of transportation or communication in interstate commerce or by the use of the mails, to publish, give publicity to, or circulate any notice, circular, advertisement, newspaper, article, letter, investment service, or communication which, though not purporting to offer a security for sale, describes such security for a consideration received or to be received, directly or indirectly, from an issuer, underwriter, or dealer, without fully disclosing the receipt, whether past or prospective, of such consideration and the amount thereof.

(c) The exemptions provided in section 3 shall not apply to the provisions of this section.

State Control of Securities

Section 18. Nothing in this title shall affect the jurisdiction of the securities commission (or any agency or office performing like functions) of any State or Territory of the United States, or the District of Columbia, over any security or any person.

Special Powers of Commission

Section 19. (a) The Commission shall have authority from time to time to make, amend, and rescind such rules and regulations as may be necessary to carry out the provisions of this title, including rules and regulations governing registration statements and prospectuses for various classes of securities and issuers, and defining accounting, technical, and trade terms used in this title. Among other things, the Commission shall have authority, for the purposes of this title, to prescribe the form or forms in which required information shall be set forth, the items or details to be shown in the balance sheet and earning statement, and the methods to be followed in the preparation of accounts, in the appraisal or valuation of assets and liabilities, in the determination of depreciation and depletion, in the differentiation of recurring and nonrecurring income, in the differentiation of investment and operating income, and in the preparation, where the Commission deems it necessary or desirable, of consolidated balance sheets or income accounts of any person directly or indirectly controlling or controlled by the issuer, or any person under direct or indirect common control with the issuer. The rules and regulations of the Commission shall be effective upon publication in the manner which the Commission shall prescribe. No provision of this title imposing any liability shall apply to any act done or omitted in good faith in conformity with any rule or regulation of the Commission, notwithstanding that such rule or regulation may, after such act or omission, be amended or rescinded or be determined by judicial or other authority to be invalid for any reason.

(b) For the purpose of all investigations which, in the opinion of the Commission, are necessary and proper for the enforcement of this title, any member of the Commission or any officer or officers designated by it are empowered to administer oaths and affirmations, subpena witnesses, take evidence, and require the production of any books, papers, or other documents which the Commission deems relevant or material to the inquiry. Such attendance of witnesses and the production of such documentary evidence may be required from any place in the

United States or any Territory at any designated place of hearing.

(c)(1) The Commission is authorized to cooperate with any association composed of duly constituted representatives of State governments whose primary assignment is the regulation of the securities business within those States, and which, in the judgment of the Commission, could assist in effectuating greater uniformity in Federal-State securities matters. The Commission shall, at its discretion, cooperate, coordinate, and share information with such an association for the purposes of carrying out the policies and projects set forth in paragraphs (2) and (3).

(2) It is the declared policy of this subsection that there should be greater Federal and State cooperation in securities matters, including—

(A) maximum effectiveness of regulation,

(B) maximum uniformity in Federal and State regulatory standards,

(C) minimum interference with the business of capital formation, and

(D) a substantial reduction in costs and paperwork to diminish the burdens of raising investment capital (particularly by small business) and to diminish the costs of the administration of the Government programs involved.

(3) The purpose of this subsection is to engender cooperation between the Commission, any such association of State securities officials, and other duly constituted securities associations in the following areas:

(A) the sharing of information regarding the registration or exemption of securities issues applied for in the various States;

(B) the development and maintenance of uniform securities forms and procedures; and

(C) the development of a uniform exemption from registration for small issuers which can be agreed upon among several States or between the States and the Federal Government. The Commission shall have the authority to adopt such an exemption as agreed upon for Federal purposes. Nothing in this Act shall be construed as authorizing preemption of State law.

(4) In order to carry out these policies and purposes, the Commission shall conduct an annual conference as well as such other meetings as are deemed necessary, to which representatives from such securities associations, securities self-regulatory organizations, agencies, and private organizations involved in capital formation shall be invited to participate.

(5) For fiscal year 1982, and for each of the three succeeding fiscal years, there are authorized to be appropriated such amounts as may be necessary and appropriate to carry out the policies, provisions, and purposes of this subsection. Any sums so appropriated shall remain available until expended.

Injunctions and Prosecution of Offenses

Section 20. (a) Whenever it shall appear to the Commission, either upon complaint or otherwise, that the provisions of this title, or of any rule or regulation prescribed under authority thereof, have been or are about to be violated, it may, in its discretion, either require or permit such person to file with it a statement in writing, under oath, or otherwise, as to all the facts and circumstances concerning the subject matter which it believes to be in the public interest to investigate, and may investigate such facts.

(b) Whenever it shall appear to the Commission that any person is engaged or about to engage in any acts or practices which constitute or will constitute a violation of the provisions of this title, or of any rule or regulation prescribed under authority thereof, it may in its discretion, bring an action in any district court of the United States, United States court of any Territory, or the United States District Court for the District of Columbia to enjoin such acts or practices, and upon a proper showing a permanent or temporary injunction or restraining order shall be granted without bond. The Commission may transmit such evidence as may be available concerning such acts or practices to the Attorney General who may, in his discretion, institute the necessary criminal proceedings under this title. Any such criminal proceeding may be brought either in the district wherein the transmittal of the prospectus or security complained of begins, or in the district wherein such prospectus or security is received.

(c) Upon application of the Commission the district courts of the United States, the United States courts of any Territory, and the United States District Court for the District of Columbia, shall also have jurisdiction to issue writs of mandamus commanding any person to comply with the provisions of this title or any order of the Commission made in pursuance thereof.

Hearings by Commission

Section 21. All hearings shall be public and may be held before the Commission or an officer or officers of the Commission designated by it, and appropriate records thereof shall be kept.

Jurisdiction of Offenses and Suits

Section 22. (a) The district courts of the United States, the United States courts of any Territory, and the United States District Court for the District of Columbia shall have jurisdiction of offenses and violations under this title and under the rules and regulations promulgated by the Commission in respect thereto, and concurrent with State and Territorial courts, of all suits in equity and actions at law brought to enforce any liability or duty created by this title. Any such suit or action may be brought in the district wherein the defendant is found or is an inhabitant or transacts business, or in the district where the offer or sale took place, if the defendant participated therein, and process in such cases may be served in any other district of which the defendant is an inhabitant or wherever the defendant may be found. Judgments and decrees so rendered shall be subject to review as provided in sections 128 and 240 of the Judicial Code, as amended (U.S.C., title 28, secs. 225 and 347). No case arising under this title and brought in any State court of competent jurisdiction shall be removed to any court of the United States. No costs shall be assessed for or against the Commission in any proceeding under this title brought by or against it in the Supreme Court or such other courts.

(b) In case of contumacy or refusal to obey a subpena issued to any person, any of the said United States courts, within the jurisdiction of which said person guilty of contumacy or refusal to obey is found or resides, upon application by the Commission may issue to such person an order requiring such person to appear before the Commission, or one of its examiners designated by it, there to produce documentary evidence if so ordered, or there to give evidence touching the matter in question; and any failure to obey such order of the court may be punished by said court as a contempt thereof.

Unlawful Representations

Section 23. Neither the fact that the registration statement for a security has been filed or is in effect nor the fact that a stop order is not in effect with respect thereto shall be deemed a finding by the Commission that the registration statement is true and accurate on its face or that it does not contain an untrue statement of fact or omit to state a material fact, or be held to mean that the Commission has in any way passed upon the merits of, or given approval to, such security. It shall be unlawful to make, or cause to be made, to any prospective purchaser any representation contrary to the foregoing provisions of this section.

Penalties

Section 24. Any person who willfully violates any of the provisions of this title, or the rules and regulations promulgated by the Commission under authority thereof, or any person who willfully, in a registration statement filed under this title, makes any untrue statement of a material fact or omits to state any material fact required to be stated therein or necessary to make the statements therein not misleading, shall upon conviction be fined not more than $10,000 or imprisoned not more than five years, or both.

Jurisdiction of Other Government Agencies Over Securities

Section 25. Nothing in this title shall relieve any person from submitting to the respective supervisory units of the Government of the United States information, reports, or other documents that are now or may hereafter be required by any provision of law.

Separability of Provisions

Section 26. If any provision of this Act, or the application of such provision to any person or circumstance, shall be held invalid, the remainder of this Act, or the application of such provision to persons or circumstances other than those as to which it is held invalid, shall not be affected thereby.

Schedule A

(1) The name under which the issuer is doing or intends to do business;

(2) the name of the State or other sovereign power under which the issuer is organized;

(3) the location of the issuer's principal business office, and if the issuer is a foreign or territorial person, the name and address of its agent in the United States authorized to receive notice;

(4) the names and addresses of the directors or persons performing similar functions, and the chief executive, financial and accounting officers, chosen or to be chosen if the issuer be a corporation, association, trust, or other entity; of all partners, if the issuer be a partnership; and of the issuer, if the issuer be an individual; and of the promoters in the case of a business to be formed, or formed within two years prior to the filing of the registration statement;

(5) the names and addresses of the underwriters;

(6) the names and addresses of all persons, if any, owning of record or beneficially, if known, more than 10 per centum of any class of stock of the issuer, or more than 10 per centum in the aggregate of the outstanding stock of the issuer as of a date within twenty days prior to the filing of the registration statement;

(7) the amount of securities of the issuer held by any person specified in paragraphs (4), (5), and (6) of this schedule, as of a date within twenty days prior to the filing of the registration statement, and, if possible, as of one year prior thereto, and the amount of the securities, for which the registration statement is filed, to which such persons have indicated their intention to subscribe;

(8) the general character of the business actually transacted or to be transacted by the issuer;

(9) a statement of the capitalization of the issuer, including the authorized and outstanding amounts of its capital stock and the proportion thereof paid up, the number and classes of shares in which such capital stock is divided, par value thereof, or if it has no par value, the stated or assigned value thereof, a description of the respective voting rights, preferences, conversion and exchange rights, rights to dividends, profits, or capital of each class, with respect to each other class, including the retirement and liquidation rights or values thereof;

(10) a statement of the securities, if any, covered by options outstanding or to be created in connection with the security to be offered, together with the names and addresses of all persons, if any, to be allotted more than 10 per centum in the aggregate of such options;

(11) the amount of capital stock of each class issued or included in the shares of stock to be offered;

(12) the amount of the funded debt outstanding and to be created by the security to be offered, with a brief description of the date, maturity, and character of such debt, rate of interest, character of amortization provisions, and the security, if any, therefor. If substitution of any security is permissible, a summarized statement of the conditions under which such substitution is permitted. If substitution is permissible without notice, a specific statement to that effect;

(13) the specific purposes in detail and the approximate amounts to be devoted to such purposes, so far as determinable, for which the security to be offered is to supply funds, and if the funds are to be raised in part from other sources, the amounts thereof and the sources thereof, shall be stated;

(14) the remuneration, paid or estimated to be paid, by the issuer or its predecessor, directly or indirectly, during the past year and ensuing year, to (a) the directors or persons performing similar functions, and (b) its officers and other persons, naming them wherever such remuneration exceeded $25,000 during any such year;

(15) the estimated net proceeds to be derived from the security to be offered;

(16) the price at which it is proposed that the security shall be offered to the public or the method by which such price is computed and any variation therefrom at which any portion of such security is proposed to be offered to any persons or classes of persons, other than the underwriters, naming them or specifying the class. A variation in price may be proposed prior to the date of the public offering of the security, but the Commission shall immediately be notified of such variation;

(17) all commissions or discounts paid or to be paid, directly or indirectly, by the issuer to the

underwriters in respect of the sale of the security to be offered. Commissions shall include all cash, securities, contracts, or anything else of value, paid, to be set aside, disposed of, or understandings with or for the benefit of any other persons in which any underwriter is interested, made, in connection with the sale of such security. A commission paid or to be paid in connection with the sale of such security by a person in which the issuer has an interest or which is controlled or directed by, or under common control with, the issuer shall be deemed to have been paid by the issuer. Where any such commission is paid the amount of such commission paid to each underwriter shall be stated;

(18) the amount or estimated amounts, itemized in reasonable detail, of expenses, other than commissions specified in paragraph (17) of this schedule, incurred or borne by or for the account of the issuer in connection with the sale of the security to be offered or properly chargeable thereto including legal, engineering, certification, authentication, and other charges;

(19) the net proceeds derived from any security sold by the issuer during the two years preceding the filing of the registration statement, the price at which such security was offered to the public, and the names of the principal underwriters of such security;

(20) any amount paid within two years preceding the filing of the registration statement or intended to be paid to any promoter and the consideration for any such payment;

(21) the names and addresses of the vendors and the purchase price of any property, or goodwill, acquired or to be acquired, not in the ordinary course of business, which is to be defrayed in whole or in part from the proceeds of the security to be offered, the amount of any commission payable to any person in connection with such acquisition, and the name or names of such person or persons, together with any expense incurred or to be incurred in connection with such acquisition, including the cost of borrowing money to finance such acquisition;

(22) full particulars of the nature and extent of the interest, if any, of every director, principal executive officer, and of every stockholder holding more than 10 per centum of any class of stock or more than 10 per centum in the aggregate of the stock of the issuer, in any property acquired, not in the ordinary course of business of the issuer, within two years preceding the filing of the registration statement or proposed to be acquired at such date;

(23) the names and addresses of counsel who have passed on the legality of the issue;

(24) dates of and parties to, and the general effect concisely stated of every material contract made, not in the ordinary course of business, which contract is to be executed in whole or in part at or after the filing of the registration statement or which contract has been made not more than two years before such filing. Any management contract or contract providing for special bonuses or profit-sharing arrangements, and every material patent or contract for a material patent right, and every contract by or with a public utility company or an affiliate thereof, providing for the giving or receiving of technical or financial advice or service (if such contract may involve a charge to any party thereto at a rate in excess of $2,500 per year in cash or securities or anything else of value), shall be deemed a material contract;

(25) a balance sheet as of a date not more than ninety days prior to the date of the filing of the registration statement showing all of the assets of the issuer, the nature and cost thereof, whenever determinable, in such detail and in such form as the Commission shall prescribe (with intangible items segregated), including any loan in excess of $20,000 to any officer, director, stockholder or person directly or indirectly controlling or controlled by the issuer, or person under direct or indirect common control with the issuer. All the liabilities of the issuer in such detail and such form as the Commission shall prescribe, including surplus of the issuer showing how and from what sources such surplus was created, all as of a date not more than ninety days prior to the filing of the registration statement. If such statement be not certified by an independent public or certified accountant, in addition to the balance sheet required to be submitted under this schedule, a similar detailed balance sheet of the assets and liabilities of the issuer, certified by an independent public or certified accountant, of a date not more than one year prior to the filing of the registration statement, shall be submitted;

(26) a profit and loss statement of the issuer showing earnings and income, the nature and

source thereof, and the expenses and fixed charges in such detail and such form as the Commission shall prescribe for the latest fiscal year for which such statement is available and for the two preceding fiscal years, year by year, or, if such issuer has been in actual business for less than three years, then for such time as the issuer has been in actual business, year by year. If the date of the filing of the registration statement is more than six months after the close of the last fiscal year, a statement from such closing date to the latest practicable date. Such statement shall show what the practice of the issuer has been during the three years or lesser period as to the character of the charges, dividends or other distributions made against its various surplus accounts, and as to depreciation, depletion, and maintenance charges, in such detail and form as the Commission shall prescribe, and if stock dividends or avails from the sale of rights have been credited to income, they shall be shown separately with a statement of the basis upon which the credit is computed. Such statement shall also differentiate between any recurring and nonrecurring income and between any investment and operating income. Such statement shall be certified by an independent public or certified accountant;

(27) if the proceeds, or any part of the proceeds, of the security to be issued is to be applied directly or indirectly to the purchase of any business, a profit and loss statement of such business certified by an independent public or certified accountant, meeting the requirements of paragraph (26) of this schedule, for the three preceding fiscal years, together with a balance sheet, similarly certified, of such business, meeting the requirements of paragraph (25) of this schedule of a date not more than ninety days prior to the filing of the registration statement or at the date such business was acquired by the issuer if the business was acquired by the issuer more than ninety days prior to the filing of the registration statement;

(28) a copy of any agreement or agreements (or, if identical agreements are used, the forms thereof) made with any underwriter, including all contracts and agreements referred to in paragraph (17) of this schedule;

(29) a copy of the opinion or opinions of counsel in respect to the legality of the issue, with a translation of such opinion, when necessary, into the English language;

(30) a copy of all material contracts referred to in paragraph (24) of this schedule, but no disclosure shall be required of any portion of any such contract if the Commission determines that disclosure of such portion would impair the value of the contract and would not be necessary for the protection of the investors;

(31) unless previously filed and registered under the provisions of this title, and brought up to date, (a) a copy of its articles of incorporation, with all amendments thereof and of its existing bylaws or instruments corresponding thereto, whatever the name, if the issuer be a corporation; (b) copy of all instruments by which the trust is created or declared, if the issuer is a trust; (c) a copy of its articles of partnership or association and all other papers pertaining to its organization, if the issuer is a partnership, unincorporated association, joint-stock company, or any other form of organization; and

(32) a copy of the underlying agreements or indentures affecting any stock, bonds, or debentures offered or to be offered.

In case of certificates of deposit, voting trust certificates, collateral trust certificates, certificates of interest or shares in unincorporated investment trusts, equipment trust certificates, interim or other receipts for certificates, and like securities, the Commission shall establish rules and regulations requiring the submission of information of a like character applicable to such cases, together with such other information as it may deem appropriate and necessary regarding the character, financial or otherwise, of the actual issuer of the securities and/or the person performing the acts and assuming the duties of depositor or manager.

*

2. SECURITIES EXCHANGE ACT OF 1934

[EDITED]

15 U.S.C.A. §§ 78a et seq.

TITLE I—REGULATION OF SECURITIES EXCHANGES

TITLE I—REGULATION OF SECURITIES EXCHANGES

Short Title

Section 1. This act may be cited as the "Securities Exchange Act of 1934."

Necessity for Regulation as Provided in This Title

Section 2. For the reasons hereinafter enumerated, transactions in securities as commonly conducted upon securities exchanges and over-the-counter markets are affected with a national public interest which makes it necessary to provide for regulation and control of such transactions and of practices and matters related thereto, including transactions by officers, directors, and principal security holders, to require appropriate reports, to remove impediments to and perfect the mechanisms of a national market system for securities and a national system for the clearance and settlement of securities transactions and the safeguarding of securities and funds related thereto, and to impose requirements necessary to make such regulation and control reasonably complete and effective, in order to protect interstate commerce, the national credit, the Federal taxing power, to protect and make more effective the national banking system and Federal Reserve System, and to insure the maintenance of fair and honest markets in such transactions:

(1) Such transactions (a) are carried on in large volume by the public generally and in large part originate outside the States in which the exchanges and over-the-counter markets are located and/or are effected by means of the mails and instrumentalities of interstate commerce; (b) constitute an important part of the current of interstate commerce; (c) involve in large part the securities of issuers engaged in interstate commerce; (d) involve the use of credit, directly affect the financing of trade, industry, and transportation in interstate commerce, and directly affect and influence the volume of interstate commerce; and affect the national credit.

(2) The prices established and offered in such transactions are generally disseminated and quoted throughout the United States and foreign countries and constitute a basis for determining and establishing the prices at which securities are bought and sold, the amount of certain taxes owing to the United States and to the several States by owners, buyers, and sellers of securities, and the value of collateral for bank loans.

(3) Frequently the prices of securities on such exchanges and markets are susceptible to manipulation and control, and the dissemination of such prices gives rise to excessive speculation, resulting in sudden and unreasonable fluctuations in the prices of securities which (a) cause alternately unreasonable expansion and unreasonable contraction of the volume of credit available for trade, transportation, and industry in interstate commerce, (b) hinder the proper appraisal of the value of securities and thus prevent a fair calculation of taxes owing to the United States and to the several States by owners, buyers, and sellers of securities, and (c) prevent the fair valuation of collateral for bank loans and/or obstruct the effective operation of the national banking system and Federal Reserve System.

(4) National emergencies, which produce widespread unemployment and the dislocation of trade, transportation, and industry, and which burden interstate commerce and adversely affect the general welfare, are precipitated, intensified, and prolonged by manipulation and sudden and unreasonable fluc-

tuations of security prices and by excessive speculation on such exchanges and markets, and to meet such emergencies the Federal Government is put to such great expense as to burden the national credit.

Definitions and Application of Title

Section 3. (a) When used in this title, unless the context otherwise requires—

(1) The term "exchange" means any organization, association, or group of persons, whether incorporated or unincorporated, which constitutes, maintains, or provides a market place or facilities for bringing together purchasers and sellers of securities or for otherwise performing with respect to securities the functions commonly performed by a stock exchange as that term is generally understood, and includes the market place and the market facilities maintained by such exchange.

(2) The term "facility" when used with respect to an exchange includes its premises, tangible or intangible property whether on the premises or not, any right to the use of such premises or property or any service thereof for the purpose of effecting or reporting a transaction on an exchange (including, among other things, any system of communication to or from the exchange, by ticker or otherwise, maintained by or with the consent of the exchange), and any right of the exchange to the use of any property or service.

(3)(A) The term "member" when used with respect to a national securities exchange means (i) any natural person permitted to effect transactions on the floor of the exchange without the services of another person acting as broker, (ii) any registered broker or dealer with which such a natural person is associated, (iii) any registered broker or dealer permitted to designate as a representative such a natural person, and (iv) any other registered broker or dealer which agrees to be regulated by such exchange and with respect to which the exchange undertakes to enforce compliance with the provisions of this title, the rules and regulations thereunder, and its own rules. For purposes of sections 6(b)(1), 6(b)(4), 6(b)(6), 6(b)(7), 6(d), 17(d), 19(d), 19(e), 19(g), 19(h), and 21 of this title, the term "member" when used with respect to a national securities exchange also means, to the extent of the rules of the exchange specified by the Commission, any person required by the Commission to comply with such rules pursuant to section 6(f) of this title.

(B) The term "member" when used with respect to a registered securities association means any broker or dealer who agrees to be regulated by such association and with respect to whom the association undertakes to enforce compliance with the provisions of this title, the rules and regulations thereunder, and its own rules.

(4) The term "broker" means any person engaged in the business of effecting transactions in securities for the account of others, but does not include a bank.

(5) The term "dealer" means any person engaged in the business of buying and selling securities for his own account, through a broker or otherwise, but does not include a bank, or any person insofar as he buys or sells securities for his own account, either individually or in some fiduciary capacity, but not as a part of a regular business.

(6) The term "bank" means (A) a banking institution organized under the laws of the United States, (B) a member bank of the Federal Reserve System, (C) any other banking institution, whether incorporated or not, doing business under the laws of any State or of the United States, a substantial portion of the business of which consists of receiving deposits or exercising fiduciary powers similar to those permitted to national banks under section 11(k) of the Federal Reserve Act, as amended, and which is supervised and examined by State or Federal authority having supervision over banks, and which is not operated for the purpose of evading the provisions of this title, and (D) a receiver, conservator, or other liquidating agent of any institution or firm included in clauses (A), (B), or (C) of this paragraph.

(7) The term "director" means any director of a corporation or any person performing similar functions with respect to any organization, whether incorporated or unincorporated.

(8) The term "issuer" means any person who issues or proposes to issue any securities; except that with respect to certificates of deposit for securities, voting-trust certificates, or collateral-trust certificates, or with respect to certificates of interest or shares in an unincorporated investment trust not having a board of directors or of the fixed, restricted management, or unit type, the term "issuer" means the person or persons performing the acts and assuming the duties of depositor or manag-

er pursuant to the provisions of the trust or other agreement or instrument under which such securities are issued; and except that with respect to equipment-trust certificates or like securities, the term "issuer" means the person by whom the equipment or property is, or is to be, used.

(9) The term "person" means a natural person, company, government, or political subdivision, agency, or instrumentality of a government.

(10) The term "security" means any note, stock, treasury stock, bond, debenture, certificate of interest or participation in any profit-sharing agreement or in any oil, gas, or other mineral royalty or lease, any collateral-trust certificate, preorganization certificate or subscription, transferable share, investment contract, voting-trust certificate, certificate of deposit, for a security, or in general, any instrument commonly known as a "security"; or any certificate of interest or participation in, temporary or interim certificate for, receipt for, or warrant or right to subscribe to or purchase, any of the foregoing; but shall not include currency or any note, draft, bill of exchange, or banker's acceptance which has a maturity at the time of issuance of not exceeding nine months, exclusive of days of grace, or any renewal thereof the maturity of which is likewise limited.

(11) The term "equity security" means any stock or similar security; or any security convertible, with or without consideration, into such a security; or carrying any warrant or right to subscribe to or purchase such a security; or any such warrant or right; or any other security which the Commission shall deem to be of similar nature and consider necessary or appropriate, by such rules and regulations as it may prescribe in the public interest or for the protection of investors, to treat as an equity security.

(12)(A) The term 'exempted security' or 'exempted securities' includes—

(i) government securities, as defined in paragraph (42) of this subsection;

(ii) municipal securities, as defined in paragraph (29) of this subsection;

(iii) any interest or participation in any common trust fund or similar fund maintained by a bank exclusively for the collective investment and reinvestment of assets contributed thereto by such bank in its capacity as trustee, executor, administrator, or guardian;

(iv) any interest or participation in a single trust fund, or a collective trust fund maintained by a bank, or any security arising out of a contract issued by an insurance company, which interest, participation, or security is issued in connection with a qualified plan as defined in subparagraph (C) of this paragraph; and

(v) such other securities (which may include, among others, unregistered securities, the market in which is predominantly intrastate) as the Commission may, by such rules and regulations as it deems consistent with the public interest and the protection of investors, either unconditionally or upon specified terms and conditions or for stated periods, exempt from the operation of any one or more provisions of this title which by their terms do not apply to an 'exempted security' or to 'exempted securities'.

(B)(i) Notwithstanding subparagraph (A)(i) of this paragraph, government securities shall not be deemed to be 'exempted securities' for the purposes of section 17A of this title.

(ii) Notwithstanding subparagraph (A)(ii) of this paragraph, municipal securities shall not be deemed to be 'exempted securities' for the purposes of sections 15, 15A (other than subsection (g)(3)), and 17A of this title.

(C) For purposes of subparagraph (A)(iv) of this paragraph, the term 'qualified plan' means (i) a stock bonus, pension, or profit-sharing plan which meets the requirements for qualification under section 401 of the Internal Revenue Code of 1954, (ii) an annuity plan which meets the requirements for the deduction of the employer's contribution under section 404(a)(2) of such Code, or (iii) a governmental plan as defined in section 414(d) of such Code which has been established by an employer for the exclusive benefit of its employees or their beneficiaries for the purpose of distributing to such employees or their beneficiaries the corpus and income of the funds accumulated under such plan, if under such plan it is impossible, prior to the satisfaction of all liabilities with respect to such employees and their beneficiaries, for any part of the corpus or income to be used for, or diverted to, purposes other than the exclusive benefit of such employees or their beneficiaries, other than any plan described in clause (i), (ii), or (iii) of this subparagraph which (I) covers employees some or all of whom are employees within the meaning of section 401(c) of such Code, or (II) is a plan funded by an annuity contract described in section 403(b) of such Code.

(13) The terms "buy" and "purchase" each include any contract to buy, purchase, or otherwise acquire.

(14) The terms "sale" and "sell" each include any contract to sell or otherwise dispose of.

(15) The term "Commission" means the Securities and Exchange Commission established by section 4 of this title.

(16) The term "State" means any State of the United States, the District of Columbia, Puerto Rico, the Canal Zone, the Virgin Islands, or any other possession of the United States.

(17) The term "interstate commerce" means trade, commerce, transportation, or communication among the several States, or between any foreign country and any State, or between any State and any place or ship outside thereof. The term includes intrastate use of (A) any facility of a national securities exchange or of a telephone or other interstate means of communication, or (B) any other interstate instrumentality.

(18) The term "person associated with a broker or dealer" or "associated person of a broker or dealer" means any partner, officer, director, or branch manager of such broker or dealer (or any person occupying a similar status or performing similar functions), or any person directly or indirectly controlling, controlled by, or under common control with such broker or dealer, or any employee of such broker or dealer, except that any person associated with a broker or dealer whose functions are solely clerical or ministerial shall not be included in the meaning of such term for purposes of section 15(b) of this title (other than paragraph (6) thereof).

(19) The terms "investment company," "affiliated person," "insurance company," "separate account", and "company" have the same meanings as in the Investment Company Act of 1940.

(20) The terms "investment adviser" and "underwriter" have the same meanings as in the Investment Advisers Act of 1940.

* * *

(26) The term "self-regulatory organization" means any national securities exchange, registered securities association, or registered clearing agency, or (solely for purposes of sections 19(b), 19(c), and 23(b) of this title) the Municipal Securities Rulemaking Board established by section 15B of this title.

* * *

(34) The term "appropriate regulatory agency" means—

* * *

(i) the Comptroller of the Currency, in the case of a national bank or a bank operating under the Code of Law for the District of Columbia.

(ii) the Board of Governors of the Federal Reserve System, in the case of any other member bank of the Federal Reserve System.

(iii) the Federal Deposit Insurance Corporation, in the case of any other bank the deposits of which are insured in accordance with the Federal Deposit Insurance Act; and

(iv) the Commission in the case of all other persons.

* * *

(38) The term "market maker" means any specialist permitted to act as a dealer, any dealer acting in the capacity of block positioner, and any dealer who, with respect to a security, holds himself out (by entering quotations in an inter-dealer communications system or otherwise) as being willing to buy and sell such security for his own account on a regular or continuous basis.

(39) A person is subject to a "statutory disqualification" with respect to membership or participation in, or association with a member of, a self-regulatory organization, if such person—

(A) has been and is expelled or suspended from membership or participation in, or barred or suspended from being associated with a member of, any self-regulatory organization, contract market designated pursuant to section 5 of the Commodity Exchange Act, or futures association registered under section 17 of such Act, or has been and is denied trading privileges on any such contract market;

(B) is subject to an order of the Commission denying, suspending for a period not exceeding twelve months, revoking his registration as a broker, dealer, or municipal securities dealer, or barring his being associated with a broker, dealer, or municipal securities dealer or is subject to an order of the Commodity Futures Trading Commission denying, suspending, or revoking his registration under the Commodity Exchange Act;

(C) by his conduct while associated with a broker, dealer, or municipal securities dealer, or while associated with an entity or person required to be registered under the Commodity Exchange Act, has been found to be a cause of any effective suspension, expulsion, or order of the character described in subparagraph (A) or (B) of this paragraph, and in entering such a suspension, expulsion, or order, the Commission or any such self-regulatory organization shall have jurisdiction to find whether or not any person was a cause thereof;

(D) has associated with him any person who is known, or in the exercise of reasonable care should be known, to him to be a person described by subparagraph (A), (B), or (C) of this paragraph; or

(E) has committed or omitted any act enumerated in subparagraph (D) or (E) of paragraph (4) of section 15(b) of this title, has been convicted of any offense specified in subparagraph (B) of such paragraph (4) within ten years of the date of the filing of an application for membership or participation in, or to become associated with a member of, such self-regulatory organization, is enjoined from any action, conduct, or practice specified in subparagraph (C) of such paragraph (4), has willfully made or caused to be made in any application for membership or participation in, or to become associated with a member of, a self-regulatory organization, report required to be filed with a self-regulatory organization, or proceeding before a self-regulatory organization, any statement which was at the time, and in the light of the circumstances under which it was made, false or misleading with respect to any material fact, or has omitted to state in any such application, report, or proceeding any material fact which is required to be stated therein.

(b) The Commission and the Board of Governors of the Federal Reserve System, as to matters within their respective jurisdictions, shall have power by rules and regulations to define technical, trade, accounting, and other terms used in this title, consistently with the provisions and purposes of this title.

* * *

Securities and Exchange Commission

Section 4. (a) There is hereby established a Securities and Exchange Commission (hereinafter referred to as the "Commission") to be composed of five commissioners to be appointed by the President by and with the advice and consent of the Senate. Not more than three of such commissioners shall be members of the same political party, and in making appointments members of different political parties shall be appointed alternately as nearly as may be practicable. No commissioner shall engage in any other business, vocation, or employment than that of serving as commissioner, nor shall any commissioner participate, directly or indirectly, in any stock-market operations or transactions of a character subject to regulation by the Commission pursuant to this title. Each Commissioner shall hold office for a term of five years and until his successor is appointed and has qualified, except that he shall not so continue to serve beyond the expiration of the next session of Congress subsequent to the expiration of said fixed term of office, and except (1) any Commissioner appointed to fill a vacancy occurring prior to the expiration of the term for which his predecessor was appointed shall be appointed for the remainder of such term, and (2) the terms of office of the Commissioners first taking office after the enactment of this title shall expire as designated by the President at the time of nomination, one at the end of one year, one at the end of two years, one at the end of three years, one at the end of four years, and one at the end of five years, after the date of the enactment of this title.

(b) The Commission is authorized to appoint and fix the compensation of such officers, attorneys, examiners, and other experts as may be necessary for carrying out its functions under this Act, without regard to the provisions of other laws applicable to the employment and compensation of officers and employees of the United States, and the Commission may, subject to the civil-service laws, appoint such other officers and employees as are necessary in the execution of its functions and fix their salaries in accordance with the Classification Act of 1923, as amended.

Transactions on Unregistered Exchanges

Section 5. It shall be unlawful for any broker, dealer, or exchange, directly or indirectly, to make use of the mails or any means or instrumentality of interstate commerce for the purpose of using any facility of an exchange within or subject to the jurisdiction of the United States to effect any transaction in a security, or to report any such transaction, unless such exchange (1) is registered as a national securities exchange under section 6 of this title, or (2) is exempted from such registration upon application by the exchange because, in the opinion of the commission, by reason of the limited volume of transactions effected on such exchange, it is not practicable and not necessary or appropriate in the public interest or for the protection of investors to require such registration.

National Securities Exchanges

Section 6. (a) An exchange may be registered as a national securities exchange under the terms and conditions hereinafter provided in this section and in accordance with the provisions of section 19(a) of this title, by filing with the Commission an application for registration in such form as the Commission, by rule, may prescribe containing the rules of the exchange and such other information and documents as the Commission, by rule, may prescribe as necessary or appropriate in the public interest or for the protection of investors.

(b) An exchange shall not be registered as a national securities exchange unless the Commission determines that—

(1) Such exchange is so organized and has the capacity to be able to carry out the purposes of this title and to comply, and (subject to any rule or order of the Commission pursuant to section 17(d) or 19(g)(2) of this title) to enforce compliance by its members and persons associated with its members, with the provisions of this title, the rules and regulations thereunder, and the rules of the exchange.

(2) Subject to the provisions of subsection (c) of this section, the rules of the exchange provide that any registered broker or dealer or natural person associated with a registered broker or dealer may become a member of such exchange and any person may become associated with a member thereof.

(3) The rules of the exchange assure a fair representation of its members in the selection of its directors and administration of its affairs and provide that one or more directors shall be representative of issuers and investors and not be associated with a member of the exchange, broker, or dealer.

(4) The rules of the exchange provide for the equitable allocation of reasonable dues, fees, and other charges among its members and issuers and other persons using its facilities.

(5) The rules of the exchange are designed to prevent fraudulent and manipulative acts and practices, to promote just and equitable principles of trade, to foster cooperation and coordination with persons engaged in regulating, clearing, settling, processing information with respect to, and facilitating transactions in securities, to remove impediments to and perfect the mechanism of a free and open market and a national market system, and, in general, to protect investors and the public interest; and are not designed to permit unfair discrimination between customers, issuers, brokers, or dealers, or to regulate by virtue of any authority conferred by this title matters not related to the purposes of this title or the administration of the exchange.

(6) The rules of the exchange provide that (subject to any rule or order of the Commission pursuant to section 17(d) or 19(g)(2) of this title) its members and persons associated with its members shall be appropriately disciplined for violation of the provisions of this title, the rules or regulations thereunder, or the rules of the exchange, by expulsion, suspension, limitation of activities, functions, and operations, fine, censure, being suspended or barred from being associated with a member, or any other fitting sanction.

(7) The rules of the exchange are in accordance with the provisions of subsection (d) of this section, and in general, provide a fair procedure for the disciplining of members and persons associated with members, the denial of membership to any person seeking membership therein, the barring of any person from becoming associ-

ated with a member thereof, and the prohibition or limitation by the exchange of any person with respect to access to services offered by the exchange or a member thereof.

(8) The rules of the exchange do not impose any burden on competition not necessary or appropriate in furtherance of the purposes of this title.

(c)(1) A national securities exchange shall deny membership to (A) any person, other than a natural person, which is not a registered broker or dealer or (B) any natural person who is not, or is not associated with, a registered broker or dealer.

(2) A national securities exchange may, and in cases in which the Commission, by order, directs as necessary or appropriate in the public interest or for the protection shall, deny membership to any registered broker or dealer or natural person associated with a registered broker or dealer, and bar from becoming associated with a member any person, who is subject to a statutory disqualification. * * *

* * *

(d)(1) In any proceeding by a national securities exchange to determine whether a member or person associated with a member should be disciplined (other than a summary proceeding pursuant to paragraph (3) of this subsection), the exchange shall bring specific charges, notify such member or person of, and give him an opportunity to defend against, such charges, and keep a record. * * *

* * *

(e)(1) On and after the date of enactment of the Securities Acts Amendments of 1975, no national securities exchange may impose any schedule or fix rates of commissions, allowances, discounts, or other fees to be charged by its members: * * *

* * *

(f) The Commission, by rule or order, as it deems necessary or appropriate in the public interest and for the protection of investors, to maintain fair and orderly markets, or to assure equal regulation, may require—

(1) any person not a member or a designated representative of a member of a national securities exchange effecting transactions on such exchange without the services of another person acting as a broker, or

(2) any broker or dealer not a member of a national securities exchange effecting transactions on such exchange on a regular basis,

to comply with such rules of such exchange as the Commission may specify.

Margin Requirements

Section 7. (a) For the purpose of preventing the excessive use of credit for the purchase or carrying of securities, the Board of Governors of the Federal Reserve System shall, prior to the effective date of this section and from time to time thereafter, prescribe rules and regulations with respect to the amount of credit that may be initially extended and subsequently maintained on any security (other than an exempted security). For the initial extension of credit, such rules and regulations shall be based upon the following standard: An amount not greater than whichever is the higher of—

(1) 55 per centum of the current market price of the security, or

(2) 100 per centum of the lowest market price of the security during the preceding thirty-six calendar months, but not more than 75 per centum of the current market price.

Such rules and regulations may make appropriate provision with respect to the carrying of under-margined accounts for limited periods and under specified conditions; the withdrawal of funds or securities; the substitution or additional purchases of securities; the transfer of accounts from one lender to another; special or different margin requirements for delayed deliveries, short sales, arbitrage transactions, and securities to which paragraph (2) of this subsection does not apply; the bases and the methods to be used in calculating loans, and margins and market prices; and similar administrative adjustments and details. For the purposes of paragraph (2) of this subsection, until July 1, 1936, the lowest price at which a security has sold on or after July 1, 1933, shall be considered as the lowest price at which such security has sold during the preceding thirty-six calendar months.

(b) Notwithstanding the provisions of subsection (a) of this section, the Board of Governors of the Federal Reserve System may, from time to time, with respect to all or specified securities or transactions, or classes of securities, or classes of transactions, by such rules and regulations (1) prescribe such lower margin requirements for the initial extension or maintenance of credit as it deems necessary or appropriate for the accommodation of commerce and industry, having due regard to the general credit situation of the country, and (2) prescribe such higher margin requirements for the initial extension or maintenance of credit as it may deem necessary or appropriate to prevent the excessive use of credit to finance transactions in securities.

(c) It shall be unlawful for any member of a national securities exchange or any broker or dealer, directly or indirectly, to extend or maintain credit or arrange for the extension or maintenance of credit to or for any customer—

(1) on any security (other than an exempted security), in contravention of the rules and regulations which the Board of Governors of the Federal Reserve System shall prescribe under subsections (a) and (b) of this section;

(2) without collateral or on any collateral other than securities, except in accordance with such rules and regulations as the Board of Governors of the Federal Reserve System may prescribe (A) to permit under specified conditions and for a limited period any such member, broker, or dealer to maintain a credit initially extended in conformity with the rules and regulations of the Board of Governors of the Federal Reserve System, and (B) to permit the extension or maintenance of credit in cases where the extension or maintenance of credit is not for the purpose of purchasing or carrying securities or of evading or circumventing the provisions of paragraph (1) of this subsection.

(d) It shall be unlawful for any person not subject to subsection (c) to extend or maintain credit or to arrange for the extension or maintenance of credit for the purpose of purchasing or carrying any security, in contravention of such rules and regulations as the Board of Governors of the Federal Reserve System shall prescribe to prevent the excessive use of credit for the purchasing or carrying of or trading in securities in circumvention of the other provisions of this section. Such rules and regulations may impose upon all loans made for the purpose of purchasing or carrying securities limitations similar to those imposed upon members, brokers, or dealers by subsection (c) of this section and the rules and regulations thereunder. This subsection and the rules and regulations thereunder shall not apply (A) to a loan made by a person not in the ordinary course of his business, (B) to a loan on an exempted security, (C) to a loan to a dealer to aid in the financing of the distribution of securities to customers not through the medium of a national securities exchange, (D) to a loan by a bank on a security other than an equity security, or (E) to such other loans as the Board of Governors of the Federal Reserve System shall, by such rules and regulations as it may deem necessary or appropriate in the public interest or for the protection of investors, exempt, either unconditionally or upon specified terms and conditions or for stated periods, from the operation of this subsection and the rules and regulations thereunder.

* * *

(f)(1) It is unlawful for any United States person, or any foreign person controlled by a United States person or acting on behalf of or in conjunction with such person, to obtain, receive, or enjoy the beneficial use of a loan or other extension of credit from any lender (without regard to whether the lender's office or place of business is in a State or the transaction occurred in whole or in part within a State) for the purpose of (A) purchasing or carrying United States securities, or (B) purchasing or carrying within the United States of any other securities, if, under this section or rules and regulations prescribed thereunder, the loan or other credit transaction is prohibited or would be prohibited if it had been made or the transaction had otherwise occurred in a lender's office or other place of business in a State.

* * *

Restrictions on Borrowing by Members, Brokers, and Dealers

Section 8. It shall be unlawful for any registered broker or dealer, member of a national securities exchange, or broker or dealer who transacts a business in securities through the medium of any member of a national securities exchange, directly or indirectly—

(a) To borrow in the ordinary course of business as a broker or dealer on any security (other than an exempted security) registered on a national securities exchange except (1) from or through a member bank of the Federal Reserve System, (2) from any nonmember bank which shall have filed with the Board of Governors of the Federal Reserve System an agreement, which is still in force and which is in the form prescribed by the Board, undertaking to comply with all provisions of this Act, the Federal Reserve Act, as amended, and the Banking Act of 1933, which are applicable to member banks and which relate to the use of credit to finance transactions in securities, and with such rules and regulations as may be prescribed pursuant to such provisions of law or for the purpose of preventing evasions thereof, or (3) in accordance with such rules and regulations as the Board of Governors of the Federal Reserve System may prescribe to permit loans between such members and/or brokers and/or dealers, or to permit loans to meet emergency needs. Any such agreement filed with the Board of Governors of the Federal Reserve System shall be subject to termination at any time by order of the Board, after appropriate notice and opportunity for hearing because of any failure by such bank to comply with the provisions thereof or with such provisions of law or rules or regulations; and, for any willful violation of such agreement, such bank shall be subject to the penalties provided for violations of rules and regulations prescribed under this title. The provisions of sections 21 and 25 of this title shall apply in the case of any such proceeding or order of the Board of Governors of the Federal Reserve System in the same manner as such provisions apply in the case of proceedings and orders of the Commission.

(b) In contravention of such rules and regulations as the Commission shall prescribe for the protection of investors to hypothecate or arrange for the hypothecation of any securities carried for the account of any customer under circumstances (1) that will permit the commingling of his securities without his written consent with the securities of any other customer, (2) that will permit such securities to be commingled with the securities of any person other than a bona fide customer, or (3) that will permit such securities to be hypothecated, or subjected to any lien or claim of the pledgee, for a sum in excess of the aggregate indebtedness of such customers in respect of such securities.

(c) To lend or arrange for the lending of any securities carried for the account of any customer without the written consent of such customer or in contravention of such rules and regulations as the Commission shall prescribe for the protection of investors.

Prohibition Against Manipulation of Security Prices

Section 9. (a) It shall be unlawful for any person, directly or indirectly, by the use of the mails or any means or instrumentality of interstate commerce, or of any facility of any national securities exchange, or for any member of a national securities exchange—

(1) For the purpose of creating a false or misleading appearance of active trading in any security registered on a national securities exchange, or a false or misleading appearance with respect to the market for any such security, (A) to effect any transaction in such security which involves no change in the beneficial ownership thereof, or (B) to enter an order or orders for the purchase of such security with the knowledge that an order or orders of substantially the same size, at substantially the same time and at substantially the same price, for the sale of any such security, has been or will be entered by or for the same or different parties, or (C) to enter any order or orders for the sale of any such security with the knowledge that an order or orders of substantially the same size, at substantially the same time, and at substantially the same price, for the purchase of such security, has been or will be entered by or for the same or different parties.

(2) To effect, alone or with one or more other persons, a series of transactions in any security registered on a national securities exchange creating actual or apparent active trading in such security or raising or depressing the price of such security, for the purpose of inducing the purchase or sale of such security by others.

(3) If a dealer or broker, or other person selling or offering for sale or purchasing or offering to purchase the security, to induce the purchase or sale of any security registered on a national securities exchange by the circulation or dissemination in the ordinary course of business of information to the effect that the price of any

such security will or is likely to rise or fall because of market operations of any one or more persons conducted for the purpose of raising or depressing the prices of such security.

(4) If a dealer or broker, or other person selling or offering for sale or purchasing or offering to purchase the security, to make, regarding any security registered on a national securities exchange, for the purpose of inducing the purchase or sale of such security, any statement which was at the time and in the light of the circumstances under which it was made, false or misleading with respect to any material fact, and which he knew or had reasonable ground to believe was so false or misleading.

(5) For a consideration, received directly or indirectly from a dealer or broker, or other person selling or offering for sale or purchasing or offering to purchase the security, to induce the purchase or sale of any security registered on a national securities exchange by the circulation or dissemination of information to the effect that the price of any such security will or is likely to rise or fall because of the market operations of any one or more persons conducted for the purpose of raising or depressing the price of such security.

(6) To effect either alone or with one or more other persons any series of transactions for the purchase and/or sale of any security registered on a national securities exchange for the purpose of pegging, fixing, or stabilizing the price of such security in contravention of such rules and regulations as the Commission may prescribe as necessary or appropriate in the public interest or for the protection of investors.

(b) It shall be unlawful for any person to effect, by use of any facility of a national securities exchange, in contravention of such rules and regulations as the Commission may prescribe as necessary or appropriate in the public interest or for the protection of investors—

(1) any transaction in connection with any security whereby any party to such transaction acquires any put, call, straddle, or other option or privilege of buying the security from or selling the security to another without being bound to do so; or

(2) any transaction in connection with any security with relation to which he has, directly or indirectly, any interest in any such put, call, straddle, option, or privilege; or

(3) any transaction in any security for the account of any person who he has reason to believe has, and who actually has, directly or indirectly, any interest in any such put, call, straddle, option, or privilege with relation to such security.

(c) It shall be unlawful for any member of a national securities exchange directly or indirectly to endorse or guarantee the performance of any put, call, straddle, option, or privilege in relation to any security registered on a national securities exchange, in contravention of such rules and regulations as the Commission may prescribe as necessary or appropriate in the public interest or for the protection of investors.

(d) The terms "put", "call", "straddle", "option", or "privilege" as used in this section shall not include any registered warrant, right, or convertible security.

(e) Any person who willfully participates in any act or transaction in violation of subsection (a), (b), or (c) of this section, shall be liable to any person who shall purchase or sell any security at a price which was affected by such act or transaction, and the person so injured may sue in law or in equity in any court of competent jurisdiction to recover the damages sustained as a result of any such act or transaction. In any such suit the court may, in its discretion, require an undertaking for the payment of the costs of such suit, and assess reasonable costs, including reasonable attorneys' fees, against either party litigant. Every person who becomes liable to make any payment under this subsection may recover contribution as in cases of contract from any person who, if joined in the original suit, would have been liable to make the same payment. No action shall be maintained to enforce any liability created under this section, unless brought within one year after the discovery of the facts constituting the violation and within three years after such violation.

(f) The provisions of this section shall not apply to an exempted security.

Regulation of the Use of Manipulative and Deceptive Devices

Section 10. It shall be unlawful for any person, directly or indirectly, by the use of any means or instrumentality of interstate commerce or of the mails, or of any facility of any national securities exchange—

(a) To effect a short sale, or to use or employ any stop-loss order in connection with the purchase or sale, of any security registered on a national securities exchange, in contravention of such rules and regulations as the Commission may prescribe as necessary or appropriate in the public interest or for the protection of investors.

(b) To use or employ, in connection with the purchase or sale of any security registered on a national securities exchange or any security not so registered, any manipulative or deceptive device or contrivance in contravention of such rules and regulations as the Commission may prescribe as necessary or appropriate in the public interest or for the protection of investors.

Trading by Members of Exchanges, Brokers, and Dealers

Section 11. (a)(1) It shall be unlawful for any member of a national securities exchange to effect any transaction on such exchange for its own account, the account of an associated person, or an account with respect to which it or an associated person thereof exercises investment discretion: Provided, however, That this paragraph shall not make unlawful—

(A) any transaction by a dealer acting in the capacity of market maker;

(B) any transaction for the account of an odd-lot dealer in a security in which he is so registered;

(C) any stabilizing transaction effected in compliance with rules under section 10(b) of this title to facilitate a distribution of a security in which the member effecting such transaction is participating;

(D) any bona fide arbitrage transaction, any bona fide hedge transaction involving a long or short position in an equity security and a long or short position in a security entitling the holder to acquire or sell such equity security, or any risk arbitrage transaction in connection with a merger, acquisition, tender offer, or similar transaction involving a recapitalization;

(E) any transaction for the account of a natural person, the estate of a natural person, or a trust (other than an investment company created by a natural person for himself or another natural person;

(F) any transaction to offset a transaction made in error;

(G) any other transaction for a member's own account provided that (i) such member is primarily engaged in the business of underwriting and distributing securities issued by other persons, selling securities to customers, and acting as broker, or any one or more of such activities, and whose gross income normally is derived principally from such business and related activities and (ii) such transaction is effected in compliance with rules of the Commission which, as a minimum, assure that the transaction is not inconsistent with the maintenance of fair and orderly markets and yields priority, parity, and precedence in execution to orders for the account of persons who are not members or associated with members of the exchange; and

(H) any other transaction of a kind which the Commission, by rule, determines is consistent with the purposes of this paragraph, the protection of investors, and the maintenance of fair and orderly markets.

(2) The Commission, by rule, as it deems necessary or appropriate in the public interest and for the protection of investors, to maintain fair and orderly markets, or to assure equal regulation of exchange markets and markets occurring otherwise than on an exchange, may regulate or prohibit:

(A) transactions on a national securities exchange not unlawful under paragraph (1) of this subsection effected by any member thereof for its own account (unless such member is acting in the capacity of market maker or odd-lot dealer), the account of an associated person, or an account with respect to which such member or an associated person thereof exercises investment discretion;

(B) transactions otherwise than on a national securities exchange effected by use of the mails or any means or instrumentality of interstate commerce by any member of a national securities exchange, broker, or dealer for the account of such member, broker, or dealer (unless such member, broker, or dealer is acting in the capacity of a market maker) the account of an associated person, or an account with respect to which such member, broker, or dealer or associated person thereof exercises investment discretion; and

(C) transactions on a national securities exchange effected by any broker or dealer not a member thereof for the account of such broker or dealer (unless such broker or dealer is acting in the capacity of market maker), the account of an associated person, or an account with respect to which such broker or dealer or associated person thereof exercises investment discretion.

(3) The provisions of paragraph (1) of this subsection insofar as they apply to transactions on a national securities exchange effected by a member thereof who was a member on May 1, 1975 shall not become effective until May 1, 1978. Nothing in this paragraph shall be construed to impair or limit the authority of the Commission to regulate or prohibit such transactions prior to May 1, 1978, pursuant to paragraph (2) of this subsection.

(b) When not in contravention of such rules and regulations as the Commission may prescribe as necessary or appropriate in the public interest and for the protection of investors, to maintain fair and orderly markets, or to remove impediments to and perfect the mechanism of a national market system, the rules of a national securities exchange may permit (1) a member to be registered as an odd-lot dealer and as such to buy and sell for his own account so far as may be reasonably necessary to carry on such odd-lot transactions, and (2) a member to be registered as a specialist. Under the rules and regulations of the Commission a specialist may be permitted to act as a broker and dealer or limited to acting as a broker or dealer. It shall be unlawful for a specialist or an official of the exchange to disclose information in regard to orders placed with such specialist which is not available to all members of the exchange, to any person other than an official of the exchange, a representative of the Commission, or a specialist who may be acting for such specialist: Provided, however, That the Commission, by rule, may require disclosure to all members of the exchange of all orders placed with specialists, under such rules and regulations as the Commission may prescribe as necessary or appropriate in the public interest or for the protection of investors. It shall also be unlawful for a specialist permitted to act as a broker and dealer to effect on the exchange as broker any transaction except upon a market or limited price order.

(c) If because of the limited volume of transactions effected on an exchange, it is in the opinion of the Commission impracticable and not necessary or appropriate in the public interest or for the protection of investors to apply any of the foregoing provisions of this section or the rules and regulations thereunder, the Commission shall have power, upon application of the exchange and on a showing that the rules of such exchange are otherwise adequate for the protection of investors, to exempt such exchange and its members from any such provision or rules and regulations.

(d) It shall be unlawful for a member of a national securities exchange who is both a dealer and a broker, or for any person who both as a broker and a dealer transacts a business in securities through the medium of a member or otherwise, to effect through the use of any facility of a national securities exchange or of the mails or of any means or instrumentality of interstate commerce, or otherwise in the case of a member, (1) any transaction in connection with which, directly or indirectly, he extends or maintains or arranges for the extension or maintenance of credit to or for a customer on any security (other than an exempted security) which was a part of a new issue in the distribution of which he participated as a member of a selling syndicate or group within thirty days prior to such transaction: *Provided,* That credit shall not be deemed extended by reason of a bona fide delayed delivery of any such security against full payment of the entire purchase price thereof upon such delivery within thirty-five days after such purchase, or (2) any transaction with respect to any security (other than an exempted security) unless, if the transaction is with a customer, he discloses to such customer in writing at or before the completion of the transaction whether he is acting as a dealer for his own account, as a broker for such customer, or as a broker for some other person.

National Market System for Securities; Securities Information Processors

Section 11A. (a)(1) The Congress finds that—

(A) The securities markets are an important national asset which must be preserved and strengthened.

(B) New data processing and communications techniques create the opportunity for more efficient and effective market operations.

(C) It is in the public interest and appropriate for the protection of investors and the maintenance of fair and orderly markets to assure—

(i) economically efficient execution of securities transactions;

(ii) fair competition among brokers and dealers, among exchange markets, and between exchange markets and markets other than exchange markets;

(iii) the availability to brokers, dealers, and investors of information with respect to quotations for and transactions in securities;

(iv) the practicability of brokers executing investors' orders in the best market; and

(v) an opportunity, consistent with the provisions of clauses (i) and (iv) of this subparagraph, for investors' orders to be executed without the participation of a dealer.

(D) The linking of all markets for qualified securities through communication and data processing facilities will foster efficiency, enhance competition, increase the information available to brokers, dealers, and investors, facilitate the offsetting of investors' orders, and contribute to best execution of such orders.

(2) The Commission is directed, therefore, having due regard for the public interest, the protection of investors, and the maintenance of fair and orderly markets, to use its authority under this title to facilitate the establishment of a national market system for securities (which may include subsystems for particular types of securities with unique trading characteristics) in accordance with the findings and to carry out the objectives set forth in paragraph (1) of this subsection. The Commission, by rule, shall designate the securities or classes of securities qualified for trading in the national market system from among securities other than exempted securities. (Securities or classes of securities so designated hereinafter in this section referred to as "qualified securities".)

(3) The Commission is authorized in furtherance of the directive in paragraph (2) of this subsection—

(A) to create one or more advisory committees pursuant to the Federal Advisory Committee Act (which shall be in addition to the National Market Advisory Board established pursuant to subsection (d) of this section) and to employ one or more outside experts;

(B) by rule or order, to authorize or require self-regulatory organizations to act jointly with respect to matters as to which they share authority under this title in planning, developing, operating, or regulating a national market system (or a subsystem thereof) or one or more facilities thereof; and

(C) to conduct studies and make recommendations to the Congress from time to time as to the possible need for modifications of the scheme of self-regulation provided for in this title so as to adapt it to a national market system.

(b)(1) Except as otherwise provided in this section, it shall be unlawful for any securities information processor unless registered in accordance with this subsection, directly or indirectly, to make use of the mails or any means or instrumentality of interstate commerce to perform the functions of a securities information processor. * * *

* * *

(c)(1) No self-regulatory organization, member thereof, securities information processor, broker, or dealer shall make use of the mails or any means or instrumentality of interstate commerce to collect, process, distribute, publish, or prepare for distribution or publication any information with respect to quotations for or transactions in any security other than an exempted security, to assist, participate in, or coordinate the distribution or publication of such information, or to effect any transaction in, or to induce or attempt to induce the purchase or sale of, any such security in contravention of such rules and regulations as the Commission shall prescribe as necessary or appropriate in the public interest, for the protection of investors, or otherwise in furtherance of the purposes of this title to—

(A) prevent the use, distribution, or publication of fraudulent, deceptive, or manipulative information with respect to quotations for and transactions in such securities;

(B) assure the prompt, accurate, reliable, and fair collection, processing, distribution, and publication of information with respect to quotations for and transactions in such securities and the fairness and usefulness of the form and content of such information;

(C) assure that all securities information processors may, for purposes of distribution and publication, obtain on fair and reasonable terms such information with respect to quotations for and transactions in such securities as is collected, processed, or prepared for distribution or publication by any exclusive processor of such information acting in such capacity;

(D) assure that all exchange members, brokers, dealers, securities information processors, and, subject to such limitations as the Commission, by rule, may impose as necessary or appropriate for the protection of investors or maintenance of fair and orderly markets, all other persons may obtain on terms which are not unreasonably discriminatory such information with respect to quotations for and transactions in such securities as is published or distributed by any self-regulatory organization or securities information processor;

(E) assure that all exchange members, brokers, and dealers transmit and direct orders for the purchase or sale of qualified securities in a manner consistent with the establishment and operation of a national market system; and

(F) assure equal regulation of all markets for qualified securities and all exchange members, brokers, and dealers effecting transactions in such securities.

(2) The Commission, by rule, as it deems necessary or appropriate in the public interest or for the protection of investors, may require any person who has effected the purchase or sale of any qualified security by use of the mails or any means or instrumentality of interstate commerce to report such purchase or sale to a registered securities information processor, national securities exchange, or registered securities association and require such processor, exchange, or association to make appropriate distribution and publication of information with respect to such purchase or sale.

(3)(A) The Commission, by rule, is authorized to prohibit brokers and dealers from effecting transactions in securities registered pursuant to section 12(b) otherwise than on a national securities exchange, if the Commission finds, on the record after notice and opportunity for hearing, that—

(i) as a result of transactions in such securities effected otherwise than on a national securities exchange the fairness or orderliness of the markets for such securities has been affected in a manner contrary to the public interest or the protection of investors;

(ii) no rule of any national securities exchange unreasonably impairs the ability of any dealer to solicit or effect transactions in such securities for his own account or unreasonably restricts competition among dealers in such securities or between dealers acting in the capacity of market makers who are specialists in such securities and such dealers who are not specialists in such securities, and

(iii) the maintenance or restoration of fair and orderly markets in such securities may not be assured through other lawful means under this title.

The Commission may conditionally or unconditionally exempt any security or transaction or any class of securities or transactions from any such prohibition if the Commission deems such exemption consistent with the public interest, the protection of investors, and the maintenance of fair and ordinary markets.

(B) For the purposes of subparagraph (A) of this paragraph, the ability of a dealer to solicit or effect transactions in securities for his own account shall not be deemed to be unreasonably impaired by any rule of an exchange fairly and reasonably prescribing the sequence in which orders brought to the exchange must be executed or which has been adopted to effect compliance with a rule of the Commission promulgated under this title.

(4) The Commission is directed to review any and all rules of national securities exchanges which limit or condition the ability of members to effect transactions in securities otherwise than on such exchanges. On or before the ninetieth day following the day of enactment of the Securities Acts Amendments of 1975, the Commission shall (i) report to the Congress the results of its review, including the effects on competition of such rules, and (ii) commence a proceeding in accordance with the provisions of section 19(c) of this title to amend any such rule imposing a burden on competition which does not appear to the Commission to be necessary or appropriate in furtherance of the purposes of this title. The Commission shall conclude any such proceeding within ninety days of the date of publication of notice of its commencement.

(5) No national securities exchange or registered securities association may limit or condition the participation of any member in any registered clearing agency.

(d)(1) Not later than one hundred eighty days after the date of enactment of the Securities Acts Amendments of 1975, the Commission shall establish a National Market Advisory Board (hereinafter in this section referred to as the "Advisory Board") to be composed of fifteen members, not all of whom shall be from the same geographical area of the United States, appointed by the Commission for a term specified by the Commission of not less than two years or more than five years. The Advisory Board shall consist of persons associated with brokers and dealers (who shall be a majority) and persons not so associated who are representative of the public and, to the extent feasible, have knowledge of the securities markets of the United States.

(2) It shall be the responsibility of the Advisory Board to formulate and furnish to the Commission its views on significant regulatory proposals made by the Commission or any self-regulatory organization concerning the establishment, operation, and regulation of the markets for securities in the United States.

(3)(A) The Advisory Board shall study and make recommendations to the Commission as to the steps it finds appropriate to facilitate the establishment of a national market system. In so doing, the Advisory Board shall assume the responsibilities of any advisory committee appointed to advise the Commission with respect to the national market system which is in existence at the time of the establishment of the Advisory Board.

(B) The Advisory Board shall study the possible need for modifications of the scheme of self-regulation provided for in this title so as to adapt it to a national market system, including the need for the establishment of a new self-regulatory organization (hereinafter in this section referred to as a "National Market Regulatory Board" or "Regulatory Board") to administer the national market system. In the event the Advisory Board determines a National Market Regulatory Board should be established, it shall make recommendations as to:

(i) the point in time at which a Regulatory Board should be established;

(ii) the composition of a Regulatory Board;

(iii) the scope of the authority of a Regulatory Board;

(iv) the relationship of a Regulatory Board to the Commission and to existing self-regulatory organizations; and

(v) the manner in which a Regulatory Board should be funded.

The Advisory Board shall report to the Congress, on or before December 31, 1976, the results of such study and its recommendations, including such recommendations for legislation as it deems appropriate.

(C) In carrying out its responsibilities under this paragraph, the Advisory Board shall consult with self-regulatory organizations, brokers, dealers, securities information processors, issuers, investors, representatives of Government agencies, and other persons interested or likely to participate in the establishment, operation, or regulation of the national market system.

(e) The Commission is authorized and directed to make a study of the extent to which persons excluded from the definitions of "broker" and "dealer" maintain accounts on behalf of public customers for buying and selling securities registered under section 12 of this title and whether such exclusions are consistent with the protection of investors and the other purposes of this title. The Commission shall report to the Congress, on or before December 31,

1976, the results of its study together with such recommendations for legislation as it deems advisable.

Registration Requirements for Securities

Section 12. (a) It shall be unlawful for any member, broker, or dealer to effect any transaction in any security (other than an exempted security) on a national securities exchange unless a registration is effective as to such security for such exchange in accordance with the provisions of this title and the rules and regulations thereunder.

(b) A security may be registered on a national securities exchange by the issuer filing an application with the exchange (and filing with the Commission such duplicate originals thereof as the Commission may require), which application shall contain—

(1) Such information, in such detail, as to the issuer and any person directly or indirectly controlling or controlled by, or under direct or indirect common control with, the issuer, and any guarantor of the security as to principal or interest or both, as the Commission may by rules and regulations require, as necessary or appropriate in the public interest or for the protection of investors, in respect of the following:

(A) the organization, financial structure and nature of the business;

(B) the terms, position, rights, and privileges of the different classes of securities outstanding;

(C) the terms on which their securities are to be, and during the preceding three years have been, offered to the public or otherwise;

(D) the directors, officers, and underwriters, and each security holder of record holding more than 10 per centum of any class of any equity security of the issuer (other than an exempted security), their remuneration and their interests in the securities of, and their material contracts with, the issuer and any person directly or indirectly controlling or controlled by, or under direct or indirect common control with, the issuer;

(E) remuneration to others than directors and officers exceeding $20,000 per annum;

(F) bonus and profit-sharing arrangements;

(G) management and service contracts;

(H) options existing or to be created in respect of their securities;

(I) material contracts, not made in the ordinary course of business, which are to be executed in whole or in part at or after the filing of the application or which were made not more than 2 years before such filing, and every material patent or contract for a material patent right shall be deemed a material contract;

(J) balance sheets for not more than the three preceding fiscal years, certified if required by the rules and regulations of the Commission by independent public accountants;

(K) profit and loss statements for not more than the three preceding fiscal years, certified if required by the rules and regulations of the Commission by independent public accountants; and

(L) any further financial statements which the Commission may deem necessary or appropriate for the protection of investors.

(2) Such copies of articles of incorporation, bylaws, trust indentures, or corresponding documents by whatever name known, underwriting arrangements, and other similar documents of, and voting trust agreements with respect to, the issuer and any person directly or indirectly controlling or controlled by, or under direct or indirect common control with, the issuer as the Commission may require as necessary or appropriate for the proper protection of investors and to insure fair dealing in the security.

(3) Such copies of material contracts, referred to in paragraph (1)(I) above, as the Commission may require as necessary or appropriate for the proper protection of investors and to insure fair dealing in the security.

(c) If in the judgment of the Commission any information required under subsection (b) is inapplicable to any specified class or classes of issuers, the Commission shall require in lieu thereof the submission of such other information of comparable character as it may deem applicable to such class of issuers.

(d) If the exchange authorities certify to the Commission that the security has been approved by the exchange for listing and registration, the registration shall become effective thirty days after the receipt of such certification by the Commission or within such shorter period of time as the Commission may determine. A security registered with a national securities exchange may be withdrawn or stricken from listing and registration in accordance with the rules of the exchange and, upon such terms as the Commission may deem necessary to impose for the protection of investors, upon application by the issuer or the exchange to the Commission; whereupon the issuer shall be relieved from further compliance with the provisions of this section and section 13 of this title and any rules or regulations under such sections as to the securities so withdrawn or stricken. An unissued security may be registered only in accordance with such rules and regulations as the Commission may prescribe as necessary or appropriate in the public interest or for the protection of investors.

(e) Notwithstanding the foregoing provisions of this section, the Commission may by such rules and regulations as it deems necessary or appropriate in the public interest or for the protection of investors, permit securities listed on any exchange at the time the registration of such exchange as a national securities exchange becomes effective, to be registered for a period ending not later than July 1, 1935, without complying with the provisions of this section.

(f)(1) Notwithstanding the foregoing provisions of this section, any national securities exchange, subject to the terms and conditions hereinafter set forth—

(A) may continue unlisted trading privileges to which a security had been admitted on such exchange prior to July 1, 1964;

(B) upon application to and approval of such application by the Commission, may extend unlisted trading privileges to any security listed and registered on any other national securities exchange; and

(C) upon application to and approval of such application by the Commission, may extend unlisted trading privileges to any security registered pursuant to section 12 of this title or which would be required to be so registered except for the exemption from registration provided in subsection (g)(2)(B) or (g)(2)(G) of that section.

If an extension of unlisted trading privileges to a security is based upon its listing and registration on another national securities exchange, such privileges shall continue in effect only so long as such security remains listed and registered on a national securities exchange.

* * *

(g)(1) Every issuer which is engaged in interstate commerce, or in a business affecting interstate commerce, or whose securities are traded by use of the mails or any means or instrumentality of interstate commerce shall—

(A) within one hundred and twenty days after the last day of its first fiscal year ended after the effective date of this subsection on which the issuer has total assets exceeding $1,000,000 and a class of equity security (other than an exempted security) held of record by seven hundred and fifty or more persons; and

(B) within one hundred and twenty days after the last day of its first fiscal year ended after two years from the effective date of this subsection on which the issuer has total assets exceeding $1,000,000 and a class of equity security (other than an exempted security) held of record by five hundred or more but less than seven hundred and fifty persons,

register such security by filing with the Commission a registration statement (and such copies thereof as the Commission may require) with respect to such security containing such information and documents as the Commission may specify comparable to that which is required in an application to register a security pursuant to subsection (b) of this section. Each such registration statement shall become effective sixty days after filing with the Commission or within such shorter period as the Commission may direct. Until such registration statement becomes effective it shall not be deemed filed for the purposes of section 18 of this title. Any issuer may register any class of equity security not required to be registered by filing a registration statement pursuant to the provisions of this paragraph. The Commission is authorized to extend the date upon which any issuer or class of issuers is required to register a security pursuant to the provisions of this paragraph.

(2) The provisions of this subsection shall not apply in respect of—

(A) any security listed and registered on a national securities exchange.

(B) any security issued by an investment company registered pursuant to section 8 of the Investment Company Act of 1940.

(C) any security, other than permanent stock, guaranty stock, permanent reserve stock, or any similar certificate evidencing nonwithdrawable capital, issued by a savings and loan association, building and loan association, cooperative bank, homestead association, or similar institution, which is supervised and examined by State or Federal authority having supervision over any such institution.

(D) any security of an issuer organized and operated exclusively for religious, educational, benevolent, fraternal, charitable, or reformatory purposes and not for pecuniary profit, and no part of the net earnings of which inures to the benefit of any private shareholder or individual.

(E) any security of an issuer which is a "cooperative association" as defined in the Agricultural Marketing Act, approved June 15, 1929, as amended, or a federation of such cooperative associations, if such federation possesses no greater powers or purposes than cooperative associations so defined.

(F) any security issued by a mutual or cooperative organization which supplies a commodity or service primarily for the benefit of its members and operates not for pecuniary profit, but only if the security is part of a class issuable only to persons who purchase commodities or services from the issuer, the security is transferable only to a successor in interest or occupancy of premises serviced or to be served by the issuer, and no dividends are payable to the holder of the security.

(G) any security issued by an insurance company if all of the following conditions are met:

(i) Such insurance company is required to and does file an annual statement with the Commissioner of Insurance (or other officer or agency performing a similar function) of its domiciliary State, and such annual statement conforms to that prescribed by the National Association of Insurance Commissioners or in the determination of such State commissioner, officer or agency substantially conforms to that so prescribed.

(ii) Such insurance company is subject to regulation by its domiciliary State of proxies, consents, or authorizations in respect of securities issued by such company and such regulation conforms to that prescribed by the National Association of Insurance Commissioners.

(iii) After July 1, 1966, the purchase and sales of securities issued by such insurance company by beneficial owners, directors, or officers of such company are subject to regulation (including reporting) by its domiciliary State substantially in the manner provided in section 16 of this title.

(H) any interest or participation in any collective trust funds maintained by a bank or in a separate account maintained by an insurance company which interest or participation is issued in connection with (i) a stock-bonus, pension, or profit-sharing plan which meets the requirements for qualification under section 401 of the Internal Revenue Code of 1954, or (ii) an annuity plan which meets the requirements for deduction of the employer's contribution under section 404(a)(2) of such Code.

(3) The Commission may by rules or regulations or, on its own motion, after notice and opportunity for hearing, by order, exempt from this subsection any security of a foreign issuer, including any certificate of deposit for such a security, if the Commission finds that such exemption is in the public interest and is consistent with the protection of investors.

(4) Registration of any class of security pursuant to this subsection shall be terminated ninety days, or such shorter period as the Commission may determine, after the issuer files a certification with the Commission that the number of holders of record of such class of security is reduced to less than three hundred persons.

* * *

(h) The Commission may by rules and regulations, or upon application of an interested person, by order, after notice and opportunity for hearing, exempt in whole or in part any issuer or class of issuers from the provisions of subsection (g) of this section or from section 13, 14, or 15(d), or may exempt from section 16 any officer, director, or beneficial owner of securities of any issuer, any security of which is required to be registered pursuant to subsection (g) hereof, upon such terms and conditions and for such period as it deems necessary or appropriate, if the Commission finds, by reason of the number of public investors, amount of trading interest in the securities, the nature and extent of the activities of the issuer, income or assets of the issuer or otherwise, that such action is not inconsistent with the public interest or the protection of investors.

* * *

(i) In respect of any securities issued by banks the deposits of which are insured in accordance with the Federal Deposit Insurance Act or institutions the accounts of which are insured by the Federal Savings and Loan Insurance Corporation, the powers, functions, and duties vested in the Commission to administer and enforce sections 12, 13, 14(a), 14(c), 14(d), 14(f), and 16, (1) with respect to national banks and banks operating under the Code of Law for the District of Columbia are vested in the Comptroller of the Currency, (2) with respect to all other member banks of the Federal Reserve System are vested in the Board of Governors of the Federal Reserve System, (3) with respect to all other insured banks are vested in the Federal Deposit Insurance Corporation, and (4) with respect to institutions the accounts of which are insured by the Federal Savings and Loan Insurance Corporation are vested in the Federal Home Loan Bank Board. The Comptroller of the Currency, the Board of Governors of the Federal Reserve System, the Federal Deposit Insurance Corporation, and the Federal Home Loan Bank Board shall have the power to make such rules and regulations as may be necessary for the execution of the functions vested in them as provided in this subsection. In carrying out their responsibilities under this subsection, the agencies named in the first sentence of this subsection shall issue substantially similar regulations to regulations and rules issued by the Commission under sections 12, 13, 14(a), 14(c), 14(d), 14(f), and 16, unless they find that implementation of substantially similar regulations with respect to insured banks and insured institutions are not necessary or appropriate in the public interest or for protection of investors, and publish such findings, and the detailed reasons therefor, in the Federal Register. Such regulations of the above-named agencies, or the reasons for failure to publish such substantially similar regulations to those of the Commission, shall be published in the Federal Register within 120 days of the date of enactment of this subsection, and, thereafter, within 60 days of any changes made by the Commission in its relevant regulations and rules.

(j) The Commission is authorized, by order, as it deems necessary or appropriate for the protection of investors to deny, to suspend the effective date of, to suspend for a period not exceeding twelve months, or to revoke the registration of a security, if the Commission finds, on the record after notice and opportunity for hearing, that the issuer of such security has failed to comply with any provision of this title or the rules and regulations thereunder. No member of a national securities exchange, broker, or dealer shall make use of the mails or any means or instrumentality of interstate commerce to effect any transaction in, or to induce the purchase or sale of, any security the registration of which has been and is suspended or revoked pursuant to the preceding sentence.

(k) If in its opinion the public interest and the protection of investors so require, the Commission is authorized summarily to suspend trading in any security (other than an exempted security) for a period not exceeding ten days, or with the approval of the President, summarily to suspend all trading on any national securities exchange or otherwise, in securities other than exempted securities, for a period not exceeding ninety days. No member of a national securities exchange, broker, or dealer shall make use of the mails or any means or instrumentality of interstate commerce to effect any transaction in, or to induce the purchase or sale of, any security in which trading is so suspended.

(*l*) It shall be unlawful for an issuer, any class of whose securities is registered pursuant to this section or would be required to be so registered except for the exemption from registration provided by subsection (g)(2)(B) or (g)(2)(G) of this section, by the use of any means or instrumentality of interstate commerce, or of the mails, to issue, either originally or upon transfer, any of such securities in a form or with a format which contravenes such rules and regulations as the Commission may prescribe as necessary or appropriate for the prompt and accurate clearance and settlement of transactions in securities. The provisions of this subsection shall not apply to variable annuity contracts or variable life policies issued by an insurance company or its separate accounts.

(m) The Commission is authorized and directed to make a study and investigation of the practice of recording the ownership of securities in the records of the issuer in other than the name of the beneficial owner of such securities and to determine (1) whether such practice is consistent with the purposes of this title, with particular reference to subsection (g) of this section and sections 13, 14, 15(d), 16, and 17A, and (2) whether steps can be taken to facilitate communications between issuers and the beneficial owners of their securities while at the same time retaining the benefits of such practice. The Commission shall report to the Congress its preliminary findings within six months after the date of enactment of the Securities Acts Amendments of 1975, and its final conclusions and recommendations within one year of such date.

Periodical and Other Reports

Section 13. (a) Every issuer of a security registered pursuant to section 12 of this title shall file with the Commission, in accordance with such rules and regulations as the Commission may prescribe as necessary or appropriate for the proper protection of investors and to insure fair dealing in the security—

(1) such information and documents (and such copies thereof) as the Commission shall require to keep reasonably current the information and documents required to be included in or filed with an application or registration statement filed pursuant to section 12, except that the Commission may not require the filing of any material contract wholly executed before July 1, 1962.

(2) such annual reports (and such copies thereof), certified if required by the rules and regulations of the Commission by independent public accountants, and such quarterly reports (and such copies thereof), as the Commission may prescribe.

Every issuer of a security registered on a national securities exchange shall also file a duplicate original of such information, documents, and reports with the exchange.

(b)(1) The Commission may prescribe, in regard to reports made pursuant to this title, the form or forms in which the required information shall be set forth, the items or details to be shown in the balance sheet and the earning statement, and the methods to be followed in the preparation of reports, in the appraisal or valuation of assets and liabilities, in the determination of depreciation and depletion, in the differentiation of recurring and nonrecurring income, in the differentiation of investment and operating income, and in the preparation, where the Commission deems it necessary or desirable, of separate and/or consolidated balance sheets or income accounts of any person directly or indirectly controlling or controlled by the issuer, or any person under direct or indirect common control with the issuer; but in the case of the reports of any person whose methods of accounting are prescribed under the provisions of any law of the United States, or any rule or regulation thereunder, the rules and regulations of the Commission with respect to reports shall not be inconsistent with the requirements imposed by such law or rule or regulation in respect of the same subject matter (except that such rules and regulations of the Commission may be inconsistent with such requirements to the extent that the Commission determines that the public interest or the protection of investors so requires).

(2) Every issuer which has a class of securities registered pursuant to section 12 of this title and every issuer which is required to file reports pursuant to section 15(d) of this title shall—

(A) make and keep books, records, and accounts, which, in reasonable detail, accurately and fairly reflect the transactions and dispositions of the assets of the issuer; and

(B) devise and maintain a system of internal accounting controls sufficient to provide reasonable assurances that—

(i) transactions are executed in accordance with management's general or specific authorization;

(ii) transactions are recorded as necessary (I) to permit preparation of financial statements in conformity with generally accepted accounting principles or any other criteria applicable to such statements, and (II) to maintain accountability for assets;

(iii) access to assets is permitted only in accordance with management's general or specific authorization; and

(iv) the recorded accountability for assets is compared with the existing assets at reasonable intervals and appropriate action is taken with respect to any differences.

(3)(A) With respect to matters concerning the national security of the United States, no duty or liability under paragraph (2) of this subsection shall be imposed upon any person acting in cooperation with the head of any Federal department or agency responsible for such matters if such act in cooperation with such head of a department or agency was done upon the specific, written directive of the head of such department or agency pursuant to Presidential authority to issue such directives. Each directive issued under this paragraph shall set forth the specific facts and circumstances with respect to which the provisions of this paragraph are to be invoked. Each such directive shall, unless renewed in writing, expire one year after the date of issuance.

(B) Each head of a Federal department or agency of the United States who issues a directive pursuant to this paragraph shall maintain a complete file of all such directives and shall, on October 1 of each year, transmit a summary of matters covered by such directives in force at any time during the previous year to the Permanent Select Committee on Intelligence of the House of Representatives and the Select Committee on Intelligence of the Senate.

(c) If in the judgment of the Commission any report required under subsection (a) is inapplicable to any specified class or classes of issuers, the Commission shall require in lieu thereof the submission of such reports of comparable character as it may deem applicable to such class or classes of issuers.

(d)(1) Any person who, after acquiring directly or indirectly the beneficial ownership of any equity security of a class which is registered pursuant to section 12 of this title, or any equity security of an insurance company which would have been required to be so registered except for the exemption contained in section 12(g)(2)(G) of this title, or any equity security issued by a closed-end investment company registered under the Investment Company Act of 1940, is directly or indirectly the beneficial owner of more than 5 per centum of such class shall, within ten days after such acquisition, send to the issuer of the security at its principal executive office, by registered or certified mail, send to each exchange where the security is traded, and file with the Commission, a statement containing such of the following information, and such additional information, as the Commission may by rules and regulations prescribe as necessary or appropriate in the public interest or for the protection of investors—

(A) the background, and identity, residence, and citizenship of, and the nature of such beneficial ownership by, such person and all other persons by whom or on whose behalf the purchases have been or are to be effected;

(B) the source and amount of the funds or other consideration used or to be used in making the purchases, and if any part of the purchase price or proposed purchase price is represented or is to be represented by funds or other consideration borrowed or otherwise obtained for the purpose of acquiring, holding, or trading such security, a description of the transaction and the names of the parties thereto, except that where a source of funds is a loan made in the ordinary course of business by a bank, as defined in section 3(a)(6) of this title, if the person filing such statement so requests, the name of the bank shall not be made available to the public;

(C) if the purpose of the purchases or prospective purchases is to acquire control of the business of the issuer of the securities, any plans or proposals which such persons may have to liquidate such issuer, to sell its assets to or merge it with any other persons, or to make any other major change in its business or corporate structure;

(D) the number of shares of such security which are beneficially owned, and the number of shares concerning which there is a right to acquire, directly or indirectly, by (i) such person, and (ii) by each associate of such person, giving the name and address of each such associate; and

(E) information as to any contracts, arrangements, or understandings with any person with respect to any securities of the issuer, including but not limited to transfer of any of the securities, joint ventures, loan or option arrangements, puts or calls, guaranties of loans, guaranties against loss or guaranties of profits, division of losses or profits, or the giving or withholding of proxies, naming the persons with whom such contracts, arrangements, or understandings have been entered into, and giving the details thereof.

(2) If any material change occurs in the facts set forth in the statements to the issuer and the exchange, and in the statement filed with the Commission, an amendment shall be transmitted to the issuer and the exchange and shall be filed with the Commission, in accordance with such rules and regulations as the Commission may prescribe as necessary or appropriate in the public interest or for the protection of investors.

(3) When two or more persons act as a partnership, limited partnership, syndicate, or other group for the purpose of acquiring, holding, or disposing of securities of an issuer, such syndicate or group shall be deemed a "person" for the purposes of this subsection.

(4) In determining, for purposes of this subsection, any percentage of a class of any security, such class shall be deemed to consist of the amount of the outstanding securities of such class, exclusive of any securities of such class held by or for the account of the issuer or a subsidiary of the issuer.

(5) The Commission, by rule or regulation or by order, may permit any person to file in lieu of the statement required by paragraph (1) of this subsection or the rules and regulations thereunder, a notice stating the name of such person, the number of shares of any equity securities subject to paragraph (1) which are owned by him, the date of their acquisition and such other information as the Commission may specify, if it appears to the Commission that such securities were acquired by such person in the ordinary course of his business and were not acquired for the purpose of and do not have the effect of changing or influencing the control of the issuer nor in connection with or as a participant in any transaction having such purpose or effect.

(6) The provisions of this subsection shall not apply to—

(A) any acquisition or offer to acquire securities made or proposed to be made by means of a registration statement under the Securities Act of 1933;

(B) any acquisition of the beneficial ownership of a security which, together with all other acquisitions by the same person of securities of the same class during the preceding twelve months, does not exceed 2 per centum of that class;

(C) any acquisition of an equity security by the issuer of such security;

(D) any acquisition or proposed acquisition of a security which the Commission, by rules or regulations or by order, shall exempt from the provisions of this subsection as not entered into for the purpose of, and not having the effect of, changing or influencing the control of the issuer or otherwise as not comprehended within the purposes of this subsection.

(e)(1) It shall be unlawful for an issuer which has a class of equity securities registered pursuant to section 12 of this title, or which is a closed-end investment company registered under the Investment Company Act of 1940, to purchase any equity security issued by it if such purchase is in contravention of such rules and regulations as the Commission, in the public interest or for the protection of investors, may adopt (A) to define acts and practices which are fraudulent, deceptive, or manipulative, and (B) to prescribe means reasonably designed to prevent such acts and practices. Such rules and regulations may require such issuer to provide holders of equity securities of such class with such information relating to the reasons for such purchase, the source of funds, the number of shares to be purchased, the price to be paid for such securities, the method of purchase, and such additional information, as the Commission deems necessary or appropriate in the public interest or for the protection of investors, or which the Commission deems to be material to a determination whether such security should be sold.

(2) For the purpose of this subsection, a purchase by or for the issuer or any person controlling, controlled by, or under common control with the issuer, or a purchase subject to control of the issuer or any such person, shall be deemed to be a purchase by the issuer. The Commission shall have power to make rules and regulations implementing this paragraph in the public interest and for the

protection of investors, including exemptive rules and regulations covering situations in which the Commission deems it unnecessary or inappropriate that a purchase of the type described in this paragraph shall be deemed to be a purchase by the issuer for purposes of some or all of the provisions of paragraph (1) of this subsection.

(3) At the time of filing such statement as the Commission may require by rule pursuant to paragraph (1) of this subsection, the person making the filing shall pay to the Commission a fee of 1/50 of 1 per centum of the value of securities proposed to be purchased. The fee shall be reduced with respect to securities in an amount equal to any fee paid with respect to any securities issued in connection with the proposed transaction under section 6(b) of the Securities Act of 1933, or the fee paid under that section shall be reduced in an amount equal to the fee paid to the Commission in connection with such transaction under this paragraph.

(f)(1) Every institutional investment manager which uses the mails, or any means or instrumentality of interstate commerce in the course of its business as an institutional investment manager and which exercises investment discretion with respect to accounts holding equity securities of a class described in section 13(d)(1) of this title having an aggregate fair market value on the last trading day in any of the preceding twelve months of at least $100,000,000 or such lesser amount (but in no case less than $10,000,000) as the Commission, by rule, may determine, shall file reports with the Commission in such form, for such periods, and at such times after the end of such periods as the Commission, by rule, may prescribe, but in no event shall such reports be filed for periods longer than one year or shorter than one quarter. Such reports shall include for each such equity security held on the last day of the reporting period by accounts (in aggregate or by type as the Commission, by rule, may prescribe) with respect to which the institutional investment manager exercises investment discretion (other than securities held in amounts which the Commission, by rule, determines to be insignificant for purposes of this subsection), the name of the issuer and the title, class, CUSIP number, number of shares or principal amount, and aggregate fair market value of each such security. Such reports may also include for accounts (in aggregate or by type) with respect to which the institutional investment manager exercises investment discretion such of the following information as the Commission, by rule, prescribes—

(A) the name of the issuer and the title, class, CUSIP number, number of shares or principal amount, and aggregate fair market value or cost or amortized cost of each other security (other than an exempted security) held on the last day of the reporting period by such accounts;

(B) the aggregate fair market value or cost or amortized cost of exempted securities (in aggregate or by class) held on the last day of the reporting period by such accounts;

(C) the number of shares of each equity security of a class described in section 13(d)(1) of this title held on the last day of the reporting period by such accounts with respect to which the institutional investment manager possesses sole or shared authority to exercise the voting rights evidenced by such securities;

(D) the aggregate purchases and aggregate sales during the reporting period of each security (other than an exempted security) effected by or for such accounts; and

(E) with respect to any transaction or series of transactions having a market value of at least $500,000 or such other amount as the Commission, by rule, may determine, effected during the reporting period by or for such accounts in any equity security of a class described in section 13(d)(1) of this title—

(i) the name of the issuer and the title, class, and CUSIP number of the security;

(ii) the number of shares or principal amount of the security involved in the transaction;

(iii) whether the transaction was a purchase or sale;

(iv) the per share price or prices at which the transaction was effected;

(v) the date or dates of the transaction;

(vi) the date or dates of the settlement of the transaction;

(vii) the broker or dealer through whom the transaction was effected;

(viii) the market or markets in which the transaction was effected; and

(ix) such other related information as the Commission, by rule, may prescribe.

* * *

(5)(A) For purposes of this subsection the term "institutional investment manager" includes any person, other than a natural person, investing in or buying and selling securities for its own account, and any person exercising investment discretion with respect to the account of any other person.

* * *

(g)(1) Any person who is directly or indirectly the beneficial owner of more than 5 per centum of any security of a class described in subsection (d)(1) of this section shall send to the issuer of the security and shall file with the Commission a statement setting forth, in such form and at such time as the Commission may, by rule, prescribe—

(A) such person's identity, residence, and citizenship; and

(B) the number and description of the shares in which such person has an interest and the nature of such interest.

(2) If any material change occurs in the facts set forth in the statement sent to the issuer and filed with the Commission, an amendment shall be transmitted to the issuer and shall be filed with the Commission, in accordance with such rules and regulations as the Commission may prescribe as necessary or appropriate in the public interest or for the protection of investors.

(3) When two or more persons act as a partnership, limited partnership, syndicate, or other group for the purpose of acquiring, holding, or disposing of securities of an issuer, such syndicate or group shall be deemed a "person" for the purposes of this subsection.

(4) In determining, for purposes of this subsection, any percentage of a class of any security, such class shall be deemed to consist of the amount of the outstanding securities of such class, exclusive of any securities of such class held by or for the account of the issuer or a subsidiary of the issuer.

(5) In exercising its authority under this subsection, the Commission shall take such steps as it deems necessary or appropriate in the public interest or for the protection of investors (A) to achieve centralized reporting of information regarding ownership, (B) to avoid unnecessarily duplicative reporting by and minimize the compliance burden on persons required to report, and (C) to tabulate and promptly make available the information contained in any report filed pursuant to this subsection in a manner which will, in the view of the Commission, maximize the usefulness of the information to other Federal and State agencies and the public.

(6) The Commission may, by rule or order, exempt, in whole or in part, any person or class of persons from any or all of the reporting requirements of this subsection as it deems necessary or appropriate in the public interest or for the protection of investors.

(h) The Commission shall report to the Congress within thirty months of the date of enactment of this subsection with respect to (1) the effectiveness of the ownership reporting requirements contained in this title and (2) the desirability and the feasibility of reducing or otherwise modifying the 5 per centum threshold used in subsections (d)(1) and (g)(1) of this section, giving appropriate consideration to—

(A) the incidence of avoidance of reporting by beneficial owners using multiple holders of record;

(B) the cost of compliance to persons required to report;

(C) the cost to issuers and others of processing and disseminating the reported information;

(D) the effect of such action on the securities markets, including the system for the clearance and settlement of securities transactions;

(E) the benefits to investors and to the public;

(F) any bona fide interests of individuals in the privacy of their financial affairs;

(G) the extent to which such reported information gives or would give any person an undue advantage in connection with activities subject to sections 13(d) and 14(d) of this title;

(H) the need for such information in connection with the administration and enforcement of this title; and

(I) such other matters as the Commission may deem relevant, including the information obtained pursuant to section 13(f) of this title.

* * *

Proxies

Section 14. (a) It shall be unlawful for any person, by the use of the mails or by any means or instrumentality of interstate commerce or of any facility of a national securities exchange or otherwise, in contravention of such rules and regulations as the Commission may prescribe as necessary or appropriate in the public interest or for the protection of investors, to solicit or to permit the use of his name to solicit any proxy or consent or authorization in respect of any security (other than an exempted security) registered pursuant to section 12 of this title.

(b)(1) It shall be unlawful for any member of a national securities exchange, or any broker or dealer registered under this title, or any bank, association, or other entity that exercises fiduciary powers, in contravention of such rules and regulations as the Commission may prescribe as necessary or appropriate in the public interest or for the protection of investors, to give, or to refrain from giving a proxy, consent, or authorization in respect of any security registered pursuant to section 12 of this title and carried for the account of a customer.

(2) With respect to banks, the rules and regulations prescribed by the Commission under paragraph (1) shall not require the disclosure of the names of beneficial owners of securities in an account held by the bank on the date of enactment of this paragraph unless the beneficial owner consents to the disclosure. The provisions of this paragraph shall not apply in the case of a bank which the Commission finds has not made a good faith effort to obtain such consent from such beneficial owners.

(c) Unless proxies, consents, or authorizations in respect of a security registered pursuant to section 12 of this title are solicited by or on behalf of the management of the issuer from the holders of record of such security in accordance with the rules and regulations prescribed under subsection (a) of this section, prior to any annual or other meeting of the holders of such security, such issuer shall, in accordance with rules and regulations prescribed by the Commission, file with the Commission and transmit to all holders of record of such security information substantially equivalent to the information which would be required to be transmitted if a solicitation were made, but no information shall be required to be filed or transmitted pursuant to this subsection before July 1, 1964.

(d)(1) It shall be unlawful for any person, directly or indirectly, by use of the mails or by any means or instrumentality of interstate commerce or of any facility of a national securities exchange or otherwise, to make a tender offer for, or a request or invitation for tenders of, any class of any equity security which is registered pursuant to section 12 of this title, or any equity security of an insurance company which would have been required to be so registered except for the exemption contained in section 12(g)(2)(G) of this title, or any equity security issued by a closed-end investment company registered under the Investment Company Act of 1940, if, after consummation thereof, such person would, directly or indirectly, be the beneficial owner of more than 5 per centum of such class, unless at the time copies of the offer or request or invitation are first published or sent or given to security holders such person has filed with the Commission a statement containing such of the information specified in section 13(d) of this title, and such additional information as the Commission may by rules and regulations prescribe as necessary or appropriate in the public interest or for the protection of investors. All requests or invitations for tenders or advertisements making a tender offer or requesting or inviting tenders of such a security shall be filed as a part of such statement and shall contain such of the information contained in such statement as the Commission may by rules and regulations prescribe. Copies of any additional material soliciting or requesting such tender offers subsequent to the initial solicitation or request shall contain such information as the Commission may by rules and regulations prescribe as necessary or appropriate in the public interest or for the protection of investors, and shall be filed with the Commission not later than the time copies of such material are first published or sent or given to security holders. Copies of all statements, in the form in which such material is furnished to security holders and the Commission, shall be sent to the issuer not later than the date such material is first published or sent or given to any security holders.

(2) When two or more persons act as a partnership, limited partnership, syndicate, or other group for the purpose of acquiring, holding, or disposing of securities of an issuer, such syndicate or group shall be deemed a "person" for purposes of this subsection.

(3) In determining, for purposes of this subsection, any percentage of a class of any security, such class shall be deemed to consist of the amount of the outstanding securities of such class, exclusive of any securities of such class held by or for the account of the issuer or a subsidiary of the issuer.

(4) Any solicitation or recommendation to the holders of such a security to accept or reject a tender offer or request or invitation for tenders shall be made in accordance with such rules and regulations as the Commission may prescribe as necessary or appropriate in the public interest or for the protection of investors.

(5) Securities deposited pursuant to a tender offer or request or invitation for tenders may be withdrawn by or on behalf of the depositor at any time until the expiration of seven days after the time definitive copies of the offer or request or invitation are first published or sent or given to security holders, and at any time after sixty days from the date of the original tender offer or request or invitation, except as the Commission may otherwise prescribe by rules, regulations, or order as necessary or appropriate in the public interest or for the protection of investors.

(6) Where any person makes a tender offer, or request or invitation for tenders, for less than all the outstanding equity securities of a class, and where a greater number of securities is deposited pursuant thereto within ten days after copies of the offer or request or invitation are first published or sent or given to security holders than such person is bound or willing to take up and pay for, the securities taken up shall be taken up as nearly as may be pro rata, disregarding fractions, according to the number of securities deposited by each depositor. The provisions of this subsection shall also apply to securities deposited within ten days after notice of an increase in the consideration offered to security holders, as described in paragraph (7), is first published or sent or given to security holders.

(7) Where any person varies the terms of a tender offer or request or invitation for tenders before the expiration thereof by increasing the consideration offered to holders of such securities, such person shall pay the increased consideration to each security holder whose securities are taken up and paid for pursuant to the tender offer or request or invitation for tenders whether or not such securities have been taken up by such person before the variation of the tender offer or request or invitation.

(8) The provisions of this subsection shall not apply to any offer for, or request or invitation for tenders of, any security—

(A) if the acquisition of such security, together with all other acquisitions by the same person of securities of the same class during the preceding twelve months, would not exceed 2 per centum of that class;

(B) by the issuer of such security; or

(C) which the Commission, by rules or regulations or by order, shall exempt from the provisions of this subsection as not entered into for the purpose of, and not having the effect of, changing or influencing the control of the issuer or otherwise as not comprehended within the purposes of this subsection.

(e) It shall be unlawful for any person to make any untrue statement of a material fact or omit to state any material fact necessary in order to make the statements made, in the light of the circumstances under which they are made, not misleading, or to engage in any fraudulent, deceptive, or manipulative acts or practices, in connection with any tender offer or request or invitation for tenders, or any solicitation of security holders in opposition to or in favor of any such offer, request, or invitation. The Commission shall, for the purposes of this subsection, by rules and regulations define, and prescribe means reasonably designed to prevent, such acts and practices as are fraudulent, deceptive, or manipulative.

(f) If, pursuant to any arrangement or understanding with the person or persons acquiring securities in a transaction subject to subsection (d) of this section or subsection (d) of section 13 of this title, any persons are to be elected or designated as directors of the issuer, otherwise than at a meeting of security holders, and the persons so elected or designated will constitute a majority of the directors of the issuer, then, prior to the time any such person takes office as a director, and in accordance with rules and regulations prescribed by the Commission, the issuer shall file with the Commission, and transmit to all holders of record of securities of the issuer who would be entitled to vote at a meeting for election of directors, information substantially equivalent to the information which would be required by subsection (a) or (c) of this section to be transmitted if such person or persons were nominees for election as directors at a meeting of such security holders.

* * *

Registration and Regulation of Brokers and Dealers

Section 15. (a)(1) It shall be unlawful for any broker or dealer which is either a person other than a natural person or a natural person not associated with a broker or dealer which is a person other than a natural person (other than such a broker or dealer whose business is exclusively intrastate and who does not make use of any facility of a national securities exchange) to make use of the mails or any means or instrumentality of interstate commerce to effect any transactions in, or to induce or attempt to induce the purchase or sale of, any security (other than an exempted security or commercial paper, bankers' acceptances, or commercial bills) unless such broker or dealer is registered in accordance with subsection (b) of this section.

(2) The Commission, by rule or order, as it deems consistent with the public interest and the protection of investors, may conditionally or unconditionally exempt from paragraph (1) of this subsection any broker or dealer or class of brokers or dealers specified in such rule or order.

(b)(1) A broker or dealer may be registered by filing with the Commission an application for registration in such form and containing such information and documents concerning such broker or dealer and any persons associated with such broker or dealer as the Commission, by rule, may prescribe as necessary or appropriate in the public interest or for the protection of investors. * * *

* * *

(3) Any provision of this title (other than section 5 and subsection (a) of this section) which prohibits any act, practice, or course of business if the mails or any means or instrumentality of interstate commerce is used in connection therewith shall also prohibit any such act, practice, or course of business by any registered broker or dealer or any person acting on behalf of such a broker or dealer, irrespective of any use of the mails or any means or instrumentality of interstate commerce in connection therewith.

(4) The Commission, by order, shall censure, place limitations on the activities, functions, or operations of, suspend for a period not exceeding twelve months, or revoke the registration of any broker or dealer if it finds, on the record after notice and opportunity for hearing, that such censure, placing of limitations, suspension, or revocation is in the public interest and that such broker or dealer, whether prior or subsequent to becoming such, or any person associated with such broker or dealer, whether prior or subsequent to becoming so associated—

(A) has willfully made or caused to be made in any application for registration or report required to be filed with the Commission or with any other appropriate regulatory agency under this title, or in any proceeding before the Commission with respect to registration, any statement which was at the time and in the light of the circumstances under which it was made false or misleading with respect to any material fact, or has omitted to state in any such application or report any material fact which is required to be stated therein.

(B) has been convicted within ten years preceding the filing of any application for registration or at any time thereafter of any felony or misdemeanor which the Commission finds—

(i) involves the purchase or sale of any security, the taking of a false oath, the making of a false report, bribery, perjury, burglary, or conspiracy to commit any such offense;

(ii) arises out of the conduct of the business of a broker, dealer, municipal securities dealer, government securities broker, government securities dealer, investment adviser, bank, insurance company, fiduciary, or any entity or person required to be registered under the Commodity Exchange Act (7 U.S.C. 1 et seq.);

(iii) involves the larceny, theft, robbery, extortion, forgery, counterfeiting, fraudulent concealment, embezzlement, fraudulent conversion, or misappropriation of funds, or securities, or

(iv) involves the violation of section 152, 1341, 1342, or 1343 or chapter 25 or 47 of title 18, United States Code

(C) is permanently or temporarily enjoined by order, judgment, or decree of any court of competent jurisdiction from acting as an investment adviser, underwriter, broker, dealer, entity or person required to be registered under the Commodity Exchange Act, municipal securities dealer, government securities broker, or government securities dealer, or as an affiliated person or employee of any investment company, bank, entity or person required to be registered under such Act, or insurance company, or from engaging in or continuing any conduct or practice in connection with any such activity, or in connection with the purchase or sale of any security.

(D) has willfully violated any provision of the Securities Act of 1933, the Investment Advisers Act of 1940, the Investment Company Act of 1940, the Commodity Exchange Act, *this title*, the rules or regulations under any of such statutes, or the rules of the Municipal Securities Rulemaking Board, or is unable to comply with any such provision;

(E) has willfully aided, abetted, counseled, commanded, induced, or procured the violation by any person of any provision of the Securities Act of 1933, the Investment Advisers Act of 1940, the Investment Company Act of 1940, the Commodity Exchange Act, this title, the rules or regulations under any of such statutes, or the rules of the Municipal Securities Rulemaking Board, or has failed reasonably to supervise, with a view to preventing violations of the provisions of such statutes, rules, and regulations, another person who commits such a violation, if such other person is subject to his supervision. For the purposes of this subparagraph (E) no person shall be deemed to have failed reasonably to supervise any other person, if—

(i) there have been established procedures, and a system for applying such procedures, which would reasonably be expected to prevent and detect, insofar as practicable, any such violation by such other person, and

(ii) such person has reasonably discharged the duties and obligations incumbent upon him by reason of such procedures and system without reasonable cause to believe that such procedures and system were not being complied with.

(F) is subject to an order of the Commission entered pursuant to paragraph (6) of this subsection (b) barring or suspending the right of such person to be associated with a broker or dealer.

(5) Pending final determination whether any registration under this subsection shall be revoked, the Commission, by order, may suspend such registration, if such suspension appears to the Commission, after notice and opportunity for hearing, to be necessary or appropriate in the public interest or for the protection of investors. Any registered broker or dealer may, upon such terms and conditions as the Commission deems necessary or appropriate in the public interest or for the protection of investors, withdraw from registration by filing a written notice of withdrawal with the Commission. If the Commission finds that any registered broker or dealer is no longer in existence or has ceased to do business as a broker or dealer, the Commission, by order, shall cancel the registration of such broker or dealer.

(6) The Commission, by order, shall censure or place limitations on the activities or functions of any person associated, or seeking to become associated, with a broker or dealer, or suspend for a period not exceeding twelve months or bar any such person from being associated with a broker or dealer, if the Commission finds, on the record after notice and opportunity for hearing, that such censure, placing of limitations, suspension, or bar is in the public interest and that such person has committed or omitted any act or omission enumerated in subparagraph (A), (D), or (E) of paragraph (4) of this subsection, has been convicted of any offense specified in subparagraph (B) of said paragraph (4) within ten years of the commencement of the proceedings under this paragraph, or is enjoined from any action, conduct, or practice specified in subparagraph (C) of said paragraph (4). It shall be unlawful for any person as to whom such an order suspending or barring him from being associated with a broker or dealer is in effect willfully to become, or to be, associated with a broker or dealer without the consent of the Commission, and it shall be unlawful

for any broker or dealer to permit such a person to become, or remain, a person associated with him without the consent of the Commission, if such broker or dealer knew, or in the exercise of reasonable care should have known, of such order.

(7) No registered broker or dealer shall effect any transaction in, or induce the purchase or sale of, any security unless such broker or dealer meets such standards of operational capability and such broker or dealer and all natural persons associated with such broker or dealer meet such standards of training, experience, competence, and such other qualifications as the Commission finds necessary or appropriate in the public interest or for the protection of investors. * * *

(8) It shall be unlawful for any registered broker or dealer to effect any transactions in, or induce or attempt to induce the purchase or sale of, any security (other than commercial paper, bankers' acceptances, or commercial bills), unless such broker or dealer is a member of a securities association registered pursuant to section 15A of this title or effects transactions in securities solely on a national securities exchange of which it is a member.

(9) The Commission by rule or order, as it deems consistent with the public interest and the protection of investors, may conditionally or unconditionally exempt from paragraph (8) of this subsection any broker or dealer or class of brokers or dealers specified in such rule or order.

(c)(1) No broker or dealer shall make use of the mails or any means or instrumentality of interstate commerce to effect any transaction in, or to induce or attempt to induce the purchase or sale of, any security (other than commercial paper, bankers' acceptances, or commercial bills) otherwise than on a national securities exchange of which it is a member by means of any manipulative, deceptive, or other fraudulent device or contrivance, and no municipal securities dealer shall make use of the mails or any means or instrumentality of interstate commerce to effect any transaction in, or to induce or attempt to induce the purchase or sale of, any municipal security by means of any manipulative, deceptive, or other fraudulent device or contrivance. The Commission shall, for the purposes of this paragraph, by rules and regulations define such devices or contrivances as are manipulative, deceptive, or otherwise fraudulent.

(2) No broker or dealer shall make use of the mails or any means or instrumentality of interstate commerce to effect any transaction in, or to induce or attempt to induce the purchase or sale of, any security (other than an exempted security or commercial paper, bankers' acceptances, or commercial bills) otherwise than on a national securities exchange of which it is a member, in connection with which such broker or dealer engages in any fraudulent, deceptive, or manipulative act or practice, or makes any fictitious quotation, and no municipal securities dealer shall make use of the mails or any means or instrumentality of interstate commerce to effect any transactions in, or to induce or attempt to induce the purchase or sale of, any municipal security in connection with which such municipal securities dealer engages in any fraudulent, deceptive, or manipulative act or practice, or makes any fictitious quotation. The Commission shall, for the purposes of this paragraph, by rules and regulations define, and prescribe means reasonably designed to prevent, such acts and practices as are fraudulent, deceptive, or manipulative and such quotations as are fictitious.

(3) No broker or dealer (other than a government securities broker or government securities dealer, except a registered broker or dealer) shall make use of the mails or any means or instrumentality of interstate commerce to effect any transaction in, or to induce or attempt to induce the purchase or sale of, any security (other than an exempted security (except a government security) or commercial paper, bankers' acceptances, or commercial bills) in contravention of such rules and regulations as the Commission shall prescribe as necessary or appropriate in the public interest or for the protection of investors to provide safeguards with respect to the financial responsibility and related practices of brokers and dealers including, but not limited to, the acceptance of custody and use of customers' securities and the carrying and use of customers' deposits or credit balances. Such rules and regulations shall (A) require the maintenance of reserves with respect to customers' deposits or credit balances, and (B) no later than September 1, 1975, establish minimum financial responsibility requirements for all brokers and dealers.

(4) If the Commission finds, after notice and opportunity for hearing, that any person subject to the provisions of section 12, 13, or subsection (d) of

section 15 of this title or any rule or regulation thereunder has failed to comply with any such provision, rule, or regulation in any material respect, the Commission may publish its findings and issue an order requiring such person, and any person who was a cause of the failure to comply due to an act or omission the person knew or should have known would contribute to the failure to comply, to comply, or to take steps to effect compliance, with such provision or such rule or regulation thereunder upon such terms and conditions and within such time as the Commission may specify in such order.

(5) No dealer (other than a specialist registered on a national securities exchange) acting in the capacity of market maker or otherwise shall make use of the mails or any means or instrumentality of interstate commerce to effect any transaction in, or to induce or attempt to induce the purchase or sale of, any security (other than an exempted security or municipal security) in contravention of such specified and appropriate standards with respect to dealing as the Commission, by rule, shall prescribe as necessary or appropriate in the public interest and for the protection of investors, to maintain fair and orderly markets, or to remove impediments to and perfect the mechanism of a national market system. Under the rules of the Commission a dealer in a security may be prohibited from acting as a broker in that security.

(6) No broker or dealer shall make use of the mails or any means or instrumentality of interstate commerce to effect any transaction in, or to induce or attempt to induce the purchase or sale of, any security (other than an exempted security, municipal security, commercial paper, bankers' acceptances, or commercial bills) in contravention of such rules and regulations as the Commission shall prescribe as necessary or appropriate in the public interest and for the protection of investors or to perfect or remove impediments to a national system for the prompt and accurate clearance and settlement of securities transactions, with respect to the time and method of, and the form and format of documents used in connection with, making settlements of and payments for transactions in securities, making transfers and deliveries of securities, and closing accounts. Nothing in this paragraph shall be construed (A) to affect the authority of the Board of Governors of the Federal Reserve System, pursuant to section 7 of this title, to prescribe rules and regulations for the purpose of preventing the excessive use of credit for the purchase or carrying of securities, or (B) to authorize the Commission to prescribe rules or regulations for such purpose.

(d) Each issuer which has filed a registration statement containing an undertaking which is or becomes operative under this subsection as in effect prior to the date of enactment of the Securities Acts Amendments of 1964, and each issuer which shall after such date file a registration statement which has become effective pursuant to the Securities Act of 1933, as amended, shall file with the Commission, in accordance with such rules and regulations as the Commission may prescribe as necessary or appropriate in the public interest or for the protection of investors, such supplementary and periodic information, documents, and reports as may be required pursuant to section 13 of this title in respect of a security registered pursuant to section 12 of this title. The duty to file under this subsection shall be automatically suspended if and so long as any issue of securities of such issuer is registered pursuant to section 12 of this title. The duty to file under this subsection shall also be automatically suspended as to any fiscal year, other than the fiscal year within which such registration statement became effective, if, at the beginning of such fiscal year, the securities of each class to which the registration statement relates are held of record by less than three hundred persons. For the purposes of this subsection, the term "class" shall be construed to include all securities of an issuer which are of substantially similar character and the holders of which enjoy substantially similar rights and privileges. The Commission may, for the purpose of this subsection, define by rules and regulations the term "held of record" as it deems necessary or appropriate in the public interest or for the protection of investors in order to prevent circumvention of the provisions of this subsection. Nothing in this subsection shall apply to securities issued by a foreign government or political subdivision thereof.

(e) The Commission, by rule, as it deems necessary or appropriate in the public interest and for the protection of investors or to assure equal regulation, may require any member of a national securities exchange not required to register under section 15 of this title and any person associated with any such member to comply with any provision of this title (other than section 15(a)) or the rules or regulations thereunder which by its terms regulates or prohibits any act, practice, or course of business by a "broker or dealer" or "registered broker or dealer" or a "person associated with a broker or dealer," respectively.

Registered Securities Associations

Section 15A. (a) An association of brokers and dealers may be registered as a national securities association pursuant to subsection (b), or as an affiliated securities association pursuant to subsection (d), under the terms and conditions hereinafter provided in this section and in accordance with the provisions of section 19(a) of this title, by filing with the Commission an application for registration in such form as the Commission, by rule, may prescribe containing the rules of the association and such other information and documents as the Commission, by rule, may prescribe as necessary or appropriate in the public interest or for the protection of investors.

(b) An association of brokers and dealers shall not be registered as a national securities association unless the commission determines that—

(1) By reason of the number and geographical distribution of its members and the scope of their transactions, such association will be able to carry out the purposes of this section.

(2) Such association is so organized and has the capacity to be able to carry out the purposes of this title and to comply, and (subject to any rule or order of the Commission pursuant to section 17(d) or 19(g)(2) of this title) to enforce compliance by its members and persons associated with its members, with the provisions of this title, the rules and regulations thereunder, the rules of the Municipal Securities Rulemaking Board, and the rules of the association.

(3) Subject to the provisions of subsection (g) of this section, the rules of the association provide that any registered broker or dealer may become a member of such association and any person may become associated with a member thereof.

(4) The rules of the association assure a fair representation of its members in the selection of its directors and administration of its affairs and provide that one or more directors shall be representative of issuers and investors and not be associated with a member of the association, broker, or dealer.

(5) The rules of the association provide for the equitable allocation of reasonable dues, fees, and other charges among members and issuers and other persons using any facility or system which the association operates or controls.

(6) The rules of the association are designed to prevent fraudulent and manipulative acts and practices, to promote just and equitable principles of trade, to foster cooperation and coordination with persons engaged in regulating, clearing, settling, processing information with respect to, and facilitating transactions in securities, to remove impediments to and perfect the mechanism of a free and open market and a national market system, and, in general, to protect investors and the public interest; and are not designed to permit unfair discrimination between customers, issuers, brokers, or dealers, to fix minimum profits, to impose any schedule or fix rates of commissions, allowances, discounts, or other fees to be charged by its members, or to regulate by virtue of any authority conferred by this title matters not related to the purposes of this title or the administration of the association.

(7) The rules of the association provide that (subject to any rule or order of the Commission pursuant to section 17(d) or 19(g)(2) of this title) its members and persons associated with its members shall be appropriately disciplined for violation of any provision of this title, the rules or regulations thereunder, the rules of the Municipal Securities Rulemaking Board, or the rules of the association, by expulsion, suspension, limitation of activities, functions, and operations, fine, censure, being suspended or barred from being associated with a member, or any other fitting sanction.

(8) The rules of the association are in accordance with the provisions of subsection (h) of this section, and, in general, provide a fair procedure for the disciplining of members and persons associated with members, the denial of membership to any person seeking membership therein, the barring of any person from becoming associated with a member thereof, and the prohibition or limitation by the association of any person with respect to access to services offered by the association or a member thereof.

(9) The rules of the association do not impose any burden on competition not necessary or appropriate in furtherance of the purposes of this title.

(10) The requirements of subsection (c), insofar as these may be applicable, are satisfied.

(11) The rules of the association include provisions governing the form and content of quotations relating to securities sold otherwise than on a national securities exchange which may be distributed or published by any member or person associated with a member, and the persons to whom such quotations may be supplied. Such rules relating to quotations shall be designed to produce fair and informative quotations, to prevent fictitious or misleading quotations, and to promote orderly procedures for collecting, distributing, and publishing quotations.

* * *

(e)(1) The rules of a registered securities association may provide that no member thereof shall deal with any nonmember professional (as defined in paragraph (2) of this subsection) except at the same prices, for the same commissions or fees, and on the same terms and conditions as are by such member accorded to the general public.

(2) For the purposes of this subsection, the term "nonmember professional" shall include (A) with respect to transactions in securities other than municipal securities, any registered broker or dealer who is not a member of any registered securities association, except such a broker or dealer who deals exclusively in commercial paper, bankers' acceptances, and commercial bills, and (B) with respect to transactions in municipal securities, any municipal securities dealer (other than a bank or division or department of a bank) who is not a member of any registered securities association and any municipal securities broker who is not a member of any such association.

(3) Nothing in this subsection shall be so construed or applied as to prevent (A) any member of a registered securities association from granting to any other member of any registered securities association any dealer's discount, allowance, commission, or special terms, in connection with the purchase or sale of securities, or (B) any member of a registered securities association or any municipal securities dealer which is a bank or a division or department of a bank from granting to any member of any registered securities association or any such municipal securities dealer any dealer's discount, allowance, commission, or special terms in connection with the purchase or sale of municipal securities: Provided, however, That the granting of any such discount, allowance, commission, or special terms in connection with the purchase or sale of municipal securities shall be subject to rules of the Municipal Securities Rulemaking Board adopted pursuant to section 15B(b)(2)(K) of this title.

(f)(1) Except as provided in paragraph (2) of this subsection, nothing in this section shall be construed to apply with respect to any transaction by a registered broker or dealer in any exempted security.

(2) A registered securities association may adopt and implement rules applicable to members of such association (A) to enforce compliance by registered brokers and dealers with applicable provisions of this title and the rules and regulations thereunder, (B) to provide that its members and persons associated with its members shall be appropriately disciplined, in accordance with subsections (b)(7), (b)(8), and (h) of this section, for violation of applicable provisions of this title and the rules and regulations thereunder, (C) to provide for reasonable inspection and examination of the books and records of registered brokers and dealers, (D) to provide for the matters described in paragraphs (b)(3), (b)(4), and (b)(5) of this section, (E) to implement the provisions of subsection (g) of this section, and (F) to prohibit fraudulent, misleading, deceptive, and false advertising.

(3) Nothing in subsection (b)(6) or (b)(11) of this section shall be construed to permit a registered securities association to make rules concerning any transaction by a registered broker or dealer in a municipal security.

* * *

(h)(1) In any proceeding by a registered securities association to determine whether a member or person associated with a member should be disciplined (other than a summary proceeding pursuant to paragraph (3) of this subsection) the association shall bring specific charges, notify such member or person of, and give him an opportunity to defend against, such charges, and keep a record. A determination by the association to impose a disciplinary sanction shall be supported by a statement setting forth—

(A) any act or practice in which such member or person associated with a member has been found to have engaged, or which such member or person has been found to have omitted;

(B) the specific provision of this title, the rules or regulations thereunder, the rules of the Municipal Securities Rulemaking Board, or the rules of the association which any such act or practice, or omission to act, is deemed to violate; and

(C) the sanction imposed and the reason therefor.

(2) In any proceeding by a registered securities association to determine whether a person shall be denied membership, barred from becoming associated with a member, or prohibited or limited with respect to access to services offered by the association or a member thereof (other than a summary proceeding pursuant to paragraph (3) of this subsection), the association shall notify such person of, and give him an opportunity to be heard upon, the specific grounds for denial, bar, or prohibition or limitation under consideration and keep a record. A determination by the association to deny membership, bar a person from becoming associated with a member, or prohibit or limit a person with respect to access to services offered by the association or a member thereof shall be supported by a statement setting forth the specific grounds on which the denial, bar, or prohibition or limitation is based.

* * *

Municipal Securities

Section 15B. (a)(1) It shall be unlawful for any municipal securities dealer (other than one registered as a broker or dealer under section 15 of this title) to make use of the mails or any means or instrumentality of interstate commerce to effect any transaction in, or to induce or attempt to induce the purchase or sale of, any municipal security unless such municipal securities dealer is registered in accordance with this subsection.

(2) A municipal securities dealer may be registered by filing with the Commission an application for registration in such form and containing such information and documents concerning such municipal securities dealer and any persons associated with such municipal securities dealer as the Commission, by rule, may prescribe as necessary or appropriate in the public interest or for the protection of investors. * * *

* * *

(b)(1) Not later than one hundred twenty days after the date of enactment of the Securities Acts Amendments of 1975, the Commission shall establish a Municipal Securities Rulemaking Board (hereinafter in this section referred to as the "Board"), to be composed initially of fifteen members appointed by the Commission, which shall perform the duties set forth in this section. The initial members of the Board shall serve as members for a term of two years, and shall consist of (A) five individuals who are not associated with any broker, dealer, or municipal securities dealer, at least one of whom shall be representative of investors in municipal securities, and at least one of whom shall be representative of issuers of municipal securities (which members are hereinafter referred to as "public representatives"); (B) five individuals who are associated with and representative of municipal securities brokers and municipal securities dealers which are not banks or subsidiaries or departments or divisions of banks (which members are hereinafter referred to as "broker-dealer representatives"); and (C) five individuals who are associated with and representative of municipal securities dealers which are banks or subsidiaries or departments or divisions of banks (which members are hereinafter referred to as "bank representatives"). Prior to the expiration of the terms of office of the initial members of the Board, an election shall be held under rules adopted by the Board (pursuant to subsection (b)(2)(B) of this section) of the members to succeed such initial members.

(2) The Board shall propose and adopt rules to effect the purposes of this title with respect to transactions in municipal securities effected by brokers, dealers, and municipal securities dealers. * *

* * *

(c)(1) No broker, dealer, or municipal securities dealer shall make use of the mails or any means or instrumentality of interstate commerce to effect any transaction in, or to induce or attempt to induce the purchase or sale of, any municipal security in contravention of any rule of the Board.

(2) The Commission, by order, shall censure, place limitations on the activities, functions, or operations, suspend for a period not exceeding twelve months, or revoke the registration of any municipal

securities dealer, if it finds, on the record after notice and opportunity for hearing, that such censure, placing of limitations, denial, suspension, or revocation, is in the public interest and that such municipal securities dealer has committed or omitted any act or omission enumerated in subparagraph (A), (D), or (E) of paragraph (4) of section 15(b) of this title, has been convicted of any offense specified in subparagraph (B) of such paragraph (4) within ten years of the commencement of the proceedings under this paragraph, or is enjoined from any action, conduct, or practice specified in subparagraph (C) of such paragraph (4).

* * *

(5) With respect to any municipal securities dealer for which the Commission is not the appropriate regulatory agency, the appropriate regulatory agency for such municipal securities dealer may sanction any such municipal securities dealer in the manner and for the reasons specified in paragraph (2) of this subsection and any person associated with such municipal securities dealer in the manner and for the reasons specified in paragraph (4) of this subsection. * * *

(d)(1) Neither the Commission nor the Board is authorized under this title, by rule or regulation, to require any issuer of municipal securities, directly or indirectly through a purchaser or prospective purchaser of securities from the issuer, to file with the Commission or the Board prior to the sale of such securities by the issuer any application, report, or document in connection with the issuance, sale, or distribution of such securities.

(2) The Board is not authorized under this title to require any issuer of municipal securities, directly or indirectly through a municipal securities broker or municipal securities dealer or otherwise, to furnish to the Board or to a purchaser or prospective purchaser of such securities any application, report, document, or information with respect to such issuer: Provided, however, That the Board may require municipal securities brokers and municipal securities dealers to furnish to the Board or purchasers or prospective purchasers of municipal securities applications, reports, documents, and information with respect to the issuer thereof which is generally available from a source other than such issuer. Nothing in this paragraph shall be construed to impair or limit the power of the Commission under any provision of this title.

Government Securities

Section 15C. (a)(1)(A) It shall be unlawful for any government securities broker or government securities dealer (other than a registered broker or dealer or a financial institution) to make use of the mails or any means or instrumentality of interstate commerce to effect any transaction in, or to induce or attempt to induce the purchase or sale of, any government security unless such government securities broker or government securities dealer is registered in accordance with paragraph (2) of this subsection.

* * *

(a)(2) A government securities broker or a government securities dealer subject to the registration requirement of paragraph (1)(A) of this subsection may be registered by filing with the Commission an application for registration in such form and containing such information and documents concerning such government securities broker or government securities dealer and any persons associated with such government securities broker or government securities dealer as the Commission, by rule, may prescribe as necessary or appropriate in the public interest or for the protection of investors.

* * *

(a)(3) Any provision of this title (other than section 5 or paragraph (1) of this subsection) which prohibits any act, practice, or course of business if the mails or any means or instrumentality of interstate commerce is used in connection therewith shall also prohibit any such act, practice, or course of business by any government securities broker or government securities dealer registered or having filed notice under paragraph (1) of this subsection or any person acting on behalf of such government securities broker or government securities dealer, irrespective of any use of the mails or any means or instrumentality of interstate commerce in connection therewith.

(a)(4) The Secretary of the Treasury (hereinafter in this section referred to as the 'Secretary'), by rule or order, upon the Secretary's own motion or upon application, may conditionally or unconditionally exempt any government securities broker or government securities dealer, or class of government securities brokers or government securities dealers, from any provision of subsection (a), (b), or (d) of this section or the rules thereunder, if the Secretary finds that such exemption is consistent with the public interest, the protection of investors, and the purposes of this title.

(b)(1) The Secretary shall propose and adopt rules to effect the purposes of this title with respect to transactions in government securities effected by government securities brokers and government securities dealers * * *

* * *

(b)(2) Rules promulgated and orders issued under this section shall—

(A) be designed to prevent fraudulent and manipulative acts and practices and to protect the integrity, liquidity, and efficiency of the market for government securities, investors, and the public interest; and

(B) not be designed to permit unfair discrimination between customers, issuers, government securities brokers, or government securities dealers, or to impose any burden on competition not necessary or appropriate in furtherance of the purposes of this title.

* * *

(b)(5) No government securities broker or government securities dealer shall make use of the mails or any means or instrumentality of interstate commerce to effect any transaction in, or to induce or attempt to induce the purchase or sale of, any government security in contravention of any rule under this section.

(c)(1) With respect to any government securities broker or government securities dealer registered or required to register under subsection (a)(1)(A) of this section—

(A) The Commission, by order, shall censure, place limitations on the activities, functions, or operations of, suspend for a period not exceeding 12 months, or revoke the registration of such government securities broker or government securities dealer, if it finds, on the record after notice and opportunity for hearing, that such censure, placing of limitations, suspension, or revocation is in the public interest and that such government securities broker or government securities dealer, or any person associated with such government securities broker or government securities dealer (whether prior or subsequent to becoming so associated), has committed or omitted any act or omission enumerated in subparagraph (A), (D), or (E) of paragraph (4) of section 15(b) of this title, has been convicted of any offense specified in subparagraph (B) of such paragraph (4) within 10 years of the commencement of the proceedings under this paragraph, or is enjoined from any action, conduct, or practice specified in subparagraph (C) of such paragraph (4).

* * *

(c)(2)(A) With respect to any government securities broker or government securities dealer which is not registered or required to register under subsection (a)(1)(A) of this section, the appropriate regulatory agency for such government securities broker or government securities dealer may, in the manner and for the reasons specified in paragraph (1)(A) of this subsection, censure, place limitations on the activities, functions, or operations of, suspend for a period not exceeding 12 months, or bar from acting as a government securities broker or government securities dealer any such government securities broker or government securities dealer, and may sanction any person associated with such government securities broker or government securities dealer in the manner and for the reasons specified in paragraph (1)(C) of this subsection.

* * *

Directors, Officers, and Principal Stockholders

Section 16. (a) Every person who is directly or indirectly the beneficial owner of more than 10 per centum of any class of any equity security (other than an exempted security) which is registered pursuant to section 12 of this title, or who is a director or an officer of the issuer of such security, shall file, at the time of the registration of such security on a national securities exchange or by the effective date of a registration statement filed pursuant to section 12(g) of this title, or within ten days after he becomes such beneficial owner, director, or officer, a statement with the Commission (and, if such security is registered on a national securities exchange, also with the exchange) of the amount of all equity securities of such issuer of which he is the beneficial owner, and within ten days after the close of each calendar month thereafter, if there has been a change in such ownership during such month, shall file with the Commission (and if such security is registered on a national securities exchange, shall also file with the exchange), a statement indicating his ownership at the close of the calendar month and such changes in his ownership as have occurred during such calendar month.

(b) For the purpose of preventing the unfair use of information which may have been obtained by such beneficial owner, director, or officer by reason of his relationship to the issuer, any profit realized by him from any purchase and sale, or any sale and purchase, of any equity security of such issuer (other than an exempted security) within any period of less than six months, unless such security was acquired in good faith in connection with a debt previously contracted, shall inure to and be recoverable by the issuer, irrespective of any intention on the part of such beneficial owner, director, or officer in entering into such transaction of holding the security purchased or of not repurchasing the security sold for a period exceeding six months. Suit to recover such profit may be instituted at law or in equity in any court of competent jurisdiction by the issuer, or by the owner of any security of the issuer in the name and in behalf of the issuer if the issuer shall fail or refuse to bring such suit within sixty days after request or shall fail diligently to prosecute the same thereafter; but no such suit shall be brought more than two years after the date such profit was realized. This subsection shall not be construed to cover any transaction where such beneficial owner was not such both at the time of the purchase and sale, or the sale and purchase, of the security involved, or any transaction or transactions which the Commission by rules and regulations may exempt as not comprehended within the purpose of this subsection.

(c) It shall be unlawful for any such beneficial owner, director, or officer, directly or indirectly, to sell any equity security of such issuer (other than an exempted security), if the person selling the security or his principal (1) does not own the security sold, or (2) if owning the security, does not deliver it against such sale within twenty days thereafter, or does not within five days after such sale deposit it in the mails or other usual channels of transportation; but no person shall be deemed to have violated this subsection if he proves that notwithstanding the exercise of good faith he was unable to make such delivery or deposit within such time, or that to do so would cause undue inconvenience or expense.

(d) The provisions of subsection (b) of this section shall not apply to any purchase and sale, or sale and purchase, and the provisions of subsection (c) of this section shall not apply to any sale, of an equity security not then or theretofore held by him in an investment account, by a dealer in the ordinary course of his business and incident to the establishment or maintenance by him of a primary or secondary market (otherwise than on a national securities exchange or an exchange exempted from registration under section 5 of this title) for such security. The Commission may, by such rules and regulations as it deems necessary or appropriate in the public interest, define and prescribe terms and conditions with respect to securities held in an investment account and transactions made in the ordinary course of business and incident to the establishment or maintenance of a primary or secondary market.

(e) The provisions of this section shall not apply to foreign or domestic arbitrage transactions unless made in contravention of such rules and regulations as the Commission may adopt in order to carry out the purposes of this section.

Accounts and Records, Reports, Examinations of Exchanges, Members, and Others

Section 17. (a)(1) Every national securities exchange, member thereof, broker or dealer who transacts a business in securities through the medium of any such member, registered securities association, registered broker or dealer, registered municipal securities dealer, registered securities information processor, registered transfer agent, and registered clearing agency and the Municipal Securities Rulemaking Board shall make and keep for prescribed periods such records, furnish such copies thereof, and make and disseminate such reports as the Commission, by rule, prescribes as necessary or appropriate in the public interest, for the protection of investors, or otherwise in furtherance of the purposes of this title.

(2) Every registered clearing agency shall also make and keep for prescribed periods such records, furnish such copies thereof, and make and disseminate such reports, as the appropriate regulatory agency for such clearing agency, by rule, prescribes as necessary or appropriate for the safeguarding of

securities and funds in the custody or control of such clearing agency or for which it is responsible.

(3) Every registered transfer agent shall also make and keep for prescribed periods such records, furnish such copies thereof, and make such reports as the appropriate regulatory agency for such transfer agent, by rule, prescribes as necessary or appropriate in furtherance of the purposes of section 17A of this title.

(b) All records of persons described in subsection (a) of this section are subject at any time, or from time to time, to such reasonable periodic, special, or other examinations by representatives of the Commission and the appropriate regulatory agency for such persons as the Commission or the appropriate regulatory agency for such persons deems necessary or appropriate in the public interest, for the protection of investors, or otherwise in furtherance of the purposes of this title: Provided, however, That the Commission shall, prior to conducting any such examination of a registered clearing agency, registered transfer agent, or registered municipal securities dealer for which it is not the appropriate regulatory agency, give notice to the appropriate regulatory agency for such clearing agency, transfer agent, or municipal securities dealer of such proposed examination and consult with such appropriate regulatory agency concerning the feasibility and desirability of coordinating such examination with examinations conducted by such appropriate regulatory agency with a view to avoiding unnecessary regulatory duplication or undue regulatory burdens for such clearing agency, transfer agent, or municipal securities dealer. Nothing in the proviso to the preceding sentence shall be construed to impair or limit (other than by the requirement of prior consultation) the power of the Commission under this subsection to examine any clearing agency, transfer agent, or municipal securities dealer or to affect in any way the power of the Commission under any other provision of this title or otherwise to inspect, examine, or investigate any such clearing agency, transfer agent, or municipal securities dealer.

* * *

(e)(1)(A) Every registered broker or dealer shall annually file with the Commission a balance sheet and income statement certified by an independent public accountant, prepared on a calendar or fiscal year basis, and such other financial statements (which shall, as the Commission specifies, be certified) and information concerning its financial condition as the Commission, by rule, may prescribe as necessary or appropriate in the public interest or for the protection of investors.

(B) Every registered broker and dealer shall annually send to its customers its certified balance sheet and such other financial statements and information concerning its financial condition as the Commission, by rule, may prescribe pursuant to subsection (a) of this section.

* * *

National System for Clearance and Settlement of Securities Transactions

Section 17A. (a)(1) The Congress finds that—

(A) The prompt and accurate clearance and settlement of securities transactions, including the transfer of record ownership and the safeguarding of securities and funds related thereto, are necessary for the protection of investors and persons facilitating transactions by and acting on behalf of investors.

(B) Inefficient procedures for clearance and settlement impose unnecessary costs on investors and persons facilitating transactions by and acting on behalf of investors.

(C) New data processing and communications techniques create the opportunity for more efficient, effective, and safe procedures for clearance and settlement.

(D) The linking of all clearance and settlement facilities and the development of uniform standards and procedures for clearance and settlement will reduce unnecessary costs and increase the protection of investors and persons facilitating transactions by and acting on behalf of investors.

(2) The Commission is directed, therefore, having due regard for the public interest, the protection of investors, the safeguarding of securities and funds, and maintenance of fair competition among brokers and dealers, clearing agencies, and transfer agents, to use its authority under this title to facilitate the establishment of a national system for the prompt and accurate clearance and settlement of transactions in securities (other than exempted se-

curities) in accordance with the findings and to carry out the objectives set forth in paragraph (1) of this subsection. The Commission shall use its authority under this title to assure equal regulation under this title of registered clearing agencies and registered transfer agents.

(b)(1) Except as otherwise provided in this section, it shall be unlawful for any clearing agency, unless registered in accordance with this subsection, directly or indirectly, to make use of the mails or any means or instrumentality of interstate commerce to perform the functions of a clearing agency with respect to any security (other than an exempted security). * * *

* * *

(c)(1) Except as otherwise provided in this section, it shall be unlawful for any transfer agent, unless registered in accordance with this section, directly or indirectly, to make use of the mails or any means or instrumentality of interstate commerce to perform the function of a transfer agent with respect to any security registered under section 12 of this title or which would be required to be registered except for the exemption from registration provided by subsection (g)(2)(B) or (g)(2)(G) of that section. * * *

(2) A transfer agent may be registered by filing with the appropriate regulatory agency for such transfer agent an application for registration in such form and containing such information and documents concerning such transfer agent as such appropriate regulatory agency may prescribe as necessary or appropriate in furtherance of the purposes of this section. * * *

* * *

(e) The Commission shall use its authority under this title to end the physical movement of securities certificates in connection with the settlement among brokers and dealers of transactions in securities consummated by means of the mails or any means or instrumentalities of interstate commerce.

Liability for Misleading Statements

Section 18. (a) Any person who shall make or cause to be made any statement in any application, report, or document filed pursuant to this title or any rule or regulation thereunder or any undertaking contained in a registration statement as provided in subsection (d) of section 15 of this title, which statement was at the time and in the light of the circumstances under which it was made false or misleading with respect to any material fact, shall be liable to any person (not knowing that such statement was false or misleading) who, in reliance upon such statement, shall have purchased or sold a security at a price which was affected by such statement, for damages caused by such reliance, unless the person sued shall prove that he acted in good faith and had no knowledge that such statement was false or misleading. A person seeking to enforce such liability may sue at law or in equity in any court of competent jurisdiction. In any such suit the court may, in its discretion, require an undertaking for the payment of the costs of such suit, and assess reasonable costs, including reasonable attorneys' fees, against either party litigant.

(b) Every person who becomes liable to make payment under this section may recover contribution as in cases of contact from any person who, if joined in the original suit, would have been liable to make the same payment.

(c) No action shall be maintained to enforce any liability created under this section unless brought within one year after the discovery of the facts constituting the cause of action and within three years after such cause of action accrued.

Registration, Responsibilities, and Oversight of Self-Regulatory Organizations

Section 19. (a)(1) The Commission shall, upon the filing of an application for registration as a national securities exchange, registered securities association, or registered clearing agency, pursuant to section 6, 15A, or 17A of this title, respectively, publish notice of such filing and afford interested persons an opportunity to submit written data, views, and arguments concerning such application. * * *

The Commission shall grant such registration if it finds that the requirements of this title and the rules and regulations thereunder with respect to the applicant are satisfied. The Commission shall deny such registration if it does not make such finding.

* * *

(b)(1) Each self-regulatory organization shall file with the Commission, in accordance with such rules as the Commission may prescribe, copies of any proposed rule or any proposed change in, addition to, or deletion from the rules of such self-regulatory organization (hereinafter in this subsection collectively referred to as a "proposed rule change") accompanied by a concise general statement of the basis and purpose of such proposed rule change. The Commission shall, upon the filing of any proposed rule change, publish notice thereof together with the terms of substance of the proposed rule change or a description of the subjects and issues involved. The Commission shall give interested persons an opportunity to submit written data, views, and arguments concerning such proposed rule change. No proposed rule change shall take effect unless approved by the Commission or otherwise permitted in accordance with the provisions of this subsection.

* * *

(c) The Commission, by rule, may abrogate, add to, and delete from (hereinafter in this subsection collectively referred to as "amend") the rules of a self-regulatory organization (other than a registered clearing agency) as the Commission deems necessary or appropriate to insure the fair administration of the self-regulatory organization, to conform its rules to requirements of this title and the rules and regulations thereunder applicable to such organization, or otherwise in furtherance of the purposes of this title * * *.

* * *

(d)(1) If any self-regulatory organization imposes any final disciplinary sanction on any member thereof or participant therein, denies membership or participation to any applicant, or prohibits or limits any person in respect to access to services offered by such organization or member thereof or if any self-regulatory organization (other than a registered clearing agency) imposes any final disciplinary sanction on any person associated with a member or bars any person from becoming associated with a member, the self-regulatory organization shall promptly file notice thereof with the appropriate regulatory agency for the self-regulatory organization and (if other than the appropriate regulatory agency for the self-regulatory organization) the appropriate regulatory agency for such member, participant, applicant, or other person. The notice shall be in such form and contain such information as the appropriate regulatory agency for the self-regulatory organization, by rule, may prescribe as necessary or appropriate in furtherance of the purposes of this title.

(2) Any action with respect to which a self-regulatory organization is required by paragraph (1) of this subsection to file notice shall be subject to review by the appropriate regulatory agency for such member, participant, applicant, or other person, on its own motion, or upon application by any person aggrieved thereby filed within thirty days after the date such notice was filed with such appropriate regulatory agency and received by such aggrieved person, or within such longer period as such appropriate regulatory agency may determine. * *

* * *

(g)(1) Every self-regulatory organization shall comply with the provisions of this title, the rules and regulations thereunder, and its own rules, and (subject to the provisions of section 17(d) of this title, paragraph (2) of this subsection, and the rules thereunder) absent reasonable justification or excuse enforce compliance—

(A) in the case of a national securities exchange, with such provisions by its members and persons associated with its members;

(B) in the case of a registered securities association, with such provisions and the provisions of the rules of the Municipal Securities Rulemaking Board by its members and persons associated with its members; and

(C) in the case of a registered clearing agency, with its own rules by its participants.

* * *

Liabilities of Controlling Persons

Section 20. (a) Every person who, directly or indirectly, controls any person liable under any provision of this title or of any rule or regulation thereunder shall also be liable jointly and severally with and to the same extent as such controlled person to any person to whom such controlled person is liable, unless the controlling person acted in good faith and did not directly or indirectly induce the act or acts constituting the violation or cause of action.

(b) It shall be unlawful for any person, directly or indirectly, to do any act or thing which it would be unlawful for such person to do under the provisions of this title or any rule or regulation thereunder through or by means of any other person.

(c) It shall be unlawful for any director or officer of, or any owner of any securities issued by, any issuer required to file any document, report, or information under this title or any rule or regulation thereunder without just cause to hinder, delay, or obstruct the making or filing of any such document, report, or information.

(d) Wherever communicating, or purchasing or selling a security while in possession of, material nonpublic information would violate, or result in liability to any purchaser or seller of the security under any provision of this title, or any rule or regulation thereunder, such conduct in connection with a purchase or sale of a put, call, straddle, option, or privilege with respect to such security or with respect to a group or index of securities including such security, shall also violate and result in comparable liability to any purchaser or seller of that security under such provision, rule, or regulation.

Investigations; Injunctions and Prosecution of Offenses

Section 21. (a) The Commission may, in its discretion, make such investigations as it deems necessary to determine whether any person has violated, is violating, or is about to violate any provision of this title, the rules or regulations thereunder, the rules of a national securities exchange or registered securities association of which such person is a member or a person associated with a member, the rules of a registered clearing agency in which such person is a participant, or the rules of the Municipal Securities Rulemaking Board, and may require or permit any person to file with it a statement in writing, under oath or otherwise as the Commission shall determine, as to all the facts and circumstances concerning the matter to be investigated. The Commission is authorized in its discretion, to publish information concerning any such violations, and to investigate any facts, conditions, practices, or matters which it may deem necessary or proper to aid in the enforcement of such provisions, in the prescribing of rules and regulations under this title, or in securing information to serve as a basis for recommending further legislation concerning the matters to which this title relates.

(b) For the purpose of any such investigation, or any other proceeding under this title, any member of the Commission or any officer designated by it is empowered to administer oaths and affirmations, subpena witnesses, compel their attendance, take evidence, and require the production of any books, papers, correspondence, memoranda, or other records which the Commission deems relevant or material to the inquiry. Such attendance of witnesses and the production of any such records may be required from any place in the United States or any State at any designated place of hearing.

(c) In case of contumacy by, or refusal to obey a subpena issued to, any person, the Commission may invoke the aid of any court of the United States within the jurisdiction of which such investigation or proceeding is carried on, or where such person resides or carries on business, in requiring the attendance and testimony of witnesses and the production of books, papers, correspondence, memoranda, and other records. And such court may issue an order requiring such person to appear before the Commission or member or officer designated by the Commission, there to produce records, if so ordered, or to give testimony touching the matter under investigation or in question; and any failure to obey such order of the court may be punished by such court as a contempt thereof. All process in any such case may be served in the judicial district whereof such person is an inhabitant or wherever he may be found. Any person who shall, without just cause, fail or refuse to attend and testify or to answer any lawful inquiry or to produce books, papers, correspondence, memoranda, and other records, if in his power so to do, in obedience to the subpena of the Commission, shall be guilty of a misdemeanor and, upon conviction, shall be subject to a fine of not more than $1,000 or to imprisonment for a term of not more than one year, or both.

(d)(1) Wherever it shall appear to the Commission that any person is engaged or is about to engage in acts or practices constituting a violation of any provision of this title, the rules or regulations thereunder, the rules of a national securities exchange or registered securities association of which such person is a member or a person associated with a member, the rules of a registered clearing agency in which such person is a participant, or the rules of the Municipal Securities Rulemaking Board, it may in its discretion bring an action in the proper district court of the United States, the United States District Court for the District of Columbia, or the United States courts of any territory or other place subject to the jurisdiction of the United States, to enjoin such acts or practices, and upon a proper showing a permanent or temporary injunction or restraining order shall be granted without bond. The Commission may transmit such evidence as may be available concerning such acts or practices as may constitute a violation of any provision of this title or the rules or regulations thereunder to the Attorney General, who may, in his discretion, institute the necessary criminal proceedings under this title.

(2)(A) Whenever it shall appear to the Commission that any person has violated any provision of this title or the rules or regulations thereunder by purchasing or selling a security while in possession of material nonpublic information in a transaction (i) on or through the facilities of a national securities exchange or from or through a broker or dealer, and (ii) which is not part of a public offering by an issuer of securities other than standardized options, the Commission may bring an action in a United States district court to seek, and the court shall have jurisdiction to impose, a civil penalty to be paid by such person, or any person aiding and abetting the violation of such person. The amount of such penalty shall be determined by the court in light of the facts and circumstances, but shall not exceed three times the profit gained or loss avoided as a result of such unlawful purchase or sale, and shall be payable into the Treasury of the United States. If a person upon whom such a penalty is imposed shall fail to pay such penalty within the time prescribed in the court's order, the Commission shall refer the matter to the Attorney General who shall recover such penalty by action in the appropriate United States district court. The actions authorized by this paragraph may be brought in addition to any other actions that the Commission or the Attorney General are entitled to bring. For purposes of section 27 of this title, actions under this paragraph shall be actions to enforce a liability or a duty created by this title. The Commission, by rule or regulation, may exempt from the provisions of this paragraph any class of persons or transactions.

(B) No person shall be subject to a sanction under subparagraph (A) of this paragraph solely because that person aided and abetted a transaction covered by such subparagraph in a manner other than by communicating material nonpublic information. Section 20(a) of this title shall not apply to an action brought under this paragraph. No person shall be liable under this paragraph solely by reason of employing another person who is liable under this paragraph.

(C) For purposes of this paragraph "profit gained" or "loss avoided" is the difference between the purchase or sale price of the security and the value of that security as measured by the trading price of the security a reasonable period after public dissemination of the nonpublic information.

(D) No action may be brought under this paragraph more than five years after the date of the purchase or sale. This paragraph shall not be construed to bar or limit in any manner any action by the Commission or the Attorney General under any other provision of this title, nor shall it bar or limit in any manner any action to recover penalties, or to seek any other order regarding penalties, imposed in an action commenced within five years of such transaction.

(e) Upon application of the Commission the district courts of the United States, the United States District Court for the District of Columbia, and the United States courts of any territory or other place subject to the jurisdiction of the United States shall have jurisdiction to issue writs of mandamus, injunctions, and orders commanding (1) any person to comply with the provisions of this title, the rules, regulations, and orders thereunder, the rules of a national securities exchange or registered securities association of which such person is a member or person associated with a member, the rules of a registered clearing agency in which such person is a participant, the rules of the Municipal Securities Rulemaking Board, or any undertaking contained in a registration statement as provided in subsection (d) of section 15 of this title, (2) any national securities exchange or registered securities association to enforce compliance by its members and persons associated with its members with the provisions of this title, the rules, regulations, and orders thereunder, and the rules of such exchange or association, or (3) any registered clearing agency to enforce compliance by its participants with the provisions of the rules of such clearing agency.

(f) Notwithstanding any other provision of this title, the Commission shall not bring any action pursuant to subsection (d) or (e) of this section against any person for violation of, or to command compliance with, the rules of a self-regulatory organization unless it appears to the Commission that (1) such self-regulatory organization is unable or unwilling to take appropriate action against such person in the public interest and for the protection of investors, or (2) such action is otherwise necessary or appropriate in the public interest or for the protection of investors.

(g) Notwithstanding the provisions of section 1407(a) of title 28, United States Code, or any other provision of law, no action for equitable relief instituted by the Commission pursuant to the securities laws shall be consolidated or coordinated with other actions not brought by the Commission, even though such other actions may involve common questions of fact, unless such consolidation is consented to by the Commission. The term "securities laws" as used herein includes the Securities Act of 1933, the Securities Exchange Act of 1934, the Public Utility Holding Company Act of 1935, the Trust Indenture Act of 1939, the Investment Company Act of 1940, the Investment Advisers Act of 1940, and the Securities Investor Protection Act of 1970.

(h)(1) The Right to Financial Privacy Act of 1978 shall apply with respect to the Commission, except as otherwise provided in this subsection.

(2) Notwithstanding section 1105 or 1107 of the Right to Financial Privacy Act of 1978, the Commission may have access to and obtain copies of, or the information contained in financial records of a customer from a financial institution without prior notice to the customer upon an ex parte showing to an appropriate United States district court that the Commission seeks such financial records pursuant to a subpena issued in conformity with the requirements of section 19(b) of the Securities Act of 1933, section 21(b) of the Securities Exchange Act of 1934, section 18(c) of the Public Utility Holding Company Act of 1935, section 42(b) of the Investment Company Act of 1940, or section 209(b) of the Investment Advisers Act of 1940, and that the Commission has reason to believe that—

(A) delay in obtaining access to such financial records, or the required notice, will result in—

(i) flight from prosecution;

(ii) destruction of or tampering with evidence;

(iii) transfer of assets or records outside the territorial limits of the United States;

(iv) improper conversion of investor assets; or

(v) impeding the ability of the Commission to identify or trace the source or disposition of funds involved in any securities transaction;

(B) such financial records are necessary to identify or trace the record or beneficial ownership interest in any security;

(C) the acts, practices or course of conduct under investigation involve—

(i) the dissemination of materially false or misleading information concerning any security, issuer, or market, or the failure to make disclosures required under the securities laws, which remain uncorrected; or

(ii) a financial loss to investors or other persons protected under the securities laws which remains substantially uncompensated; or

(D) the acts, practices or course of conduct under investigation—

(i) involve significant financial speculation in securities; or

(ii) endanger the stability of any financial or investment intermediary.

* * *

Hearings by Commission

Section 22. Hearings may be public and may be held before the Commission, any member or members thereof, or any officer or officers of the Commission designated by it, and appropriate records thereof shall be kept.

Rules, Regulations, and Orders; Annual Reports

Section 23. (a)(1) The Commission, the Board of Governors of the Federal Reserve System, and the other agencies enumerated in section 3(a)(34) of this title shall each have power to make such rules and regulations as may be necessary or appropriate to implement the provisions of this title for which they are responsible or for the execution of the functions vested in them by this title, and may for such purposes classify persons, securities, transactions, statements, applications, reports, and other matters within their respective jurisdictions, and prescribe greater, lesser, or different requirements for different classes thereof. No provision of this title imposing any liability shall apply to any act done or omitted in good faith in conformity with a rule, regulation, or order of the Commission, the Board of Governors of the Federal Reserve System, other agency enumerated in section 3(a)(34) of this title, any self-regulatory organization, notwithstanding that such rule, regulation, or order may thereafter be amended or rescinded or determined by judicial or other authority to be invalid for any reason.

(2) The Commission and the Secretary of the Treasury, in making rules and regulations pursuant to any provisions of this title, shall consider among other matters the impact any such rule or regulation would have on competition. The Commission and the Secretary of the Treasury shall not adopt any such rule or regulation which would impose a burden on competition not necessary or appropriate in furtherance of the purposes of this title. The Commission and the Secretary of the Treasury shall include in the statement of basis and purpose incorporated in any rule or regulation adopted under this title, the reasons for the Commission's or the Secretary's determination that any burden on competition imposed by such rule or regulation is necessary or appropriate in furtherance of the purposes of this title.

(3) The Commission and the Secretary in making rules and regulations pursuant to any provision of this title, considering any application for registration in accordance with section 19(a) of this title, or reviewing any proposed rule change of a self-regulatory organization in accordance with section 19(b) of this title, keep in a public file and make available for copying all written statements filed with the Commission and the Secretary and all written communications between the Commission or the Secretary and any person relating to the proposed rule, regulation, application, or proposed rule change; Provided, however, That the Commission and the Secretary shall not be required to keep in a public file or make available for copying any such statement or communication which it may withhold from the public in accordance with the provisions of section 552 of title 5, United States Code.

* * *

Public Availability of Information

Section 24. (a) For purposes of section 552 of title 5, United States Code, the term "records" includes all applications, statements, reports, contracts, correspondence, notices, and other documents filed with or otherwise obtained by the Commission pursuant to this title or otherwise.

(b) It shall be unlawful for any member, officer, or employee of the Commission to disclose to any person other than a member, officer, or employee of the Commission, or to use for personal benefit, any information contained in any application, statement, report, contract, correspondence, notice, or other document filed with or otherwise obtained by the Commission (1) in contravention of the rules and regulations of the Commission under section 552 of title 5, United States Code, or (2) in circumstances where the Commission has determined pursuant to such rules to accord confidential treatment to such information. Nothing in this subsection shall authorize the Commission to withhold information from the Congress.

Court Review of Orders and Rules

Section 25. (a)(1) A person aggrieved by a final order of the Commission entered pursuant to this title may obtain review of the order in the United States Court of Appeals for the circuit in which he resides or has his principal place of business, or for the District of Columbia Circuit, by filing in such court, within sixty days after the entry of the order, a written petition requesting that the order be modified or set aside in whole or in part.

* * *

Unlawful Representations

Section 26. No action or failure to act by the Commission or the Board of Governors of the Federal Reserve System, in the administration of this title shall be construed to mean that the particular authority has in any way passed upon the merits of, or given approval to, any security or any transaction or transactions therein, nor shall such action or failure to act with regard to any statement or report filed with or examined by such authority pursuant to this title or rules and regulations thereunder, be deemed a finding by such authority that such statement or report is true and accurate on its face or that it is not false or misleading. It shall be unlawful to make, or cause to be made, to any prospective purchaser or seller of a security any representation that any such action or failure to act by any such authority is to be so construed or has such effect.

Jurisdiction of Offenses and Suits

Section 27. The district courts of the United States, the United States District Court for the District of Columbia, and the United States courts of any Territory or other place subject to the jurisdiction of the United States shall have exclusive jurisdiction of violations of this title or the rules and regulations thereunder, and of all suits in equity and actions at law brought to enforce any liability or duty created by this title or the rules and regulations thereunder. Any criminal proceeding may be brought in the district wherein any act or transaction constituting the violation occurred. Any suit or action to enforce any liability or duty created by this title or rules and regulations thereunder, or enjoin any violation of such title or rules and regulations, may be brought in any such district or in the district wherein the defendant is found or is an inhabitant or transacts business, and process in such cases may be served in any other district of which the defendant is an inhabitant or wherever the defendant may be found. Judgments and decrees so rendered shall be subject to review as provided in sections 128 and 240 of the Judicial Code, as amended (U.S.C., title 28, secs. 225 and 347). No costs shall be assessed for or against the Commission in any proceeding under this title brought by or against it in the Supreme Court or such other courts.

Effect on Existing Law

Section 28. (a) The rights and remedies provided by this title shall be in addition to any and all other rights and remedies that may exist at law or in equity; but no person permitted to maintain a suit for damages under the provisions of this title shall recover, through satisfaction of judgment in one or more actions, a total amount in excess of his actual damages on account of the act complained of. Nothing in this title shall affect the jurisdiction of the securities commission (or any agency or officer performing like functions) of any State over any security or any person insofar as it does not conflict with the provisions of this title or the rules and regulations thereunder.

(b) Nothing in this title shall be construed to modify existing law with regard to the binding effect (1) on any member of or participant in any self-regulatory organization of any action taken by the authorities of such organization to settle disputes between its members or participants, (2) on any municipal securities dealer or municipal securities broker of any action taken pursuant to a procedure established by the Municipal Securities Rulemaking Board to settle disputes between municipal securities dealers and municipal securities brokers, or (3) of any action described in paragraph (1) or (2) on any person who has agreed to be bound thereby.

(c) The stay, setting aside, or modification pursuant to section 19(e) of this title of any disciplinary sanction imposed by a self-regulatory organization or a member thereof, person associated with a member, or participant therein, shall not affect the validity or force of any action taken as a result of such sanction by the self-regulatory organization prior to such stay, setting aside, or modification: Provided, That such action is not inconsistent with the provisions of this title or the rules or regulations thereunder. The rights of any person acting in good faith which arise out of any such action shall not be affected in any way by such stay, setting aside, or modification.

(d) No State or political subdivision thereof shall impose any tax on any change in beneficial or record ownership of securities effected through the facilities of a registered clearing agency or registered transfer agent or any nominee thereof or custodian therefor or upon the delivery or transfer of securities to or through or receipt from such agency or agent or any nominee thereof or custodian therefor, unless such change in beneficial or record ownership or such transfer or delivery or receipt would otherwise be taxable by such State or political subdivision if the facilities of such registered clearing agency, registered transfer agent, or any nominee thereof or custodian therefor were not physically located in the taxing State or political subdivision. No State or political subdivision thereof shall impose any tax on securities which are deposited in or retained by a registered clearing agency, registered transfer agent, or any nominee thereof or custodian therefor, unless such securities would otherwise be taxable by such State or political subdivision if the facilities of such registered clearing agency, registered transfer agent, or any nominee thereof or custodian therefor were not physically located in the taxing State or political subdivision.

(e)(1) No person using the mails, or any means or instrumentality of interstate commerce, in the exercise of investment discretion with respect to an account shall be deemed to have acted unlawfully or to have breached a fiduciary duty under State or Federal law unless expressly provided to the contrary by a law enacted by the Congress or any State subsequent to the date of enactment of the Securities Acts Amendments in 1975 solely by reason of his having caused the account to pay a member of an exchange, broker, or dealer an amount of commission for effecting a securities transaction in excess of the amount of commission another member of an exchange, broker, or dealer would have charged for effecting that transaction, if such person determined in good faith that such amount of commission was reasonable in relation to the value of the brokerage and research services provided by such member, broker, or dealer, viewed in terms of either that particular transaction or his overall responsibilities with respect to the accounts as to which he exercises investment discretion. This subsection is exclusive and plenary insofar as conduct is covered by the foregoing, unless otherwise expressly provided by contract: Provided, however, That nothing in this subsection shall be construed to impair or limit the power of the Commission under any other provision of this title or otherwise.

(2) A person exercising investment discretion with respect to an account shall make such disclosure of his policies and practices with respect to commissions that will be paid for effecting securities transactions, at such times and in such manner, as the appropriate regulatory agency, by rule, may prescribe as necessary or appropriate in the public interest or for the protection of investors.

(3) For purposes of this subsection a person provides brokerage and research services insofar as he—

(A) furnishes advice, either directly or through publications or writings, as to the value of securities, the advisability of investing in, purchasing, or selling securities, and the availability of securities or purchasers or sellers of securities;

(B) furnishes analyses and reports concerning issuers, industries, securities, economic factors and trends, portfolio strategy, and the performance of accounts; or

(C) effects securities transactions and performs functions incidental thereto (such as clearance, settlement, and custody) or required in connection therewith by rules of the Commission or a self-regulatory organization of which such person is a member or person associated with a member or in which such person is a participant.

Validity of Contracts

Section 29. (a) Any condition, stipulation, or provision binding any person to waive compliance with any provision of this title or of any rule or regulation thereunder, or of any rule of an exchange required thereby shall be void.

(b) Every contract made in violation of any provision of this title or of any rule or regulation thereunder, and every contract (including any contract for listing a security on an exchange) heretofore or hereafter made the performance of which involves the violation of, or the continuance of any relationship or practice in violation of, any provision of this title or any rule or regulation thereunder, shall be void (1) as regards the rights of any person who, in violation of any such provision, rule, or regulation, shall have made or engaged in the performance of any such contract, and (2) as regards the rights of any person who, not being a party to such contract, shall have acquired any right thereunder with actual knowledge of the facts by reason of which the making or performance of such contract was in violation of any such provision, rule, or regulation: *Provided,* (A) That no contract shall be void by reason of this subsection because of any violation of any rule or regulation prescribed pursuant to paragraph (2) or (3) of subsection (c) of section 15 of this title, and (B) that no contract shall be deemed to be void by reason of this subsection in any action maintained in reliance upon this subsection, by any person to or for whom any broker or dealer sells, or from or for whom any broker or dealer purchases, a security in violation of any rule or regulation prescribed pursuant to paragraph (1) of subsection (c) of section 15 of this title, unless such action is brought within one year after the discovery that such sale or purchase involves such violation and within three years after such violation.

(c) Nothing in this title shall be construed (1) to affect the validity of any loan or extension of credit (or any extension or renewal thereof) made or of any lien created prior or subsequent to the enactment of this title, unless at the time of the making of such loan or extension of credit (or extension or renewal thereof) or the creating of such lien, the person making such loan or extension of credit (or extension or renewal thereof) or acquiring such lien shall have actual knowledge of facts by reason of which the making of such loan or extension of credit (or extension or renewal thereof) or the acquisition of such lien is a violation of the provisions of this title or any rule or regulation thereunder, or (2) to afford a defense to the collection of any debt or obligation or the enforcement of any lien by any person who shall have acquired such debt, obligation, or lien in good faith for value and without actual knowledge of the violation of any provision of this title or any rule or regulation thereunder affecting the legality of such debt, obligation, or lien.

Foreign Securities Exchanges

Section 30. (a) It shall be unlawful for any broker or dealer, directly or indirectly, to make use of the mails or of any means or instrumentality of interstate commerce for the purpose of effecting on an exchange not within or subject to the jurisdiction of the United States, any transaction in any security the issuer of which is a resident of, or is organized under the laws of, or has its principal place of business in, a place within or subject to the jurisdiction of the United States, in contravention of such rules and regulations as the Commission may prescribe as necessary or appropriate in the public interest or for the protection of investors or to prevent the evasion of this title.

(b) The provisions of this title or of any rule or regulation thereunder shall not apply to any person insofar as he transacts a business in securities without the jurisdiction of the United States, unless he transacts such business in contravention of such rules and regulations as the Commission may prescribe as necessary or appropriate to prevent the evasion of this title.

Foreign Corrupt Practices by Issuers

Section 30A. (a) It shall be unlawful for any issuer which has a class of securities registered pursuant to section 12 of this title or which is required to file reports under section 15(d) of this title, or for any officer, director, employee, or agent of such issuer or any stockholder thereof acting on behalf of such issuer, to make use of the mails or any means or instrumentality of interstate commerce corruptly in furtherance of an offer, payment, promise to pay, or authorization of the payment of any money, or offer, gift, promise to give, or authorization of the giving of anything of value to—

(1) any foreign official for purposes of—

(A) influencing any act or decision of such foreign official in his official capacity, including a decision to fail to perform his official functions; or

(B) inducing such foreign official to use his influence with a foreign government or instrumentality thereof to affect or influence any act or decision of such government or instrumentality;

in order to assist such issuer in obtaining or retaining business for or with, or directing business to, any person;

(2) any foreign political party or official thereof or any candidate for foreign political office for purposes of—

(A) influencing any act or decision of such party, official, or candidate in its or his official capacity, including a decision to fail to perform its or his official functions; or

(B) inducing such party, official, or candidate to use its or his influence with a foreign government or instrumentality thereof to affect or influence any act or decision of such government or instrumentality,

in order to assist such issuer in obtaining or retaining business for or with, or directing business to, any person; or

(3) any person, while knowing or having reason to know that all or a portion of such money or thing

of value will be offered, given, or promised, directly or indirectly, to any foreign official, to any foreign political party or official thereof, or to any candidate for foreign political office, for purposes of—

(A) influencing any act or decision of such foreign official, political party, party official, or candidate in his or its official capacity, including a decision to fail to perform his or its official functions; or

(B) inducing such foreign official, political party, party official, or candidate to use his or its influence with a foreign government or instrumentality thereof to affect or influence any act or decision of such government or instrumentality,

in order to assist such issuer in obtaining or retaining business for or with, or directing business to, any person.

(b) As used in this section, the term "foreign official" means any officer or employee of a foreign government or any department, agency, or instrumentality thereof, or any person acting in an official capacity for or on behalf of such government or department, agency, or instrumentality. Such term does not include any employee of a foreign government or any department, agency, or instrumentality thereof whose duties are essentially ministerial or clerical.

Transaction Fees

Section 31. Every national securities exchange shall pay to the Commission on or before March 15 of each calendar year a fee in an amount equal to one three-hundredths of 1 per centum of the aggregate dollar amount of the sales of securities (other than bonds, debentures, and other evidences of indebtedness) transacted on such national securities exchange during each preceding calendar year to which this section applies. Every registered broker and dealer shall pay to the Commission on or before March 15 of each calendar year a fee in an amount equal to one three-hundredths of 1 per centum of the aggregate dollar amount of the sales of securities registered on a national securities exchange (other than bonds, debentures, and other evidences of indebtedness) transacted by such broker or dealer otherwise than on such an exchange during each preceding calendar year: Provided, however, That no payment shall be required for any calendar year in which such payment would be less than one hundred dollars. The Commission, by rule, may exempt any sale of securities or any class of sales of securities from any fee imposed by this section, if the Commission finds that such exemption is consistent with the public interest, the equal regulation of markets and brokers and dealers, and the development of a national market system.

Penalties

Section 32. (a) Any person who willfully violates any provision of this title (other than section 30A), or any rule or regulation thereunder the violation of which is made unlawful or the observance of which is required under the terms of this title, or any person who willfully and knowingly makes, or causes to be made, any statement in any application, report, or document required to be filed under this title or any rule or regulation thereunder or any undertaking contained in a registration statement as provided in subsection (d) of section 15 of this title, or by any self-regulatory organization in connection with an application for membership or participation therein or to become associated with a member thereof, which statement was false or misleading with respect to any material fact, shall upon conviction be fined not more than $100,000, or imprisoned not more than five years, or both, except that when such person is an exchange, a fine not exceeding $500,000 may be imposed; but no person shall be subject to imprisonment under this section for the violation of any rule or regulation if he proves that he had no knowledge of such rule or regulation.

(b) Any issuer which fails to file information, documents, or reports required to be filed under subsection (d) of section 15 of this title or any rule or regulation thereunder shall forfeit to the United States the sum of $100 for each and every day such failure to file shall continue. Such forfeiture, which shall be in lieu of any criminal penalty for such failure to file which might be deemed to arise under subsection (a) of this section, shall be payable into the Treasury of the United States and shall be recoverable in a civil suit in the name of the United States.

(c)(1) Any issuer which violates section 30A(a) of this title shall, upon conviction, be fined not more than $1,000,000.

(2) Any officer or director of an issuer, or any stockholder acting on behalf of such issuer, who willfully violates section 30A(a) of this title shall, upon conviction, be fined not more than $10,000, or imprisoned not more than five years, or both.

(3) Whenever an issuer is found to have violated section 30A(a) of this title, any employee or agent of such issuer who is a United States citizen, national, or resident or is otherwise subject to the jurisdiction of the United States (other than an officer, director, or stockholder of such issuer), and who willfully carried out the act or practice constituting such violation shall, upon conviction, be fined not more than $10,000, or imprisoned not more than five years, or both.

(4) Whenever a fine is imposed under paragraph (2) or (3) of this subsection upon any officer, director, stockholder, employee, or agent of an issuer, such fine shall not be paid, directly or indirectly, by such issuer.

Separability of Provisions

Section 33. If any provision of this act, or the application of such provision to any person or circumstances, shall be held invalid, the remainder of the act, and the application of such provision to persons or circumstances other than those as to which it is held invalid, shall not be affected thereby.

* * *

TITLE II—AMENDMENTS TO THE SECURITIES ACT OF 1933

[Sections 201 to 209 of Public No. 291, 73d Cong. (48 Stat. 905), the Securities Exchange Act of 1934, are amendments to the Securities Act of 1933.]

Section 210. Upon the expiration of sixty days after the date upon which a majority of the members of the Securities and Exchange Commission appointed under Section 4 of title I of this Act, have qualified and taken office, all powers, duties and functions of the Federal Trade Commission under the Securities Act of 1933 shall be transferred to such Commission, together with all property, books, records, and unexpended balances of appropriations used by or available to the Federal Trade Commission for carrying out its functions under the Securities Act of 1933. All proceedings, hearings, or investigations commenced or pending before the Federal Trade Commission arising under the Securities Act of 1933 shall be continued by the Securities and Exchange Commission. All orders, rules, and regulations which have been issued by the Federal Trade Commission under the Securities Act of 1933 and which are in effect shall continue in effect until modified, superseded, revoked, or repealed. All rights and interests accruing or to accrue under the Securities Act of 1933, or any provision of any regulation relating to, or out of action taken by, the Federal Trade Commission under such Act, shall be followed in all respects and may be exercised and enforced.

Section 211. The Commission is authorized and directed to make a study and investigation of the work, activities, personnel, and functions of protective and reorganization committees in connection with the reorganization, readjustment, rehabilitation, liquidation, or consolidation of persons and properties and to report the result of its studies and investigations and its recommendations to the Congress on or before January 3, 1936.

FOREIGN CORRUPT PRACTICES ACT OF 1977

Foreign Corrupt Practices by Domestic Concerns

Section 104. (a) It shall be unlawful for any domestic concern, other than an issuer which is subject to section 30A of the Securities Exchange Act of 1934, or any officer, director, employee, or agent of such domestic concern or any stockholder thereof acting on behalf of such domestic concern, to make use of the mails or any means or instrumentality of interstate commerce corruptly in furtherance of an offer, payment, promise to pay, or authorization of the payment of any money, or offer, gift, promise to give, or authorization of the giving of anything of value to—

(1) any foreign official for purposes of—

(A) influencing any act or decision of such foreign official in his official capacity, including a decision to fail to perform his official functions; or

(B) inducing such foreign official to use his influence with a foreign government or instrumentality thereof to affect or influence any act or decision of such government or instrumentality,

in order to assist such domestic concern in obtaining or retaining business for or with, or directing business to, any person;

(2) any foreign political party or official thereof or any candidate for foreign political office for purposes of—

(A) influencing any act or decision of such party, official, or candidate in its or his official capacity, including a decision to fail to perform its or his official functions; or

(B) inducing such party, official, or candidate to use its or his influence with a foreign government or instrumentality thereof to affect or influence any act or decision of such government or instrumentality,

in order to assist such domestic concern in obtaining or retaining business for or with, or directing business to, any person; or

(3) any person, while knowing or having reason to know that all or a portion of such money or thing of value will be offered, given, or promised, directly or indirectly, to any foreign official, to any foreign political party or official thereof, or to any candidate for foreign political office, for purposes of—

(A) influencing any act or decision of such foreign official, political party, party official, or candidate in his or its official capacity, including a decision to fail to perform his or its official functions; or

(B) inducing such foreign official, political party, party official, or candidate to use his or its influence with a foreign government or instrumentality thereof to affect or influence any act or decision of such government or instrumentality,

in order to assist such domestic concern in obtaining or retaining business for or with, or directing business to, any person.

(b)(1)(A) Except as provided in subparagraph (B), any domestic concern which violates subsection (a) shall, upon conviction, be fined not more than $1,000,000.

(B) Any individual who is a domestic concern and who willfully violates subsection (a) shall, upon conviction, be fined not more than $10,000, or imprisoned not more than five years, or both.

(2) Any officer or director of a domestic concern, or stockholder acting on behalf of such domestic concern, who willfully violates subsection (a) shall, upon conviction, be fined not more than $10,000, or imprisoned not more than five years, or both.

(3) Whenever a domestic concern is found to have violated subsection (a) of this section, any employee or agent of such domestic concern who is a United States citizen, national, or resident or is otherwise subject to the jurisdiction of the United States (other than an officer, director, or stockholder acting on behalf of such domestic concern), and who willfully carried out the act or practice constituting such violation shall, upon conviction, be fined not more than $10,000, or imprisoned not more than five years, or both.

(4) Whenever a fine is imposed under paragraph (2) or (3) of this subsection upon any officer, director, stockholder, employee, or agent of a domestic concern, such fine shall not be paid, directly or indirectly, by such domestic concern.

(c) Whenever it appears to the Attorney General that any domestic concern, or officer, director, employee, agent, or stockholder thereof, is engaged, or is about to engage, in any act or practice constituting a violation of subsection (a) of this section, the Attorney General may, in his discretion, bring a civil action in an appropriate district court of the United States to enjoin such act or practice, and upon a proper showing a permanent or temporary injunction or a temporary restraining order shall be granted without bond.

(d) As used in this section:

(1) The term "domestic concern" means (A) any individual who is a citizen, national, or resident of the United States; or (B) any corporation, partnership, association, joint-stock company, business trust, unincorporated organization, or sole proprietorship which has its principal place of business in the United States, or which is organized under the laws of a State of the United States or a territory, possession, or commonwealth of the United States.

(2) The term "foreign official" means any officer or employee of a foreign government or any department, agency, or instrumentality thereof, or any person acting in an official capacity for or on behalf of any such government or department, agency, or instrumentality. Such term does not include any employee of a foreign government or any department, agency, or instrumentality thereof whose duties are essentially ministerial or clerical.

(3) The term "interstate commerce" means trade, commerce, transportation, or communication among the several States, or between any foreign country and any State or between any State and any place or ship outside thereof. Such term includes the intrastate use of (A) a telephone or other interstate means of communication, or (B) any other interstate instrumentality.

*

B. SELECTED RULES

1. UNDER SECURITIES ACT OF 1933

17 C.F.R. § 230.——

GENERAL

REGULATION A—GENERAL EXEMPTION

1933 ACT RULES

REGULATION C—REGISTRATION

REGULATION D—LIMITED OFFERINGS

GENERAL

* * *

Rule 134. Communications Not Deemed a Prospectus

The term "prospectus" as defined in Section 2(10) of the Act shall not include a notice, circular, advertisement, letter, or other communication published or transmitted to any person after a registration statement has been filed if it contains only the statements required or permitted to be included therein by the following provisions of this rule:

(a) Such communication may include any one or more of the following items of information, which need not follow the numerical sequence of this paragraph:

(1) the name of the issuer of the security;

(2) the full title of the security and the amount being offered;

(3) a brief indication of the general type of business of the issuer, limited to the following:

(i) in the case of a manufacturing company, the general type of manufacturing and the principal products or classes of products manufactured;

(ii) in the case of a public utility company, the general type of services rendered and a brief indication of the area served;

* * *

(iv) in the case of any other type of company, a corresponding statement;

(4) the price of the security, or if the price is not known, the method of its determination or the probable price range as specified by the issuer or the managing underwriter;

(5) in the case of a debt security with a fixed (non-contingent) interest provision, the yield or, if the yield is not known, the probable yield range, as specified by the issuer or the managing underwriter;

(6) the name and address of the sender of the communication and the fact that he is participating, or expects to participate, in the distribution of the security;

(7) the names of the managing underwriters;

(8) the approximate date upon which it is anticipated the proposed sale to the public will commence;

(9) whether, in the opinion of counsel, the security is a legal investment for savings banks, fiduciaries, insurance companies, or similar investors under the laws of any State or Territory or the District of Columbia;

(10) whether, in the opinion of counsel, the security is exempt from specified taxes, or the extent to which the issuer has agreed to pay any tax with respect to the security or measured by the income therefrom;

(11) whether the security is being offered through rights issued to security holders, and, if so, the class of securities the holders of which will be entitled to subscribe, the subscription ratio, the actual or proposed record date, the date upon which the rights were issued or are expected to be issued, the actual or anticipated date upon which they will expire, and the approximate subscription price, or any of the foregoing;

(12) any statement or legend required by any state law or administrative authority.

* * *

(14)(i) With respect to any class of debt securities, any class of convertible debt securities or any class of preferred stock, the security rating or ratings assigned to the class of securities by any nationally recognized statistical rating organization and the name or names of the nationally recognized statistical rating organization(s) which assigned such rating(s).

(ii) For the purpose of paragraph 14(a)(i) of this section, the term "nationally recognized statistical rating organization" shall have the same meaning as used in Rule 15c3–1(c)(2)(vi)(F) under the Securities Exchange Act of 1934.

* * *

(b) Except as provided in paragraph (c), every communication used pursuant to this rule shall contain the following:

(1) if the registration statement has not yet become effective, the following statement:

"A registration statement relating to these securities has been filed with the Securities and Exchange Commission but has not yet become effective. These securities may not be sold nor may offers to buy be accepted prior to the time the registration statement becomes effective. This (communication) shall not constitute an offer to sell or the solicitation of an offer to buy nor shall there be any sale of these securities in any State in which such offer, solicitation or sale would be unlawful prior to registration or qualification under the securities laws of any such State."

(2) a statement whether the security is being offered in connection with a distribution by the issuer or by a security holder, or both, and whether the issue represents new financing or refunding or both; and

(3) the name and address of a person or persons from whom a written prospectus meeting the requirements of Section 10 of the Act may be obtained.

(c) Any of the statements or information specified in paragraph (b) may, but need not, be contained in a communication: (i) which does no more than state from whom a written prospectus meeting the requirements of Section 10 of the Act may be obtained, identify the security, state the price thereof and state by whom orders will be executed; or (ii) which is accompanied or preceded by a prospectus or a summary prospectus which meets the requirements of Section 10 of the Act at the date of such preliminary communication.

(d) A communication sent or delivered to any person pursuant to this rule which is accompanied or preceded by a prospectus which meets the requirements of Section 10 of the Act at the date of such communication, may solicit from the recipient of the communication an offer to buy the security or request the recipient to indicate, upon an enclosed or attached coupon or card, or in some other manner, whether he might be interested in the security, if the communication contains substantially the following statement:

"No offer to buy the securities can be accepted and no part of the purchase price can be received until the registration statement has become effective, and any such offer may be withdrawn or revoked, without obligation or commitment of any kind, at any time prior to notice of its acceptance given after the effective date. An indication of interest in response to this advertisement will involve no obligation or commitment of any kind."

Provided, that such statement need not be included in such a communication to a dealer if the communication refers to a prior communication to the dealer, with respect to the same security, in which the statement was included.

Rule 135. Notice of Certain Proposed Offerings

(a) For the purpose only of Section 5 of the Act, a notice given by an issuer that it proposes to make a public offering of securities to be registered under the Act shall not be deemed to offer any securities for sale if such notice states that the offering will be made only by means of a prospectus and contains no more than the following additional information:

(1) The name of the issuer;

(2) The title, amount and basic terms of the securities proposed to be offered, the amount of the offering, if any, to be made by selling security holders, the anticipated time of the offering and a brief statement of the manner and purpose of the offering without naming the underwriters;

(3) In the case of a rights offering to security holders of the issuer, the class of securities the holders of which will be entitled to subscribe to the securities proposed to be offered, the subscription ration, the proposed record date, the approximate date upon which the rights are proposed to be issued, the proposed term or expiration date of the rights and the approximate subscription price, or any of the foregoing;

(4) In the case of an offering of securities in exchange for other securities of the issuer or of another issuer, the name of the issuer and the title of the securities to be surrendered in exchange for the securities to be offered, the basis upon which the exchange may be made, or any of the foregoing;

(5) In the case of an offering to employees of the issuer or to employees of any affiliate of the issuer, the name of the employer and class or classes of employees to whom the securities are proposed to be offered, the offering price or basis of the offering and the period during which the offering is to be made, or any of the foregoing; and

(6) Any statement or legend required by State law or administrative authority.

(b) Any notice contemplated by this rule may take the form of a news release or a written communication directed to security holders or employees, as the case may be, or other published statement.

(c) Notwithstanding the provisions of paragraphs (a) and (b) of this section, in the case of a rights offering of a security listed or subject to unlisted trading privileges on a national securities exchange or quoted on the NASDAQ interdealer quotation system information with respect to the interest rate, conversion ratio and subscription price may be disseminated through the facilities of the exchange, the consolidated transaction reporting system, the NASDAQ system or the Dow Jones broad tape, provided such information is already disclosed in a registration statement on file with the Commission.

* * *

Rule 137. Definition of "Offers", "Participates", or "Participation" in Section 2(11) in Relation to Certain Publications by Persons Independent of Participants in a Distribution

The terms "offers", "participates", or "participation" in Section 2(11) shall not be deemed to apply to the publication or distribution of information, opinions or recommendations with respect to the securities of a registrant which is required to file reports pursuant to Sections 13 or 15(d) of the Securities Exchange Act of 1934 and has filed or proposes to file a registration statement under the Securities Act of 1933 if—

(a) such information, opinions and recommendations are published and distributed in the regular course of its business by a dealer which is not and does not propose to be a participant in the distribution of the security to which the registration statement relates; and

(b) such dealer receives no consideration, directly or indirectly, in connection with the publication and distribution of such information, opinions or recommendations from the registrant, a selling security holder or any participant in the distribution or any other person interested in the securities to which the registration statement relates, and such information, opinions or recommendations are not published or distributed pursuant to any arrangement or understanding, direct or indirect, with such issuer, underwriter, dealer or selling security holder; provided, however, that nothing herein shall forbid payment of the regular subscription or purchase price of the document or other written communication in which such information, opinions or recommendations appear.

Rule 138. Definition of "Offer for Sale" and "Offer to Sell" in Sections 2(10) and 5(c) in Relation to Certain Publications

(a) Where a registrant which meets all of the conditions for the use of Form S–2 or Form F–2 proposes to file, has filed or has an effective registration statement under the Act relating solely to a nonconvertible debt security or to a nonconvertible, nonparticipating preferred stock, publication or distribution in the regular course of its business by a broker or dealer of information, opinions or recommendations relating solely to common stock or to debt or preferred stock convertible into common stock of such issuer shall not be deemed to constitute an offer for sale or offer to sell the security to which such registration statement relates for purposes of sections 2(10) and 5(c) of the Act, even though such broker or dealer is or will be a participant in the distribution of the security to which such registration statement relates.

(b) Where a registrant which meets all of the conditions for the use of Form S–2 or Form F–2 proposes to file, has filed or has an effective registration statement under the Act relating solely to common stock or to debt or preferred stock convertible into common stock, the publication or distribution in the regular course of its business by a broker or dealer of information, opinions or recommendations relating solely to a nonconvertible debt security, or to a nonconvertible nonparticipating preferred stock shall not be deemed to constitute an offer for sale or offer to sell the security to which such registration statement relates for purposes of sections 2(10) and 5(c) of the Act, even though such broker or dealer is or will be a participant in the distribution of the security to which such registration statement relates.

Rule 139. Definition of "Offer for Sale" and "Offer to Sell" in Sections 2(10) and 5(c) in Relation to Certain Publications

Where a registrant which is required to file reports pursuant to section 13 or 15(d) of the Securities Exchange Act of 1934 proposes to file, has filed or has an effective registration statement under the Securities Act of 1933 relating to its securities, the publication or distribution by a broker or dealer of information, an opinion or a recommendation with respect to the registrant or any class of its securities shall not be deemed to constitute an offer for sale or offer to sell the securities registered or proposed to be registered for purposes of sections 2(10) and 5(c) of the Act, even though such broker or dealer is or will be a participant in the distribution of such securities, if the conditions of paragraph (a) or (b) have been met:

(a) The registrant meets the registrant requirements of Form S–3 or Form F–3 and the minimum float or investment grade securities provisions of either paragraph (B)(1) or (2) of General Instruction I of the respective form and such information, opinion or recommendation is contained in a publication which is distributed with reasonable regularity in the normal course of business; or

(b)(1) Such information, opinion or recommendation is contained in a publication which:

(i) Is distributed with reasonable regularity in the normal course of business and

(ii) Includes similar information, opinions or recommendations with respect to a substantial number of companies in the registrant's industry or sub-industry, or contains a comprehensive list of securities currently recommended by such broker or dealer;

(2) Such information, opinion or recommendation is given no materially greater space or prominence in such publication than that given to other securities or registrants; and

(3) An opinion or recommendation as favorable or more favorable as to the registrant or any class of its securities was published by the broker or dealer in the last publication of such broker or dealer addressing the registrant or its securities prior to the commencement of participation in the distribution.

Instructions to Rule 139.

1. For purposes of paragraph (a), a research report has not been distributed with "reasonable regularity" if it contains information, an opinion, or a recommendation concerning a company with respect to which a broker or dealer currently is not publishing research.

2. Where projections of a registrants sales or earnings are included, the publication must comply with the following in order to meet paragraphs (b)(1) and (b)(3).

A. The projections must have been published previously on a regular basis in order for the publication to meet paragraph (b)(1)(i);

B. The projections must be included with respect to either a substantial number of companies in the registrant's industry or sub-industry or all companies in a comprehensive list which is contained in the publication, and must cover the same periods with respect to such companies as with respect to the registrant, in order to meet the requirements of paragraph (b)(1)(ii); and

C. Because projections constitute opinions within the meaning of the Rule, they must come within paragraph (b)(3).

* * *

Rule 141. Definition of "Commission from an Underwriter or Dealer Not in Excess of the Usual and Customary Distributors' or Sellers' Commissions" in Section 2(11), for Certain Transactions

(a) The term "commission" in Section 2(11) shall include such remuneration, commonly known as a spread, as may be received by a distributor or dealer as a consequence of reselling securities bought from an underwriter or dealer at a price below the offering price of such securities, where such resales afford the distributor or dealer a margin of profit not in excess of what is usual and customary in such transactions.

(b) The term "commission from an underwriter or dealer" in Section 2(11) shall include commissions paid by an underwriter or dealer directly or indirectly controlling or controlled by, or under direct or indirect common control with the issuer.

(c) The term "usual and customary distributors' or sellers' commission" in Section 2(11) shall mean a commission or remuneration, commonly known as a spread, paid to or received by any person selling securities either for his own account or for the account of others, which is not in excess of the amount usual and customary in the distribution and sale of issues of similar type and size, and not in excess of the amount allowed to other persons, if any, for comparable service in the distribution of the particular issue; but such term shall not include amounts paid to any person whose function is the management of the distribution of all or a substantial part of the particular issue, or who performs the functions normally performed by an underwriter or underwriting syndicate.

* * *

Rule 144. Persons Deemed Not to Be Engaged in a Distribution and Therefore Not Underwriters

Preliminary Note to Rule 144

Rule 144 is designed to implement the fundamental purposes of the Act, as expressed in its preamble, "To provide full and fair disclosure of the character of the securities sold in interstate commerce and through the mails, and to prevent fraud in the sale thereof ..." The rule is designed to prohibit the creation of public markets in securities of issuers concerning which adequate current information is not available to the public. At the same time, where adequate current information concerning the issuer is available to the public, the rule permits the public sale in ordinary trading transactions of limited amounts of securities owned by persons controlling, controlled by or under common control with the issuer and by persons who have acquired restricted securities of the issuer.

Certain basic principles are essential to an understanding of the requirement of registration in the Act:

1. If any person utilizes the jurisdictional means to sell any non-exempt security to any other person, the security must be registered unless a statutory exemption can be found for the transaction.

2. In addition to the exemptions found in Section 3, four exemptions applicable to transactions in securities are contained in Section 4. Three of these Section 4 exemptions are clearly not available to anyone acting as an "underwriter" of securities. (The fourth, found in Section 4(4), is available only to those who act as brokers under certain limited circumstances.) An understanding of the term "underwriter" is therefore important to anyone who wishes to determine whether or not an exemption from registration is available for his sale of securities.

The term underwriter is broadly defined in Section 2(11) of the Act to mean any person who has purchased from an issuer with a view to, or offers or sells for an issuer in connection with, the distribution of any security, or participates or has a direct or indirect participation in any such undertaking, or participates or has a participation in the direct or indirect underwriting of any such undertaking. The interpretation of this definition has traditionally focused on the words "with a view to" in the phrase "purchased from an issuer with a view to ... distribution." Thus, an investment banking firm which arranges with an issuer for the public sale of its securities is clearly an "underwriter" under that Section. Individual investors who are not professionals in the securities business may also be "underwriters" within the meaning of that term as used in the Act if they act as links in a chain of transactions through which securities move from an issuer to the public. Since it is difficult to ascertain the mental state of the purchaser at the time of his acquisition, subsequent acts and circumstances have been considered to determine whether such person took with a view to distribution at the time of his acquisition. Emphasis has been placed on factors such as the length of time the person has held the securities and whether there has been an unforeseeable change in circumstances of the holder. Experience has shown, however, that reliance upon such factors as the above has not assured adequate protection of investors through the maintenance of informed trading markets and has led to uncertainty in the application of the registration provisions of the Act.

It should be noted that the statutory language of Section 2(11) is in the disjunctive. Thus, it is insufficient to conclude that a person is not an underwriter solely because he did not purchase securities from an issuer with a view to their distribution. It must also be established that the person is not offering or selling for an issuer in connection with the distribution of the securities, does not participate or have a direct or indirect participation in any such undertaking, and does not participate or have a participation in the direct or indirect underwriting of such an undertaking.

In determining when a person is deemed not to be engaged in a distribution several factors must be considered.

First, the purpose and underlying policy of the Act to protect investors requires that there be adequate current information concerning the issuer, whether the resales of securities by persons result in a distribution or are effected in trading transactions. Accordingly, the availability of the rule is conditioned on the existence of adequate current public information.

Secondly, a holding period prior to resale is essential, among other reasons, to assure that those persons who buy under a claim of a Section 4(2) exemption have assumed the economic risks of investment, and therefore are not acting as conduits for sale to the public of unregistered securities, directly or indirectly, on behalf of an issuer. It should be noted that there is nothing in Section 2(11) which places a time limit on a person's status as an underwriter. The public has the same need for protection afforded by registration whether the securities are distributed shortly after their purchase or after a considerable length of time.

A third factor, which must be considered in determining what is deemed not to constitute a "distribution," is the impact of the particular transaction or transactions on the trading markets. Section 4(1) was intended to exempt only routine trading transactions between individual investors with respect to securities already issued and not to exempt distributions by issuers or acts of other individuals who engage in steps necessary to such distributions. Therefore, a person reselling securities under Section 4(1) of the Act must sell the securities in such limited quantities and in such a manner as not to disrupt the trading markets. The larger the amount of securities involved, the more likely it is that such resales may involve methods of offering and amounts of compensation usually associated with a distribution rather than routine trading transactions. Thus, solicitation of buy orders or the payment of extra compensation are not permitted by the rule.

In summary, if the sale in question is made in accordance with *all* of the provisions of the rule, as set forth below, any person who sells restricted securities shall be deemed not to be engaged in a distribution of such securities and therefore not an underwriter thereof. The rule also provides that any person who sells restricted or other securities on behalf of a person in a control relationship with the issuer shall be deemed not to be engaged in a distribution of such securities and therefore not to be an underwriter thereof, if the sale is made in accordance with *all* the conditions of the rule.

Rule 144

(a) *Definitions.* The following definitions shall apply for the purposes of this rule.

(1) An "affiliate" of an issuer is a person that directly, or indirectly through one or more intermediaries, controls, or is controlled by, or is under common control with, such issuer.

(2) The term "person" when used with reference to a person for whose account securities are to be sold in reliance upon this rule includes, in addition to such person, all of the following persons:

(A) Any relative or spouse of such person, or any relative of such spouse, any one of whom has the same home as such person;

(B) Any trust or estate in which such person or any of the persons specified in (A) collectively own ten percent or more of the total beneficial interest or of which any of such persons serve as trustee, executor or in any similar capacity; and

(C) Any corporation or other organization (other than the issuer) in which such person or any of the persons specified in (A) are the beneficial owners collectively of ten percent or more of any class of equity securities or ten percent or more of the equity interest.

(3) The term "restricted securities" means securities that are acquired directly or indirectly from the issuer, or from an affiliate of the issuer, in a transaction or chain of transactions not involving any public offering, or securities acquired from the issuer that are subject to the resale limitations of Regulation D under the Act, or securities that are subject to the resale limitations of Regulation D and are acquired in a transaction or chain of transactions not involving any public offering.

(b) *Conditions to be Met.* Any affiliate or other person who sells restricted securities of an issuer for his own account, or any person who sells restricted or any other securities for the account of an affiliate of the issuer of such securities, shall be deemed not to be engaged in a distribution of such securities and therefore not to be an underwriter thereof within the meaning of Section 2(11) of the Act if all of the conditions of this rule are met.

(c) *Current Public Information.* There shall be available adequate current public information with respect to the issuer of the securities. Such information shall be deemed to be available only if either of the following conditions is met:

(1) *Filing of Reports.* The issuer has securities registered pursuant to Section 12 of the Securities Exchange Act of 1934, has been subject to the reporting requirements of Section 13 of that Act for a period of at least 90 days immediately preceding the sale of the securities and has filed all the reports required to be filed thereunder during the 12 months preceding such sale (or for such shorter period that the issuer was required to file such reports); or has securities registered pursuant to the Securities Act of 1933, has been subject to the reporting requirements of Section 15(d) of the Securities Exchange Act of 1934 for a period of at least 90 days immediately preceding the sale of the securities and has filed all the reports required to be filed thereunder during the 12 months preceding such sale (or for such shorter period that the issuer was required to file such reports). The person for whose account the securities are to be sold shall be entitled to rely upon a statement in whichever is the most recent report, quarterly or annual, required to be filed and filed by the issuer that such issuer has filed all reports required to be filed by Section 13 or 15(d) of the Securities Exchange Act of 1934 during the preceding 12 months (or for such shorter period that the issuer was required to file such reports) and has been subject to such filing requirements for the past 90 days, unless he knows or has reason to believe that the issuer has not complied with such requirements. Such person shall also be entitled to rely upon a written statement from the issuer that it has complied with such reporting requirements unless he knows or has reason to believe that the issuer has not complied with such requirements.

(2) *Other Public Information.* If the issuer is not subject to Section 13 or 15(d) of the Securities Exchange Act of 1934, there is publicly available the information concerning the issuer specified in clauses (1) to (14), inclusive, and clause (16) of paragraph (a)(4) of Rule 15c2–11 under that Act or, if the issuer is an insurance company, the information specified in Section 12(g)(2)(G)(i) of that Act.

(d) *Holding Period for Restricted Securities.* If the securities sold are restricted securities, the following provisions apply:

(1) *General Rule.* The person for whose account the securities are sold shall have been the beneficial owner of the securities for a period of at least two years prior to the sale and, if the securities were purchased, the full purchase price or other consideration shall have been paid or given at least two years prior to the sale.

(2) *Promissory Notes, Other Obligations or Installment Contracts.* Giving the person from whom the securities were purchased a promissory note or other obligation to pay the purchase price, or entering into an installment purchase contract with such person, shall not be deemed full payment of the purchase price unless the promissory note, obligation or contract—

(A) provides for full recourse against the purchaser of the securities;

(B) is secured by collateral, other than the securities purchased, having a fair market value at least equal to the purchase price of the securities purchased; and

(C) shall have been discharged by payment in full prior to the sale of the securities.

(3) *Short Sales, Puts or Other Options to Sell Securities.* In computing the two-year holding period the following periods shall be excluded:

(A) If the securities sold are equity securities, there shall be excluded any period during which the person for whose account they are sold had a short position in, or any put or other option to dispose of, any equity securities of the same class or any securities convertible into securities of such class; and

(B) If the securities sold are nonconvertible debt securities, there shall be excluded any period during which the person for whose account they are sold had a short position in, or any put or other option to dispose of, any nonconvertible debt securities of the same issuer.

(4) *Determination of Holding Period.* The following provisions shall apply for the purpose of determining the period securities have been held:

(A) *Stock Dividends, Splits and Recapitalizations.* Securities acquired from the issuer as a dividend or pursuant to a stock split, reverse split or recapitalization shall be deemed to have been acquired at the same time as the securities on which the dividend or, if more than one, the initial dividend was paid, the securities involved in the split or reverse split, or the securities surrendered in connection with the recapitalization;

(B) *Conversions.* If the securities sold were acquired from the issuer for a consideration consisting solely of other securities of the same issuer surrendered for conversion, the securities so acquired shall be deemed to have been acquired at the same time as the securities surrendered for conversion;

(C) *Contingent Issuance of Securities.* Securities acquired as a contingent payment of the purchase price of an equity interest in a business, or the assets of a business, sold to the issuer or an affiliate of the issuer shall be deemed to have been acquired at the time of such sale if the issuer or affiliate was then committed to issue the securities subject only to conditions other than the payment of further consideration for such securities. An agreement entered into in connection with any such purchase to remain in the employment of, or not to compete with, the issuer or affiliate or the rendering of services pursuant to such agreement shall not be deemed to be the payment of further consideration for such securities.

(D) *Pledged Securities.* Securities which are bona fide pledged by any person other than the issuer when sold by the pledgee, or by a purchaser, after a default in the obligation secured by the pledge, shall be deemed to have been acquired when they were acquired by the pledgor, except that if the securities were pledged without recourse they shall be deemed to have been acquired by the pledgee at the time of the pledge or by the purchaser at the time of purchase.

Note. Securities sold by the pledgee shall be aggregated with those sold by the pledgor, as provided in paragraph (e)(3)(B) below.

(E) *Gifts of Securities.* Securities acquired from any person, other than the issuer, by gift shall be deemed to have been acquired by the donee when they were acquired by the donor;

Note. Securities sold by the donee shall be aggregated with those sold by the donor, as provided in paragraph (e)(3)(C) below.

(F) *Trusts.* Securities acquired from the settlor of a trust by the trust or acquired from the trust by the beneficiaries thereof shall be deemed to have been acquired when they were acquired by the settlor;

Note. Securities sold by the trust shall be aggregated with those sold by the settlor of the trust, as provided in paragraph (e)(3)(D) below.

(G) *Estates.* Securities held by the estate of a deceased person or acquired from such an estate by the beneficiaries thereof shall be deemed to have been acquired when they were acquired by the deceased person, except that no holding period is required if the estate is not an affiliate of the issuer or if the securities are sold by a beneficiary of the estate who is not such an affiliate.

Notes. 1. Securities sold by the estate shall be aggregated with those sold by the deceased person, as provided in paragraph (e)(3)(E) below, if the estate is an affiliate of the issuer.

2. While there is no holding period or amount limitation for estates and beneficiaries thereof which are not affiliates of the issuer, paragraphs (c), (f), (g), (h) and (i) of the rule apply to securities sold by such persons in reliance upon the rule.

(e) *Limitation on Amount of Securities Sold.* Except as hereinafter provided, the amount of securities which may be sold in reliance upon this rule shall be determined as follows:

(1) *Sales by Affiliates.* If restricted or other securities are sold for the account of an affiliate of the issuer, the amount of securities sold, together with all sales of restricted and other securities of the same class for the account of such person within the preceding three months, shall not exceed the greater of (i) one percent of the shares or other units of the class outstanding as shown by the most recent report or statement published by the issuer, or (ii) the average weekly volume of trading in such securities reported on all national securities exchanges and/or reported through the automated quotation system of a registered securities association during the four calendar weeks preceding the filing of the notice required by paragraph (h), or, if no such notice is required, the date of receipt of the order to execute the transaction by the broker or the date of execution of the transaction directly with a market maker, or (iii) the average weekly volume of trading in such securities reported through the consolidated transaction reporting system contemplated by Rule 17a–15 under the Securities Exchange Act of 1934 during the four-week period specified in subdivision (ii) of this subparagraph.

(2) *Sales by Persons Other Than Affiliates.* The amount of restricted securities sold for the account of any person other than an affiliate of the issuer, together with all other sales of restricted securities of the same class for the account of such person within the preceding three months, shall not exceed the amount specified in paragraphs (e)(1)(i), (1)(ii) or (1)(iii) of this section, whichever is applicable, unless the conditions in paragraph (k) of this rule are satisfied.

(3) *Determination of Amount.* For the purpose of determining the amount of securities specified in paragraphs (e)(1) and (2) of this rule, the following provisions shall apply:

(i) Where both convertible securities and securities of the class into which they are convertible are sold, the amount of convertible securities sold shall be deemed to be the amount of securities of the class into which they are convertible for the purpose of determining the aggregate amount of securities of both classes sold;

(ii) The amount of securities sold for the account of a pledgee thereof, or for the account of a purchaser of the pledged securities, during any period of three months within two years after a default in the obligation secured by the pledge, and the amount of securities sold during the same three-month period for the account of the pledgor shall not exceed, in the aggregate, the amount specified in subparagraph (1) or (2) of this paragraph, whichever is applicable;

(iii) The amount of securities sold for the account of a donee thereof during any period of three months within two years after the donation, and the amount of securities sold during the same three-month period for the account of the donor, shall not exceed, in the aggregate, the amount specified in subparagraph (1) or (2) of this paragraph, whichever is applicable;

(iv) Where securities were acquired by a trust from the settlor of the trust, the amount of such securities sold for the account of the trust during any period of three months within two years after the acquisition of the securities by the trust, and the amount of securities sold during the same three-month period for the account of the settlor, shall not exceed, in the aggregate, the amount specified in subparagraph (1) or (2) of this paragraph, whichever is applicable;

(v) The amount of securities sold for the account of the estate of a deceased person, or for the account of a beneficiary of such estate, during any period of three months and the amount of securities sold during the same period for the account of the deceased person prior to his death shall not exceed, in the aggregate, the amount specified in subparagraph (1) or (2) of this paragraph, whichever is applicable, *Provided,* That no limitation on amount shall apply if the estate or beneficiary thereof is not an affiliate of the issuer;

(vi) When two or more affiliates or other persons agree to act in concert for the purpose of selling securities of an issuer, all securities of the same class sold for the account of all such persons during any period of three months shall be aggregated for the purpose of determining the limitation on the amount of securities sold;

(vii) Securities sold pursuant to an effective registration statement under the Act or pursuant to an exemption provided by Regulation A under the Act or in a transaction exempt pursuant to Section 4 of the Act and not involving any public offering need not be included in determining the amount of securities sold in reliance upon this rule.

(f) *Manner of Sale.* The securities shall be sold in "brokers' transactions" within the meaning of section 4(4) of the Act or in transactions directly with a "market maker," as that term is defined in section 3(a)(38) of the Securities Exchange Act of 1934, and the person selling the securities shall not (1) solicit or arrange for the solicitation of orders to buy the securities in anticipation of or in connection with such transaction, or (2) make any payment in connection with the offer or sale of the securities to any person other than the broker who executes the order to sell the securities. The requirements of this paragraph, however, shall not apply to securities sold for the account of the estate of a deceased person or for the account of a beneficiary of such estate provided the estate or beneficiary thereof is not an affiliate of the issuer; nor shall they apply to securities sold for the account of any person other than an affiliate of the issuer, provided the conditions of paragraph (k) of this rule are satisfied.

(g) *Brokers' Transactions.* The term "brokers' transactions" in Section 4(4) of the Act shall for the purposes of this rule be deemed to include transactions by a broker in which such broker—

(1) does no more than execute the order or orders to sell the securities as agent for the person for whose account the securities are sold; and receives no more than the usual and customary broker's commission;

(2) neither solicits nor arranges for the solicitation of customers' orders to buy the securities in anticipation of or in connection with the transaction; provided, that the foregoing shall not preclude *(i)* inquiries by the broker of other brokers or dealers who have indicated an interest in the securities within the preceding 60 days, *(ii)* inquiries by the broker of his customers who have indicated an unsolicited bona fide interest in the securities within the preceding 10 business days; or *(iii)* the publication by the broker of bid and ask quotations for the security in an inter-dealer quotation system provided that such quotations are incident to the maintenance of a bona fide inter-dealer market for the security for the broker's own account and that the broker has published bona fide bid and ask quotations for the security in an inter-dealer quotation system on each of at least twelve days within the preceding thirty calendar days with no more than four business days in succession without such two-way quotations;

Note to Subparagraph (g)(2)(ii): The broker should obtain and retain in his files written evidence of indications of bona fide unsolicited interest by his customers in the securities at the time such indications are received.

(3) after reasonable inquiry is not aware of circumstances indicating that the person for whose account the securities are sold is an underwriter with respect to the securities or that the transaction is a part of a distribution of securities of the issuer. Without limiting the foregoing, the broker shall be deemed to be aware of any facts or statements contained in the notice required by paragraph (h) below.

Notes. 1. The broker, for his own protection, should obtain and retain in his files a copy of the notice required by paragraph (h).

2. The reasonable inquiry required by paragraph (g)(3) above should include, but not necessarily be limited to, inquiry as to the following matters:

a. The length of time the securities have been held by the person for whose account they are to be sold. If practicable, the inquiry should include physical inspection of the securities;

b. The nature of the transaction in which the securities were acquired by such person;

c. The amount of securities of the same class sold during the past six months by all persons whose sales are required to be taken into consideration pursuant to paragraph (e) above;

d. Whether such person intends to sell additional securities of the same class through any other means;

e. Whether such person has solicited or made any arrangement for the solicitation of buy orders in connection with the proposed sale of securities;

f. Whether such person has made any payment to any other person in connection with the proposed sale of the securities; and

g. The number of shares or other units of the class outstanding, or the relevant trading volume.

(h) *Notice of Proposed Sale.* If the amount of securities to be sold in reliance upon the rule during any period of three months exceeds 500 shares or other units or has an aggregate sale price in excess of $10,000, three copies of a notice on Form 144 shall be filed with the Commission at its principal office in Washington, D.C.; and if such securities are admitted to trading on any national securities exchange, one copy of such notice shall also be transmitted to the principal exchange on which such securities are so admitted. The Form 144 shall be signed by the person for whose account the securities are to be sold and shall be transmitted for filing concurrently with either the placing with a broker of an order to execute a sale of securities in reliance upon this rule or the execution directly with a market maker of such a sale. Neither the filing of such notice nor the failure of the Commission to comment thereon shall be deemed to preclude the Commission from taking any action it deems necessary or appropriate with respect to the sale of the securities referred to in such notice. The requirements of this paragraph, however, shall not apply to securities sold for the account of any person other than an affiliate of the issuer, provided the conditions of paragraph (k) of this rule are satisfied.

(i) *Bona Fide Intention to Sell.* The person filing the notice required by paragraph (h) shall have a bona fide intention to sell the securities referred to therein within a reasonable time after the filing of such notice.

(j) *Non-exclusive Rule.* Although this rule provides a means for reselling restricted securities and securities held by affiliates without registration, it is not the exclusive means for reselling such securities in that manner. Therefore, it does not eliminate or otherwise affect the availability of any exemption for resales under the Securities Act that a person or entity may be able to rely upon.

(k) *Termination of Certain Restrictions on Sales of Restricted Securities by Persons Other Than Affiliates.* The requirements of paragraphs (c), (e), (f) and (h) of this rule shall not apply to restricted securities sold for the account of a person who is not an affiliate of the issuer at the time of the sale and has not been an affiliate during the preceding three months, provided the securities have been beneficially owned by the person for a period of at least three years prior to their sale. In computing the period for which securities have been beneficially owned for purposes of this provision, reference should be made to paragraph (d) of this rule.

Rule 145. Reclassifications of Securities, Mergers, Consolidations and Acquisitions of Assets

Preliminary Note to Rule 145

Rule 145 is designed to make available the protection provided by registration under the Securities Act of 1933, as amended (Act), to persons who are offered securities in a business combination of the type described in subparagraphs (a)(1), (2), and (3) of the Rule. The thrust of the Rule is that an "offer", "offer to sell", "offer for sale", or "sale" occurs when there is submitted to security holders a plan or agreement pursuant to which such holders are required to elect, on the basis of what is in substance a new investment decision, whether to accept a new or different security in exchange for their existing security. Rule 145 embodies the Commission's determination that such transactions are subject to the registration requirements of the Act, and that the previously existing "no-sale" theory of Rule 133 is no longer consistent with the statutory purposes of the Act.

Transactions for which statutory exemptions under the Act, including those contained in Sections 3(a)(9), 3(a)(10), 3(a)(11), and 4(2), are otherwise available are not affected by Rule 145.

Rule 145

Note 1: Reference is made to Rule 153A, describing the prospectus delivery required in a transaction of the type referred to in Rule 145.

Note 2: A reclassification of securities covered by Rule 145 would be exempt from registration pursuant to Sections 3(a)(9) or 3(a)(11) of the Act if the conditions of either of these sections are satisfied.

(a) *Transactions Within the Rule.* An "offer", "offer to sell", "offer for sale" or "sale" shall be deemed to be involved, within the meaning of Section 2(3) of the Act, so far as the security holders of a corporation or other person are concerned where, pursuant to statutory provisions of the jurisdiction under which such corporation or other person is organized, or pursuant to provisions contained in its certificate of incorporation or similar controlling instruments, or otherwise, there is submitted for the vote or consent of such security holders a plan or agreement for—

(1) *Reclassifications.* A reclassification of securities of such corporation or other person, other than a stock split, reverse stock split, or change in par value, which involves the substitution of a security for another security;

(2) *Mergers or Consolidations.* A statutory merger or consolidation or similar plan of acquisition in which securities of such corporation or other person held by such security holders will become or be exchanged for securities of any other person, except where the sole purpose of the transaction is to change an issuer's domicile; or

(3) *Transfers of Assets.* A transfer of assets of such corporation or other person, to another person in consideration of the issuance of securities of such other person or any of its affiliates, if:

(A) such plan or agreement provides for dissolution of the corporation or other person whose security holders are voting or consenting; or

(B) such plan or agreement provides for a pro rata or similar distribution of such securities to the security holders voting or consenting; or

(C) the board of directors or similar representatives of such corporation or other person, adopts resolutions relative to (A) or (B) above within one year after the taking of such vote or consent; or

(D) the transfer of assets is a part of a preexisting plan for distribution of such securities, notwithstanding (A), (B) or (C), above.

(b) *Communications Not Deemed to be a "Prospectus" or "Offer to Sell".* For the purpose of this rule, the term "prospectus" as defined in Section 2(10) of the Act and the term "offer to sell" in Section 5 of the Act shall not be deemed to include the following:

(1) Any written communication or other published statement which contains no more than the following information: the name of the issuer of the securities to be offered, or the person whose assets are to be sold in exchange for the securities to be offered, and the names of other parties to any transaction specified in paragraph (a); a brief description of the business of parties to such transaction; the date, time and place of the meeting of security holders to vote on or consent to any such transaction specified in paragraph (a); a brief description of the transaction to be acted upon and the basis upon which such transaction will be made; and any legend or similar statement required by State or federal law or administrative authority.

(2) Any written communication subject to and meeting the requirements of paragraph (a) of Rule 14a–12 under the Securities Exchange Act of 1934 and filed in accordance with paragraph (b) of that rule.

(c) *Persons and Parties Deemed to be Underwriters.* For purposes of this rule, any party to any transaction specified in paragraph (a), other than the issuer, or any person who is an affiliate of such party at the time any such transaction is submitted for vote or consent, who publicly offers or sells securities of the issuer acquired in connection with any such transaction, shall be deemed to be engaged in a distribution and therefore to be an underwriter thereof within the meaning of Section 2(11) of the Act. The term "party" as used in this paragraph (c) shall mean the corporations, business entities, or other persons, other than the issuer, whose assets or capital structure are affected by the transactions specified in paragraph (a).

(d) *Resale Provisions for Persons and Parties Deemed Underwriters.* Notwithstanding the provisions of paragraph (c), a person or party specified therein shall not be deemed to be engaged in a distribution and therefore not to be an underwriter of registered securities acquired in a transaction specified in paragraph (a) of this section if: (1) such securities are sold by such person or party in accordance with the provisions of paragraphs (c), (e), (f) and (g) of Rule 144; (2) such person or party is not an affiliate of the issuer and has been the beneficial owner of the securities for at least two years as determined in accordance with paragraph (d) of Rule 144, and the issuer meets the requirements of paragraph (c) of Rule 144; or (3) such person or party is not, and has not been for at least three months, an affiliate of the issuer and has been the beneficial owner of the securities for at least three years as determined in accordance with paragraph (d) of Rule 144.

(e) *Definition of "Person".* The term "person" as used in paragraphs (c) and (d) of this rule, when used with reference to a person for whose account securities are to be sold, shall have the same meaning as the definition of that term in paragraph (a)(2) of Rule 144 under the Act.

Rule 147. "Part of an Issue," "Person Resident," and "Doing Business Within" for Purposes of Section 3(a)(11)

(a) *Transactions Covered.*

Offers, offers to sell, offers for sale and sales by an issuer of its securities made in accordance with all of the terms and conditions of this rule shall be deemed to be part of an issue offered and sold only to persons resident and doing business within such state or territory, within the meaning of Section 3(a)(11) of the Act.

(b) *Part of an Issue.*

(1) For purposes of this rule, all securities of the issuer which are part of an issue shall be offered, offered for sale or sold in accordance with all of the terms and conditions of this rule.

(2) For purposes of this rule only, an issue shall be deemed not to include offers, offers to sell, offers for sale or sales of securities of the issuer pursuant to the exemptions provided by Section 3 or Section 4(2) of the Act or pursuant to a registration statement filed under the Act, that take place prior to the six month period immediately preceding or after the six month period immediately following any offers, offers for sale or sales pursuant to this rule, *provided that,* there are during either of said six month periods no offers, offers for sale or sales of securities by or for the issuer of the same or similar class as those offered, offered for sale or sold pursuant to the rule.

NOTE: In the even that securities of the same or similar class as those offered pursuant to the rule are offered, offered for sale or sold less than six months prior to or subsequent to any offer, offer for sale or sale pursuant to this rule, see Preliminary Note 3 hereof, as to which offers, offers to sell, offers for sale, or sales are part of an issue.

(c) *Nature of the Issuer.*

The issuer of the securities shall at the time of any offers and the sales be a person resident and doing business within the state or territory in which all of the offers, offers to sell, offers for sale and sales are made.

(1) The issuer shall be deemed to be a resident of the state or territory in which:

(i) it is incorporated or organized, if a corporation, limited partnership, trust or other form of business organization that is organized under state or territorial law;

(ii) its principal office is located, if a general partnership or other form of business organization that is not organized under any state or territorial law;

(iii) his principal residence is located, if an individual.

(2) The issuer shall be deemed to be doing business within a state or territory if:

(i) the issuer derived at least 80% of its gross revenues and those of its subsidiaries on a consolidated basis;

(A) for its most recent fiscal year, if the first offer of any part of the issue is made during the first six months of the issuer's current fiscal year; or

(B) for the first six months of its current fiscal year or during the twelve month fiscal period ending with such six month period, if the first offer of any part of the issue is made during the last six months of the issuer's current fiscal year

from the operation of a business or of real property located in or from the rendering of services within such state or territory; provided, however, that this provision does not apply to any issuer which has not had gross revenues in excess of $5,000 from the sale of products or services or other conduct of its business for its most recent twelve month fiscal period; and

(ii) the issuer had at the end of its most recent semi-annual fiscal period prior to the first offer of any part of the issue, at least 80 percent of its assets and those of its subsidiaries on a consolidated basis located within such state or territory;

(iii) the issuer intends to use and uses at least 80% of the net proceeds to the issuer from sales made pursuant to this rule in connection with the operation of a business or of real property, the purchase of real property located in, or the rendering of services within such state or territory; and

(iv) the principal office of the issuer is located within such state or territory.

(d) *Offerees and Purchasers: Person Resident.*

Offers, offers to sell, offers for sale and sales of securities that are part of an issue shall be made only to persons resident within the state or territory of which the issuer is a resident. For purposes of determining the residence of offerees and purchasers:

(1) A corporation, partnership, trust or other form of business organization shall be deemed to be a resident of a state or territory if, at the time of the offer and sale to it, it has its principal office within such state or territory.

(2) An individual shall be deemed to be a resident of a state or territory if such individual has, at the time of the offer and sale to him, his principal residence in the state or territory.

(3) A corporation, partnership, trust or other form of business organization which is organized for the specific purpose of acquiring part of an issue offered pursuant to this rule shall be deemed not to be a resident of a state or territory unless all of the beneficial owners of such organization are residents of such state or territory.

(e) *Limitation of Resales.*

During the period in which securities that are part of an issue are being offered and sold by the issuer, and for a period of nine months from the date of the last sale by the issuer of such securities, all resales of any part of the issue, by any person, shall be made only to persons resident within such state or territory.

NOTES: 1. In the case of convertible securities resales of either the convertible security, or if it is converted, the underlying security, could be made during the period described in paragraph (e) only to persons resident within such state or territory. For purposes of this rule a conversion in reliance on Section 3(a)(9) of the Act does not begin a new period.

2. Dealers must satisfy the requirements of Rule 15c2–11 under the Securities Exchange Act of 1934 prior to publishing any quotation for a security, or submitting any quotation for publication, in any quotation medium.

(f) *Precautions Against Interstate Offers and Sales.*

(1) The issuer shall, in connection with any securities sold by it pursuant to this rule:

(i) place a legend on the certificate or other document evidencing the security stating that the securities have not been registered under the Act and setting forth the limitations on resale contained in paragraph (e);

(ii) issue stop transfer instructions to the issuer's transfer agent, if any, with respect to the securities, or, if the issuer transfers its own securities, make a notation in the appropriate records of the issuer; and

(iii) obtain a written representation from each purchaser as to his residence.

(2) The issuer shall, in connection with the issuance of new certificates for any of the securities that are part of the same issue that are presented for transfer during the time period specified in paragraph (e), take the steps required by subsections (f)(1)(i) and (ii).

(3) The issuer shall, in connection with any offers, offers to sell, offers for sale or sales by it pursuant to this rule, disclose, in writing, the limitations on resale contained in paragraph (e) and the provisions of subsections (f)(1)(i) and (ii) and subparagraph (f)(2).

* * *

Rule 149. Definition of "Exchanged" in Section 3(a)(9), for Certain Transactions

The term "exchanged" in section 3(a)(9) shall be deemed to include the issuance of a security in consideration of the surrender by the existing security holders of the issuer, of outstanding securities of the issuer, notwithstanding the fact that the surrender of the outstanding securities may be required by the terms of the plan of exchange to be accompanied by such payment in cash by the security holder as may be necessary to effect an equitable adjustment, in respect of dividends or interest paid or payable on the securities involved in the exchange, as between such security holder and other security holders of the same class accepting the offer of exchange.

Rule 150. Definition of "Commission or Other Remuneration" in Section 3(a)(9), for Certain Transactions

The term "commission or other remuneration" in Section 3(a)(9) shall not include payments made by the issuer, directly or indirectly, to its security holders in connection with an exchange of securities for outstanding securities, when such payments are part of the terms of the offer of exchange.

* * *

Rule 152. Definition of "Transactions by an Issuer Not Involving Any Public Offering" in Section 4(2), for Certain Transactions

The phrase "transactions by an issuer not involving any public offering" in Section 4(2) shall be deemed to apply to transactions not involving any public offering at the time of said transactions although subsequently thereto the issuer decides to make a public offering and/or files a registration statement.

Rule 153. Definition of "Preceded by a Prospectus," as Used in Section 5(b)(2), in Relation to Certain Transactions

(a) The term "preceded by a prospectus," as used in Section 5(b)(2) of the Securities Act of 1933, as amended, in respect of any requirement of delivery of a prospectus to a member of a national securities exchange, on account of a transaction in a security effected on such exchange, shall mean delivery, prior to such transaction, of copies of a prospectus descriptive of such security and meeting the requirements of Section 10(a), to such exchange by the issuer or any underwriter, for the purpose of redelivery to members of such exchange upon their request, *Provided,* That as to any transaction occurring prior to the expiration of forty days after the effective date of the registration statement or the expiration of forty days after the first date upon which the security was *bona fide* offered to the public by the issuer or by or through an underwriter after such effective date, whichever is later (exclusive of the time during which a stop order issued under Section 8 is in effect as to such security):

(1) Such exchange shall theretofore have requested of the issuer or, if such request shall not have been complied with, of a "principal underwriter" (as that term is defined in Rule 405), from time to time, such number of copies of such prospectus as may have appeared reasonably necessary to comply with the requests of its members, and shall have delivered from its supply on hand a copy to any member theretofore making a written request therefor; and

(2) The issuer or any underwriter shall theretofore have furnished such exchange with such reasonable number of copies of such prospectus as may have been requested by the exchange for the purpose stated above.

(b) The term "national securities exchange," as used herein, shall mean a securities exchange registered as a national securities exchange under the Securities Exchange Act of 1934, as amended.

Rule 153A. Definition of "Preceded by a Prospectus" as Used in Section 5(b)(2) in Relation to Certain Transactions Requiring Approval of Security Holders

The term "preceded by a prospectus", as used in Section 5(b)(2) of the Act with respect to any requirement for the delivery of a prospectus to security holders of a corporation or other person, in connection with transactions of the character specified in paragraph (a) of Rule 145 under the Act, shall mean the delivery of a prospectus:

(i) prior to the vote of security holders on such transaction; or,

(ii) with respect to actions taken by consent, prior to the earliest date on which the corporate action may be taken;

to all security holders of record of such corporation or other person, entitled to vote on or consent to the proposed transaction, at their address of record on the transfer records of the corporation or other person:

* * *

Rule 158. Definitions of Certain Terms in the Last Paragraph of Section 11(a)

(a) An "earning statement" made generally available to security holders of the registrant pursuant to the last paragraph of section 11(a) of the Act shall be sufficient for the purposes of such paragraph if (1) there is included the information required for statements of income contained either (i) in Item 8 of Form 10–K, Part I, Item 1 of Form 10–Q, or Rule 14a–3(b) under the Securities Exchange Act of 1934, or (ii) in Item 17 of Form 20–F, if appropriate; and (2) the information specified in the last paragraph of section 11(a) is contained in one report or any combination of reports either (i) on Form 10–K, Form 10–Q, Form 8–K, or in the annual report to security holders pursuant to Rule 14a–3 under the Securities Exchange Act of 1934, or (ii) on Form 20–F or Form 6–K. A subsidiary issuing debt securities guaranteed by its parent will be deemed to have met the requirements of this paragraph if the parent's income statements satisfy the criteria of this paragraph and information respecting the subsidiary is included to the same extent as was presented in the registration statement. An "earning statement" not meeting the requirements of this paragraph may otherwise be sufficient for purposes of the last paragraph of section 11(a).

(b) For purposes of the last paragraph of section 11(a) only, the "earning statement" contemplated by paragraph (a) of this Rule shall be deemed to be "made generally available to its security holders" if the registrant (1) is required to file reports pursuant to section 13 or 15(d) of the Securities Exchange Act of 1934 and (2) has filed its report or reports on Form 10–K, Form 10–Q, Form 8–K, Form 20–F, or Form 6–K, or has supplied to the Commission copies of the annual report sent to security holders pursuant to Rule 14a–3(c), containing such information. A registrant may use other methods to make an earning statement "generally available to its security holders" for purposes of the last paragraph of section 11(a).

(c) For purposes of the last paragraph of section 11(a) only, the "effective date of the registration statement" is deemed to be the date of the latest to occur of (1) the effective date of the registration statement; (2) the effective date of the last post-effective amendment to the registration statement next preceding a particular sale by the registrant of registered securities to the public filed for purposes of (i) including any prospectus required by section 10(a)(3) of the Act, (ii) reflecting in the prospectus any facts or events arising after the effective date of the registration statement (or the most recent post-effective amendment thereof) which, individually or in the aggregate, represent a fundamental change in the information set forth in the registration statement, or (iii) including any material information with respect to the plan of distribution not previously disclosed in this registration statement or any material change to such information in the registration statement, or (3) the date of filing of the last report of the registrant incorporated by reference into the prospectus, and relied upon in lieu of filing a post-effective amendment for purposes of paragraphs (c)(2)(i) and (ii) of this rule, next preceding a particular sale by the registrant of registered securities to the public.

Rule 174. Delivery of Prospectus by Dealers; Exemptions under Section 4(3) of the Act

The obligations of a dealer (including an underwriter no longer acting as an underwriter in respect of the security involved in such transactions) to deliver a prospectus in transactions in a security as to which a registration statement has been filed taking place prior to the expiration of the 40 or 90 day period specified in Section 4(3) of the Act after the effective date of such registration statement or prior to the expiration of such period after the first date upon which the security was bona fide offered to the public by the issuer or by or through an underwriter after such effective date, whichever is later, shall be subject to the following provisions:

(a) No prospectus need be delivered if the registration statement is on Form F–6.

(b) No prospectus need be delivered if the issuer is subject, immediately prior to the time of filing the registration statement, to the reporting requirements of Section 13 or 15(d) of the Securities Exchange Act of 1934.

(c) Where a registration statement relates to offerings to be made from time to time no prospectus need be delivered after the expiration of the initial prospectus delivery period specified in Section 4(3) of the Act following the first bona fide offering of securities under such registration statement.

(d) Notwithstanding the foregoing the period during which a prospectus must be delivered by a dealer shall be:

(1) As specified in Section 4(3) of the Act if the registration statement was the subject of a stop order issued under Section 8 of the Act; or

(2) As the Commission may provide upon application or on its own motion in a particular case.

(e) Nothing in this section shall affect the obligation to deliver a prospectus pursuant to the provisions of Section 5 of the Act by a dealer who is acting as an underwriter with respect to the securities involved or who is engaged in a transaction as to securities constituting the whole or a part of an unsold allotment to or subscription by such dealer as a participant in the distribution of such securities by the issuer or by or through an underwriter.

Rule 175. Liability for Forward-Looking Statements by Issuers

(a) A statement within the coverage of paragraph (b) below which is made by or on behalf of an issuer or by an outside reviewer retained by the issuer shall be deemed not to be a fraudulent statement (as defined in paragraph (d) below), unless it is shown that such statement was made or reaffirmed without a reasonable basis or was disclosed other than in good faith.

(b) This rule applies to the following statements:

(1) A forward-looking statement (as defined in paragraph (c) of this section) made in a document filed with the Commission, in Part I of a quarterly report on Form 10–Q, or in an annual report to shareholders meeting the requirements of Rules 14a–3(b) and (c) or 14c–3(a) and (b) under the Securities Exchange Act of 1934, a statement reaffirming such forward-looking statement subsequent to the date the document was filed or the annual report was made publicly available, or a forward-looking statement made prior to the date the document was filed or the date the annual report was publicly available if such statement is reaffirmed in a filed document, in Part I of a quarterly report on Form 10–Q, or in an annual report made publicly available within a reasonable time after the making of such forward-looking statement; *Provided,* That (i) at the time such statements are made or reaffirmed, either the issuer is subject to the reporting requirements of section 13(a) of 15(d) of the Securities Exchange Act of 1934 and has complied with the requirements of Rule 13a–1 or 15d–1 thereunder, if applicable, to file its most recent annual report on Form 10–K or Form 20–F; or, if the issuer is not subject to the reporting requirements of section 13(a) or 15(d) of the Securities Exchange Act of 1934, the statements are made in a registration statement filed under the Securities Act of 1933 or pursuant to section 12(b) or (g) of the Securities Exchange Act of 1934, and (ii) the statements are not made by or on behalf of an issuer that is an investment company registered under the Investment Company Act of 1940; and

(2) Information which is disclosed in a document filed with the Commission, in Part I of a quarterly report on Form 10–Q or in an annual report to shareholders meeting the requirements of Rules 14a–3(b) and (c) or 14c–3(a) and (b) under the Securities Exchange Act of 1934 and which relates to (i) the effects of changing prices on the business enterprise, presented voluntarily or pursuant to Item 303 of Regulation S–K or Item 9 of Form 20–F, "Management's discussion and analysis of financial condition and results of operations," or Item 302 of Regulation S–K, "Supplementary financial information," or Rule 3–20(c) of Regulation S–X, or (ii) the value of proved oil and gas reserves (such as a standardized measure of discounted future net cash flows relating to proved oil and gas reserves as set forth in paragraphs 30–34 of Statement of Financial Accounting Standards No. 69) presented voluntarily or pursuant to Item 302 of Regulation S–K.

(c) For the purpose of this rule the term "forward looking statement" shall mean and shall be limited to:

(1) A statement containing a projection of revenues, income (loss), earnings (loss) per share, capital expenditures, dividends, capital structure or other financial items;

(2) A statement of management's plans and objectives for future operations;

(3) A statement of future economic performance contained in management's discussion and analysis of financial condition and results of operations included pursuant to Item 303 of Regulation S-K; or

(4) Disclosed statements of the assumptions underlying or relating to any of the statements described in paragraphs (c)(1), (2) or (3) above.

(d) For the purpose of this rule the term "fraudulent statement" shall mean a statement which is an untrue statement of a material fact, a statement false or misleading with respect to any material fact, an omission to state a material fact necessary to make a statement not misleading, or which constitutes the employment of a manipulative, deceptive, or fraudulent device, contrivance, scheme, transaction, act, practice, course of business, or an artifice to defraud, as those terms are used in the Securities Act of 1933 or the rules or regulations promulgated thereunder.

Rule 176. Circumstances Affecting the Determination of What Constitutes Reasonable Investigation and Reasonable Grounds for Belief Under Section 11 of the Securities Act

In determining whether or not the conduct of a person constitutes a reasonable investigation or a reasonable ground for belief meeting the standard set forth in section 11(c), relevant circumstances include, with respect to a person other than the issuer:

(a) The type of issuer;

(b) The type of security;

(c) The type of person;

(d) The office held when the person is an officer;

(e) The presence or absence of another relationship to the issuer when the person is a director or proposed director;

(f) Reasonable reliance on officers, employees, and others whose duties should have given them knowledge of the particular facts (in the light of the functions and responsibilities of the particular person with respect to the issuer and the filing);

(g) When the person is an underwriter, the type of underwriting arrangement, the role of the particular person as an underwriter and the availability of information with respect to the registrant; and

(h) Whether, with respect to a fact or document incorporated by reference, the particular person had any responsibility for the fact or document at the time of the filing from which it was incorporated.

* * *

Rule 215. Definition of "Accredited Investor" in Section 2(15)

The term "accredited investor" as used in section 2(15)(ii) of the Securities Act of 1933 shall include the following persons:

(a) Any employee benefit plan within the meaning of Title I of the Employee Retirement Income Security Act of 1974 with total assets in excess of $5,000,000;

(b) Any private business development company as defined in section 202(a)(22) of the Investment Advisers Act of 1940;

(c) Any organization described in section 501(c)(3) of the Internal Revenue Code with total assets in excess of $5,000,000;

(d) Any director, executive officer, or general partner of the issuer of the securities being offered or sold, or any director, executive officer, or general partner of a general partner of that issuer;

(e) Any person who purchases at least $150,000 of the securities being offered, where the purchaser's total purchase price does not exceed 20 percent of the purchaser's net worth at the time of sale, or joint net worth with that person's spouse, for one or any combination of the following: (1) cash, (2) securities for which market quotations are readily available, (3) an unconditional obligation to pay cash or securities for which market quotations are readily available which obligation is to be discharged within five years of the sale of the securities to the purchaser, or (4) the cancellation of any indebtedness owed by the issuer to the purchaser;

(f) Any natural person whose individual net worth, or joint net worth with that person's spouse, at the time of his purchase exceeds $1,000,000;

(g) Any natural person who had an individual income in excess of $200,000 in each of the two most recent years and who reasonably expects an income in excess of $200,000 in the current year; and

(h) Any entity in which all of the equity owners are accredited investors under paragraph (a), (b), (c), (d), (f) or (g) of Rule 215.

REGULATION A—GENERAL EXEMPTION

Rule 251. Definitions of Terms Used in This Regulation

As used in this regulation, the following terms shall have the meaning indicated:

Affiliate. An "affiliate" of an issuer is a person controlling, controlled by or under common control with such issuer.

Parent. A "parent" of a specified person is an affiliate controlling such person directly, or indirectly through one or more intermediaries.

Predecessor. A "predecessor" of an issuer is (i) a person the major portion of whose assets have been acquired directly or indirectly by the issuer, or (ii) a person from which the issuer acquired directly or indirectly the major portion of its assets.

Promoter. The term "promoter" includes—

(*a*) Any person who, acting alone or in conjunction with one or more other persons, directly or indirectly takes the initiative in founding and organizing the business or enterprise of an issuer:

(*b*) Any person who, in connection with the founding or organizing of the business or enterprise of an issuer, directly or indirectly receives in consideration of services or property, or both services and property, 10 percent or more of any class of securities of the issuer or 10 percent or more of the proceeds from the sale of any class of securities. However, a person who receives such securities or proceeds either solely as underwriting commissions or solely in consideration of property shall not be deemed a promoter within the meaning of this paragraph if such person does not otherwise take part in founding and organizing the enterprise.

Province. A "Province" is any Province or Territory of Canada.

Resident. A "resident" of a specified country is an individual resident of such country or a corporation or other organization which is incorporated or organized under the laws of such country or any of its political subdivisions.

State. A "State" is any State, Territory or insular possession of the United States, or the District of Columbia.

Underwriter. The term "underwriter" shall have the meaning given in section 2(11) of the Act.

Rule 252. Securities Exempted

(*a*) Except as hereinafter provided in this regulation, securities issued by any of the following persons shall be exempt from registration under the Act if offered in accordance with the terms and conditions of this regulation:

(1) Any corporation, unincorporated association or trust (i) which is incorporated or organized under the laws of the United States or Canada or any State or Province thereof and (ii) which has or proposes to have its principal business operations in the United States or Canada; or

(2) Any individual who is a resident of, and has or proposes to have his principal business operations in, any State or Province; or

(3) In the case of an offering to existing security holders on a pro rata basis pursuant to warrants or rights, any direct or indirect majority-owned subsidiary of any issuer specified in (1) above which has securities registered on a national securities exchange pursuant to the provisions of the Securities Exchange Act of 1934.

(*b*) No exemption under this regulation shall be available for any of the following securities:

(1) Fractional undivided interests in oil or gas rights as defined in Rule 300, or similar interests in other mineral rights;

(2) Securities of any investment company registered or required to be registered under the Investment Company Act of 1940.

(*c*) No exemption under this regulation shall be available for the securities of any issuer if such issuer, any of its predecessors or any affiliated issuer—

(1) Has filed a registration statement which is the subject of any proceeding or examination under section 8 of the Act, or is the subject of any refusal order or stop order entered thereunder within 5 years prior to the filing of the notification required by Rule 255;

(2) Is subject to pending proceedings under Rule 261 or any similar rule adopted under section 3(b) of the Act, or to an order entered thereunder within 5 years prior to the filing of such notification;

(3) Has been convicted within five years prior to the filing of such notification of any felony or misdemeanor in connection with the purchase or sale of any security or involving the making of any false filing with the Commission;

(4) Is subject to any order, judgment, or decree of any court of competent jurisdiction temporarily or preliminarily restraining or enjoining, or is subject to any order, judgment or decree of any court of competent jurisdiction, entered within five years prior to the filing of such notification, permanently restraining or enjoining, such person from engaging in or continuing any conduct or practice in connection with the purchase or sale of any security or involving the making of any false filing with the Commission; or

(5) Is subject to a United States Postal Service false representation order entered under section 3005 of title 39, United States Code, within five years prior to the filing of the notification required by Rule 255; or is subject to a temporary restraining order or preliminary injunction entered under section 3007 of title 39, United States Code, with respect to conduct alleged to have violated section 3005 of title 39, United States Code.

This paragraph (c) of Rule 252 shall not apply to any order, judgment, or decree contemplated by paragraphs (1) through (5) hereunder because of its entry against any affiliated entity before the affiliation with the issuer arose, if the affiliated entity is not in control of the issuer and if the affiliated entity and the issuer are not under the common control of a third party who was in control of the affiliated entity at the time the order, judgment, or decree was entered against it.

(d) No exemption under this regulation shall be available for the securities of any issuer, if any of its directors, officers, general partners, or beneficial owners of ten percent or more of any class of its equity securities (beneficial ownership meaning the power to vote or direct the vote and/or the power to dispose or direct the disposition of such securities), any of its promoters presently connected with it in any capacity, any underwriter of the securities to be offered, or any partner, director, or officer of any such underwriter—

(1) Has been convicted within ten years prior to the filing of the notification required by Rule 255 of any felony or misdemeanor in connection with the purchase or sale of any security, involving the making of a false filing with the Commission, or arising out of the conduct of the business of an underwriter, broker, dealer, municipal securities dealer, or investment adviser;

(2) Is subject to any order, judgment, or decree of any court of competent jurisdiction temporarily or preliminarily enjoining or restraining, or is subject to any order, judgment, or decree of any court of competent jurisdiction, entered within five years prior to the filing of such notification, permanently enjoining or restraining such person from engaging in or continuing any conduct or practice in connection with the purchase or sale of any security, involving the making of a false filing with the Commission, or arising out of the conduct of the business of an underwriter, broker, dealer, municipal securities dealer, or investment adviser;

(3) Is subject to an order of the Commission entered pursuant to section 15(b), 15B(a), or 15B(c) of the Securities Exchange Act of 1934; or is subject to an order of the Commission entered pursuant to section 203(e) or (f) of the Investment Advisers Act of 1940;

(4) Is suspended or expelled from membership in, or suspended or barred from association with a member of, an exchange registered as a national securities exchange pursuant to section 6 of the

Securities Exchange Act of 1934, an association registered as a national securities association under section 15A of the Securities Exchange Act of 1934, or a Canadian securities exchange or association for any act or omission to act constituting conduct inconsistent with just and equitable principles of trade; or

(5) Is subject to a United States Postal Service false representation order entered under section 3005 of title 39, United States Code, within five years prior to the filing of the notification required by Rule 255 or is subject to a restraining order or preliminary injunction entered under section 3007 of title 39, United States Code, with respect to conduct alleged to have violated section 3005 of title 39, United States Code.

(e) No exemption under this regulation shall be available for the securities of any issuer if any underwriter of such securities was, or was named as, an underwriter of any securities:

(1) Covered by any registration statement which is the subject of any pending proceeding or examination under section 8 of the Act, or is the subject of any refusal order or stop order entered thereunder within 5 years prior to the filing of the notification required by Rule 255; or

(2) Covered by a filing which is subject to pending proceedings under Rule 261 or any similar rule adopted under section 3(b) of the Act, or to an order entered thereunder within 5 years prior to the filing of such notification.

(f) No exemption under this regulation shall be available for the securities of an issuer which is subject to the requirements of sections 13, 14, 15(d) of the Securities Exchange Act of 1934, unless such issuer has filed all reports required by those sections to be filed during the 12 calendar months preceding the filing of the notification required by Rule 255 (or for such shorter period that the issuer was required to file such reports).

(g) Paragraph(*c*), (*d*), (*e*) or (*f*) shall not apply to the securities of any issuer if the Commission determines, upon a showing of good cause, that it is not necessary under the circumstances that the exemption be denied. Any such determination by the Commission shall be without prejudice to any other action by the Commission in any other proceeding or matter with respect to the issuer or any other person.

Rule 253. Special Requirements for Certain Offerings

(*a*) The following provisions of this rule shall apply to any offering under this regulation of securities of any issuer which—

(1) was incorporated or organized within 1 year prior to the date of filing the notification required by Rule 255 and has not had a net income from operations; or

(2) was incorporated or organized more than 1 year prior to such date and has not had a net income from operations, of the character in which the issuer intends to engage, for at least one of the last 2 fiscal years.

(*b*) If the issuer conducts or proposes to conduct its principal business operations in Canada, the securities to be offered hereunder shall be qualified or made eligible for offering in the Province in which such operations are or will be conducted. The securities of any other issuer incorporated or organized under the laws of Canada or any Province thereof shall be qualified or made eligible for offering in the Province in which the issuer has its principal office or principal place of business in Canada. All securities subject to this paragraph shall be offered in the Province in which they are qualified or made eligible for offering, concurrently with the offering in the United States. Issuers engaged in extractive or manufacturing enterprises shall be deemed to have their principal business operations in the Province in which their principal plants or other properties are located.

(*c*) In computing the amount of securities which may be offered hereunder, there shall be included, in addition to the securities specified in Rule 254—

(1) All securities issued prior to the filing of the offering statement, or proposed to be issued, for a consideration consisting in whole or in part of assets or services and held by the person to whom issued; and

(2) All securities issued to and held by or proposed to be issued, pursuant to options or otherwise, to any director, officer or promoter of the issuer, or to any underwriter, dealer or security salesman:

Provided, That such securities need not be included to the extent that effective provision is made, by escrow arrangements or otherwise, to assure that none of such securities or any interest therein will e reoffered to the public within 1 year after the commencement of the offering hereunder and that any reoffering of such securities will be made in accordance with the applicable provisions of the Act.

(*d*) None of the securities to be offered hereunder shall be offered for the account of any person other than the issuer of such securities.

(*e*) Rule 257 shall not apply to any offering of securities under this regulation by any issuer which is subject to this rule.

Rule 254. Amount of Securities Exempted

(*a*) For determining the requisite amount:

(1) The aggregate offering price of all securities of the issuer offered or sold pursuant to this regulation and any other securities offered or sold within one year prior to the commencement of the proposed offering pursuant to any other exemption under Section 3(b) of the Act or in violation of Section 5(a) of the Act shall not exceed the following amounts:

(i) $1,500,000 if the securities are offered or sold by or on behalf of the issuer, or by the estate of a decedent who owned the securities at death if offered within two years after the death of the decedent, or by affiliates of issuer; provided that the aggregate offering price of securities offered or sold by or on behalf of any one affiliate, other than an estate shall not exceed $100,000; and

(ii) $100,000 if the securities are offered or sold by or on behalf of any person other than the issuer or its affiliates; provided that the aggregate offering price of all such securities offered or sold by or on behalf of all such other persons shall not exceed $300,000 and provided that the aggregate offering price of securities offered or sold by or on behalf of an estate pursuant to this paragraph and paragraph (i) above shall not exceed $500,000.

(2) When two or more persons agree to act in concert for the purpose of selling securities of the issuer, all securities of the same class sold for the account of all such persons during any 12-month period shall be aggregated for the purpose of determining the limitation on the amount of securities sold.

(3) The following definitions shall apply for the purposes of this rule:

(A) The term "securities of the issuer" shall include securities issued by any predecessor of the issuer or by any affiliate of the issuer which was organized or became such an affiliate within the past two years.

(B) The term "person" when used with reference to a person who offers securities in reliance upon the exemption provided by this rule includes, in addition to such person, all of the following persons:

(i) Any relative or spouse of such person, or any relative of such spouse, any one of whom has the same home as such person;

(ii) Any trust or estate in which such person or any of the persons specified in (i) collectively own ten percent or more of the total beneficial interest or of which any of such persons serve as trustee, executor or in any similar capacity; and

(iii) Any corporation or other organization (other than the issuer) in which such person or any of the persons specified in (i) are the beneficial owners collectively of ten percent or more of any class of equity securities or ten percent or more of the equity interest.

(*b*) The aggregate offering price of securities which have a determinable market value shall be computed upon the basis of such market value as determined from transactions or quotations on a specified date within 15 days prior to the date of filing the offering statement or the offering price to the public, whichever is higher: *Provided,* That the aggregate gross proceeds actually received from the public for the securities offered hereunder shall not exceed the maximum aggregate offering price permitted in the particular case by paragraph *(a)* of this rule.

(*c*) Where securities which have no determinable market value are offered in exchange for outstanding securities, claims, property, or services, the aggregate offering price thereof shall be computed at the public offering price of securities of the same class for cash, or if no cash offering is to be made, then upon the basis of the value of the securities, claims, property or services to be received in exchange, as established by bona fide sales made within a reasonable time, or in the absence of such sales, upon the basis of the fair value of the securities, claims, property or services to be received in exchange, as determined by some accepted standard.

(*d*) The following securities need not be included in computing the amount of securities which may be offered under this regulation:

(1) Unsold securities the offering of which has been withdrawn with the consent of the Commission by amending the pertinent offering statement to reduce the amount stated therein as proposed to be offered;

(2) Securities acquired or to be acquired, otherwise than for distribution by a single holder of the majority of the outstanding voting stock of the issuer in connection with a pro rata offering to stockholders;

(3) In the case of an offering by an issuer to existing security holders on a pro rata basis pursuant to warrants or rights, that portion of the offering made outside of the United States and Canada;

(4) In the case of an offering of interests in an unincorporated theatrical production, interests in any affiliated unincorporated theatrical production; or

(5) In the case of an offering of interests in an unincorporated issuer organized to hold title to, lease, operate or improve specific real property, interests in any affiliated issuer organized to hold title to, lease, operate or improve other specific real property.

Rule 255. Filing of Offering Statement

(a) At least 10 days (Saturdays, Sundays and holidays excluded) prior to the date on which the initial offering or sale of any securities is to be made under this regulation, there shall be filed with the Regional Office of the Commission specified below five copies of the offering statement required by this Regulation which shall consist of Part I—Notification, Part II—Offering Circular, and Part III—Exhibits. The Commission may, however, in its discretion, authorize the commencement of the offering prior to the expiration of such 10-day period upon a written request for such authorization.

(b) The offering statement shall be signed by the issuer and each person, other than the issuer, for whose account any of the securities are to be offered. If the offering statement is signed by any person on behalf of any other person, evidence of authority to sign on behalf of such other person shall be filed with the offering statement, except where an officer of the issuer signs on behalf of the issuer. At the time of filing an offering statement, the applicant shall pay to the Commission at the Regional Office where the offering statement is filed a fee of $100.00, no part of which shall be refunded.

(c) The offering statement shall be filed with the Regional Office for the region in which the issuer's principal business operations are conducted or proposed to be conducted in the United States. The offering statement of any issuer having or proposing to have its principal business operations in Canada shall be filed with the Regional Office nearest the place where the issuer's principal business operations are conducted or proposed to be conducted, unless the offering is to be made through a principal underwriter located in the United States, in which case the offering statement shall be filed with the Regional Office for the region in which such underwriter has its principal office.

(d) An amendment to any part of the offering statement will necessitate the filing of an amended offering statement which shall be signed in the same manner as the original offering statement. Five copies of such amendment shall be filed with the same Regional Office as the original offering statement at least 10 days prior to any offering or sale of the securities subsequent to the filing of such amendment, or such shorter period as the Commission, in its discretion, may authorize upon a written request for such authorization.

(e) An offering statement or any other document filed as a part thereof may be withdrawn upon application unless the offering statement is subject to an order under Rule 261 at the time the application is filed or becomes subject to such an order within 15 days (Saturdays, Sundays and holidays excluded) thereafter, *Provided* That an offering statement may not be withdrawn after any of the securities proposed to be offered thereunder have been sold. Any such application shall be signed in the same manner and filed with the same Regional Office as the offering statement.

(f) The manually signed original (or in the case of duplicate originals, one duplicate original) of all offering statements, reports, or other documents filed shall be numbered sequentially (in addition to any internal numbering which otherwise may be present) by handwritten, typed, printed, or other legible form of notation from the cover page of the document through the last page of that document and any exhibits or attachments thereto. Further, the total number of pages contained in a numbered original shall be set forth on the first page of the document.

(g) Each offering statement shall contain an exhibit index, which should immediately precede the exhibits filed with such offering statement. The index shall list each exhibit filed and identify by handwritten, typed, printed, or other legible form of notation in the manually signed original, the page number in the sequential numbering system described in paragraph (f) of this rule where such exhibit can be found or where it is stated that the exhibit is incorporated by reference. Further, the first page of the manually signed offering statement shall list the page in the filing where the exhibit index is located.

Rule 256. Filing and Use of the Offering Circular

(*a*) Except as provided in paragraph (*c*) of this rule and in Rule 257—

(1) No written offer of securities of any issuer shall be made under this regulation unless an offering circular containing the information specified in Part II of the offering statement is concurrently given or has previously been given to the person to whom the offer is made, or has been sent to such person under such circumstances that it would normally have been received by him at or prior to the time of such written offer; and

(2) No securities of such issuer shall be sold under this regulation unless such an offering circular is furnished to the person to whom the securities are expected to be sold at least 48 hours prior to the mailing of the confirmation of sale to such person, or is sent to such person under such circumstances that it would normally be received by him 48 hours prior to his receipt of confirmation of the sale; provided however, if the issuer is required to file reports pursuant to Section 13(a) or 15(d) of the Securities Exchange Act of 1934, as amended, the offering circular may be furnished with or prior to the confirmation of sale.

(b) In the case of transactions effected on a securities exchange, delivery of the offering circular (offering statement—Part II) shall be deemed to have been made if prior to such transactions a reasonable number of copies of the offering circular have been furnished to the exchange for delivery to any person or persons requesting copies thereof.

(c) Any written advertisement or other written communication, or any radio or television broadcast, which states from whom an offering circular containing the information specified in Part II of the offering statement may be obtained and in addition contains no more than the following information may be published, distributed or broadcast at or after the commencement of the public offering to any person prior to sending or giving such person a copy of such circular:

(1) the name of the issuer of such security;

(2) the title of the security, the amount being offered, and the per-unit offering price to the public;

(3) the identity of the general type of business of the issuer; and

(4) a brief statement as to the general character and location of its property.

(d) If the offering is not completed within nine months from the date of the offering circular (offering statement—Part II) a revised offering circular shall be prepared, filed and used in accordance with these rules as for an original offering circular, except that in the case of offerings under stock purchase, savings, stock option or other similar plans for the benefit of employees, if the offering is not completed within 12 months from the date of the offering circular, a revised offering circular shall be prepared, filed and used in accordance with these rules as for an original offering circular. In no event shall an offering circular be used which is false or misleading in light of the circumstances then existing.

(e) If the original offering circular (offering statement—Part II) is revised or amended, such revised or amended circular shall be filed as an amendment to the offering statement, as provided by Rule 255(d), with the appropriate Regional Office of the Commission at least 10 days prior to its use, or such shorter period as the Commission may, in its discretion, authorize upon a written request for such authorization.

(f) Sales by a dealer (including an underwriter no longer acting as an underwriter in respect of the security involved in such transaction) of securities of an issuer not subject, immediately prior to the time of filing an offering statement, to the provisions of section 13(a) or 15(d) of the Securities Exchange Act of 1934, as amended, offered pursuant to this regulation and taking place prior to the expiration of ninety days after the first date upon which the securities were bona fide offered to the public, shall not be exempt pursuant to this regulation unless: (1) the dealer furnishes a copy of the then current offering circular (offering statement—Part II) to the purchaser prior to or with the purchaser's receipt of the confirmation of the sale; or (2) the offering circular has previously been mailed or delivered to such purchaser. Failure by a dealer to comply with the provision of this subparagraph shall not otherwise affect the availability of the exemption for any other person, including the aggregate amount of securities exempted pursuant to Rule 254.

(g) The issuer or, if there is an underwriter, the underwriter shall provide reasonable quantities of copies of the offering circular (offering statement—Part II) to any dealer on request prior to the expiration of ninety days after the first date upon which securities of such issuer were bona fide offered to the public pursuant to this regulation.

(h) An offering circular filed pursuant to paragraph (e) of this section may be distributed prior to the expiration of the 10–day waiting period for offerings provided for in Rule 255(a) and (d) and paragraph (e) of this rule and such distribution may be accompanied or followed by oral offers related thereto, provided the conditions in paragraphs (1) through (4) are met. For the purposes of this rule, any offering circular distributed prior to the expiration of the ten day waiting period is called a Preliminary Offering Circular. Such Preliminary Offering Circular may be used to meet the requirements of paragraph (a)(2) of Rule 256: *Provided,* That if a Preliminary Offering Circular is inaccurate or inadequate in any material respect, a revised Preliminary Offering Circular or an offering circular of the type referred to in paragraph (4) of this rule, shall be furnished to all persons to whom the securities are to be sold at least 48 hours prior to the mailing of any confirmation of sale to such persons, or shall be sent to such persons under such circumstances that it would normally be received by them 48 hours prior to their receipt of confirmation of the sale.

(1) Such Preliminary Offering Circular contains substantially the information required by this rule to be included in an offering circular, or contains substantially that information except for the omission of information with respect to the offering price, underwriting discounts or commissions, discounts or commissions to dealers, amount of proceeds, conversion rates, call prices, or other matters dependent upon the offering price. For issuers not subject to the reporting provisions under section 13(a) or 15(d) of the Securities Exchange Act of 1934, the disclosure on the outside front cover page of the Preliminary Offering Circular should include a bona fide estimate of the range of the maximum offering price and maximum number of shares or other units of securities to be offered or should include a bona fide estimate of the principal amount of debt securities to be offered.

(2) The outside front cover page of the Preliminary Offering Circular shall bear the caption "Preliminary Offering Circular," the date of its issuance, and the following statement which shall run along the left hand margin of the page and be printed perpendicular to the text, in boldface type at least as large as that used generally in the body of such offering circular.

An offering statement pursuant to Regulation A relating to these securities has been filed with the Securities and Exchange Commission. Information contained in this Preliminary Offering Circular is subject to completion or amendment. These securities may not be sold nor may offers to buy be accepted prior to the time an offering circular which is not designated as a Preliminary Offering Circular is delivered. This Preliminary Offering Circular shall not constitute an offer to sell or the solicitation of an offer to buy nor shall there be any sales of these securities in any state in which such offer, solicitation or sale would be unlawful prior to registration or qualification under the securities laws of any such state.

(3) The Preliminary Offering Circular relates to a proposed public offering of securities which is to be sold by or through one or more underwriters who are broker-dealers registered under section 15

of the Securities Exchange Act of 1934, each of whom has furnished a signed Consent and Certification in the form prescribed as a condition to the use of such offering circular.

(4) An offering circular which contains all of the information specified in Part II of the offering statement and which is not designated as a Preliminary Offering Circular is furnished with or prior to delivery of the confirmation of sale to any person who has been furnished with a Preliminary Offering Circular pursuant to this paragraph.

Rule 257. Offerings Not in Excess of $100,000

Except as to issues specified in paragraph (*a*) of Rule 253 and issues of assessable stock, the offering circular (offering statement—Part II) need not be filed or used in connection with an offering of securities under this regulation if the aggregate offering price of all securities of the issuer, its predecessors and affiliates offered or sold without the use of such an offering circular does not exceed $100,000 computed in accordance with Rule 254, provided the following conditions are met:

(*a*) In addition to filing Part I—Notification and Part III—Exhibits, there shall be filed as an exhibit five copies of a statement setting forth the information (other than financial statements) required by Part II—Offering Circular of the offering statement.

(*b*) No advertisement, article or other communication published in any newspaper, magazine or other periodical and no radio or television broadcast in regard to the offering shall contain more than the following information:

(1) The name of the issuer of such security;

(2) The title of the security, amount offered, and the per-unit offering price to the public;

(3) The identity of the general type of business of the issuer;

(4) A brief statement as to the general character and location of its property; and

(5) By whom orders will be filled or from whom further information may be obtained.

Rule 258. Sales Material to be Filed

Four copies of each of the following communications prepared or authorized by the issuer or anyone associated with the issuer, any of its affiliates or any principal underwriter for use in connection with the offering of any securities under this regulation shall be filed, with the office of the Commission with which the offering statement is filed, at least 5 days (exclusive of Saturdays, Sundays and holidays) prior to any use thereof, or such shorter period as the Commission, in its discretion, may authorize:

(*a*) Every advertisement, article or other communication proposed to be published in any newspaper, magazine or other periodical;

(*b*) The script of every radio or television broadcast; and

(*c*) Every letter, circular or other written communication proposed to be sent, given or otherwise communicated to more than 10 persons, except an offering circular (offering statement—Part II) filed pursuant to Rule 256(e).

Rule 259. Statement Required in All Offering Circulars

There shall be set forth on the cover page of every offering circular the following statement in capital letters printed in boldface roman type at least as large as ten-point modern type and at least two points leaded;

"THE UNITED STATES SECURITIES AND EXCHANGE COMMISSION DOES NOT PASS UPON THE MERITS OF OR GIVE ITS APPROVAL TO ANY SECURITIES OFFERED OR THE TERMS OF THE OFFERING, NOR DOES IT PASS UPON THE ACCURACY OR COMPLETENESS OF ANY OFFERING CIRCULAR OR OTHER SELLING LITERATURE. THESE SECURITIES ARE OFFERED PURSUANT TO AN EXEMPTION FROM REGISTRATION WITH THE COMMISSION; HOWEVER, THE COMMISSION HAS NOT MADE AN INDEPENDENT DETERMINATION THAT THE SECURITIES OFFERED HEREUNDER ARE EXEMPT FROM REGISTRATION."

Rule 260. Reports of Sales Hereunder

Within 30 days after the end of each 6-month period following the date of the original offering circular (offering statement—Part II) required by Rule 256, or of the statement required by Rule 257, the issuer or other person for whose account the securities are offered shall file with the Regional

Office of the Commission with which the offering statement was filed four copies of a report on Form 2–A containing the information called for by that form. A final report shall be made upon completion or termination of the offering and may be made prior to the end of the 6-month period in which the last sale is made.

Rule 261. Suspension of Exemption

(*a*) The Commission may, at any time after the filing of an offering statement, enter an order temporarily suspending the exemption, if it has reason to believe that—

(1) No exemption is available under this regulation for the securities purported to be offered hereunder or any of the terms or conditions of this regulation have not been complied with, including failure to file any report as required by Rule 260.

(2) The offering statement or any other sales literature contains any untrue statement of a material fact or omits to state a material fact necessary in order to make the statements made, in the light of the circumstances under which they are made, not misleading;

(3) The offering is being made or would be made in violation of section 17 of the Act;

(4) Any event has occurred after the filing of the offering statement which would have rendered the exemption hereunder unavailable if it had occurred prior to such filing;

(5) Any person specified in paragraph (*c*) of Rule 252 has been indicted for any crime or offense of the character specified in subparagraph (3) thereof, or any proceeding has been initiated for the purpose of enjoining any such person from engaging in or continuing any conduct or practice of the character specified in subparagraph (4) of such paragraph;

(6) Any person specified in paragraph (*d*) of Rule 252 has been indicted for any crime or offense of the character specified in subparagraph (1) thereof, or any proceeding has been initiated for the purpose of enjoining any such person from engaging in or continuing any conduct or practice of the character specified in subparagraph (2) of such paragraph; or

(7) The issuer or any promoter, officer, director or underwriter has failed to cooperate, or has obstructed or refused to permit the making of an investigation by the Commission in connection with any offering made or proposed to be made hereunder.

(*b*) Upon the entry of an order under paragraph (*a*) of this rule, the Commission will promptly give notice to the persons on whose behalf the offering statement was filed (i) that such order has been entered, together with a brief statement of the reasons for the entry of the order, and (ii) that the Commission, upon receipt of a written request within 30 days after the entry of such order, will, within 20 days after the receipt of such request, set the matter down for hearing at a place to be designated by the Commission. If no hearing is requested and none is ordered by the Commission, the order shall become permanent on the 30th day after its entry and shall remain in effect unless or until it is modified or vacated by the Commission. Where a hearing is requested or is ordered by the Commission, the Commission will, after notice of an opportunity for such hearing, either vacate the order or enter an order permanently suspending the exemption.

(*c*) The Commission may at any time after notice of an opportunity for hearing, enter an order permanently suspending the exemption for any reason upon which it could have entered a temporary suspension order under paragraph (*a*) of this rule. Any such order shall remain in effect until vacated by the Commission.

(*d*) All notices required by this rule shall be given to the person or persons on whose behalf the offering statement was filed by personal service, registered or certified mail or confirmed telegraphic notice at the addresses of such persons given in the offering statement.

Rule 262. Consent to Service of Process

(*a*) If the issuer, any of its directors or officers, any person for whose account any of the securities are to be offered, or any underwriter of the securities to be offered, is not a resident of the United States, each such nonresident person shall, at the time of filing the offering statement required by Rule 255, furnish the Commission in a form prescribed by or acceptable to it, a written irrevocable consent and power of attorney which—

(1) Designates the Securities and Exchange Commission as an agent upon whom may be served

any process, pleadings, or other papers in any civil suit or action brought against the person executing the consent and power of attorney or to which he has been joined as defendant or respondent, in any appropriate court in any place subject to the jurisdiction of the United States, where the cause of action (i) accrues on or after the effective date of this rule, and (ii) arises out of any offering made or purported to be made under this regulation or any purchase or sale of any security in connection therewith; and

(2) Stipulates and agrees that any such civil suit or action may be commenced by the service of process upon the Commission and the forwarding of a copy thereof as provided in paragraph (*b*) of this rule, and that the service as aforesaid of any such process, pleadings, or other papers upon the Commission shall be taken and held in all courts to be as valid and binding as if due personal service thereof had been made.

(*b*) Service of any process, pleadings or other papers on the Commission under his rule shall be made by delivering the requisite number of copies thereof to the Secretary of the Commission or to such other person as the Commission may authorize to act in its behalf. Whenever any process, pleadings or other papers as aforesaid are served upon the Commission, it shall promptly forward a copy thereof by registered or certified mail to the appropriate defendants at their last address of record filed with the Commission. The Commission shall be furnished a sufficient number of copies for such purpose, and one copy for its files.

Rule 263. Notice of Delayed or Suspended Offering and Sale

If within 3 business days after the issuer has received notice that the Commission has no further comments with respect to the offering statement a bona fide effort is not made to proceed with the offering and sale of the securities proposed to be offered under this regulation, or if the offering or sale of such securities is suspended by the issuer or any underwriter within 15 days after the issuer has received such notice, a notice of the delay or suspension, stating the reasons therefor, shall be filed by the issuer or underwriter with the Regional Office of the Commission with which the offering statement was filed, unless such information is set forth in the offering statement. Such notice shall be sent promptly by telegraph or air mail and if sent by telegraph shall be confirmed in writing within a reasonable time by the filing of a signed copy of the notice.

* * *

REGULATION C—REGISTRATION

Rule 400. Application of Regulation C

The rules contained in this regulation shall govern every registration of securities under the Act, except that any provision in a form, or an item of Regulation S–K referred to in such form, covering the same subject matter as any such rule shall be controlling unless otherwise specifically provided herein.

General Requirements

* * *

Rule 404. Preparation of Registration Statement

(a) A registration statement shall consist of the facing sheet of the applicable form; cross reference sheet; a prospectus containing the information called for by Part I of such form; the information, list of exhibits, undertakings and signatures required to be set forth in Part II of such form; financial statements and schedules; exhibits; any other information or documents filed as part of the registration statement; and all documents or information incorporated by reference in the foregoing (whether or not required to be filed).

(b) All general instructions, instructions to items of the form, and instructions as to financial statements, exhibits, or prospectuses are to be omitted from the registration statement in all cases.

(c) The prospectus shall contain the information called for by all of the items of Part I of the applicable form, except that unless otherwise specified, no reference need by made to inapplicable items, and negative answers to any item in Part I may be omitted. A copy of the prospectus may be filed as a part of the registration statement in lieu of furnishing the information in item-and-answer form. Wherever a copy of the prospectus is filed in lieu of information in item-and-answer form, the text of the items of the form is to be omitted from the registration statement, as well as from the prospectus, except to the extent provided in paragraph (d) of this rule.

* * *

Rule 405. Definitions of Terms

Unless the context otherwise requires, all terms used in this regulation, or in the forms for registration have the same meanings as in the Act and in the general rules and regulations. In addition, the following definitions apply, unless the context otherwise requires:

Affiliate. An "affiliate" of, or person "affiliated" with, a specified person, is a person that directly, or indirectly through one or more intermediaries, controls or is controlled by, or is under common control with, the person specified.

Amount. The term "amount," when used in regard to securities, means the principal amount if relating to evidences of indebtedness, the number of shares if relating to shares, and the number of units if relating to any other kind of security.

Associate. The term "associate," when used to indicate a relationship with any person, means (1) a corporation or organization (other than the registrant or a majority-owned subsidiary of the registrant) of which such person is an officer or partner or is, directly or indirectly, the beneficial owner of 10 percent or more of any class of equity securities, (2) any trust or other estate in which such person has a substantial beneficial interest or as to which such person serves as trustee or in a similar capacity, and (3) any relative or spouse of such person, or any relative of such spouse, who has the same home as such person or who is a director or officer of the registrant or any of its parents or subsidiaries.

Business development company. The term "business development company" refers to a company which has elected to be regulated as a business development company under sections 55 through 65 of the Investment Company Act of 1940.

Certified. The term "certified," when used in regard to financial statements, means examined and reported upon with an opinion expressed by an independent public or certified public accountant.

Charter. The term "charter" includes articles of incorporation, declarations of trust, articles of association or partnership, or any similar instrument, as amended, affecting (either with or without filing with any governmental agency) the organization or creation of an incorporated or unincorporated person.

Common equity. The term "common equity" means any class of common stock or an equivalent interest, including but not limited to a unit of beneficial interest in a trust or a limited partnership interest.

Commission. The term "Commission" means the Securities and Exchange Commission.

Control. The term "control" (including the terms "controlling," "controlled by" and "under common control with") means the possession, direct or indirect, of the power to direct or cause the direction of the management and policies of a person, whether through the ownership of voting securities, by contract, or otherwise.

Director. The term "director" means any director of a corporation or any person performing similar functions with respect to any organization whether incorporated or unincorporated.

* * *

Employee. The term "employee" does not include a director, trustee, or officer.

Employee benefit plan. The term "employee benefit plan" means any purchase, savings, option, bonus, appreciation, profit sharing, thrift, incentive, pension or similar plan solely for employees, directors, trustees or officers.

Equity security. The term "equity security" means any stock or similar security, certificate of interest or participation in any profit sharing agreement, preorganization certificate or subscription, transferable share, voting trust certificate or certificate of deposit for an equity security, limited partnership interest, interest in a joint venture, or certificate of interest in a business trust; or any security convertible, with or without consideration into such a security, or carrying any warrant or right to subscribe to or purchase such a security; or any such warrant or right; or any put, call, straddle, or other option or privilege of buying such a security from or selling such a security to another without being bound to do so.

Executive officer. The term "executive officer," when used with reference to a registrant, means its president, any vice president of the registrant in charge of a principal business unit, division or function (such as sales, administration or finance), any other officer who performs a policy making function or any other person who performs similar policy making functions for the registrant. Executive officers of subsidiaries may be deemed executive officers of the registrant if they perform such policy making functions for the registrant.

Fiscal year. The term "fiscal year" means the annual accounting period or, if no closing date has been adopted, the calendar year ending on December 31.

* * *

Managing underwriter. The term "managing underwriter" includes an underwriter (or underwriters) who, by contract or otherwise, deals with the registrant; organizes the selling effort; receives some benefit directly or indirectly in which all other underwriters similarly situated do not share in proportion to their respective interests in the underwriting; or represents any other underwriters in such matters as maintaining the records of the distribution, arranging the allotments of securities offered or arranging for appropriate stabilization activities, if any.

Material. The term "material," when used to qualify a requirement for the furnishing of information as to any subject, limits the information required to those matters to which there is a substantial likelihood that a reasonable investor would attach importance in determining whether to purchase the security registered.

* * *

Officer. The term "officer" means a president, vice president, secretary, treasurer or principal financial officer, comptroller or principal accounting officer, and any person routinely performing corresponding functions with respect to any organization whether incorporated or unincorporated.

Parent. A "parent" of a specified person is an affiliate controlling such person directly, or indirectly through one or more intermediaries.

Predecessor. The term "predecessor" means a person the major portion of the business and assets of which another person acquired in a single succession, or in a series of related successions in each of which the acquiring person acquired the major portion of the business and assets of the acquired person.

Principal underwriter. The term "principal underwriter" means an underwriter in privity of contract with the issuer of the securities as to which he is underwriter, the term "issuer" having the meaning given in sections 2(4) and 2(11) of the Act.

Promoter. (1) The term "promoter" includes—

(i) Any person who, acting alone or in conjunction with one or more other persons, directly or indirectly takes initiative in founding and organizing the business or enterprise of an issuer; or

(ii) Any person who, in connection with the founding and organizing of the business or enterprise of an issuer, directly or indirectly receives in consideration of services or property, or both services and property, 10 percent or more of any class of securities of the issuer or 10 percent or more of the proceeds from the sale of any class of such securities. However, a person who receives such securities or proceeds either solely as underwriting commissions or solely in consideration of property shall not be deemed a promoter within the meaning of this paragraph if such person does not otherwise take part in founding and organizing the enterprise.

(2) All persons coming within the definition of "promoter" in paragraph (1) of this definition may be referred to as "founders" or "organizers" or by another term provided that such term is reasonably descriptive of those persons' activities with respect to the issuer.

Prospectus. Unless otherwise specified or the context otherwise requires, the term "prospectus" means a prospectus meeting the requirements of section 10(a) of the Act.

Registrant. The term "registrant" means the issuer of the securities for which the registration statement is filed.

Share. The term "share" means a share of stock in a corporation or unit of interest in an unincorporated person.

* * *

Succession. The term "succession" means the direct acquisition of the assets comprising a going business, whether by merger, consolidation, purchase, or other direct transfer. The term does not include the acquisition of control of a business unless followed by the direct acquisition of its assets. The terms "succeed" and "successor" have meanings correlative to the foregoing.

* * *

Voting securities. The term "voting securities" means securities the holders of which are presently entitled to vote for the election of directors.

* * *

Rule 406. Confidential Treatment of Information Filed With the Commission

Preliminary Note: Confidential treatment of supplemental information or other information not required to be filed under the Act should be requested under 17 CFR § 200.83 and not under this rule.

(a) Any person submitting any information in a document required to be filed under the Act may make written objection to its public disclosure by following the procedure in paragraph (b) of this section, which shall be the exclusive means of requesting confidential treatment of information included in any document (hereinafter referred to as the "material filed") required to be filed under the Act, *except* that if the material filed is a registration statement on Form S–8 or on Form S–3, F–2 or F–3 relating to a dividend or interest reinvestment plan, or on Form S–4 or F–4 complying with General Instruction G of that Form, or if the material filed is a registration statement that does not contain a delaying amendment pursuant to Rule 473, the person shall comply with the procedure in paragraph (b) prior to the filing of the registration statement.

(b) The person shall omit from the material filed the portion thereof which it desires to keep undisclosed (hereinafter called the "confidential portion"). In lieu thereof, the person shall indicate at the appropriate place in the material filed that the confidential portion has been so omitted and filed separately with the Commission. The person shall file with the material filed:

(1) As many copies of the confidential portion, each clearly marked "Confidential Treatment", as there are copies of the material filed with the Commission. Each copy shall contain an appropriate identification of the item or other requirement involved and, notwithstanding that the confidential portion does not constitute the whole of the answer or required disclosure, the entire answer or required disclosure, *except* that in the case where the confidential portion is part of a financial statement or schedule only the particular financial statement or schedule need be included. All copies of the confidential portion shall be in the same form as the remainder of the material filed;

(2) An application making objection to the disclosure of the confidential portion. Such application shall be on a sheet or sheets separate from the confidential portion, and shall contain (i) an identification of the portion; (ii) a statement of the grounds of the objection referring to and analyzing the applicable exemption(s) from disclosure under § 200.80 of this chapter, the Commission's rule adopted under the Freedom of Information Act, and a justification of the period of time for which confidential treatment is sought; (iii) a detailed explanation of why, based on the facts and circumstances of the particular case, disclosure of the information is unnecessary for the protection of investors; (iv) a written consent to the furnishing of the confidential portion to other government agencies, offices, or bodies and to the Congress; and (v) the name, address and telephone number of the person to whom all notices and orders issued under this rule at any time should be directed.

(3) The copies of the confidential portion and the application filed in accordance with this paragraph (b) shall be enclosed in a separate envelope marked "Confidential Treatment" and addressed to the Secretary, Securities and Exchange Commission, Washington, D.C. 20549.

(c) Pending a determination as to the objection, the material for which confidential treatment has been applied will not be made available to the public.

(d) If it is determined by the Division, acting pursuant to delegated authority, that the application should be granted, an order to that effect will be entered, and a notation to that effect will be made at the appropriate place in the material filed. Such a determination will not preclude reconsideration whenever appropriate, such as upon receipt of any subsequent request under the Freedom of Information Act and, if appropriate, revocation of the confidential status of all or a portion of the information in question.

(e) If the Commission denies the application, or the Division, acting pursuant to delegated authority, denies the application and Commission review is not sought pursuant to § 201.26 of this chapter, confirmed telegraphic notice of the order of denial will be sent to the person named in the application pursuant to paragraph (b)(2)(v) of this rule. In such case, if the material filed may be withdrawn pursuant to an applicable statute, rule, or regulation, the registrant shall have the right to withdraw the material filed in accordance with the terms of the applicable statute, rule, or regulation, but without the necessity of stating any grounds for the withdrawal or of obtaining the further assent of the Commission. In the event of such withdrawal, the confidential portion will be returned to the registrant. If the material filed may not be so withdrawn, the confidential portion will be made available for public inspection in the same manner as if confidential treatment had been revoked under paragraph (h) of this rule.

(f) If a right of withdrawal pursuant to paragraph (e) of this rule is not exercised, the confidential portion will be made available for public inspection as part of the material filed, and the registrant shall amend the material filed to include all information required to be set forth in regard to such confidential portion.

(g) In any case where a prior grant of confidential treatment has been revoked, the person named in the application pursuant to paragraph (b)(2)(v) of this rule will be so informed by registered or certified mail. Pursuant to § 201.26 of this chapter, persons making objections to disclosure may petition the Commission for review of a determination by the Division revoking confidential treatment.

(h) Upon revocation of confidential treatment, the confidential portion shall be made available to the public at the time and according to the conditions specified in paragraphs (h)(1)–(2):

(1) Upon the lapse of five days after the dispatch of notice by registered or certified mail of a determination disallowing an objection, if prior to the lapse of such five days the person shall not have communicated to the Secretary of the Commission his intention to seek review by the Commission under § 201.26 of this chapter of the determination made by the Division; or

(2) If such a petition for review shall have been filed under § 1201.26 of this chapter, upon final disposition adverse to the petitioner.

(i) If the confidential portion is made available to the public, one copy thereof shall be attached to each copy of the material filed with the Commission.

Rule 408. Additional Information

In addition to the information expressly required to be included in a registration statement, there shall be added such further material information, if any, as may be necessary to make the required statements, in the light of the circumstances under which they are made, not misleading.

Rule 409. Information Unknown or Not Reasonably Available

Information required need by given only insofar as it is known or reasonably available to the registrant. If any required information is unknown and not reasonably available to the registrant, either because the obtaining thereof would involve unreasonable effort or expense, or because it rests peculiarly within the knowledge of another person not affiliated with the registrant, the information may be omitted, subject to the following conditions:

(*a*) The registrant shall give such information on the subject as it possesses or can acquire without unreasonable effort or expense, together with the sources thereof.

(*b*) The registrant shall include a statement either showing that unreasonable effort or expense would be involved or indicating the absence of any affiliation with the person within whose knowledge the information rests and stating the result of a request made to such persons for the information.

Rule 410. Disclaimer of Control

If the existence of control is open to reasonable doubt in any instance, the registrant may disclaim the existence of control and any admission thereof; in such case, however, the registrant shall state the material facts pertinent to the possible existence of control.

Rule 411. Incorporation by Reference

(a) *Prospectus.* Except as provided by this rule or unless otherwise provided in the appropriate form, information shall not be incorporated by reference in a prospectus. Where a summary or outline of the provisions of any document is required in the prospectus, the summary or outline may incorporate by reference particular items, sections or paragraphs of any exhibit and may be qualified in its entirety by such reference.

* * *

Rule 412. Modified or Superseded Documents

(a) Any statement contained in a document incorporated or deemed to be incorporated by reference shall be deemed to be modified or superseded for purposes of the registration statement or the prospectus to the extent that a statement contained in the prospectus or in any other subsequently filed document which also is or is deemed to be incorporated by reference modifies or replaces such statement.

(b) The modifying or superseding statement may, but need not, state that it has modified or superseded a prior statement or include any other information set forth in the document which is not so modified or superseded. The making of a modifying or superseding statement shall not be deemed an admission that the modified or superseded statement, when made, constituted an untrue statement of a material fact, an omission to state a material fact necessary to make a statement not misleading, or the employment of a manipulative, deceptive, or fraudulent device, contrivance, scheme, transaction, act, practice, course of business or artifice to defraud, as those terms are used in the Act, the Securities Exchange Act of 1934, the Public Utility Holding Company Act of 1935, the Investment Company Act of 1940, or the rules and regulations thereunder.

(c) Any statement so modified shall not be deemed in its unmodified form to constitute part of the registration statement or prospectus for purposes of the Act. Any statement so superseded shall not be deemed to constitute a part of the registration statement or the prospectus for purposes of the Act.

Rule 413. Registration of Additional Securities

Except as provided in sections 24(e)(1) and 24(f) of the Investment Company Act of 1940, the registration of additional securities of the same class as other securities for which a registration statement is already in effect shall be effected through a separate registration statement relating to the additional securities.

* * *

Rule 415. Delayed or Continuous Offering and Sale of Securities

(a) Securities may be registered for an offering to be made on a continuous or delayed basis in the future. *Provided,* That—

(1) The registration statement pertains only to:

(i) Securities which are to be offered or sold solely by or on behalf of a person or persons other than the registrant, a subsidiary of the registrant or a person of which the registrant is a subsidiary;

(ii) Securities which are to be offered and sold pursuant to a dividend or interest reinvestment plan or an employee benefit plan of the registrant;

(iii) Securities which are to be issued upon the exercise of outstanding options, warrants or rights;

(iv) Securities which are to be issued upon conversion of other outstanding securities;

(v) Securities which are pledged as collateral;

(vi) Securities which are registered on Form F–6;

(vii) Mortgage related securities, including such securities as mortgage backed debt and mortgage participation or pass through certificates;

(viii) Securities which are to be issued in connection with business combination transactions;

(ix) Securities the offering of which will be commenced promptly, will be made on a continuous basis and may continue for a period in excess of 30 days from the date of initial effectiveness; or

(x) Securities registered (or qualified to be registered) on Form S–3 or Form F–3 which are to be offered and sold on a continuous or delayed basis by or on behalf of the registrant, a subsidiary of the registrant or a person of which the registrant is a subsidiary.

(2) Securities in paragraphs (a)(1)(viii) through (x) may only be registered in an amount which, at the time the registration statement becomes effective, is reasonably expected to be offered and sold within two years from the initial effective date of the registration.

(3) The registrant furnishes the undertakings required by Item 512(a) of Regulation S-K.

(4) In the case of a registration statement pertaining to an at the market offering of equity securities by or on behalf of the registrant:

(i) The offering comes within paragraph (a)(1)(x); (ii) where voting stock is registered, the amount of securities registered for such purposes must not exceed 10% of the aggregate market value of the registrant's outstanding voting stock held by non-affiliates of the registrant (calculated as of a date within 60 days prior to the date of filing); (iii) the securities must be sold through an underwriter or underwriters, acting as principal(s) or as agent(s) for the registrant; and (iv) the underwriter or underwriters must be named in the prospectus which is part of the registration statement. As used in this paragraph, the term "at the market offering" means an offering of securities into an existing trading market for outstanding shares of the same class at other than a fixed price on or through the facilities of a national securities exchange or to or through a market maker otherwise than on an exchange.

(b) This section shall not apply to any registration statement pertaining to securities issued by a face-amount certificate company or redeemable securities issued by an open-end management company or unit investment trust under the Investment Company Act of 1940 or any registration statement filed by any foreign government or political subdivision thereof.

Rule 418. Supplemental Information

(a) The Commission or its staff may, where it is deemed appropriate, request supplemental information concerning the registrant, the registration statement, the distribution of the securities, market activities and underwriters' activities. Such information includes, but is not limited to, the following items which the registrant should be prepared to furnish promptly upon request:

(1)(i) Any reports or memoranda which have been prepared for external use by the registrant or a principal underwriter, as defined in Rule 405, in connection with the proposed offering;

(ii) A statement as to the actual or proposed use and distribution of the reports or memoranda specified in paragraph (a)(1)(i) of this section, identifying each class of persons who have received or will receive such reports or memoranda and the number of copies distributed to each such class;

(2) In the case of a registration statement relating to a business combination as defined in Rule 145(a), exchange offer, tender offer or similar transaction, any feasibility studies, management analyses, fairness opinions or similar reports prepared by or for any of the parties to the subject transaction in connection with such transaction;

(3) Except in the case of a registrant eligible to use Form S–2 or Form S–3 any engineering, management or similar reports or memoranda relating to broad aspects of the business, operations or products of the registrant, which have been prepared within the past twelve months for or by the registrant, any affiliate of the registrant or any principal underwriter, as defined in Rule 405, of the securities being registered except for:

(i) Reports solely comprised of recommendations to buy, sell or hold the securities of the registrant, unless such recommendations have changed within the past six months; and

(ii) Any information contained in documents already filed with the Commission.

(4) Where there is a registration of an "offering at the market," as defined in Rule 10b–7 under the Securities Exchange Act of 1934, of more than 10 percent of the securities outstanding, where the offering includes securities owned by officers, directors or affiliates of the registrant and where there is no underwriting agreement, information (i) concerning contractual arrangements between selling security holders of a limited group or of several groups of related shareholders to comply with the anti-manipulation rules until the offering by all members of the group is completed and to inform the exchange, brokers and selling security holders when the distribution by the members of the group is over; or (ii) concerning the registrant's efforts to notify members of a large group of unrelated sell-

ers of the applicable Commission rules and regulations;

(5) Where the registrant recently has introduced a new product or has begun to do business in a new industry segment or has made public its intentions to introduce a new product or to do business in a new industry segment, and this action requires the investment of a material amount of the assets of the registrant or otherwise is material, copies of any studies prepared for the registrant by outside persons or any internal studies, documents, reports or memoranda the contents of which were material to the decision to develop the product or to do business in the new segment including, but not limited to, documents relating to financial requirements and engineering, competitive, environmental and other considerations, but excluding technical documents;

(6) Where reserve estimates are referred to in a document, a copy of the full report of the engineer or other expert who estimated the reserves; and

(7) With respect to the extent of the distribution of a preliminary prospectus, information concerning:

(i) The date of the preliminary prospectus distributed;

(ii) The dates or approximate dates of distribution;

(iii) The number of prospective underwriters and dealers to whom the preliminary prospectus was furnished;

(iv) The number of prospectuses so distributed;

(v) The number of prospectuses distributed to others, identifying them in general terms; and

(vi) The steps taken by such underwriters and dealers to comply with the provisions of Rule 15c2–8 under the Securities Exchange Act of 1934.

(b) Supplemental information described in paragraph (a) of this section shall not be required to be filed with or deemed part of the registration statement. The information shall be returned to the registrant upon request, provided that:

(1) Such request is made at the time such information is furnished to the staff;

(2) The return of such information is consistent with the protection of investors; and

(3) The return of such information is consistent with the provisions of the Freedom of Information Act [5 U.S.C. 552].

* * *

Form and Contents of Prospectuses

Rule 421. Presentation of Information in Prospectuses

(a) The information required in a prospectus need not follow the order of the items or other requirements in the form. Such information shall not, however, be set forth in such fashion as to obscure any of the required information or any information necessary to keep the required information from being incomplete or misleading. Where an item requires information to be given in a prospectus in tabular form it shall be given in substantially the tabular form specified in the item.

(b) The information set forth in a prospectus should be presented in a clear, concise and understandable fashion. All information contained in a prospectus shall be set forth under appropriate captions or headings reasonably indicative of the principal subject matter set forth thereunder. Except as to financial statements and other tabular data, all information set forth in a prospectus shall be divided into reasonably short paragraphs or sections.

(c) All information required to be included in a prospectus shall be clearly understandable without the necessity of referring to the particular form or to the general rules and regulations. Except as to financial statements and information required in a tabular form, the information set forth in a prospectus may be expressed in condensed or summarized form. In lieu of repeating information in the form of notes to financial statements, references may be made to other parts of the prospectus where such information is set forth.

* * *

Rule 423. Date of Prospectuses

Except for a form of preliminary prospectus used after the effective date of the registration statement and prior to the opening of bids as permitted by Rule 445(c), each prospectus used after the effective date of the registration statement shall be dated approximately as of such effective date; provided, however, that a revised or amended prospectus used thereafter need only bear the approximate date of its issuance. Each supplement to a prospectus shall be dated separately the approximate date of its issuance.

Rule 424. Filing of Prospectuses—Number of Copies

(*a*) Five copies of every form of prospectus sent or given to any person prior to the effective date of the registration statement which varies from the form or forms of prospectus included in the registration statement as filed pursuant to Rule 402(*a*) shall be filed as a part of the registration statement not later than the date such form of prospectus is first sent or given to any person: Provided, however, That an investment company advertisement which is deemed to be a prospectus pursuant to Rule 434D and which is required to be filed pursuant to this paragraph shall not be filed as part of the registration statement.

(*b*) Within 5 days after the effective date of a registration statement or the commencement of a public offering after the effective date of a registration statement, whichever occurs later, 10 copies of each form of prospectus used after the effective date in connection with such offering shall be filed with the Commission in the exact form in which it was used: *Provided, however,* That this paragraph shall not apply in respect of a form of prospectus contained in a registration statement and relating solely to securities offered at competitive bidding which prospectus is intended for use prior to the opening of bids.

(*c*) After the effective date of the registration statement, no prospectus which purports to comply with section 10 of the Act and which varies from any form of prospectus filed pursuant to paragraph (b) of this Rule shall be used until 10 copies thereof have been filed with, or mailed for filing to, the Commission, together with 5 copies of a cross reference sheet similar to that previously filed, if changed: *Provided, however,* That this paragraph shall not apply in respect of a form of prospectus contained in a registration statement and relating solely to securities offered at competitive bidding which prospectus is intended for use prior to the opening of bids.

(*d*) Every prospectus consisting of a radio or television broadcast shall be reduced to writing. Five copies of every such prospectus shall be filed with the Commission at least 5 days before it is broadcast or otherwise issued to the public.

(*e*) Each copy of a prospectus filed under this rule shall contain in the upper right corner of the cover page the paragraph of this rule under which the filing is made and the file number of the registration statement to which the prospectus relates. The information required by this paragraph may be set forth in longhand, provided it is legible.

* * *

Rule 427. Contents of Prospectus Used After Nine Months

There may be omitted from any prospectus used more than 9 months after the effective date of the registration statement any information previously required to be contained in the prospectus insofar as later information covering the same subjects, including the latest available certified financial statement, as of a date not more than 16 months prior to the use of the prospectus is contained therein.

* * *

Rule 430. Prospectus for Use Prior to Effective Date

A form of prospectus filed as a part of the registration statement shall be deemed to meet the requirements of section 10 of the Act for the purpose of section 5(b)(1) thereof prior to the effective date of the registration statement, provided such form of prospectus contains substantially the information required by the Act and the rules and regulations thereunder to be included in a prospectus meeting the requirements of section 10(a) of the Act for the securities being registered, or contains substantially that information except for the omission of information with respect to the offering price, underwriting discounts or commissions, discounts or commissions to dealers, amount of proceeds, conversion rates, call prices, or other matters dependent upon the offering price. Every such form of prospectus shall be deemed to have been filed as a part of the registration statement for the purpose of section 7 of the Act.

Rule 431. Summary Prospectuses

(a) A summary prospectus prepared and filed as a part of a registration statement in accordance with this rule shall be deemed to be a prospectus permitted under section 10(b) of the Act for the purpose of section 5(b)(1) of the Act if the form used for registration of the securities to be offered provides for the use of a summary prospectus * *.

(b) A summary prospectus shall contain the information specified in the instructions as to summary prospectuses in the form used for registration of the securities to be offered. Such prospectus may include any other information the substance of which is contained in the registration statement except as otherwise specifically provided in the instructions as to summary prospectuses in the form used for registration. It shall not include any information the substance of which is not contained in the registration statement except that a summary prospectus may contain any information specified in Rule 134(a). No reference need be made to inapplicable terms and negative answers to any item of the form may be omitted.

(c) All information included in a summary prospectus, other than the statement required by paragraph (e) of this section, may be expressed in such condensed or summarized form as may be appropriate in the light of the circumstances under which the prospectus is to be used. The information need not follow the numerical sequence of the items of the form used for registration. Every summary prospectus shall be dated approximately as of the date of its first use.

* * *

Rule 432. Additional Information Required to be Included in Prospectuses Relating to Tender Offers

Notwithstanding the provisions of any form for the registration of securities under the Act, any prospectus relating to securities to be offered in connection with a tender offer for, or a request or invitation for tenders of, securities which is subject to section 14(d) of the Securities Exchange Act of 1934 shall include all of the information, not otherwise required to be included therein, required by Rule 14d–6(e)(1) to be included in all such tender offers, requests or invitations, published or sent or given to the holders of such securities.

* * *

Written Consents

* * *

Rule 436. Consents Required in Special Cases

(a) If any portion of the report or opinion of an expert or counsel is quoted or summarized as such in the registration statement or in a prospectus, the written consent of the expert or counsel shall be filed as an exhibit to the registration statement and shall expressly state that the expert or counsel consents to such quotation or summarization.

(b) If it is stated that any information contained in the registration statement has been reviewed or passed upon by any persons and that such information is set forth in the registration statement upon the authority of or in reliance upon such persons as experts, the written consents of such persons shall be filed as exhibits to the registration statement.

(c) Notwithstanding the provisions of paragraph (b) of this section, a report on unaudited interim financial information (as defined in paragraph (d) of this rule) by an independent accountant who has conducted a review of such interim financial information shall not be considered a part of a registration statement prepared or certified by an accountant or a report prepared or certified by an accountant within the meaning of sections 7 and 11 of the Act.

(d) The term "report on unaudited interim financial information" shall mean a report which consists of the following: (1) a statement that the review of interim financial information was made in accordance with established professional standards for such reviews; (2) an identification of the interim financial information reviewed; (3) a description of the procedures for a review of interim financial information; (4) a statement that a review of interim financial information is substantially less in scope than an examination in accordance with generally accepted auditing standards, the objective of which is an expression of opinion regarding the financial statements taken as a whole, and, accordingly, no such opinion is expressed; and (5) a statement about whether the accountant is aware of any material modifications that should be made to the accompanying financial information so that it conforms with generally accepted accounting principles.

(e) Where a counsel is named as having acted for the underwriters or selling security holders, no consent will be required by reason of his being named as having acted in such capacity.

(f) Where the opinion of one counsel relies upon the opinion of another counsel, the consent of the counsel whose prepared opinion is relied upon need not be furnished.

(g)(1) Notwithstanding the provisions of paragraphs (a) and (b) of this rule, the security rating assigned to a class of debt securities, a class of convertible debt securities, or a class of preferred stock by a nationally recognized statistical rating organization shall not be considered a part of a registration statement prepared or certified by a person within the meaning of sections 7 and 11 of the Act.

(2) For the purpose of paragraph (g)(1) of this rule, the term "nationally recognized statistical rating organization" shall have the same meaning as used in Rule 15c3–1(c)(2)(vi)(F).

* * *

Rule 439. Consent to Use of Material Incorporated by Reference

If the Act or the rules and regulations of the Commission require the filing of a written consent to the use of any material in connection with the registration statement, such consent shall be filed as an exhibit to the registration statement even though the material is incorporated therein by reference. Where the filing of a written consent is required with respect to material incorporated in the registration statement by reference, which is to be filed subsequent to the effective date of the registration statement, such consent shall be filed as an amendment to the registration statement no later than the date on which such material is filed with the Commission, unless express consent to incorporation by reference is contained in the material to be incorporated by reference.

* * *

Filings; Fees; Effective Date

Rule 455. Place of Filing

All registration statements and other papers filed with the Commission shall be filed at its principal office, except for statements on Form S–18 and except as otherwise provided in Rule 445. Registration statements on Form S–18 may be filed with the Commission either at its principal office or at the Commission's regional offices as specified in General Instruction B to Form S–18. Such material may be filed by delivery to the Commission through the mails or otherwise.

* * *

Rule 459. Calculation of Effective Date

Saturdays, Sundays, and holidays shall be counted in computing the effective date of registration statements under section 8(a) of the Act. In the case of statements which become effective on the 20th day after filing, the 20th day shall be deemed to begin at the expiration of 19 periods of 24 hours each from 5:30 p.m. Eastern Standard Time or Eastern Daylight Saving Time, whichever is in effect at the principal office of the Commission on the date of filing.

Rule 460. Distribution of Preliminary Prospectus

(a) Pursuant to the statutory requirement that the Commission in ruling upon requests for acceleration of the effective date of a registration statement shall have due regard to the adequacy of the information respecting the issuer theretofore available to the public, the Commission may consider whether the persons making the offering have taken reasonable steps to make the information contained in the registration statement conveniently available to underwriters and dealers who it is reasonably anticipated will be invited to participate in the distribution of the security to be offered or sold.

(b) As a minimum, reasonable steps to make the information conveniently available would involve the distribution, to each underwriter and dealer who it is reasonably anticipated will be invited to participate in the distribution of the security, a reasonable time in advance of the anticipated effective date of the registration statement, of as many copies of the proposed form of preliminary prospectus permitted by Rule 430 as appears to be reasonable to secure adequate distribution of the preliminary prospectus.

(c) The granting of acceleration will not be conditioned upon

(1) The distribution of a preliminary prospectus in any state where such distribution would be illegal; or

(2) The distribution of a preliminary prospectus (i) in the case of a registration statement relating solely to securities to be offered at competitive bidding, provided the undertaking in Item 512(d)(1) of Regulation S–K is included in the registration statement and distribution of prospectuses pursuant to such undertaking is made prior to the publication or distribution of the invitation for bids, or (ii) in the case of a registration statement relating to a security issued by a face-amount certificate company or a redeemable security issued by an open-end management company or unit investment trust if any other security of the same class is currently being offered or sold, pursuant to an effective registration statement by the issuer or by or through an underwriter, or (iii) in the case of an offering of subscription rights unless it is contemplated that the distribution will be made through dealers and the underwriters intend to make the offering during the stockholders' subscription period, in which case copies of the preliminary prospectus must be distributed to dealers prior to the effective date of the registration statement in the same fashion as is required in the case of other offerings through underwriters, or (iv) in the case of a registration statement pertaining to a security to be offered pursuant to an exchange offer or transaction described in Rule 145.

Rule 461. Acceleration of Effective Date

(a) Requests for acceleration of the effective date of a registration statement shall be made in writing by the registrant and the managing underwriters of the proposed issue, or, if there are no managing underwriters, by the principal underwriters of the proposed issue, and shall state the date upon which it is desired that the registration statement shall become effective. If, by reason of the expected arrangements in connection with the offering, it is to be requested that the registration statement shall become effective at a particular hour of the day, the Commission must be advised to that effect not later than the second business day before the day which it is desired that the registration statement shall become effective. A person's request for acceleration will be considered confirmation of such person's awareness of the person's obligations under the Act. Not later than the time of filing the last amendment prior to the effective date of the registration statement, the registrant shall inform the Commission as to whether or not the amount of compensation to be allowed or paid to the underwriters and any other arrangements among the registrant, the underwriters and other broker-dealers participating in the distribution, as described in the registration statement, have been reviewed to the extent required by the National Association of Securities Dealers, Inc. and such Association has issued a statement expressing no objections to the compensation and other arrangements.

(b) Having due regard to the adequacy of information respecting the registrant theretofore available to the public, to the facility with which the nature of the securities to be registered, their relationship to the capital structure of the registrant issuer and the rights of holders thereof can be understood, and to the public interest and the protection of investors, as provided in section 8(a) of the Act, it is the general policy of the Commission, upon request, as provided in paragraph (a) of this section, to permit acceleration of the effective date of the registration statement as soon as possible after the filing of appropriate amendments, if any. In determining the date on which a registration statement shall become effective, the following are included in the situations in which the Commission considers that the statutory standards of section 8(a) may not be met and may refuse to accelerate the effective date:

(1) Where there has not been a bona fide effort to make the prospectus reasonably concise and readable, so as to facilitate an understanding of the information required or permitted to be contained in the prospectus.

(2) Where the form of preliminary prospectus, which has been distributed by the issuer or underwriter, is found to be inaccurate or inadequate in any material respect, until the Commission has received satisfactory assurance that appropriate correcting material has been sent to all underwriters and dealers who received such preliminary prospectus or prospectuses in quantity sufficient for their

information and the information of others to whom the inaccurate or inadequate material was sent.

(3) Where the Commission is currently making an investigation of the issuer, a person controlling the issuer, or one of the underwriters, if any, of the securities to be offered, pursuant to any of the Acts administered by the Commission.

(4) Where one or more of the underwriters, although firmly committed to purchase securities covered by the registration statement, is subject to and does not meet the financial responsibility requirements of Rule 15c3–1 under the Securities Exchange Act of 1934. For the purposes of this paragraph underwriters will be deemed to be firmly committed even though the obligation to purchase is subject to the usual conditions as to receipt of opinions of counsel, accountants, etc., the accuracy of warranties or representations, the happening of calamities or the occurrence of other events the determination of which is not expressed to be in the sole or absolute discretion of the underwriters.

(5) Where there have been transactions in securities of the registrant by persons connected with or proposed to be connected with the offering which may have artificially affected or may artificially affect the market price of the security being offered.

(6) Where the amount of compensation to be allowed or paid to the underwriters and any other arrangements among the registrant, the underwriters and other broker-dealers participating in the distribution, as described in the registration statement, if required to be reviewed by the National Association of Securities Dealers, Inc. (NASD), have been reviewed by the NASD and the NASD has not issued a statement expressing no objections to the compensation and other arrangements.

(7) Where, in the case of a significant secondary offering at the market, the registrant, selling security holders and underwriters have not taken sufficient measures to insure compliance with Rules 10b–2, 10b–6, and 10b–7 under the Securities Exchange Act of 1934.

(c) Insurance against liabilities arising under the Act, whether the cost of insurance is borne by the registrant, the insured or some other person, will not be considered a bar to acceleration, unless the registrant is a registered investment company or a business development company and the cost of such insurance is borne by other than an insured officer or director of the registrant. In the case of such a registrant, the Commission may refuse to accelerate the effective date of the registration statement when the registrant is organized or administered pursuant to any instrument (including a contract for insurance against liabilities arising under the Act) that protects or purports to protect any director or officer of the company against any liability to the company or its security holders to which he or she would otherwise be subject by reason of willful misfeasance, bad faith, gross negligence or reckless disregard of the duties involved in the conduct of his or her office.

* * *

Rule 463. Report of Sales of Securities and Use of Proceeds Therefrom

(a) Except as hereinafter provided in this rule, within 10 days after the end of the first three-month period following the effective date of the first registration statement filed under the Act by an issuer, and within 10 days after the end of each six-month period following such three-month period, such issuer shall file with the Commission four copies of a report on Form SR containing the information required by that form. A final report shall be filed within 10 days after the later of (1) the application of the offering proceeds or (2) the termination of the offering. A report on Form SR shall be filed at the same office of the Commission where the registration statement to which it relates was filed.

(b) A successor issuer shall comply with paragraph (a) of this section only to the extent that filings on Form SR are required with respect to the first effective registration statement of the predecessor issuer.

(c) For purposes of this section:

(1) The term "offering proceeds" shall not include any amount(s) received for the account(s) of any selling security holder(s).

(2) The term "application" shall not include the temporary investment of proceeds by the issuer pending final application.

* * *

Amendments; Withdrawals

Rule 470. Formal Requirements for Amendments

Except for telegraphic amendments filed pursuant to Rule 473, amendments to a registration statement shall be filed under cover of an appropriate facing sheet, shall be numbered consecutively in the order in which filed, and shall indicate on the facing sheet the applicable registration form on which the amendment is prepared and the file number of the registration statement.

* * *

Rule 473. Delaying Amendments

(a) An amendment in the following form filed with a registration statement, or as an amendment to a registration statement which has not become effective, shall be deemed, for the purpose of section 8(a) of the Act, to be filed on such date or dates as may be necessary to delay the effective date of such registration statement (1) until the registrant shall file a further amendment which specifically states as provided in paragraph (b) of this rule that such registration statement shall thereafter become effective in accordance with section 8(a) of the Act, or (2) until the registration statement shall become effective on such date as the Commission, acting pursuant to section 8(a), may determine:

> "The registrant hereby amends this registration statement on such date or dates as may be necessary to delay its effective date until the registrant shall file a further amendment which specifically states that this registration statement shall thereafter become effective in accordance with section 8(a) of the Securities Act of 1933 or until the registration statement shall become effective on such date as the Commission acting pursuant to said section 8(a), may determine."

(b) An amendment which for the purpose of paragraph (a)(1) of this section specifically states that a registration statement shall thereafter become effective in accordance with section 8(a) of the Act, shall be in the following form:

> "This registration statement shall hereafter become effective in accordance with the provisions of section 8(a) of the Securities Act of 1933."

(c) An amendment pursuant to paragraph (a) of this rule which is filed with a registration statement shall be set forth on the facing page thereof following the calculation of the registration fee. Any such amendment filed after the filing of the registration statement, any amendment altering the proposed date of public sale of the securities being registered, or any amendment filed pursuant to paragraph (b) of this rule may be made by telegram or letter. Each such telegraphic amendment shall be confirmed in writing within a reasonable time by the filing of a signed copy of the amendment. Such confirmation shall not be deemed an amendment.

(d) No amendments pursuant to paragraph (a) of this rule may be filed with a registration statement on Form S–8 or on Form S–3 relating to a dividend or interest reinvestment plan; or on Form S–4 or F–4 complying with General Instruction F of that Form.

* * *

Rule 477. Withdrawal of Registration Statement or Amendment

(a) Except as provided in paragraph (b) of this section, any registration statement or any amendment or exhibit thereto may be withdrawn upon application if the Commission, finding such withdrawal consistent with the public interest and the protection of investors, consents thereto.

(b) Any application for withdrawal of a registration statement filed on Form S–8 or on Form S–3, F–2 or F–3 relating to a dividend or interest reinvestment plan; or on Form S–4 or F–4 complying with General Instruction F of that Form and/or any pre-effective amendment thereto, will be deemed granted upon filing if such filing is made prior to the effective date.

(c) The application for withdrawal under either paragraphs (a) or (b) of this rule, shall be signed and shall state fully the grounds upon which made. The fee paid upon the filing of the registration statement will not be returned to the registrant. The papers comprising the registration statement or amendment thereto shall not be removed from the files of the Commission but an order with the date f the granting of such withdrawal shall be included in the file for the registration statement in the following manner: "Withdrawn upon the request of the registrant, the Commission consenting thereto."

* * *

REGULATION D—LIMITED OFFERINGS

Preliminary Notes

1. The following rules relate to transactions exempted from the registration requirements of section 5 of the Securities Act of 1933 (the "Act"). Such transactions are not exempt from the antifraud, civil liability, or other provisions of the federal securities laws. Issuers are reminded of their obligation to provide such further material information, if any, as may be necessary to make the information required under this regulation, in light of the circumstances under which it is furnished, not misleading.

2. Nothing in these rules obviates the need to comply with any applicable state law relating to the offer and sale of securities. Regulation D is intended to be a basic element in a uniform system of federal-state limited offering exemptions consistent with the provisions of sections 18 and 19(c) of the Act. In those states that have adopted Regulation D, or any version of Regulation D, special attention should be directed to the applicable state laws and regulations, including those relating to registration of persons who receive remuneration in connection with the offer and sale of securities, to disqualification of issuers and other persons associated with offerings based on state administrative orders or judgments, and to requirements for filings of notices of sales.

3. Attempted compliance with any rule in Regulation D does not act as an exclusive election; the issuer can also claim the availability of any other applicable exemption. For instance, an issuer's failure to satisfy all the terms and conditions of Rule 506 shall not raise any presumption that the exemption provided by section 4(2) of the Act is not available.

4. These rules are available only to the issuer of the securities and not to any affiliate of that issuer or to any other person for resales of the issuer's securities. The rules provide an exemption only for the transactions in which the securities are offered or sold by the issuer, not for the securities themselves.

5. These rules may be used for business combinations that involve sales by virtue of Rule 145(a) or otherwise.

6. In view of the objectives of these rules and the policies underlying the Act, Regulation D is not available to any issuer for any transaction or chain of transactions that, although in technical compliance with these rules, is part of a plan or scheme to evade the registration provisions of the Act. In such cases, registration under the Act is required.

7. Offers and sales of securities to foreign persons made outside the United States effected in a manner that will result in the securities coming to rest abroad generally need not be registered under the Act. See Release No. 33–4708 (July 9, 1964). This interpretation may be relied on for such offers and sales even if coincident offers and sales are made under Regulation D inside the United States. Thus, for example, persons who are not citizens or residents of the United States would not be counted in the calculation of the number of purchasers. Similarly, proceeds from sales to foreign purchasers would not be included in the aggregate offering price. The provisions of this note, however, do not apply if the issuer elects to rely solely on Regulation D for offers or sales to foreign persons.

Rule 501. Definitions and Terms Used in Regulation D

As used in Regulation D, the following terms shall have the meaning indicated:

(a) *Accredited investor.* "Accredited investor" shall mean any person who comes within any of the following categories, or who the issuer reasonably believes comes within any of the following categories, at the time of the sale of the securities to that person:

(1) Any bank as defined in section 3(a)(2) of the Act whether acting in its individual or fiduciary capacity; insurance company as defined in section

2(13) of the Act; investment company registered under the Investment Company Act of 1940 or a business development company as defined in section 2(a)(48) of that Act; Small Business Investment Company licensed by the U.S. Small Business Administration under section 301(c) or (d) of the Small Business Investment Act of 1958; employee benefit plan within the meaning of Title I of the Employee Retirement Income Security Act of 1974, if the investment decision is made by a plan fiduciary, as defined in section 3(21) of such Act, which is either a bank, insurance company, or registered investment adviser, or if the employee benefit plan has total assets in excess of $5,000,000;

(2) Any private business development company as defined in section 202(a)(22) of the Investment Advisers Act of 1940;

(3) Any organization described in Section 501(c)(3) of the Internal Revenue Code with Total assets in excess of $5,000,000;

(4) Any director, executive officer, or general partner of the issuer of the securities being offered or sold, or any director, executive officer, or general partner of a general partner of that issuer;

(5) Any person who purchases at least $150,000 of the securities being offered, where the purchaser's total purchase price does not exceed 20 percent of the purchaser's net worth at the time of sale, or joint net worth with that person's spouse, for one or any combination of the following: (i) cash, (ii) securities for which market quotations are readily available, (iii) an unconditional obligation to pay cash or securities for which market quotations are readily available which obligation is to be discharged within five years of the sale of the securities to the purchaser, or (iv) the cancellation of any indebtedness owed by the issuer to the purchaser;

(6) Any natural person whose individual net worth, or joint net worth with that person's spouse, at the time of his purchase exceeds $1,000,000;

(7) Any natural person who had an individual income in excess of $200,000 in each of the two most recent years and who reasonably expects an income in excess of $200,000 in the current year; and

(8) Any entity in which all of the equity owners are accredited investors under paragraph (a)(1), (2), (3), (4), (6), or (7) of Rule 501.

(b) *Affiliate.* An "affiliate" of, or person "affiliated" with, a specified person shall mean a person that directly, or indirectly through one or more intermediaries, controls or is controlled by, or is under common control with, the person specified.

(c) *Aggregate offering price.* "Aggregate offering price" shall mean the sum of all cash, services, property, notes, cancellation of debt, or other consideration received by an issuer for issuance of its securities. Where securities are being offered for both cash and non-cash consideration, the aggregate offering price shall be based on the price at which the securities are offered for cash. If securities are not offered for cash, the aggregate offering price shall be based on the value of the consideration as established by bona fide sales of that consideration made within a reasonable time, or, in the absence of sales, on the fair value as determined by an accepted standard.

(d) *Business combination.* "Business combination" shall mean any transaction of the type specified in paragraph (a) of Rule 145 under the Act and any transaction involving the acquisition by one issuer, in exchange for all or a part of its own or its parent's stock, of stock of another issuer if, immediately after the acquisition, the acquiring issuer has control of the other issuer (whether or not it had control before the acquisition).

(e) *Calculation of number of purchasers.* For purposes of calculating the number of purchasers under Rule 505(b) and Rule 506(b) only, the following shall apply:

(1) The following purchasers shall be excluded:

(i) Any relative, spouse or relative of the spouse of a purchaser who has the same principal residence as the purchaser;

(ii) Any trust or estate in which a purchaser and any of the persons related to him as specified in paragraph (e)(1)(i) or (e)(1)(iii) of Rule 501 collectively have more than 50 percent of the beneficial interest (excluding contingent interests);

(iii) Any corporation or other organization of which a purchaser and any of the persons related to him as specified in paragraph (e)(1)(i) or (e)(1)(ii) of Rule 501 collectively are beneficial owners of more than 50 percent of the equity securities (excluding directors' qualifying shares) or equity interests; and

(iv) Any accredited investor.

(2) A corporation, partnership or other entity shall be counted as one purchaser. If, however, that entity is organized for the specific purpose of acquiring the securities offered and is not an accredited investor under paragraph (a)(8) of Rule 501, then each beneficial owner of equity securities or equity interests in the entity shall count as a separate purchaser for all provisions of Regulation D.

Note: The issuer must satisfy all the other provisions of Regulation D for all purchasers whether or not they are included in calculating the number of purchasers. Clients of an investment adviser or customers of a broker or dealer shall be considered the "purchasers" under Regulation D regardless of the amount of discretion given to the investment adviser or broker or dealer to act on behalf of the client or customer.

(f) *Executive officer.* "Executive officer" shall mean the president, any vice president in charge of a principal business unit, division or function (such as sales, administration or finance), any other officer who performs a policy making function, or any other person who performs similar policy making functions for the issuer. Executive officers of subsidiaries may be deemed executive officers of the issuer if they perform such policy making functions for the issuer.

(g) *Issuer.* The definition of the term "issuer" in section 2(4) of the Act shall apply, except that in the case of a proceeding under the Federal Bankruptcy Code, the trustee or debtor in possession shall be considered the issuer in an offering under a plan of reorganization, if the securities are to be issued under the plan.

(h) *Purchaser representative.* "Purchaser representative" shall mean any person who satisfies all of the following conditions or who the issuer reasonably believes satisfies all of the following conditions:

(1) Is not an affiliate, director, officer or other employee of the issuer, or beneficial owner of 10 percent or more of any class of the equity securities or 10 percent or more of the equity interest in the issuer, except where the purchaser is:

(i) A relative of the purchaser representative by blood, marriage or adoption and not more remote than a first cousin;

(ii) A trust or estate in which the purchaser representative and any persons related to him as specified in paragraph (h)(1)(i) or (h)(1)(iii) of Rule 501 collectively have more than 50 percent of the beneficial interest (excluding contingent interest) or of which the purchaser representative serves as trustee, executor, or in any similar capacity; or

(iii) A corporation or other organization of which the purchaser representative and any persons related to him as specified in paragraph (h)(1)(i) or (h)(1)(ii) of Rule 501 collectively are the beneficial owners of more than 50 percent of the equity securities (excluding directors' qualifying shares) or equity interests;

(2) Has such knowledge and experience in financial and business matters that he is capable of evaluating, alone, or together with other purchaser representatives of the purchaser, or together with the purchaser, the merits and risks of the prospective investment;

(3) Is acknowledged by the purchaser in writing, during the course of the transaction, to be his purchaser representative in connection with evaluating the merits and risks of the prospective investment; and

(4) Discloses to the purchaser in writing prior to the acknowledgment specified in paragraph (h)(3) of Rule 501 any material relationship between himself or his affiliates and the issuer or its affiliates that then exists, that is mutually understood to be contemplated, or that has existed at any time during the previous two years, and any compensation received or to be received as a result of such relationship.

Note 1: A person acting as a purchaser representative should consider the applicability of the registration and antifraud provisions relating to brokers and dealers under the Securities Exchange Act of 1934 ("Exchange Act") and relating to investment advisers under the Investment Advisers Act of 1940.

Note 2: The acknowledgment required by paragraph (h)(3) and the disclosure required by paragraph (h)(4) of Rule 501 must be made with specific reference to each prospective investment. Advance blanket acknowledgment, such as for "all securities transactions" or "all private placements," is not sufficient.

Note 3: Disclosure of any material relationships between the purchaser representative or his affiliates and the issuer or its affiliates does not relieve the purchaser representative of his obligation to act in the interest of the purchaser.

Rule 502. General Conditions to be Met

The following conditions shall be applicable to offers and sales made under Regulation D:

(a) *Integration.* All sales that are part of the same Regulation D offering must meet all of the terms and conditions of Regulation D. Offers and sales that are made more than six months before the start of a Regulation D offering or are made more than six months after completion of a Regulation D offering will not be considered part of that Regulation D offering, so long as during those six month periods there are no offers or sales of securities by or for the issuer that are of the same or a similar class as those offered or sold under Regulation D, other than those offers or sales of securities under an employee benefit plan as defined in Rule 405 under the Act.

Note: The term "offering" is not defined in the Act or in Regulation D. If the issuer offers or sells securities for which the safe harbor rule in paragraph (a) of Rule 502 is unavailable, the determination as to whether separate sales of securities are part of the same offering (*i.e.* are considered "integrated") depends on the particular facts and circumstances. Generally, transactions otherwise meeting the requirements of an exemption will not be integrated with simultaneous offerings being made outside the United States effected in a manner that will result in the securities coming to rest abroad. See Release No. 33–4708 (July 9, 1964).

The following factors should be considered in determining whether offers and sales should be integrated for purposes of the exemptions under Regulation D:

(a) Whether the sales are part of a single plan of financing;

(b) Whether the sales involve issuance of the same class of securities;

(c) Whether the sales have been made at or about the same time;

(d) Whether the same type of consideration is received; and

(e) Whether the sales are made for the same general purpose. *See* Release No. 33–4552 (November 6, 1962).

(b) *Information requirements.*

(1) *When information must be furnished.*

(i) If the issuer sells securities either under Rule 504 or only to accredited investors, paragraph (b) of Rule 502 does not require that specific information be furnished to purchasers.

(ii) If the issuer sells securities under Rule 505 or Rule 506 to any purchaser that is not an accredited investor, the issuer shall furnish the information specified in paragraph (b)(2) of Rule 502 to all purchasers during the course of the offering and prior to sale.

(2) *Type of information to be furnished.*

(i) If the issuer is not subject to the reporting requirements of section 13 or 15(d) of the Exchange Act, the issuer shall furnish the following information, to the extent material to an understanding of the issuer, its business, and the securities being offered:

(A) *Offerings up to $5,000,000.* The same kind of information as would be required in Part I of Form S–18, except that only the financial statements for the issuer's most recent fiscal year must be certified by an independent public or certified accountant. If Form S–18 is not available to an issuer, then the issuer shall furnish the same kind of information as would be required in Part I of a registration statement filed under the Act on the form that the issuer would be entitled to use, except that only the financial statements for the most recent two fiscal years prepared in accordance with generally accepted accounting principles shall be furnished and only the financial statements for the issuer's most recent fiscal year shall be certified by an independent public or certified accountant. If an issuer, other than a limited partnership, cannot obtain audited financial statements without unreasonable effort or expense, then only the issuer's balance sheet, which shall be dated within 120 days of the start of the offering, must be audited. If the issuer is a limited partnership and cannot obtain the required financial statements without unreasonable effort or expense, it may furnish financial statements that have been prepared on the basis of federal income tax requirements and examined and reported on in accordance with generally accepted auditing standards by an independent public or certified accountant.

(B) *Offerings over $5,000,000.* The same kind of information as would be required in Part I of a registration statement filed under the Act on the form that the issuer would be entitled to use. If an issuer, other than a limited partnership, cannot obtain audited financial statements without unreasonable effort or expense, then only the issuer's balance sheet, which shall be dated within 120 days of the start of the offering, must be audited. If the issuer is a limited partnership and cannot obtain the required financial statements without unreasonable effort or expense, it may furnish financial statements that have been prepared on the basis of federal income tax requirements and examined and reported on in accordance with generally accepted auditing standards by an independent public or certified accountant.

(C) If the issuer is a foreign private issuer eligible to use Form 20–F, the issuer shall disclose the same kind of information required to be included in a registration statement filed under the Act on the form that the issuer would be entitled to use. The financial statements need be certified only to the extent required by paragraph (b)(2)(i)(A) or (B) as appropriate.

(ii) If the issuer is subject to the reporting requirements of section 13 or 15(d) of the Exchange Act, the issuer shall furnish the information specified in paragraph (b)(2)(ii)(A) or (b)(2)(ii)(B), and in either event the information specified in paragraph (b)(2)(ii)(C) of Rule 502:

(A) The issuer's annual report to shareholders for the most recent fiscal year, if such annual report meets the requirements of Rule 14a–3 or Rule 14c–3 under the Exchange Act, the definitive proxy statement filed in connection with that annual report, and, if requested by the purchaser in writing, a copy of the issuer's most recent Form 10–K under the Exchange Act.

(B) The information contained in an annual report on Form 10–K under the Exchange Act or in a registration statement on Form S–1 under the Act or on Form 10 under the Exchange Act, whichever filing is the most recent required to be filed.

(C) The information contained in any reports or documents required to be filed by the issuer under sections 13(a), 14(a), 14(c), and 15(d) of the Exchange Act since the distribution or filing of the report or registration statement specified in paragraph (A) or (B), and a brief description of the securities being offered, the use of the proceeds from the offering, and any material changes in the issuer's affairs that are not disclosed in the documents furnished.

(D) If the issuer is a foreign private issuer eligible to use Form 20–F, the issuer may provide in lieu of the information specified in paragraphs (b)(2)(ii)(A) or (B) of this section, the information contained in its most recent filing on Form 20–F or Form F–1.

(iii) Exhibits required to be filed with the Commission as part of a registration statement or report, other than an annual report to shareholders or parts of that report incorporated by reference in a Form 10–K report, need not be furnished to each purchaser if the contents of the exhibits are identified and the exhibits are made available to the purchaser, upon his written request, prior to his purchase.

(iv) At a reasonable time prior to the purchase of securities by any purchaser that is not an accredited investor in a transaction under Rule 505 or Rule 506, the issuer shall furnish the purchaser a brief description in writing of any written information concerning the offering that has been provided by the issuer to any accredited investor. The issuer shall furnish any portion or all of this information to the purchaser, upon his written request, prior to his purchase.

(v) The issuer shall also make available to each purchaser at a reasonable time prior to his purchase of securities in a transaction under Rule 505 or Rule 506 the opportunity to ask questions and receive answers concerning the terms and conditions of the offering and to obtain any additional information which the issuer possesses or can acquire without unreasonable effort or expense that is necessary to verify the accuracy of information furnished under paragraph (b)(2)(i) or (ii) of Rule 502.

(vi) For business combinations, in addition to information required by paragraph (b)(2) of Rule 502, the issuer shall provide to each purchaser at the time the plan is submitted to security holders, or, with an exchange, during the course of the transaction and prior to sale, written information about any terms or arrangements of the proposed transaction that are materially different from those for all other security holders.

(c) *Limitation on manner of offering.* Except as provided in Rule 504(b)(1), neither the issuer nor any person acting on its behalf shall offer or sell the securities by any form of general solicitation or general advertising, including, but not limited to, the following:

(1) Any advertisement, article, notice or other communication published in any newspaper, magazine, or similar media or broadcast over television or radio; and

(2) Any seminar or meeting whose attendees have been invited by any general solicitation or general advertising.

(d) *Limitations on resale.* Except as provided in Rule 504(b)(1), securities acquired in a transaction under Regulation D shall have the status of securities acquired in a transaction under section 4(2) of the Act and cannot be resold without registration under the Act or an exemption therefrom. The issuer shall exercise reasonable care to assure that the purchasers of the securities are not underwriters within the meaning of section 2(11) of the Act, which reasonable care shall include, but not be limited to, the following:

(1) Reasonable inquiry to determine if the purchaser is acquiring the securities for himself or for other persons;

(2) Written disclosure to each purchaser prior to sale that the securities have not been registered under the Act and, therefore, cannot be resold unless they are registered under the Act or unless an exemption from registration is available; and

(3) Placement of a legend on the certificate or other document that evidences the securities stating that the securities have not been registered under the Act and setting forth or referring to the restrictions on transferability and sale of the securities.

Rule 503. Filing of Notice of Sales

(a) The issuer shall file with the Commission five copies of a notice on Form D at the following times:

(1) No later than 15 days after the first sale of securities in an offering under Regulation D;

(2) Every six months after the first sale of securities in an offering under Regulation D, unless the final notice required by paragraph (a)(3) of Rule 503 has been filed; and

(3) No later than 30 days after the last sale of securities in an offering under Regulation D.

(b) If the offering is completed within the 15 day period described in paragraph (a)(1) of Rule 503 and if the notice is filed no later than the end of that period but after the completion of the offering, then only one notice need be filed to comply with paragraphs (a)(1) and (3) of Rule 503.

(c) One copy of every notice on Form D shall be manually signed by a person duly authorized by the issuer.

(d) If sales are made under Rule 505, the notice shall contain an undertaking by the issuer to furnish to the Commission, upon the written request of its staff, the information furnished by the issuer under Rule 502(b)(2) to any purchaser that is not an accredited investor.

(e) If more than one notice for an offering is required to be filed under paragraph (a) of Rule 503, notices after the first notice need only report the issuer's name and the information required by Part C and any material change in the facts from those set forth in Parts A and B of the first notice.

(f) A notice on Form D shall be considered filed with the Commission under paragraph (a) of Rule 503:

(1) As of the date on which it is received at the Commission's principal office in Washington, D.C.; or

(2) As of the date on which the notice is mailed by means of United States registered or certified mail to the Commission's Office of Small Business Policy, Division of Corporation Finance, at the Commission's principal office in Washington, D.C., if the notice is delivered to such office after the date on which it is required to be filed.

Rule 504. Exemption for Limited Offers and Sales of Securities Not Exceeding $500,000

(a) *Exemption.* Offers and sales of securities that satisfy the conditions in paragraph (b) of Rule 504 by an issuer that is not subject to the reporting requirements of section 13 or 15(d) of the Exchange Act and that is not an investment company shall be exempt from the provisions of section 5 of the Act under section 3(b) of the Act.

(b) *Conditions to be met.*

(1) *General conditions.* To qualify for exemption under Rule 504, offers and sales must satisfy the terms and conditions of Rules 501 through 503, except that the provisions of Rule 502(c) and (d) shall not apply to offers and sales of securities under Rule 504 that are made exclusively in one or more states each of which provides for the registration of the securities and requires the delivery of a disclosure document before sale and that are made in accordance with those state provisions.

(2) *Specific condition.*

(i) *Limitation on aggregate offering price.* The aggregate offering price for an offering of securities under Rule 504, as defined in Rule 501(c), shall not exceed $500,000, less the aggregate offering price for all securities sold within the twelve months before the start of and during the offering of securities under Rule 504 in reliance on any exemption under section 3(b) of the Act or in violation of section 5(a) of the Act.

Note 1: The calculation of the aggregate offering price is illustrated as follows:

Example 1. If an issuer sold $200,000 of its securities on June 1, 1982 under Rule 504 and an additional $100,000 on September 1, 1982, the issuer would be permitted to sell only $200,000 more under Rule 504 until June 1, 1983. Until that date the issuer must count both prior sales towards the $500,000 limit. However, if the issuer made its third sale on June 1, 1983, the issuer could then sell $400,000 of its securities because the June 1, 1982 sale would not be within the preceding twelve months.

Example 2. If an issuer sold $100,000 of its securities on June 1, 1982 under Rule 504 and an additional $4,500,000 on December 1, 1982 under Rule 505, the issuer could not sell any of its securities under Rule 504 until December 1, 1983. Until then the issuer must count the December 1, 1982 sale towards the limit of $500,000 within the preceding twelve months.

Note 2: If a transaction under Rule 504 fails to meet the limitation on the aggregate offering price, it does not affect the availability of Rule 504 for the other transactions considered in applying such limitation. For example, if the issuer in *Example 1* made its third sale on May 31, 1983, in the amount of $250,000, Rule 504 would not be available for that sale, but the exemption for the prior two sales would be unaffected.

Rule 505. Exemption for Limited Offers and Sales of Securities Not Exceeding $5,000,000

(a) *Exemption.* Offers and sales of securities that satisfy the conditions in paragraph (b) of Rule 505 by an issuer that is not an investment company shall be exempt from the provisions of section 5 of the Act under section 3(b) of the Act.

(b) *Conditions to be met.*

(1) *General conditions.* To qualify for exemption under Rule 505, offers and sales must satisfy the terms and conditions of Rules 501 through 503.

(2) *Specific conditions.*

(i) *Limitation on aggregate offering price.* The aggregate offering price for an offering of securities under Rule 505, as defined in Rule 501(c), shall not exceed $5,000,000, less the aggregate offering price for all securities sold within the twelve months before the start of and during the offering of securities under Rule 505 in reliance on any exemption under section 3(b) of the Act or in violation of section 5(a) of the Act.

Note: The calculation of the aggregate offering price is illustrated as follows:

Example 1. If an issuer sold $2,000,000 of its securities on June 1, 1982 under Rule 505 and an additional $1,000,000 on September 1, 1982, the issuer would be permitted to sell only $2,000,000 more under Rule 505 until June 1, 1983. Until that date the issuer must count both prior sales towards the $5,000,000 limit. However, if the issuer made its third sale on June 1, 1983, the issuer could then sell $4,000,000 of its securities because the June 1, 1982 sale would not be within the preceding twelve months.

Example 2. If an issuer sold $500,000 of its securities on June 1, 1982 under Rule 504 and an additional $4,500,000 on December 1, 1982 under Rule 505, then the issuer could not sell any of its securities under Rule 505 until June 1, 1983. At that time it could sell an additional $500,000 of its securities.

(ii) *Limitation on number of purchasers.* The issuer shall reasonably believe that there are no more than 35 purchasers of securities from the issuer in any offering under Rule 505.

Note: See Rule 501(e) for the calculation of the number of purchasers and Rule 502(a) for what may or may not constitute an offering under this section.

(iii) *Disqualifications.* No exemption under Rule 505 shall be available for the securities of any issuer described in Rule 252(c), (d), (e), or (f) of Regulation A, except that for purposes of Rule 505 only:

(A) The term "filing of the notification required by Rule 255" as used in Rule 252(c), (d), (e) and (f) shall mean the first sale of securities under Rule 505;

(B) The term "underwriter" as used in Rule 252(d) and (e) shall mean a person that has been or will be paid directly or indirectly remuneration for solicitation of purchasers in connection with sales of securities under Rule 505; and

(C) Paragraph (b)(2)(iii) of Rule 505 shall not apply to any issuer if the Commission determines, upon a showing of good cause, that it is not necessary under the circumstances that the exemption be denied. Any such determination shall be without prejudice to any other action by the Commission in any other proceeding or matter with respect to the issuer or any other person.

Rule 506. Exemption for Limited Offers and Sales Without Regard to Dollar Amount of Offering

(a) *Exemption.* Offers and sales of securities by an issuer that satisfy the conditions in paragraph (b) of Rule 506 shall be deemed to be transactions not involving any public offering within the meaning of section 4(2) of the Act.

(b) *Conditions to be met.*

(1) *General conditions.* To qualify for exemption under Rule 506, offers and sales must satisfy all the terms and conditions of Rules 501 through 503.

(2) *Specific conditions.*

(i) *Limitation on number of purchasers.* The issuer shall reasonably believe that there are no more than 35 purchasers of securities from the issuer in any offering under Rule 506.

Note: See Rule 501(e) for the calculation of the number of purchasers and Rule 502(a) for what may or may not constitute an offering under Rule 506.

(ii) *Nature of purchasers.* The issuer shall reasonably believe immediately prior to making any sale that each purchaser who is not an accredited investor either alone or with his purchaser representative(s) has such knowledge and experience in financial and business matters that he is capable of evaluating the merits and risks of the prospective investment.

2. UNDER SECURITIES EXCHANGE ACT OF 1934

17 C.F.R. § 240. ——

MANIPULATION AND DECEPTION

1934 ACT RULES

SOLICITATION OF PROXIES

TENDER OFFERS

OVER–THE–COUNTER MARKETS

MANIPULATION AND DECEPTION

Rule 10b–1. Prohibition of Use of Manipulative or Deceptive Devices or Contrivances With Respect to Certain Securities Exempted From Registration

The term manipulative or deceptive device or contrivance, as used in section 10(b), is hereby defined to include any act or omission to act with respect to any security exempted from the operation of section 12(a) pursuant to a rule which specifically provides that this rule shall be applicable to such security, if such act or omission to act would have been unlawful under section 9(a), or any rule or regulation heretofore or hereafter prescribed thereunder, if done or omitted to be done with respect to a security registered on a national securities exchange, and the use of any means or instrumentality of interstate commerce or of the mails or of any facility of any national securities exchange to use or employ any such device or contrivance in connection with the purchase or sale of any such security is hereby prohibited.

Rule 10b–2. Solicitation of Purchases on an Exchange to Facilitate a Distribution of Securities

(*a*) No person, participating or otherwise financially interested in the primary or secondary distribution of any security of any issuer, shall, by the use of any means or instrumentality of interstate commerce or of the mails, or of any facility of any national securities exchange:

(1) Pay or offer or agree to pay, directly or indirectly, to any person any compensation for soliciting another to purchase any security of the same issuer on a national securities exchange, or for purchasing any security of the same issuer on any such exchange for any account other than the account of the person who pays or is to pay such compensation; or

(2) Sell, offer to sell or induce an offer to buy such security, or deliver such security after sale, if, in connection with such distribution, such person has paid, or has offered or agreed to pay, directly or indirectly, to any person, any compensation for soliciting another to purchase any security of the same issuer on any national securities exchange, or for purchasing any security of the same issuer on any such exchange for any account other than the account of the person who has paid or is to pay such compensation.

(b) No person, participating or otherwise financially interested in the primary or secondary distribution of any security of any issuer, shall cause a purchase or sale of any security of the same issuer on a national securities exchange by paying or offering or agreeing to pay, directly or indirectly, to any person any compensation for soliciting another to purchase such security on any such exchange, or for purchasing such security on any such exchange for any account other than the account of the person who pays or is to pay such compensation.

(*c*) The provisions of this rule shall not apply with respect to any compensation paid or offered or agreed to be paid by a broker or dealer to any person regularly employed by him whose ordinary duties include the solicitation or execution of orders for the purchase or sale of securities, if such compensation represents only ordinary compensation either in the form of salary or the usual and customary commissions paid to such person for the discharge by such person of such duties in the regular course of his employment.

(*d*)(1) The provisions of this rule shall not apply to any transaction involving the payment of compensation pursuant to the terms of an effective plan authorizing the payment of such compensation in connection with a distribution of securities, which plan has been filed with the Commission by a national securities exchange, provided that the person paying such compensation does not know or have reasonable grounds to believe, at the time he pays or offer or agrees to pay such compensation, that transactions connected with such distribution are being carried out in violation of such plan.

(2) For the purposes of this rule a plan filed with the Commission by a national securities exchange shall not become effective unless the Commission, having due regard for the public interest and for the protection of investors, declares the plan to be effective. The Commission in its declaration may impose such terms and conditions relating to the provisions of the plan and the period of its effective-

ness as it deems necessary or appropriate in the ublic interest or for the protection of investors.

Rule 10b–3. Employment of Manipulative and Deceptive Devices, by Brokers or Dealers

(a) It shall be unlawful for any broker or dealer, directly or indirectly, by the use of any means or instrumentality of interstate commerce, or of the mails, or of any facility of any national securities exchange, to use or employ, in connection with the purchase or sale of any security otherwise than on a national securities exchange, any act, practice, or course of business defined by the Commission to be included within the term "manipulative, deceptive, or other fraudulent device or contrivance", as such term is used in section 15(c)(1) of the act.

(b) It shall be unlawful for any municipal securities dealer directly or indirectly, by the use of any means or instrumentality of interstate commerce, or of the mails, or of any facility of any national securities exchange, to use or employ, in connection with the purchase or sale of any municipal security, any act, practice, or course of business defined by the Commission to be included within the term "manipulative, deceptive, or other fraudulent device or contrivance," as such term is used in Section 15(c)(1) of the act.

Rule 10b–4. Short Tendering of Securities

(a) *Definitions.* For purposes of this section:

(1) A person shall be deemed to own a subject security or an equivalent security if neither he nor his agent has entered into an arrangement or agreement (other than one for the lending of securities or the writing of a standardized call option) whereby any other person may tender that security or be deemed to own it and (i) he or his agent has title to it, or (ii) he has purchased, or has entered into an unconditional contract, binding on both parties thereto, to purchase it but has not yet received it, or (iii) he has a standardized call option and has exercised that option, or (iv) in the case of a subject security he has converted, exchanged, or exercised an equivalent security that he owned (within the meaning of (i) or (ii) above). For the purpose of determining ownership as of the end of the proration period, securities that have been tendered and not withdrawn are deemed to be owned as of the end of the proration period. *Provided, however,* that a person shall be deemed to own a security for purposes of this rule only to the extent that he has a net long position in such security.

(2) The term "equivalent security" means (i) any security (including any option, warrant, or other right to purchase the subject security), issued by the person whose securities are the subject of the offer, that is immediately convertible into, or exchangeable or exercisable for, a subject security, or (ii) any other right or option (other than a standardized call option) that entitles the holder thereof to acquire a subject security, but only if the holder thereof reasonably believes that the maker or writer of the right or option has title to and possession of the subject security and upon exercise will promptly deliver the subject security.

(3) The term "subject security" means a security that is the subject of any tender offer or request or invitation for tenders.

(4) For purposes of this rule, a person shall be deemed to "tender" a security if he (i) delivers a subject security pursuant to an offer, (ii) causes such delivery to be made, (iii) guarantees delivery of a subject security pursuant to a tender offer, (iv) causes a guarantee of such delivery to be given by another person, or (v) uses any other method by which acceptance of a tender offer may be made.

(5) A person's net long position, as that term is used in paragraph (a)(1) of this rule, shall be reduced by the number of shares of subject securities deliverable upon exercise of any standardized call option that the person has written on or after the date that a tender offer is first publicly announced or otherwise made known by the bidder to holders of the security to be acquired, if the exercise price of such option is lower than the highest tender offer price or stated amount of the consideration offered for the subject security. If one or more other tender offers for the same security are ongoing on such date, the announcement date for purposes of this paragraph shall be that of the first announced offer.

(6) The term "standardized call option" means any call option that is traded on an exchange, or for which quotation information is disseminated in an electronic interdealer quotation system of a registered national securities association.

(b) It shall constitute a "manipulative or deceptive device or contrivance" and a "fraudulent, deceptive, or manipulative act or practice" as those terms are used in sections 10(b) and 14(e) of the Act, respectively, for any person acting alone or in concert with others, directly or indirectly, to tender any subject security in a partial offer:

(1) For his own account unless at the time of tender, and at the end of the proration period or period during which securities are accepted by lot (including any extensions thereof), he owns (i) the subject security and will deliver or cause to be delivered such security for the purpose of tender to the person making the offer within the period specified in the offer, or (ii) an equivalent security and, upon the acceptance of his tender will acquire the subject security by conversion, exchange, or exercise of such equivalent security to the extent of such acceptance and, within the period specified in the offer, will deliver or cause to be delivered the subject security so acquired for the purpose of tender to the person making the offer; or

(2) For the account of another person unless the person making the tender (i) possesses the subject security or an equivalent security, or (ii) has a reasonable belief that, upon information furnished by the person on whose behalf the tender is made, such person owns the subject security or an equivalent security and will promptly deliver the subject security or such equivalent security for the purpose of tender to the person making the tender.

(3) If the same security has been tendered in response to any other partial offer, unless such other tender has been withdrawn.

(c) This rule shall not apply to a partial offer where tenders are not accepted either by lot or on a *pro rata* basis for a specified period.

(d) This rule shall not prohibit any transaction or transactions if the Commission, upon written request or upon its own motion, exempt such transaction or transactions, either unconditionally or on specified terms and conditions, as not constituting a manipulative or deceptive device or contrivance or fraudulent, deceptive, or manipulative act or practice comprehended within the purpose of this rule.

Rule 10b–5. Employment of Manipulative and Deceptive Devices

It shall be unlawful for any person, directly or indirectly, by the use of any means or instrumentality of interstate commerce, or of the mails, or of any facility of any national securities exchange,

(1) to employ any device, scheme, or artifice to defraud,

(2) to make any untrue statement of a material fact or to omit to state a material fact necessary in order to make the statements made, in the light of the circumstances under which they were made, not misleading, or

(3) to engage in any act, practice, or course of business which operates or would operate as a fraud or deceit upon any person,

in connection with the purchase or sale of any security.

Rule 10b–6. Prohibitions Against Trading by Persons Interested in a Distribution

(a) It shall be unlawful for any person,

(1) Who is an underwriter or prospective underwriter in a particular distribution of securities, or

(2) Who is the issuer or other person on whose behalf such a distribution is being made, or

(3) Who is a broker, dealer, or other person who has agreed to participate or is participating in such a distribution, or

(4) Who is an "affiliated purchaser" as that term is defined in paragraph (c)(6) of this section, directly or indirectly, by the use of any means or instrumentality of interstate commerce, or of the mails, or of any facility of any national securities exchange, either alone or with one or more other persons, to bid for or purchase for any account in which he has a beneficial interest, any security which is the subject of such distribution, or any security of the same class and series, or any right to purchase any such security, or to attempt to induce any person to purchase any such security or right, until after he has completed his participation in such distribution: *Provided, however,* That this section shall not prohibit the following, if not engaged in for the purpose of creating actual, or apparent, active trading in or raising the price of any such security:

(i) Transactions in connection with the distribution effected otherwise than on a securities exchange with the issuer or other person or persons on whose behalf such distribution is being made or among underwriters, prospective underwriters or other persons who have agreed to participate or are participating in such distribution;

(ii) Unsolicited privately negotiated purchases, each involving at least a block of such security, that are not effected from or through a broker or dealer; or

(iii) Purchases by an issuer effected more than forty days after the effective date of the registration statement covering the securities being distributed, or in the case of an unregistered distribution, more than forty days after the commencement of offers or sales of the securities being distributed, for the purpose of satisfying a sinking fund or similar obligation to which it is subject and which becomes due as of a date that does not exceed twelve months from the date of purchase; or

(iv) Odd-lot transactions and round-lot transactions that offset odd-lot transactions previously or simultaneously executed or reasonably anticipated in the usual course of business by a person who acts in the capacity of an odd-lot dealer; or

(v) Brokerage transactions:

(A) Not involving solicitation of the customer's order, or

(B) Involving solicitation of the customer's order (*1*) in the case of securities qualified under paragraph (a)(4)(xi)(A) of this section, prior to the later of two business days before the commencement of offers or sales of the securities to be distributed or the time the broker-dealer becomes a participant in the distribution, or (*2*) in the case of other securities, prior to the later of nine business days before the commencement of offers or sales of the securities to be distributed or the time the broker-dealer becomes a participant in the distribution; or

(vi) Offers to sell or the solicitation of offers to buy the securities being distributed (including securities or rights acquired in stabilizing) or securities or rights offered as principal by the person making such offer to sell or solicitation; or

(vii) The exercise of any right or conversion privilege, set forth in the instrument governing a security, to acquire any security directly from the issuer, or the exercise of standardized call options that were acquired prior to the time a person became a participant in the distribution; or

(viii) Stabilizing transactions not in violation of Rule 10b–7; or

(ix) Bids for or purchases of rights not in violation of Rule 10b–8; or

(x) Transactions effected on a national securities exchange in accordance with the provisions of a plan filed by such exchange under Rule 10b–2(d) and declared effective by the Commission; or

(xi) Bids or purchases by an underwriter, prospective underwriter, or dealer, or by an affiliated purchaser, if all such bids or purchases are made:

(A) In the case of stock with a minimum price of five dollars per share and a minimum public float of 400,000 shares, or any security of the same class and series as such stock, or any right to purchase any such security, except for the exercise of standardized call options, prior to the later of two business days before the commencement of offers or sales of the securities to be distributed or the time such person becomes a participant in the distribution, or

(B) In the case of the exercise of standardized call options of securities qualified under paragraph (a)(4)(xi)(A) of this rule, which call options were acquired after the time such person becomes a participant in the distribution, prior to five business days before the commencement of offers or sales of the securities to be distributed, or

(C) In the case of other securities, prior to the later of nine business days before the commencement of offers or sales of the securities to be distributed or the time such person becomes a participant in the distribution, or

(D) In the case of unsolicited purchases, prior to the later of the date of commencement of offers or sales of the securities to be distributed or the time such person becomes a participant in the distribution; or

(xii) Bids or purchases by an issuer or other person on whose behalf a distribution is being made or by an affiliated purchaser (as defined in paragraph (c)(6) of this rule), if all such bids or purchases are made:

(A) In the case of stock with a minimum price of five dollars per share and minimum public float of 400,000 shares, or any security of the same class and series as such stock, or any right to purchase any such security, except for the exercise of standardized call options, prior to two business days before commencement of offers or sales of the securities to be distributed, or

(B) In the case of the exercise of standardized call options on securities qualified under paragraph (a)(4)(xii)(A) of this rule, which call options were acquired after the time that such person becomes a distribution participant, prior to five business days before the commencement of offers or sales of the securities to be distributed, or

(C) In the case of other securities, prior to nine business days before the commencement of offers or sales of the securities to be distributed, or

(D) In the case of unsolicited purchases, prior to the date of commencement of offers or sales of the securities to be distributed; or

(xiii) Transactions in nonconvertible debt securities or nonconvertible preferred securities: *Provided, however,* That at least one nationally recognized statistical rating organization, as that term is used in Rule 15c3-1 under the Act, has rated both the nonconvertible securities being distributed and those to be purchased in one of its generic rating categories that signifies investment grade.

(b) The distribution of a security (1) which is immediately exchangeable for or convertible into another security, or (2) which entitles the holder thereof immediately to acquire another security, shall be deemed to include a distribution of such other security within the meaning of this rule.

(c) The following shall be applicable for the purposes of this rule:

(1) The term "underwriter" means a person who has agreed with an issuer or other person on whose behalf a distribution is to be made (i) to purchase securities for distribution or (ii) to distribute securities for or on behalf of such issuer or other person or (iii) to manage or supervise a distribution of securities for or on behalf of such issuer or other person.

(2) The term "prospective underwriter" means a person (i) who has decided to submit a bid to become an underwriter of securities as to which the issuer or other person on whose behalf the distribution is to be made, has issued, directly or indirectly, an invitation for bids, or (ii) who has reached an understanding, with the issuer or other person on whose behalf a distribution is to be made, that he will become an underwriter, whether or not the terms and conditions of the underwriting have been agreed upon.

(3) A person shall be deemed to have completed his participation in a particular distribution as follows: (i) the issuer or other person on whose behalf such distribution is being made, when such distribution is completed; (ii) an underwriter, when he has distributed his participation, including all other securities of the same class acquired in connection with the distribution, and any stabilization arrangements and trading restrictions with respect to such distribution to which he is a party have been terminated: *Provided, however,* That an underwriter will not be deemed to have completed his participation if he has obtained an option in connection with that distribution pursuant to which he purchases from the issuer an additional amount of securities not necessary to cover any syndicate short position that remains in connection with that distribution; (iii) any other person, when he has distributed his participation. A person, including an underwriter or dealer, shall be deemed for purposes of this paragraph (c)(3) to have distributed securities acquired by him for investment.

(4) The term "plan" shall include any bonus, profit-sharing, pension, retirement, thrift, savings, incentive, stock purchase, stock ownership, stock appreciation, stock option, dividend reinvestment or similar plan for employees or shareholders of an issuer or its subsidiaries.

(5) For purposes of this section only, the term "distribution" means an offering of securities, whether or not subject to registration under the Securities Act of 1933, that is distinguished from ordinary trading transactions by the magnitude of the offering and the presence of special selling efforts and selling methods.

(6)(i) The term "affiliated purchaser" means:

(A) a person, directly or indirectly, acting in concert with a distribution participant in connection with the acquisition or distribution of any security which is the subject of such distribution, or any security of the same class and series, or any right to purchase any such security, or

(B) an affiliate who, directly or indirectly, controls the purchases of such securities by a distribution participant, whose purchases are controlled by a distribution participant, or whose purchases are under common control with those of a distribution participant, or

(C) an affiliate that is a broker or a dealer, *Provided, however,* That this paragraph (C) shall not include a broker or a dealer whose business consists solely of effecting transactions in "exempted securities" as defined in Section 3(a)(12) of the Act, or

(D) an affiliate (other than a broker or a dealer) that regularly purchases securities, through a broker-dealer or otherwise, for its own account or for the account of others, or recommends or exercises investment discretion with respect to the purchase or sale of securities: *Provided, however,* That this paragraph (D) shall not apply to an affiliate that satisfies the following conditions: (*1*) the affiliate is a separate and distinct organizational entity from, with no officers (or persons performing similar functions) or employees (other than clerical, ministerial, or support personnel) in common with, the distribution participant; (*2*) The affiliate and the distribution participant have separate employee compensation arrangements; and (*3*) The affiliate's bids for, purchases of, and inducements to purchase the securities subject to this section are made in the ordinary course of its business.

(ii) For purposes of this paragraph (c)(6), the term "distribution participant" means

(A) the issuer or other person on whose behalf the distribution is being made, and

(B) an underwriter, prospective underwriter, dealer, broker, or other person who has agreed to participate or is participating in the distribution.

(7) For purposes of paragraphs (a)(3)(xi) and (xii) of this rule, the "minimum price" will be computed (i) in the case of a stock for which last sale information is reported pursuant to Rule 11Aa3–1 under the Act, by use of the average of the closing prices so reported during a two consecutive calendar week period commencing within thirty business days prior to the commencement of offers or sales of the securities to be distributed, (ii) in the case of stocks listed and registered on a national securities exchange for which last sale information is not available pursuant to Rule 11Aa3–1, by use of the average of the closing prices for such stock on such exchange during such period, or (iii) in the case of all other stocks, by use of the average of the best independent bids or the best independent closing bids during such period. For purposes of such paragraphs, the "minimum public float" will be computed by the total number of shares, of the stock outstanding minus shares held by officers, directors, and any persons who, directly or indirectly, are the owners of ten percent or more of the stock in distribution.

(d) The provisions of this rule shall not apply to any of the following securities: (1) "exempted securities" as defined in Section 3(a)(12) of the Act, including securities issued, or guaranteed both as to principal and interest, by the International Bank for Reconstruction and Development; or (2) face-amount certificates issued by a face-amount certificate company, or redeemable securities issued by an open-end management company or a unit investment trust. Any terms used in clause (2) of this paragraph (d) which are defined in the Investment Company Act of 1940 shall have the meanings specified in such Act.

(e) The provisions of this rule shall not apply to any distribution of securities by an issuer or a subsidiary of an issuer to employees or shareholders of the issuer or its subsidiaries, or to a trustee or other person acquiring such securities for the account of such employees or shareholders pursuant to a plan, as that term is defined in paragraph (c)(4) of this section.

(f) The provisions of this rule shall not apply to bids for or purchases of any security of an issuer, any security of the same class and series as such security, or any security immediately convertible into, or exchangeable or exercisable for, any such security solely because the issuer or a subsidiary of such issuer has outstanding securities which are immediately convertible into, or exchangeable or exercisable for, such security.

(g) A bid for or purchase of any security made or effected by or for a plan shall be deemed to be a purchase by the issuer unless the bid is made, or the purchase is effected, by an agent independent of the issuer, as that term is defined in Rule 10b–18(a)(6) under the Act.

(h) This rule shall not prohibit any transaction or transactions if the Commission, upon written request or upon its own motion, exempts such transaction or transactions, either unconditionally or on specified terms and conditions, as not constituting a manipulative or deceptive device or contrivance comprehended within the purpose of this rule.

Rule 10b–7. Stabilizing to Facilitate a Distribution

(a) Scope of Rule. The provisions of this rule shall apply to any person who, either alone or with one or more other persons, directly or indirectly, stabilizes the price of a security to facilitate an offering of any security. It shall constitute a "manipulative or deceptive device or contrivance," as used in section 10(b) of the Act, for any such person, directly or indirectly, by the use of any means or instrumentality of interstate commerce, or of the mails, or of any facility of any national securities exchange, to effect, either alone or with one or more other persons, any transaction or series of transactions prohibited by thus rule.

(b) Definitions. Unless the context clearly indicates otherwise, for the purposes of this rule the following terms shall have the meaning indicated:

(1) The term "offering at the market" shall mean an offering in which it is contemplated that any offering price set in any calendar day will be increased more than once during such day.

(2) The term "transaction" shall mean a bid or a purchase.

(3) The terms "stabilize," "stabilizes," "stabilizing" or "stabilized" shall mean the placing of any bid, or the effecting of any purchase, for the purpose of pegging, fixing or stabilizing the price of any security: *Provided, however,* That a bid shall not constitute a stabilizing bid unless or until it is shown in the market.

(c) Transactions Must Be Necessary. No stabilizing bid or purchase shall be made except for the purpose of preventing or retarding a decline in the open market price of a security.

(d) Priority Must Be Granted. Any person placing or transmitting a bid which he knows is for the purpose of stabilizing the price of any security shall disclose the purpose of such bid to the person with whom it is placed or to whom it is transmitted. Any person placing a stabilizing bid or effecting a stabilizing purchase on a securities exchange shall grant priority to any independent bid at the same price irrespective of the size of such independent bid or the time when it is entered. Any person placing a stabilizing bid or effecting a stabilizing purchase otherwise than on a securities exchange shall grant priority to any independent bid at the same price placed with or transmitted to him irrespective of the size of such independent bid or the time when it is entered.

(e) Control of Stabilizing. No sole distributor or syndicate or group stabilizing the price of a security nor any member or members of such syndicate or group shall maintain more than one stabilizing bid in any one market at the same price at the same time: *Provided, however,* That more than one such bid at the same price may be maintained otherwise than on a securities exchange by or for the account of such distributor, syndicate or group.

(f) Stabilizing at Prices Resulting From Unlawful Activity. No stabilizing shall be initiated at a price which the stabilizer knows or has reason to know is the result of activity which is fraudulent, manipulative, or deceptive under the Act or any rule or regulation thereunder.

(g) Stabilizing Prohibited in Offerings at the Market. No person shall effect any stabilizing transaction to facilitate any offering at the market.

(h) Stabilizing Securities Traded in More Than One Market. If a security is traded in more than one market, stabilizing shall not be initiated at any price which would be unlawful in the market which is the principal market for such security in the United States open for trading at the time when such stabilizing is initiated: *Provided, however,* That if the principal market for such security in the United States is a securities exchange, stabilizing may be initiated in any market after the close of such exchange at the price at which stabilizing could have been initiated on such exchange at the close thereof unless the person stabilizing knows or has reason to know that other persons have offered or sold such security at a lower price after such close, except that special prices available to any group or class of persons (including employees or holders of warrants or rights) shall not limit the stabilizing price.

(i) Entering Stabilizing Bid on Exchange Prior to Opening. No person shall place a stabilizing bid on a securities exchange prior to the time the opening quotations for the security on such exchange are available, unless he has been and is lawfully stabilizing such security at such price: *Provided,*

however, That a stabilizing bid may be made immediately prior to the opening of a securities exchange at a price not in excess of the price at which stabilizing could have been initiated on such exchange at the previous close thereof, unless the person stabilizing knows or has reason to know that other persons have offered or sold such security at a lower price after such close, except that special prices available to any group or class of persons (including employees or holders of warrants or rights) shall not limit the stabilizing price.

(j) Stabilizing Levels. (1) Except as provided in subparagraphs (2), (3) and (4) of this paragraph (*j*), no person shall (A) begin to stabilize a security at a price higher than the highest current independent bid price for such security or (B) raise the price at which he is stabilizing. If no bona fide market for the security being distributed exists at the time stabilizing is initiated, stabilizing may be initiated at a price not in excess of the public offering price.

(2) If the principal market for a security is a securities exchange and stabilizing is initiated on such exchange the initial stabilizing bid or purchase may be made at a price not in excess of the last independent sale price on such exchange if (A) the security has been traded on such exchange on the day when stabilizing is begun, on either of the 2 preceding calendar days, or on the last preceding business day, and (B) the current asked price is equal to or above the last independent sale price. If both conditions (A) and (B) are not met, no person shall begin to stabilize the security at a price in excess of the highest current independent bid price for such security: *Provided, however,* That if a stabilizing bid has been entered at such independent bid price and the first sale thereafter on the exchange is an independent sale at a higher price, the security may be stabilized at a price not in excess of such independent sale price.

(3) If a stabilizing bid or purchase is made before the initial public offering price of the security to be distributed is determined, and such offering price is higher than such stabilizing bid or purchase price, then stabilizing may be resumed after determination of such public offering price at the price at which it could then be initiated: *Provided, however,* That special prices available to any group or class of persons (including employees or holders of warrants or rights) shall not constitute the initial public offering price for purposes of this subparagraph (3).

(4) A stabilizing bid lawful when made may be continuously maintained or reduced irrespective of changes in the independent bid, asked or sale price of such security: *Provided, however,* That no stabilizing shall be done at a price higher than the price at which stabilizing is being done in the principal market for such security. Except as provided in subparagraph (3) of this paragraph (*j*), if stabilizing is discontinued for less than 3 business days it shall not be resumed in connection with the same distribution except at the lower of the two following prices: (A) the last lawful stabilizing price, or (B) the price at which stabilizing could then be initiated. If no stabilizing purchases have been effected for 3 consecutive business days then stabilizing may be continued or resumed at the price at which it could then be initiated.

(5) No person shall stabilize a security at a price above the price at which such security is currently being distributed: *Provided, however,* That special prices available to any group or class of persons (including employees or holders of warrants or rights) shall not limit the stabilizing price.

(6) If a security goes ex-dividend, ex-rights, or ex-distribution, the price at which such security is being stabilized shall be reduced by an amount equal to the value of the dividend, right, or distribution, computed to the nearest trading differential: *Provided, however,* That if the dividend, right or distribution has a value of not more than 50 percent of the minimum price differential, the stabilizing price need not be reduced.

(7) When two or more securities are being offered as a unit, the component securities shall not be stabilized at prices the sum of which exceeds the offering price of the unit: *Provided, however,* That special prices available to any group or class of persons (including employees or holders of warrants or rights) shall not limit the stabilizing price.

(8) If a security is being called or redeemed it shall be unlawful to stabilize such security at a price above such call or redemption price plus accruals, if any: *Provided, however,* That if such security is immediately convertible into or exchangeable for another security or securities, and if the amount of such other security or securities (into which it is convertible or for which it is exchangeable) multiplied by their highest lawful stabilizing price exceeds the call or redemption price plus accruals,

then the security may be stabilized at a price not in excess of such price, to the nearest trading differential.

(k) Disclosure of Stabilizing. Any person subject to this rule who sells to, or purchases for the account of, any person, any security or any right or warrant to subscribe to any such security, where the price of such security, right or warrant has been stabilized, shall give or send to such person, at or before the completion of each transaction entered into while the distribution is in progress, written notice that stabilizing purchases may be or have been effected. If, however, at or before the completion of the transaction, the purchaser receives a prospectus, offering circular, confirmation or other writing containing a statement similar to that comprising the legend provided for in Item 502(d) of Regulation S–K, then no other written notice with respect to stabilizing need be given to such purchaser.

(l) Reporting Requirements. A person subject to this rule shall keep the information and make the notification required by Rule 17a–2 even though he is not subject to that rule as a broker, dealer, or member of a national securities exchange.

(m) Limitation of Liability. Whenever any act done or omitted by any person subject to this rule would involve a violation of such rule only if some other person had previously done or omitted to do some other act, the act or omission of such first-mentioned person shall not involve a violation unless such first-mentioned person knew or had reason to know that such other person had previously done or omitted to do such other act.

(n) Exempted Securities. The provisions of this rule shall not apply to "exempted securities," as defined in section 3(a)(12) of the Act, including securities issued, or guaranteed both as to principal and interest, by the International Bank for Reconstruction and Development.

(o) Exempted Transactions. This rule shall not prohibit any transaction or transactions if the Commission, upon written request or upon its own motion, exempts such transaction or transactions, either unconditionally or on specified terms and conditions, as not constituting a manipulative or deceptive device or contrivance comprehended within the purpose of this rule.

Rule 10b–8. Distributions Through Rights

(a) Scope of Rule. It shall constitute a "manipulative or deceptive device or contrivance" as used in section 10(b) of the Act for any person participating in a distribution of securities being offered through rights issued on a pro-rata basis to security holders, directly or indirectly, by the use of any means or instrumentality of interstate commerce, or of the mails, or of any facility of any national securities exchange, to do any act prohibited by this rule prior to the expiration of the rights * * *.

[Substance of prohibitions omitted.]

* * *

Rule 10b–10. Confirmation of Transactions

(a) It shall be unlawful for any broker or dealer to effect for or with the account of a customer any transaction in, or to induce the purchase or sale by such customer of, any security (other than U.S. Savings Bonds or municipal securities) unless such broker or dealer, at or before completion of such transaction, gives or sends to such customer written notification disclosing—

(1) whether he is acting as agent for such customer, as agent for some other person, as agent for both such customer and some other person, or as principal for his own account;

(2) the date and time of the transaction (or the fact that the time of the transaction will be furnished upon written request of such customer) and the identity, price and number of shares or units (or principal amount) of such security purchased or sold by such customer; and

(3) in the case of any transaction in a debt security subject to redemption before maturity, a statement to the effect that such debt security may be redeemed in whole or in part before maturity, that such a redemption could affect the yield represented and that additional information is available upon request; and

(4) in the case of a transaction in a debt security effected exclusively on the basis of a dollar price

(i) The dollar price at which the transaction was effected, and

(ii) The yield to maturity calculated from the dollar price; *Provided, however,* that this paragraph (ii) shall not apply to a transaction in a debt security with a maturity date that may be extended by the issuer thereof, with a variable interest rate payable thereon, or a participation interest in notes secured by liens upon real estate continuously subject to prepayment; and

(5) in the case of a transaction in a debt security effected on the basis of yield

(i) The yield at which the transaction was effected, including the percentage amount and its characterization (*e.g.*, current yield, yield to maturity, or yield to call) and if effected at yield to call, the type of call, the call date and call price;

(ii) The dollar price calculated from the yield at which the transaction was effected; and

(iii) If effected on a basis other than yield to maturity and the yield to maturity is lower than the represented yield, the yield to maturity as well as the represented yield; *Provided, however,* that this paragraph (iii) shall not apply to a transaction in a debt security with a maturity date that may be extended by the issuer thereof, with a variable interest rate payable thereon, or a participation interest in notes secured by liens upon real estate continuously subject to prepayment; and

(6) whether any odd-lot differential or equivalent fee has been paid by such customer in connection with the execution of an order for an odd-lot number of shares or units (or principal amount) of a security and that the amount of any such differential or fee will be furnished upon oral or written request; *Provided, however,* That such disclosure need not be made if the differential or fee is included in the remuneration disclosed, or exempted from disclosure, pursuant to paragraph (a)(7)(ii); and

(7) if he is acting as agent for such customer, for some other person, or for both such customer and some other person,

(i) the name of the person from whom the security was purchased, or to whom it was sold, for such customer or the fact that such information will be furnished upon written request of such customer; and

(ii) the amount of any remuneration received or to be received by him from such customer in connection with the transaction unless remuneration paid by such customer is determined, pursuant to a written agreement with such customer, otherwise than on a transaction basis; and

(iii) the source and amount of any other remuneration received or to be received by him in connection with the transaction; *provided, however,* that if, in the case of a purchase, the broker was not participating in a distribution, or in the case of a sale, was not participating in a tender offer, the written notification may state whether any other remuneration has been or will be received and that the source and amount of such other remuneration will be furnished upon written request of such customer; and

(8) if he is acting as principal for his own account—

(i)(A) If he is not a market maker in that security and, if, after having received an order to buy from such customer, he purchased the security from another person to offset a contemporaneous sale to such customer or, after having received an order to sell from such customer, he sold the security to another person to offset a contemporaneous purchase from such a customer, the amount of any mark-up, mark-down, or similar remuneration received in an equity security; or

(B) In any other case of a transaction in a reported security, the trade price reported in accordance with an effective transaction reporting plan, the price to the customer in the transaction, and the difference, if any, between the reported trade price and the price to the customer.

(ii) in the case of a transaction in an equity security, whether he is a market maker in that security (otherwise than by reason of his acting as a block positioner in that security).

* * *

Rule 10b-13. Prohibiting Other Purchases During Tender Offer or Exchange Offer

(*a*) No person who makes a cash tender offer or exchange offer for any equity security shall, directly or indirectly, purchase, or make any arrangement to purchase, any such security (or any other security which is immediately convertible into or exchangeable for such security), otherwise than pursuant to such tender offer or exchange offer, from the time such tender offer or exchange offer is publicly announced or otherwise made known by such person to holders of the security to be required until the expiration of the period, including any extensions thereof, during which securities tendered pursuant to such tender offer or exchange offer may by the terms of such offer be accepted or rejected: *Provided, however,* That if such person is the owner of another security which is immediately convertible into or exchangeable for the security which is the subject of the offer, his subsequent exercise of his right of conversion or exchange with respect to such other security shall not be prohibited by this rule.

(*b*) The term "exchange offer" as used in this rule shall include a tender offer for, or request or invitation for tenders of, any security in exchange for any consideration other than for all cash.

(*c*) The provisions of this rule shall not apply to a purchase of a security of the same class as that which is the subject of a cash tender offer or exchange offer (or of any other security which is immediately convertible into or exchangeable for such security) if such purchase is made by the issuer, by participating employees of the issuer or the employees of its subsidiaries, or by the trustee or other person acquiring such security for the account of such employees, pursuant to (1) a stock option plan involving only "qualified stock options," or qualifying as an "employee stock purchase plan" as those terms are defined in sections 422 and 423 of the Internal Revenue Code of 1954, as amended, or "restricted stock options" as defined in section 424(b) of the Internal Revenue Code of 1954, as amended: *Provided, however,* That for the purposes of this paragraph an option which meets all of the conditions of that section other than the date of issuance shall be deemed to be "restricted stock options"; or (2) a savings, investment, pension or other stock purchase plan providing for both (A) periodic payments (or payroll deductions) for acquisition of securities by or on behalf of participating employees and (B) periodic purchases of the securities by participating employees, or the person acquiring them for the account of such employees.

(*d*) This rule shall not prohibit any transaction or transactions if the Commission, upon written request or upon its own motion, exempts such transaction or transactions, either unconditionally or on specified terms or conditions, as not constituting a manipulative or deceptive device or contrivance or a fraudulent, or deceptive or manipulative act or practice comprehended within the purpose of this rule.

Rule 10b–16. Disclosure of Credit Terms in Margin Transactions

(a) It shall be unlawful for any broker or dealer to extend credit, directly or indirectly, to any customer in connection with any securities transaction unless such broker or dealer has established procedures to assure that each customer

(1) is given or sent at the time of opening the account, a written statement or statements disclosing (i) the conditions under which an interest charge will be imposed; (ii) the annual rate or rates of interest that can be imposed; (iii) the method of computing interest; (iv) if rates of interest are subject to change without prior notice, the specific conditions under which they can be changed; (v) the method of determining the debit balance or balances on which interest is to be charged and whether credit is to be given for credit balances in cash accounts; (vi) what other charges resulting from the extension of credit, if any, will be made and under what conditions; and (vii) the nature of any interest or lien retained by the broker or dealer in the security or other property held as collateral and the conditions under which additional collateral can be required; *provided, however,* that the requirements of this Paragraph (a)(1) will be met in any case where the account is opened by telephone if the information required to be disclosed is orally communicated to the customer at that time and the required written statement or statements are sent to the customer immediately thereafter; and *provided, further,* that in the case of customers to whom credit is already being extended on the effective date of this Rule, the written statement or statements required hereunder must be given or sent to said customers within 90 days after the effective date of this Rule; and

(2) is given or sent a written statement or statements, at least quarterly, for each account in which credit was extended, disclosing (i) the balance at the beginning of the period; the date, amount and a brief description of each debit and credit entered during such period; the closing balance; and, if interest is charged for a period different from the period covered by the statement, the balance as of the last day of the interest period; (ii) the total interest charge for the period during which interest is charged (or, if

interest is charged separately for separate accounts, the total interest charge for each such account), itemized to show the dates on which the interest period began and ended; the annual rate or rates of interest charged and the interest charge for each such different annual rate of interest; and either each different debit balance on which an interest calculation was based or the average debit balance for the interest period, except that if an average debit balance is used, a separate average debit balance must be disclosed for each interest rate applied; and (iii) all other charges resulting from the extension of credit in that account; *provided, however,* that if the interest charge disclosed on a statement is for a period different from the period covered by the statement, there must be printed on the statement appropriate language to the effect that it should be retained for use in conjunction with the next statement containing the remainder of the required information; and *provided further,* that in the case of "equity funding programs" registered under the Securities Act of 1933, the requirements of this Paragraph (a)(2) will be met if the broker or dealer furnishes to the customer, within one month after each extension of credit, a written statement or statements containing the information required to be disclosed under this Paragraph (a)(2).

(b) It shall be unlawful for any broker or dealer to make any changes in the terms and conditions under which credit charges will be made (as described in the initial statement made under Paragraph (a) of this Rule), unless the customer shall have been given not less than thirty (30) days written notice of such changes, except that no such prior notice shall be necessary where such changes are required by law; *provided, however,* that if any change for which prior notice would otherwise be required under this paragraph results in a lower interest charge to the customer than would have been imposed before the change, notice of such change may be given within a reasonable time after the effective date of the change.

* * *

Rule 10b–18. Purchases of Certain Equity Securities by the Issuer and Others

(a) *Definitions.* Unless the context otherwise requires, all terms used in this section shall have the same meaning as in the Act. In addition, unless the context otherwise requires, the following definitions shall apply:

(1) The term "affiliate" means any person that directly or indirectly controls, is controlled by, or is under common control with, the issuer;

(2) The term "affiliated purchaser" means

(i) A person acting in concert with the issuer for the purpose of acquiring the issuer's securities; or

(ii) An affiliate who, directly or indirectly, controls the issuer's purchases of such securities, whose purchases are controlled by the issuer or whose purchases are under common control with those of the issuer;

Provided, however, That the term "affiliated purchaser" shall not include a broker, dealer, or other person solely by reason of his making Rule 10b–18 bids or effecting Rule 10b–18 purchases on behalf of the issuer and for its account and shall not include an officer or director of the issuer solely by reason of his participation in the decision to authorize Rule 10b–18 bids or Rule 10b–18 purchases by or on behalf of the issuer;

(3) The term "Rule 10b–18 purchase" means a purchase of common stock of an issuer by or for the issuer or any affiliated purchaser of the issuer, but does not include any purchase of such stock

(i) Effected by or for an issuer plan by an agent independent of the issuer;

(ii) If it is a fractional interest in a security, evidenced by a script certificate, order form, or similar document;

(iii) Pursuant to a merger, acquisition, or similar transaction involving a recapitalization;

(iv) Which is subject to Rule 13e–1 under the Act;

(v) Pursuant to a tender offer that is subject to Rule 13e–4 under the Act or specifically excepted therefrom;

(vi) Pursuant to a tender offer that is subject to Section 14(d) of the Act and the rules and regulations thereunder.

(4) The term "Rule 10b–18 bid" means

(i) A bid for securities that, if accepted,

or

(ii) A limit order to purchase securities that, if executed would result in a Rule 10b–18 purchase;

(5) The term "issuer plan" means any bonus, profit-sharing, pension, retirement, thrift, savings, incentive, stock purchase, stock option, stock ownership, dividend reinvestment or similar plan for employees or security holders of the issuer or any affiliate;

(6) The term "agent independent of the issuer" means a trustee or other person who is independent of the issuer. The agent shall be deemed to be independent of the issuer only if

(i) The agent is not an affiliate of the issuer; and

(ii) Neither the issuer nor any affiliate of the issuer exercises any direct or indirect control or influence over the times when, or the prices at which, the independent agent may purchase the issuer's common stock for the issuer plan, the amounts of the security to be purchased, the manner in which the security is to be purchased, or the selection of a broker or dealer (other than the independent agent itself) through which purchases may be executed; *Provided, however,* That the issuer or its affiliate will not be deemed to have such control or influence solely because it revises not more than once in any three-month period the basis for determining the amount of its contributions to the issuer plan or the basis for determining the frequency of its allocations to the issuer plan, or any formula specified in the plan that determines the amount of shares to be purchased by the agent;

(7) The term "consolidated system" means the consolidated transaction reporting system contemplated by Rule 11Aa3–1;

(8) The term "reported security" means any security as to which last sale information is reported in the consolidated system;

(9) The term "exchange traded security" means any security, except a reported security, that it listed, or admitted to unlisted trading privileges, on a national securities exchange;

(10) The term "NASDAQ security" means any security, except a reported security, as to which bid and offer quotations are reported in the automated quotation system ("NASDAQ") operated by the National Association of Securities Dealers, Inc. ("NASD");

(11) The term "trading volume" means

(i) With respect to a reported security, the average daily trading volume for the security reported in the consolidated system in the four calendar weeks preceding the week in which the Rule 10b–18 purchase is to be effected or the Rule 10b–18 bid is to be made;

(ii) With respect to an exchange traded security, the average of the aggregate daily trading volume, including the daily trading volume reported on all exchanges on which the security is traded and, if such security is also a NASDAQ security, the daily trading volume for such security made available by the NASD, for the four calendar weeks preceding the week in which the Rule 10b–18 purchase is to be effected or the Rule 10b–18 bid is to be made;

(iii) With respect to a NASDAQ security that is not an exchange traded security, the average daily trading volume for such security made available by the NASD for the four calendar weeks preceding the week in which the Rule 10b–18 purchase is to be effected or the Rule 10b–18 bid is to be made; *Provided, however,* That such trading volume under paragraph (a)(11)(i), (ii) and (iii) shall not include any Rule 10b–18 purchase of a block by or for the issuer or any affiliated purchaser of the issuer;

(12) The term "purchase price" means the price paid per share

(i) For a reported security, or an exchange traded security on a national securities exchange, exclusive of any commission paid to a broker acting as agent, or commission equivalent, mark-up, or differential paid to a dealer;

(ii) For a NASDAQ security, or a security that is not a reported security or a NASDAQ security, otherwise than on a national securities exchange, inclusive of any commission equivalent, mark-up, or differential paid to a dealer;

(13) The term "round lot" means 100 shares or other customary unit of trading for a security;

(14) The term "block" means a quantity of stock that either

(i) Has a purchase price of $200,000 or more; or

(ii) Is at least 5,000 shares and has a purchase price of at least $50,000; or

(iii) Is at least 20 round lots of the security and totals 150 percent or more of the trading volume for that security or, in the event that trading volume data are unavailable, is at least 20 round lots of the security and totals at least one-tenth of one percent (.001) of the outstanding shares of the security, exclusive of any shares owned by any affiliate; *Provided, however,* That a block under paragraph (a)(14)(i), (ii) and (iii) shall not include any amount that a broker or a dealer, acting as principal, has accumulated for the purpose of sale or resale to the issuer or to any affiliated purchaser of the issuer if the issuer or such affiliated purchaser knows or has reason to know that such amount was accumulated for such purpose, nor shall it include any amount that a broker or dealer has sold short to the issuer or to any affiliated purchaser of the issuer if the issuer or such affiliated purchaser knows or has reason to know that the sale was a short sale.

(b) *Conditions to be met.*

In connection with a Rule 10b–18 purchase, or with a Rule 10b–18 bid that is made by the use of any means or instrumentality of interstate commerce or of the mails, or of any facility of any national securities exchange, an issuer, or an affiliated purchaser of the issuer, shall not be deemed to have violated Section 9(a)(2) of the Act or Rule 10b–5 under the Act, solely by reason of the time or price at which its Rule 10b–18 bids or Rule 10b–18 purchases are made or the amount of such bids or purchases or the number of brokers or dealers used in connection with such bids or purchases if the issuer or affiliated purchaser of the issuer

(1) (*One broker or dealer*) Effects all Rule 10b–18 purchases from or through only one broker on any single day, or, if a broker is not used, with only one dealer on a single day, and makes or causes to be made all Rule 10b–18 bids to or through only one broker on any single day, or, if a broker is not used, to only one dealer on a single day; *Provided, however,* That

(i) This paragraph (b)(1) shall not apply to Rule 10b–18 purchases which are not solicited by or on behalf of the issuer or affiliated purchaser; and

(ii) Where Rule 10b–18 purchases or Rule 10b–18 bids are made by or on behalf of more than one affiliated purchaser of the issuer (or the issuer and one or more of its affiliated purchasers) on a single day, this paragraph (b)(1) shall apply to all such bids and purchases in the aggregate; and

(2) (*Time of purchases*) Effects all Rule 10b–18 purchases from or through a broker or dealer

(i) In a reported security, (A) such that the purchaser would not constitute the opening transaction in the security reported in the consolidated system; and (B) if the principal market of such security is an exchange, at a time other than during the one-half hour before the scheduled close of trading on the principal market; and (C) if the purchase is to be made on an exchange, at a time other than during the one-half hour before the scheduled close of trading on the national securities exchange on which the purchase is to be made; and (D) if the purchase is to be made otherwise than on a national securities exchange, at a time other than during the one-half hour before the termination of the period in which last sale prices are reported in the consolidated system;

(ii) In any exchange traded security, on any national securities exchange, (A) such that the Rule 10b–18 purchase would not constitute the opening transaction in the security on such exchange; and (B) at a time other than during the one-half hour before the schedule close of trading on the exchange;

(iii) In any NASDAQ security, otherwise than on a national securities exchange, if a current independent bid quotation for the security is reported in Level 2 of NASDAQ; and

(3) (*Price of purchases*) Effects all Rule 10b–18 purchases from or through a broker or dealer at a purchase price, or makes or causes to be made all Rule 10b–18 bids to or through a broker or dealer at a price

(i) For a reported security, that is not higher than the published bid, as that term is defined in Rule 11Ac1–1(a)(9) under the Act, that is the highest current independent published bid or the last independent sale price reported in the consolidated system, whichever is higher;

(ii) On a national securities exchange, for an exchange traded security, that is not higher than the current independent bid quotation or the last independent sale price on that exchange, whichever is higher;

(iii) Otherwise than on a national securities exchange for a NASDAQ security, that is not higher than the lowest current independent offer quotation reported in Level 2 of NASDAQ; or

(iv) Otherwise than on a national securities exchange, for a security that is not a reported security or a NASD security, that is not higher than the lowest current independent offer quotation, determined on the basis of reasonable inquiry; and

(4) (*Volume of purchases*) Effects from or through a broker or dealer all Rule 10b–18 purchases other than block purchases

(i) Of a reported security, an exchange traded security or a NASDAQ security, in an amount that, when added to the amounts of all other Rule 10b–18 purchases, other than block purchases, from or through a broker or dealer effected by or for the issuer or any affiliated purchaser of the issuer on that day, does not exceed the higher of (A) one round lot or (B) the number of round lots closest to 25 percent of the trading volume for the security;

(ii) Of any other security, in an amount that (A) when added to the amounts of all other Rule 10b–18 purchases, other than block purchases, from or through a broker or dealer effected by or for the issuer or any affiliated purchaser of the issuer on that day, does not exceed one round lot or (B) when added to the amounts of all other Rule 10b–18 purchases other than block purchases from or through a broker or dealer effected by or for the issuer or any affiliated purchaser of the issuer during the day and the preceding five business days, does not exceed 1/20th of one percent (0.0005) of the outstanding shares of the security, exclusive of shares known to be owned beneficially by affiliates.

(c) No presumption shall arise that an issuer or affiliated purchaser of an issuer has violated Sections 9(a)(2) or 10(b) of the Act or Rule 10b–5 under the Act if the Rule 10b–18 bids or Rule 10b–18 purchases of such issuer or affiliated purchaser do not meet the conditions specified in paragraphs (b)(1)–(4) of this section.

REGISTRATION OF SECURITIES

Rule 12g–1. Exemption From Section 12(g)

An issuer shall be exempt from the requirement to register any class of equity securities pursuant to section 12(g)(1) if on the last day of its most recent fiscal year the issuer had total assets not exceeding $5 million and, with respect to a foreign private issuer, such securities were not quoted in an automated inter-dealer quotation system.

REPORTS OF ISSUERS

Rule 13a–1. Requirement of Annual Reports

Every issuer having securities registered pursuant to Section 12 of the Act shall file an annual report on the appropriate form authorized or prescribed therefor for each fiscal year after the last full fiscal year for which financial statements were filed in its registration statement.

* * *

Rule 13a–11. Current Reports on Form 8–K

* * * [E]very registrant subject to Rule 13a–1 shall file a current report on Form 8–K within the period specified in that form, unless substantially the same information as that required by Form 8–K has been previously reported by the registrant.

* * *

Rule 13a–13. Quarterly Reports on Form 10–Q

* * * [E]very issuer which has securities registered pursuant to Section 12 of the Act and which is required to file annual reports pursuant to Section 13 of the Act on Form 10–K, * * * shall file a quarterly report on Form 10–Q, within the period specified in General Instruction A to that form, for each of the first three fiscal quarters of each fiscal year of the issuer, commencing with the first such fiscal quarter which ends after securities of the issuer become so registered.

* * *

REPORTS BY BENEFICIAL OWNERS

Rule 13d–1. Filing of Schedules 13D and 13G

(a) Any person who, after acquiring directly or indirectly the beneficial ownership of any equity security of a class which is specified in paragraph (d) of this section, is directly or indirectly the beneficial owner of more than 5 percent of such class shall, within 10 days after such acquisition, send to the issuer of the security at its principal executive office, by registered or certified mail, and to each exchange where the security is traded, and file with the Commission, a statement containing the information required by Schedule 13D. Six copies of the statement, including all exhibits, shall be filed with the Commission.

(b)(1) A person who would otherwise be obligated under paragraph (a) of this section to file a statement on Schedule 13D may, in lieu thereof, file with the Commission, within 45 days after the end of the calendar year in which such person became so obligated, six copies, including all exhibits, of a short form statement on Schedule 13G and send one copy each of such schedule to the issuer of the security at its principal executive office, by registered or certified mail, and to the principal national securities exchange where the security is traded: *Provided,* That it shall not be necessary to file a Schedule 13G unless the percentage of the class of equity security specified in paragraph (d) of this section beneficially owned as of the end of the calendar year is more than 5 percent: *And provided further,* That:

(i) Such person has acquired such securities in the ordinary course of his business and not with the purpose nor with the effect of changing or influencing the control of the issuer, nor in connection with or as a participant in any transaction having such purpose or effect, including any transaction subject to Rule 13d-3(b);

* * *

(2) Any person relying on Rules 13d-1(b)(1) and 13d-2(b) shall, in addition to filing any statements required thereunder, file a statement on Schedule 13G, within ten days after the end of the first month in which such person's direct or indirect beneficial ownership exceeds ten percent of a class of equity securities specified in Rule 13d-1(c) * * *

(3)(i) Notwithstanding paragraphs (b)(1) and (2) of this section and Rule 13d-2(b) a person shall immediately become subject to Rules 13d-1(a) and 13d-2(a) and shall promptly, but not more than 10 days later, file a statement on Schedule 13D if such person:

(A) Has reported that it is the beneficial owner of more than five percent of a class of equity securities in a statement on Schedule 13G pursuant to paragraph (b)(1) or (b)(2) of this section, or is required to report such acquisition but has not yet filed the schedule;

(B) Determines that it no longer has acquired or holds such securities in the ordinary course of business or not with the purpose nor with the effect of changing or influencing the control of the issuer, nor in connection with or as a participant in any transaction having such purpose or effect, including any transaction subject to Rule 13d-3(b); and

(C) Is at that time the beneficial owner of more than five percent of a class of equity securities described in Rule 13d-1(c).

(ii) For the ten day period immediately following the date of the filing of a Schedule 13D pursuant to this paragraph (b)(3), such person shall not: (A) Vote or direct the voting of the securities described in paragraph (b)(3)(i)(A); nor, (B) Acquire an additional beneficial ownership interest in any equity securities of the issuer of such securities, nor of any person controlling such issuer.

(4) Any person who has reported an acquisition of securities in a statement on Schedule 13G pursuant to paragraph (b)(1) or (b)(2) of this section and thereafter ceases to be a person specified in paragraph (b)(1)(ii) of this section shall immediately become subject to Rules 13d-1(a) and 13d-2(a) and shall file, within ten days thereafter a statement on Schedule 13D, in the event such person is a beneficial owner at that time of more than five percent of the class of equity securities.

(c) Any person who, as of December 31, 1978, or as of the end of any calendar year thereafter, is directly or indirectly the beneficial owner of more than 5 percent of any equity security of a class specified in paragraph (d) of this section and who is not required to file a statement under paragraph (a) of this section by virtue of the exemption provided by Section 13(d)(6)(A) or (B) of the Act, or because such beneficial ownership was acquired prior to December 22, 1970, or because such person otherwise (except for the exemption provided by Section 13(d)(6)(c) of the Act) is not required to file such statement, shall, within 45 days after the end of the calendar year in which such person became obligated to report under this paragraph, send to the issuer of the security at its principal executive office, by registered or certified mail, and file with the Commission a statement containing the information required by Schedule 13G. Six copies of the statement, including all exhibits, shall be filed with the Commission.

* * *

Rule 13d–2. Filing of Amendments to Schedule 13D or 13G

(a) Schedule 13D—If any material change occurs in the facts set forth in the statement required by Rule 13d–1(a), including, but not limited to, any material increase or decrease in the percentage of the class beneficially owned, the person or persons who were required to file such statement shall promptly file or cause to be filed with the Commission and send or cause to be sent to the issuer at its principal executive office, by registered or certified mail, and to each exchange on which the security is traded an amendment disclosing such change. An acquisition or disposition of beneficial ownership of securities in an amount equal to one percent or more of the class of securities shall be deemed "material" for purposes of this rule; acquisitions or dispositions of less than such amounts may be material, depending upon the facts and circumstances. Six copies of each such amendment shall be filed with the Commission.

* * *

Rule 13d–3. Determination of Beneficial Owner

(a) For the purposes of section 13(d) and 13(g) of the Act a beneficial owner of a security includes any person who, directly or indirectly, through any contract, arrangement, understanding, relationship, or otherwise has or shares:

(1) *Voting power* which includes the power to vote, or to direct the voting of, such security; and/or

(2) *Investment power* which includes the power to dispose, or to direct the disposition, of such security.

(b) Any person who, directly or indirectly, creates or uses a trust, proxy, power of attorney, pooling arrangement or any other contract, arrangement, or device with the purpose or effect of divesting such person of beneficial ownership of a security or preventing the vesting of such beneficial ownership as part of a plan or scheme to evade the reporting requirements of section 13(d) or 13(g) of the Act shall be deemed for purposes of such section to be the beneficial owner of such security.

(c) All securities of the same class beneficially owned by a person, regardless of the form which such beneficial ownership takes, shall be aggregated in calculating the number of shares beneficially owned by such person.

(d) Notwithstanding the provisions of paragraphs (a) and (c) of this rule:

(1)(i) A person shall be deemed to be the beneficial owner of a security, subject to the provisions of paragraph (b) of this rule, if that person has the right to acquire beneficial ownership of such security, as defined in Rule 13d–3(a), within sixty days, including but not limited to any right acquired: (A) through the exercise of any option, warrant or right; (B) through the conversion of a security; (C) pursuant to the power to revoke a trust, discretionary account, or similar arrangement; or (D) pursuant to the automatic termination of a trust, discretionary account or similar arrangement; provided, however, any person who acquires a security or power specified in paragraphs (A), (B) or (C), above, with the purpose or effect of changing or influencing the control of the issuer, or in connection with or as a participant in any transaction having such purpose or effect, immediately upon such acquisition shall be deemed to be the beneficial owner of the securities which may be acquired through the exercise or conversion of such security or power. Any securities not outstanding which are subject to such options, warrants, rights or conversion privileges shall be deemed to be outstanding for the purpose of computing the percentage of outstanding securities of the class owned by such person but shall not be deemed to be outstanding for the purpose of computing the percentage of the class by any other person.

(ii) Paragraph (i) remains applicable for the purpose of determining the obligation to file with respect to the underlying security even though the option, warrant, right or convertible security is of a class of equity security, as defined in Rule 13d–1(c), and may therefore give rise to a separate obligation to file.

(2) A member of a national securities exchange shall not be deemed to be a beneficial owner of securities held directly or indirectly by it on behalf of another person solely because such member is

the record holder of such securities and, pursuant to the rules of such exchange, may direct the vote of such securities, without instruction, on other than contested matters or matters that may affect substantially the rights or privileges of the holders of the securities to be voted, but is otherwise precluded by the rules of such exchange from voting without instruction.

(3) A person who in the ordinary course of business is a pledgee of securities under a written pledge agreement shall not be deemed to be the beneficial owner of such pledged securities until the pledgee has taken all formal steps necessary which are required to declare a default and determines that the power to vote or to direct the vote or to dispose or to direct the disposition of such pledged securities will be exercised, provided that:

(i) The pledgee agreement is bona fide and was not entered into with the purpose nor with the effect of changing or influencing the control of the issuer, nor in connection with any transaction having such purpose or effect, including any transaction subject to Rule 13d–3(b);

(ii) The pledgee is a person specified in Rule 13d–1(b)(ii), including persons meeting the conditions set forth in paragraph (G) thereof; and

(iii) The pledgee agreement, prior to default, does not grant to the pledgee:

(A) The power to vote or to direct the vote of the pledged securities; or

(B) The power to dispose or direct the disposition of the pledged securities, other than the grant of such power(s) pursuant to a pledge agreement under which credit is extended subject to Regulation T and in which the pledgee is a broker or dealer registered under section 15 of the Act.

(4) A person engaged in business as an underwriter of securities who acquires securities through his participation in good faith in a firm commitment underwriting registered under the Securities Act of 1933 shall not be deemed to be the beneficial owner of such securities until the expiration of forty days after the date of such acquisition.

Rule 13d–4. Disclaimer of Beneficial Ownership

Any person may expressly declare in any statement filed that the filing of such statement shall not be construed as an admission that such person is, for the purposes of section 13(d), or 13(g) of the Act, the beneficial owner of any securities covered by the statement.

Rule 13d–5. Acquisition of Securities

(a) A person who becomes a beneficial owner of securities shall be deemed to have acquired such securities for purposes of section 13(d)(1) of the Act, whether such acquisition was through purchase or otherwise. However, executors or administrators of a decedent's estate generally will be presumed not to have acquired beneficial ownership of the securities in the decedent's estate until such time as such executors or administrators are qualified under local law to perform their duties.

(b)(1) When two or more persons agree to act together for the purpose of acquiring, holding, voting or disposing of equity securities of an issuer, the group formed thereby shall be deemed to have acquired beneficial ownership, for purposes of sections 13(d) and 13(g) of the Act, as of the date of such agreement, of all equity securities of that issuer beneficially owned by any such persons.

(2) Notwithstanding the previous paragraph, a group shall be deemed not to have acquired any equity securities beneficially owned by the other members of the group solely by virtue of their concerted actions relating to the purchase of equity securities directly from an issuer in a transaction not involving a public offering: *Provided,* That:

(i) All the members of the group are persons specified in Rule 13d–1(b)(1)(ii);

(ii) The purchase is in the ordinary course of each member's business and not with the purpose nor with the effect of changing or influencing control of the issuer, nor in connection with or as a participant in any transaction having such purpose or effect, including any transaction subject to Rule 13d–3(b);

(iii) There is no agreement among, or between any members of the group to act together with respect to the issuer or its securities except for the purpose of facilitating the specific purchase involved; and

(iv) The only actions among or between any members of the group with respect to the issuer or its securities subsequent to the closing date of the non-public offering are those which are necessary to conclude ministerial matters directly related to the completion of the offer or sale of the securities.

Rule 13d-6. Exemption of Certain Acquisitions

The acquisition of securities of an issuer by a person who, prior to such acquisition, was a beneficial owner of more than five percent of the outstanding securities of the same class as those acquired shall be exempt from section 13(d) of the Act: *Provided,* That:

(a) The acquisition is made pursuant to preemptive subscription right in an offering made to all holders of securities of the class to which the preemptive subscription rights pertain;

(b) Such person does not acquire additional securities except through the exercise of his pro rata share of the preemptive subscription rights; and

(c) The acquisition is duly reported if required, pursuant to section 16(a) of the Act and the rules and regulations thereunder.

REPURCHASES BY ISSUERS

Rule 13e-1. Purchase of Securities by Issuer Thereof

When a person other than the issuer makes a tender offer for, or request or invitation for tenders of, any class of equity securities of an issuer subject to Section 13(e) of the Act, and such person has filed a statement with the Commission pursuant to Rule 14d-1 and the issuer has received notice thereof, such issuer shall not thereafter, during the period such tender offer, request or invitation continues, purchase any equity securities of which it is the issuer unless it has complied with both of the following conditions:

(a) The issuer has filed with the Commission eight copies of a statement containing the information specified below with respect to the proposed purchases:

(1) The title and amount of securities to be purchased, the names of the persons or classes of persons from whom, and the market in which, the securities are to be purchased, including the name of any exchange on which the purchase is to be made;

(2) The purpose for which the purchase is to be made and whether the securities are to be retired, held in the treasury of the issuer or otherwise disposed of, indicating such disposition; and

(3) The source and amount of funds or other consideration used or to be used in making the purchases, and if any part of the purchase price or proposed purchase price is represented by funds or other consideration borrowed or otherwise obtained for the purpose of acquiring, holding, or trading the securities, a description of the transaction and the names of the parties thereto.

(b) The issuer has at any time within the past six months sent or given to its equity security holders the substance of the information contained in the statement required by subparagraph (a).

Provided, however, that any issuer making such purchases which commenced prior to July 30, 1968 shall, if such purchases continue after such date comply with the provisions of this rule on or before August 12, 1968.

Rule 13e-3. Going Private Transactions by Certain Issuers or Their Affiliates

(a) *Definitions.* Unless indicated otherwise or the context requires, all terms used in this section and in Schedule 13E-3 shall have the same meaning as in the Act or elsewhere in the General Rules and Regulations thereunder. In addition, the following definitions apply:

(1) An "affiliate" of an issuer is a person that directly or indirectly through one or more intermediaries controls, is controlled by, or is under common control with such issuer. For the purposes of this section only, a person who is not an affiliate of an issuer at the commencement of such person's tender offer for a class of equity securities of such issuer will not be deemed an affiliate of such issuer prior to the stated termination of such tender offer and any extensions thereof;

(2) The term "purchase" means any acquisition for value including, but not limited to, (i) any acquisition pursuant to the dissolution of an issuer subsequent to the sale or other disposition of substantially all the assets of such issuer to its affiliate, (ii) any

acquisition pursuant to a merger, (iii) any acquisition of fractional interests in connection with a reverse stock split, and (iv) any acquisition subject to the control of an issuer or an affiliate of such issuer;

(3) A "Rule 13e-3 transaction" is any transaction or series of transactions involving one or more of the transactions described in paragraph (a)(3)(i) of this section which has either a reasonable likelihood or a purpose of producing, either directly or indirectly, any of the effects described in paragraph (a)(3)(ii) of this section;

(i) The transactions referred to in paragraph (a)(3) of this section are:

(A) A purchase of any equity security by the issuer of such security or by an affiliate of such issuer;

(B) A tender offer for or request or invitation for tenders of any equity security made by the issuer of such class of securities or by an affiliate of such issuer; or

(C) A solicitation subject to Regulation 14A of any proxy, consent or authorization of, or a distribution subject to Regulation 14C of information statements to, any equity security holder by the issuer of the class of securities or by an affiliate of such issuer, in connection with: a merger, consolidation, reclassification, recapitalization, reorganization or similar corporate transaction of an issuer or between an issuer (or its subsidiaries) and its affiliate; a sale of substantially all the assets of an issuer to its affiliate or group of affiliates; or a reverse stock split of any class of equity securities of the issuer involving the purchase of fractional interests.

(ii) The effects referred to in paragraph (a)(4) of this section are:

(A) Causing any class of equity securities of the issuer which is subject to Section 12(g) or Section 15(d) of the Act to be held of record by less than 300 persons; or

(B) Causing any class of equity securities of the issuer which is either listed on a national securities exchange or authorized to be quoted in an inter-dealer quotation system of a registered national securities association to be neither listed on any national securities exchange nor authorized to be quoted on an inter-dealer quotation system of any registered national securities association.

(4) An "unaffiliated security holder" is any security holder of an equity security subject to a Rule 13e-3 transaction who is not an affiliate of the issuer of such security.

(b) *Application of Section to an Issuer (or an Affiliate of Such Issuer) Subject to Section 12 of the Act.*

(1) It shall be a fraudulent, deceptive or manipulative act or practice, in connection with a Rule 13e-3 transaction, for an issuer which has a class of equity securities registered pursuant to Section 12 of the Act or which is a closed-end investment company registered under the Investment Company Act of 1940, or an affiliate of such issuer, directly or indirectly.

(i) To employ any device, scheme or artifice to defraud any person;

(ii) To make any untrue statement of a material fact or to omit to state a material fact necessary in order to make the statements made, in light of the circumstances under which they were made, not misleading; or

(iii) To engage in any act, practice or course of business which operates or would operate as a fraud or deceit upon any person.

(2) As a means reasonably designed to prevent fraudulent, deceptive or manipulative acts or practices in connection with any Rule 13e-3 transaction, it shall be unlawful for an issuer which has a class of equity securities registered pursuant to Section 12 of the Act, or an affiliate of such issuer, to engage, directly or indirectly, in a Rule 13e-3 transaction unless:

(i) Such issuer or affiliate complies with the requirements of paragraphs (d), (e) and (f) of this Section; and

(ii) The Rule 13e-3 transaction is not in violation of paragraph (b)(1) of this section.

(c) *Application of Section to an Issuer (or an Affiliate of Such Issuer) Subject to Section 15(d) of the Act.*

(1) It shall be unlawful as a fraudulent, deceptive or manipulative act or practice for an issuer which is required to file periodic reports pursuant to Section 15(d) of the Act, or an affiliate of such issuer, to engage, directly or indirectly, in a Rule 13e-3 transaction unless such issuer or affiliate

complies with the requirements of paragraphs (d), (e) and (f) of this section.

(2) An issuer or affiliate which is subject to paragraph (c)(1) of this section and which is soliciting proxies or distributing information statements in connection with a transaction described in paragraph (a)(3)(i)(A) of this section may elect to use the timing procedures for conducting a solicitation subject to Regulation 14A or a distribution subject to Regulation 14C in complying with paragraphs (d), (e) and (f) of this section, *provided that* if an election is made, such solicitation or distribution is conducted in accordance with the requirements of the respective regulations, including the filing of preliminary copies of soliciting materials or an information statement at the time specified in Regulation 14A or 14C, respectively.

(d) *Material Required to be Filed.*

The issuer or affiliate engaging in a Rule 13e-3 transaction shall, in accordance with the General Instructions to the Rule 13e-3 Transaction Statement on Schedule 13E-3:

(1) File with the Commission eight copies of such schedule, including all exhibits thereto;

(2) Report any material change in the information set forth in such schedule by promptly filing with the Commission eight copies of an amendment on such schedule; and

(3) Report the results of the Rule 13e-3 transaction by filing with the Commission promptly but no later than ten days (ten business days if Rule 13e-4 is applicable) after the termination of such transaction eight copies of a final amendment to such schedule.

(e) *Disclosure of Certain Information.*

(1) The issuer or affiliate engaging in the Rule 13e-3 transaction, in addition to any other information required to be disclosed pursuant to any other applicable rule or regulation under the federal securities laws, shall disclose to security holders of the class of equity securities which is the subject of the transaction, in the manner prescribed by paragraph (f) of this section, the information required by Items 1, 2, 3, 4, 5, 6, 10, 11, 12, 13, 14, 15 and 16 of Schedule 13E-3, or a fair and adequate summary thereof, and Items 7, 8 and 9 and include in the document which contains such information the exhibit required by Item 17(e) of such Schedule. If the Rule 13e-3 transaction involves (i) a transaction subject to Regulation 14A or 14C of the Act, (ii) the registration of securities pursuant to the Securities Act of 1933 and the General Rules and Regulations promulgated thereunder, or (iii) a tender offer subject to Regulation 14D or Rule 13e-4, such information shall be included in the proxy statement, the information statement, the registration statement or the tender offer for or request or invitation for tenders of securities published, sent or given to security holders, respectively.

(2) If any material change occurs in the information previously disclosed to security holders of the class of equity securities which is the subject of the transaction, the issuer or affiliate shall promptly disclose such change to such security holders in the manner prescribed by paragraph (f)(iii) of this section.

(3) Any document transmitted to such security holders which contains the information required by paragraph (e)(1) of this section shall:

(i) set forth prominently the information required by Items 7, 8 and 9 of the Rule 13e-3 Transaction Statement on Schedule 13E-3 in a Special Factors section to be included in the forepart of such document; and

(ii) set forth on the outside front cover page, in capital letters printed in bold face roman type at least as large as ten point modern type and at least two points leaded, the statement in paragraph (e)(3)(ii)(A) of this section, if the Rule 13e-3 transaction does not involve a prospectus, or the statement in paragraph (e)(3)(ii)(B) of this section, if the Rule 13e-3 transaction involves a prospectus, and in the latter case such statement shall be used in lieu of that required by Item 501(c)(5) of Regulation S-K.

(A) THIS TRANSACTION HAS NOT BEEN APPROVED OR DISAPPROVED BY THE SECURITIES AND EXCHANGE COMMISSION NOR HAS THE COMMISSION PASSED UPON THE FAIRNESS OR MERITS OF SUCH TRANSACTION NOR UPON THE ACCURACY OR ADEQUACY OF THE INFORMATION CONTAINED IN THIS DOCUMENT. ANY REPRESENTATION TO THE CONTRARY IS UNLAWFUL.

(B) NEITHER THIS TRANSACTION NOR THESE SECURITIES HAVE BEEN APPROVED OR DISAPPROVED BY THE SECURITIES AND EXCHANGE COMMISSION, THE COMMISSION

HAS NOT PASSED UPON THE FAIRNESS OR MERITS OF THIS TRANSACTION NOR UPON THE ACCURACY OR ADEQUACY OF THE INFORMATION CONTAINED IN THIS PROSPECTUS. ANY REPRESENTATION TO THE CONTRARY IS UNLAWFUL.

Instructions. 1. Negative responses to any item of Schedule 13E–3 need not be included in the information disseminated to security holders unless otherwise indicated.

2. Although the financial information necessary to present a fair and adequate summary of Item 14 of Schedule 13E–3 may vary depending on the facts and circumstances involved, the following historical and pro forma summary financial information normally will be sufficient for purposes of paragraph (e) of this section:

(a) The following summary financial information for (i) the two most recent fiscal years and (ii) the latest year-to-date interim period and corresponding interim period of the preceding year:

Income Statement:

Net sales and operating revenues and other revenues

Income before extraordinary items

Net income

Balance Sheet (at end of period):

Working capital

Total assets

Total assets less deferred research and development charges and excess of cost of assets acquired over book value

Shareholder's equity

Per Share:

Income per common share before extraordinary items

Extraordinary items

Net income per common share (and common share equivalents, if applicable)

Net income per share on a fully diluted basis

(b) Ratio of earnings to fixed charges for the same periods required by 2(a) above;

(c) Book value per share as of the most recent fiscal year end and as of the date of the latest interim balance sheet; and

(d) If material, pro forma data for the summarized financial information described in 2(a), (b), and (c) above, disclosing the effect of the transaction, should be provided for the most recent fiscal year and latest year-to-date interim period.

If the information required by Item 14 is summarized, appropriate instructions should be included stating how more complete financial information can be obtained.

(f) *Dissemination of disclosure.* (1) If the Rule 13e–3 transaction involves a purchase as described in paragraph (a)(3)(i)(A) of this section or a vote, consent, authorization, or distribution of information statements as described in paragraph (a)(3)(i)(C) of this section, the issuer or affiliate engaging in the Rule 13e–3 transaction shall:

(i) Provide the information required by paragraph (e) of this section: (A) in accordance with the provisions of any applicable federal or state law, but in no event later than 20 days prior to: any such purchase; any such vote, consent or authorization; or with respect to the distribution of information statements, the meeting date, or if corporate action is to be taken by means of the written authorization or consent of security holders, the earliest date on which corporate action may be taken, *Provided, however,* That if the purchase subject to this section is pursuant to a tender offer excepted from Rule 13e–4 by paragraph (g)(5) of Rule 13e–4, the information required by paragraph (e) of this section shall be disseminated in accordance with paragraph (e) of Rule 13e–4 no later than 10 business days prior to any purchase pursuant to such tender offer, (B) to each person who is a record holder of a class of equity security subject to the Rule 13e–3 transaction as of a date not more than 20 days prior to the date of dissemination of such information.

(ii) If the issuer or affiliate knows that securities of the class of securities subject to the Rule 13e–3 transaction are held of record by a broker, dealer, bank or voting trustee or their nominees, such issuer or affiliate shall (unless Rule 14a–3(d) or 14c–7 is applicable) furnish the number of copies of the information required by paragraph (e) of this section that are requested by such persons (pursuant to inquiries by or on behalf of the issuer or affiliate), instruct such persons to forward such information to the beneficial owners of such securities in a timely manner and undertake to pay the reasonable expenses incurred by such persons in forwarding such information; and

(iii) Promptly disseminate disclosure of material changes to the information required by paragraph (d) of this section in a manner reasonably calculated to inform security holders.

(2) If the Rule 13e–3 transaction is a tender offer or a request or invitation for tenders of equity securities which is subject to Regulation 14D or Rule 13e–4, the tender offer containing the information required by paragraph (e) of this section, and any material change with respect thereto, shall be published, sent or given in accordance with Regulation 14D or Rule 13e–4, respectively, to security holders of the class of securities being sought by the issuer or affiliate.

(g) *Exceptions.* This section shall not apply to:

(1) Any Rule 13e–3 transaction by or on behalf of a person which occurs within one year of the date of termination of a tender offer in which such person was the bidder and became an affiliate of the issuer as a result of such tender offer *provided* that the consideration offered to unaffiliated security holders in such Rule 13e–3 transaction is at least equal to the highest consideration offered during such tender offer and *provided further* that:

(i) If such tender offer was made for any or all securities of a class of the issuer;

(A) Such tender offer fully disclosed such person's intention to engage in a Rule 13e–3 transaction, the form and effect of such transaction and, to the extent known, the proposed terms thereof; and

(B) Such Rule 13e–3 transaction is substantially similar to that described in such tender offer; or

(ii) If such tender offer was made for less than all the securities of a class of the issuer:

(A) Such tender offer fully disclosed a plan of merger, a plan of liquidation or a similar binding agreement between such person and the issuer with respect to a Rule 13e–3 transaction; and

(B) Such Rule 13e–3 transaction occurs pursuant to the plan of merger, plan of liquidation or similar binding agreement disclosed in the bidder's tender offer.

(2) Any Rule 13e–3 transaction in which the security holders are offered or receive only an equity security *provided* That:

(i) such equity security has substantially the same rights as the equity security which is the subject of the Rule 13e–3 transaction including, but not limited to, voting, dividends, redemption and liquidation rights except that this requirement shall be deemed to be satisfied if unaffiliated security holders are offered common stock;

(ii) such equity security is registered pursuant to section 12 of the Act or reports are required to be filed by the issuer thereof pursuant to section 15(d) of the Act; and

(iii) if the security which is the subject of the Rule 13e–3 transaction was either listed on a national securities exchange or authorized to be quoted in an inter-dealer quotation system of a registered national securities association, such equity security is either listed on a national securities exchange or authorized to be quoted in an inter-dealer quotation system of a registered national securities association.

(3) Transactions by a holding company registered under the Public Utility Holding Company Act of 1935 in compliance with the provisions of that Act;

(4) Redemptions, calls or similar purchases of an equity security by an issuer pursuant to specific provisions set forth in the instrument(s) creating or governing that class of equity securities; or

(5) Any solicitation by an issuer with respect to a plan of reorganization under Chapter X of the Bankruptcy Act, as amended, if made after the entry of an order approving such plan pursuant to section 174 of that Act and after, or concurrently with, the transmittal of information concerning such plan as required by section 175 of the Act.

Rule 13e–4. Tender Offers by Issuers

(a) *Definitions.* Unless the context otherwise requires, all terms used in this section and in Schedule 13E–4 shall have the same meaning as in the Act or elsewhere in the General Rules and Regulations thereunder. In addition, the following definitions shall apply:

(1) The term "issuer" means any issuer which has a class of equity security registered pursuant to

section 12 of the Act, or which is required to file periodic reports pursuant to section 15(d) of the Act, or which is a closed-end investment company registered under the Investment Company Act of 1940.

(2) The term "issuer tender offer" refers to a tender offer for, or a request or invitation for tenders of, any class of equity security, made by the issuer of such class of equity security or by an affiliate of such issuer.

(3) As used in this section and in Schedule 13E–4, the term "business day" means any day, other than Saturday, Sunday or a federal holiday, and shall consist of the time period from 12:01 a.m. through 12:00 midnight Eastern Time. In computing any time period under this Rule or Schedule 13E–4, the date of the event that begins the running of such time period shall be included *except that* if such event occurs on other than a business day such period shall begin to run on and shall include the first business day thereafter.

(4) The term "commencement" means the date an issuer tender offer is first published, sent or given to security holders.

(5) The term "termination" means the date after which securities may not be tendered pursuant to an issuer tender offer.

(6) The term "security holders" means holders of record and beneficial owners of securities of the class of equity security which is the subject of an issuer tender offer.

(7) The term "security position listing" means, with respect to the securities of any issuer held by a registered clearing agency in the name of the clearing agency or its nominee, a list of those participants in the clearing agency on whose behalf the clearing agency holds the issuer's securities and of the participants' respective positions in such securities as of a specified date.

(b)(1) It shall be a fraudulent, deceptive or manipulative act or practice, in connection with an issuer tender offer, for an issuer or an affiliate of such issuer, in connection with an issuer tender offer:

(i) to employ any device, scheme or artifice to defraud any person;

(ii) to make any untrue statement of a material fact or to omit to state a material fact necessary in order to make the statements made, in the light of the circumstances under which they were made, not misleading; or

(iii) to engage in any act, practice or course of business which operates or would operate as a fraud or deceit upon any person.

(2) As a means reasonably designed to prevent fraudulent, deceptive or manipulative acts or practices in connection with any issuer tender offer, it shall be unlawful for an issuer or an affiliate of such issuer to make an issuer tender offer unless:

(i) such issuer or affiliate complies with the requirements of paragraphs (c), (d), (e) and (f) of this section; and

(ii) the issuer tender offer is not in violation of paragraph (b)(1) of this section.

(c) *Material Required to be Filed.* The issuer or affiliate making the issuer tender offer shall, in accordance with the General Instructions to the Issuer Tender Offer Statement on Schedule 13E–4:

(1) File with the Commission ten copies of such schedule, including all exhibits thereto, prior to or as soon as practicable on the date of commencement of the issuer tender offer;

(2) Report any material change in the information set forth in such schedule by promptly filing with the Commission ten copies of an amendment on such schedule;

(3) Report the results of the issuer tender offer by filing with the Commission no later than ten business days after the termination of the issuer tender offer ten copies of a final amendment to such schedule.

(d) *Disclosure of Certain Information.*

(1) The issuer or affiliate making the issuer tender offer shall publish, send or give to security holders in the manner prescribed in paragraph (e)(1) of this section a statement containing the following information:

(i) the scheduled termination date of the issuer tender offer and whether it may be extended;

(ii) the specified dates prior to which, and after which, persons who tender securities pursuant to the issuer tender offer may withdraw their securities pursuant to paragraph (f)(2) of this section;

(iii) if the issuer tender offer is for less than all the securities of a class, the exact dates of the period during which securities will be accepted on a pro rata basis pursuant to paragraph (f)(3) of this section and the manner in which securities will be accepted for payment and in which securities may be withdrawn; and

(iv) the information required by Items 1 through 8 of Schedule 13E-4 for a fair and adequate summary thereof: *Provided, however,* That if the issuer tender offer involves the registration of securities pursuant to the Securities Act of 1933 and the General Rules and Regulations promulgated thereunder, any prospectus relating to such securities shall include all of the information, not otherwise required to be included therein, required by this paragraph.

(2) If any material change occurs in the information previously disclosed to security holders, the issuer or affiliate shall disclose promptly such change in the manner prescribed by paragraph (e)(2) of this section.

If the information required by Item 7 is summarized, appropriate instructions should be included stating how more complete financial information can be obtained.

* * *

(3) If an issuer or an affiliate publishes, sends or gives the issuer tender offer to security holders by means of a summary publication in the manner prescribed in paragraph (e)(1)(iii) of this section, the summary advertisement shall not contain a transmittal letter pursuant to which securities which are sought in the issuer tender offer may be tendered, and shall disclose only the following information:

(i) the identity of the issuer or affiliate making the issuer tender offer;

(ii) the amount and class of securities being sought and the price being offered;

(iii) the information required by paragraphs (d)(1)(i)-(iii) of this section;

(iv) a statement of the purpose of the issuer tender offer;

(v) appropriate instructions for security holders regarding how to obtain promptly, at the expense of the issuer or affiliate making the issuer tender offer, the statement required by paragraph (d)(1) of this section; and

(vi) a statement that the information contained in the statement required by paragraph (d)(1) of this section is incorporated by reference.

(e) *Dissemination of Tender Offers.*

(1) The issuer or affiliate making the issuer tender offer will be deemed to have published, sent or given the issuer tender offer to security holders if such issuer or affiliate complies fully with one or more of the following methods of dissemination. Depending on the facts and circumstances involved, and for purposes of paragraphs (e)(1)(i) and (e)(1)(iii) of this section, adequate publication of the issuer tender offer may require publication in a newspaper with a national circulation or may require only publication in a newspaper with metropolitan or regional circulation or may require publication in a combination thereof.

(i) *Dissemination of cash issuer tender offers by long-form publication:*

By making adequate publication in a newspaper or newspapers, on the date of commencement of the issuer tender offer, of the statement required by paragraph (d)(1) of this section.

(ii) *Dissemination of any issuer tender offer by use of shareholder and other lists:*

(A) By mailing the statement required by paragraph (d)(1) of this section to each security holder whose name appears on the most recent shareholder list of the issuer;

(B) By contacting each participant named on the most recent security position listing of any clearing agency within the possession or access of the issuer or affiliate making the tender offer, and making inquiry of each such participant as to the approximate number of beneficial owners of the securities for which the issuer tender offer is made which are held by such participant;

(C) By furnishing to each such participant a sufficient number of copies of the statement required by paragraph (d)(1) of this section for transmittal to the beneficial owners; and

(D) By agreeing to reimburse promptly each such participant for reasonable expenses incurred by it in forwarding such statement to the beneficial owners.

(iii) *Dissemination of certain cash issuer tender offers by summary publication:*

(A) If the issuer tender offer is not subject to Rule 13e-3, by making adequate publication in a newspaper or newspapers, on the date of commencement of the issuer tender offer, of a summary advertisement containing the information required by paragraph (d)(3) of this section; and

(B) By mailing or otherwise furnishing promptly the statement required by paragraph (d)(1) of this section and a transmittal letter to any security holder who requests either a copy of such statement or a transmittal letter.

(2) If a material change occurs in the information published, sent or given to security holders, the issuer or affiliate shall disseminate promptly disclosure of such change in a manner reasonably calculated to inform security holders of such change.

(f) *Manner of Making Tender Offer.*

(1) The issuer tender offer, unless withdrawn, shall remain open until the expiration of:

(i) At least twenty business days from its commencement; and

(ii) At least ten business days from the date that notice of an increase or decrease in the percentage of the class of securities being sought or the consideration offered or the dealer's soliciting fee to be given is first published, sent or given to security holders.

Provided, however, That, for purposes of this paragraph, the acceptance for payment by the issuer or affiliate of an additional amount of securities not to exceed two percent of the class of securities that is the subject of the tender offer shall not be deemed to be an increase. For purposes of this paragraph, the percentage of a class of securities shall be calculated in accordance with section 14(d)(3) of the Act.

(2) The issuer or affiliate making the issuer tender offer shall permit securities tendered pursuant to the issuer tender offer to be withdrawn:

(i) At any time during the period such issuer tender offer remains open; and

(ii) If not yet accepted for payment, after the expiration of forty business days from the commencement of the issuer tender offer.

(3) If the issuer or affiliate makes a tender offer for less than all of the outstanding equity securities of a class, and if a greater number of securities is tendered pursuant thereto then the issuer or affiliate is bound or willing to take up and pay for, the securities taken up and paid for shall be taken up and paid for as nearly as may be pro rata, disregarding fractions, according to the number of securities tendered by each security holder during the period such offer remains open; *Provided, however,* That this provision shall not prohibit the issuer or affiliate making the issuer tender offer from:

(i) accepting all securities tendered by persons who own, beneficially or of record, an aggregate of not more than a specified number which is less than one hundred shares of such security and who tender all their securities, before prorating securities tendered by others; or

(ii) accepting by lot securities tendered by security holders who tender all securities held by them and who, when tendering their securities, elect to have either all or none or at least a minimum amount or none accepted, if the issuer or affiliate first accepts all securities tendered by security holders who do not so elect;

(4) In the event the issuer or affiliate making the issuer tender offer increases the consideration offered after the issuer tender offer has commenced, such issuer or affiliate shall pay such increased consideration to all security holders whose tendered securities are accepted for payment by such issuer or affiliate.

(5) The issuer or affiliate making the tender offer shall either pay the consideration offered, or return the tendered securities, promptly after the termination or withdrawal of the tender offer.

(6) Until the expiration of at least ten business days after the date of termination of the issuer tender offer, neither the issuer nor any affiliate shall make any purchases, otherwise than pursuant to the tender offer, of:

(i) any security which is the subject of the issuer tender offer, or any security of the same class and series, or any right to purchase any such securities; and

(ii) in the case of an issuer tender offer which is an exchange offer any security being offered pursuant to such exchange offer, or any security of the same class and series, or any right to purchase any such security.

(7) The time periods for the minimum offering periods pursuant to this section shall be computed on a concurrent as opposed to a consecutive basis.

(8) No issuer or affiliate shall make a tender offer unless:

(i) The tender offer is open to all security holders of the class of securities subject to the tender offer; and

(ii) The consideration paid to any security holder pursuant to the tender offer is the highest consideration paid to any other security holder during such tender offer.

(9) Paragraph (f)(8)(i) of this rule shall not:

(i) Affect dissemination under paragraph (e) of this rule; or

(ii) Prohibit an issuer or affiliate from making a tender offer excluding all security holders in a state where the issuer or affiliate is prohibited from making the tender offer by administrative or judicial action pursuant to a state statute after a good faith effort by the issuer or affiliate to comply with such statute.

(10) Paragraph (f)(8)(ii) of this rule shall not prohibit the offer of more than one type of consideration in a tender offer, provided that:

(i) Security holders are afforded equal right to elect among each of the types of consideration offered; and

(ii) The highest consideration of each type paid to any security holder is paid to any other security holder receiving that type of consideration.

(11) If the offer and sale of securities constituting consideration offered in an issuer tender offer is prohibited by the appropriate authority of a state after a good faith effort by the issuer or affiliate to register or qualify the offer and sale of such securities in such state:

(i) The issuer or affiliate may offer security holders in such state an alternative form of consideration; and

(ii) Paragraph (f)(10) of this rule shall not operate to require the issuer or affiliate to offer or pay the alternative form of consideration to security holders in any other state.

(g) This rule shall not apply to:

(1) Calls or redemptions of any security in accordance with the terms and conditions of its governing instruments;

(2) Offers to purchase securities evidenced by a scrip certificate, order form or similar document which represents a fractional interest in a share of stock or similar security;

(3) Offers to purchase securities pursuant to a statutory procedure for the purchase of dissenting security holders' securities;

(4) Any tender offer which is subject to section 14(d) of the Act;

(5) Offers to purchase from security holders who own as of a specified date prior to the announcement of the offer an aggregate of not more than a specified number of shares that is less than one hundred: *Provided however,* That: (i) the offer complies with paragraph (f)(8)(i) of this rule with respect to security holders who own a number of shares equal to or less than the specified number of shares as of the specified date, except that an issuer can elect to exclude participants in an issuer's plan as that term is defined in Rule 10B–6(c)(4) under the Act, and (ii) the offer complies with paragraph (f)(8)(ii) of this rule or the consideration paid pursuant to the offer is determined on the basis of a uniformly applied formula based on the market price of the subject security;

(6) An issuer tender offer made solely to effect a rescission offer: *Provided, however,* That the offer is registered under the Securities Act of 1933, and the consideration is equal to the price paid by each security holder, plus legal interest if the issuer elects to or is required to pay legal interest; or

(7) Any other transaction or transactions, if the Commission, upon written request or upon its own motion, exempts such transaction or transactions, either unconditionally, or on specified terms and conditions, as not constituting a fraudulent, deceptive or manipulative act or practice comprehended within the purpose of this section.

REPORTS BY INSTITUTIONAL MANAGERS

Rule 13f–1. Reporting by Institutional Investment Managers of Information With Respect to Accounts Over Which They Exercise Investment Discretion

(a) Every institutional investment manager which exercises investment discretion with respect to accounts holding section 13(f) securities, as defined in paragraph (c) of this section, having an aggregate fair market value on the last trading day of any month of any calendar year of at least $100,000,000 shall file a report on Form 13F with the Commission within 45 days after the last day of such calendar year and within 45 days after the last day of each of the first three calendar quarters of the subsequent calendar year.

(b) For the purposes of this rule, "investment discretion" has the meaning set forth in section 3(a)(35) of the Act. An institutional investment manager shall also be deemed to exercise "investment discretion" with respect to all accounts over which any person under its control exercises investment discretion.

(c) For purposes of this rule "section 13(f) securities" shall mean equity securities of a class described in section 13(d)(1) of the Act that are admitted to trading on a national securities exchange or quoted on the automated quotation system of a registered securities association. In determining what classes of securities are section 13(f) securities, an institutional investment manager may rely on the most recent list of such securities published by the Commission pursuant to section 13(f)(3) of the Act. Only securities of a class on such list shall be counted in determining whether an institutional investment manager must file a report under this rule and only those securities shall be reported in such report. Where a person controls the issuer of a class of equity securities which are "section 13(f) securities" as defined in this rule, those securities shall not be deemed to be "section 13(f) securities" with respect to the controlling person, provided that such person does not otherwise exercise investment discretion with respect to accounts with fair market value of at least $100,000,000 within the meaning of paragraph (a) of this section.

* * *

SOLICITATION OF PROXIES

Rule 14a-1. Definitions

Unless the context otherwise requires, all terms used in this regulation have the same meanings as in the Act or elsewhere in the General Rules and Regulations thereunder. In addition, the following definitions apply unless the context otherwise requires:

(a) *Associate.* The term "associate" used to indicate a relationship with any person, means (1) any corporation or organization (other than the issuer or a majority owned subsidiary of the issuer) of which such person is an officer or partner or is, directly or indirectly, the beneficial owner of 10 percent or more of any class of equity securities, (2) any trust or other estate in which such person has a substantial beneficial interest or as to which such person serves as trustee or in a similar fiduciary capacity, and (3) any relative or spouse of such person, or any relative of such spouse, who has the same home as such person or who is a director or officer of the issuer or any of its parents or subsidiaries.

(b) *Entity that exercises fiduciary powers.* The term "entity that exercises fiduciary powers" means any entity that holds securities in nominee name or otherwise on behalf of a beneficial owner but does not include a clearing agency registered pursuant to Section 17A of the Act or a broker or a dealer.

(c) *Last fiscal year.* The term "last fiscal year" of the issuer means the last fiscal year of the issuer ending prior to the date of the meeting for which proxies are to be solicited.

(d) *Proxy.* The term "proxy" includes every proxy, consent or authorization within the meaning of Section 14(a) of the Act. The consent or authorization may take the form of failure to object or to dissent.

(e) *Proxy statement.* The term "proxy statement" means the statement required by Rule 14a-3(a), whether or not contained in a single document.

(f) *Record date.* The term "record date" means the date as of which the record holders of securities entitled to vote at a meeting or by written consent or authorization shall be determined.

(g) *Record holder.* For purposes of Rules 14a-13, 14b-1 and 14b-2, the term "record holder" means any broker, dealer, voting trustee, bank, association or other entity that exercises fiduciary powers which holds securities of record in nominee name or otherwise or as a participant in a clearing agency registered pursuant to Section 17A of the Act.

(h) *Registrant.* The term "registrant" means the issuer of the securities in respect of which proxies are to be solicited.

(i) *Respondent bank.* For purposes of Rules 14a-13, 14b-1 and 14b-2, the term "respondent bank" means any bank, association or other entity that exercises fiduciary powers which holds securities on behalf of beneficial owners and deposits such securities for safekeeping with another bank, association or other entity that exercises fiduciary powers.

(j) *Solication.* (1) The terms "solicit" and "solicitation" include:

(i) Any request for a proxy whether or not accompanied by or included in a form of proxy;

(ii) Any request to execute or not to execute, or to revoke, a proxy; or

(iii) The furnishing of a form of proxy or other communication to security holders under circumstances reasonably calculated to result in the procurement, withholding or revocation of a proxy.

(2) The terms do not apply, however, to the furnishing of a form of proxy to a security holder upon the unsolicited request of such security holder, the performance by the registrant of acts required by Rule 14a-7, or the performance by any person of ministerial acts on behalf of a person soliciting a proxy.

Rule 14a-2. Solicitations to Which Rules 14a-3 to 14a-13 Apply

Rules 14a-3 to 14a-13 apply to every solicitation of a proxy with respect to securities registered pursuant to section 12 of the Act, whether or not trading in such securities has been suspended, except that:

(a) Rules 14a-3 to 14a-13 do not apply to the following:

(1) Any solicitation by a person in respect to securities carried in his name or in the name of his nominee (otherwise than as voting trustee) or held in his custody, if such person—

(i) Receives no commission or remuneration for such solicitation, directly or indirectly, other than reimbursement of reasonable expenses.

(ii) Furnishes promptly to the person solicited a copy of all soliciting material with respect to the same subject matter or meeting received from all persons who shall furnish copies thereof for such purpose and who shall, if requested, defray the reasonable expenses to be incurred in forwarding such material, and

(iii) In addition, does no more than impartially instruct the person solicited to forward a proxy to the person, if any, to whom the person solicited desires to give a proxy, or impartially request from the person solicited instructions as to the authority to be conferred by the proxy and state that a proxy will be given if no instructions are received by a certain date.

(2) Any solicitation by a person in respect of securities of which he is the beneficial owner;

(3) Any solicitation involved in the offer and sale of securities registered under the Securities Act of 1933: *Provided,* That this paragraph shall not apply to securities to be issued in any transaction of the character specified in paragraph (a) of Rule 145 under that Act;

(4) Any solicitation with respect to a plan of reorganization under Chapter 11 of the Bankruptcy Reform Act of 1978, as amended, if made after the entry of an order approving the written disclosure statement concerning a plan of reorganization pursuant to section 1125 of said Act and after, or concurrently with, the transmittal of such disclosure statement as required by section 1125 of said Act;

(5) Any solicitation which is subject to Rule 62 under the Public Utility Holding Company Act of 1935; and

(6) Any solicitation through the medium of a newspaper advertisement which informs security holders of a source from which they may obtain copies of a proxy statement, form of proxy and any other soliciting material and does no more than (i) name the registrant, (ii) state the reason for the advertisement, and (iii) identify the proposal or proposals to be acted upon by security holders.

(b) Rules 14a-3 to 14a-8 and Rules 14a-10 to 14a-13 do not apply to the following:

(1) Any solicitation made otherwise than on behalf of the registrant, where the total number of persons solicited is not more than ten; and

(2) The furnishing of proxy voting advice by any person (the "advisor") to any other person with whom the advisor has a business relationship, if:

(i) The advisor renders financial advice in the ordinary course of his business;

(ii) The advisor discloses to the recipient of the advice any significant relationship with the registrant, or any of its affiliates, or a shareholder proponent of the matter on which advice is given, as well as any material interest of the advisor in such matter;

(iii) The advisor receives no special commission or remuneration for furnishing the proxy voting advice from any person other than a recipient of the advice and other persons who receive similar advice under this subsection; and

(iv) The proxy voting advice is not furnished on behalf of any person soliciting proxies or on behalf of a participant in an election subject to the provisions of Rule 14a-11.

Rule 14a-3. Information to be Furnished to Security Holders

(a) No solicitation subject to this regulation shall be made unless each person solicited is concurrently furnished or has previously been furnished with a written proxy statement containing the information specified in Schedule 14A or with a written proxy statement included in a registration statement filed under the Securities Act of 1933 on Form S-4 or F-4 or N-14 and containing the information specified in such Form.

(b) If the solicitation is made on behalf of the registrant, and relates to an annual meeting of security holders at which directors are to be elected, each proxy statement furnished pursuant to paragraph (a) shall be accompanied or preceded by an annual report to security holders as follows:

(1) The report shall include, for the registrant and its subsidiaries consolidated, audited balance sheets as of the end of the two most recent fiscal years and audited statements of income and changes in financial position for each of the three most recent fiscal years prepared in accordance with Regulation S-X, except that the provisions of Article 3, other than §§ 3-03(e), 3-04 and 3-20 and Article 11 shall not apply. Any financial statement schedules or exhibits or separate financial statements which may otherwise be required in filings with the Commission may be omitted. Investment companies registered under the Investment Company Act of 1940 need include financial statements only for the last fiscal year except for statements of changes in net assets which are to be filed for the two most recent fiscal years. If the financial statements of the registrant and its subsidiaries consolidated in the annual report filed or to be filed with the Commission are not required to be audited, the financial statements required by this paragraph may be unaudited.

* * *

(2) Financial statements and notes thereto shall be presented in roman type at least as large and as legible as 10-point modern type. If necessary for convenient presentation, the financial statements may be in roman type as large and as legible as 8-point modern type. All type shall be leaded at least 2-point.

(3) The report shall contain the supplementary financial information required by Item 302 of Regulation S-K.

(4) The report shall contain information concerning changes in and disagreements with accountants on accounting and financial disclosure required by Item 304 of Regulation S-K.

(5)(i) The report shall contain the selected financial data required by Item 301 of Regulation S-K.

(ii) The report shall contain management's discussion and analysis of financial condition and results of operations required by Item 303 of Regulation S-K.

(6) The report shall contain a brief description of the business done by the registrant and its subsidiaries during the most recent fiscal year which will, in the opinion of management, indicate the general nature and scope of the business of the issuer and its subsidiaries.

(7) The report shall contain information relating to the registrant's industry segments, classes of similar products or services, foreign and domestic operations and export sales required by paragraphs (b), (c)(1)(i) and (d) of Item 101 of Regulation S-K.

(8) The report shall identify each of the registrant's directors and executive officers, and shall indicate the principal occupation or employment of each such person and the name and principal business of any organization by which such person is employed.

(9) The report shall contain the market price of and dividends on the registrant's common equity and related security holder matters required by Item 201 of Regulation S-K.

(10) The registrant's proxy statement, or the report, shall contain an undertaking in bold face or otherwise reasonably prominent type to provide without charge to each person solicited, upon the written request of any such person, a copy of the registrant's annual report on Form 10-K, including the financial statements and the financial statement schedules, required to be filed with the Commission pursuant to Rule 13a-1 under the Act for the registrant's most recent fiscal year, and shall indicate the name and address (including title or department) of the person to whom such a written request is to be directed. In the discretion of management, a registrant need not undertake to furnish without charge copies of all exhibits to its Form 10-K provided that the copy of the annual report on Form 10-K furnished without charge to requesting security holders is accompanied by a list briefly describing all the exhibits not contained therein and indicating that the registrant will furnish any exhibit upon the payment of a specified reasonable fee which fee shall be limited to the registrant's reasonable expenses in furnishing such exhibit. If the registrant's annual report to security holders complies with all of the disclosure requirements of Form 10-K and is filed with the Commission in satisfaction of its Form 10-K filing requirements, such registrant need not furnish a separate Form 10-K to security holders who receive a copy of such annual report.

Note: Pursuant to the undertaking required by paragraph (b)(10) of this rule, a registrant shall furnish a copy of its annual report on Form 10-K to a beneficial owner of its securities upon receipt of a written request from such person. Each request must set forth a good faith representation that, as of the record date for the solicitation requiring the furnishing of the annual report to security holders pursuant to paragraph (b) of this section, the person making the request was a beneficial owner of securities entitled to vote.

(11) Subject to the foregoing requirements, the report may be in any form deemed suitable by management and the information required by paragraphs (b)(5) to (b)(10) of this rule may be presented in an appendix or other separate section of the report, provided that the attention of security holders is called to such presentation.

Note: Registrants are encouraged to utilize tables, schedules, charts, and graphic illustrations to present financial information in an understandable manner. Any presentation of financial information must be consistent with the data in the financial statements contained in the report and, if appropriate, should refer to relevant portions of the financial statements and notes thereto.

(12) Paragraphs (b)(5) through (b)(11) of this rule shall not apply to an investment company registered under the Investment Company Act of 1940. Subject to the requirements of paragraphs (b)(1) through (b)(4) of this rule, the annual report to security holders of such investment company may be in any form deemed suitable by management.

(13) Paragraph (b) of this section shall not apply, however, to solicitations made on behalf of the registrant before the financial statements are available if a solicitation is being made at the same time in opposition to the registrant and if the registrant's proxy statement includes an undertaking in bold face type to furnish such annual report to all persons being solicited at least 20 calendar days before the date of the meeting or, if the solicitation refers to a written consent or authorization in lieu of a meeting, at least 20 calendar days prior to the earliest date on which it may be used to effect corporate action.

(c) Seven copies of the report sent to security holders pursuant to this rule shall be mailed to the Commission, solely for its information, not later than the date on which such report is first sent or given to security holders or the date on which preliminary copies of solicitation material are filed with the Commission pursuant to Rule 14a-6(a), whichever date is later. The report is not deemed to be "soliciting material" or to be "filed" with the Commission or subject to this regulation otherwise than as provided in this Rule, or to the liabilities of section 18 of the Act, except to the extent that the registrant specifically requests that it be treated as a part of the proxy soliciting material or incorporates it in the proxy statement or other filed report by reference.

Note: To assist the staff, managements of registrants are requested to indicate in a letter transmitting to the Commission copies of their annual reports to security holders or in a separate letter at or about the time the annual report is furnished to the Commission, whether the financial statements in the report reflect a change from the preceding year in any accounting principles or practices or in the method of applying any such principles or practices.

(d) An annual report to security holders prepared on an integrated basis pursuant to General Instruction H to Form 10–K may also be submitted in satisfaction of this rule. When filed as the annual report on Form 10–K, responses to the Items of that form are subject to section 18 of the Act notwithstanding paragraph (c).

(e) Notwithstanding paragraphs (a) and (b) of this section:

(1) A registrant is not required to send an annual report to a security holder of record having the same address as another security holder of record, provided that (i) such security holders are not holding such registrant's securities in nominee name, (ii) at least one report is sent to a holder of record at that address and (iii) the holders of record to whom a report is not sent agree thereto in writing; and

(2) Unless state law requires otherwise, a registrant is not required to send an annual report or proxy statement to a security holder if: (i) an annual report and a proxy statement for two consecutive annual meetings; or (ii) all, and at least two, payments (if sent by first class mail) of dividends or interest on securities during a twelve month period have been mailed to such security holder's address and have been returned undeliverable. If any such security holder delivers or causes to be delivered to the registrant written notice setting forth his then current address for security holder communications purposes, the registrant's obligation to deliver an annual report or a proxy statement under this section is reinstated.

Rule 14a–4. Requirements as to Proxy

(a) The form of proxy (1) shall indicate in bold-face type whether or not the proxy is solicited on behalf of the registrant's board of directors or, if provided other than by a majority of the board of directors, shall indicate in bold-face type the identity of the persons on whose behalf the solicitation is made; (2) shall provide a specifically designated blank space for dating the proxy card; and (3) shall identify clearly and impartially each matter or group of related matters intended to be acted upon, whether proposed by the registrant or by security holders. No reference need be made, however, to proposals as to which discretionary authority is conferred pursuant to paragraph (c) of this section.

(b)(1) Means shall be provided in the form of proxy whereby the person solicited is afforded an opportunity to specify by boxes a choice between approval or disapproval of, or abstention with respect to, each matter or group of related matters referred to therein as intended to be acted upon, other than elections to office. A proxy may confer discretionary authority with respect to matters as to which a choice is not specified by the security holder provided that the form of proxy states in bold-face type how it is intended to vote the shares represented by the proxy in each such case.

(2) A form of proxy which provides for the election of directors shall set forth the names of persons nominated for election as directors. Such form of proxy shall clearly provide any of the following means for security holders to withhold authority to vote for each nominee:

(i) a box opposite the name of each nominee which may be marked to indicate that authority to vote for such nominee is withheld; or

(ii) an instruction in bold-face type which indicates that the security holder may withhold authority to vote for any nominee by lining through or otherwise striking out the name of any nominee; or

(iii) designated blank spaces in which the shareholder may enter the names of nominees with respect to whom the shareholder chooses to withhold authority to vote; or

(iv) any other similar means, provided that clear instructions are furnished indicting how the shareholder may withhold authority to vote for any nominee.

Such form of proxy also may provide a means for the security holder to grant authority to vote for the nominees set forth, as a group, provided that there is a similar means for the security holder to withhold authority to vote for such group of nominees. Any such form of proxy which is executed by the security holder in such manner as not to withhold authority to vote for the election of any nominee shall be deemed to grant such authority, provided that the form of proxy so states in bold-face type.

Instructions. 1. Paragraph (2) does not apply in the case of a merger, consolidation or other plan if the election of directors is an integral part of the plan.

2. If applicable state law gives legal effect to votes cast against a nominee, then in lieu of, or in addition to, providing a means for security holders to withhold authority to vote, the registrant should provide a similar means for security holders to vote against each nominee.

(c) A proxy may confer discretionary authority to vote with respect to any of the following matters:

(1) Matters which the persons making the solicitation do not know, a reasonable time before the solicitation, are to be presented at the meeting, if a specific statement to that effect is made in the proxy statement or form of proxy;

(2) Approval of the minutes of the prior meeting if such approval does not amount to ratification of the action taken at that meeting;

(3) The election of any person to any office for which a bona fide nominee is named in the proxy statement and such nominee is unable to serve or for good cause will not serve.

(4) Any proposal omitted from the proxy statement and form of proxy pursuant to Rule 14a-8 or 14a-9.

(5) Matters incident to the conduct of the meeting.

(d) No proxy shall confer authority (1) to vote for the election of any person to any office for which a bona fide nominee is not named in the proxy statement, (2) to vote at any annual meeting other than the next annual meeting (or any adjournment thereof) to be held after the date on which the proxy statement and form of proxy are first sent or given to security holders, (3) to vote with respect to more than one meeting (and any adjournment thereof) or more than one consent solicitation, or (4) to consent to or authorize any action other than the action proposed to be taken in the proxy statement or matters referred to in paragraph (c) of this rule. A person shall not be deemed to be a bona fide nominee and he shall not be named as such unless he has consented to being named in the proxy statement and to serve if elected.

(e) The proxy statement or form of proxy shall provide, subject to reasonable specified conditions, that the shares represented by the proxy will be voted and that where the person solicited specifies by means of a ballot provided pursuant to paragraph (b) a choice with respect to any matter to be acted upon, the shares will be voted in accordance with the specifications so made.

Rule 14a-5. Presentation of Information in Proxy Statement

(a) The information included in the proxy statement shall be clearly presented and the statements made shall be divided into groups according to subject matter and the various groups of statements shall be preceded by appropriate headings. The order of items and sub-items in the schedule need not be followed. Where practicable and appropriate, the information shall be presented in tabular form. All amounts shall be stated in figures. Information required by more than one applicable item need not be repeated. No statement need be made in response to any item or sub-item which is inapplicable.

(b) Any information required to be included in the proxy statement as to terms of securities or other subject matter which from a standpoint of practical necessity must be determined in the future may be stated in terms of present knowledge and intention. To the extent practicable, the authority to be conferred concerning each such matter shall be confined within limits reasonably related to the need for discretionary authority. Subject to the foregoing, information which is not known to the persons on whose behalf the solicitation is to be made and which it is not reasonably within the power of such persons to ascertain or procure may be omitted, if a brief statement of the circumstances rendering such information unavailable is made.

(c) Any information contained in any other proxy soliciting material which has been furnished to each person solicited in connection with the same meeting or subject matter may be omitted from the proxy statement, if a clear reference is made to the particular document containing such information.

(d) All printed proxy statements shall be in roman type at least as large and as legible as 10-point modern type, except that to the extent necessary for convenient presentation financial statements and other tabular data, but not the notes thereto, may be in roman type at least as large and as legible as 8-point modern type. All such type shall be leaded at least 2 points.

(e) All proxy statements shall disclose, under an appropriate caption, the date by which proposals of security holders intended to be presented at the next annual meeting must be received by the issuer for inclusion in the issuer's proxy statement and form of proxy relating to that meeting, such date to be calculated in accordance with the provisions of Rule 14a-8(a)(3)(i). If the date of the next annual meeting is subsequently advanced by more than 30 calendar days or delayed by more than 90 calendar days from the date of the annual meeting to which the proxy statement relates, the registrant shall, in a timely manner, inform security holders of such change, and the date by which proposals of security holders must be received, by any means reasonably calculated to so inform them.

Rule 14a-6. Material Required to be Filed

(a) *Preliminary proxy statement.* Five preliminary copies of the proxy statement and form of proxy and any other soliciting material to be furnished to security holders concurrently therewith shall be filed with the Commission at least 10 calendar days prior to the date definitive copies of such material are first sent or given to security holders, or such shorter period prior to that date as the Commission may authorize upon a showing of good cause therefor;

Note 1.—The filing of revised material does not recommence the ten day time period unless the revised material contains material revisions or material new proposal(s) that constitute a fundamental change in the proxy material.

Note 2.—The officials responsible for the preparation of the preliminary material should make every effort to verify the accuracy and completeness of the information required by the applicable rules. The preliminary material should be filed with the Commission at the earliest practicable date.

(b) *Preliminary additional materials.* Five preliminary copies of any additional soliciting material relating to the same meeting or subject matter furnished to security holders subsequent to the proxy statement shall be filed with the Commission at least 2 business days prior to the date copies of such material are first sent or given to security holders, or such shorter period prior to such date as the Commission may authorize upon a showing of good cause therefor.

(c) *Definitive proxy statement.* Eight definitive copies of the proxy statement, form of proxy and all other soliciting material, in the form in which such material is furnished to security holders, shall be filed with, or mailed for filing to, the Commission not later than the date such material is first sent or given to any security holders. Three copies of such material shall at the same time be filed with, or mailed for filing to, each national securities exchange upon which any class of securities of the registrant is listed and registered.

(d) *Personal solicitation materials.* If the solicitation is to be made in whole or in part by personal solicitation, three copies of all written instructions or other material which discusses or reviews, or comments upon the merits of, any matter to be acted upon and which is furnished to the individuals making the actual solicitation for their use directly or indirectly in connection with the solicitation shall be filed with the Commission by the person on whose behalf the solicitation is made at least five calendar days prior to the date copies of such material are first sent or given to such individuals, or such shorter period prior to that date as the Commission may authorize upon a showing of good cause therefor.

(e) *Release dates.* All preliminary material filed pursuant to paragraph (a) or (b) of this rule shall be accompanied by a statement of the date on which definitive copies therefor filed pursuant to paragraph (c) of this rule are intended to be released to security holders. All definitive material filed pursuant to paragraph (c) of this rule shall be accompanied by a statement of the date on which copies of such material have been released to security holders, or, if not released, the date on which copies thereof are intended to be released. All material filed pursuant to paragraph (d) of this rule shall be accompanied by a statement of the date on which copies thereof are intended to be released to the individual who will make the actual solicitation.

(f) *Public availability of information.* All copies of preliminary material filed pursuant to this Regulation shall be clearly marked "Preliminary

Copies," shall be for the information of the Commission only and shall not be deemed available for public inspection until definitive material has been filed with the Commission except that such material may be disclosed to any department or agency of the United States Government and to the Congress, and the Commission may make such inquiries or investigation in regard to the material as may be necessary for an adequate review thereof by the Commission.

(g) *Communications not required to be filed.* Copies of replies to inquiries from security holders requesting further information and copies of communications which do no more than request that forms of proxy theretofore solicited be signed and returned need not be filed pursuant to this rule.

(h) *Speeches, press releases and scripts.* Notwithstanding the provisions of paragraphs (a) and (b) of this rule, of Rules 14a-11(e) and 14a-12(b), copies of soliciting material in the form of speeches, press releases and radio or television scripts may, but need not, be filed with the Commission prior to use or publication. Definitive copies, however, shall be filed with or mailed for filing to the Commission as required by paragraph (c) of this rule not later than the date such material is used or published. The provisions of paragraphs (a) and (b) of this rule and of Rules 14a-11(e) and 14a-12(b) shall apply, however, to any reprints or reproductions of all or any part of such material.

(i) *Revised material.* Where any proxy statement, form of proxy or other material filed pursuant to this rule is amended or revised, two of the copies of such amended or revised material filed pursuant to this rule (or in the case of investment companies registered under the Investment Company Act of 1940, three of such copies) shall be marked to indicate clearly and precisely the changes effected therein. If the amendment or revision alters the text of the material the changes in such text shall be indicated by means of underscoring or in some other appropriate manner.

(j) *Fees.* At the time of filing the preliminary proxy solicitation material, the persons upon whose behalf the solicitation is made, other than companies registered under the Investment Company Act of 1940, or where an application or declaration under the Public Utility Holding Company Act of 1935 is involved, shall pay to the Commission the following applicable fee: (1) For preliminary proxy material which solicits proxies for election of directors or other business for which a stockholder vote is necessary, but apparently no controversy is involved, a fee of $125; (2) for proxy material where a contest as set forth in Rule 14a-11 is involved, a fee of $500 from each party to the controversy; and (3) for proxy material involving acquisitions, mergers, spin offs, consolidations or proposed sales or other dispositions of substantially all the assets of the company, a fee established in accordance with Rule 0-11 shall be paid. No refund shall be given.

(k) *Merger proxies.* Notwithstanding the foregoing provisions of this section, any proxy statement, form of proxy or other soliciting material included in a registration statement filed under the Securities Act of 1933 on Form N-14, S-4 or F-4 shall be deemed filed both for the purposes of that Act and for the purposes of this section, but separate copies of such material need not be furnished pursuant to this rule nor shall any fee be required under paragraph (j) of this rule. However, any additional soliciting material used after the effective date of the registration statement on Form N-14, S-4 or F-4 shall be filed in accordance with this rule, unless separate copies of such material are required to be filed as an amendment of such registration statement.

(*l*) *Computing time periods.* In computing time periods beginning with the filing date specified in Regulation 14A, the filing date shall be counted as the first day of the time period and midnight of the last day shall constitute the end of the specified time period.

Rule 14a-7. Mailing Communications for Security Holders

If the registrant has made or intends to make any solicitation subject to this regulation, the registrant shall perform such of the following acts as may be duly requested in writing with respect to the same subject matter or meeting by any security holder who is entitled to vote on such matter or to vote at such meeting and who shall defray the reasonable expenses to be incurred by the registrant in the performance of the act or acts requested.

(a) The registrant shall mail or otherwise furnish to such security holder the following information as promptly as practicable after the receipt of such request:

(1) A statement of the approximate number of holders of record of any class of securities, any of the holders of which have been or are to be solicited on behalf of the registrant, or any group of such holders which the security holder shall designate.

(2) If the registrant has made or intends to make, through bankers, brokers or other persons any solicitation of the beneficial owners of securities of any class, a statement of the approximate number of such beneficial owners, or any group of such owners which the security holder shall designate.

(3) An estimate of the cost of mailing a specified proxy statement, form of proxy or other communication to such holders, including insofar as known or reasonably available, the estimated handling and mailing costs of the bankers, brokers or other persons specified in (2) above.

(b)(1) Copies of any proxy statement, form of proxy or other communication furnished by the security holder shall be mailed by the registrant to such of the holders of record specified in (a)(1) above as the security holder shall designate. The registrant shall also mail to each banker, broker, or other person specified in (a)(2) above a sufficient number of copies of such proxy statement, form of proxy or other communication as will enable the banker, broker, or other person to furnish a copy thereof to each beneficial owner solicited or to be solicited through him.

(2) Any such material which is furnished by the security holder shall be mailed with reasonable promptness by the registrant after receipt of a tender of the material to be mailed, of envelopes or other containers therefor and of postage or payment for postage. The registrant need not, however, mail any such material which relates to any matter to be acted upon at an annual meeting of security holders prior to the earlier of (i) a day corresponding to the first date on which the registrant proxy soliciting material was released to security holders in connection with the last annual meeting of security holders, or (ii) the first day on which solicitation is made on behalf of the registrant. With respect to any such material which relates to any matter to be acted upon by security holders otherwise than at an annual meeting, such material need not be mailed prior to the first day on which solicitation is made on behalf of the registrant.

(3) The registrant shall not be responsible for such proxy statement, form of proxy or other communication.

(c) In lieu of performing the acts specified above, the registrant may, at its option, furnish promptly to such security holder a reasonably current list of the names and addresses of such of the holders of record specified in (a)(1) above as the security holder shall designate, and a list of the names and addresses of such of the bankers, brokers or other persons specified in (a)(2) above as the security holder shall designate together with a statement of the approximate number of beneficial owners solicited or to be solicited through each such banker, broker or other person and a schedule of the handling and mailing costs of each such banker, broker or other person, if such schedule has been supplied to the registrant. The foregoing information shall be furnished promptly upon the request of the security holder or at daily or other reasonable intervals as it becomes available to the registrant.

Rule 14a–8. Proposals of Security Holders

(a) If any security holder of a registrant notifies the registrant of his intention to present a proposal for action at a forthcoming meeting of the registrant's security holders, the registrant shall set forth the proposal in its proxy statement and identify it in its form of proxy and provide means by which security holders can make the specification required by Rule 14a–4(b). Notwithstanding the foregoing, the registrant shall not be required to include the proposal in its proxy statement or form of proxy unless the security holder (hereinafter, the "proponent") has complied with the requirements of this paragraph and paragraphs (b) and (c) of this Rule:

(1) *Eligibility.* (i) At the time he submits the proposal, the proponent shall be a record or beneficial owner of at least 1% or $1000 in market value of securities entitled to be voted on the proposal at the meeting and have held such securities for at least one year, and he shall continue to own such securities through the date on which the meeting is held. If the registrant requests documentary support for a proponent's claim that he is the beneficial

owner of at least $1000 in market value of such voting securities of the registrant or that he has been a beneficial owner of the securities for one or more years, the proponent shall furnish appropriate documentation within 14 calendar days after receiving the request. In the event the registrant includes the proponent's proposal in its proxy soliciting material for the meeting and the proponent fails to comply with the requirement that he continuously hold such securities through the meeting date, the registrant shall not be required to include any proposals submitted by the proponent in its proxy material for any meeting held in the following two calendar years.

(ii) Proponents who deliver written proxy materials to holders of more than 25 percent of a class of the registrant's outstanding securities entitled to vote with respect to the same meeting of security holders will be ineligible to use the provisions of Rule 14a–8 for the inclusion of a proposal in the registrant's proxy materials. In the event the registrant includes a proponent's proposal in its proxy material and the proponent thereafter delivers written proxy materials to the holders of more than 25 percent of a class of the registrant's outstanding securities entitled to vote with respect to such meeting, the registrant shall not be required to include any proposals submitted by that proponent in its proxy soliciting materials for any meeting held in the following two calendar years.

(2) *Notice and Attendance at the Meeting.* At the time he submits a proposal, a proponent shall provide the registrant in writing with his name, address, the number of the registrant's voting securities that he holds of record or beneficially, the dates upon which he acquired such securities, and documentary support for a claim of beneficial ownership. A proposal may be presented at the meeting either by the proponent or his representative who is qualified under state law to present the proposal on the proponent's behalf at the meeting. In the event that the proponent or his representative fails, without good cause, to present the proposal for action at the meeting, the registrant shall not be required to include any proposals submitted by the proponent in its proxy soliciting material for any meeting held in the following two calendar years.

(3) *Timeliness.* The proponent shall submit his proposal sufficiently far in advance of the meeting so that it is received by the registrant within the following time periods.

(i) *Annual Meetings.* A proposal to be presented at an annual meeting shall be received at the registrant's principal executive offices not less than 120 calendar days in advance of the date of the registrant's proxy statement released to security holders in connection with the previous year's annual meeting of security holders except that if no annual meeting was held in the previous year or the date of the annual meeting has been changed by more than 30 calendar days from the date contemplated at the time of the previous year's proxy statement, a proposal shall be received by the registrant a reasonable time before the solicitation is made.

(ii) *Other Meetings.* A proposal to be presented at any meeting other than an annual meeting specified in paragraph (a)(3)(i) of this section shall be received a reasonable time before the solicitation is made.

NOTE: In order to curtail controversy as to the date on which a proposal was received by the registrant, it is suggested that proponents submit their proposals by Certified Mail-Return Receipt Requested.

(4) *Number of Proposals.* The proponent may submit no more than one proposal and an accompanying supporting statement for inclusion in the registrant's proxy materials for a meeting of security holders. If the proponent submits more than one proposal, or if he fails to comply with the 500 word limit mentioned in paragraph (b)(1) of this rule, he shall be provided the opportunity to reduce the items submitted by him to the limits required by this rule, within 14 calendar days of notification of such limitations by the registrant.

(b)(1) *Supporting Statement.* The registrant, at the request of the proponent, shall include in its proxy statement a statement of the proponent in support of the proposal, which statement shall not include the name and address of the proponent. A proposal and its supporting statement in the aggregate shall not exceed 500 words. The supporting statement shall be furnished to the registrant at the time that the proposal is furnished, and the registrant shall not be responsible for such statement and the proposal to which it relates.

(2) *Identification of Proponent.* The proxy statement shall also include either the name and address of the proponent and the number of shares of the voting security held by the proponent or a statement that such information will be furnished by the registrant to any person, orally or in writing as requested, promptly upon the receipt of any oral or written request therefor.

(c) The registrant may omit a proposal and any statement in support thereof from its proxy statement and form of proxy under any of the following circumstances:

(1) If the proposal is, under the laws of the registrant's domicile, not a proper subject for action by security holders:

NOTE: Whether a proposal is a proper subject for action by security holders will depend on the applicable state law. Under certain states' laws, a proposal that mandates certain action by the registrant's board of directors may not be a proper subject matter for shareholder action, while a proposal recommending or requesting such action of the board may be proper under such state law;

(2) If the proposal, if implemented, would require the registrant to violate any state law or federal law of the United States, or any law of any foreign jurisdiction to which the registrant is subject, except that this provision shall not apply with respect to any foreign law compliance with which would be violative of any state or federal law of the United States;

(3) If the proposal or the supporting statement is contrary to any of the Commission's proxy rules and regulations, including Rule 14a-9 which prohibits false or misleading statements in proxy soliciting materials;

(4) If the proposal relates to the redress of a personal claim or grievance against the registrant or any other person, or if it is designed to result in a benefit to the proponent or to further a personal interest, which benefit or interest is not shared with the other security holders at large;

(5) If the proposal relates to operations which account for less than 5 percent of the registrant's total assets at the end of its most recent fiscal year, and for less than 5 percent of its net earnings and gross sales for its most recent fiscal year, and is not otherwise significantly related to the registrant's business;

(6) If the proposal deals with a matter beyond the registrant's power to effectuate;

(7) If the proposal deals with a matter relating to the conduct of the ordinary business operations of the registrant;

(8) If the proposal relates to an election to office;

(9) If the proposal is counter to a proposal to be submitted by the registrant at the meeting;

(10) If the proposal has been rendered moot;

(11) If the proposal is substantially duplicative of a proposal previously submitted to the registrant by another proponent, which proposal will be included in the registrant's proxy material for the meeting;

(12) If the proposal deals with substantially the same subject matter as a prior proposal submitted to security holders in the registrant's proxy statement and form of proxy relating to any annual or special meeting of security holders held within the preceding five calendar years, it may be omitted from the registrant's proxy materials relating to any meeting of security holders held within three calendar years after the latest such previous submission:

Provided, That

(i) If the proposal was submitted at only one meeting during such preceding period, it received less than three percent of the total number of votes cast in regard thereto; or

(ii) If the proposal was submitted at only two meetings during such preceding period, it received at the time of its second submission less than six percent of the total number of votes cast in regard thereto; or

(iii) If the prior proposal was submitted at three or more meetings during such preceding period, it received at the time of its latest submission less than 10 percent of the total number of votes cast in regard thereto; or

(13) If the proposal relates to specific amounts of cash or stock dividends.

(d) Whenever the registrant asserts, for any reason, that a proposal and any statement in support thereof received from a proponent may properly be omitted from its proxy statement and form of proxy, it shall file with the Commission, not later than 60 calendar days prior to the date the preliminary copies of the proxy statement and form of proxy are filed pursuant to Rule 14a-6(a) or such shorter period prior to such date as the Commission or its staff may permit, six copies of the following items: (1) The proposal; (2) any statement in support thereof as received from the proponent; (3) a statement of the reasons why the registrant deems such omission to be proper in the particular case; and (4) where such reasons are based on matters of law, a supporting opinion of counsel. The registrant shall at the same time, if it has not already done so, notify the proponent of its intention to omit the proposal from its proxy statement and form of proxy and shall forward to him a copy of the statement of reasons why the registrant deems the omission of the proposal to be proper and a copy of such supporting opinion of counsel.

(e) If the registrant intends to include in the proxy statement a statement in opposition to a proposal received from a proponent, it shall, not later than ten calendar days prior to the date the preliminary copies of the proxy statement and form of proxy are filed pursuant to Rule 14a-6(a), or, in the event that the proposal must be revised to be includable, not later than five calendar days after receipt by the registrant of the revised proposal promptly forward to the proponent a copy of the statement in opposition to the proposal.

In the event the proponent believes that the statement in opposition contains materially false or misleading statements within the meaning of Rule 14a-9 and the proponent wishes to bring this matter to the attention of the Commission, the proponent promptly should provide the staff with a letter setting forth the reasons for this view and at the same time promptly provide the registrant with a copy of such letter.

Rule 14a-9. False or Misleading Statements

(*a*) No solicitation subject to this regulation shall be made by means of any proxy statement, form of proxy, notice of meeting or other communication, written or oral, containing any statement which, at the time and in the light of the circumstances under which it is made, is false or misleading with respect to any material fact, or which omits to state any material fact necessary in order to make the statements therein not false or misleading or necessary to correct any statement in any earlier communication with respect to the solicitation of a proxy for the same meeting or subject matter which has become false or misleading.

(*b*) The fact that a proxy statement, form of proxy or other soliciting material has been filed with or examined by the Commission shall not be deemed a finding by the Commission that such material is accurate or complete or not false or misleading, or that the Commission has passed upon the merits of or approved any statement contained therein or any matter to be acted upon by security holders. No representation contrary to the foregoing shall be made.

Note. The following are some examples of what, depending upon particular facts and circumstances, may be misleading within the meaning of this section:

(a) Predictions as to specific future market values.

(b) Material which directly or indirectly impugns character, integrity or personal reputation, or directly or indirectly makes charges concerning improper, illegal or immoral conduct or associations, without factual foundation.

(c) Failure to so identify a proxy statement, form of proxy and other soliciting material as to clearly distinguish it from the soliciting material of any other person or persons soliciting for the same meeting or subject matter.

(d) Claims made prior to a meeting regarding the results of a solicitation.

* * *

Rule 14a-10. Prohibition of Certain Solicitations

No person making a solicitation which is subject to Rules 14a-1 to 14a-10 shall solicit:

(a) any undated or post-dated proxy, or

(b) any proxy which provides that it shall be deemed to be dated as of any date subsequent to the date on which it is signed by the security holder.

Rule 14a-11. Special Provisions Applicable to Election Contests

(a) *Solicitations to which this section applies.* This section applies to any solicitation subject to Rules 14a-1 to 14a-11 by any person or group of persons for the purpose of opposing a solicitation subject to Rules 14a-1 to 14a-11 by any other person or group of persons with respect to the election or removal of directors at any annual or special meeting of security holders.

(b) *Participant or participant in a solicitation.* For purposes of this rule the terms "participant" and "participant in a solicitation" include the following:

(1) The registrant;

(2) Any director of the registrant, and any nominee for whose election as a director proxies are solicited;

(3) Any committee or group which solicits proxies, any member of such committee or group, and any person whether or not named as a member who acting alone or with one or more other persons directly or indirectly takes the initiative, or engages, in organizing, directing, or arranging for the financing of, any such committee or group;

(4) Any person who finances or joins with another to finance the solicitation of proxies, except persons who contribute not more than $500 and who are not otherwise participants;

(5) Any person who lends money or furnishes credit or enters into any other arrangements, pursuant to any contract or understanding with a participant, for the purpose of financing or otherwise inducing the purchase, sale, holding or voting of securities of the issuer by any participant or other persons, in support of or in opposition to a participant; except that such terms do not include a bank, broker or dealer who, in the ordinary course of business, lends money or executes orders for the purchase or sale of securities and who is not otherwise a participant; and

(6) Any other person who solicits proxies. The foregoing terms do not, however, include (i) any person or organization retained or employed by a participant to solicit security holders and whose activities are limited to the performance of his duties in the course of such employment; (ii) any person who merely transmits proxy soliciting material or performs other ministerial or clerical duties; (iii) any person employed by a participant in the capacity of attorney, accountant, or advertising public relations or financial adviser, and whose activities are limited to the performance of his duties in the course of such employment; (iv) any person regularly employed as an officer or employee of the issuer or any of its subsidiaries who is not otherwise a participant; or (v) any officer or director of, or any person regularly employed by, any other participant, if such officer, director or employee is not otherwise a participant.

(c) *Filing of information required by Schedule 14B.* (1) No solicitation subject to this section shall be made by any person other than the registrant unless at least five business days prior thereto, or such shorter period as the Commission may authorize upon a showing of good cause therefor, there has been filed, with the Commission and with each national securities exchange upon which any security of the registrant is listed and registered, by or on behalf of each participant in such solicitation, a statement in triplicate containing the information specified by Schedule 14B.

(2) Within five business days after a solicitation subject to this section is made by the registrant, or such longer period as the Commission may authorize upon a showing of good cause therefor, there shall be filed, with the Commission and with each national securities exchange upon which any security of the registrant is listed and registered, by or on behalf of each participant in such a solicitation, other than the registrant, a statement in triplicate containing the information specified by Schedule 14B.

(3) If any solicitation on behalf of the registrant or any other person has been made, or if proxy material is ready for distribution, prior to a solicitation subject to this section in opposition thereto, a statement in triplicate containing the information specified in Schedule 14B shall be filed by or on behalf of each participant in such prior solicitation, other than the registrant, as soon as reasonably practicable after the commencement of the solicitation in opposition thereto, with the Commission and with each national securities exchange on which any security of the registrant is listed and registered.

(4) If, subsequent to the filing of the statements required by paragraphs (c)(1), (2), and (3) of this

section, additional persons become participants in a solicitation subject to this section, there shall be filed, with the Commission and each appropriate exchange, by or on behalf of each such person a statement in duplicate containing the information specified by Schedule 14B, within three business days after such person becomes a participant, or such longer period as the Commission may authorize upon a showing of good cause therefor.

(5) If any material change occurs in the facts reported in any statement filed by or on behalf of any participant, and appropriate amendment to such statement shall be filed promptly with the Commission and each appropriate exchange.

(6) Each statement and amendment thereto filed pursuant to this paragraph shall be part of the official public files of the Commission and for purposes of this regulation shall be deemed a communication subject to the provisions of Rule 14a-9.

(d) *Solicitations prior to furnishing required written proxy statement.* Notwithstanding the provisions of Rule 14a-3(a), a solicitation subject to this section may be made prior to furnishing security holders a written proxy statement containing the information specified in Schedule 14A with respect to such solicitation: *Provided,* That—

(1) The statements required by paragraph (c) of this section are filed by or on behalf of each participant in such solicitation.

(2) No form of proxy is furnished to security holders prior to the time the written proxy statement required by Rule 14a-3(a) is furnished to security holders: *Provided, however,* That this paragraph (d)(2) shall not apply where a proxy statement then meeting the requirements of Schedule 14A has been furnished to security holders by or on behalf of the person making the solicitation.

(3) At least the information specified in Items 2(a) and 3(a) of the statement required by paragraph (c) of this section to be filed by each participant, or an appropriate summary thereof, is included in each communication sent or given to security holders in connection with the solicitation.

(4) A written proxy statement meeting the requirements of this regulation is sent or given to security holders at the earliest practicable date.

(e) *Solicitations prior to furnishing required written proxy statement; filing requirements.* Three copies of any soliciting material proposed to be sent or given to security holders prior to the furnishing of the written proxy statement required by Rule 14a-3(a) shall be filed with the Commission in preliminary form, at least five business days prior to the date definitive copies of such material are first sent or given to security holders, or such shorter period as the Commission may authorize upon a showing of good cause therefor.

(f) *Application of this section to annual report.* Notwithstanding the provisions of Rule 14a-3(b) and (c) three copies of any portion of the annual report referred to in Rule 14a-3(b) which comments upon or refers to any solicitation subject to this section, or to any participant in any such solicitation, other than the solicitation by the issuer, shall be filed with the Commission as proxy material subject to Rules 14a-1 to 14a-11. Such portion of the annual report shall be filed with the Commission in preliminary form at least five business days prior to the date copies of the report are first sent or given to security holders.

(g) *Application of Rule 14a-6.* The provisions of paragraphs (c), (d), (e), (f) and (g) of Rule 14a-6 shall apply to the extent pertinent, to soliciting material subject to paragraphs (e) and (f) of this section.

(h) *Use of reprints or reproductions.* In any solicitation subject to this section, soliciting material which includes, in whole or part, any reprints or reproductions of any previously published material shall:

(1) State the name of the author and publication, the date of prior publication, and identify any person who is quoted without being named in the previously published material.

(2) Except in the case of a public official document or statement, state whether or not the consent of the author and publication has been obtained to the use of the previously published material as proxy soliciting material.

(3) If any participant using the previously published material, or anyone on his behalf, paid, directly or indirectly, for the preparation or prior publication of the previously published material, or has made or proposes to make any payments or give any other consideration in connection with the publication or republication of such material, state the circumstances.

Rule 14a–12. Solicitation Prior to Furnishing Required Proxy Statement

(a) Notwithstanding the provisions of Rule 14a–3(a), a solicitation (other than one subject to Rule 14a–11) may be made prior to furnishing security holders a written proxy statement meeting the requirements of Rule 14a–3(a) if—

(1) The solicitation is made in opposition to a prior solicitation or an invitation for tenders or other publicized activity, which is successful, could reasonably have the effect of defeating the action proposed to be taken at the meeting;

(2) No form of proxy is furnished to security holders prior to the time the written proxy statement required by Rule 14a–3(a) is furnished to security holders: *Provided, however,* That this paragraph (a)(2) shall not apply where a proxy statement then meeting the requirements of Rule 14a–3(a) has been furnished to security holders by or on behalf of the person making the solicitation;

(3) The identity of the person or persons by or on whose behalf the solicitation is made and a description of their interests direct or indirect, by security holdings or otherwise, are set forth in each communication sent or given to security holders in connection with the solicitation, and

(4) A written proxy statement meeting the requirements of this regulation is sent or given to security holders at the earliest practicable date.

(b) Three copies of any soliciting material proposed to be sent or given to security holders prior to the furnishing of the written proxy statement required by Rule 14a–3(a) shall be filed with the Commission in preliminary form at least 5 business days prior to the date definitive copies of such material are first sent or given to security holders, or such shorter period as the Commission may authorize upon a showing of good cause therefor.

Rule 14a–13. Obligation of Registrants in Communicating With Beneficial Owners

(a) If the registrant knows that securities of any class entitled to vote at a meeting (or by written consents or authorizations if no meeting is held) with respect to which the registrant intends to solicit proxies, consents or authorizations are held of record by a broker, dealer, voting trustee, bank, association, or other entity that exercises fiduciary powers in nominee name or otherwise, the registrant shall:

(1) By first class mail or other equally prompt means: (i) inquire of each such record holder: (A) whether other persons are the beneficial owners of such securities and if so, the number of copies of the proxy and other soliciting material necessary to supply such material to such beneficial owners; (B) in the case of an annual (or special meeting in lieu of the annual) meeting, or written consents in lieu of such meeting, at which directors are to be elected, the number of copies of the annual report to security holders necessary to supply such report to beneficial owners to whom such reports are to be distributed by such record holder or its nominee and not by the registrant; and (C) if the record holder has an obligation under Rule 14b–1(c) or 14b–2(e)(2) and (3), whether an agent has been designated to act on its behalf in fulfilling such obligation and, if so, the name and address of such agent; and (ii) indicate to each such record holder: (A) whether the registrant, pursuant to paragraph (c) of this rule, intends to distribute the annual report to security holders to beneficial owners of its securities whose names, addresses and securities positions are disclosed pursuant to Rules 14b–1(c) and 14b–2(e)(2) and (3); and (B) the record date;

(2) Upon receipt of a record holder's or respondent bank's response indicating, pursuant to Rule 14b–2(a)(1), the names and addresses of its respondent banks, within one business day after the date such response it received, make an inquiry of and give notification to each such respondent bank in the same manner required by paragraph (a)(1) of this rule;

(3) Make the inquiry required by paragraph (a)(1) of this rule at least 20 business days prior to the record date of the meeting of security holders, or (i) if such inquiry is impracticable 20 business days prior to the record date of a special meeting, as many days before the record date of such meeting as is practicable or, (ii) if consents or authorization are solicited, and such inquiry is impracticable 20 business days before the earliest date on which they may be used to effect corporate action, as many days before that date as is practicable, or (iii) at such later time as the rules of a national securities exchange on which the class of securities in question is listed may permit for good cause shown; *Provided, however,* that if a record holder or re-

spondent bank has informed the registrant that a designated office(s) or department(s) is to receive such inquiries, the inquiry shall be made to such designated office(s) or department(s);

(4) Supply, in a timely manner, each record holder and respondent bank of whom the inquiries required by paragraphs (a)(1) and (a)(2) of this rule are made with copies of the proxy, other proxy soliciting material, and/or the annual report to security holders, in such quantities, assembled in such form and at such place(s), as the record holder or respondent bank may reasonably request in order to send such material to each beneficial owner of securities who is to be furnished with such material by the record holder or respondent bank; and

(5) Upon the request of any record holder or respondent bank that is supplied with proxy soliciting material and/or annual reports to security holders pursuant to paragraph (a)(4) of this rule, pay its reasonable expenses for completing the mailing of such material to beneficial owners.

Note 1.—If the registrant's list of security holders indicates that some of its securities are registered in the name of a clearing agency registered pursuant to section 17A of the Act (*e.g.* "Cede & Co." nominee for the Depository Trust Company), the registrant shall make appropriate inquiry of the clearing agency and thereafter of the participants in such clearing agency who may hold on behalf of a beneficial owner or respondent bank, and shall comply with the above paragraph with respect to any such participant (*see* Rule 14a–1(g)).

Note 2.—The attention of registrants is called to the fact that each broker, dealer, bank, association and other entity that exercises fiduciary powers has an obligation pursuant to Rules 14b–1(b), 14b–2(b) and, with respect to brokers and dealers, applicable self-regulatory organization requirements to obtain and forward, within the time periods prescribed therein. (a) proxies (or in lieu thereof requests for voting instructions) and proxy soliciting materials to all beneficial owners on whose behalf it holds securities, and (b) annual reports to security holders to all beneficial owners on whose behalf it holds securities, unless the registrant has notified the record holder or respondent bank that it has assumed responsibility to mail such material to beneficial owners whose names, addresses and securities positions are disclosed pursuant to Rules 14b–1(c) and 14b–2(e)(2) and (3).

(b) Any registrant requesting pursuant to Rules 14b–1(c) and 14b–2(e)(2) and (3) a list of names, addresses and securities positions of beneficial owners of its securities who either have consented or have not objected to disclosure of such information shall:

(1) By first class mail or other equally prompt means, inquire of each record holder and each respondent bank identified to the registrant pursuant to Rule 14b–2(e)(1) whether such record holder or respondent bank holds the registrant's securities on behalf of any respondent banks and, if so, the name and address of each such respondent bank;

(2) Request such list to be compiled as of a date no earlier than five business days after the date the registrant's request is received by the record holder or respondent bank; *Provided, however,* that if the record holder or respondent bank has informed the registrant that a designated office(s) or department(s) is to receive such requests, the request shall be made to such designated office(s) or department(s);

(3) Make such request to all brokers, dealers, banks, associations and other entities that exercise fiduciary powers;

(4) Use the information furnished in response to such request exclusively for purposes of corporate communications; and

(5) Upon the request of any record holder or respondent bank to whom such request is made, pay the reasonable expenses, both direct and indirect, of providing beneficial owner information.

Note—A registrant will be deemed to have satisfied its obligations under paragraph (b) of this section by requesting consenting and non-objecting beneficial owner lists from a designated agent acting on behalf of the record holder or respondent bank and paying to that designated agent the reasonable expenses of providing the beneficial owner information.

(c) A registrant, at its option, may mail its annual report to security holders to the beneficial owners whose identifying information is provided by record holders and respondent banks, pursuant to Rules 14b–1(c) and 14b–2(e)(2) and (3), provided that such registrant notifies the record holders and respondent banks, at the time it makes the inquiry required by paragraph (a) of this rule, that the registrant will mail the annual report to security holders to the beneficial owners so identified.

Rule 14b–1. Obligation of Registered Brokers and Dealers in Connection With the Prompt Forwarding of Certain Communications to Beneficial Owners

A broker or dealer registered under section 15 of the Act shall:

(a) Respond, by first class mail or other equally prompt means, directly to the registrant no later than seven business days after the date it receives an inquiry made in accordance with Rule 14a–13(a) by indicating, by means of a search card or otherwise: (1) The approximate number of its customers who are beneficial owners of the registrant's securities that are held of record by the broker, dealer or its nominee;

(2) The number of its customers who are beneficial owners of the registrant's securities who have objected to disclosure of their names, addresses and securities positions if the registrant has indicated, pursuant to Rule 14a-13(a)(1)(ii)(A), that it will distribute the annual report to security holders to beneficial owners of its securities whose names, addresses and securities positions are disclosed pursuant to paragraph (c) of this section; and

(3) The identity of its designated agent, if any, acting on its behalf in fulfilling its obligations under paragraph (c) of this section;

Provided, however, that if the broker or dealer has informed the registrant that a designated office(s) or department(s) is to receive such inquiries, receipt for purposes of paragraph (a) of this section shall mean receipt by such designated office(s) or department(s);

(b) Upon receipt of the proxy, other proxy soliciting material, and/or annual reports to security holders, forward such materials to its customers who are beneficial owners of the registrant's securities no later than five business days after the receipt of the proxy material or annual reports, and

(c) Through its agent or directly: (1) Provide the registrant, upon the registrant's request, with the names, addresses and securities positions, compiled as of a date specified in the registrant's request which is no earlier than five business days after the date the registrant's request is received, of its customers who are beneficial owners of the registrant's securities and who have not objected to disclosure of such information; *Provided, however,* that if the broker or dealer has informed the registrant that a designated office(s) or department(s) is to receive such requests, receipt shall mean receipt by such designated office(s) or department(s); and (2) transmit the data specified in paragraph (c)(1) of this rule to the registrant no later than five business days after the record date or other date specified by the registrant.

Note 1.—Where a broker or dealer employs a designated agent to act on its behalf in performing the obligations imposed on the broker or dealer by paragraph (c) of this rule, the five business day time period for determining the date as of which the beneficial owner information is to be compiled is calculated from the date the designated agent receives the registrant's request. In complying with the registrant's request for beneficial owner information under paragraph (c) of this rule, a broker or dealer need only supply the registrant with the names, addresses and securities positions of non-objecting beneficial owners.

Note 2.—If a broker or dealer receives a registrant's request less than five business days before the requested compilation date, it must provide a list compiled as of a date that is no more than five business days after receipt and transmit the list within five business days after the compilation date.

(d) A broker or dealer need not satisfy (1) its obligations under paragraphs (b) and (c) of this rule if a registrant does not provide assurance of reimbursement of the broker's or dealer's reasonable expenses, both direct and indirect, incurred in connection with performing the obligations imposed by paragraphs (b) and (c) of this rule; or (2) its obligation under paragraph (b) of this rule to forward annual reports to non-objecting beneficial owners identified by the broker or dealer, through its agent or directly, pursuant to paragraph (c) of this rule if the registrant notifies the broker or dealer pursuant to Rule 14a–13(c) that the registrant will mail the annual report to such non-objecting beneficial owners, identified by the broker or dealer and delivered in a list to the registrant pursuant to paragraph (c) of this rule.

Rule 14b–2. Obligation of Banks, Associations and Other Entities That Exercise Fiduciary Powers in Connection With the Prompt Forwarding of Certain Communications to Beneficial Owners

A bank, association or other entity that exercises fiduciary powers:

(a)(1) Shall respond, by first class mail or other equally prompt means, directly to the registrant no later than one business day after the date it receives an inquiry made in accordance with Rule 14a–13(a) by indicating the name and address of each of its respondent banks, if any; and

(2) Shall respond, by first class mail or other equally prompt means, directly to the registrant no later than seven business days after the date it receives an inquiry made in accordance with Rule 14a–13(a) by indicating, by means of a search card or otherwise: (i) the approximate number of beneficial owners of the registrant's securities;

(ii) If the registrant has indicated, pursuant to Rule 14a–13(a)(1)(ii)(A), that it will distribute the annual report to security holders to beneficial owners of its securities whose names, addresses and securities positions are disclosed pursuant to Rule 14b–2(e)(2) and (3): (A) with respect to customer accounts opened on or before December 28, 1986, the number of beneficial owners of the registrant's securities who have affirmatively consented to disclosure of their names, addresses and securities positions; and (B) with respect to customer accounts opened after December 28, 1986, the number of beneficial owners of the registrant's securities who have not objected to disclosure of their names, addresses and securities positions; and (iii) the identity of its designated agent, if any, acting on its behalf in fulfilling its obligations under paragraph (e)(2) and (3) of this rule;

Provided, however, that if the record holder or respondent bank has informed the registrant that a designated office(s) or department(s) is to receive such inquiries, receipt for purposes of paragraph (a)(1) and (2) of this rule shall mean receipt by such designated office(s) or department(s);

(b) Within three business days after the record date, shall: (1) Execute an omnibus proxy, including a power of substitution, in favor of its respondent banks and forward such proxy to the registrant; and (2) furnish a notice to each respondent bank in whose favor an omnibus proxy has been executed that it has executed such a proxy, including a power of substitution, in its favor pursuant to paragraph (b)(1) of this section;

(c) Upon receipt of the proxy, other proxy soliciting material, and/or annual reports to security holders shall forward to each beneficial owner on whose behalf it holds securities, no later than five business days after the date it receives such material: (1) Either: (i) A properly executed proxy: (A) indicating the number of securities held for such beneficial owner; (B) bearing the beneficial owner's account number or other form of identification, together with instructions as to the procedures to vote the securities; (C) briefly stating which other proxies, if any, are required to permit securities to be voted under the terms of the instrument creating that voting power or applicable state law; and (D) being accompanied by an envelope addressed to the registrant or its agent, if not provided by the registrant; or (ii) a request for voting instructions (for which registrant's form of proxy may be used and which shall be voted by the record holder or respondent bank in accordance with instructions received), together with an envelope addressed to the record holder or respondent bank; and (2) other proxy soliciting material and/or annual report to security holders;

(d) Need not comply with the requirements of paragraphs (b) and/or (c) of this rule if: (1) On or before July 1, 1988, it makes a written application to the Commission for a waiver from either or both paragraphs, which application sets forth alternative procedures that will reasonably assure that beneficial owners will receive proxies, other proxy soliciting material and/or annual reports to security holders in a timely fashion; (2) the Commission finds such waiver, subject to any suitable terms or conditions, necessary or appropriate in the public interest and consistent with the protection of beneficial owners and the purposes of the Act and, in its discretion, approves such application; and (3) the record holder or respondent bank, in satisfaction of its obligations under paragraphs (b) and/or (c) of this rule, complies with any terms or conditions specified by the Commission in approving such application;

(e) Shall: (1) Respond, by first class mail or other equally prompt means, directly to the registrant no later than one business day after the date it receives an inquiry made in accordance with Rule 14a-13(b)(1) by indicating the name and address of each of its respondent banks, if any; (2) through its agent or directly, provide the registrant, upon the registrant's request and within the time specified in paragraph (e)(3) of this rule, with the names, addresses and securities position, compiled as of a date specified in the registrant's request which is no earlier than five business days after the date the registrant's request is received, of: (i) with respect to customer accounts opened on or before December 28, 1986, beneficial owners of the registrant's securities on whose behalf it holds securities who have affirmatively consented to disclosure of such information, subject to paragraph (h) of this rule; and (ii) with respect to customer accounts opened after December 28, 1986, beneficial owners of the registrant's securities on whose behalf it holds securities who have not objected to disclosure of such information; *Provided, however,* that if the record holder or respondent bank has informed the registrant that a designated office(s) or department(s) is to receive such requests, receipt for purposes of paragraphs (e)(1) and (2) of this rule shall mean receipt by such designated office(s) or department(s); and (3) through its agent or directly, transmit the data specified in paragraph (e)(2) of this rule to the registrant no later than five business days after the date specified by the registrant.

Note 1.—Where a record holder bank or respondent bank employs a designated agent to act on its behalf in performing the obligations imposed on it by paragraph (e)(2) and (3) of this rule, the five business day time period for determining the date as of which the beneficial owner information is to be compiled is calculated from the date the designated agent receives the registrant's request. In complying with the registrant's request for beneficial owner information under paragraph (e)(2) and (3) of this section, a record holder bank or respondent bank need only supply the registrant with the names, addresses and securities positions of affirmatively consenting and non-objecting beneficial owners.

Note 2.—If a record holder bank or respondent bank receives a registrant's request less than five business days before the requested compilation date, it must provide a list compiled as of a date that is no more than five business days after receipt and transmit the list within five business days after the compilation date.

(f) Need not satisfy: (1) Its obligations under paragraphs (b), (c), (e) and (h) of this rule if a registrant does not provide assurance of reimbursement of its reasonable expenses, both direct and indirect, incurred in connection with performing the obligations imposed by paragraphs (b), (c), (e) and (h) of this rule; or (2) its obligation under paragraph (c) of this rule to forward annual reports to consenting and non-objecting beneficial owners identified pursuant to paragraph (e)(2) of this rule if the registrant notifies the record holder or respondent bank pursuant to Rule 14a-13(c) that the registrant will mail the annual report to beneficial owners whose names, addresses and securities positions are disclosed pursuant to Rule 14b-2(e)(2) and (3).

(g) For purposes of determining the fees which may be charged to registrants pursuant to Rule 14a-13(b)(5) and paragraph (f)(1) of this rule for performing obligations under paragraphs (b), (c), (e) and (h) of this rule, an amount no greater than that permitted to be charged by brokers or dealers for reimbursement of their reasonable expenses, both direct and indirect, incurred in connection with performing the obligations imposed by paragraphs (b) and (c) of Rule 14b-1 shall be deemed to be reasonable.

(h) For customer accounts opened on or before December 28, 1986, unless it has made a good faith effort to obtain affirmative consent to disclosure of beneficial owner information pursuant to paragraph (e)(2) of this rule, such information as to beneficial owners who do not object to disclosure of such information. A good faith effort to obtain affirmative consent to disclosure of beneficial owner information shall include, but shall not be limited to, making an inquiry: (1) Phrased in neutral language, explaining the purpose of the disclosure and the limitations on the registrant's use thereof; (2) either in at least one mailing separate from other account mailings or in repeated mailings; and (3) in a mailing that includes a return card, postage paid enclosure.

(i) For purposes of this section, the term "beneficial owner" includes any person who has or shares, pursuant to an instrument, agreement or otherwise, the power to vote, or to direct the voting of a security.

Note 1.—If more than one person shares voting power, the provisions of the instrument creating that voting power shall govern with respect to whether consent to disclosure of beneficial owner information has been given.

Note 2.—If more than one person shares voting power or if the instrument creating that voting power provides that such power shall be exercised by different persons depending on the nature of the corporate action involved, all persons entitled to exercise such power shall be deemed beneficial owners; *Provided, however,* that only one such beneficial owner need be designated among the beneficial owners to receive proxies, other proxy soliciting material and/or annual reports to security holders, if the person so designated assumes the obligation to disseminate, in a timely manner, such materials to the other beneficial owners.

TENDER OFFERS

Rule 14d-1. Scope of and Definitions Applicable to Regulations 14D and 14E

(a) *Scope.* Regulation 14D (Rules 14d-1 through 14d-101) shall apply to any tender offer which is subject to section 14(d)(1) of the Act, including, but not limited to, any tender offer for securities of a class described in that section which is made by an affiliate of the issuer of such class. Regulation 14E (Rules 14e-1 and 14e-2) shall apply to a tender offer for securities (other than exempted securities) unless otherwise noted therein.

(b) *Definitions.* Unless the context otherwise requires, all terms used in Regulation 14D and Regulation 14E have the same meaning as in the Act and in Rule 12b-2 promulgated thereunder. In addition, for purposes of sections 14(d) and 14(e) of the Act and Regulations 14D and 14E, the following definitions apply:

(1) The term "bidder" means any person who makes a tender offer or on whose behalf a tender offer is made: *Provided, however,* That the term does not include an issuer which makes a tender offer for securities of any class of which it is the issuer;

(2) The term "subject company" means any issuer of securities which are sought by a bidder pursuant to a tender offer;

(3) The term "security holders" means holders of record and beneficial owners of securities which are the subject of a tender offer;

(4) The term "beneficial owner" shall have the same meaning as that set forth in Rule 13d-3: *Provided, however,* That, except with respect to Rule 14d-3, Rule 14d-9(d) and Item 6 of Schedule 14D-1, the term shall not include a person who does not have or share investment power or who is deemed to be a beneficial owner by virtue of Rule 13d-3(d)(1);

(5) The term "tender offer material" means:

(i) The bidder's formal offer, including all the material terms and conditions of the tender offer and all amendments thereto;

(ii) The related transmittal letter (whereby securities of the subject company which are sought in the tender offer may be transmitted to the bidder or its depositary) and all amendments thereto; and

(iii) Press releases, advertisements, letters and other documents published by the bidder or sent or given by the bidder to security holders which, directly or indirectly, solicit, invite or request tenders of the securities being sought in the tender offer;

(6) The term "business day" means any day, other than Saturday, Sunday or a federal holiday, and shall consist of the time period from 12:01 a.m. through 12:00 midnight Eastern time. In computing any time period under section 14(d)(5) of section 14(d)(6) of the Act or under Regulation 14D or Regulation 14E, the date of the event which begins the running of such time period shall be included *except that* if such event occurs on other than a business day such period shall begin to run on and shall include the first business day thereafter; and

(7) The term "security position listing" means, with respect to securities of any issuer held by a registered clearing agency in the name of the clearing agency or its nominee, a list of those participants in the clearing agency on whose behalf the clearing agency holds the issuer's securities and of the participants' respective positions in such securities as of a specified date.

Rule 14d-2. Date of Commencement of a Tender Offer

(a) *Commencement.* A tender offer shall commence for the purposes of section 14(d) of the Act and the rules promulgated thereunder at 12:01 a.m. on the date when the first of the following events occurs:

(1) The long form publication of the tender offer is first published by the bidder pursuant to Rule 14d-4(a)(1);

(2) The summary advertisement of the tender offer is first published by the bidder pursuant to Rule 14d-4(a)(2);

(3) The summary advertisement or the long form publication of the tender offer is first published by the bidder pursuant to Rule 14d-4(a)(3);

(4) Definitive copies of a tender offer, in which the consideration offered by the bidder consists of securities registered pursuant to the Securities Act of 1933, are first published or sent or given by the bidder to security holders; or

(5) The tender offer is first published or sent or given to security holders by the bidder by any means not otherwise referred to in paragraphs (a)(1) through (a)(4) of this section.

(b) *Public announcement.* A public announcement by a bidder through a press release, newspaper advertisement or public statement which includes the information in paragraph (c) of this section with respect to a tender offer in which the consideration consists solely of cash and/or securities exempt from registration under section 3 of the Securities Act of 1933 shall be deemed to constitute the commencement of a tender offer under paragraph (a)(5) of this section *except that* such tender offer shall not be deemed to be first published or sent or given to security holders by the bidder under paragraph (a)(5) of this section on the date of such public announcement if within five business days of such public announcement, the bidder either:

(1) Makes a subsequent public announcement stating that the bidder has determined not to continue with such tender offer, in which event paragraph (a)(5) of this section shall not apply to the initial public announcement; or

(2) Complies with Rule 14d-3(a) and contemporaneously disseminates the disclosure required by Rule 14d-6 to security holders pursuant to Rule 14d-4 or otherwise in which event:

(i) The date of commencement of such tender offer under paragraph (a) of this section will be determined by the date the information required by Rule 14d-6 is first published or sent or given to security holders pursuant to Rule 14d-4 or otherwise; and

(ii) Notwithstanding paragraph (b)(2)(i) of this section, section 14(d)(7) of the Act shall be deemed to apply to such tender offer from the date of such public announcement.

(c) *Information.* The information referred to in paragraph (b) of this section is as follows:

(1) The identity of the bidder;

(2) The identity of the subject company; and

(3) The amount and class of securities being sought and the price or range of prices being offered therefor.

(d) *Announcements not resulting in commencement.* A public announcement by a bidder through a press release, newspaper advertisement or public statement which only discloses the information in paragraphs (d)(1) through (d)(3) of this section concerning a tender offer in which the consideration consists solely of cash and/or securities exempt from registration under section 3 of the Securities Act of 1933 shall not be deemed to constitute the commencement of a tender offer under paragraph (a)(5) of this section.

(1) The identity of the bidder;

(2) The identity of the subject company; and

(3) A statement that the bidder intends to make a tender offer in the future for a class of equity securities of the subject company which statement does not specify the amount of securities of such class to be sought or the consideration to be offered therefor.

(e) *Announcement made pursuant to Rule 135.* A public announcement by a bidder through a press release, newspaper advertisement or public statement which discloses only the information in Rule 135(a)(4) concerning a tender offer in which the consideration consists solely or in part of securities to be registered under the Securities Act of 1933 shall not be deemed to constitute the commencement of a tender offer under paragraph (a)(5) of this section: *Provided,* That such bidder files a registration statement with respect to such securities promptly after such public announcement.

Rule 14d-3. Filing and Transmission of Tender Offer Statement

(a) *Filing and transmittal.* No bidder shall make a tender offer if, after consummation thereof, such bidder would be the beneficial owner of more than 5 percent of the class of the subject company's securities for which the tender offer is made, unless as soon as practicable on the date of the commencement of the tender offer such bidder:

(1) Files with the Commission ten copies of a Tender Offer Statement on Schedule 14D-1 (Rule 14d-100), including all exhibits thereto;

(2) Hand delivers a copy of such Schedule 14D-1, including all exhibits thereto:

(i) To the subject company at its principal executive office; and

(ii) To any other bidder, which has filed a Schedule 14D-1 with the Commission relating to a tender offer which has not yet terminated for the same class of securities of the subject company, at such bidder's principal executive office or at the address of the person authorized to receive notices and communications (which is disclosed on the cover sheet of such other bidder's Schedule 14D-1);

(3) Gives telephonic notice of the information required by Rule 14d-6(e)(2)(i) and (ii) and mails by means of first class mail a copy of such Schedule 14D-1, including all exhibits thereto:

(i) To each national securities exchange where such class of the subject company's securities is registered and listed for trading (which may be based upon information contained in the subject company's most recent Annual Report on Form 10-K filed with the Commission unless the bidder has reason to believe that such information is not current) which telephonic notice shall be made when practicable prior to the opening of each such exchange; and

(ii) To the National Association of Securities Dealers, Inc. ("NASD") if such class of the subject company's securities is authorized for quotation in the NASDAQ interdealer quotation system.

(b) *Additional materials.* The bidder shall file with the Commission ten copies of any additional tender offer materials as an exhibit to the Schedule 14D-1 required by this section, and if a material change occurs in the information set forth in such Schedule 14D-1, ten copies of an amendment to Schedule 14D-1 (each of which shall include all exhibits other than those required by Item 11(a) of Schedule 14D-1) disclosing such change and shall send a copy of such additional tender offer material or such amendment to the subject company and to any exchange and/or the NASD, as required by paragraph (a) of this section, promptly but not later than the date such additional tender offer material or such change is first published or sent or given to security holders.

(c) *Certain announcements.* Notwithstanding the provisions of paragraph (b) of this section, if the additional tender offer material or an amendment to Schedule 14D-1 discloses only the number of shares deposited to date, and/or announces an extension of the time during which shares may be tendered, then the bidder may file such tender offer material or amendment and send a copy of such tender offer material or amendment to the subject company, any exchange and/or the NASD, as required by paragraph (a) of this section, promptly after the date such tender offer material is first published or sent or given to security holders.

Rule 14d-4. Dissemination of Certain Tender Offers

(a) *Materials deemed published or sent or given.* A tender offer in which the consideration consists solely of cash and/or securities exempt from registration under section 3 of the Securities Act of 1933 shall be deemed "published or sent or given to security holders" within the meaning of section 14(d)(1) of the Act if the bidder complies with all of the requirements of any one of the following subparagraphs: *Provided, however,* That any such tender offers may be published or sent or given to security holders by other methods, but with respect to summary publication, and the use of stockholder lists and security position listings pursuant to Rule 14d-5, paragraphs (a)(2) and (a)(3) of this section are exclusive.

(1) *Long-form publication.* The bidder makes adequate publication in a newspaper or newspapers of long-form publication of the tender offer.

(2) *Summary publication.* (i) If the tender offer is not subject to Rule 13e-3, the bidder makes adequate publication in a newspaper or newspapers

of a summary advertisement of the tender offer; and

(ii) Mails by first class mail or otherwise furnishes with reasonable promptness the bidder's tender offer materials to any security holder who requests such tender offer materials pursuant to the summary advertisement or otherwise.

(3) *Use of stockholder lists and security position listings.* Any bidder using stockholder lists and security position listings pursuant to Rule 14d–5 shall comply with paragraphs (a)(1) or (a)(2) of this section on or prior to the date of the bidder's request for such lists or listing pursuant to Rule 14d–5(a).

(b) *Adequate publication.* Depending on the facts and circumstances involved, adequate publication of a tender offer pursuant to this section may require publication in a newspaper with a national circulation or may only require publication in a newspaper with metropolitan or regional circulation or may require publication in a combination thereof: *Provided, however,* That publication in all editions of a daily newspaper with a national circulation shall be deemed to constitute adequate publication.

(c) *Publication of changes.* If a tender offer has been published or sent or given to security holders by one or more of the methods enumerated in paragraph (a) of this section, a material change in the information published or sent or given to security holders shall be promptly disseminated to security holders in a manner reasonably designed to inform security holders of such change; *Provided, however,* That if the bidder has elected pursuant to Rule 14d–5(f)(1) of this section to require the subject company to disseminate amendments disclosing material changes to the tender offer materials pursuant to Rule 14d–5, the bidder shall disseminate material changes in the information published or sent or given to security holders at least pursuant to Rule 14d–5.

Rule 14d–5. Dissemination of Certain Tender Offers by the Use of Stockholder Lists and Security Position Listings

(a) *Obligations of the subject company.* Upon receipt by a subject company at its principal executive offices of a bidder's written request, meeting the requirements of paragraph (e) of this section, the subject company shall comply with the following sub-paragraphs.

(1) The subject company shall notify promptly transfer agents and any other person who will assist the subject company in complying with the requirements of this section of the receipt by the subject company of a request by a bidder pursuant to this section.

(2) The subject company shall promptly ascertain whether the most recently prepared stockholder list, written or otherwise, within the access of the subject company was prepared as of a date earlier than ten business days before the date of the bidder's request and, if so, the subject company shall promptly prepare or cause to be prepared a stockholder list as of the most recent practicable date which shall not be more than ten business days before the date of the bidder's request.

(3) The subject company shall make an election to comply and shall comply with all of the provisions of either paragraph (b) or paragraph (c) of this section. The subject company's election once made shall not be modified or revoked during the bidder's tender offer and extensions thereof.

(4) No later than the second business day after the date of the bidder's request, the subject company shall orally notify the bidder, which notification shall be confirmed in writing, of the subject company's election made pursuant to paragraph (a)(3) of this section. Such notification shall indicate (i) the approximate number of security holders of the class of securities being sought by the bidder and, (ii) if the subject company elects to comply with paragraph (b) of this section, appropriate information concerning the location for delivery of the bidder's tender offer materials and the approximate direct costs incidental to the mailing to security holders of the bidder's tender offer materials computed in accordance with paragraph (g)(2) of this section.

(b) *Mailing of tender offer materials by the subject company.* A subject company which elects pursuant to paragraph (a)(3) of this section to comply with the provisions of this paragraph shall perform the acts prescribed by the following subparagraphs.

(1) The subject company shall promptly contact each participant named on the most recent security position listing of any clearing agency within the access of the subject company and make inquiry of

each such participant as to the approximate number of beneficial owners of the subject company securities being sought in the tender offer held by each such participant.

(2) No later than the third business day after delivery of the bidder's tender offer materials pursuant to paragraph (g)(1) of this section, the subject company shall begin to mail or cause to be mailed by means of first class mail a copy of the bidder's tender offer materials to each person whose name appears as a record holder of the class of securities for which the offer is made on the most recent stockholder list referred to in paragraph (a)(2) of this section. The subject company shall use its best efforts to complete the mailing in a timely manner but in no event shall such mailing be completed in a substantially greater period of time than the subject company would complete a mailing to security holders of its own materials relating to the tender offer.

(3) No later than the third business day after the delivery of the bidder's tender offer materials pursuant to paragraph (g)(1) of this section, the subject company shall begin to transmit or cause to be transmitted a sufficient number of sets of the bidder's tender offer materials to the participants named on the security position listings described in paragraph (b)(1) of this section. The subject company shall use its best efforts to complete the transmittal in a timely manner, but in no event shall such transmittal be completed in a substantially greater period of time than the subject company would complete a transmittal to such participants pursuant to security position listings of clearing agencies of its own material relating to the tender offer.

(4) The subject company shall promptly give oral notification to the bidder, which notification shall be confirmed in writing, of the commencement of the mailing pursuant to paragraph (b)(2) of this section and of the transmittal pursuant to paragraph (b)(3) of this section.

(5) During the tender offer and any extension thereof the subject company shall use reasonable efforts to update the stockholder list and shall mail or cause to be mailed promptly following each update a copy of the bidder's tender offer materials (to the extent sufficient sets of such materials have been furnished by the bidder) to each person who has become a record holder since the later of (i) the date of preparation of the most recent stockholder list referred to in paragraph (a)(2) of this section or (ii) the last preceding update.

(6) If the bidder has elected pursuant to paragraph (f)(1) of this section to require the subject company to disseminate amendments disclosing material changes to the tender offer materials pursuant to this section, the subject company, promptly following delivery of each such amendment, shall mail or cause to be mailed a copy of each such amendment to each record holder whose name appears on the shareholder list described in paragraphs (a)(2) and (b)(5) of this section and shall transmit or cause to be transmitted sufficient copies of such amendment to each participant named on security position listings who received sets of the bidder's tender offer materials pursuant to paragraph (b)(3) of this section.

(7) The subject company shall not include any communication other than the bidder's tender offer materials or amendments thereto in the envelopes or other containers furnished by the bidder.

(8) Promptly following the termination of the tender offer, the subject company shall reimburse the bidder the excess, if any, of the amounts advanced pursuant to paragraph (f)(3)(iii) over the direct cost incidental to compliance by the subject company and its agents in performing the acts required by this section computed in accordance with paragraph (g)(2) of this section.

(c) *Delivery of stockholder lists and security position listings.* A subject company which elects pursuant to paragraph (a)(3) of this section to comply with the provisions of this paragraph shall perform the acts prescribed by the following subparagraphs.

(1) No later than the third business day after the date of the bidder's request, the subject company shall furnish to the bidder at the subject company's principal executive office a copy of the names and addresses of the record holders on the most recent stockholder list referred to in paragraph (a)(2) of this section and a copy of the names and addresses of participants identified on the most recent security position listing of any clearing agency which is within the access of the subject company.

(2) If the bidder has elected pursuant to paragraph (f)(1) of this section to require the subject company to disseminate amendments disclosing material changes to the tender offer materials, the

subject company shall update the stockholder list by furnishing the bidder with the name and address of each record holder named on the stockholder list, and not previously furnished to the bidder, promptly after such information becomes available to the subject company during the tender offer and any extensions thereof.

(d) *Liability of subject company and others.* Neither the subject company nor any affiliate or agent of the subject company nor any clearing agency shall be:

(1) Deemed to have made a solicitation or recommendation respecting the tender offer within the meaning of section 14(d)(4) based solely upon the compliance or noncompliance by the subject company or any affiliate or agent of the subject company with one or more requirements of this section;

(2) Liable under any provision of the Federal securities laws to the bidder or to any security holder based solely upon the inaccuracy of the current names or addresses on the stockholder list or security position listing, unless such inaccuracy results from a lack of reasonable care on the part of the subject company or any affiliate or agent of the subject company;

(3) Deemed to be an "underwriter" within the meaning of section (2)(11) of the Securities Act of 1933 for any purpose of that Act or any rule or regulation promulgated thereunder based solely upon the compliance or noncompliance by the subject company or any affiliate or agent of the subject company with one or more of the requirements of this section;

(4) Liable under any provision of the Federal securities laws for the disclosure in the bidder's tender offer materials, including any amendment thereto, based solely upon the compliance or noncompliance by the subject company or any affiliate or agent of the subject company with one or more of the requirements of this section.

(e) *Content of the bidder's request.* The bidder's written request referred to in paragraph (a) of this section shall include the following:

(1) The identity of the bidder;

(2) The title of the class of securities which is the subject of the bidder's tender offer;

(3) A statement that the bidder is making a requestion to the subject company pursuant to paragraph (a) of this section for the use of the stockholder list and security position listings for the purpose of disseminating a tender offer to security holders;

(4) A statement that the bidder is aware of and will comply with the provisions of paragraph (f) of this section;

(5) A statement as to whether or not it has elected pursuant to paragraph (f)(1) of this section to disseminate amendments disclosing material changes to the tender offer materials pursuant to this section; and

(6) The name, address and telephone number of the person whom the subject company shall contact pursuant to paragraph (a)(4) of this section.

(f) *Obligations of the bidder.* Any bidder who requests that a subject company comply with the provisions of paragraph (a) of this section shall comply with the following subparagraphs:

(1) The bidder shall make an election whether or not to require the subject company to disseminate amendments disclosing material changes to the tender offer materials pursuant to this section, which election shall be included in the request referred to in paragraph (a) of this section and shall not be revocable by the bidder during the tender offer and extensions thereof.

(2) With respect to a tender offer subject to section 14(d)(1) of the Act in which the consideration consists solely of cash and/or securities exempt from registration under section 3 of the Securities Act of 1933, the bidder shall comply with the requirements of Rule 14d–4(a)(3).

(3) If the subject company elects to comply with paragraph (b) of this section,

(i) The bidder shall promptly deliver the tender offer materials after receipt of the notification from the subject company as provided in paragraph (a)(4) of this section;

(ii) The bidder shall promptly notify the subject company of any amendment to the bidder's tender offer materials requiring compliance by the subject company with paragraph (b)(6) of this section and shall promptly deliver such amendment to the subject company pursuant to paragraph (g)(1) of this section;

(iii) The bidder shall advance to the subject company an amount equal to the approximate cost of conducting mailings to security holders computed in accordance with paragraph (g)(2) of this section;

(iv) The bidder shall promptly reimburse the subject company for the direct costs incidental to compliance by the subject company and its agents in performing the acts required by this section computed in accordance with paragraph (g)(2) of this section which are in excess of the amount advanced pursuant to paragraph (f)(2)(iii) of this section; and

(v) The bidder shall mail by means of first class mail or otherwise furnish with reasonable promptness the tender offer materials to any security holder who requests such materials.

(4) If the subject company elects to comply with paragraph (c) of this section,

(i) The subject company shall use the stockholder list and security position listings furnished to the bidder pursuant to paragraph (c) of this section exclusively in the dissemination of tender offer materials to security holders in connection with the bidder's tender offer and extensions thereof;

(ii) The bidder shall return the stockholder lists and security position listings furnished to the bidder pursuant to paragraph (c) of this section promptly after the termination of the bidder's tender offer;

(iii) The bidder shall accept, handle and return the stockholder lists and security position listings furnished to the bidder pursuant to paragraph (c) of this section to the subject company on a confidential basis;

(iv) The bidder shall not retain any stockholder list or security position listing furnished by the subject company pursuant to paragraph (c) of this section, or any copy thereof, nor retain any information derived from any such list or listing or copy thereof after the termination of the bidder's tender offer;

(v) The bidder shall mail by means of first class mail, at its own expense, a copy of its tender offer materials to each person whose identity appears on the stockholder list as furnished and updated by the subject company pursuant to paragraphs (c)(1) and (c)(2) of this section;

(vi) The bidder shall contact the participants named on the security position listing of any clearing agency, make inquiry of each participant as to the approximate number of sets of tender offer materials required by each such participant, and furnish, at its own expense, sufficient sets of tender offer materials and any amendment thereto to each such participant for subsequent transmission to the beneficial owners of the securities being sought by the bidder;

(vii) The bidder shall mail by means of first class mail or otherwise furnish with reasonable promptness the tender offer materials to any security holder who requests such materials; and

(viii) The bidder shall promptly reimburse the subject company for direct costs incidental to compliance by the subject company and its agents in performing the acts required by this section computed in accordance with paragraph (g)(2) of this section.

(g) *Delivery of materials, computation of direct costs.*

(1) Whenever the bidder is required to deliver tender offer materials or amendments to tender offer materials, the bidder shall deliver to the subject company at the location specified by the subject company in its notice given pursuant to paragraph (a)(4) of this section a number of sets of the materials or of the amendment, as the case may be, at least equal to the approximate number of security holders specified by the subject company in such notice, together with appropriate envelopes or other containers therefor: *Provided, however,* That such delivery shall be deemed not to have been made unless the bidder has complied with paragraph (f)(3)(iii) of this section at the time the materials or amendments, as the case may be, are delivered.

(2) The approximate direct cost of mailing the bidder's tender offer materials shall be computed by adding (i) the direct cost incidental to the mailing of the subject company's last annual report to shareholders (excluding employee time), less the costs of preparation and printing of the report, and postage, plus (ii) the amount of first class postage required to mail the bidder's tender offer materials. The approximate direct costs incidental to the mailing of the amendments to the bidder's tender offer materials shall be computed by adding (iii) the estimated direct costs of preparing mailing labels, of updating shareholder lists and of third party handling charges plus (iv) the amount of first class postage required to mail the bidder's amendment. Direct

costs incidental to the mailing of the bidder's tender offer materials and amendments thereto when finally computed may include all reasonable charges paid by the subject company to third parties for supplies or services, including costs attendant to preparing shareholder lists, mailing labels, handling the bidder's materials, contacting participants named on security position listings and for postage, but shall exclude indirect costs, such as employee time which is devoted to either contesting or supporting the tender offer on behalf of the subject company. The final billing for direct costs shall be accompanied by an appropriate accounting in reasonable detail.

Rule 14d-6. Disclosure Requirements With Respect to Tender Offers

(a) *Information required on date of commencement.*

(1) *Long-form publication.* If a tender offer is published, sent or given to security holders on the date of commencement by means of long-form publication pursuant to Rule 14d-4(a)(1), such long-form publication shall include the information required by paragraph (e)(1) of this section.

(2) *Summary publication.* If a tender offer is published, sent or given to security holders on the date of commencement by means of summary publication pursuant to Rule 14d-4(a)(2),

(i) The summary advertisement shall contain and shall be limited to, the information required by paragraph (e)(2) of this section; and

(ii) The tender offer materials furnished by the bidder upon the request of any security holder shall include the information required by paragraph (e)(1) of this section.

(3) *Use of stockholder lists and security position listings.* If a tender offer is published or sent or given to security holders on the date of commencement by the use of stockholder lists and security position listings pursuant to Rule 14d-4(a)(3),

(i) Either (A) the summary advertisement shall contain, and shall be limited to the information required by paragraph (e)(2) of this section, or (B) if long form publication of the tender offer is made, such long form publication shall include the information required by paragraph (e)(1) of this section; and

(ii) The tender offer materials transmitted to security holders pursuant to such lists and security position listings and furnished by the bidder upon the request of any security holder shall include the information required by paragraph (e)(1) of this section.

(4) *Other tender offers.* If a tender offer is published or sent or given to security holders other than pursuant to Rule 14d-4(a), the tender offer materials which are published or sent or given to security holders on the date of commencement of such offer shall include the information required by paragraph (e)(1) of this section.

(b) *Information required in summary advertisement made after commencement.* A summary advertisement published subsequent to the date of commencement of the tender offer shall include at least the information specified in paragraphs (e)(1)(i)–(iv) and (e)(2)(iv) of this section.

(c) *Information required in other tender offer materials published after commencement.* Except for summary advertisements described in paragraph (b) of this section and tender offer materials described in paragraphs (a)(2)(ii) and (a)(3)(ii) of this section, additional tender offer materials published, sent or given to security holders subsequent to the date of commencement shall include the information required by paragraphs (e)(1) and may omit any of the information required by paragraphs (e)(1)(v)–(viii) of this section which has been previously furnished by the bidder in connection with the tender offer.

(d) *Material changes.* A material change in the information published or sent or given to security holders shall be promptly disclosed to security holders in additional tender offer materials.

(e) *Information to be included.*

(1) *Long-form publication and tender offer materials.* The information required to be disclosed by paragraphs (a)(1), (a)(2)(ii), (a)(3)(i)(B) and (a)(4) of this section shall include the following:

(i) The identity of the holder;

(ii) The identity of the subject company;

(iii) The amount of class of securities being sought and the type and amount of consideration being offered therefor;

(iv) The scheduled expiration date of the tender offer, whether the tender offer may be extended and, if so, the procedures for extension of the tender offer;

(v) The exact dates prior to which, and after which, security holders who deposit their securities will have the right to withdraw their securities pursuant to section 14(d)(5) of the Act and Rule 14d-7 and the manner in which shares will be accepted for payment and in which withdrawal may be effected;

(vi) If the tender offer is for less than all the outstanding securities of a class of equity securities and the bidder is not obligated to purchase all of the securities tendered, the period or periods, and in the case of the period from the commencement of the offer, the date of the expiration of such period during which the securities will be taken up pro rata pursuant to Section 14(d)(6) of the Act or Rule 14d-8, and the present intention or plan of the bidder with respect to the tender offer in the event of an over-subscription by security holders;

(vii) The disclosure required by Items 1(c); 2 (with respect to persons other than the bidder, excluding sub-items (b) and (d)); 3; 4; 5; 6; 7; 8; and 10 of Schedule 14D-1 or a fair and adequate summary thereof; *Provided, however,* That negative responses to any such item or sub-item or Schedule 14D-1 need not be included; and

(viii) The disclosure required by Item 9 of Schedule 14D-1 or a fair and adequate summary thereof. (Under normal circumstances, the following summary financial information for the period covered by the financial information furnished in response to Item 9 will be a sufficient summary. If the information required by Item 9 is summarized, appropriate instructions shall be included stating how complete financial information can be obtained).

Income Statement:

Net sales and operating revenues and other revenues

Income before extraordinary items

Net income

Balance sheet (at end of period):

Working capital

Total assets

Total assets less deferred research and development charges and excess cost of assets acquired over book value

Total indebtedness

Shareholders' equity

Per Share:

Income per common share before extraordinary items

Extraordinary items

Net income per common share (and common share equivalents, if applicable)

Net income per share on a fully diluted basis

* * *

(2) *Summary publication.* The information required to be disclosed by paragraphs (a)(2)(i) and (a)(3)(i)(A) of this section in a summary advertisement is as follows:

(i) The information required by paragraph (e)(1)(i) through (vi) of this section;

(ii) If the tender offer is for less than all the outstanding securities of a class of equity securities, a statement as to whether the purpose or one of the purposes of the tender offer is to acquire or influence control of the business of the subject company;

(iii) A statement that the information required by paragraph (e)(1)(vii) of this section is incorporated by reference into the summary advertisement;

(iv) Appropriate instructions as to how security holders may obtain promptly, at the bidder's expense, the bidder's tender offer materials; and

(v) In a tender offer published or sent or given to security holders by the use of stockholder lists and security position listings pursuant to Rule 14d-4(a)(3), a statement that a request is being made for such lists and listings and that tender offer materials will be mailed to record holders and will be furnished to brokers, banks and similar persons whose name appears or whose nominee appears on the list of stockholders or, if applicable, who are listed as participants in a clearing agency's security position listing for subsequent transmittal to beneficial owners of such securities.

(3) *No transmittal letter.* Neither the initial summary advertisement nor any subsequent sum-

mary advertisement shall include a transmittal letter (whereby securities of the subject company which are sought in the tender offer may be transmitted to the bidder or its depository) or any amendment thereto.

Rule 14d-7. Additional Withdrawal Rights

(a) *Rights.* In addition to the provisions of Rule 14(d)(5) of the Act, any person who has deposited securities pursuant to a tender offer has the right to withdraw any such securities during the period such offer, request or invitation remains open.

(b) *Notice of withdrawal.* Notice of withdrawal pursuant to this section shall be deemed to be timely upon the receipt by the bidder's depositary of a written notice of withdrawal specifying the name(s) of the tendering stockholder(s), the number or amount of the securities to be withdrawn and the name(s) in which the certificate(s) is (are) registered, if different from that of the tendering security holder(s). A bidder may impose other reasonable requirements, including certificate numbers and a signed request for withdrawal accompanied by a signature guarantee, as conditions precedent to the physical release of withdrawn securities.

Rule 14d-8. Exemption From Statutory Pro Rata Requirement

Notwithstanding the pro rata provisions of Section 14(d)(6) of the Act, if any person makes a tender offer or request or invitation for tenders, for less than all of the outstanding equity securities of a class, and if a greater number of securities are deposited pursuant thereto than such person is bound or willing to take up and pay for, the securities taken up and paid for shall be taken up and paid for as nearly as may be pro rata, disregarding fractions, according to the number of securities deposited by each depositor during the period such offer, request or invitation remains open.

Rule 14d-9. Solicitation/Recommendation Statements With Respect to Certain Tender Offers

(a) *Filing and transmittal of recommendation statement.* No solicitation or recommendation to security holders shall be made by any person described in paragraph (d) of this section with respect to a tender offer for such securities unless as soon as practicable on the date such solicitation or recommendation is first published or sent or given to security holders such person complies with the following subparagraphs.

(1) Such person shall file with the Commission eight copies of a Tender Offer Solicitation/Recommendation Statement on Schedule 14D-9, including all exhibits thereto; and

(2) If such person is either the subject company or an affiliate of the subject company,

(i) Such person shall hand deliver a copy of the Schedule 14D-9 to the bidder at its principal office or at the address of the person authorized to receive notices and communications (which is set forth on the cover sheet of the bidder's Schedule 14D-1 filed with the Commission; and

(ii) Such person shall give telephonic notice (which notice to the extent possible shall be given prior to the opening of the market) of the information required by Items 2 and 4(a) of Schedule 14D-9 and shall mail a copy of the Schedule to each national securities exchange where the class of securities is registered and listed for trading and, if the class is authorized for quotation in the NASDAQ interdealer quotation system, to the National Association of Securities Dealers, Inc. ("NASD").

(3) If such person is neither the subject company nor an affiliate of the subject company,

(i) Such person shall mail a copy of the schedule to the bidder at its principal office or at the address of the person authorized to receive notices and communications (which is set forth on the cover sheet of the bidder's Schedule 14D-1 filed with the Commission); and

(ii) Such person shall mail a copy of the Schedule to the subject company at its principal office.

(b) *Amendments.* If any material change occurs in the information set forth in the Schedule 14D-9 required by this section, the person who filed such Schedule 14D-9 shall:

(1) File with the Commission eight copies of an amendment on Schedule 14D-9 disclosing such change promptly, but not later than the date such material is first published, sent or given to security holders; and

(2) Promptly deliver copies and give notice of the amendment in the same manner as that specified in

paragraph (a)(2) or paragraph (a)(3) of this section, whichever is applicable; and

(3) Promptly disclose and disseminate such change in a manner reasonably designed to inform security holders of such change.

(c) *Information required in solicitation or recommendation.* Any solicitation or recommendation to holders of a class of securities referred to in section 14(d)(1) of the Act with respect to a tender offer for such securities shall include the name of the person making such solicitation or recommendation and the information required by Items 1, 2, 3(b), 4, 6, 7 and 8 of Schedule 14D–9 or a fair and adequate summary thereof: *Provided, however,* That such solicitation or recommendation may omit any of such information previously furnished to security holders of such class of securities by such person with respect to such tender offer.

(d) *Applicability*

(1) Except as is provided in paragraphs (d)(2) and (e) of this section, this section shall only apply to the following persons:

(i) The subject company, any director, officer, employee, affiliate or subsidiary of the subject company;

(ii) Any record holder or beneficial owner of any security issued by the subject company, by the bidder, or by any affiliate of either the subject company or the bidder; and

(iii) Any person who makes a solicitation or recommendation to security holders on behalf of any of the foregoing or on behalf of the bidder other than by means of a solicitation or recommendation to security holders which has been filed with the Commission pursuant to this section or Rule 14d–3.

(2) Notwithstanding paragraph (d)(1) of this section, this section shall not apply to the following persons:

(i) A bidder who has filed a Schedule 14D–1 pursuant to Rule 14d–3;

(ii) Attorneys, banks, brokers, fiduciaries or investment advisers who are not participating in a tender offer in more than a ministerial capacity and who furnish information and/or advice regarding such tender offer to their customers or clients on the unsolicited request of such customers or clients or solely pursuant to a contract or a relationship providing for advice to the customer or client to whom the information and/or advice is given.

(e) *Stop-look-and-listen communication.* This section shall not apply to the subject company with respect to a communication by the subject company to its security holders which only:

(1) Identifies the tender offer by the bidder;

(2) States that such tender offer is under consideration by the subject company's board of directors and/or management;

(3) States that on or before a specified date (which shall be no later than 10 business days from the date of commencement of such tender offer) the subject company will advise such security holders of (i) whether the subject company recommends acceptance or rejection of such tender offer; expresses no opinion and remains neutral toward such tender offer; or is unable to take a position with respect to such tender offer and (ii) the reason(s) for the position taken by the subject company with respect to the tender offer (including the inability to take a position); and

(4) Requests such security holders to defer making a determination whether to accept or reject such tender offer until they have been advised of the subject company's position with respect thereto pursuant to paragraph (e)(3) of this section.

(f) *Statement of management's position.* A statement by the subject company of its position with respect to a tender offer which is required to be published or sent or given to security holders pursuant to Rule 14e–2 shall be deemed to constitute a solicitation or recommendation within the meaning of this section and section 14(d)(4) of the Act.

Rule 14e–1. Unlawful Tender Offer Practices

As a means reasonably designed to prevent fraudulent, deceptive or manipulative acts or practices within the meaning of section 14(e) of the Act, no person who makes a tender offer shall:

(a) Hold such tender offer open for less than twenty business days from the date such tender offer is first published or sent or given to security holders;

(b) Increase or decrease the percentage of the class of securities being sought or the consideration offered or the dealer's soliciting fee to be given in a tender offer unless such tender remains open for at least ten business days from the date that notice of such increase or decrease is first published or sent or given to security holders:

Provided, however, That, for purposes of this paragraph, the acceptance for payment by the bidder of an additional amount of securities not to exceed two percent of the class of securities that is the subject of the tender offer shall not be deemed to be an increase. For purposes of this paragraph, the percentage of a class of securities shall be calculated in accordance with Rule 14(d)(3) of the Act.

(c) Fail to pay the consideration offered or return the securities deposited by or on behalf of security holders promptly after the termination or withdrawal of a tender offer;

(d) Extend the length of a tender offer without issuing a notice of such extension by press release or other public announcement, which notice shall include disclosure of the approximate number of securities deposited to date and shall be issued no later than the earlier of (i) 9:00 a.m. Eastern time, on the next business day after the scheduled expiration date of the offer or (ii), if the class of securities which is the subject of the tender offer is registered on one or more national securities exchanges, the first opening of any one of such exchanges on the next business day after the scheduled expiration date of the offer.

Rule 14e-2. Position of Subject Company With Respect to a Tender Offer

(a) *Position of subject company.* As a means reasonably designed to prevent fraudulent, deceptive or manipulative acts or practices within the meaning of section 14(e) of the Act, the subject company, no later than 10 business days from the date the tender offer is first published or sent or given, shall publish, send or give to security holders a statement disclosing that the subject company:

(1) Recommends acceptance or rejection of the bidder's tender offer;

(2) Expresses no opinion and is remaining neutral toward the bidder's tender offer; or

(3) Is unable to take a position with respect to the bidder's tender offer.

Such statement shall also include the reason(s) for the position (including the inability to take a position) disclosed therein.

(b) *Material change.* If any material change occurs in the disclosure required by paragraph (a) of this section, the subject company shall promptly publish, send or give a statement disclosing such material change to security holders.

Rule 14e-3. Transactions in Securities on the Basis of Material, Nonpublic Information in the Context of Tender Offers

(a) If any person has taken a substantial step or steps to commence, or has commenced, a tender offer (the "offering person"), it shall constitute a fraudulent, deceptive or manipulative act or practice within the meaning of section 14(e) of the Act for any other person who is in possession of material information relating to such tender offer which information he knows or has reason to know is nonpublic and which he knows or has reason to know has been acquired directly or indirectly from (1) the offering person, (2) the issuer of the securities sought or to be sought by such tender offer, or (3) any officer, director, partner or employee or any other person acting on behalf of the offering person or such issuer, to purchase or sell or cause to be purchased or sold any of such securities or any securities convertible into or exchangeable for any such securities or any option or right to obtain or to dispose of any of the foregoing securities, unless within a reasonable time prior to any purchase or sale such information and its source are publicly disclosed by press release or otherwise.

(b) A person other than a natural person shall not violate paragraph (a) of this section if such person shows that:

(1) The individual(s) making the investment decision on behalf of such person to purchase or sell any security described in paragraph (a) or to cause any such security to be purchased or sold by or on behalf of others did not know the material, nonpublic information; and

(2) Such person had implemented one or a combination of policies and procedures, reasonable under the circumstances, taking into consideration the nature of the person's business, to ensure that individual(s) making investment decision(s) would not vio-

late paragraph (a), which policies and procedures may include, but are not limited to, (i) those which restrict any purchase, sale and causing any purchase and sale of any such security or (ii) those which prevent such individual(s) from knowing such information.

(c) Notwithstanding anything in paragraph (a) to the contrary, the following transactions shall not be violations of paragraph (a) of this section:

(1) Purchase(s) of any security described in paragraph (a) by a broker or by another agent on behalf of an offering person; or

(2) Sale(s) by any person of any security described in paragraph (a) to the offering person.

(d)(1) As a means reasonably designed to prevent fraudulent, deceptive or manipulative acts or practices within the meaning of section 14(e) of the Act, it shall be unlawful for any person described in paragraph (d)(2) of this section to communicate material, nonpublic information relating to a tender offer to any other person under circumstances in which it is reasonably foreseeable that such communication is likely to result in a violation of this section except that this paragraph shall not apply to a communication made in good faith,

(i) To the officers, directors, partners or employees of the offering person, to its advisors or to other persons, involved in the planning, financing, preparation or execution of such tender offer;

(ii) To the issuer whose securities are sought or to be sought by such tender offer, to its officers, directors, partners, employees or advisors or to other persons, involved in the planning, financing, preparation or execution of the activities of the issuer with respect to such tender offer; or

(iii) To any person pursuant to a requirement of any statute or rule or regulation promulgated thereunder.

(d)(2) The persons referred to in paragraph (d)(1) of this section are:

(i) The offering person or its officers, directors, partners, employees or advisors;

(ii) The issuer of the securities sought or to be sought by such tender offer or its officers, directors, partners, employees or advisors;

(iii) Anyone acting on behalf of the persons in paragraph (d)(2)(i) or the issuer or persons in paragraph (d)(2)(ii); and

(iv) Any person in possession of material information relating to a tender offer which information he knows or has reason to know is nonpublic and which he knows or has reason to know has been acquired directly or indirectly from any of the above.

Rule 14f–1. Change in Majority of Directors

If, pursuant to any arrangement or understanding with the person or persons acquiring securities in a transaction subject to sections 13(d) or 14(d) of the Act, any persons are to be elected or designated as directors of the issuer, otherwise than at a meeting of security holders, and the persons so elected or designated will constitute a majority of the directors of the issuer, then, not less than 10 days prior to the date any such person takes office as a director, or such shorter period prior to that date as the Commission may authorize upon a showing of good cause therefor, the issuer shall file with the Commission and transmit to all holders of record of securities of the issuer who would be entitled to vote at a meeting for election of directors, information substantially equivalent to the information which would be required by Items 6(a), (d), (e), and (f), 7, and 8 of Schedule 14A of Regulation 14A to be transmitted if such person or persons were nominees for election as directors at a meeting of such security holders. Eight copies of such information shall be filed with the Commission.

OVER–THE–COUNTER MARKETS

* * *

Rule 15c1–2. Fraud and Misrepresentation

(*a*) The term "manipulative, deceptive, or other fraudulent device or contrivance," as used in section 15(c)(1) of the Act, is hereby defined to include any act, practice, or course of business which operates or would operate as a fraud or deceit upon any person.

(*b*) The term "manipulative, deceptive or other fraudulent device or contrivance," as used in section 15(c)(1) of the Act, is hereby defined to include any untrue statement of a material fact and any omission to state a material fact necessary in order to make the statements made, in the light of the circumstances under which they are made, not misleading, which statement or omission is made with knowledge or reasonable grounds to believe that it is untrue or misleading.

(*c*) The scope of this rule shall not be limited by any specific definitions of the term "manipulative, deceptive, or other fraudulent device or contrivance" contained in other rules adopted pursuant to section 15(c)(1) of the Act.

Rule 15c1-3. Misrepresentation by Brokers and Dealers as to Registration

The term "manipulative, deceptive or other fraudulent device or contrivance," as used in section 15(c)(1) of the Act, is hereby defined to include any representation by a broker or dealer that the registration of a broker or dealer, pursuant to section 15(b) * * * or the failure of the Commission to deny or revoke such registration, indicates in any way that the Commission has passed upon or approved the financial standing, business, or conduct of such registered broker or dealer or the merits of any security or any transaction or transactions therein.

Rule 15c1-5. Disclosure of Control

The term "manipulative, deceptive, or other fraudulent device or contrivance," as used in section 15(c)(1) of the Act, is hereby defined to include any act of any broker or dealer controlled by, controlling, or under common control with, the issuer of any security, designed to effect with or for the account of a customer any transaction in, or to induce the purchase or sale by such customer of, such security unless such broker or dealer, before entering into any contract with or for such customer for the purchase or sale of such security, discloses to such customer the existence of such control, and unless such disclosure, if not made in writing, is supplemented by the giving or sending of written disclosure at or before the completion of the transaction.

Rule 15c1-6. Disclosure of Interest in Distribution

The term "manipulative, deceptive, or other fraudulent device or contrivance," as used in section 15(c)(1) of the Act, is hereby defined to include any act of any broker who is acting for a customer or for both such customer and some other person, or of any dealer who receives or has promise of receiving a fee from a customer for advising such customer with respect to securities, designed to effect with or for the account of such customer any transaction in, or to induce the purchase or sale by such customer of, any security in the primary or secondary distribution of which such broker or dealer is participating or is otherwise financially interested unless such broker or dealer at or before the completion of each such transaction, gives or sends to such customer written notification of the existence of such participation or interest.

Rule 15c1-7. Discretionary Accounts

(*a*) The term "manipulative, deceptive, or other fraudulent device or contrivance," as used in section 15(c)(1) of the Act, is hereby defined to include any act of any broker or dealer designed to effect with or for any customer's account in respect to which such broker or dealer or his agent or employee is vested with any discretionary power any transactions of purchase or sale which are excessive in size or frequency in view of the financial resources and character of such account.

(*b*) The term "manipulative, deceptive, or other fraudulent device or contrivance," as used in section 15(c)(1) of the Act, is hereby defined to include any act of any broker or dealer designed to effect with or for any customer's account in respect to which such broker or dealer or his agent or employee is vested with any discretionary power any transaction of purchase or sale unless immediately after effecting such transaction such broker or dealer makes a record of such transaction which record includes the name of such customer, the name, amount, and price of the security, and the date and time when such transaction took place.

Rule 15c1-8. Sales at the Market

The term "manipulative, deceptive, or other fraudulent device or contrivance," as used in section 15(c)(1) of the Act, is hereby defined to include any representation made to a customer by a broker or dealer who is participating or otherwise financially interested in the primary or secondary distribution of any security which is not admitted to trading on a national securities exchange that such security is being offered to such customer "at the market" or at a price related to the market price unless such broker or dealer knows or has reasonable grounds to believe that a market for such security exists other than that made, created, or controlled by him, or by any person for whom he is acting or with whom he is associated in such distribution, or by any person controlled by, controlling or under common control with him.

* * *

Rule 15c2–8. Delivery of Prospectus

(a) It shall constitute a deceptive act or practice, as those terms are used in Section 15(c)(2) of the Act, for a broker or dealer to participate in a distribution of securities with respect to which a registration statement has been filed under the Securities Act of 1933 unless he complies with the requirements set forth in paragraphs (b) through (g) below. For the purposes of this rule a broker or dealer participating in the distribution shall mean any underwriter and any member or proposed member of the selling group.

(b) In connection with an issue of securities, the issuer of which has not previously been required to file reports pursuant to sections 13(a) or 15(d) of the Securities Exchange Act of 1934, unless such issuer has been exempted from the requirement to file reports thereunder pursuant to section 12(h) of the Act, such broker or dealer shall deliver a copy of the preliminary prospectus to any person who is expected to receive a confirmation of sale at least 48 hours prior to the mailing of such confirmation.

(c) Such broker or dealer shall take reasonable steps to furnish to any person who makes written request for a preliminary prospectus between the filing date and a reasonable time prior to the effective date of the registration statement to which such prospectus relates, a copy of the latest preliminary prospectus on file with the Commission. Reasonable steps shall include receiving an undertaking by the managing underwriter or underwriters to mail such copy to the address given in the requests.

(d) Such broker or dealer shall take reasonable steps to comply promptly with the written request of any person for a copy of the final prospectus relating to such securities during the period between the effective date of the registration statement and the later of either the termination of such distribution, or the expiration of the applicable 40 or 90 day period under Section 4(3) of the Securities Act of 1933. Reasonable steps shall include receiving an undertaking by the managing underwriter or underwriters to mail such copy to the address given in the requests. (The 40–day period referred to above shall be deemed to apply for purposes of this rule irrespective of the provisions of paragraph (b) of Rule 174 under the Securities Act of 1933).

(e) Such broker or dealer shall take reasonable steps (i) to make available a copy of the preliminary prospectus relating to such securities to each of his associated persons who is expected, prior to the effective date, to solicit customers' orders for such securities before the making of any such solicitation by such associated persons and (ii) to make available to each such associated person a copy of any amended preliminary prospectus promptly after the filing thereof.

(f) Such broker or dealer shall take reasonable steps to make available a copy of the final prospectus relating to such securities to each of his associated persons who is expected, after the effective date, to solicit customers' orders for such securities prior to the making of any such solicitation by such associated persons, unless a preliminary prospectus which is substantially the same as the final prospectus except for matters relating to the price of the stock has been so made available.

(g) If the broker or dealer is a managing underwriter of such distribution, he shall take reasonable steps to see to it that all other brokers or dealers participating in such distribution are promptly furnished with sufficient copies, as requested by them, of each preliminary prospectus, each amended preliminary prospectus and the final prospectus to enable them to comply with paragraphs (b), (c), (d) and (e) above.

(h) If the broker or dealer is a managing underwriter of such distribution, he shall take reasonable steps to see that any broker or dealer participating in the distribution or trading in the registered security is furnished reasonable quantities of the final prospectus relating to such securities, as requested by him, in order to enable him to comply with the prospectus delivery requirements of Section 5(b)(1) and (2) of the Securities Act of 1933.

(i) This rule shall not require the furnishing of prospectuses in any state where such furnishing would be unlawful under the laws of such state;

provided, however, that this provision is not to be construed to relieve a broker-dealer from complying with the requirements of Section 5(b)(1) and (2) of the Securities Act of 1933. Prospectuses shall not be furnished pursuant to this rule while the registration statement is subject to an examination, proceeding, or stop order pursuant to Section 8 of the Securities Act of 1933.

* * *

Rule 15c2-11. Initiation or Resumption of Quotations Without Specified Information

(a) It shall be a fraudulent, manipulative, and deceptive practice within the meaning of Section 15(c)(2) of the Act, for a broker or dealer to publish any quotation for a security or, directly or indirectly, to submit any such quotation for publication, in any quotation medium (as defined in this rule) unless:

(1) the issuer has filed a registration statement under the Securities Act of 1933, other than a registration statement on Form F-6, which became effective less than 90 calendar days prior to the day on which such broker or dealer publishes or submits the quotation to the quotation medium, *provided* that such registration statement has not thereafter been the subject of a stop order which is still in effect when the quotation is published or submitted, and such broker or dealer has in his records a copy of the prospectus specified by Section 10(a) of the Securities Act of 1933; or

(2) the issuer has filed a notification under Regulation A under the Securities Act of 1933 which became effective less than 40 calendar days prior to the day on which such broker or dealer publishes or submits the quotation to the quotation medium, *provided* that the offering circular provided for under Regulation A has not thereafter become the subject of a suspension order which is still in effect when the quotation is published or submitted, and such broker or dealer has in his records a copy of such offering circular; or

(3)(A) the issuer is required to file reports pursuant to Section 13 or 15(d) of the Act, or is the issuer of a security covered by Section 12(g)(2)(B) or (G) of the Act, and

(B) the broker or dealer has a reasonable basis for believing that the issuer is current in filing the reports required to be filed at regular intervals pursuant to Section 13 of 15(d) of the Act, or, in the case of insurance companies exempted from Section 12(g) of the Act by subparagraph 12(g)(2)(G) thereof, the annual statement referred to in Section 12(g)(2)(G)(i) of the Act; and

(C) the broker or dealer has in his records the issuer's most recent annual report filed pursuant to Section 13 of 15(d) of the Act, or the annual statement in the case of an insurance company not subject to Section 12(g) of the Act, together with any other reports required to be filed at regular intervals under such provisions of the Act which have been filed by the issuer after such annual report or annual statement; or

(4)(i) The issuer is exempt from Section 12(g) of the Act by reason of compliance with the provisions of Rule 12g3-2(b), and

(ii) The broker or dealer wishing to submit for publication a quotation for such security has in his records, and makes reasonably available upon request to any person expressing an interest in a proposed transaction in the security with such broker or dealer, the information furnished to the Commission pursuant to Rule 12g3-2(b) since the beginning of the issuer's last fiscal year, which the broker or dealer has no reasonable basis for believing is not true and correct and which was obtained by him from sources that he has a reasonable basis for believing are reliable; or

(5) Such broker or dealer has in his records, and shall make reasonably available upon request to any person expressing an interest in a proposed transaction in the security with such broker or dealer, the following information (which shall be reasonably current in relation to the day the quotation is submitted), which he has no reasonable basis for believing is not true and correct or reasonably current, and which was obtained by him from sources which he has a reasonable basis for believing are reliable: (1) the exact name of the issuer and its predecessor (if any); (2) the address of its principal executive offices; (3) the state of incorporation, if it is a corporation; (4) the exact title and class of the security; (5) the par or stated value of the security; (6) the number of shares or total amount of the securities outstanding as of the end of the issuer's most recent fiscal year; (7) the name and address of the transfer agent; (8) the nature of the issuer's

business; (9) the nature of products or services offered; (10) the nature and extent of the issuer's facilities; (11) the name of the chief executive officer and members of the board of directors; (12) the issuer's most recent balance sheet and profit and loss and retained earnings statements; (13) similar financial information for such part of the two preceding fiscal years as the issuer or its predecessor has been in existence; (14) whether the broker or dealer or any associated person is affiliated, directly or indirectly with the issuer; (15) whether the quotation is being published or submitted on behalf of any other broker or dealer, and, if so, the name of such broker or dealer; and, (16) whether the quotation is being submitted or published directly or indirectly on behalf of the issuer, or any director, officer or any person, directly or indirectly the beneficial owner of more than 10 per cent of the outstanding units or shares of any equity security of the issuer, and, if so, the name of such person, and the basis for any exemption under the federal securities laws for any sales of such securities on behalf of such person. If such information is made available to others upon request pursuant to this subparagraph, such delivery, unless otherwise represented, shall not constitute a representation by such broker or dealer that such information is true and correct, but shall constitute a representation by such broker or dealer that the information is reasonably current in relation to the day the quotation is submitted, that he has no reasonable basis for believing the information is not true and correct, and that the information was obtained from sources which he has a reasonable basis for believing are reliable. This paragraph (a)(5) shall not apply to any security of an issuer included in paragraph (a)(3) of this rule unless a report or statement of such issuer described in paragraph (a)(3) of this rule is not reasonably available to the broker or dealer. A report or statement of an issuer described in paragraph (a)(3) of this rule shall be "reasonably available" when such report or statement is filed with the Commission.

(b) With respect to any security the quotation of which is within the provisions of this rule, the broker or dealer submitting or publishing such quotation shall maintain in his records information regarding all circumstances involved in the submission of publication of such quotation, including the identity of the person or persons for whom the quotation is being submitted or published and any information regarding the transaction provided to the broker or dealer by such person or persons.

(c) The broker or dealer shall maintain in writing as part of his records the information described in paragraphs (a) and (b), and any other information (including adverse information) regarding the issuer which comes to his knowledge or possession before the publication or submission of the quotation, and preserve such records for the periods specified in Rule 17a-4.

(d) For any security of an issuer included in paragraph (a)(4), the broker or dealer submitting the quotation shall furnish to the inter-dealer-quotation-system (as defined below), in such form as such system shall prescribe, at least 2 days before the quotation is published or submitted, the information regarding the security and the issuer which such broker or dealer is required to maintain pursuant to said paragraph (a)(4).

(e) For purposes of this rule:

(1) "Quotation medium" shall mean any "inter-dealer quotation system" or any publication or electronic communications network or other device which is used by brokers or dealers to make known to others their interest in transactions in any security, including offers to buy or sell at a stated price or otherwise, or invitations of offers to buy or sell.

(2) "Inter-dealer quotation system" shall mean any system of general circulation to brokers or dealers which regularly disseminates quotations of identified brokers or dealers.

(3) Except as otherwise specified in this rule, "quotation" shall mean any bid or offer at a specified price with respect to a security, or any indication of interest by a broker or dealer in receiving bids or offers from others for a security, or any indication by a broker or dealer that he wishes to advertise his general interest in buying or selling a particular security.

(4) "Issuer," in the case of quotations represented by American Depositary Receipts, shall mean the issuer of the deposited shares represented by such American Depositary Receipts.

(f) The provisions of this rule shall not apply to:

(1) The publication or submission of a quotation respecting a security admitted to trading on

a national securities exchange and which is traded on such an exchange on the same day as, or on the business day next preceding, the day the quotation is published or submitted.

(2) The publication or submission by a broker or dealer, solely on behalf of a customer (other than a person acting as or for a dealer), of a quotation that represents the customer's indication of interest and does not involve the solicitation of the customer's interest; *Provided, however,* That this paragraph (f)(2) shall not apply to a quotation consisting of both a bid and an offer, each of which is at a specified price, unless the quotation medium specifically identifies the quotation as representing such an unsolicited customer interest.

(3)(i) The publication or submission, in an interdealer quotation system that specifically identifies as such unsolicited customer indications of interest of the kind described in paragraph (f)(2) of this rule, of a quotation respecting a security which has been the subject of quotations (exclusive of any identified customer interests) in such a system on each of at least 12 days within the previous 30 calendar days, with no more than 4 business days in succession without a quotation; or

(ii) The publication or submission, in an interdealer quotation system that does not so identify any such unsolicited customer indications of interest, of a quotation respecting a security which has been the subject of both bid and ask quotations in an interdealer quotation system at specified prices on each of at least 12 days within the previous 30 calendar days, with no more than 4 business days in succession without such a two-way quotation;

(iii) A dealer acting in the capacity of market maker, as defined in Rule 3(a)(38) of the Act, that has published or submitted a quotation respecting a security in an interdealer quotation system and such quotation has qualified for an exception provided in this paragraph (f)(3), may continue to publish or submit quotations for such security in the interdealer quotation system without compliance with this section unless and until such dealer ceases to submit or publish a quotation or ceases to act in the capacity of market maker respecting such security.

(4) The publication or submission of a quotation respecting a municipal security.

(5) The publication or submission of a quotation respecting a security that is authorized for quotation in an interdealer quotation system sponsored and governed by the rules of a registered securities association, and such authorization is not suspended, terminated or prohibited.

(g) The requirement in subparagraph (a)(5) that the information with respect to the issuer be "reasonably current" will be presumed to be satisfied, unless the broker or dealer has information to the contrary, if:

(1) the balance sheet is as of a date less than 16 months before the publication or submission of the quotation, the statements of profit and loss and retained earnings are for the 12 months preceding the date of such balance sheet, and if such balance sheet is not as of a date less than 6 months before the publication or submission of the quotation, it shall be accompanied by additional statements of profit and loss and retained earnings for the period from the date of such balance sheet to a date less than 6 months before the publication or submission of the quotation.

(2) other information regarding the issuer specified in subparagraph (a)(5) is as of a date within 12 months prior to the publication or submission of the quotation.

(h) This rule shall not prohibit any publication or submission of any quotation if the Commission, upon written request or upon its own motion, exempts such quotation either unconditionally or on specified terms and conditions, as not constituting a fraudulent, manipulative or deceptive practice comprehended within the purpose of this rule.

REPORTS OF DIRECTORS, OFFICERS, AND PRINCIPAL STOCKHOLDERS

Rule 16a–1. Filing of Statements

(a) Initial statements of beneficial ownership of equity securities required by Section 16(a) of the Act shall be filed on Form 3. Statements of changes in such beneficial ownership required by that section shall be filed on Form 4. All such statements shall be prepared and filed in accordance with the requirements of the applicable form.

* * *

(b) A person who is already filing statements pursuant to Section 16(a) with respect to securities registered pursuant to either Section 12(b) or 12(g) of the Act need not file an additional statement on Form 3:

(1) When an additional class of equity securities of the same issuer becomes registered pursuant to the same subsection of the Act; or

(2) If any class of equity securities is registered pursuant to Section 12(b), when another class of equity securities of the same issuer becomes registered pursuant to Section 12(g); or

(3) When such person assumes another or an additional relationship to the issuer; for example, when an officer becomes a director.

(c) Any issuer which has equity securities listed on more than one national securities exchange may designate one such exchange as the only exchange with which reports pursuant to Section 16(a) of the Act need be filed. Such designation shall be made in writing and shall be filed with the Commission and with each national securities exchange on which any equity security of the issuer is listed. After the filing of such designation the securities of such issuer shall be exempted with respect to the filing of statements pursuant to Section 16(a) of the Act with any exchange other than the designated exchange.

(d) Any director or officer who is required to file a statement on Form 4 with respect to any change in his beneficial ownership of equity securities which occurs within 6 months after he became a director or officer of the issuer of such securities, or within 6 months after equity securities of such issuer first became registered pursuant to Section 12 of the Act, shall include in the first such statement the information called for by Form 4 with respect to all changes in his beneficial ownership of equity securities of such issuer which occurred within 6 months prior to the date of the changes which requires the filing of such statement.

(e) Any person who has ceased to be a director or officer of an issuer which has equity securities registered pursuant to Section 12 of the Act, or who is a director or officer of an issuer at the time it ceased to have any equity securities so registered, shall file a statement on Form 4 with respect to any change in his beneficial ownership of equity securities of such issuer which shall occur on or after the date on which he ceased to be such director or officer, or the date on which the issuer ceased to have any equity securities so registered, as the case may be, if such change shall occur within 6 months after any change in his beneficial ownership of such securities prior to such date. The statement on Form 4 shall be filed within 10 days after the end of the month in which the reported change in beneficial ownership occurs.

Rule 16a-2. Ownership of More Than 10 Percent of a Class of Equity Securities

(a) In determining, for the purpose of section 16(a) of the Act, whether a person is the beneficial owner, directly or indirectly, of more than 10 percent of any class of equity securities, such class shall be deemed to consist of the total amount of such class outstanding, exclusive of any securities of such class held by or for the account of the issuer or a subsidiary of the issuer. However, for the purpose of determining percentage ownership of voting trust certificates or certificates of deposit for equity securities, the class of voting trust certificates or certificates of deposit shall be deemed to consist of the amount of voting trust certificates or certificates of deposit issuable with respect to the total amount of outstanding equity securities of the class which may be deposited under the voting trust agreement or deposit agreement in question, whether or not all of such outstanding securities have been so deposited. For the purpose of this rule a person acting in good faith may rely on the information contained in the latest consolidated financial statement in a registration statement or annual report filed with the Commission under the Act with respect to the amount of securities of the class outstanding or in the case of voting trust certificates or certificates of deposit the amount thereof issuable.

(b) In determining for the purpose of section 16(a) of the Act whether a person is the beneficial owner, directly or indirectly, of more than 10 percent of any class of equity securities, such person shall be deemed to be the beneficial owner of securities of such class which such person has the right to acquire through the exercise of presently exercisable options, warrants or rights or through the conversion of presently convertible securities. The securities subject to such options, warrants, rights or conversion privileges held by a person shall be deemed to be outstanding for the purpose of computing, in accordance with paragraph (*a*), the percentage of outstanding securities of the class owned by such person but shall not be deemed outstanding for the purpose of computing the percentage of the class owned by any other person. This paragraph shall not be construed to relieve any person of any duty to comply with section 16(a) of the Act with respect to any equity securities consisting of options, warrants, rights or convertible securities which are otherwise subject as a class to that section.

Rule 16a-3. Disclaimer of Beneficial Ownership

Any person filing a statement may expressly declare therein that the filing of such statement shall not be construed as an admission that such person is, for the purpose of section 16 of the Act, the beneficial owner of any equity securities covered by the statement.

Rule 16a-4. Exemptions From Sections 16(a) and 16(b) of the Act

(a) During the period of 12 months following their appointment and qualification, securities held by the following persons shall be exempt from sections 16(a) and 16(b) of the act:

(1) Executors or administrators of the estate of a decedent;

(2) Guardians or committees for an incompetent; and

(3) Receivers, trustees in bankruptcy, assignees for the benefit of creditors, conservators, liquidating agents, and other similar persons duly authorized by law to administer the estate or assets of other persons.

(b) After the 12-month period following their appointment or qualification the foregoing persons shall be required to file reports with respect to the securities held by the estates which they administer under section 16(a) and shall be liable for profits realized from trading in such securities pursuant to section 16(b) only when the estate being administered is a beneficial owner of more than 10 percent of any class of equity security (other than an otherwise exempted security) which is registered pursuant to section 12 of the act.

(c) Securities reacquired by or for the account of an issuer and held by it for its account shall be exempt from sections 16(a) and 16(b) during the time they are held by the issuer.

(d) Securities reacquired by or for account of the issuer and held by it or for its account.

* * *

Rule 16a-6. Certain Transactions Subject to Section 16(a)

(a) The granting, acquisition or disposition of any presently exercisable put, call, option, or other right or obligation to buy securities from, or sell securities to, another person, or any expiration or cancellation thereof, shall be deemed to effect such a change in the beneficial ownership of the securities to which the right or obligation relates as to require the filing of a statement pursuant to section 16(a) of the Act reflecting such change in beneficial ownership.

Notes. 1. If any such right or obligation is not initially exercisable, the granting and acquisition thereof shall be reported in a statement filed for the month in which it became exercisable, unless the filing of such statement is otherwise not required.

2. The right of a pledgee or borrower of securities to sell the pledged or borrowed securities is not an option or right to sell securities within the meaning of this section. However, the sale of the pledged or borrowed securities by the pledgee or borrower shall be reported by the pledgor or lender.

3. The right to acquire securities, or the obligation to dispose of securities, in connection with a merger or consolidation involving the issuer of the securities is not a right or obligation to buy or sell securities within the meaning of this section.

(b) For the purpose of section 16(a) of the Act both the grantor and the holder of any presently exercisable put, call, option, or other right or obligation to buy or sell securities shall be deemed to be beneficial owners of the securities subject to such right or obligation until it is exercised or canceled or expires.

(c) Notwithstanding the foregoing, a statement need not be filed pursuant to section 16(a) of the Act.

(1) By any person with respect to the acquisition, expiration, surrender to the issuer, or cancellation of any non-transferable stock option or stock appreciation right granted by the issuer of the securities to which the option or right relates pursuant to a plan which meets the conditions specified in Rule 16b-3(a), (b), (c), (d) and (e) of this chapter, or

(2) By any issuer with respect to any put, call, option or other right or obligation to buy or sell securities of which it is the issuer. As used in this paragraph (c), the term "plan" shall have the meaning assigned to it in paragraph (d) of Rule 16b-3.

Note. An option, otherwise nontransferable, is deemed to be nontransferable even though it may be disposed of by will or by descent and distribution upon the death of the holder.

(d) Nothing in this section shall be deemed to exempt any person from the duty to file the statements required upon the exercise of any put, call, option or other right or obligation to buy or sell securities.

* * *

Rule 16a-9. Exemption for Small Transactions

(*a*) Any acquisition of securities shall be exempt from section 16(a) where:

(1) The person effecting the acquisition does not within 6 months thereafter effect any disposition, otherwise than by way of gift, of securities of the same class, and

(2) The person effecting such acquisition does not participate in acquisitions or in dispositions of securities of the same class having a total market value in excess of $10,000 for any 6 months period during which the acquisition occurs.

(*b*) Any acquisition or disposition of securities by way of gift, where the total amount of such gifts does not exceed $10,000 in market value for any 6 months period, shall be exempt from section 16(a) and may be excluded from the computations prescribed in paragraph (*a*)(2).

(*c*) Any person exempted by paragraphs (*a*) or (*b*) of this rule shall include in the first report filed by him after a transaction within the exemption a statement showing his acquisitions and dispositions for each 6 months period or portion thereof which has elapsed since his last filing.

Rule 16a-10. Exemption From Section 16(b) of Transactions Which Need Not Be Reported Under Section 16(a)

Any transaction which has been or shall be exempted by the Commission from the requirements of section 16(a) shall, insofar as it is otherwise subject to the provisions of section 16(b), be likewise exempted from section 16(b).

* * *

EXEMPTION OF CERTAIN TRANSACTIONS FROM SECTION 16(b)

Rule 16b-1. Exemption From Section 16(b) of Certain Transactions by Registered Investment Companies

Any transaction of purchase and sale, or sale and purchase, of a security shall be exempt from the operation of section 16(b) of the act, as not comprehended within the purpose of that section, if the transaction is effected by an investment company registered under the Investment Company Act of 1940 and both the purchase and sale of such security have been exempted from the provisions of section 17(a) of the Investment Company Act of 1940 by an order of the Commission entered pursuant to section 17(b) of the act.

Rule 16b-2. Exemption From Section 16(b) of Certain Transactions Effected in Connection With a Distribution

(a) Any transaction of purchase and sale, or sale and purchase, of a security which is effected in connection with the distribution of a substantial block of securities shall be exempt from the provisions of section 16(b) of the Act, to the extent specified in this rule, as not comprehended within the purpose of said section, upon the following conditions:

(1) The person effecting the transaction is engaged in the business of distributing securities and is participating in good faith, in the ordinary course

of such business, in the distribution of such block of securities;

(2) The security involved in the transaction is (A) a part of such block of securities and is acquired by the person effecting the transaction, with a view to the distribution thereof, from the issuer or other person on whose behalf such securities are being distributed or from a person who is participating in good faith in the distribution of such block of securities or (B) a security purchased in good faith by or for the account of the person effecting the transaction for the purpose of stabilizing the market price of securities of the class being distributed or to cover an over-allotment or other short position created in connection with such distribution; and

(3) Other persons not within the purview of section 16(b) of the Act are participating in the distribution of such block of securities on terms at least as favorable as those on which such person is participating and to an extent at least equal to the aggregate participation of all persons exempted from the provisions of section 16(b) of the Act by this rule. However, the performance of the functions of manager of a distributing group and the receipt of a bona fide payment for performing such functions shall not preclude an exemption which would otherwise be available under this rule.

(b) The exemption of a transaction pursuant to this rule with respect to the participation therein of one party thereto shall not render such transaction exempt with respect to participation of any other party therein unless such other party also meets the conditions of this rule.

Rule 16b-3. Exemption From Section 16(b) of Certain Transactions Occurring Under Employee Benefit Plans

The following transactions by a director or officer shall be exempt from the operation of section 16(b) of the Act if they occur pursuant to a plan which satisfies the conditions of this rule: the acquisition of shares of stock, except that stock acquired upon the exercise of an option, warrant or right shall be exempt only to the extent indicated in the final clause of this sentence; the acquisition, expiration, cancellation or surrender to the issuer of a stock option or stock appreciation right; the surrender or delivery to the issuer of shares of its stock as payment for the exercise of a stock option for shares of the same class; and the acquisition upon the exercise of a stock option of shares of stock equal to the number of shares of the same class surrendered or delivered to the issuer as payment for the exercise of the option. The conditions of this rule that a plan must satisfy in order for the above transactions to be exempt are as follows:

(a) *Approval by security holders.* The plan has been approved, directly or indirectly, (1) by the affirmative votes of the holders of a majority of the securities of the issuer present, or represented, and entitled to vote at a meeting duly held in accordance with the applicable laws of the state or other jurisdiction in which the issuer was incorporated, or (2) by the written consent of the holders of a majority of the securities of the issuer entitled to vote: *Provided, however,* That if such vote or written consent was not solicited substantially in accordance with the rules and regulations, if any, in effect under section 14(a) of the Act at the time of such vote or written consent, the issuer shall furnish in writing to the holders of record of the securities entitled to vote for the plan substantially the same information concerning the plan which would be required by the rules and regulations in effect under section 14(a) of the Act at the time such information is furnished, if proxies to be voted with respect to the approval or disapproval of the plan were then being solicited, on or prior to the date of the first annual meeting of security holders held subsequent to the later of (i) the first registration of an equity security under section 12 of the Act or (ii) the acquisition of an equity security for which exemption is claimed. Such written information may be furnished by mail to the last known address of the security holders of record within 30 days prior to the date of mailing. Four copies of such written information shall be filed with, or mailed for filing to, the Commission not later than the date on which it is first sent or given to security holders of the issuer. For the purposes of this paragraph, the term "issuer" includes a predecessor corporation if the plan or obligations to participate thereunder were assumed by the issuer in connection with the succession. In addition, any amendment to the plan shall be similarly approved if the amendment would:

(A) Materially increase the benefits accruing to participants under the plan;

(B) Materially increase the number of securities which may be issued under the plan; or

(C) Materially modify the requirements as to eligibility for participation in the plan.

(b) *Disinterested administrators.* If the selection of any director or officer of the issuer to whom stock may be allocated or to whom stock options or stock appreciation rights may be granted pursuant to the plan, or the determination of the number of maximum number of shares of stock which may be allocated to any such director or officer or which may be covered by stock options or stock appreciation rights granted to any such director or officer pursuant to the plan is subject to the discretion of any person, then such discretion shall be exercised only as follows:

* * *

(e) *Cash Settlements of Stock Appreciation Rights.* Any transaction involving the exercise and cancellation of a stock appreciation right issued pursuant to a plan (whether or not the transaction also involves the related surrender and cancellation of a stock option), and the receipt of cash in complete or partial settlement of that right, shall be exempt from the operation of section 16(b) of the Act, as not comprehended within the purpose of that section, if all the following conditions are met:

(1) *Information about the issuer.* (i) The issuer of the stock appreciation right has been subject to the reporting requirements of section 13 of the Act for at least a year prior to the transaction and has filed all reports and statements required to be filed pursuant to that section during that year.

(ii) The issuer of the stock appreciation right on a regular basis does release for publication quarterly and annual summary statements of sales and earnings. This condition shall be deemed satisfied if the specified financial data appears (A) on a wire service, (B) in a financial news service, (C) in a newspaper of general circulation, or (D) is otherwise made publicly available.

(2) *Limitation on the right and any related option.* Neither the stock appreciation right nor any related stock option shall have been exercised during the first six months of their respective terms, except that this limitation shall not apply in the event death or disability of the grantee occurs prior to the expiration of the six-month period.

(3) *Administration of the plan.* (i) The plan shall be administered by either the board of directors, a majority of which are disinterested persons and a majority of the directors acting on plan matters are disinterested persons, or by a committee or three or more persons, all of whom are disinterested persons;

(ii) The board or committee shall have sole discretion either;

(A) To determine the form in which payment of the right will be made (i.e., cash, securities, or any combination thereof), or

(B) To consent to or disapprove the election of the participant to receive cash in full or partial settlement of the right. Such consent or disapproval may be given at any time after the election to which it relates.

(iii) Any election by the participant to receive cash in full or partial settlement of the stock appreciation right, as well as any exercise by him of his stock appreciation right for such cash, shall be made during the period beginning on the third business day following the date of release of the financial data specified in paragraph (e)(1)(ii) of this section and ending on the twelfth business day following such date. This paragraph (e)(3)(iii), however, shall not apply to any exercise by the participant of a stock appreciation right for cash where the date of exercise:

(A) Is automatic or fixed in advance under the plan;

(B) Is at least six months beyond the date of grant of the stock appreciation right; and

(C) Is outside the control of the participant.

(4) *Compliance with other conditions of Rule 16b–3.* The plan under which the stock appreciation rights and any related options are granted shall meet the conditions specified above in Rule 16b–3(a), (b), (c) and (d).

(5) *Limit of the exemption.* Nothing in this paragraph (e) provides an exemption from section 16(b) for the acquisition of stock upon the exercise of a stock appreciation right or a stock option.

* * *

Rule 16b–6. Exemption of Long-Term Profits Incident to Sales Within Six Months of the Exercise of an Option

(a) To the extent specified in paragraph (*b*) of this rule the Commission hereby exempts as not comprehended within the purposes of section 16(b) of the Act any transaction or transactions involving the purchase and sale or sale and purchase of any equity security where such purchase is pursuant to the exercise of an option or similar right either (1) acquired more than 6 months before its exercise, or (2) acquired pursuant to the terms of an employment contract entered into more than 6 months before its exercise.

(b) In respect of transactions specified in paragraph (*a*) the profits inuring to the issuer shall not exceed the difference between the proceeds of sale and the lowest market price of any security of the same class within 6 months before or after the date of sale. Nothing in this rule shall be deemed to enlarge the amount of profit which would inure to the issuer in the absence of this rule.

(c) The Commission also hereby exempts, as not comprehended within the purposes of section 16(b) of the Act, the disposition of a security, purchased in a transaction specified in paragraph (*a*), pursuant to a plan or agreement for merger or consolidation, or reclassification of the issuers' securities, or for the exchange of its securities for the securities of another person which has acquired its assets or which is in control, as defined in section 368(c) of the Internal Revenue Code of 1954, of a person which has acquired its assets, where the terms of such plan or agreement are binding upon all stockholders of the issuer except to the extent that dissenting stockholders may be entitled, under statutory provisions or provisions contained in the certificate of incorporation, to receive the appraised or fair value of their holdings.

(d) The exemptions provided by this rule shall not apply to any transaction made unlawful by section 16(c) of the Act or by any rules and regulations thereunder.

(e) The burden of establishing market price of a security for the purpose of this rule shall rest upon the person claiming the exemption.

(f) The exemption granted pursuant to this rule shall apply to any liability under section 16(b) existing at or after the effective date of this rule, but shall not be deemed to affect judgments rendered prior to that date.

Rule 16b-7. Exemption From Section 16(b) of Certain Acquisitions and Dispositions of Securities Pursuant to Mergers or Consolidations

(a) The following transactions shall be exempt from the provisions of section 16(b) as not comprehended within the purpose of said subsection:

(1) The acquisition of a security of a company, pursuant to a merger or consolidation, in exchange for a security of a company which, prior to said merger or consolidation, owned 85 percent or more of the equity securities of all other companies involved in the merger or consolidation except, in the case of consolidation, the resulting company;

(2) The disposition of a security, pursuant to a merger or consolidation of a company which, prior to said merger or consolidation, owned 85 percent or more of the equity securities of all other companies involved in the merger or consolidation except, in the case of consolidations, the resulting company;

(3) The acquisition of a security of a company, pursuant to a merger or consolidation, in exchange for a security of a company which, prior to said merger or consolidation, held over 85 percent of the combined assets of all the companies undergoing merger or consolidation, computed according to their book values prior to the merger or consolidation as determined by reference to their most recent available financial statements for a 12-month period prior to the merger or consolidation.

(4) The disposition of a security, pursuant to a merger or consolidation, of a company which, prior to said merger or consolidation, held over 85 percent of the combined assets of all the companies undergoing merger or consolidation, computed according to their book values prior to the merger or consolidation, as determined by reference to their most recent available financial statements for a 12-month period prior to the merger or consolidation.

(b) A merger within the meaning of this rule shall include the sale or purchase of substantially all the assets of one company by another in exchange for stock which is then distributed to the security holders of the company which sold its assets.

(c) Notwithstanding the foregoing, if an officer, director or stockholder shall make any purchase (other than a purchase exempted by this rule or any other rule under section 16(b) of the Act) of a security in any company involved in the merger or consolidation and any sale (other than a sale exempted by this rule or any other rule under section 16(b) of the Act) of a security in any other company involved in the merger or consolidation within any period of less than 6 months during which the merger or consolidation took place the exemption provided by this rule shall be unavailable to such officer, director, or stockholder to the extent of such purchase and sale.

* * *

Rule 16b–9. Exemption From Section 16(b) of Transactions Involving the Conversion of Equity Securities

(a) Any acquisition or disposition of an equity security involved in the conversion of an equity security which, by its terms or pursuant to the terms of the corporate charter or other governing instruments, is convertible immediately or after a stated period of time into another equity security of the same issuer, shall be exempt from the operation of section 16(b) of the Act: *Provided, however,* That this rule shall not apply to the extent that there shall have been either (i) a purchase of any equity security of the class convertible (including any acquisition of or change in a conversion privilege) and a sale of any equity security of the class issuable upon conversion, or (ii) a sale of any equity security of the class convertible and any purchase of any equity security issuable upon conversion (otherwise than in a transaction involved in such conversion or in a transaction exempted by any other rule under section 16(b)) within a period of less than 6 months which includes the date of conversion.

(b) For the purpose of this rule, an equity security shall not be deemed to be acquired or disposed of upon conversion of an equity security if the terms of the equity security converted require the payment or entail the receipt, in connection with such conversion, of cash or other property (other than equity securities involved in the conversion) equal in value at the time of conversion to more than 15 percent of the value of the equity security issued upon conversion.

(c) For the purpose of this rule, an equity security shall be deemed convertible if it is convertible at the option of the holder or of some other person or by operation of the terms of the security or the governing instruments.

Rule 16b–11. Exemption From Section 16(b) of Certain Transactions Involving the Sale of Subscription Rights

(a) Any sale of a subscription right to acquire any subject security of the same issuer shall be exempt from the provision of section 16(b) (of the act), to the extent prescribed in this section, as not comprehended within the purpose of said section of the act, if:

(1) Such subscription right is acquired, directly or indirectly, from the issuer without the payment of consideration;

(2) Such subscription right by its terms expires within 45 days after the issuance thereof;

(3) Such subscription right by its term is issued on a pro rata basis to all holders of the beneficiary security of the issuer; and

(4) A registration statement under the Securities Act of 1933 (15 U.S.C. 77) is in effect as to each subject security or the applicable terms of any exemption from such registration have been met in respect to each subject security.

(b) When used within this section the following terms shall have the meaning indicated.

(1) The term "subscription right" means any warrant or certificate evidencing a right to subscribe to or otherwise acquire an equity security.

(2) The term "beneficiary security" means a security registered pursuant to section 12 (of the act) to the holders of which a subscription right is granted.

(3) The term "subject security" means a security which is the subject of a subscription right.

(c) Notwithstanding anything contained herein to the contrary, if a person purchases subscription rights for cash or other consideration, then a sale by such person of subscription rights otherwise exempted by this section will not be so exempted to the extent of such purchases within the 6-month period preceding or following such sale.

* * *

*

C. SELECTED FORMS AND SCHEDULES

1. UNDER SECURITIES ACT OF 1933

FORM S–1

Registration Statement Under The Securities Act of 1933

GENERAL INSTRUCTIONS

I. Eligibility Requirements for Use of Form S–1

This Form shall be used for the registration under the Securities Act of 1933 ("Securities Act") of securities of all registrants for which no other form is authorized or prescribed, except that this Form shall not be used for securities of foreign governments or political sub-divisions thereof.

II. Application of General Rules and Regulations

A. Attention is directed to the General Rules and Regulations under the Securities Act, particularly those comprising Regulation C thereunder. That Regulation contains general requirements regarding the preparation and filing of the registration statement.

B. Attention is directed to Regulation S–K for the requirements applicable to the content of the nonfinancial statement portions of registration statements under the Securities Act. Where this Form directs the registrant to furnish information required by Regulation S–K and the item of Regulation S–K so provides, information need only be furnished to the extent appropriate.

III. Exchange Offers

If any of the securities being registered are to be offered in exchange for securities of any other issuer the prospectus shall also include the information which would be required by Item 11 if the securities of such other issuer were registered on this Form. There shall also be included the information concerning such securities of such other issuer which would be called for by Item 9 if such securities were being registered. In connection with this instruction, reference is made to Rule 409.

PART I. INFORMATION REQUIRED IN PROSPECTUS

Item 1. Forepart of the Registration Statement and Outside Front Cover Page of Prospectus

Set forth in the forepart of the registration statement and on the outside front cover page of the prospectus the information required by Item 501 of Regulation S–K.

Item 2. Inside Front and Outside Back Cover Pages of Prospectus

Set forth on the inside front cover page of the prospectus or, where permitted, on the outside back cover page, the information required by Item 502 of Regulation S–K.

Item 3. Summary Information, Risk Factors and Ratio of Earnings to Fixed Charges

Furnish the information required by Item 503 of Regulation S–K.

Item 4. Use of Proceeds

Furnish the information required by Item 504 of Regulation S–K.

Item 5. Determination of Offering Price

Furnish the information required by Item 505 of Regulation S–K.

Item 6. Dilution

Furnish the information required by Item 506 of Regulation S–K.

Item 7. Selling Security Holders

Furnish the information required by Item 507 of Regulation S–K.

Item 8. Plan of Distribution

Furnish the information required by Item 508 of Regulation S–K.

Item 9. Description of Securities to be Registered

Furnish the information required by Item 202 of Regulation S–K.

Item 10. Interests of Named Experts and Counsel

Furnish the information required by Item 509 of Regulation S–K.

Item 11. Information With Respect to the Registrant

Furnish the following information with respect to the registrant:

(a) Information required by Item 101 of Regulation S–K, description of business;

(b) Information required by Item 102 of Regulation S–K, description of property;

(c) Information required by Item 103 of Regulation S–K, legal proceedings;

(d) Where common equity securities are being offered, information required by Item 201 of Regulation S–K, market price of and dividends on the registrant's common equity and related stockholder matters;

(e) Financial statements meeting the requirements of Regulation S–K.

(f) Information required by Item 301 of Regulation S–K, selected financial data;

(g) Information required by Item 302 of Regulation S–K, supplementary financial information;

(h) Information required by Item 303 of Regulation S–K, management's discussion and analysis of financial condition and results of operations;

(i) Information required by Item 304 of Regulation S–K, changes in and disagreements with accountants on accounting and financial disclosure;

(j) Information required by Item 401 of Regulation S–K, directors and executive officers;

(k) Information required by Item 402 of Regulation S–K, executive compensation;

(*l*) Information required by Item 403 of Regulation S–K, security ownership of certain beneficial owners and management; and

(m) Information required by Item 404 of Regulation S–K, certain relationships and related transactions.

Item 12. Disclosure of Commission Position on Indemnification for Securities Act Liabilities

Furnish the information required by Item 510 of Regulation S–K.

PART II. INFORMATION NOT REQUIRED IN PROSPECTUS

Item 13. Other Expenses of Issuance and Distribution

Furnish the information required by Item 511 of Regulation S–K.

Item 14. Indemnification of Directors and Officers

Furnish the information required by Item 702 of Regulation S–K.

Item 15. Recent Sales of Unregistered Securities

Furnish the information required by Item 701 of Regulation S–K.

Item 16. Exhibits and Financial Statement Schedules

(a) Subject to the rules regarding incorporation by reference, furnish the exhibits as required by Item 601 of Regulation S–K.

(b) Furnish the financial statement schedules required by Regulation S–K and Item 11(e) of this Form. These schedules shall be lettered or numbered in the manner described for exhibits in paragraph (a).

Item 17. Undertakings

Furnish the undertakings required by Item 512 of Regulation S–K.

FORM S–2

Registration Statement Under the Securities Act of 1933 of Certain Issuers

GENERAL INSTRUCTIONS

I. Eligibility Requirements for Use of Form S–2

Any registrant which meets the following conditions may use this Form for registration of securities under the Securities Act of 1933 ("Securities Act") which are offered or to be offered in any transaction other than an exchange offer for securities of another person:

A. The registrant is organized under the laws of the United States or any State or Territory or the District of Columbia and has its principal business operations in the United States or its territories.

B. The registrant has a class of securities registered pursuant to Section 12(b) of the Securities Exchange Act of 1934 ("Exchange Act") or has a class of equity securities registered pursuant to section 12(g) of the Exchange Act or is required to file reports pursuant to section 15(d) of the Exchange Act.

C. The registrant: (1) has been subject to the requirements of section 12 or 15(d) of the Exchange Act and has filed all the material required to be filed pursuant to section 13, 14 or 15(d) for a period of at least thirty-six calendar months immediately preceding the filing of the registration statement on this Form; and (2) has filed in a timely manner all reports required to be filed during the twelve calendar months and any portion of a month immediately preceding the filing of the registration statement * * *.

D. Neither the registrant nor any of its consolidated or unconsolidated subsidiaries have, since the end of their last fiscal year for which certified financial statements of the registrant and its consolidated subsidiaries were included in a report filed pursuant to section 13(a) or 15(d) of the Exchange Act: (a) failed to pay any dividend or sinking fund installment on preferred stock; or (b) defaulted (i) on any installment or installments on indebtedness for borrowed money, or (ii) on any rental on one or more long term leases, which defaults in the aggregate are material to the financial position of the registrant and its consolidated and unconsolidated subsidiaries, taken as a whole.

PART I. INFORMATION REQUIRED IN PROSPECTUS

Item 1. Forepart of the Registration Statement and Outside Front Cover Page of Prospectus

Set forth in the forepart of the registration statement and on the outside front cover page of the prospectus the information required by Item 501 of Regulation S–K.

Item 2. Inside Front and Outside Back Cover Pages of Prospectus

Set forth on the inside front cover page of the prospectus or, where permitted, on the outside back cover page, the information required by Item 502 of Regulation S–K.

Item 3. Summary Information, Risk Factors and Ratio of Earnings to Fixed Charges

Furnish the information required by Item 503 of Regulation S–K.

Item 4. Use of Proceeds

Furnish the information required by Item 504 of Regulation S–K.

Item 5. Determination of Offering Price

Furnish the information required by Item 505 of Regulation S–K.

Item 6. Dilution

Furnish the information required by Item 506 of Regulation S–K.

Item 7. Selling Security Holders

Furnish the information required by Item 507 of Regulation S–K.

Item 8. Plan of Distribution

Furnish the information required by Item 508 of Regulation S–K.

Item 9. Description of Securities to be Registered

Furnish the information required by Item 202 of Regulation S–K.

Item 10. Interests of Named Experts and Counsel

Furnish the information required by Item 509 of Regulation S–K.

Item 11. Information with Respect to the Registrant

Furnish the information required by either paragraph (a) or paragraph (b) of this item. * * *

(a) If the registrant elects to deliver this prospectus together with its latest annual report to security holders, which at the time of original preparation met the requirements of either Rule 14a–3 or Rule 14c–3, or a complete and legible facsimile of its latest annual report to security holders:

(1) Indicate that the prospectus is accompanied by the registrant's latest annual report to security holders.

(2) Provide financial and other information with respect to the registrant in the form required by Part I of Form 10–Q as of the end of the most recent fiscal quarter which ended after the end of the latest fiscal year for which certified financial statements were included in the latest report to security holders and more than forty-five days prior to the effective date of this registration statement (or as of a more recent date) by one of the following means:

(i) Including such information in the prospectus; or

(ii) Providing without charge to each person to whom a prospectus is delivered a copy of the registrant's latest Form 10–Q; or

(iii) Providing without charge to each person to whom a prospectus is delivered a copy of the registrant's latest quarterly report which was delivered to its shareholders and which included the required financial information.

(3) If not reflected in the registrant's latest annual report to security holders, provide the information required by Rule 3.05 and Article 11 of Regulation S–K.

(4) Describe any and all material changes in the registrant's affairs which have occurred since the end of the latest fiscal year for which certified financial statements were included in the latest annual report to security holders and which were not described in a Form 10–Q or quarterly report delivered with the prospectus in accordance with paragraph (a)(2)(ii) or (iii) of this item.

Instruction. Where the registrant elects to deliver its annual report to security holders, Form 10–Q or quarterly report together with the prospectus, each document must be delivered with the preliminary prospectus, but need not be redelivered with the final prospectus if the recipient has already been given the document along with the preliminary prospectus.

(b) If the registrant does not elect to deliver its latest annual report to security holders:

(1) Furnish a brief description of the business done by the registrant and its subsidiaries during the most recent fiscal year as required by Rule 14a–3 to be included in annual reports to security holders. The description also should take into account changes in its business which have occurred between the end of the last fiscal year and the effective date of the registration statement.

(2) Include financial statements and information as required by Rule 14a-3(b)(1) to be included in annual reports to security holders as well as: (i) The interim financial information required by Rule 10-01 of Regulation S-K for a filing on Form 10-Q; (ii) any information required by Rules 3.05 and Article 11 of Regulation S-K; and (iii) any financial information required because of a material disposition of assets outside the normal course of business. * * *

(3) Furnish information relating to industry segments, classes or similar products or services, foreign and domestic operations, and export sales required by paragraphs (b), (c)(1)(i) and (d) of Item 101 of Regulation S-K.

(4) Where common equity securities are being offered, furnish information required by Item 201 of Regulation S-K, market price and dividends on the registrant's common stock and related stockholder matters.

(5) Furnish selected financial data required by Item 301 of Regulation S-K.

(6) Furnish supplementary financial information required by Item 302 of Regulation S-K.

(7) Furnish management's discussion and analysis of the registrant's financial condition and results of operations required by Item 303 of Regulation S-K.

(8) Furnish information concerning changes in and disagreements with accountants on accounting and financial disclosure required by Item 304 of Regulation S-K.

Item 12. Incorporation of Certain Information by Reference

(a) The documents listed in (1), (2), and, if applicable, the portions of the documents listed in (3) and (4) below shall be specifically incorporated by reference into the prospectus, by means of a statement to that effect in the prospectus listing all such documents. In lieu of incorporating portions of the documents listed in (3) and (4) below, the registrant may incorporate by reference its entire annual or quarterly report to security holders.

(1) The registrant's latest Form 10-K filed pursuant to Section 13(a) or 15(d) of the Exchange Act which contains certified financial statements for the registrant's latest fiscal year for which a Form 10-K was required to have been filed.

(2) All other reports filed pursuant to Section 13(a) or 15(d) of the Exchange Act since the end of the fiscal year covered by the annual report referred to in (1) above.

(3) If the registrant elects to deliver its latest annual report to security holders, pursuant to Item 11(a)(1) of this Form:

(i) description of business furnished in accordance with the provisions of Rule 14a-3(b)(6) under the Exchange Act;

(ii) financial statements and information furnished in accordance with the provisions of Rule 14a-3(b)(1);

(iii) information relating to industry segments, classes of similar products or services, foreign and domestic operations, and export sales furnished as required by paragraphs (b), (c)(1)(i) and (d) of Item 101 of Regulation S-K;

(iv) where common equity securities are being offered, market price and dividends on the registrant's common equity and related stockholder matters furnished as required by Item 201 of Regulation S-K;

(v) selected financial data furnished as required by Item 301 of Regulation S-K;

(vi) supplementary financial information furnished as required by Item 302 of Regulation S-K;

(vii) management's discussion and analysis of financial condition and results of operations furnished as required by Item 303 of Regulation S-K; and

(viii) information concerning disagreements with accountants on accounting and financial disclosure furnished as required by Item 304 of Regulation S-K;

(4) If the registrant elects, pursuant to Item 11(a)(2)(iii) of this Form, to provide a copy of its latest quarterly report which was delivered to shareholders, the financial information equivalent to that required to be presented in Part I of Form 10-Q.

Instruction. Attention is directed to Rule 439 regarding consent to use of material incorporated by reference.

(b) The registrant may also state, if it so chooses, that specifically described portions of its annual or quarterly report to security holders, other than those portions required to be incorporated by reference pursuant to paragraphs (a)(3) and (4) above, are not part of the registration statement. In such case, the description of portions which are not incorporated by reference or which are excluded shall be made with clarity and in reasonable detail.

Item 13. Disclosure of Commission Position on Indemnification for Securities Act Liabilities

Furnish the information required by Item 510 of Regulation S–K.

PART II. INFORMATION NOT REQUIRED IN PROSPECTUS

Item 14. Other Expenses of Issuance and Distribution

Furnish the information required by Item 511 of Regulation S–K.

Item 15. Indemnification of Directors and Officers

Furnish the information required by Item 702 of Regulation S–K.

Item 16. Exhibits

Subject to the rules regarding incorporation by reference, furnish the exhibits required by Item 601 of Regulation S–K.

Item 17. Undertakings

Furnish the undertakings required by Item 312 of Regulation S–K.

FORM S–3

Registration Statement Under the Securities Act of 1933 of Securities of Certain Issuers Offered Pursuant to Certain Types of Transactions

GENERAL INSTRUCTIONS

I. Eligibility Requirements for Use of Form S–3.

This instruction sets forth registrant requirements and transaction requirements for the use of Form S–3. Any registrant which meets the Requirements of I.A. below ("Registrant Requirements") may use this Form for the registration of securities under the Securities Act of 1933 ("Securities Act") which are offered in any transaction specified in I.B. below ("Transaction Requirement") provided that the requirements applicable to the specified transaction are met.

A. Registrant Requirements.

All registrants must meet the following conditions in order to use this Form S–3 for registration under the Securities Act of securities offered in the transactions specified in I.B. below:

1. The registrant is organized under the laws of the United States or any State or Territory or the District of Columbia and has its principal business operations in the United States or its territories.

2. The registrant has a class of securities registered pursuant to Section 12(b) of the Securities Exchange Act of 1934 ("Exchange Act") or a class of equity securities registered pursuant to Section 12(g) of the Exchange Act or is required to file reports pursuant to Section 15(d) of the Exchange Act.

3. The registrant: (a) has been subject to the requirements of Section 12 or 15(d) of the Exchange Act and has filed all the material required to be filed pursuant to Sections 13, 14 or 15(d) for a period of at least thirty-six calendar months immediately preceding the filing of the registration statement on this Form; and (b) has filed in a timely manner all reports required to be filed during the twelve calendar months and any portion of a month immediately preceding the filing of the registration statement and, if the registrant has used (during the twelve calendar months and any portion of a month immediately preceding the filing of the registra-

tion statement) Rule 12b-25(b) under the Exchange Act with respect to a report or a portion of a report, that report or portion thereof has actually been filed within the time period prescribed by the Rule.

4. Neither the registrant nor any of its consolidated or unconsolidated subsidiaries have, since the end of the last fiscal year for which certified financial statements of the registrant and its consolidated subsidiaries were included in a report filed pursuant to Section 13(a) or 15(d) of the Exchange Act: (a) failed to pay any dividend or sinking fund installment on preferred stock; or (b) defaulted (i) on any installment or installments on indebtedness for borrowed money, or (ii) on any rental on one or more long term leases, which defaults in the aggregate are material to the financial position of the registrant and its consolidated and unconsolidated subsidiaries, taken as a whole.

* * *

(B) Transaction Requirements.

Security offerings meeting any of the following conditions and made by registrants meeting the Registrant Requirements above may be registered on this Form:

1. **Primary And Secondary Offerings By Certain Registrants.** Securities to be offered for cash by or on behalf of a registrant, or outstanding securities to be offered for cash for the account of any person other than the registrant, including securities acquired by standby underwriters in connection with the call or redemption by the registrant of warrants or a class of convertible securities; *provided* that the aggregate market value of the voting stock held by non-affiliates of the registrant is $150 million or more, or alternatively, the aggregate market value of the voting stock held by non-affiliates of the registrant is $100 million or more and the registrant has had an annual trading volume of such stock of 3 million shares or more.

Instructions. The aggregate market value of the registrant's outstanding voting stock shall be computed by use of the price at which the stock was last sold, or the average of the bid and asked prices of such stock, as of a date within 60 days prior to the date of filing. Annual trading volume shall be the volume of shares traded in any continuous twelve month period ended within 60 days prior to the date of filing. See the definition of "affiliate" in Securities Act Rule 405.

2. **Primary Offerings of Certain Debt and Non-convertible Preferred Securities.** Non-convertible debt and preferred securities to be offered for cash by or on behalf of a registrant, provided such securities are "investment grade securities," as defined below. A non-convertible debt or preferred security is an "investment grade security" if, at the time of effectiveness of the registration statement, at least one nationally recognized statistical rating organization (as that term is used in Rule 15c3-1(c)(2)(vi)(F) under the Securities Exchange Act of 1934) has rated the security in one of its generic rating categories which signifies investment grade; typically, the four highest rating categories (within which there may be sub-categories or gradations indicating relative standing) signify investment grade.

3. **Transactions Involving Secondary Offerings.** Outstanding securities to be offered for the account of any person other than the issuer, including securities acquired by standby underwriters in connection with the call or redemption by the issuer of warrants or a class of convertible securities, if securities of the same class are listed and registered on a national securities exchange or are quoted on the automated quotation system of a national securities association.

* * *

PART I. INFORMATION REQUIRED IN PROSPECTUS

Item 1. Forepart of the Registration Statement and Outside Front Cover Page of Prospectus.

Set forth in the forepart of the registration statement and on the outside front cover page of the prospectus the information required by Item 501 of Regulation S-K.

Item 2. Inside Front and Outside Back Cover Pages of Prospectus.

Set forth on the inside front cover page of the prospectus or, where permitted, on the outside back cover page, the information required by Item 502 of Regulation S-K.

Item 3. Summary Information, Risk Factors and Ratio of Earnings to Fixed Charges.

Furnish the information required by Item 503 of Regulation S–K.

Item 4. Use of Proceeds.

Furnish the information required by Item 504 of Regulation S–K.

Item 5. Determination of Offering Price.

Furnish the information required by Item 505 of Regulation S–K.

Item 6. Dilution.

Furnish the information required by Item 506 of Regulation S–K.

Item 7. Selling Security Holders.

Furnish the information required by Item 507 of Regulation S–K.

Item 8. Plan of Distribution.

Furnish the information required by Item 508 of Regulation S–K.

Item 9. Description of Securities to be Registered.

Furnish the information required by Item 202 of Regulation S–K unless capital stock is to be registered and securities of the same class are registered pursuant to Section 12 of the Exchange Act.

Item 10. Interests of Named Experts and Counsel.

Furnish the information required by Item 509 of Regulation S–K.

Item 11. Material Changes.

(a) Describe any and all material changes in the registrant's affairs which have occurred since the end of the latest fiscal year for which certified financial statements were included in the latest annual report to security holders and which have not been described in a report on Form 10–Q or Form 8–K filed under the Exchange Act.

(b) Include in the prospectus, if not incorporated by reference therein from the reports filed under the Exchange Act specified in Item 12(a), a proxy or information statement filed pursuant to Section 14 of the Exchange Act, or a prospectus previously filed pursuant to Rule 424(b) or (c) under the Securities Act or a Form 8–K filed during either of the two preceding fiscal years; (i) information required by Rule 3.05 and Article 11 of Regulation S–X; (ii) restated financial statements prepared in accordance with Regulation S–X if there has been a change in accounting principles or a correction of an error where such change or correction requires a material retroactive restatement of financial statements; (iii) restated financial statements prepared in accordance with Regulation S–X where one or more business combinations accounted for by the pooling of interest method of accounting have been consummated subsequent to the most recent fiscal year and the acquired businesses, considered in the aggregate, are significant pursuant to Rule 11–01(b); or (iv) any financial information required because of a material disposition of assets outside the normal course of business.

Item 12. Incorporation of Certain Information by Reference.

(a) The documents listed in (1) and (2) below shall be specifically incorporated by reference into the prospectus, by means of a statement to that effect in the prospectus listing all such documents.

(1) the registrant's latest annual report on Form 10–K filed pursuant to Section 13(a) or 15(d) of the Exchange Act which contains financial statements for the registrant's latest fiscal year for which a Form 10–K was required to have been filed;

(2) all other reports filed pursuant to Section 13(a) or 15(d) of the Exchange Act since the end of the fiscal year covered by the annual report referred to in (1) above; and

(3) if capital stock is to be registered and securities of the same class are registered under Section 12, of the Exchange Act, the description of such class of securities which is contained in a registration statement filed under the Exchange Act, including any amendment or reports filed for the purpose of updating such description.

(b) The prospectus shall also state that all documents subsequently filed by the registrant pursuant to Sections 13(a), 13(c), 14 or 15(d) of the Exchange Act, prior to the termination of the offering, shall be deemed to be incorporated by reference into the prospectus.

Instruction. Attention is directed to Rule 439 regarding consent to use of material incorporated by reference.

Item 13. Disclosure of Commission Position on Indemnification for Securities Act Liabilities.

Furnish the information required by Item 510 of Regulation S-K.

PART II. INFORMATION NOT REQUIRED IN PROSPECTUS

Item 14. Other Expenses of Issuance and Distribution.

Furnish the information required by Item 511 of Regulation S-K.

Item 15. Indemnification of Directors and Officers.

Furnish the information required by Item 702 of Regulation S-K.

Item 16. Exhibits.

Subject to the rules regarding incorporation by reference, furnish the exhibits required by Item 601 of Regulation S-K.

Item 17. Undertakings.

Furnish the undertakings required by Item 512 of Regulation S-K.

FORM S-4

For Registration of Securities Issued in Business Combination Transactions

GENERAL INSTRUCTIONS

A. Rule as to Use of Form S-4.

1. This Form may be used for registration under the Securities Act of 1933 ("Securities Act") of securities to be issued (1) in a transaction of the type specified in paragraph (a) of Rule 145; (2) in a merger in which the applicable state law would not require the solicitation of the votes or consents of all of the security holders of the company being acquired; (3) in an exchange offer for securities of the issuer or another entity; (4) in a public reoffering or resale of any such securities acquired pursuant to this registration statement; or (5) in more than one of the kinds of transaction listed in (1) through (4) registered on one registration statement.

* * *

E. Compliance with Exchange Act Rules.

1. If a corporation or other person submits a proposal to its security holders entitled to vote on, or consent to, the transaction which the securities being registered are to be issued, and such person's submission to its security holders is subject to Regulation 14A or 14C under the Exchange Act, then the provisions of such Regulations shall apply in all respects to such person's submission, except that (a) the prospectus may be in the form of a proxy or information statement and may contain the information required by this Form in lieu of that required by Schedule 14A or 14C of Regulation 14A or 14C under the Exchange Act; and (b) copies of the preliminary and definitive proxy or information statement, form of proxy or other material filed as a part of the registration statement shall be deemed filed pursuant to such person's obligations under such Regulations.

2. If the proxy or information material sent to security holders is not subject to Regulation 14A or 14C, all such material shall be filed as a part of the registration statement at the time the statement is filed or as an amendment thereto prior to the use of such material.

3. If the transaction in which the securities being registered are to be issued is subject to Section 13(e), 14(d) or 14(e) of the Exchange Act, the provisions of those sections and the rules and regulations thereunder shall apply to the transaction in addition to the provisions of this Form.

* * *

PART I. INFORMATION REQUIRED IN THE PROSPECTUS

A. Information About The Transaction

Item 1. Forepart of Registration Statement and Outside Front Cover Page of Prospectus.

Set forth in the forepart of the registration statement and on the outside front cover page of the prospectus the information required by Item 501 of Regulation S–K.

Item 2. Inside Front and Outside Back Cover Pages of Prospectus.

Set forth on the inside front cover page of the prospectus or, where permitted, on the outside back cover page, the information required by Item 502 of Regulation S–K. In addition, on the inside front cover page include the following statement in bold face type, where applicable:

This prospectus incorporates documents by reference which are not presented herein or delivered herewith. These documents are available upon request from (name, address and telephone number to which a request is to be directed). In order to ensure timely delivery of the documents, any request should be made by (date five business days prior to the date on which the final investment decision must be made.)

Item 3. Risk Factors, Ratio of Earnings to Fixed Charges and Other Information.

Provide in the forepart of the prospectus a summary containing the information required by Item 503 of Regulation S–K and the following:

(a) The name, complete mailing address (including the Zip Code), and telephone number (including the area code) of the principal executive offices of the registrant and the company being acquired;

(b) A brief description of the general nature of the business conducted by the registrant and by the company being acquired;

(c) A brief description of the transaction in which the securities being registered are to be offered;

(d) The information required by Item 301 of Regulation S–K (selected financial data) for (i) the registrant; (ii) the company being acquired; and (iii) if material, the registrant, on a pro forma basis, giving effect to the transaction. To the extent the information is required to be presented in the prospectus pursuant to Items 12, 14, 16 or 17, it need not be repeated pursuant to this Item;

(e) In comparative columnar form, historical and pro forma per share data of the registrant and historical and equivalent pro forma per share data of the company being acquired for the following items:

(1) Book value per share as of the date financial data is presented pursuant to Item 301 of Regulation S–K (selected financial data);

(2) Cash dividends declared per share for the periods for which financial data is presented pursuant to Item 301 of Regulation S–K (selected financial data);

(3) Income (loss) per share from continuing operations for the periods for which financial data is presented pursuant to Item 301 of Regulation S–K (selected financial data).

* * *

(f) In comparative columnar form, the market value of securities of the company being acquired (on an historical and equivalent per share basis) and the market value of the securities of the registrant (on an historical basis) as of the date preceding public announcement of the proposed transaction, or, if no such public announcement was made, as of the day preceding the day the agreement with respect to the transaction was entered into;

(g) With respect to the registrant and the company being acquired, a brief statement comparing the percentage of outstanding shares entitled to vote held by directors, executive officers and their affiliates and the vote required for approval of the proposed transaction;

(h) A statement as to whether any federal or state regulatory requirements must be complied with or approval must be obtained in connection with the transaction, and if so, the status of such compliance or approval;

(i) A statement about whether or not dissenters' rights of appraisal exist, including a cross-reference to the information provided pursuant to Item 18 or 19 of this Form; and

(j) A brief statement about the tax consequences of the transaction, or if appropriate, consisting of a cross-reference to the information provided pursuant to Item 4 of this Form.

Item 4. Terms of the Transaction.

(a) Furnish a summary of the material features of the proposed transaction. The summary shall include, where applicable:

(1) A brief summary of the terms of the acquisition agreement;

(2) The reasons of the registrant and of the company being acquired for engaging in the transaction;

(3) The information required by Item 202 of Regulation S-K, description of registrant's securities, unless: (i) the registrant would meet the requirements for use of Form S-3, (ii) capital stock is to be registered and (iii) securities of the same class are registered under Section 12 of the Exchange Act and (i) listed for trading or admitted to unlisted trading privileges on a national securities exchange; or (ii) are securities for which bid and offer quotations are reported in an automated quotations system operated by a national securities association;

(4) An explanation of any material differences between the rights of security holders of the company being acquired and the rights of holders of the securities being offered;

(5) A brief statement as to the accounting treatment of the transaction; and

(6) The federal income tax consequences of the transaction.

(b) If a report, opinion or appraisal materially relating to the transaction has been received from an outside party, and such report, opinion or appraisal is referred to in the prospectus, furnish the same information as would be required by Item 9(b)(1) through (6) of Schedule 13E-3.

(c) Incorporate the acquisition agreement by reference into the prospectus by means of a statement to that effect.

Item 5. Pro Forma Financial Information.

Furnish financial information required by Article 11 of Regulation S-X with respect to this transaction.

* * *

Item 6. Material Contacts with the Company Being Acquired.

Describe any past, present or proposed material contracts, arrangements, understandings, relationships, negotiations or transactions during the periods for which financial statements are presented or incorporated by reference pursuant to Part I.B. or C. of this Form between the company being acquired or its affiliates and the registrant or its affiliates, such as those concerning: a merger, consolidation or acquisition; a tender offer or other acquisition of securities; an election of directors; or a sale or other transfer of a material amount of assets.

Item 7. Additional Information Required for Reoffering by Persons and Parties Deemed to Be Underwriters.

If any of the securities are to be reoffered to the public by any person or party who is deemed to be an underwriter thereof, furnish the following information in the prospectus, at the time it is being used for the reoffer of the securities to the extent it is not already furnished therein:

(a) The information required by Item 507 of Regulation S-K, selling security holders; and

(b) Information with respect to the consummation of the transaction pursuant to which the securities were acquired and any material change in the registrant's affairs subsequent to the transaction.

Item 8. Interests of Named Experts and Counsel.

Furnish the information required by Item 509 of Regulation S-K.

Item 9. Disclosure of Commission Position on Indemnification for Securities Act Liabilities.

Furnish the information required by Item 510 of Regulation S-K.

B. Information About The Registrant

Item 10. Information with Respect to S-3 Registrants.

If the registrant meets the requirements for use of Form S-3 and elects to furnish information in accordance with the provisions of this Item, furnish information as required below:

(a) Describe any and all material changes in the registrant's affairs that have occurred since the end of the latest fiscal year for which audited financial statements were included in the latest annual report to security holders and that have not been described in a report on Form 10–Q or Form 8–K filed under the Exchange Act.

* * *

Item 11. Incorporation of Certain Information by Reference.

If the registrant meets the requirements of Form S–3 and elects to furnish information in accordance with the provisions of Item 10 of this Form:

(a) Incorporate by reference into the prospectus, by means of a statement to that effect listing all documents so incorporated, the documents listed in paragraphs (1), (2) and, if applicable, (3) below.

(1) The registrant's latest annual report on Form 10–K filed pursuant to Section 13(a) or 15(d) of the Exchange Act which contains financial statements for the registrant's latest fiscal year for which a Form 10–K was required to be filed;

(2) All other reports filed pursuant to Section 13(a) or 15(d) of the Exchange Act since the end of the fiscal year covered by the annual report referred to in Item 11(a)(1) of this Form; * * *

Item 12. Information with Respect to S–2 or S–3 Registrants.

If the registrant meets the requirements for use of Form S–2 or S–3 and elects to comply with this Item, furnish the information required by either paragraph (a) or (b) of this Item. * * *

(a) If the registrant elects to deliver this prospectus together with its latest annual report to security holders, which at the time of original preparation met the requirements of either Rule 14a–3 or 14c–3, or a complete and legible facsimile of its latest annual report to security holders:

(1) Indicate that the prospectus is accompanied by the registrant's latest annual report to security holders.

(2) Provide financial and other information with respect to the registrant in the form required by Part I of Form 10–Q as of the end of the most recent fiscal quarter which ended after the end of the last fiscal year * * *

(4) Describe any and all material changes in the registrant's affairs that have occurred since the end of the latest fiscal year * * *

(b) If the registrant does not elect to deliver its latest annual report to security holders:

(1) Furnish a brief description of the business done by the registrant and its subsidiaries during the most recent fiscal year as required by Rule 14a–3 to be included in an annual report to security holders. The description also should take into account changes in the registrant's business that have occurred between the end of the latest fiscal year and the effective date of the registration statement.

(2) Include financial statements and information as required by Rule 14a–3(b)(1) (240.14a–3(b)(1) of this chapter) to be included in an annual report to security holders.

* * *

(3) Furnish the information required by the following:

(i) Item 101(b), (c)(1)(i) and (d) of Regulation S–K, industry segments, classes of similar products or services, foreign and domestic operations and export sales;

(ii) where common equity securities are being offered, Item 201 of Regulation S–K, market price of and dividends on the registrant's common equity and related stockholder matters;

(iii) Item 301 or Regulation S–K, selected financial data;

(iv) Item 302 of Regulation S–K, supplementary financial information;

(v) Item 303 of Regulation S–K, management's discussion and analysis of financial condition and results of operations; and

(vi) Item 304 of Regulation S–K, changes in and disagreements with accountants on accounting and financial disclosure.

Item 13. Incorporation of Certain Information by Reference.

If the registrant meets the requirements of Form S-2 or S-3 and elects to furnish information in accordance with the provisions of Item 12 of this Form:

(a) Incorporate by reference into the prospectus, by means of a statement to that effect in the prospectus listing all documents so incorporated, the documents listed in paragraphs (1) and (2) of this Item * * *

(b) The registrant also may state, if it so chooses, that specifically described portions of its annual or quarterly report to security holders, other than those portions required to be incorporated by reference pursuant to paragraphs (a)(3) and (4) of this Item, are not part of the registration statement. In such case, the description of portions that are not incorporated by reference or that are excluded shall be made with clarity and in reasonable detail.

Item 14. Information with Respect to Registrants Other Than S-3 or S-2 Registrants.

If the registrant does not meet the requirements for use of Form S-2 or S-3, or otherwise elects to comply with this Item in lieu of Item 10 or 12, furnish the information required by:

(a) Item 101 of Regulation S-K, description of business;

(b) Item 102 of Regulation S-K, description of property;

(c) Item 103 of Regulation S-K, legal proceedings;

(d) Where common equity securities are being issued, Item 201 of Regulation S-K, market price of and dividends on the registrant's common equity and related stockholder matters;

(e) Financial statements meeting the requirements of Regulation S-X, (schedules required by Regulation S-X shall be filed as "Financial Statement Schedules" pursuant to Item 21 of this Form), as well as financial information required by Rule 3-05 and Article 11 of Regulation S-X with respect to transactions other than that pursuant to which the securities being registered are to be issued;

(f) Item 301 of Regulation S-K, selected financial data;

(g) Item 302 of Regulation S-K, supplementary financial information;

(h) Item 303 of Regulation S-K management's discussion and analysis of financial condition and results of operations; and

(i) Item 304 of Regulation S-K, disagreements with accountants on accounting and financial disclosure.

C. Information About The Company Being Acquired

Item 15. Information with Respect to S-3 Companies.

If the company being acquired meets the requirements for use of Form S-3 and compliance with this Item is elected, furnish the information that would be required by Items 10 and 11 of this Form if securities of such company were being registered.

Item 16. Information with Respect to S-2 or S-3 Companies.

If the company being acquired meets the requirements for use of Form S-2 or S-3 and compliance with this Item is elected, furnish the information that would be required by Items 12 and 13 of this Form if securities of such company were being registered.

Item 17. Information with Respect to Companies Other Than S-3 or S-2 Companies.

If the company being acquired does not meet the requirements for use of Form S-2 or S-3, or compliance with this Item is otherwise elected in lieu of Item 15 or 16, furnish the information required by paragraph (a) or (b) of this Item, whichever is applicable.

(a) If the company being acquired is subject to the reporting requirements of Section 13(a) or 15(d) of the Exchange Act, or compliance with this subparagraph in lieu of subparagraph (b) of this Item is selected, furnish the information that would be required by Item 14 of this Form if the securities of such company were being registered; * * *

(b) If the company being acquired is not subject to the reporting requirements of either Section 13(a) or 15(d) of the Exchange Act; or, because of Section

12(i) of the Exchange Act, has not furnished an annual report to security holders pursuant to Rule 14a–3 or Rule 14c–3 for its latest fiscal year; furnish the information that would be required by the following if securities of such company were being registered:

(1) a brief description of the business done by the company which indicates the general nature and scope of the business;

(2) Item 201 of Regulation S–K, market price of and dividends on the registrant's common equity and related stockholder matters;

(3) Item 301 of Regulation S–K, selected financial data;

(4) Item 302 of Regulation S–K, supplementary financial information;

(5) Item 303 of Regulation S–K, management's discussion and analysis of financial condition and results of operations;

(6) Item 304(b) of Regulation S–K, changes in and disagreements with accountants on accounting and financial disclosure.

(7) financial statements as would have been required to be included in an annual report furnished to security holders pursuant to Rules 14a–3(b)(1) and (b)(2) or Rules 14c–3(a)(1) and (a)(2), had the company being acquired been required to prepare such a report; * * *

(8) the quarterly financial and other information as would have been required had the company being acquired been required to file Part I of Form 10–Q for the most recent quarter for which such a report would have been on file at the time the registration statement becomes effective or for a period ending as of a more recent date.

* * *

D. Voting and Management Information

Item 18. Information if Proxies, Consents or Authorizations are to be Solicited.

(a) If proxies, consents or authorizations are to be solicited, furnish the following information, except as provided by paragraph (b) of this Item:

(1) The information required by Item 1 of Schedule 14A, date, time and place information;

(2) The information required by Item 2 of Schedule 14A, revocability of proxy;

(3) The information required by Item 3 of Schedule 14A, dissenters' rights of appraisal;

(4) The information required by Item 4 of Schedule 14A, persons making the solicitation;

(5) With respect to both the registrant and the company being acquired, the information required by:

(i) Item 5 of Schedule 14A, interest of certain persons in matters to be acted upon; and

(ii) Item 6 of Schedule 14A, voting securities and principal holders thereof;

(6) The information required by Item 21 of Schedule 14A, vote required for approval; and

(7) With respect to each person who will serve as a director or an executive officer of the surviving or acquiring company, the information required by:

(i) Item 401 of Regulation S–K, directors and executive officers;

(ii) Item 402 of Regulation S–K, executive compensation; and

(iii) Item 404 of Regulation S–K, certain relationships and related transactions.

(b) If the registrant or the company being acquired meets the requirements for use of Form S–2 or S–3, any information required by paragraphs (a)(4)(ii) and (7) of this Item with respect to such company may be incorporated by reference from its latest annual report on Form 10–K.

Item 19. Information if Proxies, Consents or Authorizations are not to be Solicited or in an Exchange Offer.

(a) If the transaction is an exchange offer or if proxies, consents or authorizations are not to be solicited, furnish the following information, except as provided by paragraph (c) of this Item;

(1) The information required by Item 2 of Schedule 14C, statement that proxies are not to be solicited;

(2) The date, time and place of the meeting of security holders, unless such information is otherwise disclosed in material furnished to security holders with the prospectus;

(3) The information required by Item 3 of Schedule 14A, dissenters' rights of appraisal;

(4) With respect to both the registrant and the company being acquired, a brief description of any material interest, direct or indirect, by the security holdings or otherwise, of affiliates of the registrant and of the company being acquired, in the proposed transactions;

Instruction.

This subparagraph shall not apply to any interest arising from the ownership of securities of the registrant where the security of the registrant where the security holder receives no extra or special benefit not shared on a pro rata basis by all other holders of the same class.

(5) With respect to both the registrant and the company being acquired, the information required by Item 6 of Schedule 14A, voting securities and principal holders thereof;

(6) The information required by Item 21 of Schedule 14A, vote required for approval; and

(7) With respect to each person who will serve as a director or an executive officer of the surviving or acquiring company, the information required by:

(i) Item 401 of Regulation S–K, directors and executive officers;

(ii) Item 402 of Regulation S–K, executive compensation; and

(iii) Item 404 of Regulation S–K, certain relationships and related transactions.

(b) If the transaction is an exchange offer, furnish the information required by paragraphs (a)(4), (a)(5), (a)(6) and (a)(8) of this Item, except as provided by paragraph (c) of this Item.

(c) If the registrant or the company being acquired meets the requirements for use of Form S–2 or S–3, any information required by paragraphs (a)(5) and (18) of this Item with respect to such company may be incorporated by reference from its latest annual report on Form 10–K.

PART II. INFORMATION NOT REQUIRED IN PROSPECTUS

Item 20. Indemnification of Directors and Officers.

Furnish the information required by Item 702 of Regulation S–K.

Item 21. Exhibits and Financial Statement Schedules.

(a) Subject to the rules regarding incorporation by reference, furnish the exhibits as required by Item 601 of Regulation S–K.

* * *

FORM S–18

Registration Statement Under the Securities Act of 1933 for Certain Offerings Not in Excess of $5,000,000

GENERAL INSTRUCTIONS

I. Rule as to Use of Form S–18.

A. This form is to be used for the registration of securities not to exceed an aggregate offering price of $7.5 million which are to be sold for cash, installments for cash and/or cash assessments and assumptions by partners of partnership debt, by the registrant, or for the account of security holders in accordance with paragraph B, provided such registrant:

(1) Is organized under the laws of the United States or Canada or any State or Province thereof, and has or proposes to have its principal business operations in the United States, if a domestic issuer, or Canada or the United States if a Canadian issuer;

(2) Is not subject to the reporting provisions of the Securities Exchange Act of 1934 pursuant to Sections 12 or 15(d) of that Act;

(3) Is not an investment company;

(4) Is not an insurance company which is exempt from the provisions of Section 12 of the Securities Exchange Act of 1934 in reliance upon Section 12(g)(2)(G) thereof; and

(5) Is not a majority owned subsidiary of a registrant which does not meet the qualifications for use of the form, as specified herein.

B. This form may be used for the registration of securities to be sold for the account of any person other than the registrant, provided: (i) the aggregate offering price of such securities does not exceed $1.5 million and (ii) the aggregate offering price of such securities together with the aggregate offering price of any securities to be sold by the registrant does not exceed $7.5 million.

C. For purposes of computing the $7.5 million ceiling specified above, there shall be included in the aggregate offering price of the securities registered herein, the aggregate offering price of all securities sold: (i) by the registrant within one year prior to the commencement of the proposed offering in violation of Section 5(a) of the Securities Act; (ii) by the registrant within one year prior to the commencement of the proposed offering pursuant to a registration statement filed on Form S–18; and (iii) which would be deemed integrated with the proposed offering. In computing the $7.5 million ceiling, the aggregate price of all securities sold which fall in more than one of the above described categories need by counted only once.

D. Notwithstanding the provisions of paragraph (A)(2), a registrant which has had a prior offering on Form S–18 may, during the remainder of the fiscal year in which the prior registration statement was made effective, use the form to register additional securities until the offering limit as computed in paragraph C has been met.

II. Place of Filing

A. At the election of the registrant, all registration statements on Form S–18 and related papers filed with the Commission shall be filed either at its principal office in Washington, D.C., or in the Regional Office for the region in which the registrant's principal business operations are conducted, or are proposed to be conducted. The registration statement of any registrant having or proposing to have its principal business operations in Canada may be filed with the Regional Office nearest the place where the registrant's principal business operations are conducted, or are proposed to be conducted; *Provided, however,* That if the offering is to be made through a principal underwriter located in the United States, the offering statement may be filed with the Regional Office for the region in which such underwriter has its principal office. Such material may be filed by delivery to the Commission through the mails or otherwise. Questions concerning the appropriate place of filing may be directed to the Commission's Regional Offices.

B. The Commission will endeavor to process Form S–18 registration statements at the place of filing. However, due to workload or other special consideration, the Commission may refer processing to a different Commission office.

C. All post-effective amendments to the Form S–18 registration statement shall be filed in the office where the corresponding Form S–18 registration statement was declared effective.

* * *

PART I. INFORMATION REQUIRED IN PROSPECTUS

Item 1. Forepart of the Registration Statement and Outside Front Cover Page of Prospectus.

Set forth in the forepart of the registration statement and on the outside front cover page of the prospectus the information required by Item 501 of Regulation S–K.

Item 2. Inside Front and Outside Back Cover Pages of Prospectus.

Set forth on the inside front cover page of the prospectus or, where permitted, on the outside back cover page, the information required by Item 502 of Regulation S–K.

Item 3. Summary Information and Risk Factors.

Furnish the information required by Item 503(a), (b), and (c) of Regulation S–K.

Item 4. Use of Proceeds.

Furnish the information required by Item 504 of Regulation S–K.

Item 5. Determination of Offering Price.

Furnish the information required by Item 505 of Regulation S–K.

Item 6. Dilution.

Furnish the information required by Item 506 of Regulation S-K.

Item 7. Selling Security Holders.

Furnish the information required by Item 507 of Regulation S-K.

Item 8. Plan of Distribution.

Furnish the information required by Item 508 of Regulation S-K, except the information specified in Item 508(c)(1), (3), and (d).

Item 9. Legal Proceedings.

Furnish the information required by Item 103 of Regulation S-K.

Item 10. Directors and Executive Officers.

Furnish the information required by Item 401 of Regulation S-K.

Item 11. Security Ownership of Certain Beneficial Owners and Management.

Furnish the information required by Item 403 of Regulation S-K.

Item 12. Description of the Securities To Be Registered.

Furnish the information required by Item 202 of Regulation S-K.

Item 13. Interest of Named Experts and Counsel.

Furnish the information required by Item 509 of Regulation S-K.

Item 14. Statement as to Indemnification.

Furnish the information required by Item 510 of Regulation S-K.

Item 15. Organization Within 5 Years.

If the registrant was organized within the past 5 years, furnish the following information:

(a) State the names of the promoters, the nature and amount of anything of value (including money, property, contracts, options or rights of any kind) received or to be received by each promoter directly or indirectly from the registrant, and the nature and amount of any assets, services or other consideration therefor received or to be received by the registrant. The term "promoter" is defined in Rule 405 under the Act.

(b) As to any assets acquired or to be acquired by the registrant from a promoter, state the amount at which acquired or to be acquired and the principle followed or to be followed in determining the amount. Identify the persons making the determination and state their relationship, if any, with the registrant or any promoter. If the assets were acquired by the promoter within two years prior to their transfer to the registrant, state the cost thereof to the promoter.

(c) List all parents of the registrant showing the basis of control and as to each parent, the percentage of voting securities owned or other basis of control by its immediate parent if any.

> *Instruction.* Include the registrant and show the percentage of its voting securities owned or other basis of control by its immediate parent.

Item 16. Description of Business.

(a) *General development of business.* Describe the general development of the business of the registrant, its subsidiaries and any predecessor(s) during the past five years, or such shorter period as the registrant may have been engaged in business. Information shall be disclosed for earlier periods if material to an understanding of the general development of the business.

(1) In describing developments, information shall be given as to matters such as the following: the year in which the registrant was organized and its form of organization; the nature and results of any bankruptcy, receivership or similar proceedings with respect to the registrant or any of its significant subsidiaries; the nature and results of any other material reclassification, merger or consolidation of the registrant or any of its significant subsidiaries; the acquisition or disposition of any material amount of assets otherwise than in the ordinary course of business; and any material changes in the mode of conducting the business.

> *Instruction.* The following requirement in paragraph (2) applies only to registrants (includ-

ing predecessors) which have not received revenue from operations during each of the three fiscal years immediately prior to the filing of the registration statement.

(2) Describe, if formulated, the registrant's plan of operation for the remainder of the fiscal year, if the registration statement is filed prior to the end of the registrant's second fiscal quarter. Describe, if formulated, the registrant's plan of operation for the remainder of the fiscal year and for the first six months of the next fiscal year if the registration statement is filed subsequent to the end of the second fiscal quarter. If such information is not available, the reasons for its not being available shall be stated. Disclosure relating to any plan should include such matters as:

(i) A statement in narrative form indicating the registrant's opinion as to the period of time that the proceeds from the offering will satisfy cash requirements and whether in the next six months it will be necessary to raise additional funds to meet the expenditures required for operating the business of the registrant. The specific reasons for such opinion shall be set forth and categories of expenditures and sources of cash resources shall be identified; however, amounts of expenditure and cash resources need not be provided. In addition, if the narrative statement is based on a cash budget, such budget should be furnished to the Commission as supplemental information, but not as a part of the registration statement.

(ii) An explanation of material product research and development to be performed during the period covered in the plan.

(iii) Any anticipated material acquisition of plant and equipment and the capacity thereof.

(iv) Any anticipated material changes in number of employees in the various departments such as research and development, production, sales or administration.

(v) Other material areas which may be peculiar to the registrant's business.

(b) *Narrative description of business.*

(1) Describe the business done and intended to be done by the registrant and its subsidiaries. Such description should include, if material to an understanding of the registrant's business, a discussion of:

(a) the principal products produced and services rendered and the principal markets for and methods of distribution of such products and services.

(b) the status of a product or service if the issuer has made public information about a new product or service which would require the investment of a material amount of the assets of the registrant or is otherwise material.

(c) the estimated amount spent during each of the last two fiscal years on company-sponsored research and development activities determined in accordance with generally accepted accounting principles. In addition, state the estimated dollar amount spent during each of such years on material customer-sponsored research activities relating to the development of new products, services or techniques or the improvement of existing products, services or techniques.

(d) the number of persons employed by the registrant indicating the number employed full time.

(e) the material effects that compliance with Federal, State and local provisions which have been enacted or adopted regulating the discharge of materials into the environment, or otherwise relating to the protection of the environment, may have upon the capital expenditures, earnings and competitive position of the registrant and its subsidiaries. The registrant shall disclose any material estimated capital expenditures for environmental control facilities for the remainder of its current fiscal year and for such further periods as the registrant may deem material.

(2) The registrant should also describe those distinctive or special characteristics of the registrant's operations or industry which may have a material impact upon the registrant's future financial performance. Examples of factors which might be discussed include dependence on one or a few major customers or suppliers (including suppliers of raw materials or financing), existing or probable governmental regulation, expiration of material labor contracts or patents, trademarks, licenses, franchises, concessions or royalty agreements, unusual competitive conditions in the industry, cyclicality of the industry and anticipated raw material or energy shortages to the extent management may not be able to secure a continuing source of supply.

(c) *Segment data.* If the registrant is required to include segment information in its financial statements, such information may be disclosed in the description of business or in the financial statements. If such information is included in the financial statements, an appropriate cross reference shall be included in the description of business.

Item 17. Description of Property.

State briefly the location and general character of the principal plants, and other materially important physical properties of the registrant and its subsidiaries. If any such property is not held in fee or is held subject to any major encumbrance, so state and briefly describe how held.

Instruction. What is required is information essential to an investor's appraisal of the securities being registered. Such information should be furnished as will reasonably inform investors as to the suitability, adequacy, productive capacity and extent of utilization of the facilities used in the enterprise. Detailed descriptions of the physical characteristics of individual properties or legal descriptions by metes and bounds are not required and should not be given.

* * *

Item 18. Interest of Management and Others in Certain Transactions.

Describe briefly any transactions during the previous two years or any presently proposed transactions, to which the registrant or any of its subsidiaries was or is to be a party, in which any of the following persons had or is to have a direct or indirect material interest, naming such person and stating his relationship to the issuer, the nature of his interest in the transaction and, where practicable, the amount of such interest:

(1) Any director or executive officer of the issuer;

(2) Any nominee for election as a director;

(3) Any security holder named in answer to Item 11; or

(4) Any member of the immediate family of any of the foregoing persons.

Instructions. 1. See Instruction 2 to Item 20(a)(1). No information need be given in response to this item as to any remuneration or other transaction reported in response to Item 20 or specifically excluded from Item 20.

2. No information need be given in answer to this item as to any transaction where:

(a) the rates or charges involved in the transaction are determined by competitive bids, or the transaction involves the rendering of services as a common or contract carrier, or public utility, at rates or charges fixed in conformity with law or governmental authority;

(b) the transaction involves services as a bank depositary of funds, transfer agent, registrar, trustee under a trust indenture, or similar services;

(c) the amount involved in the transaction or a series of similar transactions, including all periodic installments in the case if any lease or other agreement providing for periodic payments or installments, does not exceed $60,000; or

(d) the interest of the specified person arises solely from the ownership of securities of the issuer and the specified person receives no extra or special benefit not shared on a pro rata basis by all holders of securities of the class.

3. It should be noted that this item calls for disclosure of indirect, as well as direct, material interests in transactions. A person who has a position or relationship with a firm, corporation, or other entity, which engages in a transaction with the issuer or its subsidiaries may have an indirect interest in such transaction by reason of such position or relationship. However, a person shall be deemed not to have a material indirect interest in a transaction within the meaning of this item where:

(a) the interest arises only (i) from such person's position as a director of another corporation or organization (other than a partnership) which is a party to the transaction, or (ii) from the direct or indirect ownership by such person and all other persons specified in subparagraphs (1) through (3) above, in the aggregate, of less than a 10 percent equity interest in another person (other than a partnership) which is a party to the transaction, or (iii) from both such position and ownership.

(b) the interest arises only from such person's position as a limited partner in a partnership in which he and all other persons specified in (1) through (4) above had an interest of less than 10 percent; or

(c) the interest of such person arises solely from the holding of an equity interest (including a limited partnership interest but excluding a general partnership interest) or a creditor interest in another person which is a party to the transaction with the issuer or any of its subsidiaries and the transaction is not material to such other person.

4. Include the name of each person whose interest in any transaction is described and the nature of the relationships by reason of which such interest is required to be described. The amount of the interest of any specified person shall be computed without regard to the amount of the profit or loss involved in the transaction. Where it is not practicable to state the approximate amount of the interest, the approximate amount involved in the transaction shall be disclosed.

5. Information should be included as to any material underwriting discounts and commissions upon the sale of securities by the registrant where any of the specified persons was or is to be a principal underwriter or is a controlling person, or member, of a firm which was or is to be a principal underwriter. Information need not be given concerning ordinary management fees paid by underwriters to a managing underwriter pursuant to an agreement among underwriters the parties to which do not include the registrant or its subsidiaries.

6. As to any transaction involving the purchase or sale of assets by or to the registrant or any subsidiary, otherwise than in the ordinary course of business, state the cost of the assets to the purchaser and if acquired by the seller within two years prior to the transaction, the cost thereof to the seller.

7. Information shall be furnished in answer to this item with respect to transactions not excluded above which involve remuneration from the registrant or its subsidiaries, directly or indirectly, to any of the specified persons for services in any capacity unless the interest of such persons arises solely from the ownership individually and in the aggregate of less than 10% of any class of equity securities of another corporation furnishing the services to the registrant or its subsidiaries.

8. The foregoing instructions specify certain transactions and interests as to which information may be omitted in answering this item. There may be situations where, although the foregoing instructions do not expressly authorize nondisclosure, the interest of a specified person in the particular transaction or series of transactions is not a material interest. In that case, information regarding such interest and transaction is not required to be disclosed in response to this item. The materiality of any interest or transaction is to be determined on the basis of the significance of the information to investors in light of all of the circumstances of the particular transaction. The importance of the interest to the person having the interest, the relationship of the parties to the transaction to each other and the amount involved in the transaction are among the factors to be considered in determining the significance of the information to investors.

Item 19. Certain Market Information.

Furnish the information required by Item 201(a)(2) of Regulation S–K.

Item 20. Executive Compensation.

(a)(1) *Cash compensation.* Furnish, in substantially the tabular form specified, all cash compensation paid to the following persons through the latest practicable date for services rendered in all capacities to the registrant and its subsidiaries during the registrant's last fiscal year.

(i) Each of the registrant's five most highly compensated executive officers whose cash compensation required to be disclosed pursuant to this paragraph exceeds $60,000, naming each person; and

(ii) All executive officers as a group, stating the number of persons in the group without naming them.

Cash Compensation Table

A	B	C
Name of individual or number in group	Capacities in which served	Cash compensation

Instructions. 1. The Cash Compensation Table shall include: (i) all cash bonuses to be paid for services rendered during the last fiscal year unless such amounts have not been allocated at such time as the registration statement is filed, and (ii) all compensation that would have been paid in cash but for the fact the payment of such compensation was deferred.

2. Paragraph (a) applies to any person who was an executive officer of the registrant at any time during the period specified. However, information need not be given for any portion of the period during which such person was not an executive officer of the registrant, provided a statement to that effect is made.

(b)(1) *Compensation pursuant to plans.* Describe briefly all plans, pursuant to which cash or non-cash compensation was paid or distributed during the last fiscal year, stating such amounts, and all plans pursuant to which cash or non-cash is proposed to be paid or distributed in the future, to the named individuals and group specified in paragraph (a) of this section. Information need not be given with respect to any group life, health, hospitalization, medical reimbursement or relocation plans that do not discriminate, in scope, terms, or operation in favor of officers or directors of the registrant and that are available generally to all salaried employees. Information relating to pension or retirement benefits need not be disclosed if the amounts to be paid are computed on an actuarial basis under any plan which provides for fixed benefits in the event of retirement at a specified age or after a specified number of years of service.

(2) *Stock option plans.* In addition to providing the information required by paragraph (b)(1) of this section, furnish:

(i) With respect to stock options granted during the last fiscal year: (A) the title and aggregate amount of securities subject to options; (B) the average per share exercise price; and (C) if such option exercise price was less than 100 percent of the market value of the security on the date of grant, such fact and the market price on such date.

(ii) With respect to stock options exercised during the last fiscal year, regardless of the year such options were granted, the net value realized upon such exercise, calculated by subtracting the exercise price from the market value.

(c) *Other compensation.* Describe, stating amounts, any other compensation not covered by paragraphs (a) or (b) of this section, such as personal benefits, securities or property, that was paid or distributed during the last fiscal year to the named individuals and group specified in paragraph (a) of this section unless:

(1) With respect to any named individual, the aggregate amount of such other compensation is the lesser of $25,000 or 10 percent of the compensation reported in the Cash Compensation Table of such person pursuant to paragraph (a) of this section or

(2) With respect to the group, the aggregate amount of such other compensation is the lesser of $25,000 times the number of persons in the group or

10 percent of the compensation reported in the Cash Compensation Table for the group pursuant to paragraph (a) of this section and a statement to that effect is made.

Instruction. Compensation within paragraph (c) shall be valued on the basis of the registrant's and subsidiaries' aggregate incremental cost.

(d) *Compensation of directors.* Describe briefly, stating amounts, all compensation received by directors of the registrant for all services as a director.

Item 21. Financial Statements.

(a) General

(1) The financial statements of the registrant, or the registrant and its predecessors or any businesses to which the registrant is a successor, which are to be filed as part of the registration statement shall be prepared in accordance with generally accepted accounting principles (GAAP) in the United States or in the case of a Canadian registrant, a reconciliation to such U.S. GAAP shall be included in a note or schedule to the financial statements.

(2) Regulations S–X Form and Content of Requirements for Financial Statements, shall not apply to the preparation of such financial statements, except that the report and qualifications of the independent accountant shall comply with the requirements of Article 2 of Regulation S–X, and registrants engaged in oil and gas producing activities shall follow the financial accounting and reporting standards specified in Article 4–10 of Regulation S–X with respect to such activities.

* * *

(3) The Commission may, upon the informal written request of the registrant, and where consistent with the protection of investors, permit the omission of one or more of the financial statements herein required or the filing in substitution therefor of appropriate statements of comparable character. The Commission may also by informal written notice require the filing of other financial statements in addition to, or in substitution for, the statements herein required in any case where such statements are necessary or appropriate for as adequate presentation of the financial condition of any person whose financial statements are required, or whose statements are otherwise necessary for the protection of investors.

(b) Consolidated Balance Sheets

(1) The registrant and its subsidiaries consolidated shall file an audited balance sheet as of the end of the most recent fiscal year, or as of a date within 135 days of the date of filing the registration statement if the registrant (including predecessors) existed for a period less than one fiscal year.

(2) When the filing date of the registration statement falls after 134 days subsequent to the end of the registrant's most recent fiscal year a balance sheet as of an interim date within 135 days of the filing date also shall be included in the registration statement. Such balance sheet need not be audited and may be in condensed form.

(c) Consolidated Statements of Income, Changes in Financial Condition and Stockholder's Equity

(1) There shall be filed for the registrant and its subsidiaries consolidated, statements of income, changes in financial position and stockholders equity for each of the two fiscal years preceding the date of the most recent audited balance sheet being filed (or for such shorter period as the registrant has been in business), and for the interim period, if any, between the end of the most recent fiscal year and the date of the most recent balance sheet being filed. These statements should be audited to the date of the most recent audited balance sheet being filed. Any interim financial statements may be in condensed form.

(2) If an income statement is filed for an interim period there shall also be filed, except for registrants in the development stage as defined by GAAP, an income statement for a comparable period of the prior year.

(3) In connection with any unaudited statement for an interim period a statement shall be made that all adjustments necessary to a fair statement of the results for such period have been included. If all such adjustments are of a normal recurring nature, a statement to that effect shall be made; otherwise, there shall be furnished information describing in appropriate detail the nature and amount of any adjustments other than normal recurring adjustments entering into the determination of the results shown.

* * *

PART II. INFORMATION NOT REQUIRED IN PROSPECTUS

Item 22. Indemnification of Directors and Officers.

Furnish the information called for Item 702 of Regulation S-K.

Item 23. Other Expenses of Issuance and Distribution.

Furnish the information called for by Item 511 of Regulation S-K.

Item 24. Recent Sales of Unregistered Securities.

Furnish the information called for by Item 701 of Regulation S-K.

Item 25. Exhibits.

Furnish the exhibits as required by Item 601 of Regulation S-K.

Item 26. Undertakings.

Furnish the undertakings required by Item 512 of Regulation S-K.

*

2. UNDER SECURITIES EXCHANGE ACT OF 1934

FORM 8–K

CURRENT REPORT

Pursuant to Section 13 or 15(d) of The Securities Exchange Act of 1934 For the Month of ______, 19__

GENERAL INSTRUCTIONS

A. Rule as to Use of Form 8–K.

Form 8–K shall be used for current reports under Section 13 or 15(d) of the Securities Exchange Act of 1934, filed pursuant to Rule 13a–11 or Rule 15d–11.

B. Events to be Reported and Time for Filing of Reports.

1. A report on this form is required to be filed upon the occurrence of any one or more of the events specified in Items 1–4 and 6 of this form. Reports of events specified in those items are to be filed within 15 days after the occurrence of the earliest such event reported.

2. Since a report on this form pursuant to Item 5 is optional, there is correspondingly no mandatory time for filing. Registrants are encouraged, however, to file promptly after the occurrence of any event therein reported.

3. If substantially the same information as that required by this form has been previously reported by the registrant, an additional report of the information on this form need not be made. The term "previously reported" is defined in Rule 12b–2.

4. When considering current reporting on this form, particularly of other events of importance pursuant to Item 5, registrants should have due regard for the accuracy, completeness and currency of the information in registration statements filed under the Securities Act of 1933 which incorporate by reference information in reports filed pursuant to the Securities Exchange Act of 1934, including reports on this form.

* * *

F. Incorporation by Reference.

If the registrant makes available to its stockholders or otherwise publishes, within the period prescribed for filing the report, a press release or other document or statement containing information meeting some or all of the requirements of this form, the information called for may be incorporated by reference to such published document or statement, in answer or partial answer to any item or items of this form, provided copies thereof are filed as an exhibit to the report on this form.

INFORMATION TO BE INCLUDED IN THE REPORT

Item 1. Changes in Control of Registrant.

(a) If, to the knowledge of management, a change in control of the registrant has occurred, state the name of the person(s) who acquired such control; the amount and the source of the consideration used by such person(s); the basis of the control; the date and a description of the transaction(s) which resulted in the change in control; the percentage of voting securities of the registrant now beneficially owned directly or indirectly by the person(s) who acquired control; and the identity of the person(s) from whom control was assumed. If the source of all or any part of the consideration used is a loan made in the ordinary course of business by a bank as defined by Section 3(a)(6) of the Act, the identity of such bank shall be omitted provided a request for confidentiality has been made pursuant to Section 13(d)(1)(B) of the Act by the person(s) who acquired control. In lieu thereof, the material shall indicate that disclosure of the identity of the bank has been so omitted and filed separately with the Commission.

Instructions. 1. State the terms of any loans or pledges obtained by the new control group for the purpose of acquiring control, and the names of the lenders or pledgees.

2. Any arrangements or understandings among members of both the former and new control groups and their associates with respect to election of directors or other matters should be described.

(b) Furnish the information required by Item 403(c) of Regulation S–K.

Item 2. Acquisition or Disposition of Assets.

If the registrant or any of its majority-owned subsidiaries has acquired or disposed of a significant amount of assets, otherwise than in the ordinary course of business, furnish the following information:

(a) The date and manner of acquisition or disposition and a brief description of the assets involved, the nature and amount of consideration given or received therefor, the principle followed in determining the amount of such consideration, the identity of the persons from whom the assets were acquired or to whom they were sold and the nature of any material relationship between such persons and the registrant or any of its affiliates, any director or officer of the registrant, or any associate of such director or officer. If the transaction being reported is an acquisition, identify the source(s) of the funds used unless all or any part of the consideration used is a loan made in the ordinary course of business by a bank as defined by Section 3(a)(6) of the Act in which the identity of such bank shall be omitted provided a request for confidentiality has been made pursuant to Section 13(d)(1)(B) of the Act. In lieu thereof, the material shall indicate that the identity of the bank has been so omitted and filed separately with the Commission.

(b) If any assets so acquired by the registrant or its subsidiaries constituted plant, equipment or other physical property, state the nature of the business in which the assets were used by the persons from whom acquired and whether the registrant intends to continue such use or intends to devote the assets to other purposes, indicating such other purposes.

* * *

Item 3. Bankruptcy or Receivership.

If a receiver, fiscal agent or similar officer has been appointed for a registrant or its parent, in a proceeding under the Bankruptcy Act or in any other proceeding under State or Federal law in which a court or governmental agency has assumed jurisdiction over substantially all of the assets or business of the registrant or its parent, or if such jurisdiction has been assumed by leaving the existing directors and officers in possession but subject to the supervision and orders of a court or governmental body, identify the proceeding, the court or governmental body, the date jurisdiction was assumed, the identity of the receiver, fiscal agent or similar officer and the date of his appointment.

* * *

Item 4. Changes in Registrant's Certifying Accountant.

If an independent accountant who was previously engaged as the principal accountant to audit the registrant's financial statements resigns (or indicates he declines to stand for re-election after the completion of the current audit) or is dismissed as the registrant's principal accountant, or another independent accountant is engaged as principal accountant, or another independent accountant on whom the principal accountant expressed reliance in his report regarding a significant subsidiary resigns (or formally indicates he declines to stand for re-election after the completion of the current audit) or is dismissed or another independent accountant is engaged to audit that subsidiary:

(a) State the date of such resignation (or declination to stand for re-election), dismissal or engagement.

(b) State whether in connection with the audits of the two most recent fiscal years and any subsequent interim period preceding such resignation, dismissal or engagement there were any disagreements with the former accountant on any matter of accounting principles or practices, financial statement disclosure, or auditing scope or procedure, which disagreements if not resolved to the satisfaction of the former accountant would have caused him to make reference in connection with his report to the subject matter of the disagreement(s); also, describe each such disagreement. The disagreements required to be reported in response to the preceding sentence include both those resolved to the former accountant's satisfaction and those not resolved to the former accountant's satisfaction. Disagreements contemplated by this rule are those which occur at the decision making level; i.e., between personnel of the registrant responsible for presentation of its financial statements and personnel of the accounting firm responsible for rendering its report.

(c) State whether the principal accountant's report on the financial statements for any of the past two years contained an adverse opinion or a disclaimer of opinion or was qualified as to uncertainty, audit scope, or accounting principles; also describe the nature of each such adverse opinion, disclaimer of opinion, or qualification.

(d) The registrant shall request the former accountant to furnish the registrant with a letter addressed to the Commission stating whether he agrees with the statements made by the registrant in response to this item and, if not, stating the respects in which he does not agree. The registrant shall file copies of the former accountant's letter as an exhibit to the report on this form. If the former accountant's letter is unavailable at the time of filing, it shall be filed within thirty days thereafter.

(e) State whether the decision to change accountants was recommended or approved by:

(1) any audit or similar committee of the Board of Directors, if the issuer has such a committee; or

(2) the Board of Directors, if the issuer has no such committee.

Item 5. Other Events.

The registrant may, at its option, report under this item any events, with respect to which information is not otherwise called for by this form, that the registrant deems of importance to security holders.

Item 6. Resignations of Registrant's Directors.

(a) If a director has resigned or declined to stand for re-election to the board of directors since the date of the last annual meeting of shareholders because of a disagreement with the registrant on any matter relating to the registrant's operations, policies or practices, and if the director has furnished the registrant with a letter describing such disagreement and requesting that the matter be disclosed, the registrant shall state the date of such resignation or declination to stand for re-election and summarize the director's description of the disagreement.

(b) If the registrant believes that the description provided by the director is incorrect or incomplete, it may include a brief statement presenting its views of the disagreement.

(c) The registrant shall file a copy of the director's letter as an exhibit with all copies of the Form 8-K required to be filed pursuant to general Instruction E.

* * *

FORM 10–K

Annual Report Pursuant to Section 13 or 15(d) of The Securities Exchange Act of 1934

GENERAL INSTRUCTIONS

A. Rule as to Use of Form 10–K.

This Form shall be used for annual reports pursuant to Section 13 or 15(d) of the Securities Exchange Act of 1934 (the "Act") for which no other form is prescribed. Reports on this form shall be filed within 90 days after the end of the fiscal year covered by the report. However, all schedules required by Article 12 of Regulation S–K may, at the option of the registrant, be filed as an amendment to the report not later than 120 days after the end of the fiscal year covered by the report. Such amendment shall be filed under cover of Form 8.

* * *

D. Signature and Filing of Report.

(1) Three complete copies of the report, including financial statements, financial statement schedules, exhibits, and all other papers and documents filed as a part thereof, and five additional copies which need not include exhibits, shall be filed with the Commission. At least one complete copy of the report, including financial statements, financial statement schedules, exhibits, and all other papers and documents filed as a part thereof, shall be filed with each exchange on which any class of securities of the registrant is registered. At least one complete copy of the report filed with the Commission and one such copy filed with each exchange shall be manually signed. Copies not manually signed shall bear typed or printed signatures.

(2)(a) The report shall be signed by the registrant, and on behalf of the registrant by its principal executive officer or officers, its principal financial officer, its controller or principal accounting officer, and by at least the majority of the board of directors or persons performing similar functions. Where the registrant is a limited partnership, the report shall be signed by the majority of the board of directors of any corporate general partner who signs the report. (b) The name of each person who signs the report shall be typed or printed beneath his signature. Any person who occupies more than one of the specified positions shall indicate each capacity in which he signs the report. Attention is directed to Rule 12b–11 concerning manual signatures and signatures pursuant to powers of attorney.

* * *

G. Information to be Incorporated by Reference.

(1) Attention is directed to Rule 12b–23 which provides for the incorporation by reference of information contained in certain documents in answer or partial answer to any item of a report.

(2) The information called for by Parts I and II of this Form (Items 1 through 9 or any portion thereof) may, at the registrant's option, be incorporated by reference from the registrant's annual report to security holders furnished to the Commission pursuant to Rule 14a–3(b) or Rule 14c–3(b) or from the registrant's annual report to security holders, even if not furnished to the Commission pursuant to Rule 14a–3(b) or Rule 14c–3(a), provided such annual report contains the information required by Rule 14a–3.

> **Note:** In order to fulfill the requirements of Part I of Form 10–K, the incorporated portion of the annual report to security holders must contain the information required by Items 1–3 of Form 10–K, to the extent applicable.

(3) The information called for by Part III (Items 10, 11, 12 and 13) shall be incorporated by reference from the registrant's definitive proxy statement (filed or to be filed pursuant to Regulation 14A) or definitive information statement (filed or to be filed pursuant to Regulation 14C) which involves the election of directors, if such definitive proxy statement or information statement is filed with the Commission not later than 120 days after the end of the fiscal year covered by the Form 10–K. However, if such definitive proxy or information statement is not filed with the Commission in the 120-day period, the items comprising the Part III information must be filed as part of the Form 10–K, or as an amendment to the Form 10–K under cover of Form 8, not later than the end of the 120-day period. It should be noted that the information regarding executive officers required by Item 401 of Regula-

tion S–K may be included in Part I of Form 10–K under an appropriate caption. See Instruction 4 to Item 401(b) of Regulation S–K.

* * *

H. Integrated Reports to Security Holders.

Annual reports to security holders may be combined with the required information of Form 10–K and will be suitable for filing with the Commission if the following conditions are satisfied:

(1) The combined report contains full and complete answers to all items required by Form 10–K. When responses to a certain item of required disclosure are separated within the combined report, an appropriate cross-reference should be made. If the information required by Part III of Form 10–K is omitted by virtue of General Instruction G, a definitive proxy or information statement shall be filed.

(2) The cover page and the required signatures are included. As appropriate, a cross-reference sheet should be filed indicating the location of information required by the items of the Form.

I. Registrants Filing on Form S–18.

If the registrant is subject to the reporting requirements of Section 15(d) of the Exchange Act and such obligation arises solely because the registrant has filed a registration statement on Form S–18 which has become effective during the last fiscal year, the registrant may comply with the disclosure requirements of Form S–18 Item 16, Description of Business; Item 18, Interest of Management and Others in Certain Transactions; and Item 20, Remuneration of Directors and Officers, in lieu of complying with the disclosure requirements of Item 1, Business; Item 11, Management Remuneration; and Item 13, Certain Relationships and Related Transactions, herein. Item 6 of this Form, Selected Financial Data, may be omitted at the election of such registrant.

* * *

PART I

[See General Instruction G(2).]

Item 1. Business.

Furnish the information required by Item 101 of Regulation S–K except that the discussion of the development of the registrant's business need only include developments since the beginning of the fiscal year for which this report is filed.

Item 2. Properties.

Furnish the information required by Item 102 of Regulation S–K.

Item 3. Legal Proceedings.

(a) Furnish the information required by Item 103 of Regulation S–K.

(b) As to any proceeding that was terminated during the fourth quarter of the fiscal year covered by this report, furnish information similar to that required by Item 103 of Regulation S–K, including the date of termination and a description of the disposition thereof with respect to the registrant and its subsidiaries.

Item 4. Submission of Matters to a Vote of Security Holders.

If any matter was submitted during the fourth quarter of the fiscal year covered by this report to a vote of security holders, through the solicitation of proxies or otherwise, furnish the following information:

(a) The date of the meeting and whether it was an annual or special meeting.

(b) If the meeting involved the election of directors, the name of each director elected at the meeting and the name of each other director whose term of office as a director continued after the meeting.

(c) A brief description of each other matter voted upon at the meeting and the number of affirmative votes and the number of negative votes cast with respect to each such matter.

(d) A description of the terms of any settlement between the registrant and any other participant (as defined in Rule 14a–11 of Regulation 14A under the Act) terminating any solicitation subject to Rule 14a–11, including the cost or anticipated cost to the registrant.

Instructions:

1. If any matter has been submitted to a vote of security holders otherwise than at a meeting of such security holders, corresponding information

with respect to such submission shall be furnished. The solicitation of any authorization or consent (other than a proxy to vote at a stockholders' meeting) with respect to any matter shall be deemed a submission of such matter to a vote of security holders within the meaning of this item.

2. Paragraph (a) need be answered only if paragraph (b) or (c) is required to be answered.

3. Paragraph (b) need not be answered if (i) proxies for the meeting were solicited pursuant to Regulation 14A under the Act, (ii) there was no solicitation in opposition to the management's nominees as listed in the proxy statement, and (iii) all of such nominees were elected. If the registrant did not solicit proxies and the board of directors as previously reported to the Commission was re-elected in its entirety, a statement to that effect in answer to paragraph (b) will suffice as an answer thereto.

4. Paragraph (c) need not be answered as to procedural matters or as to the selection or approval of auditors.

5. If the registrant has furnished to its security holders proxy soliciting material containing the information called for by paragraph (d), the paragraph may be answered by reference to the information contained in such material.

6. If the registrant has published a report containing all of the information called for by this item, the item may be answered by a reference to the information contained in such report.

PART II

[See General Instruction G(2).]

Item 5. Market for Registrant's Common Equity and Related Stockholder Matters.

Furnish the information required by Item 201 of Regulation S–K.

Item 6. Selected Financial Data.

Furnish the information required by Item 301 of Regulation S–K.

Item 7. Management's Discussion and Analysis of Financial Condition and Results of Operation.

Furnish the information required by Item 303 of Regulation S–K.

Item 8. Financial Statements and Supplementary Data.

Furnish financial statements meeting the requirements of Regulation S–X and the supplementary financial information required by Item 302 of Regulation S–K. Financial statements of the registrant and its subsidiaries consolidated [as required by Rule 14a–3(b)] shall be filed under this item. Other financial statements and schedules required under Regulation S–X may be filed as "Financial Statement Schedules" pursuant to Item 13, Exhibits, Financial Statement Schedules, and Reports on Form 8–K, of this Form.

* * *

Item 9. Disagreements on Accounting and Financial Disclosure.

Furnish the information required by Item 304 of Regulation S–K.

PART III

[See General Instruction G(3).]

Item 10. Directors and Executive Officers of the Registrant.

Furnish the information required by Item 401 of Regulation S–K.

Item 11. Executive Compensation.

Furnish the information required by Item 402 of Regulation S–K.

Item 12. Security Ownership of Certain Beneficial Owners and Management.

Furnish the information required by Item 403 of Regulation S–K.

Item 13. Certain Relationships and Related Transactions.

Furnish the information required by Item 404 of Regulation S–K.

PART IV

Item 14. Exhibits, Financial Statement Schedules, and Reports on Form 8–K.

(a) List the following documents filed as a part of the report:

1. All financial statements.

2. Those financial statement schedules required to be filed by Item 8 of this Form, and by paragraph (b) below.

(b) Those exhibits required by Item 601 of Regulation S–K and by paragraph (c) below. Where any financial statement, financial statement schedule, or exhibit is incorporated by reference, the incorporation by reference shall be set forth in the list required by this item. For purposes of all rules concerning incorporation by reference a financial statement schedule shall constitute an "exhibit." See Rule 12b 23.

(c) Registrants shall file, as exhibits to this Form, the exhibits required by Item 601 of Regulation S–K.

* * *

FORM 10–Q

For Quarterly Reports Under Section 13 or 15(d) of the Securities Exchange Act of 1934

GENERAL INSTRUCTIONS

A. Rule as to Use of Form 10–Q.

(a) Form 10–Q shall be used for quarterly reports under Section 13 or 15(d) of the Securities Exchange Act of 1934, filed pursuant to Rule 13a–13 or Rule 15d–13.

(b) A report on this form shall be filed within 45 days after the end of each of the first three fiscal quarters of each fiscal year. No report need be filed for the fourth quarter of any fiscal year.

* * *

E. Integrated Reports to Security Holders.

Quarterly reports to security holders may be combined with the required information of Form 10–Q and will be suitable for filing with the Commission if the following conditions are satisfied:

1. The combined report contains full and complete answers to all items required by Part I of this form. When responses to a certain item of required disclosure are separated within the combined report, an appropriate cross-reference should be made.

2. If not included in the combined report, the cover page, appropriate responses to Part II, and the required signatures shall be included in the Form 10–Q. Additionally, as appropriate, a cross-reference sheet should be filed indicating the location of information required by the items of the form.

F. Filed Status of Information Presented.

1. Pursuant to Rule 13a–13(d) and Rule 15d–13(d), the information presented in satisfaction of the requirements of Items 1 and 2 of Part I of this form, whether included directly in a report on this form, incorporated therein by reference from a report, document or statement filed as an exhibit to Part I of this form pursuant to Instruction D(1) above, included in an integrated report pursuant to Instruction E above, or contained in a statement regarding computation of per share earnings or a letter regarding a change in accounting principles filed as an exhibit to Part I pursuant to Item 601 of Regulation S–K, except as provided by Instruction F(2) below, shall not be deemed filed for the purpose of Section 18 of the Act or otherwise subject to the liabilities of that section of the Act but shall be subject to the other provisions of the Act.

2. Information presented in satisfaction of the requirements of this form other than those of Items (1) and (2) of Part I shall be deemed filed for the purpose of Section 18 of the Act; except that, where information presented in response to Item (1) or (2) of Part I (or as an exhibit thereto) is also used to satisfy Part II requirements through incorporation by reference, only that portion of Part I (or exhibit thereto) consisting of the information required by Part II shall be deemed so filed.

PART I. FINANCIAL INFORMATION

Item 1. Financial Statements.

Provide the information required by Rule 10–01 of Regulation S–X.

Item 2. Management's Discussion and Analysis of Financial Condition and Results of Operations.

Furnish the information required by Item 303 of Regulation S–K.

PART II. OTHER INFORMATION

Item 1. Legal Proceedings.

Furnish the information required by Item 103 of Regulation S–K. As to such proceedings which have been terminated during the period covered by the report, provide similar information, including the date of termination and a description of the disposition thereof with respect to the registrant and its subsidiaries.

Instruction. A legal proceeding need only be reported in the 10–Q filed for the quarter in which it first became a reportable event and in subsequent quarters in which there have been material developments. Subsequent Form 10–Q filings in the same fiscal year in which a legal proceeding or a material development is reported should reference any previous reports in that year.

Item 2. Changes in Securities.

(a) If the constituent instruments defining the rights of the holders of any class of registered securities have been materially modified, give the title of the class of securities involved and state briefly the general effect of such modification upon the rights of holders of such securities.

(b) If the rights evidenced by any class of registered securities have been materially limited or qualified by the issuance or modification of any other class of securities, state briefly the general effect of the issuance or modification of such other class of securities upon the rights of the holders of the registered securities.

Instruction. Working capital restrictions and other limitations upon the payment of dividends are to be reported hereunder.

Item 3. Defaults upon Senior Securities.

(a) If there has been any material default in the payment of principal, interest, a sinking or purchase fund installment, or any other material default not cured within 30 days, with respect to any indebtedness of the registrant or any of its significant subsidiaries exceeding 5 percent of the total assets of the registrant and its consolidated subsidiaries, identify the indebtedness and state the nature of the default. In the case of such a default in the payment of principal, interest, or a sinking or purchase fund installment, state the amount of the default and the total arrearage on the date of filing this report.

Instruction. This paragraph refers only to events which have become defaults under the governing instruments, *i.e.,* after the expiration of any period of grace and compliance with any notice requirements.

(b) If any material arrearage in the payment of dividends has occurred or if there has been any other material delinquency not cured within 30 days, with respect to any class of preferred stock of the registrant which is registered or which ranks prior to any class of registered securities, or with respect to any class of preferred stock of any significant subsidiary of the registrant, give the title of the class and state the nature of the arrearage or delinquency. In the case of an arrearage in the payment of dividends, state the amount and the total arrearage on the date of filing this report.

Instruction. Item 3 need not be answered as to any default or arrearage with respect to any class of securities all of which is held by, or for the account of, the registrant or its totally held subsidiaries.

Item 4. Submission of Matters to a Vote of Security Holders.

If any matter has been submitted to a vote of security holders, through the solicitation of proxies or otherwise, furnish the following information:

(a) The date of the meeting and whether it was an annual or special meeting.

(b) If the meeting involved the election of directors, state the name of each director elected at the meeting and the name of each other director whose term of office as a director continued after the meeting.

(c) A brief description of each other matter voted upon at the meeting and state the number of affirmative votes and the number of negative votes cast with respect to each such matter.

(d) Describe the terms of any settlement between the registrant and any other participant (as defined in Rule 14a–11 of Regulation 14A under the Act) terminating any solicitation subject to Rule 14a–11, including the cost or anticipated cost to the registrant.

Instructions. 1. If any matter has been submitted to a vote of security holders otherwise than at a meeting of such security holders, corresponding information with respect to such submission shall be furnished. The solicitation of any authorization or consent (other than a proxy to vote at a stockholders' meeting) with respect to any matter shall be deemed a submission of such matter to a vote of security holders within the meaning of this item.

2. Paragraph (a) need be answered only if paragraph (b) or (c) is required to be answered.

3. Paragraph (b) need not be answered if (i) proxies for the meeting were solicited pursuant to Regulation 14 under the Act, (ii) there was no solicitation in opposition to the management's nominees as listed in the proxy statement, and (iii) all of such nominees were elected. If the registrant did not solicit proxies and the board of directors as previously reported to the Commission was re-elected in its entirety, a statement to that effect in answer to paragraph (b) will suffice as an answer thereto.

4. Paragraph (c) need not be answered as to procedural matters or as to the selection or approval of auditors.

5. If the registrant has furnished to its security holders proxy soliciting material containing the information called for by paragraph (d), the paragraph may be answered by reference to the information contained in such material.

6. If the registrant has published a report containing all of the information called for by this item, the item may be answered by a reference to the information contained in such report.

* * *

Item 5. Other Information.

The registrant may, at its option, report under this item any information, not previously reported in a report on Form 8–K, with respect to which information is not otherwise called for by this form. If disclosure of such information is made under this item, it need not be repeated in a report on Form 8–K which would otherwise be required to be filed with respect to such information or in a subsequent report on Form 10–Q.

Item 6. Exhibits and Reports on Form 8–K.

(a) Furnish the exhibits required by Item 601 of Regulation S–K.

(b) Reports on Form 8–K. State whether any reports on Form 8–K have been filed during the quarter for which this report is filed, listing the items reported, any financial statements filed, and the dates of any such reports.

SCHEDULE 13D

Information to be Included in Statements Filed Pursuant to Rule 13d–1(a) and Amendments Thereto Filed Pursuant to Rule 13d–2(a)

Item 1. Security and Issuer.

State the title of the class of equity securities to which this statement relates and the name and address of the principal executive offices of the issuer of such securities.

Item 2. Identity and Background.

If the person filing this statement or any person enumerated in Instruction C of this statement is a corporation, general partnership, limited partnership, syndicate or other group of persons, state its name, the state or other place of its organization, its principal business, the address of its principal business, the address of its principal office and the information required by (d) and (e) of this Item. If the person filing this statement or any person enumerated in Instruction C is a natural person, provide the information specified in (a) through (f) of this Item with respect to such person(s).

(a) Name;

(b) Residence or business address;

(c) Present principal occupation or employment and the name, principal business and address of any corporation or other organization in which such employment is conducted;

(d) Whether or not, during the last five years, such person has been convicted in a criminal proceeding (excluding traffic violations or similar misdemeanors) and, if so, give the dates, nature of conviction, name and location of court, any penalty imposed, or other disposition of the case;

(e) Whether or not, during the last five years, such person was a party to a civil proceeding of a judicial or administrative body of competent jurisdiction and as a result of such proceeding was or is subject to a judgment, decree or final order enjoining future violations of, or prohibiting or mandating activities subject to, federal or state securities laws or finding any violation with respect to such laws; and, if so, identify and describe such proceedings and summarize the terms of such judgment, decree or final order; and

(f) Citizenship.

Item 3. Source and Amount of Funds or Other Consideration.

State the source and the amount of funds or other consideration used or to be used in making the purchases, and if any part of the purchase price is or will be represented by funds or other consideration borrowed or otherwise obtained for the purpose of acquiring, holding, trading or voting the securities, a description of the transaction and the names of the parties thereto. Where material, such information should also be provided with respect to prior acquisitions not previously reported pursuant to this regulation. If the source of all or any part of the funds is a loan made in the ordinary course of business by a bank, as defined in Section 3(a)(6) of the Act, the name of the bank shall not be made available to the public if the person at the time of filing the statement so requests in writing and files such request, naming such bank, with the Secretary of the Commission. If the securities were acquired other than by purchase, describe the method of acquisition.

Item 4. Purpose of Transaction.

State the purpose or purposes of the acquisition of securities of the issuer. Describe any plans or proposals which the reporting persons may have which relate to or would result in:

(a) The acquisition by any person of additional securities of the issuer, or the disposition of securities of the issuer;

(b) An extraordinary corporate transaction, such as a merger, reorganization or liquidation, involving the issuer or any of its subsidiaries;

(c) A sale or transfer of a material amount of assets of the issuer or any of its subsidiaries;

(d) Any change in the present board of directors or management of the issuer, including any plans or proposals to change the number or term of directors or to fill any existing vacancies on the board;

(e) Any material change in the present capitalization or dividend policy of the issuer;

(f) Any other material change in the issuer's business or corporate structure, including but not limited to, if the issuer is a registered closed-end investment company, any plans or proposals to make any changes in its investment policy for which a vote is required by section 13 of the Investment Company Act of 1940;

(g) Changes in the issuer's charter, bylaws or instruments corresponding thereto or other actions which may impede the acquisition of control of the issuer by any person:

(h) Causing a class of securities of the issuer to be delisted from a national securities exchange or to cease to be authorized to be quoted in an inter-dealer quotation system of a registered national securities association;

(i) A class of equity securities of the issuer becoming eligible for termination of registration pursuant to Section 12(g)(4) of the Act; or

(j) Any action similar to any of those enumerated above.

Item 5. Interest in Securities of the Issuer.

(a) State the aggregate number and percentage of the class of securities identified pursuant to Item 1 (which may be based on the number of securities outstanding as contained in the most recently available filing with the Commission by the issuer unless the filing person has reason to believe such information is not current) beneficially owned (identifying those shares which there is a right to acquire) by each person named in Item 2. The above mentioned information should also be furnished with respect to persons who, together with any of the persons named in Item 2, comprise a group within the meaning of Section 13(d)(3) of the Act;

(b) For each person named in response to paragraph (a), indicate the number of shares as to which there is sole power to vote or to direct the vote, shared power to vote or to direct the vote, sole power to dispose or to direct the disposition, or shared power to dispose or to direct the disposition. Provide the applicable information required by Item 2 with respect to each person with whom the power to vote or to direct the vote or to dispose or direct the disposition is shared;

(c) Describe any transactions in the class of securities reported on that were effected during the past sixty days or since the most recent filing on Schedule 13D, whichever is less, by the persons named in response to paragraph (a).

Instruction. The description of a transaction required by Item 5(c) shall include, but not necessarily be limited to: (1) the identity of the person covered by Item 5(c) who effected the transaction; (2) the date of the transaction; (3) the amount of securities involved; (4) the price per share or unit; and (5) where and how the transaction was effected.

(d) If any other person is known to have the right to receive or the power to direct the receipt of dividends from, or the proceeds from the sale of, such securities, a statement to that effect should be included in response to this item and, if such interest relates to more than five percent of the class, such person should be identified. A listing of the shareholders of an investment company registered under the Investment Company Act of 1940 or the beneficiaries of an employee benefit plan, pension fund or endowment fund is not required.

(e) If applicable, state the date on which the reporting person ceased to be the beneficial owner of more than five percent of the class of securities.

Instruction. For computations regarding securities which represent a right to acquire an underlying security, see Rule 13d–3(d)(1) and the note thereto.

Item 6. Contracts, Arrangements, Understandings or Relationships With Respect to Securities of the Issuer.

Describe any contracts, arrangements, understandings or relationships (legal or otherwise) among the persons named in Item 2 and between such persons and any person with respect to any securities of the issuer, including but not limited to transfer or voting of any of the securities, finder's fees, joint ventures, loan or option arrangements, put or calls, guarantees of profits, division of profits or loss, or the giving or withholding of proxies, naming the persons with whom such contracts, arrangements, understandings or relationships have been entered into. Include such information for any of the securities that are pledged or otherwise subject to a contingency the occurrence of which would give another person voting power or investment power over such securities except that disclosure of standard default and similar provisions contained in loan agreements need not be included.

Item 7. Material to be Filed as Exhibits.

The following shall be filed as exhibits: copies of written agreements relating to the filing of joint acquisition statements as required by Rule 13d–1(f) and copies of all written agreements, contracts, arrangements, understandings, plans or proposals relating to (1) the borrowing of funds to finance the acquisition as disclosed in Item 3; (2) the acquisition of issuer control, liquidation, sale of assets, merger, or change in business or corporate structure or any other matter as disclosed in Item 4; and (3) the transfer or voting of the securities, finder's fees, joint ventures, options, puts, calls, guarantees of loans, guarantees against loss or of profit, or the giving or withholding of any proxy as disclosed in Item 6.

SCHEDULE 13E–3

Transaction Statement Pursuant to Section 13(e) and Rule 13e–3

GENERAL INSTRUCTIONS

A. Depending on the type of Rule 13e–3 transaction, this statement shall be filed with the Commission:

1. Concurrently with the filing of "Preliminary Copies" of soliciting materials or an information statement pursuant to Regulations 14A or 14C under the Act;

2. Concurrently with the filing of a registration statement under the Securities Act of 1933;

3. As soon as practicable on the date a tender offer is first published, sent or given to security holders; or

4. At least 30 days prior to any purchase of any securities of the class of securities subject to the Rule 13e–3 transaction, if the transaction does not involve a solicitation, an information statement, the registration of securities or a tender offer, as described in 1, 2 or 3 of this Instruction.

5. If the Rule 13e–3 transaction involves a series of transactions, the issuer or affiliate shall file this statement at the time indicated in 1–4 of this general instruction for the first transaction of such series and shall promptly amend this schedule with respect to each subsequent transaction in such series.

* * *

Item 1. Issuer and Class of Security Subject to the Transaction.

(a) State the name of the issuer of the class of equity security which is the subject of the Rule 13e–3 transaction and the address of its principal executive offices.

(b) State the exact title, the amount of securities outstanding of the class of security which is the subject of the Rule 13e–3 transaction as of the most recent practicable date and the approximate number of holders of record of such class as of the most recent practicable date.

(c) Identify the principal market in which such securities are being traded and, if the principal market is an exchange, state the high and low sales prices for such securities as reported in the consolidated transaction reporting system or, if not so reported, on such principal exchange for each quarterly period during the past two years. If the principal market is not an exchange, state the range of high and low bid quotations for each quarterly period during the past two years, the source of such quotations and, if there is currently no established trading market for such securities (excluding limited or sporadic quotations); furnish a statement to that effect.

(d) State the frequency and amount of any dividends paid during the past two years with respect to such class of securities and briefly describe any restriction on the issuer's present or future ability to pay such dividends.

Instruction: If the person filing this statement is an affiliate of the issuer, the information required by Item 1(d) should be furnished to the extent known by such affiliate after making reasonable inquiry.

(e) If the issuer and/or affiliate filing this statement has made an underwritten public offering of such securities for cash during the past three years which was registered under the Securities Act of 1933 or exempt from registration thereunder pursuant to Regulation A, state the date of such offering, the amount of securities offered, the offering price per share (which should be appropriately adjusted for stock splits, stock dividends, etc.) and the aggregate proceeds received by such issuer and/or such affiliate.

(f) With respect to any purchases of such securities made by the issuer or affiliate since the commencement of the issuer's second full fiscal year preceding the date of this schedule, state the amount of such securities purchased, the range of prices paid for such securities and the average purchase price for each quarterly period of the issuer during such period.

Instruction: The information required by Item 1(f) need not be given with respect to purchases of such securities by a person prior to the time such person became an affiliate.

Item 2. Identity and Background.

If the person filing this statement is the issuer of the class of equity securities which is the subject of the Rule 13e–3 transaction, make a statement to that effect. If this statement is being filed by an affiliate of the issuer which is other than a natural person or if any person enumerated in Instruction C to this statement is a corporation, general partnership, limited partnership, syndicate or other group of persons, state its name, the state or other place of its organization, its principal business, the address of its principal executive offices and provide the information required by (e) and (f) of this Item. If this statement is being filed by an affiliate of the issuer who is a natural person or if any person enumerated in Instruction C of this statement is a natural person, provide the information required by (a) through (g) of this Item with respect to such person(s).

(a) Name;

(b) Residence or business address;

(c) Present principal occupation or employment and the name, principal business and address of any corporation or other organization in which such employment or occupation is conducted;

(d) Material occupations, positions, offices or employments during the last 5 years, giving the starting and ending dates of each and the name, principal business and address of any business corporation or other organization in which such occupation, position, office or employment was carried on;

(e) Whether or not, during the last 5 years, such person has been convicted in a criminal proceeding (excluding traffic violations or similar misdemeanors) and, if so give the dates, nature of conviction, name and location of court, and penalty imposed or other disposition of the case;

(f) Whether or not, during the last 5 years, such person was a party to a civil proceeding of a judicial or administrative body of competent jurisdiction and as a result of such proceeding was or is subject to a judgment, decree or final order enjoining further violations of, or prohibiting activities subject to, federal or state securities laws or finding any violation of such laws; and, if so, identify and describe such proceeding and summarize the terms of such judgment, decree or final order;

Instruction: While negative answers to Items 2(e) and 2(f) are required in this schedule, they need not be furnished to security holders.

(g) Citizenship(s).

Item 3. Past Contacts, Transactions or Negotiations.

(a) If this schedule is filed by an affiliate of the issuer of the class of securities which is the subject of the Rule 13e–3 transaction:

(1) Briefly state the nature and approximate amount (in dollars) of any transaction, other than those described in Item 3(b) of this schedule, which has occurred since the commencement of the issuer's second full fiscal year preceding the date of this schedule between such affiliate (including subsidiaries of the affiliate and those persons enumerated in Instruction C of this schedule) and the issuer: *Provided, however,* That no disclosure need be made with respect to any transaction if the aggregate amount involved in such transaction was

less than one percent of the issuer's consolidated revenues (which may be based upon information contained in the most recently available filing with the Commission by the issuer unless such affiliate has reason to believe otherwise) (i) for the fiscal year in which such transaction occurred or (ii) for the portion of the current fiscal year which has occurred, if the transaction occurred in such year; and

(2) Describe any contacts, negotiations or transactions which have been entered into or which have occurred since the commencement of the issuer's second full fiscal year preceding the date of this schedule between such affiliate (including subsidiaries of the affiliate and those persons enumerated in Instruction C of this schedule) and the issuer concerning: a merger, consolidation or acquisition; a tender offer for or other acquisition of securities of any class of the issuer; an election of directors of the issuer; or a sale or other transfer of a material amount of assets of the issuer or any of its subsidiaries.

(b) Describe any contacts or negotiations concerning the matters referred to in Item 3(a)(2) which have been entered into or which have occurred since the commencement of the issuer's second full fiscal year preceding the date of this schedule (i) between any affiliates of the issuer of the class of securities which is the subject of the Rule 13e–3 transaction; or (ii) between such issuer or any of its affiliates and any person who is not affiliated with the issuer and who would have a direct interest in such matters. Identify the person who initiated such contacts or negotiations.

Item 4. Terms of the Transaction.

(a) State the material terms of the Rule 13e–3 transaction.

(b) Describe any term or arrangement concerning the Rule 13e–3 transaction relating to any security holder of the issuer which is not identical to that relating to other security holders of the same class of securities of the issuer.

Item 5. Plans or Proposals of the Issuer or Affiliate.

Describe any plan or proposal of the issuer or affiliate regarding activities or transactions which are to occur after the Rule 13e–3 transaction which relate to or would result in:

(a) An extraordinary corporate transaction, such as a merger, reorganization or liquidation, involving the issuer or any of its subsidiaries;

(b) A sale or transfer of a material amount of assets of the issuer or any of its subsidiaries;

(c) Any change in the present board of directors or management of the issuer including, but not limited to, any plan or proposal to change the number or term of directors, to fill any existing vacancy on the board or to change any material term of the employment contract of any executive officer;

(d) Any material change in the present dividend rate or policy or indebtedness or capitalization of the issuer;

(e) Any other material change in the issuer's corporate structure or business;

(f) A class of equity securities of the issuer becoming eligible for termination of registration pursuant to Section 12(g)(4) of the Act; or

(g) The suspension of the issuer's obligation to file reports pursuant to Section 15(d) of the Act.

Item 6. Source and Amounts of Funds or Other Consideration.

(a) State the source and total amount of funds or other consideration to be used in the Rule 13e–3 transaction.

(b) Furnish a reasonably itemized statement of all expenses incurred or estimated to be incurred in connection with the Rule 13e–3 transaction including, but not limited to, filing fees, legal, accounting and appraisal fees, solicitation expenses and printing costs and state whether or not the issuer has paid or will be responsible for paying any or all of such expenses.

(c) If all or any part of such funds or other consideration is, or is expected to be, directly or indirectly borrowed for the purpose of the Rule 13e–3 transaction,

(1) Provide a summary of each such loan agreement containing the identity of the parties, the term, the collateral, the stated and effective interest rates, and other material terms or conditions; and

(2) Briefly describe any plans or arrangements to finance or repay such borrowings, or, if no such plans or arrangements have been made, make a statement to that effect.

(d) If the source of all or any part of the funds to be used in the Rule 13e–3 transaction is a loan made in the ordinary course of business by a bank as defined by Section 3(a)(6) of the Act and Section 13(d) or 14(d) is applicable to such transaction, the name of such bank shall not be made available to the public if the person filing the statement so requests in writing and files such request, naming such bank, with the Secretary of the Commission.

Item 7. Purpose(s), Alternatives, Reasons and Effects.

(a) State the purpose(s) for the Rule 13e–3 transaction.

(b) If the issuer or affiliate considered alternative means to accomplish such purpose(s), briefly describe such alternative(s) and state the reason(s) for their rejection.

(c) State the reasons for the structure of the Rule 13e–3 transaction and for undertaking such transaction at this time.

(d) Describe the effects of the Rule 13e–3 transaction on the issuer, its affiliates and unaffiliated security holders, including the federal tax consequences.

Instructions: (1) Conclusory statements will not be considered sufficient disclosure in response to Item 7.

(2) The description required by Item 7(d) should include a reasonably detailed discussion of the benefits and detriments of the Rule 13e–3 transaction to the issuer, its affiliates and unaffiliated security holders. The benefits and detriments of the Rule 13e–3 transaction should be quantified to the extent practicable.

(3) If this statement is filed by an affiliate of the issuer, the description required by Item 7(d) should include but not be limited to, the effect of the Rule 13e–3 transaction on the affiliate's interest in the net book value and net earnings of the issuer in terms of both dollar amounts and percentages.

Item 8. Fairness of the Transaction.

(a) State whether the issuer or affiliate filing this schedule reasonably believes that the Rule 13e–3 transaction is fair or unfair to unaffiliated security holders. If any director dissented to or abstained from voting on the Rule 13e–3 transaction, identify each such director, and indicate, if known, after making reasonable inquiry, the reasons for each dissent or abstention.

Instruction: A statement that the issuer or affiliate has no reasonable belief as to the fairness of the Rule 13e–3 transaction to unaffiliated security holders will not be considered sufficient disclosure in response to Item 8(a).

(b) Discuss in reasonable detail the material factors upon which the belief stated in Item 8(a) is based and, to the extent practicable, the weight assigned to each such factor. Such discussion should include an analysis of the extent, if any, to which such belief is based on the factors set forth in instruction (1) to paragraph (b) of this Item, paragraphs (c), (d), and (e) of this Item, and Item 9.

Instructions: (1) The factors which are important in determining the fairness of a transaction to unaffiliated security holders and the weight, if any, which should be given to them in a particular context will vary. Normally such factors will include, among others, those referred to in paragraphs (c), (d) and (e) of this Item and whether the consideration offered to unaffiliated security holders constitutes fair value in relation to:

(i) current market prices

(ii) historical market prices

(iii) net book value

(iv) going concern value

(v) liquidation value

(vi) the purchase price paid in previous purchases disclosed in Item 1(f) of Schedule 13e–3

(vii) any report, opinion, or appraisal described in Item 9 and

(viii) firm offers of which the issuer or affiliate is aware made by any unaffiliated person, other than the person filing this statement, during the preceding eighteen months for (A) the merger or consolidation of the issuer into or with such person or of such person into or with the issuer, (B) the sale or other transfer of all or any substantial part of the assets of the issuer or (C) securities of the issuer which would enable the holder thereof to exercise control of the issuer.

(2) Conclusory statements, such as "The Rule 13e–3 transaction is fair to unaffiliated security holders in relation to net book value, going concern value and future prospects of the issuer" will not be considered sufficient disclosure in response to Item 8(b).

(c) State whether the transaction is structured so that approval of at least a majority of unaffiliated security holders is required.

(d) State whether a majority of directors who are not employees of the issuer has retained an unaffiliated representative to act solely on behalf of unaffiliated security holders for the purposes of negotiating the terms of the Rule 13e–3 transaction and/or preparing a report concerning the fairness of such transaction.

(e) State whether the Rule 13e–3 transaction was approved by a majority of the directors of the issuer who are not employees of the issuer.

(f) If any offer of the type described in instruction (viii) to Item 8(b) has been received, describe such offer and state the reason(s) for its rejection.

Item 9. Reports, Opinions, Appraisals and Certain Negotiations.

(a) State whether or not the issuer or affiliate has received any report, opinion (other than an opinion of counsel) or appraisal from an outside party which is materially related to the Rule 13e–3 transaction including, but not limited to, any such report, opinion or appraisal relating to the consideration or the fairness of the consideration to be offered to security holders of the class of securities which is the subject of the Rule 13e–3 transaction or the fairness of such transaction to the issuer or affiliate or to security holders who are not affiliates.

(b) With respect to any report, opinion or appraisal described in Item 9(a) or with respect to any negotiation or report described in Item 8(d) concerning the terms of the Rule 13e–3 transaction:

(1) Identify such outside party and/or unaffiliated representative;

(2) Briefly describe the qualifications of such outside party and/or unaffiliated representative;

(3) Describe the method of selection of such outside party and/or unaffiliated representative;

(4) Describe any material relationship between (i) the outside party, its affiliates, and/or unaffiliated representative, and (ii) the issuer or its affiliates, which existed during the past two years or is mutually understood to be contemplated and any compensation received or to be received as a result of such relationship;

(5) If such report, opinion or appraisal relates to the fairness of the consideration, state whether the issuer or affiliate determined the amount of consideration to be paid or whether the outside party recommended the amount of consideration to be paid.

(6) Furnish a summary concerning such negotiation report, opinion or appraisal which shall include, but not be limited to, the procedures followed; the findings and recommendations; the bases for and methods of arriving at such findings and recommendations; instructions received from the issuer or affiliate; and any limitation imposed by the issuer or affiliate; and any limitation imposed by the issuer or affiliate on the scope of the investigation.

Instruction: The information called for by subitem 9(b)(1), (2) and (3) should be given with respect to the firm which provides the report, opinion or appraisal rather than the employees of such firm who prepared it.

(c) Furnish a statement to the effect that such report, opinion or appraisal shall be made available for inspection and copying at the principal executive offices of the issuer or affiliate during its regular business hours by any interested equity security holder of the issuer or his representative who has been so designated in writing. This statement may also provide that a copy of such report, opinion or appraisal will be transmitted by the issuer or affiliate to any interested equity security holder of the issuer or his representative who has been so designated in writing upon written request and at the expense of the requesting security holder.

Item 10. Interest in Securities of the Issuer.

(a) With respect to the class of equity security to which the Rule 13e–3 transaction relates, state the aggregate amount and percentage of securities beneficially owned (identifying those securities for which there is a right to acquire) as of the most recent practicable date by the person filing this statement (unless such person is the issuer), by any pension, profit sharing or similar plan of the issuer or affiliate, by each person enumerated in Instruction C of this Schedule or by any associate or majority owned subsidiary of the issuer or affiliate giving the name and address of any such associate or subsidiary.

Instructions: 1. For the purpose of this Item, beneficial ownership shall be determined in accordance with Rule 13d–3 under the Exchange Act.

2. The information required by this paragraph should be given with respect to officers, directors and associates of the issuer to the extent known after making reasonable inquiry.

(b) Describe any transaction in the class of equity securities of the issuer which is the subject of a Rule 13e–3 transaction that was effected during the past 60 days by the issuer of such class or by the persons named in response to paragraph (a) of this Item.

Instructions: 1. The description of a transaction required by Item 10(b) shall include, but not necessarily be limited to: (i) the identity of the person covered by Item 10(b) who effected the transaction; (ii) the date of the transaction; (iii) the amount of securities involved; (iv) the price per security; and (v) where and how the transaction was effected.

2. If the information required by Item 10(b) is available to the person filing this statement at the time this statement is initially filed with the Commission, the information shall be included in the initial filing. However, if the information is not available to such person at the time of such initial filing, it shall be filed with the Commission promptly but in no event later than seven days (or 2 business days with respect to a tender subject to Regulation 14D or 10 business days with respect to a tender offer subject to Rule 13e–4) after the date of such filing and, if material, disclosed to security holders of the issuer pursuant to Rule 13e–3(e), and disseminated to them in a manner reasonably calculated to inform security holders.

Item 11. Contracts, Arrangements or Understandings with Respect to the Issuer's Securities.

Describe any contract, arrangement, understanding or relationship (whether or not legally enforceable) in connection with the Rule 13e–3 transaction between the person filing this statement (including any person enumerated in Instruction C of this schedule) and any person with respect to any securities of the issuer (including, but not limited to, any contract, arrangement, understanding or relationship concerning the transfer or the voting of any such securities, joint ventures, loan or option arrangements, puts or calls, guaranties of loans, guaranties against loss or the giving or withholding of proxies, consents or authorizations), naming the persons with whom such contracts, arrangements, understandings or relationships have been entered into and giving the material provisions thereof. Include such information for any of such securities that are pledged or otherwise subject to a contingency, the occurrence of which would give another person the power to direct the voting or disposition of such securities, except that disclosure of standard default and similar provisions contained in loan agreements need not be included.

Item 12. Present Intention and Recommendation of Certain Persons with Regard to the Transaction.

(a) To the extent known by the person filing this statement after making reasonable inquiry, furnish a statement of present intention with regard to the Rule 13e–3 transaction indicating whether or not any executive officer, director or affiliate of the issuer or any person enumerated in Instruction C of this statement will tender or sell securities of the issuer owned or held by such person and/or how such securities, and securities with respect to which such person holds proxies, will be voted and the reasons therefor.

Instruction: If the information required by Item 12(a) is available to the person filing this statement at the time this statement is initially filed with the Commission, the information shall be included in the initial filing. However, if the information is not available to such person at the time of such initial filing, it shall be filed with the Commission promptly but in no event later than seven days (or two business days with respect to a tender offer subject to Regulation 14D or ten business days with respect to a tender offer subject to Rule 13e–4) after the date of such filing and, if material, disclosed to security holders of the issuer pursuant to Rule 13e–3(e), and disseminated to them in a manner reasonably calculated to inform security holders.

(b) To the extent known by the person filing this statement after making reasonable inquiry, state whether any person named in paragraph (a) of this item has made a recommendation in support of or opposed to the Rule 13e–3 transaction and the reasons for such recommendation. If no recommendation has been made by such persons, furnish a statement to that effect.

Item 13. Other Provisions of the Transaction.

(a) State whether or not appraisal rights are provided under applicable state law or under the issuer's articles of incorporation or will be voluntarily accorded by the issuer or affiliate to security holders in connection with the Rule 13e–3 transaction and, if so, summarize such appraisal rights. If appraisal rights will not be available under the applicable state law, to security holders who object to the transaction, briefly outline the rights which may be available to such security holders under such law.

(b) If any provision has been made by the issuer or affiliate in connection with the Rule 13e–3 transaction to allow unaffiliated security holders to obtain access to the corporate files of the issuer or affiliate or to obtain counsel or appraisal services at the expense of the issuer or affiliate, describe such provision.

(c) If the Rule 13e–3 transaction involves the exchange of debt securities of the issuer or affiliate for the equity securities held by security holders of the issuer who are not affiliates, describe whether or not the issuer or affiliate will take steps to provide or assure that such securities are or will be eligible for trading on any national securities exchange or an automated inter-dealer quotation system.

Item 14. Financial Information.

(a) Furnish the following financial data concerning the issuer:

(1) Audited financial statements for the two fiscal years required to be filed with the issuer's most recent annual report under sections 13 and 15(d) of the Act;

(2) Unaudited balance sheets and comparative year-to-date income statements and statements of changes in financial position and related earnings per share amounts required to be included in the issuer's most recent quarterly report filed pursuant to the Act;

(3) Ratio of earnings to fixed charges for the two most recent fiscal years and the interim periods provided under Item 14(a)(2); and

(4) Book value per share as of the most recent fiscal year end and as of the date of the latest interim balance sheet provided under Item 14(a)(2).

(b) If material, provide pro forma data disclosing the effect of the Rule 13e–3 transaction on:

(1) The issuer's balance sheet as of the most recent fiscal year end and the latest interim balance sheet provided under Item 14(a)(2);

(2) The issuer's statement of income, earnings per share amounts, and ratio of earnings to fixed charges for the most recent fiscal year and the latest interim period provided under Item 14(a)(2); and

(3) The issuer's book value per share as of the most recent fiscal year end and as of the latest interim balance sheet date provided under Item 14(a)(2).

Item 15. Persons and Assets Employed, Retained or Utilized.

(a) Identify and describe the purpose for which any officer, employee, class of employees or corporate asset of the issuer (excluding corporate assets which are proposed to be used as consideration for purchases of securities which are disclosed in Item 6 of this schedule) has been or is proposed to be employed, availed of or utilized by the issuer or affiliate in connection with the Rule 13e–3 transaction.

(b) Identify all persons and classes of persons (excluding officers, employees and class of employees who have been identified in Item 15(a) of this schedule) employed, retained or to be compensated by the person filing this statement, or by any person on behalf of the person filing this statement, to make solicitations or recommendations in connection with the Rule 13e-3 transaction and provide a summary of the material terms of such employment, retainer or arrangement for compensation.

* * *

SCHEDULE 13E-4

Issuer Tender Offer Statement Pursuant to Section 13(e)(1)

Item 1. Security and Issuer.

(a) State the name of the issuer and the address of its principal executive office;

(b) State the exact title and the amount of securities outstanding of the class of security being sought as of the most recent practicable date; the exact amount of such securities being sought and the consideration being offered therefor; whether any such securities are to be purchased from any officer, director or affiliate of the issuer, and the details of each such transaction; and

(c) Identify the principal market in which such securities are being traded and, if the principal market is an exchange, state the high and low sales prices for such securities as reported in the consolidated transaction reporting system or, if not so reported, on such principal exchange for each quarterly period during the past two years. If the principal market is not an exchange, state the range of high and low bid quotations for each quarterly period during the past two years, the source of such quotations, and if there is currently no established trading market for such securities (excluding limited or sporadic) furnish a statement to that effect.

(d) State the name and address of the person filing this statement, if other than the issuer, and the nature of the affiliation between such person and the issuer.

Item 2. Source and Amount of Funds or Other Consideration.

(a) State the source and total amount of funds or other consideration for the purchase of the maximum amount of securities for which the tender offer is being made.

(b) If all or any part of such funds or other consideration is, or is expected to be borrowed, directly or indirectly, for the purpose of the tender offer:

(1) Provide a summary of each such loan agreement or arrangement containing the identity of the parties, the term, the collateral, the stated and effective interest rates, and other material terms or conditions relative to such loan agreement; and

(2) Briefly describe any plans or arrangements to finance or repay such borrowings, or if no such plans or arrangements have been made, make a statement to that effect.

Item 3. Purpose of the Tender Offer and Plans or Proposals of the Issuer or Affiliate.

State the purpose of purposes of the tender offer, and whether the securities are to be retired, held in the treasury of the issuer, or otherwise disposed of, indicating such disposition, and any plans or proposals which relate to or would result in:

(a) The acquisition by any person of additional securities of the issuer, or the disposition of securities of the issuer;

(b) An extraordinary corporate transaction, such as a merger, reorganization or liquidation, involving the issuer or any of its subsidiaries;

(c) A sale or transfer of a material amount of assets of the issuer or any of its subsidiaries;

(d) Any change in the present board of directors or management of the issuer including, but not limited to, any plans or proposals to change the number or the term of directors, to fill any existing vacancy on the board or to change any material term of the employment contract of any executive officer;

(e) Any material change in the present dividend rate or policy, or indebtedness or capitalization of the issuer;

(f) Any other material change in the issuer's corporate structure or business, including, if the issuer is a registered closed-end investment company, any plans or proposals to make any changes in its investment policy for which a vote would be required by Section 13 of the Investment Company Act of 1940;

(g) Changes in the issuer's charter, bylaws or instruments corresponding thereto or other actions which may impede the acquisition of control of the issuer by any person;

(h) Causing a class of equity security of the issuer to be delisted from a national securities exchange or to cease to be authorized to be quoted in an inter-dealer quotation system of a registered national securities association;

(i) A class of equity security of the issuer becoming eligible for termination of registration pursuant to Section 12(g)(4) of the Act; or

(j) The suspension of the issuer's obligation to file reports pursuant to Section 15(d) of the Act.

Item 4. Interest in Securities of the Issuer.

Describe any transaction in the class of subject security that was effected during the past 40 business days by the issuer or the person filing this statement, by any person referred to in Instruction C of this schedule or by any associate or subsidiary of any such person, including any executive officer or director of any such subsidiary.

Instructions: 1. The description of a transaction required by this Item shall include, but not necessarily be limited to: (1) the identity of the person covered by this Item who effected the transaction; (2) the date of the transaction; (3) the amount of securities involved; (4) the price per security; and (5) where and how the transaction was effected.

2. If the information required by this Item is available to the person filing this statement at the time this statement is initially filed with the Commission, the information should be included in the initial filing. However, if the information is not available to such person at the time of such initial filing, it shall be filed with the Commission promptly but in no event later than ten business days after such date of the filing and, if material, should be disclosed to security holders of the issuer in a manner reasonably calculated to inform security holders.

Item 5. Contracts, Arrangements, Understandings or Relations With Respect to the Issuer's Securities.

Describe any contract, arrangement, understanding or relationship relating, directly or indirectly, to the tender offer (whether or not legally enforceable) between the person filing this statement (including any person enumerated in Instruction C of this schedule) and any person with respect to any securities of the issuer (including, but not limited to, any contract, arrangement, understanding or relationship concerning the transfer or the voting of any such securities, joint ventures, loan or option arrangements, puts or calls, guaranties of loans, guaranties against loss, or the giving or withholding of proxies, consents or authorizations) naming the persons with whom such contracts, arrangements, understandings or relationships have been entered into and giving the material provisions thereof. Include such information for any of such securities that are pledged or otherwise subject to a contingency, the occurrence of which would give another person the power to direct the voting or disposition of such securities, except that disclosure of standard default and similar provisions contained in loan agreements need not be included.

Item 6. Persons Retained, Employed or to be Compensated.

Identify all persons and classes of persons employed, retained or to be compensated by the person filing this statement, or by any person on behalf of the person filing this statement, to make solicitations or recommendations in connection with the tender offer, and provide a summary of the material terms of such employment, retainer or arrangement for compensation.

Item 7. Financial Information.

(a) If material, furnish the following financial data of the issuer:

(1) Audited financial statements for the two fiscal years required to be filed with the issuer's most recent annual report under Sections 13 and 15(d) of the Act;

(2) Unaudited balance sheets and comparative year-to-date income statements and statements of changes in financial position and related earnings

per share amounts required to be included in the issuer's most recent quarterly report filed pursuant to the Act;

(3) Ratio of earnings to fixed charges for the two most recent fiscal years and the interim periods provided under Item 7(a)(2); and

(4) Book value per share as of the most recent fiscal year end and as of the date of the latest interim balance sheet provided under Item 7(a)(2).

(b) If material, provide pro forma data disclosing the effect of the tender offer on:

(1) The issuer's balance sheet as of the most recent fiscal year end and the latest interim balance sheet provided under Item 7(a)(2);

(2) The issuer's statement of income, earnings per share amounts, and ratio of earnings to fixed charges for the most recent fiscal year and the latest interim period provided under Item 7(a)(2); and

(3) The issuer's book value per share as of the most recent fiscal year end and as of the latest interim balance sheet date provided under Item 7(a)(2).

Item 8. Additional Information.

If material to a decision by a security holder whether to sell, tender or hold securities being sought in the tender offer, furnish information including, but not limited to, the following:

(a) Any present or proposed contracts, arrangements, understandings or relationships between the issuer and its executive officers, directors or affiliates (other than any contract, arrangement or understanding required to be disclosed pursuant to Item 5 of this schedule);

(b) Any applicable regulatory requirements which must be complied with or approvals which must be obtained in connection with the tender offer;

(c) The applicability of the margin requirements of Section 7 of the Act and the regulation promulgated thereunder;

(d) Any material pending legal proceedings relating to the tender offer, including the name and location of the court or agency in which the proceedings are pending, the date instituted, the principal parties thereto and a brief summary of the proceedings and the relief sought; and

Instruction: In connection with sub-item (d), a copy of any document relating to a major development (such as pleadings, an answer, complaint, temporary restraining order, injunction, opinion, judgment or order) in a material pending legal proceeding should be furnished promptly to the Commission on a supplemental basis.

(e) Such additional material information, if any, as may be necessary to make the required statements, in light of the circumstances under which they are made, not materially misleading.

SCHEDULE 14A

Information Required in Proxy Statement

Notes. A. Where any item calls for information with respect to any matter to be acted upon and such matter involves other matters with respect to which information is called for by other items of this schedule, the information called for by such other items shall also be given. For example, where a solicitation of security holders is for the purpose of approving the authorization of additional securities which are to be used to acquire another specified company, and the registrants' security holders will not have a separate opportunity to vote upon the transaction, the solicitation to authorize the securities is also a solicitation with respect to the acquisition. Under those facts, information required by Items 11, 13, and 14 shall be furnished.

B. Where any item calls for information with respect to any matter to be acted upon at the meeting, such item need be answered in the registrant's soliciting material only with respect to proposals to be made by or on behalf of the issuer.

C. Except as otherwise specifically provided, where any item calls for information for a specified period in regard to directors, officers or other persons holding specified positions or relationships, the information shall be given in regard to any person who held any of the specified positions or relationships at any time during the period. However, information need not be included for any portion of the period during which such person did not hold any such position or relationship provided a statement to that effect is made.

Item 1. Date, time and place information

(a) State the date, time and place of the meeting of security holders, and the complete mailing address, including ZIP Code, of the principal executive offices of the registrant, unless such information is otherwise disclosed in material furnished to security holders with or preceding the proxy statement. If action is to be taken by written consent, state the date by which consents are to be submitted if state law requires that such a date be specified or if the person soliciting intends to set a date.

(b) On the first page of the proxy statement, state the approximate date on which the proxy statement and form of proxy are first sent or given to security holders.

(c) Furnish the information required to be in the proxy statement by Rule 14a–5(e).

Item 2. Revocability of Proxy

State whether or not the person giving the proxy has the power to revoke it. If the right of revocation before the proxy is exercised is limited or is subject to compliance with any formal procedure, briefly describe such limitation or procedure.

Item 3. Dissenters' Rights of Appraisal

Outline briefly the rights of appraisal or similar rights of dissenters with respect to any matter to be acted upon and indicate any statutory procedure required to be followed by dissenting security holders in order to perfect such rights. Where such rights may be exercised only within a limited time after the date of adoption of a proposal, the filing of a charter amendment or other similar act, state whether the persons solicited will be notified of such date.

Instruction. Indicate whether a security holder's failure to vote against a proposal will constitute a waiver of his appraisal or similar rights and whether a vote against a proposal will be deemed to satisfy any notice requirements under State law with respect to appraisal rights. If the State law is unclear, state what position will be taken in regard to these matters.

Item 4. Persons Making the Solicitation

(a) *Solicitations not subject to Rule 14a–11.* (1) If the solicitation is made by the registrant, so state. Give the name of any director of the registrant who has informed the issuer in writing that he intends to oppose any action intended to be taken by the registrant and indicate the action which he intends to oppose.

(2) If the solicitation is made otherwise than by the registrant, so state and give the names of the persons by whom and on whose behalf it is made.

(3) If the solicitation is to be made otherwise than by the use of the mails, describe the methods to be employed. If the solicitation is to be made by specially engaged employees or paid solicitors, state (i) the material features of any contract or arrangement for such solicitation and identify the parties, and (ii) the cost or anticipated cost thereof.

(4) State the names of the persons by whom the cost of solicitation has been or will be borne, directly or indirectly.

(b) *Solicitations subject to Rule 14a–11.* (1) State by whom the solicitation is made and describe the methods employed and to be employed to solicit security holders.

(2) If regular employees of the registrant or any other participant in a solicitation have been or are to be employed to solicit security holders, describe the class or classes of employees to be so employed, and the manner and nature of their employment for such purpose.

(3) If specially engaged employees, representatives or other persons have been or are to be employed to solicit security holders, state (i) the material features of any contract or arrangement for such solicitation and identify the parties (ii) the cost or anticipated cost thereof, and (iii) the approximate number of such employees or employees of any other person (naming such other person) who will solicit security holders.

(4) State the total amount estimated to be spent and the total expenditures to date for, in furtherance of, or in connection with the solicitation of security holders.

(5) State by whom the cost of the solicitation will be borne. If such cost to be borne initially by any person other than the registrant, state whether reimbursement will be sought from the registrant, and, if so, whether the question of such reimbursement will be submitted to a vote of security holders.

(6) If any such solicitation is terminated pursuant to a settlement between the registrant and any other participant in such solicitation, describe the terms of such settlement, including the cost or anticipated cost thereof to the registrant.

Instructions. 1. With respect to solicitations subject to Rule 14a–11, costs and expenditures within the meaning of this item 3 shall include fees for attorneys, accountants, public relations or financial advisers, solicitors, advertising, printing, transportation, litigation and other costs incidental to the solicitation, except that the registrant may exclude the amount of such costs represented by the amount normally expended for a solicitation for an election of directors in the absence of a contest, and costs represented by salaries and wages of regular employees and officers, provided a statement to the effect is included in the proxy statement.

2. The information required pursuant to paragraph (6) of item 3(b) should be included in any amended or revised proxy statement or other soliciting materials relating to the same meeting or subject matter furnished to security holders by the registrant subsequent to the date of settlement.

Item 5. Interest of Certain Persons in Matters to be Acted Upon

(a) *Solicitations not subject to Rule 14a–11.* Describe briefly any substantial interest, direct or indirect, by security holdings or otherwise, of each of the following persons in any matter to be acted upon, other than elections to office:

(1) If the solicitation is made on behalf of registrant, each person who has been a director or officer of the registrant at any time since the beginning of the last fiscal year.

(2) If the solicitation is made otherwise than on behalf of registrant, each person on whose behalf the solicitation is made.

Any person who would be a participant in a solicitation for purposes of Rule 14a–11 as defined in paragraph (b)(3), (4), (5) and (6) thereof shall be deemed a person on whose behalf the solicitation is made for purposes of this paragraph (a).

(3) Each nominee for election as a director of the registrant.

(4) Each associate of the foregoing persons.

Instruction. Except in the case of a solicitation subject to this regulation made in opposition to another solicitation subject to this regulation, this sub-item (a) shall not apply to any interest arising from the ownership of securities of the registrant where the security holder receives no extra or special benefit not shared on a pro rata basis by all other holders of the same class.

(b) *Solicitations subject to Rule 14a–11.* (1) Describe briefly any substantial interest, direct or indirect, by security holdings or otherwise, of each participant as defined in Rule 14a–11(b)(2), (3), (4), (5) and (6), in any matter to be acted upon at the meeting, and include with respect to each participant the information, or a fair and adequate summary thereof, required by Items 2(a), 2(d), 3, 4(b) and 4(c) of Schedule 14B.

(2) With respect to any person, other than a director or officer of the registrant acting solely in that capacity, who is a party to an arrangement or understanding pursuant to which a nominee for election as director is proposed to be elected, describe any substantial interest, direct or indirect, by security holdings or otherwise, that he has in any matter to be acted upon at the meeting, and furnish the information called for by Item 4(b) and (c) of Schedule 14B.

Item 6. Voting Securities and Principal Holders Thereof

(a) State as to each class of voting securities of the registrant entitled to be voted at the meeting, the number of shares outstanding and the number of votes to which each class is entitled.

(b) Give the date as of which the record of security holders entitled to vote at the meeting will be determined. If the right to vote is not limited to security holders of record on that date, indicate the conditions under which other security holders may be entitled to vote.

(c) If action is to be taken with respect to the election of directors and if the persons solicited have cumulative voting rights: (1) Make a statement that they have such rights, (2) briefly describe such rights, (3) state briefly the conditions precedent to the exercise thereof, and (4) if discretionary authority to cumulate votes is solicited, so indicate.

(d) Furnish the information required by Item 403(a) of Regulation S–K to the extent known by the persons on whose behalf the solicitation is made.

(e) Furnish the information required by Item 403(b) of Regulation S–K.

(f) If, to the knowledge of the persons on whose behalf the solicitation is made, a change in control of the registrant has occurred since the beginning of its last fiscal year, state the name of the person(s) who acquired such control, the amount and the source of the consideration used by such person or persons; the basis of the control, the date and a description of the transaction(s) which resulted in the change of control and the percentage of voting securities of the registrant now beneficially owned directly or indirectly by the person(s) who acquired control; and the identity of the person(s) from whom control was assumed. If the source of all or any part of the consideration used is a loan made in the ordinary course of business by a bank as defined by section 3(a)(6) of the Act, the identity of such bank shall be omitted provided a request for confidentiality has been made pursuant to section 13(d)(1)(B) of the Act by the person(s) who acquired control. In lieu thereof, the material shall indicate that the identity of the bank has been so omitted and filed separately with the Commission.

Instructions. 1. State the terms of any loans or pledges obtained by the new control group for the purpose of acquiring control, and the names of the lenders or pledgees.

2. Any arrangements or understandings among members of both the former and new control groups and their associates with respect to election of directors or other matters should be described.

Item 7. Directors and Executive Officers

If action is to be taken with respect to election of directors, furnish the following information, in tabular form to the extent practicable. However, if the solicitation is made on behalf of persons other than the registrant, the information required need be furnished only as to nominees of the persons making the solicitation.

(a) The information required by Instruction 4 to Item 103 of Regulation S–K with respect to directors and executive officers.

(b) The information required by Items 401 and 404(a) and (c) of Regulation S–K.

(c) With respect to issuers other than investment companies registered under the Investment Company Act of 1940, furnish the information required by Item 404(b) of Regulation S–K.

(d) With respect to investment companies registered under the Investment Company Act of 1940, indicate by an asterisk any nominee or director who is or would be an "interested person" within the meaning of section 2(a)(19) of the Investment Company Act of 1940 and briefly describe the relationships by reason of which such person is deemed an "interested person."

(e)(1) State whether or not the registrant has standing audit, nominating and compensation committees of the Board of Directors, or committees performing similar functions. If the registrant has such committees, however designated, identify each committee member, state the number of committee meetings held by each such committee during the last fiscal year and describe briefly the functions performed by such committees. In the case of investment companies registered under the Investment Company Act of 1940, indicate by an asterisk whether that member is an "interested person" as defined in section 2(a)(19) of that Act. Information concerning compensation committees is not required of registered investment companies whose management functions are performed by external managers.

(2) If the registrant has a nominating or similar committee, state whether the committee will consider nominees recommended by shareholders and, if so, describe the procedures to be followed by shareholders in submitting such recommendations.

(f) State the total number of meetings of the board of directors (including regularly scheduled and special meetings) which were held during the last full fiscal year. Name each incumbent director who during the last full fiscal year attended fewer than 75 percent of the aggregate of (1) the total number of meetings of the board of directors (held during the period for which he has been a director) and (2) the total number of meetings held by all committees of the board on which he served (during the periods that he served).

(g) If a director has resigned or declined to stand for re-election to the board of directors since the date of the last annual meeting of shareholders because of a disagreement with the issuer on any matter relating to the issuer's operations, policies or practices, and if the director has furnished the issuer with a letter describing such disagreement and requesting that the matter be disclosed, the issuer shall state the date of resignation or declination to stand for re-election and summarize the director's description of the disagreement.

If the issuer believes that the description provided by the director is incorrect or incomplete, it may include a brief statement presenting its views of the disagreement.

Item 8. Compensation of Directors and Executive Officers

(See Note C at the beginning of Schedule 14A.)

Furnish the information required by Item 402 of Regulation S–K if action is to be taken with regard to (i) the election of directors (ii) any bonus, profit sharing or other compensation plan, contract or arrangement in which any director, nominee for election as a director, or officer of the registrant will participate, (iii) any pension or retirement plan in which any such person will participate or (iv) the granting or extension to any such person of any options, warrants or rights to purchase any securities, other than warrants or rights issued to security holders as such, on a pro rata basis. However, if the solicitation is made on behalf of persons other than the registrant, the information required need be furnished only as to nominee of the persons making the solicitation and associates of such nominees.

Item 9. Independent Public Accountants

If the solicitation is made on behalf of the registrant and relates to (1) the annual (or special meeting in lieu of annual) meeting of security holders at which directors are to be elected, or a solicitation of consents or authorizations in lieu of such meeting or (2) the election, approval or ratification of the registrant's accountant, furnish the following information describing the registrant's relationship with its independent public accountant:

(a) The name of the principal accountant selected or being recommended to security holders for election approval or ratification for the current year. If no accountant has been selected or recommended, so state and briefly describe the reasons therefor.

(b) The name of the principal accountant for the fiscal year most recently completed if different from the accountant selected or recommended for the current year or if no accountant has yet been selected or recommended for the current year.

(c) The proxy statement shall indicate (1) whether or not representatives of the principal accountant for the current year and for the most recently completed fiscal year are expected to be present at the security holders' meeting, (2) whether or not they will have the opportunity to make a statement if they desire to do so and (3) whether or not such representatives are expected to be available to respond to appropriate questions.

(d) If a change or changes in accountants have taken place since the date of the proxy statement for the most recent annual meeting of security holders (or, if this is the first meeting for which a proxy statement is required, within 12 months prior to, and any period subsequent to, the date of the end of the most recent fiscal year), notwithstanding any previous disclosure, provide the information required by Item 304(a) of Regulation S–K.

Item 10. Compensation Plans

If action is to be taken with respect to any plan pursuant to which cash or noncash compensation may be paid, furnish the following information with respect to any such plan.

(a) *All Plans.*

(1) Describe briefly the material features of the plan, identify each class of persons who will be eligible to participate therein, indicate the approximate number of persons in each such class and state the basis of such participation.

(2) State the benefits or amounts which will be received by or allocated to each of the following under the plan, if such benefits or amounts are determinable: (i) each person (stating name and position) specified in paragraph (a)(1)(i) of Item 402 of Regulation S–K; (ii) all current executive officers as a group; (iii) all directors who are not executive

officers as a group; (iv) all employees as a group. If such benefits or amounts are not determinable, state the benefits or amounts which would have been received by or allocated to each of the following for the last fiscal year if the plan had been in effect, if such benefits or amounts may be determined: (i) each person (stating name and position) specified in paragraph (a)(1)(i) 402 of Regulation S–K; (ii) all current executive officers as a group; (iii) all directors who are not executive officers as a group; (iv) all employees as a group.

(3) Furnish the information called for by Item 402(b) of Regulation S–K with respect to all compensation plans now in effect or in effect during the last three years except that information called for in subparagraphs (b)(1)(vi) and (vii) and (b)(4) of Item 402(b) of Regulation S–K should be furnished with respect to the last three fiscal years of the following: (i) each person (stating name and position) specified in Item 402(a)(1)(i) of Regulation S–K; (ii) all current executive officers as a group; (iii) all directors who are not executive officers as a group, if such persons may participate in the plan; and (iv) all employees as a group, if such persons may participate in the plan. Such information is in lieu of the information otherwise called for by Item 402(b) of Regulation S–K in connection with the disclosure required by Item 8 of this schedule.

(4) If the plan to be acted upon can be amended, otherwise than by a vote of security holders, to increase the cost thereof to the registrant or to alter the allocation of the benefits as between the groups specified in paragraph (a)(3), state the nature of the amendments which can be so made.

(b) *Specific Plans.*

(1) With respect to any pension or retirement plan submitted for security holder action, state: (i) the approximate total amount necessary to fund the plan with respect to past services, the period over which such amount is to be paid and the estimated annual payments necessary to pay the total amount over such period; and (ii) the estimated annual payment to be made with respect to current services. In the case of a pension or retirement plan, information called for by paragraph (a)(2) of this Item may be furnished in the format specified by paragraphs (b)(2) and (3) of Item 402 of Regulation S–K.

(2) With respect to options, warrants or rights submitted for security holder action; (i) state: (A) the title and amount of securities called for or to be called for by such options, warrants or rights; (B) the prices, expiration dates and other material conditions upon which the options, warrants or rights may be exercised; (C) the consideration received or to be received by the registrant or subsidiary for the granting or extension of the options, warrants or rights; (D) the market value of the securities called for or to be called for by the options, warrants or rights as of the latest practicable date; and (E) in the case of options, the federal income tax consequences of the issuance and exercise of such options to the recipient and the registrant; and (ii) state separately the amount of such options by the following persons if such benefits or amounts are determinable: (A) each person (stating name and position) specified in paragraph (a)(1)(i) of Item 402 of Regulation S–K; (B) all current executive officers as a group; (C) all directors who are not executive officers as a group; (D) each nominee for election as a director; (E) each associate of any of such directors, executive officers or nominees; (F) each other person who received or is to receive 5 percent of such options, warrants or rights; and (G) all employees as a group.

Instructions. 1. The term "plan" as used in this Item means any plan as defined in Instruction 3 of paragraph (b) of Item 402 of Regulation S–K.

2. If action is to be taken with respect to a material amendment or modification of an existing plan, the item shall be answered with respect to the plan as proposed to be amended or modified and shall indicate any material differences from the existing plan.

3. If the plan to be acted upon is set forth in a written document, three copies thereof shall be filed with the Commission at the time preliminary copies of the proxy statement and form of proxy are filed pursuant to paragraph (a) of Rule 14a–6.

4. Paragraphs (a)(3) and (b)(2)(ii) do not apply to warrants or rights to be issued to security holders as such on a pro rata basis.

5. The Commission should be informed, as supplemental information, when the proxy statement in preliminary form is filed, as to when the options, warrants or rights and the shares called for thereby will be registered under the Securities Act or, if

such registration is not contemplated, the section of the Securities Act or rule of the Commission under which exemption from such registration is claimed and the facts relied upon to make the exemption available.

Item 11. Authorization or Issuance of Securities Otherwise Than for Exchange

If action is to be taken with respect to the authorization or issuance of any securities otherwise than for exchange for outstanding securities of the issuer, furnish the following information:

(a) State the title and amount of securities to be authorized or issued.

(b) Furnish the information required by Item 202 of Regulation S–K. If the terms of the securities cannot be stated or estimated with respect to any or all of the securities to be authorized, because no offering thereof is contemplated in the proximate future, and if no further authorization by security holders for the issuance thereof is to be obtained, it should be stated that the terms of the securities to be authorized, including dividend or interest rates, conversion prices, voting rights, redemption prices, maturity dates, and similar matters will be determined by the board of directors. If the securities are additional shares of common stock of a class outstanding, the description may be omitted except for a statement of the preemptive rights, if any. Where the statutory provisions with respect to preemptive rights are so indefinite or complex that they cannot be stated in summarized form, it will suffice to make a statement in the form of an opinion of counsel as to the existence and extent of such rights.

(c) Describe briefly the transaction in which the securities are to be issued, including a statement as to (1) the nature and approximate amount of consideration received or to be received by the registrant, and (2) the approximate amount devoted to each purpose so far as determinable for which the net proceeds have been or are to be used. If it is impracticable to describe the transaction in which the securities are to be issued, state the reason, indicate the purpose of the authorization of the securities, and state whether further authorization for the issuance of the securities by a vote of security holders will be solicited prior to such issuance.

(d) If the securities are to be issued otherwise than in a general public offering for cash, state the reasons for the proposed authorization or issuance and the general effect thereof upon the rights of existing security holders.

Item 12. Modification or Exchange of Securities

If action is to be taken with respect to the modification of any class of securities of the registrant, or the issuance or authorization for issuance of securities of the registrant in exchange for outstanding securities of the registrant, furnish the following information:

(a) If outstanding securities are to be modified, state the title and amount thereof. If securities are to be issued in exchange for outstanding securities, state the title and amount of securities to be so issued, the title and amount of outstanding securities to be exchanged therefor and the basis of the exchange.

(b) Describe any material differences between the outstanding securities and the modified or new securities in respect of any of the matters concerning which information would be required in the description of the securities in an application on the appropriate form for their registration on a national securities exchange.

(c) State the reasons for the proposed modification or exchange and the general effect thereof upon the rights of existing security holders.

(d) Furnish a brief statement as to arrears in dividends or as to defaults in principal or interest in respect to the outstanding securities which are to be modified or exchanged and such other information as may be appropriate in the particular case to disclose adequately the nature and effect of the proposed action.

(e) Outline briefly any other material features of the proposed modification or exchange. If the plan of proposed action is set forth in a written document, file copies thereof with the Commission in accordance with Rule 14a–6.

(f) Furnish the information required by Item 13(a) of this schedule.

Instruction. If the existing security is presently listed and registered on a national securities exchange, state whether it is intended to apply for listing and registration of the new or reclassified security on such exchange or any other exchange. If it is not intended to make such application, state the effect of the termination of such listing and registration.

Item 13. Financial and Other Information

(*See* Notes D and E at the beginning of this Schedule.)

(a) Information required. If action is to be taken with respect to any matter specified in Item 11 or 12, furnish the following information:

(1) Financial statements meeting the requirements of Regulation S–X, including financial information required by Rule 3–05 and Article 11 of Regulation S–X with respect to transactions other than that pursuant to which action is to be taken as described in this proxy statement;

(2) Item 302 of Regulation S–K, supplementary financial information;

(3) Item 303 of Regulation S–K, management's discussion and analysis of financial condition and results of operations;

(4) Item 304 of Regulation S–K, changes in and disagreements with accountants on accounting and financial disclosure; and

(5) A statement as to whether or not representatives of the principal accountants for the current year and for the most recently completed fiscal year:

(i) are expected to be present at the security holders' meeting;

(ii) will have the opportunity to make a statement if they desire to do so; and

(iii) are expected to be available to respond to appropriate questions.

(b) Incorporation by reference. The information required pursuant to paragraph (a) of this Item may be incorporated by reference into the proxy statement as follows:

(1) S–3 registrants. If the registrant meets the requirements of Form S–3 (*see* Note E of this Schedule), it may incorporate by reference to previously-filed documents any of the information required by paragraph (a) of this Item, provided that the requirements of paragraph (c) are met. When the registrant meets the requirements of Form S–3 and has elected to furnish the required information by incorporation by reference, the registrant may elect to update the information so incorporated by reference to information in subsequently-filed documents.

(2) All registrants. The registrant may incorporate by reference any of the information required by paragraph (a) of this Item, provided that the information is contained in an annual report to security holders or a previously-filed statement or report, such report or statement is delivered to security holders with the proxy statement and the requirements of paragraph (c) are met.

(c) Certain conditions applicable to incorporation by reference. Registrants eligible to incorporate by reference into the proxy statement the information required by paragraph (a) of this Item in the manner specified by paragraphs (b)(1) and (b)(2) may do so only if:

(1) the information is not required to be included in the proxy statement pursuant to the requirement of another Item;

(2) the proxy statement identifies on the last page(s) the information incorporated by reference; and

(3) the material incorporated by reference substantially meets the requirements of this Item or the appropriate portions of this Item.

Instructions to Item 13 1. Notwithstanding the provisions of this Item, any or all of the information required by paragraph (a) of this Item, not material for the exercise of prudent judgment in regard to the matter to be acted upon may be omitted. In the usual case the information is deemed material to the exercise of prudent judgment where the matter to be acted upon is the authorization or issuance of a material amount of senior securities, but the information is not deemed material where the matter to be acted upon is the authorization or issuance of common stock, otherwise than in an exchange, merger, consolidation, acquisition or similar transaction, the authorization of preferred stock without present intent to issue or the authorization of preferred stock for issuance for cash in an amount constituting fair value.

2. In order to facilitate compliance with Rule 2–02(a) of Regulation S–X, one copy of the definitive proxy statement filed with the Commission shall

include a manually signed copy of the accountant's report. If the financial statements are incorporated by reference, a manually signed copy of the accountant's report shall be filed with the definitive proxy statement.

3. Notwithstanding the provisions of Regulation S–X, no schedules other than those prepared in accordance with Rules 12–15, 12–28 and 12–29 (or, for management investment companies, Rules 12–12 through 12–14) of that regulation need be furnished in the proxy statement.

4. Unless registered on a national securities exchange or otherwise required to furnish such information, registered investment companies need not furnish the information required by paragraphs (a)(2) or (3) of this Item.

5. If the registrant submits preliminary proxy material incorporating by reference financial statements required by this Item, the registrant should furnish a draft of the financial statements if the document from which they are incorporated has not been filed with or furnished to the Commission.

Item 14. Mergers, Consolidations, Acquisitions and Similar Matters

(*See* Notes A, D and E at the beginning of this Schedule.)

If action is to be taken with respect to any transaction involving (i) the merger or consolidation of the registrant into or with any other person or of any other person into or with the registrant, (ii) the acquisition by the registrant or any of its security holders of securities of another person, (iii) the acquisition by the registrant of any other going business or of the assets thereof, (iv) the sale or other transfer of all or any substantial part of the assets of the registrant, or (v) the liquidation or dissolution of the registrant, furnish the following information:

(a) Information about the transaction. Furnish the following information concerning the registrant and (unless otherwise indicated) each other person: which is to be merged into the registrant or into or with which the registrant is to be merged or consolidated; the business or assets of which are to be acquired; which is the issuer of securities to be acquired by the registrant in exchange for all or a substantial part of the registrant's assets; or which is the issuer of securities to be acquired by the registrant or its security holders:

(1) The name, complete mailing address (including the ZIP Code) and telephone number (including the area code) of the principal executive offices.

(2) A brief description of the general nature of the business conducted by the other person.

(3) A summary of the material features of the proposed transaction. If the transaction is set forth in a written document, file three copies thereof with the Commission at the time preliminary copies of the proxy statement and form of proxy are filed pursuant to Rule 14a–6(a). The summary shall include, where applicable:

(i) a brief summary of the terms of the transaction agreement;

(ii) the reasons for engaging in the transaction;

(iii) an explanation of any material differences in the rights of security holders of the registrant as a result of this transaction;

(iv) a brief statement as to the accounting treatment of the transaction; and

(v) the federal income tax consequences of the transaction.

(4) A brief statement as to dividends in arrears or defaults in principal or interest in respect of any securities of the registrant or of such other person and as to the effect of the transaction thereon and such other information as may be appropriate in the particular case to disclose adequately the nature and effect of the proposed action.

(5) The information required by Item 301 of Regulation S–K (selected financial data) for (i) the registrant; (ii) the other person; and (iii) if material, the registrant or the other person on a pro forma basis, giving effect to the transaction.

(6) In comparative columnar form, historical and pro forma per share data of the registrant and historical and equivalent pro forma per share data of the other person for the following items:

(i) book value per share as of the date financial data is presented pursuant to Item 301 of Regulation S–K (selected financial data);

(ii) cash dividends declared per share for the periods for which financial data is presented pursuant to Item 301 of Regulation S–K (selected financial data); and

(iii) income (loss) per share from continuing operations for the periods for which financial data is presented pursuant to Item 301 of Regulation S–K (selected financial data).

Instruction to paragraph (a)(6). For a business combination accounted for as a purchase, the pro forma and equivalent pro forma income (loss) from continuing operations per share and equivalent pro forma cash dividends declared per share shall be presented only for the most recent fiscal year and interim period. Equivalent pro forma per share amounts shall be calculated by multiplying the pro forma income (loss) per share before non-recurring charges or credits directly attributable to the transaction, pro forma book value per share, and the pro forma dividends per share of the registrant by the exchange ratio so that the per share amounts are equated to the respective values for one share of the other person.

(7) Financial information required by Article 11 of Regulation S–X with respect to this transaction.

Instructions to paragraph (a)(7). 1. Any other Article 11 information that is presented (rather than incorporated by reference) pursuant to other Items of this schedule shall be presented together with the information provided pursuant to paragraph (a)(7), but the presentation shall clearly distinguish between this transaction and any other.

2. If pro forma financial information with respect to all other transactions is incorporated by reference pursuant to paragraph (b) of this Item, only the pro forma results need be presented as part of the pro forma financial information required by this Item.

(8) A statement as to whether any federal or state regulatory requirements must be complied with or approval must be obtained in connection with the transaction and if so the status of such compliance or approval.

(9) If a report, opinion or appraisal materially relating to the transaction has been received from an outside party, and such report, opinion or appraisal is referred to in the proxy statement, furnish the same information as would be required by Item 9(b)(1) through (6) of Schedule 13E–3.

(10) A description of any past, present or proposed material contracts, arrangements, understandings, relationships, negotiations or transactions during the periods for which financial statements are presented or incorporated by reference pursuant to this Item between the other person or its affiliates and the registrant or its affiliates such as those concerning a merger, consolidation or acquisition; a tender offer or other acquisition of securities; any election of directors; or a sale or other transfer of a material amount of assets.

(11) As to each class of securities of the registrant or of the other person which is admitted to trading on a national securities exchange or with respect to which a market otherwise exists, and which will be materially affected by the transaction, state the high and low sale prices (or in the absence of trading in a particular period, the range of the bid and asked prices) as of the date preceding public announcement of the proposed transaction, or if no such public announcement was made, as of the day preceding the day the agreement or resolution with respect to the action was made.

(12) A statement as to whether or not representatives of the principal accountants for the current year and for the most recently completed fiscal year

(i) are expected to be present at the security holders' meeting;

(ii) will have the opportunity to make a statement if they desire to do so; and

(iii) are expected to be available to respond to appropriate questions.

(b) Information about the registrant and the other person. Furnish the information specified below for the registrant and for the other person designated in paragraph (a) of this Item, if applicable (hereinafter all references to the registrant should be read to include a reference to such other person unless the context otherwise indicates):

(1) Information with respect to S–3 registrants. If the registrant meets the requirements of Form S–3 (See Note E to this Schedule) and elects to furnish information in accordance with the provisions of this paragraph, furnish information as required below.

(i) Describe any and all material changes in the registrant's affairs that have occurred since the end of the latest fiscal year for which audited financial statements were included in the latest annual report to security holders and that have not been described in a report on Form 10–Q or Form 8–K filed under the Exchange Act;

(ii) Include in the proxy statement, if not incorporated by reference from the reports filed under the Exchange Act specified in paragraph (b)(1)(iii) of this Item, from a proxy or information statement filed pursuant to section 14 of the Exchange Act, from a prospectus previously filed pursuant to Rule 424 under the Securities Act or from a Form 8–K filed during either of the two preceding fiscal years:

(A) Financial information required by Rule 3–05 and Article 11 of Regulation S–X with respect to transactions other than that pursuant to which action is to be taken as described in this proxy statement.

(B) Restated financial statements prepared in accordance with Regulation S–X, if there has been a change in accounting principles or a correction of an error where such change or correction requires a material retroactive restatement of financial statements;

(C) Restated financial statements prepared in accordance with Regulation S–X where one or more business combinations accounted for by the pooling of interest method of accounting have been consummated subsequent to the most recent fiscal year and the acquired businesses, considered in the aggregate, are significant pursuant to Rule 11–01(b) of Regulation S–X; or

(D) Any financial information required because of a material disposition of assets outside the normal course of business.

(iii) Incorporate by reference into the proxy statement the documents listed in paragraphs (A) and (B) below:

(A) The registrant's latest annual report on Form 10–K filed pursuant to section 13(a) or 15(d) of the Exchange Act which contains financial statements for the registrant's latest fiscal year for which a Form 10–K was required to be filed;

(B) All other reports filed pursuant to section 13(a) or 15(d) of the Exchange Act since the end of the fiscal year covered by the annual report referred to in paragraph (b)(1)(iii)(A) of this Item.

(iv) The proxy statement also shall state on the last page(s) that all documents subsequently filed by the registrant pursuant to sections 13(a), 13(c), 14 or 15(d) of the Exchange Act, prior to one of the following dates, whichever is applicable, shall be deemed to be incorporated by reference into the proxy statement:

(A) If a meeting of security holders is to be held, the date on which such meeting is held;

(B) If a meeting of security holders is not to be held, the date on which the consents or authorizations are used to effect the proposed action.

(2) *Information with respect to S–2 or S–3 registrants.*

(i) *Information required to be furnished.* If the registrant meets the requirements of Form S–2 or Form S–3 (*See* Note E of this Schedule) and elects to comply with this paragraph, furnish the information required by either paragraph (A) or (B) of this paragraph. However, the registrant shall not provide information in the manner allowed by paragraph (A) of this paragraph, if the financial statements in the registrant's latest annual report to security holders do not reflect: restated financial statements prepared in accordance with Regulation S–X if there has been a change in accounting principles or a correction of an error where such change or correction requires a material retroactive restatement of financial statements; restated financial statements prepared in accordance with Regulation S–X where one or more business combinations accounted for by the pooling of interest method of accounting have been consummated subsequent to the most recent fiscal year and the acquired businesses, considered in the aggregate, are significant pursuant to Rule 11–01(b) of Regulation S–X; or any financial information required because of a material disposition of assets outside of the normal course of business.

(A) If the registrant elects to furnish information pursuant to this paragraph (b)(2)(i)(A) and delivers the proxy statement together with its latest annual report to security holders which, at the time of original preparation met the requirements of either Rule 14a–3 or 14c–3, or a complete and legible facsimile of such latest annual report to security holders:

(*1*) Indicate that the proxy statement is accompanied by the registrant's latest annual report to security holders.

(*2*) Provide financial and other information with respect to the registrant in the form required by Part I of Form 10–Q as of the end of the most recent fiscal quarter which ended after the end of the latest fiscal year for which audited financial statements were included in the latest report to security holders and more than 45 days prior to the date the proxy statement is filed in definitive form (or as of a more recent date) by one of the following means:

(i) Including such information in the proxy statement;

(ii) Providing without charge to each person to whom a proxy statement is delivered a copy of the registrant's latest Form 10–Q; or

(iii) Providing without charge to each person to whom a proxy statement is delivered a copy of the registrant's latest quarterly report that was delivered to its security holders and that included the required financial information.

(*3*) If not reflected in the registrant's latest annual report to security holders, provide information required by Rule 3–05 and Article 11 of Regulation S–X with respect to transactions other than that as to which action is to be taken as described in the proxy statement.

(*4*) Describe any and all material changes in the registrant's affairs that have occurred between the end of the latest fiscal year for which audited financial statements were included in the latest annual report to security holders and the date the definitive proxy statement is filed and that were not described in a Form 10–Q or quarterly report delivered with the proxy statement in accordance with paragraph (b)(2)(i)(A)(*2*)(ii) or (iii).

(B) If the registrant does not elect to furnish information and delivers its latest annual report to security holders pursuant to paragraph (b)(2)(i)(A):

(*1*) Furnish a brief description of the business done by the registrant and its subsidiaries during the most recent fiscal year as required by Rule 14a–3 to be included in an annual report to security holders. The description also should take into account changes in the registrant's business that have occurred between the end of the last fiscal year and the filing of definitive proxy materials.

(*2*) Include financial statements and information as required by Rule 14a–3(b)(1) to be included in an annual report to security holders. In addition, provide:

(*i*) The interim financial information required by Rule 10–01 of Regulation S–X for a report on Form 10–Q;

(*ii*) Financial information required by Rule 3–05 and Article 11 of Regulation S–X with respect to transactions other than that as to which action is to be taken as described in this proxy statement;

(*iii*) Restated financial statements prepared in accordance with Regulation S–X if there has been a change in accounting principles or a correction of an error where such change or correction requires a material retroactive restatement of financial statements;

(*iv*) Restated financial statements prepared in accordance with Regulation S–X where one or more business combinations accounted for by the pooling of interest method of accounting have been consummated subsequent to the most recent fiscal year and the acquired businesses, considered in the aggregate, are significant pursuant to Rule 11–01(b) of Regulation S–X; and

(*v*) Any financial information required because of a material disposition of assets outside of the normal course of business.

(*3*) Furnish the information required by the following:

(*i*) Item 101(b), (c)(1)(i) and (d) of Regulation S–K, industry segments, classes of similar products or services, foreign and domestic operations and import sales;

(*ii*) Item 102 of Regulation S–K for any property involved in the transaction, if such disclosure is material to the security holder's understanding of the transaction;

(*iii*) Item 201 of Regulation S–K, market price of and dividends on the registrant's common equity and related stockholder matters;

(*iv*) Item 301 of Regulation S–K, selected financial data;

(*v*) Item 302 of Regulation S–K, supplementary financial information;

(*vi*) Item 303 of Regulation S–K, management's discussion and analysis of financial condition and results of operations; and (*vii*) Item 304 of Regulation S–K, changes in and disagreements with accountants on accounting and financial disclosure.

(ii) *Incorporation of certain information by reference.*

If the registrant meets the requirements of Form S–2 or S–3 (*See* Note E of this Schedule) and elects to furnish information in accordance with the provisions of paragraph (b)(2)(i) of this Item:

(A) Incorporate by reference into the proxy statement the document listed in paragraphs (1) and (2) below and, if applicable, the portions of the documents listed in paragraphs (3) and (4) below.

(*1*) The registrant's latest annual report on Form 10–K filed pursuant to section 13(a) or 15(d) of the Exchange Act which contains audited financial statements for the registrant's latest fiscal year for which a Form 10–K was required to be filed.

(*2*) All other reports filed pursuant to section 13(a) or 15(d) of the Exchange Act since the end of the fiscal year covered by the annual report referred to in paragraph (a)(2)(i)(A)(*1*).

(*3*) If the registrant elects to deliver its latest annual report to security holders pursuant to paragraph (b)(2)(i)(A) of this Item, the information furnished in accordance with the following:

(*i*) Item 101(b), (c)(1)(i) and (d) of Regulation S–K, industry segments, classes of similar products or services, foreign and domestic operations and export sales;

(*ii*) Item 201 of Regulation S–K, market price of and dividends on the registrant's common equity and related stockholder matters;

(*iii*) Item 301 of Regulation S–K, selected financial data;

(*iv*) Item 302 of Regulation S–K, supplementary financial information;

(*v*) Item 303 of Regulation S–K, management's discussion and analysis of financial condition and results of operations; and

(vi) Item 304 of Regulation S–K, changes in and disagreements with accountants on accounting and financial disclosure.

(*4*) If the registrant elects, pursuant to paragraph (b)(2)(i)(A)(*2*)(*iii*) of this Item, to provide a copy of its latest quarterly report which was delivered to security holders, financial information equivalent to that required to be presented in Part I of Form 10–Q.

(B) The registrant also may state, if it so chooses, that specifically described portions of its annual or quarterly report to security holders, other than those portions required to be incorporated by reference pursuant to paragraphs (b)(2)(ii)(A)(*3*) and (*4*) of this Item, are not part of the proxy statement. In such case, the description of portions that are not incorporated by reference or that are excluded shall be made with clarity and in reasonable detail.

(3) *Information with respect to registrants other than S–2 or S–3 registrants.* (i) If the registrant does not meet the requirements of Form S–2 or S–3 (*See* Note E of this Schedule), or elects to comply with this paragraph (b)(3) in lieu of (b)(1) or (b)(2), furnish the following information:

(A) In addition to the brief description of the other person's business required to be in the proxy statement by paragraph (a)(2) of this Item, a brief description of the business done by the registrant and the other person and their subsidiaries during the most recent fiscal year as required by Rule 14a–3 to be included in an annual report to security holders. The description also shall take into account changes in the business that have occurred between the end of the latest fiscal year and the date the definitive proxy statement is filed.

(B) Information relating to industry segments, classes of similar products or services, foreign and domestic operations and export sales required by paragraph (b), (c)(1)(i) and (d) of Item 101 of Regulation S–K.

(C) Information relating to property required by Item 102 of Regulation S–K shall be provided for any property involved in the plan described pursuant to this Item, if such disclosure is material to the security holder's understanding of the transaction.

(D) Information required by Item 201 of Regulation S–K, market price of an dividends on the registrants' common equity and related stockholder matters.

(E) Financial statements meeting the requirements of Regulation S–X, including financial information required by Rule 3–05 and Article 11 of Regulation S–X with respect to transactions other than that as to which action is to be taken as escribed in this proxy statement.

(F) Item 301 of Regulation S–K, selected financial data;

(G) Item 302 of Regulation S–K, supplementary financial information;

(H) Item 303 of Regulation S–K, management's discussion and analysis of financial condition and results of operations; and

(I) Item 304 of Regulation S–K, changes in and disagreements with accountants on accounting and financial disclosure.

(ii) If the other person is not subject to the reporting requirements of either section 13(a) or 15(d) of the Exchange Act; or, because of section 12(i) of the Exchange Act, has not furnished an annual report to security holders pursuant to Rule 14a–3 or Rule 14c–3 for its latest fiscal year, furnish:

(A) the financial statements that would have been required to be included in an annual report to security holders pursuant to Rules 14a–3(b)(1) and (b)(2) had the company been required to furnish such a report; *provided, however,* that the balance sheet for the year preceding the latest full fiscal year and the income statements for the two years preceding the latest full year need not be audited if they have not previously been audited. In any case, such financial statements need be audited only to the extent practicable.

(B) the quarterly financial and other information that would have been required had the company been required to file Part I of Form 10–Q (§ 249.-308a) for the most recent quarter for which such a report would have been on file at the time the proxy statement is mailed or for a period ending as of a more recent date.

(C) the information required by paragraphs (b)(3)(i)(A)–(D) and (F)–(I) of this Item.

(c) *Additional method of incorporation by reference.* In lieu of the provision of information about the registrant and the other person required in paragraph (b) of this Item, the registrant may incorporate by reference into the proxy statement the information required by paragraph (b)(3) of this Item if it is contained in an annual report sent to security holders pursuant to the requirement of Rule 14a–3 with respect to the same meeting or solicitation of consents or authorizations as that to which the proxy statement relates, provided such information substantially meets the requirements of paragraph (b)(3) of this Item or the appropriate portions of paragraph (b)(3) of this Item.

Instructions to Item 14. 1. In order to facilitate compliance with Rule 2–02(a) of Regulation S–X, one copy of the definitive proxy statement filed with the Commission shall include a manually signed copy of the accountant's report. If the financial statements are incorporated by reference, a manually signed copy of the accountant's report shall be filed with the definitive proxy statement.

2. Notwithstanding the provisions of this Item, any or all of the required financial statements and related information which are not material for the exercise of prudent judgment in regard to the matter to be acted upon may be omitted.

3. If the registrant or any of its securities or assets are to be acquired by the other person, the information regarding the other person that is required by this Item, other than information required by paragraphs (a)(1)–(3) and (a)(8)–(11) of this Item, need be provided only to the extent that: (1) the registrant or its security holders who are entitled to vote or give an authorization or consent with regard to the action will become or remain security holders of the other person; or (2) such information is otherwise material to an informed voting decision.

4. If the plan being voted on involves only the registrant and one or more of its totally held subsidiaries and does not involve a liquidation of the registrant or a spinoff, the information required by this Item, other than information required by paragraphs (a)(1)–(4) and (a)(8)–(11) of this Item, may be omitted.

5. Notwithstanding the provisions of Regulation S–X, no schedules other than those prepared in accordance with Rules 12–15, 12–28 and 12–29 (or, for management investment companies, Rules 12–12 through 12–14) of that regulation need be furnished in the proxy statement.

6. Unless registered on a national securities exchange or otherwise required to furnish such information, registered investment companies need not furnish the information required by paragraphs (a)(5), (b)(3)(i)(F), (G) or (H) of this Item.

7. If the registrant submits preliminary proxy material incorporating by reference financial statements required by this Item, the registrant should furnish a draft of the financial statements if the document from which they are incorporated has not been filed with or furnished to the Commission.

Item 15. Acquisition or Disposition of Property

If action is to be taken with respect to the acquisition or disposition of any property, furnish the following information:

(a) Describe briefly the general character and location of the property.

(b) State the nature and amount of consideration to be paid or received by the registrant or any subsidiary. To the extent practicable, outline briefly the facts bearing upon the question of the fairness of the consideration.

(c) State the name and address of the transferer or transferee, as the case may be, and the nature of any material relationship of such person to the issuer or any affiliate of the issuer.

(d) Outline briefly any other material features of the contract or transaction.

Item 16. Restatement of Accounts

If action is to be taken with respect to the restatement of any asset, capital, or surplus account of the registrant, furnish the following information:

(a) State the nature of the restatement and the date as of which it is to be effective.

(b) Outline briefly the reasons for the restatement and for the selection of the particular effective date.

(c) State the name and amount of each account (including any reserve accounts) affected by the restatement and the effect of the restatement thereon. Tabular presentation of the amounts shall be made when appropriate, particularly in the case of recapitalizations.

(d) To the extent practicable, state whether and the extent, if any, to which, the restatement will, as of the date thereof, alter the amount available for distribution to the holders of equity securities.

Item 17. Action with Respect to Reports

If action is to be taken with respect to any report of the registrant or of its directors, officers or committees or any minutes of meeting of its stockholders, furnish the following information:

(a) State whether or not such action is to constitute approval or disapproval of any of the matters referred to in such reports or minutes.

(b) Identify each of such matters which it is intended will be approved or disapproved, and furnish the information required by the appropriate item or items of this schedule with respect to each such matter.

Item 18. Matters Not Required to be Submitted

If action is to be taken with respect to any matter which is not required to be submitted to a vote of security holders, state the nature of such matter, the reasons for submitting it to a vote of security holders and what action is intended to be taken by the registrant in the event of a negative vote on the matter by the security holders.

Item 19. Amendment of Charter, Bylaws or Other Documents

If action is to be taken with respect to any amendment of the registrant's charter, bylaws or other documents as to which information is not required above, state briefly the reasons for and the general effect of such amendment.

Instructions. 1. Where the matter to be acted upon is the classification of directors, state whether vacancies which occur during the year may be filled by the board of directors to serve only until the next annual meeting or may be so filled for the remainder of the full term.

2. Attention is directed to the discussion of disclosure regarding anti-takeover and similar proposals in Release No. 34–15230 (Oct. 13, 1978).

Item 20. Other Proposed Action

If action is to be taken with respect to any matter not specifically referred to above, describe briefly the substance of each such matter in substantially the same degree of detail as is required by Items 5 to 19, inclusive, above.

Item 21. Vote Required for Approval

As to each matter which is to be submitted to a vote of security holders, other than elections to office or the selection or approval of auditors, state the vote required for its approval.

SCHEDULE 14B

Information to be Included in Statements Filed by or on Behalf of a Participant (Other than the Issuer) pursuant to Rule 14a–11(c)

Instructions. 1. The item numbers and captions of the items shall be included but the text of the items may be omitted if the answers thereto are so prepared as to indicate clearly the coverage of the items. Answer every item. If an item is inapplicable or the answer is in the negative, so state. The information called for by Items 2(a) and 3(a) or a fair summary thereof is required to be included in all preliminary soliciting by Rule 14a–11(d)(3).

2. If the participant is a partnership, corporation, association or other business entity, the information called for by Items 2, 3 and 4(b) and (c) shall be given with respect to each partner, officer and director of such entity, and each person controlling such entity, who is not a participant.

Item 1. Issuer

State the name and address of the registrant.

Item 2. Identity and Background

(a) State the following:

(1) Your name and business address.

(2) Your present principal occupation or employment and the name, principal business and address of any corporation or other organization in which such employment is carried on.

(b) State the following:

(1) Your residence address.

(2) Information as to all material occupations, positions, offices or employments during the last ten years, giving starting and ending dates of each and the name, principal business and address of any business corporation or other business organization in which each such occupation, position, office or employment was carried on.

(c) State whether or not you are or have been a participant in any other proxy contest involving this or other registrants within the past ten years. If so, identify the principals, the subject matter and your relationship to the parties and the outcome.

(d) State whether or not, during the past ten years, you have been convicted in a criminal proceeding (excluding traffic violations or similar misdemeanors) and, if so, give dates, nature of conviction, name and location of court, and penalty imposed or other disposition of the case. A negative answer to this sub-item need not be included in the proxy statement or other proxy soliciting material.

Item 3. Interests in Securities of the Issuer

(a) State the amount of each class of securities of the registrant which you own beneficially, directly or indirectly.

(b) State the amount of each class of securities of the registrant which you own of record but not beneficially.

(c) State with respect to all securities of the registrant purchased or sold within the past 2 years, the dates on which they were purchased or sold and the amount purchased or sold on each such date.

(d) If any part of the purchase price or market value of any of the shares specified in paragraph (c) is represented by funds borrowed or otherwise obtained for the purpose of acquiring or holding such securities, so state and indicate the amount of the indebtedness as of the latest practicable date. If such funds were borrowed or obtained otherwise than pursuant to a margin account or bank loan in the regular course of business of a bank, broker or dealer, briefly describe the transaction, and state the names of the parties.

(e) State whether or not you are, or were within the past year, a party to any contract, arrangements or understandings with any person with respect to any securities of the registrant, including, but not limited to joint ventures, loan or option arrangements, puts or calls, guarantees against loss or guarantees of profit, division of losses or profits, or the giving or withholding of proxies. If so, name the parties to such contracts, arrangements or understandings and give the details thereof.

(f) State the amount of securities of the registrant owned beneficially, directly or indirectly, by each of your associates and the name and address of each such associate.

(g) State the amount of each class of securities of any parent or subsidiary of the registrant which you own beneficially, directly or indirectly.

Instruction. For purposes of this item, beneficial ownership shall be determined in accordance with Rule 13d–2 under the Act.

Item 4. Further Matters

(a) Describe the time and circumstances under which you became a participant in the solicitation and state the nature and extent of your activities or proposed activities as a participant.

(b) Furnish for yourself and your associates the information required by Item 404(a) of Regulation S–K.

(c) State whether or not you or any of your associates have any arrangement or understanding with any person—

(1) With respect to any future employment by the registrant or its affiliates; or

(2) With respect to any future transactions to which the registrant or any of its affiliates will or may be a party.

If so, describe such arrangement or understanding and state the names of the parties thereto.

(d) State the total amount contributed and proposed to be contributed by you in furtherance of the solicitation, directly or indirectly, if such amount exceeds or will exceed $500 in the aggregate.

SCHEDULE 14D–1

Tender Offer Statement Pursuant to Section 14(d)(1) of the Securities Exchange Act of 1934

* * *

Item 1. Security and Subject Company

(a) State the name of the subject company and the address of its principal executive offices;

(b) State the exact title and the number of shares outstanding of the class of equity securities being sought (which may be based upon information contained in the most recently available filing with the Commission by the subject company unless the bidder has reason to believe such information is not current), the exact amount of such securities being sought and the consideration being offered therefor; and

(c) Identify the principal market in which such securities are traded and state the high and low sales prices for such securities in such principal market (or, in the absence thereof, the range of high and low bid quotations) for each quarterly period during the past two years.

Item 2. Identity and Background

If the person filing this statement or any person enumerated in Instruction C of this statement is a corporation, partnership, limited partnership, syndicate or other group of persons, state its name, the state or other place of its organization, its principal business, the address of its principal office and the information required by (e) and (f) of this Item. If the person filing this statement or any person enumerated in Instruction C is a natural person, provide the information specified in (a) through (g) of this Item with respect to such person(s).

(a) Name;

(b) Residence or business address;

(c) Present principal occupation or employment and the name, principal business and address of any corporation or other organization in which such employment or occupation is conducted;

(d) Material occupations, positions, offices or employments during the last 5 years, giving the starting and ending dates of each and the name, principal business and address of any business corporation or other organization in which such occupation, position, office or employment was carried on;

Instruction. If a person has held various positions with the same organization, or if a person holds comparable positions with multiple related organizations, each and every position need not be specifically disclosed.

(e) Whether or not, during the last 5 years, such person has been convicted in a criminal proceeding (excluding traffic violations or similar misdemeanors) and, if so, give the dates, nature of conviction, name and location of court, and penalty imposed or other disposition of the case;

Instruction. While a negative answer to this sub-item is required in this schedule, it need not be furnished to security holders.

(f) Whether or not, during the last 5 years, such person was a party to a civil proceeding of a judicial or administrative body of competent jurisdiction and as a result of such proceeding was or is subject to a judgment, decree or final order enjoining future violations of, or prohibiting activities subject to federal or state securities laws or finding any violation of such laws; and, if so, identify and describe such proceeding and summarize the terms of such judgment, decree or final order; and

Instruction. While a negative answer to this sub-item is required in this schedule, it need not be furnished to security holders.

(g) Citizenship(s).

Item 3. Past Contacts, Transactions or Negotiations with the Subject Company

(a) Briefly state the nature and approximate amount (in dollars) of any transaction, other than those described in Item 3(b) of this schedule, which has occurred since the commencement of the subject company's third full fiscal year preceding the date of this schedule, between the person filing this schedule (including those persons enumerated in Instruction C of this schedule) and:

(1) the subject company or any of its affiliates which are corporations: *Provided, However,* That no disclosure need be made with respect to any transaction if the aggregate amount involved in such transaction was less than one percent of the subject company's consolidated revenues (which may be based upon information contained in the most recently available filing with the Commission by the subject company, unless the bidder has reason to believe otherwise) (i) for the fiscal year in which such transaction occurred or, (ii) for the portion of the current fiscal year which has occurred, if the transaction occurred in such year; and

(2) the executive officers, directors or affiliates of the subject company which are not corporations if the aggregate amount involved in such transaction or in a series of similar transactions, including all periodic installments in the case of any lease or other agreement providing for periodic payments or installments, exceeds $40,000.

(b) Describe any contacts, negotiations or transactions which have occurred since the commencement of the subject company's third full fiscal year preceding the date of this schedule between the bidder or its subsidiaries (including those persons enumerated in Instruction C of this schedule) and the subject company or its affiliates concerning: a merger, consolidation or acquisition; a tender offer or other acquisition of securities; an election of directors; or a sale or other transfer of a material amount of assets.

Item 4. Source and Amount of Funds or Other Consideration

(a) State the source and the total amount of funds or other consideration for the purchase of the maximum number of securities for which the tender offer is being made.

(b) If all or any part of such funds or other consideration are or are expected to be, directly or indirectly, borrowed for the purpose of the tender offer:

(1) Provide a summary of each loan agreement or arrangement containing the identity of the parties, the term, the collateral, the stated and effective interest rates, and other material terms or conditions relative to such loan agreement; and

(2) Briefly describe any plans or arrangements to finance or repay such borrowings, or if no such plans or arrangements have been made, make a statement to that effect.

(c) If the source of all or any part of the funds to be used in the tender offer is a loan made in the ordinary course of business by a bank as defined by section 3(a)(6) of the Act, the name of such bank shall not be made available to the public if the person filing the statement so requests in writing and files such request, naming such bank, with the Secretary of the Commission.

Item 5. Purpose of the Tender Offer and Plans or Proposals of the Bidder

State the purpose or purposes of the tender offer for the subject company's securities. Describe any plans or proposals which relate to or would result in:

(a) An extraordinary corporate transaction, such as a merger, reorganization or liquidation, involving the subject company or any of its subsidiaries;

(b) A sale or transfer of a material amount of assets of the subject company or any of its subsidiaries;

(c) Any change in the present board of directors or management of the subject company including, but not limited to, any plans or proposals to change the number or the term of directors or to fill any existing vacancies on the board;

(d) Any material change in the present capitalization or dividend policy of the subject company;

(e) Any other material change in the subject company's corporate structure or business, including, if the subject company is a registered closed-end investment company, any plans or proposals to make any changes in its investment policy for which a vote would be required by section 13 of the Investment Company Act of 1940;

(f) Causing a class of securities of the subject company to be delisted from a national securities exchange or to cease to be authorized to be quoted in an inter-dealer quotation system of a registered national securities association; or

(g) A class of equity securities of the subject company becoming eligible for termination of registration pursuant to section 12(g)(4) of the Act.

Item 6. Interest in Securities of the Subject Company

(a) State the aggregate number and percentage of the class represented by such shares (which may be based on the number of shares outstanding as contained in the most recently available filing with the Commission by the subject company unless the bidder has reason to believe such information is not current), beneficially owned (identifying those shares for which there is a right to acquire) by each person named in Item 2 of this schedule and by each associate and majority-owned subsidiary of such person giving the name and address of any such associate or subsidiary.

(b) Describe any transaction in the class of securities reported on that was effected during the past 60 days by the persons named in response to paragraph (a) of this item or by any executive officer, director or subsidiary of such person.

Instructions. 1. The description of a transaction required by item 6(b) shall include, but not necessarily be limited to: 1) the identity of the person covered by Item 6(b) who effected the transactions; 2) the date of the transaction; 3) the amount of securities involved; 4) the price per share; and 5) where and how the transaction was effected.

2. If the information required by Item 6(b) of this schedule is available to the bidder at the time this statement is initially filed with the Commission pursuant to Rule 14d-3(a)(1), such information should be included in such initial filing. However, if such information is not available to the bidder at the time of such initial filing, it shall be filed with the Commission promptly but in no event later than two business days after the date of such filing and, if material, shall be disclosed in a manner reasonably designed to inform security holders. The procedure specified by this instruction is provided for the purpose of maintaining the confidentiality of the tender offer in order to avoid possible misuse of inside information.

Item 7. Contracts, Arrangements, Understandings or Relationships with Respect to the Subject Company's Securities

Describe any contract, arrangement, understanding or relationship (whether or not legally enforceable) between the bidder (including those persons enumerated in Instruction C to this schedule) and any person with respect to any securities of the subject company, (including, but not limited to, any contract, arrangement, understanding or relationship concerning the transfer or the voting of any of such securities, joint ventures, loan or option arrangements, puts or calls, guaranties of loans, guaranties against loss, or the giving or withholding of proxies) naming the persons with whom such contracts, arrangements, understandings or relationships have been entered into and giving the material provisions thereof. Include such information for any of such securities that are pledged or otherwise subject to a contingency, the occurrence of which would give another person the power to direct the voting or disposition of such securities, except that disclosure of standard default and similar provisions contained in loan agreements need not be included.

Item 8. Persons Retained, Employed or to be Compensated

Identify all persons and classes of persons employed, retained or to be compensated by the bidder, or by any person on the bidder's behalf, to make solicitations or recommendations in connection with the tender offer and describe briefly the terms of such employment, retainer or arrangement for compensation.

Item 9. Financial Statement of Certain Bidders

Where the bidder is other than a natural person and the bidder's financial condition is material to a decision by a security holder of the subject company whether to sell, tender or hold securities being sought in the tender offer, furnish current, adequate financial information concerning the bidder *Provided* That if the bidder is controlled by another entity which is not a natural person and has been formed for the purpose of making the tender offer, furnish current, adequate financial information concerning such parent.

Instructions. 1. The facts and circumstances concerning the tender offer, particularly the terms of the tender offer, may influence a determination as to whether disclosure of financial information is material. However, once the materiality requirement is applicable, the adequacy of the financial information will depend primarily on the nature of the bidder.

In order to provide guidance in making this determination, the following types of financial information will be deemed adequate for purposes of this item for the type of bidder specified: (a) financial statements prepared in compliance with Form 10 as amended for a domestic bidder which is otherwise eligible to use such form; and (b) financial statements prepared in accordance with Item 17 of Form 20–F for a foreign bidder which is otherwise eligible to use such form.

2. If the bidder is subject to the periodic reporting requirements of section 13(a) or 15(d) of the Act, financial statements contained in any document filed with the Commission may be incorporated by reference in this schedule solely for the purposes of this schedule *Provided* That such financial statements substantially meet the requirements of this item; an express statement is made that such financial statements are incorporated by reference; the matter incorporated by reference is clearly identified by page, paragraph, caption or otherwise; and an indication is made where such information may be inspected and copies obtained. Financial statements which are required to be presented in comparative form for two or more fiscal years or periods shall not be incorporated by reference unless the material incorporated by reference includes the entire period for which the comparative data is required to be given.

3. If the bidder is not subject to the periodic reporting requirements of the Act, the financial statements required by this item need not be audited if such audited financial statements are not available or obtainable without unreasonable cost or expense and a statement is made to that effect disclosing the reasons therefor.

Item 10. Additional Information

If material to a decision by a security holder whether to sell, tender or hold securities being sought in the tender offer, furnish information as to the following:

(a) Any present or proposed material contracts, arrangements, understandings or relationships between the bidder or any of its executive officers, directors, controlling persons or subsidiaries and the subject company or any of its executive officers, directors, controlling persons or subsidiaries (other than any contract, arrangement or understanding required to be disclosed pursuant to Item 3 or 7 of this schedule);

(b) To the extent known by the bidder after reasonable investigation, the applicable regulatory requirements which must be complied with or approvals which must be obtained in connection with the tender offer;

(c) The applicability of anti-trust laws;

(d) The applicability of the margin requirements of section 7 of the Act and the regulations promulgated thereunder;

(e) Any material pending legal proceedings relating to the tender offer including the name and location of the court or agency in which the proceedings are pending, the date instituted, the principal parties thereto and a brief summary of the proceedings; and

Instruction. In connection with this sub-item, a copy of any document relating to a major development (such as pleadings, an answer, complaint, temporary restraining order, injunction, opinion, judgment or order) in a material pending legal proceeding should be promptly furnished to the Commission on a supplemental basis.

(f) Such additional material information, if any, as may be necessary to make the required statements, in light of the circumstances under which they are made, not materially misleading.

Item 11. Material to be Filed as Exhibits

Furnish a copy of:

(a) Tender offer material which is published, sent or given to security holders by or on behalf of the bidder in connection with the tender offer;

(b) Any loan agreement referred to in Item 4 of this schedule;

Instruction. The identity of any bank which is a party to a loan agreement need not be disclosed if the person filing the statement has requested that the identity of such bank not be made available to the public pursuant to Item 4 of this schedule.

(c) Any document setting forth the terms of any contracts, arrangements, understandings or relationships referred to in Item 7 or 10(a) of this schedule;

(d) Any written opinion prepared by legal counsel at the bidder's request and communicated to the bidder pertaining to the tax consequences of the tender offer;

(e) In an exchange offer where securities of the bidder have been or are to be registered under the Securities Act of 1933, the prospectus containing the information required to be included therein by Rule 432 of that Act;

(f) If any oral solicitations of security holders is to be made by or on behalf of the bidder, any written instruction, form or other material which is furnished to the persons making the actual oral solicitation for their use, directly or indirectly, in connection with the tender offer.

SCHEDULE 14D–9

Solicitation/Recommendation Statement Pursuant to Section 14(d)(4) of the Securities Exchange Act of 1934

Instructions. Eight copies of this statement, including all exhibits, should be filed with the Commission.

General Instructions: A. The item numbers and captions of the items shall be included but the text of the items is to be omitted. The answers to the items shall be so prepared as to indicate clearly the coverage of the items without referring to the text of the items. Answer every item. If an item is inapplicable or the answer is in the negative so state.

B. Information contained in exhibits to the statement may be incorporated by reference in answer or partial answer to any item or sub-item of the statement unless it would render such answer misleading, incomplete, unclear or confusing. Material incorporated by reference shall be clearly identified in the reference by page, paragraph, caption or otherwise. An express statement that the specified matter is incorporated by reference shall be made at the particular place in the statement where the information is required. A copy of any information or a copy of the pertinent pages of a document containing such information which is incorporated by reference shall be submitted with this statement as an exhibit and shall be deemed to be filed with the Commission for all purposes of the Act.

Item 1. Security and Subject Company

State the title of the class of equity securities to which this statement relates and the name and the address of the principal executive offices of the subject company.

Item 2. Tender Offer of the Bidder

Identify the tender offer to which this statement relates, the name of the bidder and the address of its principal executive offices or, if the bidder is a natural person, the bidder's residence or business address (which may be based on the bidder's Schedule 14D–1 filed with the Commission).

Item 3. Identity and Background

(a) State the name and business address of the person filing this statement.

(b) If material, describe any contract, agreement, arrangement or understanding and any actual or potential conflict of interest between the person filing this statement or its affiliates and: (1) the subject company, its executive officers, directors or affiliates; or (2) the bidder, its executive officers, directors or affiliates.

Instruction. If the person filing this statement is the subject company and if the materiality requirement of Item 3(b) is applicable to any contract, agreement, arrangement or understanding between the subject company or any affiliate of the subject company and any executive officer or director of the subject company, it shall not be necessary to include a description thereof in this statement, or in any solicitation or recommendation published, sent or given to security holders if such information, or information which does not differ materially from such information, has been disclosed in any proxy statement, report or other communication sent within one year of the filing date of this statement by the subject company to the then holders of the securities and has been filed with the Commission: *Provided* That this statement and the solicitation or recommendation published, sent or given to security holders shall contain specific reference to such proxy statement, report or other communication and that a copy of the pertinent portion(s) thereof is filed as an exhibit to this statement.

Item 4. The Solicitation or Recommendation

(a) State the nature of the solicitation or the recommendation. If this statement relates to a recommendation, state whether the person filing this statement is advising security holders of the securities being sought by the bidder to accept or reject the tender offer or to take other action with respect to the tender offer and, if so, furnish a description of such other action being recommended. If the person filing this statement is the subject company and a recommendation is not being made, state whether the subject company is either expressing no opinion and is remaining neutral toward the tender offer or is unable to take a position with respect to the tender offer.

(b) State the reason(s) for the position (including the inability to take a position) stated in (a) of this Item.

Instruction. Conclusory statements such as "The tender offer is in the best interest of shareholders," will not be considered sufficient disclosure in response to Item 4(b).

Item 5. Persons Retained, Employed or to Be Compensated

Identify any person or class of persons employed, retained or to be compensated by the person filing this statement or by any person on its behalf, to make solicitations or recommendations to security holders and describe briefly the terms of such employment, retainer or arrangement for compensation.

Item 6. Recent Transactions and Intent with Respect to Securities

(a) Describe any transaction in the securities referred to in Item 1 which was effected during the past 60 days by the person(s) named in response to Item 3(a) and by any executive officer, director, affiliate or subsidiary of such person(s).

(b) To the extent known by the person filing this statement, state whether the persons referred to in Item 6(a) presently intend to tender to the bidder, sell or hold securities of the class of securities being sought by the bidder which are held of record or beneficially owned by such persons.

Item 7. Certain Negotiations and Transactions by the Subject Company

(a) If the person filing this statement is the subject company, state whether or not any negotiation is being undertaken or is underway by the subject company in response to the tender offer which relates to or would result in:

(1) An extraordinary transaction such as a merger or reorganization, involving the subject company or any subsidiary of the subject company;

(2) A purchase, sale or transfer of a material amount of assets by the subject company or any subsidiary of the subject company;

(3) A tender offer for or other acquisition of securities by or of the subject company; or

(4) Any material change in the present capitalization or dividend policy of the subject company.

Instruction. If no agreement in principle has yet been reached, the possible terms of any transaction or the parties thereto need not be disclosed if in the opinion of the Board of Directors of the subject company such disclosure would jeopardize continuation of such negotiations. In such event, disclosure that negotiations are being undertaken or are underway and are in the preliminary stages will be sufficient.

(b) Describe any transaction, board resolution, agreement in principle, or a signed contract in response to the tender offer, other than one described pursuant to Item 3(b) of this statement, which relates to or would result in one or more of the matters referred to in Item 7(a)(1), (2), (3) or (4).

Item 8. Additional Information to Be Furnished

Furnish such additional information, if any, as may be necessary to make the required statements, in light of the circumstances under which they are made, not materially misleading.

Item 9. Material to Be Filed as Exhibits

Furnish a copy of:

(a) Any written solicitation or recommendation which is published or sent or given to security holders in connection with the solicitation or recommendation referred to in Item 4.

(b) If any oral solicitation or recommendation to security holders is to be made by or on behalf of the person filing this statement, any written instruction, or other material which is furnished to the persons making the actual oral solicitation or recommendation for their use, directly or indirectly, in connection with the solicitation or recommendation.

(c) Any contract, agreement, arrangement or understanding described in Item 3(b) or the pertinent portion(s) of any proxy statement, report or other communication referred to in Item 3(b).

*

3. REGULATION S–K

Standard Instruction for Filing Forms Under Securities Act of 1933 and Securities Exchange Act of 1934

Subpart 1—General

Subpart 100—Business

Subpart 200—Securities of the Registrant

Subpart 300—Financial Information

Subpart 400—Management and Certain Security Holders

Subpart 500—Registration Statement and Prospectus Provisions

Subpart 1—General

(a) *Application of Regulation S–K.*

This part (together with the General Rules and Regulations under the Securities Act of 1933, ("Securities Act") and the Securities Exchange Act of 1934, as amended ("Exchange Act"), the Interpretative Releases under these Acts and the forms under these Acts) states the requirements applicable to the content of the non-financial statement portions of:

(1) Registration statements under the Securities Act to the extent provided in the forms to be used for registration under such Act; and

(2) Registration statements under section 12, annual or other reports under sections 13 and 15(d), annual reports to security holders and proxy and information statements under section 14 of the Exchange Act, and any other documents required to be filed under the Exchange Act, to the extent provided in the forms and rules under such Act.

(b) *Commission policy on projections.* The Commission encourages the use in documents specified in Rule 175 under the Securities Act and Rule 3b–6 under the Exchange Act of management's projections of future economic performance that have a reasonable basis and are presented in an appropriate format. The guidelines set forth herein represent the Commission's views on important factors to be considered in formulating and disclosing such projections.

(1) *Basis for projections.* The Commission believes that management must have the option to present in Commission filings its good faith assessment of a registrant's future performance. Management, however, must have a reasonable basis for such an assessment. Although a history of operations or experience in projecting may be among the factors providing a basis for management's assessment, the Commission does not believe that a registrant always must have had such a history or experience in order to formulate projections with a reasonable basis. An outside review of management's projections may furnish additional support for having a reasonable basis for a projection. If management decides to include a report of such a review in a Commission filing, there also should be disclosure of the qualifications of the reviewer, the extent of the review, the relationship between the reviewer and the registrant, and other material factors concerning the process by which any outside review was sought or obtained. Moreover, in the case of a registration statement under the Securities Act, the reviewer would be deemed an expert and an appropriate consent must be filed with the registration statement.

(2) *Format for projections.* In determining the appropriate format for projections included in Commission filings, consideration must be given to, among other things, the financial items to be projected, the period to be covered, and the manner of presentation to be used. Although traditionally projections have been given for three financial items generally considered to be of primary importance to investors (revenues, net income (loss) and earnings (loss) per share), projection information need not necessarily be limited to these three items. However, management should take care to assure that the choice of items projected is not susceptible of misleading inferences through selective projection of only favorable items. Revenues, net income (loss) and earnings (loss) per share usually are presented together in order to avoid any misleading inferences that may arise when the individual items reflect contradictory trends. There may be instanc-

es, however, when it is appropriate to present earnings (loss) from continuing operations, or income (loss) before extraordinary items in addition to or in lieu of net income (loss). It generally would be misleading to present sales or revenue projections without one of the foregoing measures of income. The period that appropriately may be covered by a projection depends to a large extent on the particular circumstances of the company involved. For certain companies in certain industries, a projection covering a two or three year period may be entirely reasonable. Other companies may not have a reasonable basis for projections beyond the current year. Accordingly, management should select the period most appropriate in the circumstances. In addition, management, in making a projection, should disclose what, in its opinion, is the most probable specific amount or the most reasonable range for each financial item projected based on the selected assumptions. Ranges, however, should not be so wide as to make the disclosures meaningless. Moreover, several projections based on varying assumptions may be judged by management to be more meaningful than a single number or range and would be permitted.

(3) *Investor understanding.* (i) When management chooses to include its projections in a Commission filing, the disclosures accompanying the projections should facilitate investor understanding of the basis for and limitations of projections. In this regard investors should be cautioned against attributing undue certainty to management's assessment, and the Commission believes that investors would be aided by a statement indicating management's intention regarding the furnishing of updated projections. The Commission also believes that investor understanding would be enhanced by disclosure of the assumptions which in management's opinion are most significant to the projections or are the key factors upon which the financial results of the enterprise depend and encourages disclosure of assumptions in a manner that will provide a framework for analysis of the projection.

(ii) Management also should consider whether disclosure of the accuracy or inaccuracy of previous projections would provide investors with important insights into the limitations of projections. In this regard, consideration should be given to presenting the projections in a format that will facilitate subsequent analysis of the reasons for differences between actual and forecast results. An important benefit may arise from the systematic analysis of variances between projected and actual results on a continuing basis, since such disclosure may highlight for investors the most significant risk and profit-sensitive areas in a business operation.

(iii) With respect to previously issued projections, registrants are reminded of their responsibility to make full and prompt disclosure of material facts, both favorable and unfavorable, regarding their financial condition. This responsibility may extend to situations where management knows or has reason to know that its previously disclosed projects no longer have a reasonable basis.

(iv) Since a registrant's ability to make projections with relative confidence may vary with all the facts and circumstances, the responsibility for determining whether to discontinue or to resume making projections is best left to management. However, the Commission encourages registrants not to discontinue or to resume projections in Commission filings without a reasonable basis.

(c) *Commission policy on security ratings.*

In view of the importance of security ratings ("ratings") to investors and the marketplace, the Commission permits registrants to disclose, on a voluntary basis, ratings assigned by rating organizations to classes of debt securities, convertible debt securities and preferred stock in registration statements and periodic reports. In addition, the Commission permits, pursuant to Rule 134(a)(14) under the Securities Act, voluntary disclosure of ratings assigned by any nationally recognized statistical rating organizations ("NRSROs") in certain communications deemed not to be a prospectus ("tombstone advertisements").

Set forth herein are the Commission's views on important matters to be considered in disclosing security ratings.

(1) *Securities Act filings.*

(i) If a registrant includes in a registration statement filed under the Securities Act any rating(s) assigned to a class of securities, it should consider including: (A) any other rating intended for public dissemination assigned to such class by a NRSRO ("additional NRSRO rating") that is available on the date of the initial filing of the document and that is materially different from any rating disclosed; and

(B) the name of each rating organization whose rating is disclosed; each such rating organization's definition or description of the category in which it rated the class of securities; the relative rank of each rating within the assigning rating organization's overall classification system; and a statement informing investors that a security rating is not a recommendation to buy, sell or hold securities, that it may be subject to revision or withdrawal at any time by the assigning rating organization, and that each rating should be evaluated independently of any other rating. The registrant also should include the written consent of any rating organization that is not a NRSRO whose rating is included. With respect to the written consent of any NRSRO whose rating is included, see Rule 436(g) under the Securities Act.

(ii) If a change in a rating already included is available subsequent to the filing of the registration statement, but prior to its effectiveness, the registrant should consider including such rating change in the final prospectus. If the rating change is material or if a materially different rating from any disclosed becomes available during this period, the registrant should consider amending the registration statement to include the rating change or additional rating and recirculating the preliminary prospectus.

(iii) If a materially different additional NRSRO rating or a material change in a rating already included becomes available during any period in which offers or sales are being made, the registrant should consider disclosing such additional rating or rating change by means of a post-effective amendment or sticker to the prospectus pursuant to Rule 424(c) under the Securities Act, unless, in the case of a registration statement on Form S-3, it has been disclosed in a document incorporated by reference into the registration statement subsequent to its effectiveness and prior to the termination of the offering.

(2) *Exchange Act filings.*

(i) If a registrant includes in a registration statement or periodic report filed under the Exchange Act any rating(s) assigned to a class of securities, it should consider including the information specified in paragraphs (1)(i)(A) and (B) of this section.

(ii) If there is a material change in the rating(s) assigned by any NRSRO(s) to any outstanding class(es) of securities of a registrant subject to the reporting requirements of section 13(a) or 15(d) of the Exchange Act, the registrant should consider filing a report on Form 8-K or other appropriate report under the Exchange Act disclosing such rating change.

Subpart 100—Business

Item 101. Description of Business

(a) *General development of business.* Describe the general development of the business of the registrant, its subsidiaries and any predecessor(s) during the past five years, or such shorter period as the registrant may have been engaged in business. Information shall be disclosed for earlier period if material to an understanding of the general development of the business.

(1) In describing developments, information shall be given as to matters such as the following: the year in which the registrant was organized and its form of organization; the nature and results of any bankruptcy, receivership or similar proceedings with respect to the registrant or any of its significant subsidiaries; the nature and results of any other material reclassification, merger or consolidation of the registrant or any of its significant subsidiaries; the acquisition or disposition of any material amount of assets otherwise than in the ordinary course of business; and any material changes in the mode of conducting the business.

(2) Registrants, (i) filing a registration statement on Form S-1 under the Securities Act or on Form 10 under the Exchange Act, (ii) not subject to the reporting requirements of section 13(a) or 15(d) of the Exchange Act immediately prior to the filing of such registration statement, and (iii) that (including predecessors) have not received revenue from operations during each of the three fiscal years immediately prior to the filing of registration statement, shall provide the following information: (A) if the registration statement is filed prior to the end of the registrant's second fiscal quarter, a description of the registrant's plan of operation for the remainder of the fiscal year, or (B) if the registration statement is filed subsequent to the end of the registrant's second fiscal quarter, a description of the registrant's plan of operation for the remainder of the fiscal year and for the first six months of the next fiscal year. If such information is not avail-

able, the reasons for its not being available shall be stated. Disclosure relating to any plan shall include such matters as:

(1) In the case of a registration statement on Form S-1, a statement in narrative form indicating the registrant's opinion as to the period of time that the proceeds from the offering will satisfy cash requirements and whether in the next six months it will be necessary to raise additional funds to meet the expenditures required for operating the business of the registrant; the specific reasons for such opinion shall be set forth and categories of expenditures and sources of cash resources shall be identified; however, amounts of expenditures and cash resources need not be provided; in addition, if the narrative statement is based on a cash budget, such budget shall be furnished to the Commission as supplemental information, but not as part of the registration statement;

(2) An explanation of material product research and development to be performed during the period covered in the plan;

(3) Any anticipated material acquisition of plant and equipment and the capacity thereof;

(4) Any anticipated material changes in number of employees in the various departments such as research and development, production, sales or administration; and

(5) Other material areas which may be peculiar to the registrant's business.

(b) *Financial information about industry segments.* State for each of the registrant's last three fiscal years or for each fiscal year the registrant has been engaged in business, whichever period is shorter, the amounts of revenue (with sales to unaffiliated customers and sales or transfers to other industry segments of the registrant shown separately), operating profit or loss and identifiable assets attributed to each of the registrant's industry segments. * * * To the extent that financial information included pursuant to this paragraph (b) complies with generally accepted accounting principles, the registrant may include in its financial statements a cross reference to this data in lieu of presenting duplicative information about its segments in the financial statements; conversely, a registrant may cross reference to the financial statements.

(1) The prior period information shall be restated retroactively in the following circumstances, unless not material, with appropriate disclosure of the nature and effect of the restatement:

(i) When the financial statement of the registrant as a whole have been restated retroactively; or (ii) When there has been a change in the way the registrant's products or services are grouped into industry segments and such change affects the segment information being reported; restatement is not required when a registrant's reportable segments change solely as a result of a change in the nature of its operations or as a result of a segment losing or gaining in significance.

(2) If the registrant includes, or is required by Article 3 of Regulation S-X to include, interim financial statements, discuss any facts relating to the performance of any of the segments during the period which, in the opinion of management, indicate that the three year segment financial data may not be indicative of current or future operations of the segment. Comparative financial information shall be included to the extent necessary to the discussion.

(c) *Narrative description of business.* (1) Describe the business done and intended to be done by the registrant and its subsidiaries, focusing upon the registrant's dominant industry segment or each reportable industry segment about which financial information is presented in the financial statements. To the extent material to an understanding of the registrant's business taken as a whole, the description of each such segment shall include the information specified in paragraphs (c)(1)(i) through (x) of this Item. The matters specified in paragraphs (c)(1)(xi) through (xiii) of this Item shall be discussed with respect to the registrant's business in general; where material, the industry segments to which these matters are significant shall be identified.

(i) The principal products produced and services rendered by the registrant in the industry segment and the principal markets for, and methods of distribution of, the segment's principal products and services. In addition, state for each of the last three fiscal years the amount or percentage of total revenue contributed by any class of similar products or services which accounted for 10 percent or more of consolidated revenue in any of the last three fiscal years or 15 percent or more of consolidated revenue, if total revenue did not exceed $50,000,000 during any of such fiscal years.

(ii) A description of the status of a product or segment (e.g. whether in the planning stage, whether prototypes exist, the degree to which product design has progressed or whether further engineering is necessary), if there has been a public announcement of, or if the registrant otherwise has made public information about, a new product or industry segment that would require the investment of a material amount of the assets of the registrant or that otherwise is material. This paragraph is not intended to require disclosure of otherwise nonpublic corporate information the disclosure of which would affect adversely the registrant's competitive position.

(iii) The sources and availability of raw materials.

(iv) The importance to the industry segment and the duration and effect of all patents, trade marks, licenses, franchises and concessions held.

(v) The extent to which the business of the industry segment is or may be seasonal.

(vi) The practices of the registrant and the industry (respective industries) relating to working capital items (e.g., where the registrant is required to carry significant amounts of inventory to meet rapid delivery requirements of customers or to assure itself of a continuous allotment of goods from suppliers; where the registrant provides rights to return merchandise; or where the registrant has provided extended payment terms to customers).

(vii) The dependence of the segment upon a single customer, or a few customers, the loss of any one or more of which would have a material adverse effect on the segment. The name of any customer and its relationship, if any, with the registrant or its subsidiaries shall be disclosed if sales to the customer by one or more segments are made in an aggregate amount equal to 10 percent or more of the registrant's consolidated revenues and the loss of such customer would have a material adverse effect on the registrant and its subsidiaries taken as a whole. The names of other customers may be included, unless in the particular case the effect of including the names would be misleading. For purposes of this paragraph, a group of customers under common control or customers that are affiliates of each other shall be regarded as a single customer.

(viii) The dollar amount of backlog orders believed to be firm, as of a recent date and as of a comparable date in the preceding fiscal year, together with an indication of the portion thereof not reasonably expected to be filled within the current fiscal year, and seasonal or other material aspects of the backlog. (There may be included as firm orders government orders that are firm but not yet funded and contracts awarded but not yet assigned, provided an appropriate statement is added to explain the nature of such orders and the amount thereof. The portion of orders already included in sales or operating revenues on the basis of percentage of completion or program accounting shall be excluded.)

(ix) A description of any material portion of the business that may be subject to renegotiation of profits or termination of contracts or subcontracts at the election of the Government.

(x) Competitive conditions in the business involved including, where material, the identity of the particular markets in which the registrant competes, an estimate of the number of competitors and the registrant's competitive position, if known or reasonably available to the registrant. Separate consideration shall be given to the principal products or services or classes of products or services of the segment, if any. Generally, the names of competitors need not be disclosed. The registrant may include such names, unless in the particular case the effect of including the names would be misleading. Where, however, the registrant knows or has reason to know that one or a small number of competitors is dominant in the industry it shall be identified. The principal methods of competition (e.g., price, service, warranty or product performance) shall be identified, and positive and negative factors pertaining to the competitive position of the registrant, to the extent that they exist, shall be explained if known or reasonably available to the registrant.

(xi) If material, the estimated amount spent during each of the last three fiscal years on company-sponsored research and development activities determined in accordance with generally accepted accounting principles. In addition, state, if material, the estimated dollar amount spent during each of such years on customer-sponsored research activities relating to the development of new products, services or techniques or the improvement of existing products, services or techniques.

(xii) Appropriate disclosure also shall be made as to the material effects that compliance with Federal, State and local provisions which have been enacted or adopted regulating the discharge of materials into the environment, or otherwise relating to the protection of the environment, may have upon the capital expenditures, earnings and competitive position of the registrant and its subsidiaries. The registrant shall disclose any material estimated capital expenditures for environmental control facilities for the remainder of its current fiscal year and its succeeding fiscal year and for such further periods as the registrant may deem material.

(xiii) The number of persons employed by the registrant.

(d) *Financial information about foreign and domestic operations and export sales.* (1) State for each of the registrant's last three fiscal years, or for each fiscal year the registrant has been engaged in business, whichever period is shorter, the amounts of revenue (with sales to unaffiliated customers and sales or transfers to other geographic areas shown separately), operating profit or loss and identifiable assets attributable to each of the registrant's geographic areas and the amount of export sales in the aggregate or by appropriate geographic area to which the sales are made. (See Appendix B to this Item for a suggested tabular format for presentation of this information.) To the extent that financial information included pursuant to this paragraph (d) complies with generally accepted accounting principles, the registrant may include in its financial statements a cross-reference to this data in lieu of presenting duplicative data in its financial statements; conversely a registrant may cross-reference to the financial statements. The prior period information shall be retroactively restated in the following circumstances, unless not material, with appropriate disclosure of the nature and effect of the restatement:

(i) When the financial statements of the registrant as a whole have been retroactively restated, or

(ii) When there has been a change in the way a registrant's foreign operations are grouped into geographic areas and such change affects the geographic area information being reported. Restatement is not required when a registrant's geographic areas change as a result of a change in the nature of operations or as a result of an area losing or gaining in significance.

(2) Any risks attendant to the foreign operations and any dependence of one or more of the registrant's industry segments upon such foreign operations shall be described unless it would be more appropriate for this matter to be discussed in connection with the description of one or more of the registrant's industry segments pursuant to paragraph (c) of this Item.

(3) If the registrant includes, or is required by Article 3 of Regulation S–X to include, interim financial statements, discuss any facts relating to the information furnished pursuant to this paragraph (d) that, in the opinion of management, indicate that the three year financial data for foreign and domestic operations or export sales may not be indicative of current or future operations. Comparative information shall be included to the extent necessary to the discussion.

Instructions to Item 101. 1. In determining what information about the industry segments is material to an understanding of the registrant's business taken as a whole and therefore required to be disclosed pursuant to paragraph (c) of this Item, the registrant should take into account both quantitative and qualitative factors such as the significance of the matter to the registrant (e.g., whether a matter with a relatively minor impact on the registrant's business is represented by management to be important to its future profitability), the pervasiveness of the matter (e.g., whether it affects or may affect numerous items in the segment information), and the impact of the matter (e.g., whether it distorts the trends reflected in the segment information). Situations may arise when information should be disclosed about a segment, although the information in quantitative terms may not appear significant to the registrant's business taken as a whole.

2. The determination whether information about foreign and domestic operations and export sales is required in the document for a particular year shall be based upon an evaluation of interperiod comparability. For instance, interperiod comparability most likely would require that foreign

and domestic operations and export sales that have been significant in the past and are expected to be significant in the future be regarded as reportable even though they are not significant in the current fiscal year.

3. The Commission, upon written request of the registrant and where consistent with the protection of investors, may permit the omission of any of the information required by this Item or the furnishing in substitution thereof of appropriate information of comparable character.

Item 102. Description of Property

State briefly the location and general character of the principal plants, mines and other materially important physical properties of the registrant and its subsidiaries. In addition, identify the industry segment(s) that use the properties described. If any such property is not held in fee or is held subject to any major encumbrance, so state and describe briefly, how held.

Instructions to Item 102. 1. What is required is such information as reasonably will inform investors as to the suitability, adequacy, productive capacity and extent of utilization of the facilities by the registrant. Detailed descriptions of the physical characteristics of individual properties or legal descriptions by metes and bounds are not required and shall not be given.

2. In determining whether properties should be described, the registrant should take into account both quantitative and qualitative factors. See Instruction 1 to Item 101 of Regulation S-K.

3. In the case of an extractive enterprise, material information shall be given as to production, reserves, locations, development and the nature of the registrant's interest. If individual properties are of major significance to an industry segment:

A. More detailed information concerning these matters shall be furnished; and

B. Appropriate maps shall be used to disclose location data of significant properties except in cases for which numerous maps would be required.

4. A. If reserve estimates are referred to in the document, the staff of the Office of Engineering, Division of Corporation Finance of the Commission, shall be consulted. That Office may request that a copy of the full report of the engineer or other expert who estimated the reserves be furnished as supplemental information and not as part of the filing. See Rule 418 of Regulation C and Rule 12b-4 of Regulation 12B with respect to the submission to, and return by, the Commission of supplemental information.

B. If the estimates of reserves, or any estimated valuation thereof, are represented as being based on estimates prepared or reviewed by independent consultants, those independent consultants shall be named in the document.

5. Estimates of oil or gas reserves other than proved or, in the case of other extractive reserves, estimates other than proved or probable reserves, and any estimated values of such reserves shall not be disclosed in any document publicly filed with the Commission unless such information is required to be disclosed in the document by foreign or state law; provided, however, that where such estimates previously have been provided to a person (or any of its affiliates) that is offering to acquire, merge or consolidate with the registrant or otherwise to acquire the registrant's securities, such estimates may be included in documents relating to such acquisition.

6. The definitions in § 210.4-10(a) of Regulation S-X shall apply to this Item with respect to oil and gas operation.

Item 103. Legal Proceedings

Describe briefly any material pending legal proceedings, other than ordinary routine litigation incidental to the business, to which the registrant or any of its subsidiaries is a party or of which any of their property is the subject. Include the name of the court or agency in which the proceedings are pending, the date instituted, the principal parties thereto, a description of the factual basis alleged to underlie the proceeding and the relief sought. Include similar information as to any such proceedings known to be contemplated by governmental authorities.

Instructions to Item 103. If the business ordinarily results in actions for negligence or other claims, no such action or claim need be described unless it departs from the normal kind of such actions.

2. No information need be given with respect to any proceeding that involves primarily a claim for

damages if the amount involved exclusive of interest and costs, does not exceed 10 percent of the current assets of the registrant and its subsidiaries on a consolidated basis. However, if any proceeding presents in large degree the same issues as other proceedings pending or known to be contemplated, the amount involved in such other proceedings shall be included in computing such percentage.

3. Notwithstanding Instructions 1 and 2, any material bankruptcy, receivership, or similar proceeding with respect to the registrant or any of its significant subsidiaries shall be described.

4. Any material proceedings to which any director, officer or affiliate of the registrant, any owner of record or beneficially of more than five percent of any class of voting securities of the registrant, or any associate of any such director, officer, affiliate of the registrant, or security holder is a party adverse to the registrant or any of its subsidiaries or has a material interest adverse to the registrant or any of its subsidiaries also shall be described.

5. Notwithstanding the foregoing, an administrative or judicial proceeding (including for purposes of A and B of this Instruction proceedings which present in large degree the same issues) arising under any Federal, State or local provisions that have been enacted or adopted regulating the discharge of materials into the environment or otherwise relating to the protection of the environment shall not be deemed "ordinary routine litigation incidental to the business" and shall be described if:

A. Such proceeding is material to the business or financial condition of the registrant;

B. Such proceeding involves primarily a claim for damages, or involves potential monetary sanctions, capital expenditures, deferred charges or charges to income and the amount involved, exclusive of interest and costs, exceeds 10 percent of the current assets of the registrant and its subsidiaries on a consolidated basis; or

C. A governmental authority is a party to such proceeding and such proceeding involves potential monetary sanctions, unless the registrant reasonably believes that such proceeding will result in no monetary sanctions, or in money sanctions exclusive of interest and costs of less than $100,000; provided, however, that such proceedings which are similar in nature may be grouped and described generically.

Subpart 200—Securities of the Registrant

Item 201. Market Price of and Dividends on the Registrant's Common Equity and Related Stockholder Matters

(a) *Market information.* (1)(i) Identify the principal United States market or markets in which each class of the registrant's common equity is being traded. Where there is no established public trading market for a class of common equity, furnish a statement to that effect. For purposes of this Item the existence of limited or sporadic quotations should not of itself be deemed to constitute an "established public trading market." In the case of foreign registrants, also identify the principal established foreign public trading market, if any, for each class of the registrant's common equity.

(ii) If the principal United States market for such common equity is an exchange, state the high and low sales prices for the equity for each full quarterly period within the two most recent fiscal years and any subsequent interim period for which financial statements are included, or are required to be included by Article 3 of Regulation S–X, as reported in the consolidated transaction reporting system or, if not so reported, as reported on the principal exchange market for such equity.

(iii) If the principal United States market for such common equity is not an exchange, state the range of high and low bid information for the equity for each full quarterly period within the two most recent fiscal years and any subsequent interim period for which financial statements are included, or are required to be included by Article 3 of Regulation S–X, as regularly quoted in the automated quotation system of a registered securities association, or where the equity is not quoted in such a system, the range of reported high and low bid quotations, indicating the source of such quotations. Indicate, as applicable, that such over-the-counter market quotations reflect interdealer prices, without retail mark-up, mark-down, or commission and may not necessarily represent actual transactions. Where there is an absence of an established public trading market, reference to quotations shall be qualified by appropriate explanation.

(iv) Where a foreign registrant has identified a principal established foreign trading market for its common equity pursuant to paragraph (a)(1) of this Item, also provide market price information comparable, to the extent practicable, to that required for the principal United States market, including the source of such information. Such prices shall be stated in the currency in which they are quoted. The registrant may translate such prices into United States currency at the currency exchange rate in effect on the date the price disclosed was reported on the foreign exchange. If the primary United States market for the registrant's common equity trades using American Depositary Receipts, the United States prices disclosed shall be on that basis.

(v) If the information called for by this Item is being presented in a registration statement filed pursuant to the Securities Act or a proxy or information statement filed pursuant to the Exchange Act, the document also shall include price information as of the latest practicable date, and, in the case of securities to be issued in connection with an acquisition, business combination or other reorganization, as of the date immediately prior to the public announcement of such transaction.

(2) If the information called for by this paragraph (a) is being presented in a registration statement on Form S–1 or Form S–18 under the Securities Act or on Form 10 under the Exchange Act relating to a class of common equity for which at the time of filing there is no established United States public trading market, indicate the amounts of common equity (i) that is subject to outstanding options or warrant to purchase, or securities convertible into, common equity of the registrant; (ii) that could be sold pursuant to Rule 144 under the Securities Act or that the registrant has agreed to register under the Securities Act for sale by security holders; or (iii) that is being, or has been publicly proposed to be, publicly offered by the registrant (unless such common equity is being offered pursuant to an employee benefit plan or dividend reinvestment plan), the offering of which could have a material effect on the market price of the registrant's common equity.

(b) *Holders.* (1) Set forth the approximate number of holders of each class of common equity of the registrants as of the latest practicable date.

(2) If the information called for by this paragraph (b) is being presented in a registration statement filed pursuant to the Securities Act or a proxy statement or information statement filed pursuant to the Exchange Act that relates to an acquisition, business combination or other reorganization, indicate the effect of such transaction on the amount and percentage of present holdings of the registrant's common equity owned beneficially by (i) any person (including any group as that term is used in section 13(d)(3) of the Exchange Act) who is known to the registrant to be the beneficial owner of more than five percent of any class of the registrant's common equity and (ii) each director and nominee and (iii) all directors and officers as a group and the registrant's present commitments to such persons with respect to the issuance of shares of any class of its common equity.

(c) *Dividends.* (1) State the frequency and amount of any cash dividends declared on each class of its common equity by the registrant for the two most recent fiscal years and any subsequent interim period for which financial statements are required to be presented by § 210.3 of Regulation S–X. Where there are restrictions (including, where appropriate, restrictions on the ability of registrant's subsidiaries to transfer funds to the registrant in the form of cash dividends, loans or advances) that currently materially limit the registrant's ability to pay such dividends or that the registrant reasonably believes are likely to limit materially the future payment of dividends on the common equity so state and either (i) describe briefly (where appropriate quantify such restrictions), or (ii) cross reference to the specific discussion of such restrictions in the Management's Discussion and Analysis of financial condition and operating results prescribed by Item 303 of Regulation S–K and the description of such restrictions required by Regulation S–X in the registrant's financial statements.

(2) Where registrants have a record of paying no cash dividends although earnings indicate an ability to do so, they are encouraged to consider the question of their intention to pay cash dividends in the foreseeable future and, if no such intention exists, to make a statement of that fact in the filing. Registrants which have a history of paying cash dividends also are encouraged to indicate whether they currently expect that comparable cash dividends will continue to be paid in the future and, if

not, the nature of the change in the amount or rate **of cash** dividend payments.

Instructions to Item 201. 1. Registrants, the common equity of which is listed for trading on more than one securities exchange registered under the Exchange Act, are required to indicate each such exchange pursuant to paragraph (a)(1)(i) of this Item; such registrants, however, need only report one set of price quotations pursuant to paragraph (a)(1)(ii) of this Item; where available, these shall be the prices as reported in the consolidated transaction reporting system and, where the prices are not so reported, the prices on the most significant (in terms of volume) securities exchange for such shares.

2. Market prices and dividends reported pursuant to this Item shall be adjusted to give retroactive effect to material changes resulting from stock dividends, stock splits and reverse stock splits.

3. The computation of the approximate number of holders of registrant's common equity may be based upon the number of record holders or also may include individual participants in security position listings. See Rule 17Ad–8 under the Exchange Act. The method of computation that is chosen shall be indicated.

4. If the registrant is a foreign issuer, describe briefly:

A. Any governmental laws, decrees or regulations in the country in which the registrant is organized that restrict the export or import of capital including, but not limited to, foreign exchange controls, or that affect the remittance of dividends or other payments to nonresidential holders of the registrant's common equity; and

B. All taxes, including withholding provisions, to which United States common equity holders are subject under existing laws and regulations of the foreign country in which the registrant is organized. Include a brief description of pertinent provisions of any reciprocal tax treaty between such foreign country and the United States regarding withholding. If there is no such treaty, so state.

5. If the registrant is a foreign private issuer whose common equity of the class being registered is wholly or partially in bearer form, the response to this Item shall so indicate together with as much information as the registrant is able to provide with respect to security holdings in the United States. If the securities being registered trade in the United States in the form of American Depositary Receipts or similar certificates, the response to this Item shall so indicate together with the name of the depositary issuing such receipts and the number of shares or other units of the underlying security representing the trading units in such receipts.

Item 202. Description of Registrant's Securities

Note: If the securities being described have been accepted for listing on an exchange, the exchange may be identified. The document should not however, convey the impression that the registrant may apply successfully for listing of the securities on an exchange or that, in the case of an underwritten offering, the underwriters may request the registrant to apply for such listing, unless there is reasonable assurance that the securities to be offered will be acceptable to a securities exchange for listing.

(a) *Capital stock.* If capital stock is to be registered, state the title of the class and describe such of the matters listed in paragraphs (a)(1) through (5) as are relevant. A complete legal description of the securities need not be given.

(1) Outline briefly: (i) dividend rights; (ii) terms of conversion; (iii) sinking fund provisions; (iv) redemption provisions; (v) voting rights, including any provisions specifying the vote required by security holders to take action; (vi) any classification of the Board of Directors, and the impact of such classification where cumulative voting is permitted or required; (vii) liquidation rights; (viii) preemption rights; and (ix) liability to further calls or to assessment by the registrant and for liabilities of the registrant imposed on its stockholders under state statutes (e.g., to laborers, servants or employees of the registrant), unless such disclosure would be immaterial because the financial resources of the registrant or other factors make it improbable that liability under such state statutes would be imposed; (x) any restriction on alienability of the securities to be registered; and (xi) any provision discriminating against any existing or prospective holder of such securities as a result of such security holder owning a substantial amount of securities.

(2) If the rights of holders of such stock may be modified otherwise than by a vote of a majority or

more of the shares outstanding, voting as a class, so state and explain briefly.

(3) If preferred stock is to be registered, describe briefly any restriction on the repurchase or redemption of shares by the registrant while there is any arrearage in the payment of dividends or sinking fund installments. If there is no such restriction, so state.

(4) If the rights evidenced by, or amounts payable with respect to, the shares to be registered are, or may be, materially limited or qualified by the rights of any other authorized class of securities, include the information regarding such other securities as will enable investors to understand such limitations or qualifications. No information need be given, however, as to any class of securities all of which will be retired, provided appropriate steps to ensure such retirement will be completed prior to or upon delivery by the registrant of the shares.

(5) Describe briefly or cross-reference to a description in another part of the document, any provision of the registrant's charter or by-laws that would have an effect of delaying, deferring or preventing a change in control of the registrant and that would operate only with respect to an extraordinary corporate transaction involving the registrant [or any of its subsidiaries], such as a merger, reorganization, tender offer, sale or transfer of substantially all of its assets, or liquidation. Provisions and arrangements required by law or imposed by governmental or judicial authority need not be described or discussed pursuant to this paragraph (a)(5). Provisions or arrangements adopted by the registrant to effect, or further, compliance with laws or governmental or judicial mandate are not subject to the immediately preceding sentence where such compliance did not require the specific provisions or arrangements adopted.

(b) *Debt securities.* If debt securities are to be registered, state the title of such securities, the principal amount being offered, and, if a series, the total amount authorized and the total amount outstanding as of the most recent practicable date; and describe such of the matter listed in paragraphs (b)(1) through (10) as are relevant. A complete legal description of the securities need not be given. For purposes solely of this Item, debt securities that differ from one another only as to the interest rate or maturity shall be regarded as securities of the same class. Outline briefly:

(1) Provisions with respect to maturity, interest, conversion, redemption, amortization, sinking fund, or retirement;

(2) Provisions with respect to the kind and priority of any lien securing the securities, together with a brief identification of the principal properties subject to such lien;

(3) Provisions with respect to the subordination of the rights of holders of the securities to other security holders or creditors of the registrant; where debt securities are designated as subordinated in accordance with Instruction 1 to this Item, set forth in the aggregate amount of outstanding indebtedness as of the most recent practicable date that by the terms of such debt securities would be senior to such subordinated debt and describe briefly any limitations on the issuance of such additional senior indebtedness or state that there is no such limitation;

(4) Provisions restricting the declaration of dividends or requiring the maintenance of any asset ratio or the creation or maintenance of reserves;

(5) Provisions restricting the incurrence of additional debt or the issuance of additional securities; in the case of a secured debt, whether the securities being registered are to be issued on the basis of unbonded bondable property, the deposit of cash or otherwise; as of the most recent practicable date, the approximate amount of unbonded bondable property available as a basis for the issuance of bonds; provisions permitting the withdrawal of cash deposited as a basis for the issuance of bonds; and provisions permitting the release or substitution of assets securing the issue; *Provided, however,* That provisions permitting the release of assets upon the deposit of equivalent funds or the pledge of equivalent property, the release of property no longer required in the business, obsolete property, or property taken by eminent domain or the application of insurance moneys, and other similar provisions need not be described;

(6) The general type of event that constitutes a default and whether or not any periodic evidence is required to be furnished as to the absence of default or as to compliance with the terms of the indenture;

(7) Provisions relating to modification of the terms of the security or the rights of security holders;

(8) If the rights evidenced by the securities to be registered are, or may be, materially limited or qualified by the rights of any other authorized class of securities, the information regarding such other securities as will enable investors to understand the rights evidenced by the securities to the extent not otherwise disclosed pursuant to this Item; no information need be given, however, as to any class of securities all of which will be retired, provided appropriate steps to ensure such retirement will be completed prior to or upon delivery by the registrant of the securities;

(9) If debt securities are to be offered at a price such that they will be deemed to be offered at an "original issue discount" as defined in section 1273 of the Internal Revenue Code, or if a debt security is sold in a package with another security and the allocation of the offering price between the two securities may have the effect of offering the debt security at such an original issue discount, the tax effects thereof pursuant to sections 1271–1278; and

(10) The name of the trustee(s) and the nature of any material relationship with the registrant or with any of its affiliates; the percentage of securities of the class necessary to require the trustee to take action; and what indemnification the trustee may require before proceeding to enforce the lien.

(c) *Warrants and rights.* If the securities described are to be offered pursuant to warrants or rights state:

(1) The amount of securities called for by such warrants or rights;

(2) The period during which and the price at which the warrants or rights are exercisable;

(3) The amount of warrants or rights outstanding;

(4) Provisions for changes to or adjustments in the exercise price; and

(5) Any other material terms of such rights or warrants.

(d) *Other securities.* If securities other than capital stock, debt, warrants or rights are to be registered, include a brief description (comparable to that required in paragraphs (a), (b) and (c) of Item 202) of the rights evidenced thereby.

(e) *Market information for securities other than common equity.* If securities other than common equity are to be registered and there is an established public trading market for such securities (as that term is used in Item 201 of Regulation S-K) provide market information with respect to such securities comparable to that required by paragraph (a) of Item 201 of Regulation S-K.

(f) *American Depositary Receipts.* If Depositary Shares represented by American Depositary Receipts are being registered, furnish the following information:

(1) The name of the depositary and the address of its principal executive office.

(2) State the title of the American Depositary Receipts and identify the deposited security. Describe briefly the terms of deposit, including the provisions, if any, with respect to: (i) the amount of deposited securities represented by one unit of American Depositary Receipts; (ii) the procedure for voting, if any, the deposited securities; (iii) the collection and distribution of dividends; (iv) the transmission of notices, reports and proxy soliciting material; (v) the sale or exercise of rights; (vi) the deposit or sale of securities resulting from dividends, splits or plans of reorganization; (vii) amendment, extension or termination of the deposit; (viii) rights of holders of receipts to inspect the transfer books of the depositary and the list of holders of receipts; (ix) restrictions upon the right to deposit or withdraw the underlying securities; (x) limitation upon the liability of the depositary.

(3) Describe all fees and charges which may be imposed directly or indirectly against the holder of the American Depositary Receipts, indicating the type of service, the amount of fee or charges and to whom paid.

Instructions to Item 202.

1. Wherever the title of securities is required to be stated, there shall be given such information as will indicate the type and general character of the securities, including the following:

A. In the case of shares, the par or stated value, if any; the rate of dividends, if fixed, and whether cumulative or non-cumulative; brief indication of the preference, if any; and if convertible or redeemable, a statement to that effect;

B. In the case of debt, the rate of interest; the date of maturity or, if the issue matures serially, a brief indication of the serial maturities, such as "maturing serially from 1955 to 1960"; if the payment of principal or interest is contingent, an appropriate indication of such contingency; a brief indication of the priority of the issue; and, if convertible or callable, a statement to that effect; or

C. In the case of any other kind of security, appropriate information of comparable character.

2. If the registrant is a foreign registrant, include (to the extent not disclosed in the document pursuant to Item 201 of Regulation S-K or otherwise) in the description of the securities:

A. A brief description of any limitations on the right of nonresident or foreign owners to hold or vote such securities imposed by foreign law or by the charter or other constituent document of the registrant, or if no such limitations are applicable, so state;

B. A brief description of any governmental laws, decree or regulations in the country in which the registrant is organized affecting the remittance of dividends, interest and other payments to nonresident holders of the securities registered;

C. A brief outline of all taxes, including withholding provisions, to which United States security holders are subject under existing laws and regulations of the foreign country in which the registrant is organized; and

D. A brief description of pertinent provisions of any reciprocal tax treaty between such foreign country and the United States regarding withholding or, if there is no such treaty, so state.

3. Section 305(a)(2) of the Trust Indenture Act of 1939, as amended ("Trust Indenture Act"), shall not be deemed to require the inclusion in a registration statement or in a prospectus of any information not required by this Item.

4. Where convertible securities or stock purchase warrants are being registered that are subject to redemption or call, the description of the conversion terms of the securities or material terms of the warrants shall disclose:

A. Whether the right to convert or purchase the securities will be forfeited unless it is exercised before the date specified in a notice of the redemption or call;

B. The expiration or termination date of the warrants;

C. The kinds, frequency and timing of notice of the redemption or class, including the cities or newspapers in which notice will be published (where the securities provide for a class of newspapers or group of cities in which the publication may be made at the discretion of the registrant, the registrant should describe such provision); and

D. In the case of bearer securities, that investors are responsible for making arrangements to prevent loss of the right to convert or purchase in the event of redemption or call, for example, by reading the newspapers in which the notice of redemption or call may be published.

5. The response to paragraph (f) shall include information with respect to fees and charges in connection with (A) the deposit or substitution of the underlying securities; (B) receipt and distribution of dividends; (C) the sale or exercise of rights; (D) the withdrawal of the underlying security; and (E) the transferring, splitting or grouping of receipts. Information with respect to the right to collect the fees and charges against dividends received and deposited securities shall be included in response to this item.

Subpart 300—Financial Information

Item 301. Selected Financial Data

Furnish in comparative columnar form the selected financial data for the registrant referred to below, for

(a) Each of the last five fiscal years of the registrant (or for the life of the registrant and its predecessors, if less), and

(b) Any additional fiscal years necessary to keep the information from being misleading.

Instructions to Item 301. 1. The purpose of the selected financial data shall be to supply in a convenient and readable format selected financial data which highlight certain significant trends in the registrant's financial condition and results of operations.

2. Subject to appropriate variation to conform to the nature of the registrant's business, the following items shall be included in the table of financial data; net sales or operating revenue; income (loss) from continuing operations; income (loss) from continuing operations per common share; total assets; long-term obligations and redeemable preferred stock (including long-term debt, capital leases, and redeemable preferred stock as defined in § 210.5–02.28(a) of Regulation S–X); and cash dividends declared per common share. Registrants may include additional items which they believe would enhance an understanding of and would highlight other trends in their financial condition and results of operations.

Briefly describe, or cross-reference to a discussion thereof, factors such as accounting changes, business combinations or dispositions of business operations, that materially affect the comparability of the information reflected in selected financial data. Discussion of, or reference to, any material uncertainties should also be included where such matters might cause the data reflected herein not to be indicative of the registrant's future financial condition or results of operations.

3. Those registrants that are required to provide five-year summary information in accordance with Statement of Financial Accounting Standard No. 33, "Financial Reporting and Changing Prices," or inflation adjustments pursuant to Rule 3–20(c) of Regulation S–X may combine such information with the selected financial data appearing pursuant to this Item.

4. All references to the registrant in the table of selected financial data and in this Item shall mean the registrant and its subsidiaries consolidated.

5. If interim period financial statements are included, or are required to be included by Article 3 of Regulation S–X, registrants should consider whether any or all of the selected financial data need to be updated for such interim periods to reflect a material change in the trends indicated; where such updating information is necessary, registrants shall provide the information on a comparative basis unless not necessary to an understanding of such updating information.

6. A foreign private issuer shall disclose also the following information in all filings containing financial statements:

A. In the forepart of the document and as of the latest practicable date, the exchange rate into U.S. currency of the foreign currency in which the financial statements are denominated;

B. A history of exchange rates for the five most recent years and any subsequent interim period for which financial statements are presented setting forth the rates for period end, the average rates, and the range of high and low rates for each year; and

C. If equity securities are being registered, a five year summary of dividends per share stated in both the currency in which the financial statements are denominated and United States currency based on the exchange rates at each respective payment date.

7. A foreign private issuer shall present the selected financial data in the same currency as its financial statements. The issuer may present the selected financial data on the basis of the accounting principles used in its primary financial statements but in such case shall present this data also on the basis of any reconciliations of such data to United States generally accepted accounting principles and Regulation S–X made pursuant to Rule 4–01 of Regulation S–X.

8. For purposes of this rule, the rate of exchange means the noon buying rate in New York City for cable transfers in foreign currencies as certified for customs purposes by the Federal Reserve Bank of New York. The average rate means the average of the exchange rates on the last day of each month during a year.

Item 302. Supplementary Financial Information

(a) *Selected quarterly financial data.* Registrants specified in paragraph (a)(5) of this Item shall provide the information specified below.

(1) Disclosure shall be made of net sales, gross profit (net sales less costs and expenses associated directly with or allocated to products sold or services rendered), income (loss) before extraordinary items and cumulative effect of a change in accounting, per share data based upon such income (loss), and net income (loss), for each full quarter within

the two most recent fiscal years and any subsequent interim period for which financial statements are included or are required to be included by Article 3 of Regulation S–X.

(2) When the data supplied pursuant to this paragraph (a) vary from the amounts previously reported on the Form 10–Q filed for any quarter, such as would be the case when a pooling of interest occurs or where an error is corrected, reconcile the amounts given with those previously reported and describe the reason for the difference.

(3) Describe the effect of any disposals of segments of a business, and extraordinary, unusual or infrequently occurring items recognized in each full quarter within the two most recent fiscal years and any subsequent interim period for which financial statements are included or are required to be included by Article 3 of Regulation S–X, as well as the aggregate effect and the nature of year-end or other adjustments which are material to the results of the quarter.

(4) If the financial statements to which this information relates have been reported on by an accountant, appropriate professional standards and procedures, as enumerated in the Statements of Auditing Standards issued by the Auditing Standards Board of the American Institute of Certified Public Accountants, shall be followed by the reporting accountant with regard to the data required by this paragraph (a).

(5) This paragraph (a) applies to any registrant, except a foreign private issuer eligible to use Form 20–F, that meets both of the following tests:

(i) First test. The registrant:

(A) Has securities registered pursuant to section 12(b) of the Exchange Act (other than mutual life insurance companies); or

(B) Is an insurance company that is subject to the reporting requirements of section 15(d) of the Exchange Act and has securities which also meet the criteria set forth in paragraphs (C)(1) and (C)(2) immediately following; or

(C) Has securities registered pursuant to section 12(g) of the Exchange Act which also

(1) Are quoted on the National Association of Securities Dealers Automated Quotation System, and

(2) Meet the following criteria:

(i) Three or more dealers stand willing to, and do in fact, make a market in such stock, including making regularly published bona fide bids and offers for such stock for their own accounts; or the stock is registered on a securities exchange that is exempted by the Commission from registration as a national securities exchange pursuant to section 5 of the Exchange Act; for purposes of this paragraph, the insertion of quotations into the National Association of Securities Dealers Automated Quotation System by three or more dealers on at least 10 business days during the six month period immediately preceding the fiscal year for which the financial statements are required shall satisfy the requirement that three dealers be making a market;

(ii) There continue to be 800 or more holders of record, as defined in Rule 12g5–1, under the Exchange Act, of the stock who are not officers, directors, or beneficial owners of 10 percent or more of the stock;

(iii) The registrant continues to be a United States corporation;

(iv) There are 300,000 or more of such securities outstanding in addition to shares held beneficially by officers, directors, or beneficial owners of more than 10 percent of the stock; and

(v) In addition, the registrant shall meet two of the three following requirements:

(A) The shares described in paragraph (5)(i)(C)(2)(iv) of this Item continue to have a market value of at least $2.5 million;

(B) The minimum representative bid price of such stock is at least $5 per share; or

(C) The registrant continues to have at least $2.5 million of capital, surplus, and undivided profits.

Instructions to Paragraph (a)(5)(i)(C)(2)(v). 1. The computation required by paragraphs (v)(A) and (v)(B) shall be based on the average of the closing representative bid prices as reported by the National Association of Securities Dealers Automated Quotation System in accordance with Rule 11Ac1–2 under the Exchange Act for the 20 business days immediately preceding the fiscal year for which the financial statements are required.

2. The computation required by paragraph (v)(C) shall be as at the last business day of the

fiscal year immediately preceding the fiscal year for which the financial statements are required.

(ii) Second test. The registrant and its consolidated subsidiaries (A) have had a net income after taxes but before extraordinary items and the cumulative effect of a change in accounting of at least $250,000 for each of the last three fiscal years; or (B) had total assets of at least $200,000,000 for the last fiscal year end.

(b) *Information on the effects of changing prices.* Information on the effects of changing prices on business enterprises shall be presented by registrants subject to the reporting provisions of Statements of Financial Accounting Standards Nos. 33, 39, 40, 41, and 46. "Financial Reporting and Changing Prices," in accordance with the specific provisions of those Statements. Registered investment companies are excluded from these standards by Statement of Financial Accounting Standard No. 54 "Financial Reporting and Changing Prices: Investment Companies."

* * *

Item 303. Management's Discussion and Analysis of Financial Condition and Results of Operations

(a) *Full fiscal years.* Discuss registrant's financial condition, changes in financial condition and results of operations. The discussion shall provide information as specified in paragraphs (a)(1), (2) and (3) with respect to liquidity, capital resources and results of operations and also shall provide such other information that the registrant believes to be necessary to an understanding of its financial condition, changes in financial condition and results of operations. Discussions of liquidity and capital resources may be combined whenever the two topics are interrelated. Where in the registrant's judgment a discussion of segment information or of other subdivisions of the registrant's business would be appropriate to an understanding of such business, the discussion shall focus on each relevant, reportable segment or other subdivision of the business and on the registrant as a whole.

(1) *Liquidity.* Identify any known trends or any known demands, commitments, events or uncertainties that will result in or that are reasonably likely to result in the registrant's liquidity increasing or decreasing in any material way. If a material deficiency is identified, indicate the course of action that the registrant has taken or proposes to take to remedy the deficiency. Also identify and separately describe internal and external sources of liquidity, and briefly discuss any material unused sources of liquid assets.

(2) *Capital resources.* (i) Describe the registrant's material commitments for capital expenditures as of the end of the latest fiscal period, and indicate the general purpose of such commitments and the anticipated source of funds needed to fulfill such commitments.

(ii) Describe any known material trends, favorable or unfavorable, in the registrant's capital resources. Indicate any expected material changes in the mix and relative cost of such resources. The discussion shall consider changes between equity, debt and any off-balance sheet financing arrangements.

(3) *Results of operations.* (i) Describe any unusual or infrequent events or transactions or any significant economic changes that materially affected the amount of reported income from continuing operations and, in each case, indicate the extent to which income was so affected. In addition, describe any other significant components of revenues or expenses that, in the registrant's judgment, should be described in order to understand the registrant's results of operations.

(ii) Describe any known trends or uncertainties that have had or that the registrant reasonably expects will have a material favorable or unfavorable impact on net sales or revenues or income from continuing operations. If the registrant knows of events that will cause a material change in the relationship between costs and revenues (such as known future increases in costs of labor or materials or price increases or inventory adjustments), the change in the relationship shall be disclosed.

(iii) To the extent that the financial statements disclose material increases in net sales or revenues, provide a narrative discussion of the extent to which such increases are attributable to increases in prices or to increases in the volume or amount of goods or services being sold or to the introduction of new products or services.

(iv) For the three most recent fiscal years of the registrant, or for those fiscal years beginning after December 25, 1979, or for those fiscal years in which the registrant has been engaged in business, whichever period is shortest, discuss the impact of inflation and changing prices on the registrant's net sales and revenues and on income from continuing operations.

Instructions to Paragraph 303(a). 1. The registrant's discussion and analysis shall be of the financial statements and of other statistical data that the registrant believes will enhance a reader's understanding of its financial condition, changes in financial condition and results of operations. Generally, the discussion shall cover the three year period covered by the financial statements and shall use year-to-year comparisons or any other formats that in the registrant's judgment enhance a reader's understanding. However, where trend information is relevant, reference to the five year selected financial data appearing pursuant to Item 301 of Regulation S–K may be necessary.

2. The purpose of the discussion and analysis shall be to provide to investors and other users information relevant to an assessment of the financial condition and results of operations of the registrant as determined by evaluating the amounts and certainty of cash flows from operations and from outside sources. The information provided pursuant to this Item need only include that which is available to the registrant without undue effort or expense and which does not clearly appear in the registrant's financial statements.

3. The discussion and analysis shall focus specifically on material events and uncertainties known to management that would cause reported financial information not to be necessarily indicative of future operating results or of future financial condition. This would include descriptions and amounts of (A) matters that would have an impact on future operations and have not had an impact in the past, and (B) matters that have had an impact on reported operations and are not expected to have an impact upon future operations.

4. Where the consolidated financial statements reveal material changes from year to year in one or more line items, the causes for the changes shall be described to the extent necessary to an understanding of the registrant's businesses as a whole; *Provided, however,* That if the causes for a change in one line item also relate to other line items, no repetition is required and a line-by-line analysis of the financial statements as a whole is not required or generally appropriate. Registrants need not recite the amounts of changes from year to year which are readily computable from the financial statements. The discussion shall not merely repeat numerical data contained in the consolidated financial statements.

5. The term "liquidity" as used in this Item refers to the ability of an enterprise to generate adequate amounts of cash to meet the enterprise's needs for cash. Except where it is otherwise clear from the discussion, the registrant shall indicate those balance sheet conditions or income or cash flow items which the registrant believes may be indicators of its liquidity condition. Liquidity generally shall be discussed on both a long-term and short-term basis. The issue of liquidity shall be discussed in the context of the registrant's own business or businesses. For example a discussion of working capital may be appropriate for certain manufacturing, industrial or related operations but might be inappropriate for a bank or public utility.

6. Where financial statements presented or incorporated by reference in the registration statement are required by § 210.4–08(e)(3) of Regulation S–X to include disclosure of restrictions on the ability of both consolidated and unconsolidated subsidiaries to transfer funds to the registrant in the form of cash dividends, loans or advances, the discussion of liquidity shall include a discussion of the nature and extent of such restrictions and the impact such restrictions have had and are expected to have on the ability of the parent company to meet its cash obligations.

7. Registrants are encouraged, but not required, to supply forward-looking information. This is to be distinguished from presently known data which will impact upon future operating results, such as known future increases in costs of labor or materials. This latter data may be required to be disclosed. Any forward-looking information supplied is expressly covered by the safe harbor rule for projections. See Rule 175 under the Securities Act, Rule 3b–8 under the Exchange Act and Securities Act Release No. 8084 (June 25, 1979).

8. Registrants that are required to provide narrative explanations of supplementary information disclosed in accordance with paragraph 37 of Statement of Financial Accounting Standards No. 33,

"Financial Reporting and Changing Prices," (SFAS 33) may combine such explanations with the registrant's discussion and analysis required pursuant to this Item or may supply such information separately. If such statement is combined, the supplementary information required by SFAS 33 shall be located in reasonable proximity to the discussion and analysis. If such statement is not combined, the discussion of the impact of inflation otherwise required by this Item may be omitted but an appropriate cross reference to the explanation required by paragraph 37 of SFAS 33 shall be made. Foreign registrants normally are not subject to SFAS 33. If a foreign registrant otherwise discusses information on the effects of changing prices, then such information shall be given.

9. Registrants that are not required to provide supplementary information in accordance with SFAS 33 (including foreign private registrants) may discuss the effects of inflation and changes in prices in whatever manner appears appropriate under the circumstances. Although voluntary compliance with SFAS 33 is encouraged, it is not required. All that is required is a brief textual presentation of management's views. No specific numerical financial data need be presented.

10. All references to the registrant in the discussion and in this Item shall mean the registrant and its subsidiaries consolidated.

11. Foreign private registrants also shall discuss briefly any pertinent governmental economic, fiscal, monetary, or political policies or factors that have materially affected or could materially affect, directly or indirectly, their operations or investments by United States nationals.

12. If the registrant is a foreign private issuer, the discussion shall focus on the primary financial statements presented in the registration statement or report. There shall be a reference to the reconciliation to United States generally accepted accounting principles, and a discussion of any aspects of the difference between foreign and United States generally accepted accounting principles, not discussed in the reconciliation, that the registrant believes is necessary for an understanding of the financial statements as a whole.

(b) *Interim periods.* If interim period financial statements are included or are required to be included by Article 3 of Regulation S-X, a management's discussion and analysis of the financial condition and results of operations shall be provided so as to enable the reader to assess material changes in financial condition and results of operations between the periods specified in paragraphs (b)(1) and (2) of this Item. The discussion and analysis shall include a discussion of material changes in those items specifically listed in paragraph (a) of this Item, except that the impact of inflation and changing prices on operations for interim periods need not be addressed.

(1) *Material changes in financial condition.* Discuss any material changes in financial condition from the end of the preceding fiscal year to the date of the most recent interim balance sheet provided. If the interim financial statements include an interim balance sheet as of the corresponding interim date of the preceding fiscal year, any material changes in financial condition from that date to the date of the most recent interim balance sheet provided also shall be discussed. If discussions of changes from both the end and the corresponding interim date of the preceding fiscal year are required, the discussions may be combined at the discretion of the registrant.

(2) *Material changes in results of operations.* Discuss any material changes in the registrant's results of operations with respect to the most recent fiscal year-to-date period for which an income statement is provided and the corresponding year-to-date period of the preceding fiscal year. If the registrant is required to or has elected to provide an income statement for the most recent fiscal quarter, such discussion also shall cover material changes with respect to that fiscal quarter and the corresponding fiscal quarter in the preceding fiscal year. In addition, if the registrant has elected to provide an income statement for the twelve month period ended as of the date of the most recent interim balance sheet provided, the discussion also shall cover material changes with respect to that twelve month period and the twelve month period ended as of the corresponding interim balance sheet date of the preceding fiscal year. Notwithstanding the above, if for purposes of a registration statement a registrant subject to paragraph (b) of Rule 3-03 of Regulation S-X provides a statement of income for the twelve month period ended as of the date of the most recent interim balance sheet provided in lieu of the interim income statements otherwise required,

the discussion of material changes in that twelve month period will be in respect to the preceding fiscal year rather than the corresponding preceding period.

Instructions to Paragraph (b) of Item 303. 1. If interim financial statements are presented together with financial statements for full fiscal years, the discussion of the interim financial information shall be prepared pursuant to this paragraph (b) and the discussion of the full fiscal year's information shall be prepared pursuant to paragraph (a) of this Item. Such discussions may be combined.

2. In preparing the discussion and analysis required by this paragraph (b), the registrant may presume that users of the interim financial information have read or have access to the discussion and analysis required by paragraph (a) for the preceding fiscal year.

3. The discussion and analysis required by this paragraph (b) is required to focus only on material changes. Where the interim financial statements reveal material changes from period to period in one or more significant line items, the causes for the changes shall be described if they have not already been disclosed; *Provided, however,* That if the causes for a change in one line item also relate to other line items, no repetition is required. Registrants need not recite the amounts of changes from period to period which are readily computable from the financial statements. The discussion shall not merely repeat numerical data contained in the financial statements. The information provided shall include that which is available to the registrant without undue effort or expense and which does not clearly appear in the registrant's condensed interim financial statements.

4. The registrant's discussion of material changes in results of operations shall identify any significant elements of the registrant's income or loss from continuing operations which do not arise from or are not necessarily representative of the registrant's ongoing business.

5. The registrant shall discuss any seasonal aspects of its business which have had a material effect upon its financial condition or results of operation.

6. Registrants are encouraged but are not required to discuss forward-looking information. Any forward-looking information supplied is expressly covered by the safe harbor rule for projections. See Rule 175 under the Securities Act, Rule 3B–6 under the Exchange Act and Securities Act Release No. 6084 (June 25, 1979).

Item 304. Disagreements With Accountants on Accounting and Financial Disclosure

If, (a) within the twenty-four months prior to the date of the most recent financial statements, a Form 8–K under the Exchange Act reporting a change of accountants has been filed, (b) included in such Form 8–K there was a reported disagreement on any matter of accounting principles or practices or financial statement disclosure, (c) during the fiscal year in which the change in accountants took place or during the subsequent fiscal year there have been any transactions or events similar to those which involved the reported disagreement, and (d) such transactions or events were material and were accounted for or disclosed in a manner different from that which the former accountants apparently would have concluded was required, state the existence and nature of the disagreement and also state the effect on the financial statements if the method had been followed which the former accountants apparently would have concluded was required. These disclosures need not be made if the method asserted by the former accountants ceases to be generally accepted because of authoritative standards or interpretations subsequently issued.

Subpart 400—Management and Certain Security Holders

Item 401. Directors and Executive Officers

(a) *Identification of directors.* List the names and ages of all directors of the registrant and all persons nominated or chosen to become directors; indicate all positions and offices with the registrant held by each such person; state his term of office as director and any period(s) during which he has served as such; describe briefly any arrangement or understanding between him and any other person(s) (naming such person(s)) pursuant to which he was or is to be selected as a director or nominee.

Instructions to Paragraph (a) of Item 401. 1. Do not include arrangements or understandings with directors or officers of the registrant acting solely in their capacities as such.

2. No nominee or person chosen to become a director who has not consented to act as such shall be named in response to this Item. In this regard, with respect to proxy statements, see Rule 14a–4(d) under the Exchange Act.

3. If the information called for by this paragraph (a) is being presented in a proxy or information statement, no information need be given respecting any director whose term of office as a director will not continue after the meeting to which the statement relates.

4. With regard to proxy statements in connection with action to be taken concerning the election of directors, if fewer nominees are named than the number fixed by or pursuant to the governing instruments, state the reasons for this procedure and that the proxies cannot be voted for a greater number of persons than the number of nominees named.

5. With regard to proxy statements in connection with action to be taken concerning the election of directors, if the solicitation is made by persons other than management, information shall be given as to nominees of the persons making the solicitation. In all other instances, information shall be given as to directors and persons nominated for election or chosen by management to become directors.

(b) *Identification of executive officers.* List the names and ages of all executive officers of the registrant and all persons chosen to become executive officers; indicate all positions and offices with the registrant held by each such person; state his term of office as officer and the period during which he has served as such and describe briefly any arrangement or understanding between him and any other person(s) (naming such person) pursuant to which he was or is to be selected as an officer.

Instructions to Paragraph (b) of Item 401. 1. Do not include arrangements or understandings with directors or officers of the registrant acting solely in their capacities as such.

2. No person chosen to become an executive officer who has not consented to act as such shall be named in response to this Item.

3. The information regarding executive officers called for by this Item need not be furnished in proxy or information statements prepared in accordance with Schedule 14A under the Exchange Act by those registrants relying on general instruction G of Form 10–K under the Exchange Act, *Provided,* That such information is furnished in a separate item captioned "Executive officers of the registrant," and included in part 1 of the registrant's annual report on Form 10–K.

(c) *Identification of certain significant employees.* Where the registrant employs persons such as production managers, sales managers, or research scientists who are not executive officers but who make or are expected to make significant contributions to the business of the registrant, such persons shall be identified and their background disclosed to the same extent as in the case of executive officers. Such disclosure need not be made if the registrant was subject to section 13(a) or 15(d) of the Exchange Act or was exempt from section 13(a) by section 12(g)(2)(G) of such Act immediately prior to the filing of the registration statement, report, or statement to which this Item is applicable.

(d) *Family relationships.* State the nature of any family relationship between any director, executive officer, or person nominated or chosen by the registrant to become a director or executive officer.

Instruction to Paragraph 401(d). The term "family relationship" means any relationship by blood, marriage, or adoption, not more remote than first cousin.

(e) *Business experience.* (1) *Background.* Give a brief account of the business experience during the past five years of each director, executive officer, person nominated or chosen to become a director or executive officer, and each person named in answer to paragraph (c) of this Item, including his principal occupations and employment during that period and the name and principal business of any corporation or other organization in which such occupations and employment were carried on, and whether such corporation or organization is a parent, subsidiary or other affiliate of the registrant. When an executive officer or person named in response to paragraph (c) of Item 401 has been employed by the registrant or a subsidiary of the registrant for less than five years, a brief explanation shall be included as to the nature of the responsibility undertaken by the individual in prior positions to provide adequate disclosure of his prior business experience. What is required is information relating to the level of his professional competence which may include, depending upon the circumstances, such specific information as the size of the operation supervised.

(2) *Directorships.* Indicate any other directorships held by each director or person nominated or chosen to become a director in any company with a class of securities registered pursuant to section 12 of the Exchange Act or subject to the requirements of section 15(d) of such Act or any company registered as an investment company under the Investment Company Act of 1940, as amended, naming such company.

(f) *Involvement in certain legal proceedings.* Describe any of the following events that occurred during the past five years and that are material to an evaluation of the ability or integrity of any director, person nominated to become a director or executive officer of the registrant:

(1) A petition under the Federal bankruptcy laws or any state insolvency law was filed by or against, or a receiver, fiscal agent or similar officer was appointed by a court for the business or property of such person, or any partnership in which he was a general partner at or within two years before the time of such filing, or any corporation or business association of which he was an executive officer at or within two years before the time of such filing;

(2) Such person was convicted in a criminal proceeding or is a named subject of a pending criminal proceeding (excluding traffic violations and other minor offenses);

(3) Such person was the subject of any order, judgment, or decree, not subsequently reversed, suspended or vacated, of any court of competent jurisdiction, permanently or temporarily enjoining him from, or otherwise limiting, the following activities:

(i) Acting as a futures commission merchant, introducing broker, commodity trading advisor, commodity pool operator, floor broker, leverage transaction merchant, any other person regulated by the Commodity Futures Trading Commission, or an associated person of any of the foregoing, or as an investment adviser, underwriter, broker or dealer in securities, or as an affiliated person, director or employee of any investment company, bank, savings and loan association or insurance company, or engaging in or continuing any conduct or practice in connection with such activity;

(ii) Engaging in any type of business practice; or

(iii) Engaging in any activity in connection with the purchase or sale of any security or commodity or in connection with any violation of Federal or State securities laws or Federal commodities laws;

(4) Such person was the subject of any order, judgment or decree, not subsequently reversed, suspended or vacated, of any Federal or State authority barring, suspending or otherwise limiting for more than 60 days the right of such person to engage in any activity described in paragraph (f)(3)(i) of this Item, or to be associated with persons engaged in any such activity; or

(5) Such person was found by a court of competent jurisdiction in a civil action or by the Commission to have violated any Federal or State securities law, and the judgment in such civil action or finding by the Commission has not been subsequently reversed, suspended, or vacated.

(6) Such person was found by a court of competent jurisdiction in a civil action or by the Commodities Futures Trading Commission to have violated any Federal commodities law, and the judgment in such civil action or finding by the Commodities Futures Trading Commission has not been subsequently reversed, suspended or vacated.

Instructions to Paragraph (f) of Item 401. 1. For purposes of computing the five year period referred to in this paragraph, the date of a reportable event shall be deemed the date on which the final order, judgment or decree was entered, or the date on which any rights of appeal from preliminary orders, judgments, or decrees have lapsed. With respect to bankruptcy petitions, the computation date shall be the date of filing for uncontested petitions or the date upon which approval of a contested petition became final.

2. If any event specified in this paragraph (f) has occurred and information in regard thereto is omitted on the grounds that it is not material, the registrant may furnish to the Commission, at time of filing (or at time preliminary materials are filed pursuant to Rule 14a-6 or 14c-5 under the Exchange Act, as supplemental information and not as part of the registration statement, report, or proxy

or information statement, materials to which the omission relates, a description of the event and a statement of the reasons for the omission of information in regard thereto.

3. The registrant is permitted to explain any mitigating circumstances associated with events reported pursuant to this paragraph.

4. If the information called for by this paragraph (f) is being presented in a proxy or information statement, no information need be given respecting any director whose term of office as a director will not continue after the meeting to which the statement relates.

(g) *Promoters and control persons.*

(1) Registrants, which have not been subject to the reporting requirements of Section 13(a) or 15(d) of the Exchange Act for the twelve months immediately prior to the filing of the registration statement, report, or statement to which this Item is applicable, and which were organized within the last five years, shall describe with respect to any promoter, any of the events enumerated in paragraphs (f)(1) through (f)(6) of this section that occurred during the past five years and that are material to a voting or investment decision.

(2) Registrants, which have not been subject to the reporting requirements of Section 13(a) or 15(d) of the Exchange Act for the twelve months immediately prior to the filing of the registration statement, report, or statement to which this Item is applicable, shall describe with respect to any control person, any of the events enumerated in paragraphs (f)(1) through (f)(6) of this section that occurred during the past five years and that are material to a voting or investment decision.

Instructions to Paragraph (g) of Item 401. 1. Instructions 1. through 3. to paragraph (f) shall apply to this paragraph (g).

2. Paragraph (g) shall not apply to any subsidiary of a registrant which has been reporting pursuant to Section 13(a) or 15(d) of the Exchange Act for the twelve months immediately prior to the filing of the registration statement, report or statement.

Item 402. Executive Compensation

(a)(1) *Cash compensation.* Furnish, in substantially the tabular form specified, all cash compensation paid to the following persons through the latest practicable date for services rendered in all capacities to the registrant and its subsidiaries during the registrant's last fiscal year:

(i) *Five executive officers.* Each of the registrant's five most highly compensated executive officers whose cash compensation required to be disclosed pursuant to this paragraph exceeds $60,000, naming each such person; and

(ii) *All executive officers.* All executive officers as a group, stating the number of persons in the group without naming them.

(2) *Bonuses and deferred compensation.* The Cash Compensation Table also shall include:

(i) All cash bonuses to be paid to the named individuals and group for services rendered in all capacities to the registrant and its subsidiaries during the last fiscal year unless such amounts have not been allocated at such time as compensation disclosure is filed;

(ii) All cash bonuses paid during the last fiscal year for services rendered in all capacities to the registrant and its subsidiaries in a previous fiscal year, less any amount relating to the same contract, agreement, plan or arrangement included in the Cash Compensation Table for a prior fiscal year and less any amount that would have been so included but for the fact that the individual was not included in the Cash Compensation Table, as a named individual or as a member of the group, for such prior fiscal year; and

(iii) All compensation that would have been paid in cash to the named individuals and group for services rendered in all capacities to the registrant and its subsidiaries during the last fiscal year but for the fact that the payment of such compensation was deferred.

CASH COMPENSATION TABLE

(A)	(B)	(C)
Name of individual or number in group	Capacities in which served	Cash compensation

Instructions to Item 402(a). 1. *Cash Compensation Table.* (A) The registrant may include additional columns in the Cash Compensation Table. For example, the registrant may segregate cash bonuses and deferred compensation from cash salaries and fees.

(B) Amounts deferred pursuant to Section 401(k) of the Internal Revenue Code are to be included in paragraph (a) for the fiscal year during which they are accrued.

(C) Registrants need list in Column (B) of the Cash Compensation Table only those principal capacities served by each of the identified individuals. The cash compensation disclosed, however, must include cash compensation received in *all* capacities.

2. *Persons covered.* (A) Paragraph (a) of this Item applies to any individual who was an executive officer of the registrant at any time during the last fiscal year. Information need not be disclosed, however, for any portion of the period during which such individual was not an executive officer of the registrant, provided a statement to that effect is made. With respect to an individual who becomes for the first time an individual whose compensation is to be reported in the Cash Compensation Table, it is not necessary to report compensation that would have been reported in the Table had the individual been included in prior years.

(B) Registrants should be flexible in determining which individuals should be named in the Cash Compensation Table in order to ensure that disclosure is made with respect to key policy making members of management. Consideration should be given to the question of whether an individual's level of executive responsibilities, viewed in conjunction with such individual's actual level of cash compensation is such that the registrant reasonably may conclude that the person is among its five most highly compensated, key policy making executive officers. Under this standard, it may be appropriate, in certain circumstances, to include an executive officer of a subsidiary in the Cash Compensation Table.

(C) In certain circumstances, it may be appropriate for a registrant not to include in the Cash Compensation Table an individual who is one of the registrant's five most highly compensated executive officers. Among the factors that should be considered in determining not to name an individual are: (i) The distribution or accrual of an unusually large amount of cash compensation (such as a bonus or commission) that is not part of a recurring arrangement and is unlikely to continue; and (ii) the payment of amounts of cash compensation relating to overseas assignments that may be attributed predominantly to such assignments.

(b)(1) *Compensation pursuant to plans.* Describe briefly all plans, pursuant to which cash or non-cash compensation was paid or distributed during the last fiscal year, or is proposed to be paid or distributed in the future, to the named individuals and group specified in paragraph (a) of this section. Information need not be given with respect to any group life, health, hospitalization, medical reimbursement or relocation plans that do not discriminate, in scope, terms, or operation, in favor of officers or directors of the registrant and that are available generally to all salaried employees. The description of each plan shall include the following, except that the description of any defined benefit or actuarial plans need not include the information specified in paragraphs (b)(1)(vi) and (b)(1)(vii) of this section and the description of any stock option and stock appreciation right plan need not include the information specified in paragraph (b)(1)(vii) of this section:

(i) A summary of how the plan operates and who is covered by the plan;

(ii) The criteria used to determine amounts payable, including any performance formula or measure;

(iii) The time periods over which the measurement of benefits will be determined;

(iv) Payment schedules;

(v) Any recent material amendments to the plan;

(vi) Amounts paid or distributed pursuant to the plan to the named individuals and the group during the last fiscal year less any amount relating to the same plan which previously has been disclosed as accrued pursuant to paragraph (b)(1)(vii) of this section or a predecessor provision; and

(vii) Amounts accrued pursuant to the plan for the accounts of the named individuals and group during the last fiscal year, the distribution or unconditional vesting of which are not subject to future events.

(2) *Pension table.* As to defined benefit and actuarial plans, other than any defined benefit or actuarial plan under which benefits are not determined primarily by final compensation (or average final compensation) and years of service, include, as the payment schedule required by paragraph (b)(1)(iv) of this section, a separate Pension Table showing estimated annual benefits payable upon retirement (including amounts attributable to any defined benefit supplementary or excess pension award plans) to persons in specified compensation and years-of-service classifications. In addition, in furnishing the information required by paragraphs (b)(1)(i)–(v) of this section, include:

(i) The compensation covered by the plan, including the relationship of such covered compensation to the compensation reported in the Cash Compensation Table pursuant to paragraph (a) of this section, and state the current compensation covered by the plan for any individuals named in the Cash Compensation Table whose covered compensation differs substantially (by more than 10 percent) from that set forth in the Cash Compensation Table;

(ii) The estimated credited years of service for each of the individuals named in the Cash Compensation Table; and

(iii) A statement as to the basis upon which benefits are computed (*e.g.*, straight life annuity amounts) and whether or not the benefits listed in the Pension Table are subject to any deduction for Social Security or other offset amounts.

EXAMPLE OF PENSION TABLE

Remuneration	Years of service				
	15	20	25	30	35
125,000...	xxx	xxx	xxx	xxx	xxx
150,000...	xxx	xxx	xxx	xxx	xxx
175,000...	xxx	xxx	xxx	xxx	xxx
200,000...	xxx	xxx	xxx	xxx	xxx
225,000...	xxx	xxx	xxx	xxx	xxx

(3) *Alternative pension plan disclosure.* In furnishing the information required by paragraphs (b)(1)(i)–(v) of this Item with respect to defined benefit or actuarial plans under which benefits are not determined primarily by final compensation (or average final compensation) and years of service, include:

(i) The formula by which benefits are determined; and

(ii) The estimated annual benefits payable upon retirement at normal retirement age for each of the individuals named in the Cash Compensation Table pursuant to paragraph (a) of this Item.

(4) *Stock option and stock appreciation right plans.* In addition to providing the information required by paragraphs (b)(1)(i)–(vi) of this Item, furnish:

(i) With respect to stock options granted during the last fiscal year: (A) the title and aggregate amount of securities subject to options; (B) the average per share exercise price; and (C) if such option exercise price was less than 100 percent of the market value of the security on the date of grant, such fact and the market price on such date. The title and aggregate amount of such securities subject to options, if any, which are in tandem with stock appreciation rights should be set forth separately.

(ii) With respect to the exercise or realization of options or stock appreciation rights held in tandem with options, state the net value of securities (market value less any exercise price) or cash realized during the last fiscal year.

(iii) With respect to plans pursuant to which stock appreciation rights not in tandem with options were granted during the last fiscal year: (A) the number of rights granted; and (B) the average per share base price thereof.

(iv) With respect to the exercise or realization of stock appreciation rights not in tandem with options, state the net value of the shares (market price) or cash realized during the last fiscal year.

Instructions to Item 402(b). 1. *Format.* With the exception of those pension plans disclosed pursuant to paragraph 402(b)(2), the registrant may use either a narrative, tabular or other format or combination of formats provided the information so disclosed is clear and understandable. Disclosure required by paragraph (b)(2), pertaining to certain defined benefit and actuarial plans, is required to be presented in the Pension Table format set forth in that paragraph.

2. *Cash paid pursuant to plans.* The cash compensation paid pursuant to a plan need not be disclosed as amounts paid or distributed pursuant to paragraph (b)(1)(vi) of this Item if such compensation was included in the Cash Compensation Table pursuant to paragraph (a) of this section and a statement to that effect is made. Similarly, the cash compensation deferred under a deferred compensation plan need not be disclosed as amounts accrued pursuant to paragraph (b)(1)(vii) of this Item if such compensation was included in the Cash Compensation Table and a statement to that effect is made.

3. *Definition of "plan".* The term "plan" includes, but is not limited to the following: any plan, contract, authorization or arrangement, whether or not set forth in any formal documents, pursuant to which the following may be received: cash, stock, restricted stock, phantom stock, stock options, stock appreciation rights, stock options in tandem with stock appreciation rights, warrants, convertible securities, performance units and performance shares. A plan may be applicable to one person.

4. *Pension levels.* Compensation set forth in the Pension Table pursuant to paragraph (b)(2) of this section shall allow for reasonable increases in existing compensation levels; alternatively, registrants may present as the highest compensation level in the Pension Table an amount equal to 120 percent of the amount of covered compensation of the most highly compensated individual named in the Cash Compensation Table pursuant to paragraph (a) of this Item.

5. *Definition of "normal retirement age".* The term "normal retirement age" means normal retirement age as defined in a pension or similar plan or, if not defined therein, the earliest time at which a participant may retire without any benefit reduction because of age.

(c) *Other compensation.* Describe, stating amounts, any other compensation not covered by paragraphs (a) or (b) of this section that was paid or distributed during the last fiscal year to the named individuals and group specified in paragraph (a) of this section unless:

(1) With respect to any named individual, the aggregate amount of such other compensation is the lesser of $25,000 or 10 percent of the compensation reported in the Cash Compensation Table for such person pursuant to paragraph (a) of this section or

(2) With respect to the group, the aggregate amount of such other compensation is the lesser of $25,000 times the number of persons in the group or 10 percent of the compensation reported in the Cash Compensation Table for the group pursuant to paragraph (a) of this section and a statement to that effect is made.

Instructions to Item 402(c). 1. *Scope.* Compensation to be disclosed pursuant to this paragraph may include, among other things: (a) personal benefits or; (b) securities or property that were paid or distributed other than pursuant to a plan. It does not, in any event, include cash, which is to be disclosed pursuant to either paragraph (a) or (b).

2. *Threshold.* If the amount of other compensation for a named individual or the group exceeds the established thresholds, the entire amount of such other compensation must be disclosed pursuant to this paragraph.

3. *Valuation.* Compensation within paragraph (c) shall be valued on the basis of the registrant's and subsidiaries' aggregate incremental cost.

(d) *Compensation of directors.*

(1) *Standard arrangements.* Describe any standard arrangement, stating amounts, pursuant to which directors of the registrant are compensated for all services as a director, including any additional amounts payable for committee participation or special assignments.

(2) *Other arrangements.* Describe any other arrangements pursuant to which any director of the registrant was compensated during the registrant's last fiscal year for services as a director, stating the amount paid and the name of the director.

(e) *Termination of employment and change of control arrangement.* Describe any compensatory plan or arrangement, including payments to be received from the registrant, with respect to any individual named in the Cash Compensation Table pursuant to paragraph (a) of this section for the latest or then next preceding fiscal year if such a plan or arrangement results or will result from the resignation, retirement or any other termination of such individual's employment with the registrant and its subsidiaries or from a change in control of the registrant or a change in the individual's responsibilities following a change in control and the amount involved, including all periodic payments or installments, exceeds $60,000.

General Instructions to Item 402. 1. *Foreign private issuers.* A non-Canadian foreign private issuer may respond to all of Item 402 by indicating the aggregate payments or benefits paid or to be paid to all executive officers as a group unless such registrants disclose to their security holders or otherwise make public the information specified in this section for individually named executive officers, in which case such information also shall be disclosed.

2. *Transactions with third parties.* This section includes transactions between the registrant and a third party where the primary purpose of the transaction is to furnish compensation to any named individual or the group specified in paragraph (a) of this section. No information need be given in response to any paragraph of this section as to any such transaction if the transaction has been reported in response to Item 404 of Regulation S-K.

3. *Exclusions.* No information need be given pursuant to this Item with respect to interest on deferred compensation provided that the rate of interest does not exceed prevailing market interest rates either: (1) at the time the interest is accrued or (2) at the time the plan pursuant to which the compensation is deferred was established. Similarly, dividends awarded on restricted stock need not be disclosed provided that the restricted stock is not of a particular class available only to certain employees on a discriminatory basis.

Item 403. Security Ownership of Certain Beneficial Owners and Management

(a) *Security ownership of certain beneficial owners.* Furnish the following information, as of the most recent practicable date, in substantially the tabular form indicated, with respect to any person (including any "group" as that term is used in section 13(d)(3) of the Exchange Act) who is known to the registrant to be the beneficial owner of more than five percent of any class of the registrant's voting securities. The address given in column (2) may be a business, mailing or residence address. Show in column (3) the total number of shares beneficially owned and in column (4) the percentage of class so owned. Of the number of shares shown in column (3), indicate by footnote or otherwise the amount known to be shares with respect to which such listed beneficial owner has the right to acquire beneficial ownership, as specified in Rule 13d-3(d)(1) under the Exchange Act.

(1) Title of class	(2) Name and address of beneficial owner	(3) Amount and nature of beneficial ownership	(4) Percent of class

(b) *Security ownership of management.* Furnish the following information, as of the most recent practicable date, in substantially the tabular form indicated, as to each class of equity securities of the registrant or any of its parents or subsidiaries other than directors' qualifying shares, beneficially owned by all directors and nominees, naming them, and directors and officers of the registrant as a group, without naming them. Show in column (3) the total number of shares beneficially owned and in column (4) the percent of class so owned. Of the number of shares shown in column (3), indicate, by footnote or otherwise, the amount of shares with respect to which such persons have the right to acquire beneficial ownership as specified in Rule 13d-3(d)(1) under the Exchange Act.

(1) Title of class	(2) Name of beneficial owner	(3) Amount and nature of beneficial ownership	(4) Percent of class

(c) *Changes in control.* Describe any arrangements, known to the registrant, including any pledge by any person of securities of the registrant or any of its parents, the operation of which may at a subsequent date result in a change in control of the registrant.

Instructions to Item 403. 1. The percentages are to be calculated on the basis of the amount of outstanding securities, excluding securities held by or for the account of the registrant or its subsidiaries, plus securities deemed outstanding pursuant to Rule 13d–3(d)(1) under the Exchange Act [17 CFR 240.13d–3(d)(1)]. For purposes of paragraph (b), if the percentage of shares beneficially owned by any director or nominee, or by all directors and officers of the registrant as a group, does not exceed one percent of the class so owned, the registrant may, in lieu of furnishing a precise percentage, indicate this fact by means of an asterisk and explanatory footnote or other similar means.

2. For the purposes of this Item, beneficial ownership shall be determined in accordance with Rule 13d–3 under the Exchange Act. Include such additional subcolumns or other appropriate explanation of column (3) necessary to reflect amounts as to which the beneficial owner has (A) sole voting power, (B) shared voting power, (C) sole investment power, or (D) shared investment power.

3. The registrant shall be deemed to know the contents of any statements filed with the Commission pursuant to section 13(d) or 13(g) of the Exchange Act. When applicable, a registrant may rely upon information set forth in such statements unless the registrant knows or has reason to believe that such information is not complete or accurate or that a statement or amendment should have been filed and was not.

4. For purposes of furnishing information pursuant to paragraph (a) of this Item, the registrant may indicate the source and date of such information.

5. Where more than one beneficial owner is known to be listed for the same securities, appropriate disclosure should be made to avoid confusion. *For purposes of paragraph (b), in computing the aggregate number of shares owned by directors and officers of the registrant as a group, the same shares shall not be counted more than once.*

6. Paragraph (c) of this Item does not require a description of ordinary default provisions contained in the charter, trust indentures or other governing instruments relating to securities of the registrant.

7. Where the holder(s) of voting securities reported pursuant to paragraph (a) hold more than five percent of any class of voting securities of the registrant pursuant to any voting trust or similar agreement, state the title of such securities, the amount held or to be held pursuant to the trust or agreement (if not clear from the table) and the duration of the agreement. Give the names and addresses of the voting trustees and outline briefly their voting rights and other powers under the trust or agreement.

Item 404. Certain Relationships and Related Transactions

(a) *Transactions with management and others.* Describe briefly any transaction, or series of similar transactions, since the beginning of the registrant's last fiscal year, or any currently proposed transaction, or series of similar transactions, to which the registrant or any of its subsidiaries was or is to be a party, in which the amount involved exceeds $60,000 and in which any of the following persons had, or will have, a direct or indirect material interest, naming such person and indicating the person's relationship to the registrant, the nature of such person's interest in the transaction(s), the amount of such transaction(s) and, where practicable, the amount of such person's interest in the transaction(s):

(1) Any director or executive officer of the registrant;

(2) Any nominee for election as a director;

(3) Any security holder who is known to the registrant to own of record or beneficially more than five percent of any class of the registrant's voting securities; and

(4) Any member of the immediate family of any of the foregoing persons.

Instructions to Paragraph (a) of Item 404. 1. The materiality of any interest is to be determined on the basis of the significance of the information to investors in light of all the circumstances of the particular case. The importance of the interest to the person having the interest, the relationship of the parties to the transaction with each other and the amount involved in the transactions are among the factors to be considered in determining the significance of the information to investors.

2. For purposes of paragraph (a), a person's immediate family shall include such person's spouse; parents; children; siblings; mothers and fathers-in-law; sons and daughters-in-law; and brothers and sisters-in-law.

3. In computing the amount involved in the transaction or series of similar transactions, include all periodic installments in the case of any lease or other agreement providing for periodic payments or installments.

4. The amount of the interest of any person specified in paragraphs (a)(1) through (4) shall be computed without regard to the amount of the profit or loss involved in the transaction(s).

5. In describing any transaction involving the purchase or sale of assets by or to the registrant or any of its subsidiaries, otherwise than in the ordinary course of business, state the cost of the assets to the purchaser and, if acquired by the seller within two years prior to the transaction, the cost thereof to the seller. Indicate the principle followed in determining the registrant's purchase or sale price and the name of the person making such determination.

6. Information shall be furnished in answer to paragraph (a) with respect to transactions that involve remuneration from the registrant or its subsidiaries, directly or indirectly, to any of the persons specified in paragraphs (a)(1) through (4) for services in any capacity unless the interest of such person arises solely from the ownership individually and in the aggregate of less than ten percent of any class of equity securities of another corporation furnishing the services to the registrant or its subsidiaries.

7. No information need be given in answer to paragraph (a) as to any transactions where:

A. The rates or charges involved in the transaction are determined by competitive bids, or the transaction involves the rendering of services as a common or contract carrier, or public utility, at rates or charges fixed in conformity with law or governmental authority;

B. The transaction involves services as a bank depositary of funds, transfer agent, registrar, trustee under a trust indenture, or similar services; or

C. The interest of the person specified in paragraphs (a)(1) through (4) arises solely from the ownership of securities of the registrant and such person receives no extra or special benefit not shared on a pro rata basis.

8. Paragraph (a) requires disclosure of indirect, as well as direct, material interests in transactions. A person who has a position or relationship with a firm, corporation, or other entity that engages in a transaction with the registrant or its subsidiaries may have an indirect interest in such transaction by reason of such position or relationship. Such an interest, however, shall not be deemed "material" within the meaning of paragraph (a) where:

A. The interest arises only (i) from such person's position as a director of another corporation or organization which is a party to the transaction; or (ii) from the direct or indirect ownership by such person and all other persons specified in paragraphs (a)(1) through (4), in the aggregate, of less than a ten percent equity interest in another person (other than a partnership) which is a party to the transaction; or (iii) from both such position and ownership;

B. The interest arises only from such person's position as a limited partner in a partnership in which the person and all other persons specified in paragraphs (a)(1) through (4) have an interest of less than ten percent; or

C. The interest of such person arises solely from the holding of an equity interest (including a limited partnership interest, but excluding a general partnership interest) or a creditor interest in another person that is a party to the transaction with the registrant or any of its subsidiaries, and the transaction is not material to such other person.

9. There may be situations where, although these instructions do not expressly authorize nondisclosure, the interest of a person specified in paragraphs (a)(1) through (4) in a particular transaction or series of transactions is not a direct or indirect material interest. In that case, information regarding such interest and transaction is not required to be disclosed in response to this paragraph.

(b) *Certain business relationships.* Describe any of the following relationships regarding directors or nominees for director that exist, or have existed during the registrant's last fiscal year, indicating the identity of the entity with which the registrant has such a relationship, the name of the nominee or director affiliated with such entity and the nature of such nominee's or director's affiliation, the relationship between such entity and the registrant and the amount of the business done between the registrant and the entity during the registrant's last full fiscal year or proposed to be done during the registrant's current fiscal year:

(1) If the nominee or director is, or during the last fiscal year has been, an executive officer of, or owns, or during the last fiscal year has owned, of record or beneficially in excess of ten percent equity interest in, any business or professional entity that has made during the registrant's last full fiscal year, or proposes to make during the registrant's current fiscal year, payments to the registrant or its subsidiaries for property or services in excess of five percent of (i) the registrant's consolidated gross revenues for its last full fiscal year, or (ii) the other entity's consolidated gross revenues for its last full fiscal year;

(2) If the nominee or director is, or during the last fiscal year has been, an executive officer of, or owns, or during the last fiscal year has owned, of record or beneficially in excess of ten percent equity interest in, any business or professional entity to which the registrant or its subsidiaries has made during the registrant's last full fiscal year, or proposes to make during the registrant's current fiscal year, payments for property or services in excess of five percent of (i) the registrant's consolidated gross revenues for its last full fiscal year, or (ii) the other entity's consolidated gross revenues for its last full fiscal year;

(3) If the nominee or director is, or during the last fiscal year has been, an executive officer of, or owns, or during the last fiscal year has owned, of record or beneficially in excess of ten percent equity interest in, any business or professional entity to which the registrant or its subsidiaries was indebted at the end of the registrant's last full fiscal year in an aggregate amount in excess of five percent of the registrant's total consolidated assets at the end of such fiscal year;

(4) If the nominee or director is, or during the last fiscal year has been, a member of, or of counsel to, a law firm that the issuer has retained during the last fiscal year or proposes to retain during the current fiscal year; *Provided, however,* that the dollar amount of fees paid to a law firm by the registrant need not be disclosed if such amount does not exceed five percent of the law firm's gross revenues for that firm's last full fiscal year;

(5) If the nominee or director is, or during the last fiscal year has been, a partner or executive officer of any investment banking firm that has performed services for the registrant, other than as a participating underwriter in a syndicate, during the last fiscal year or that the registrant proposes to have performed services during the current year; *Provided, however,* that the dollar amount of compensation received by an investment banking firm need not be disclosed if such amount does not exceed five percent of the investment banking firm's consolidated gross revenues for that firm's last full fiscal year; or

(6) Any other relationships that the registrant is aware of between the nominee or director and the registrant that are substantially similar in nature and scope to those relationships listed in paragraphs (b)(1) through (5).

Instructions to Paragraph (b) of Item 404. 1. In order to determine whether payments or indebtedness exceed five percent of the consolidated gross revenues of any entity, other than the registrant, it is appropriate to rely on information provided by the nominee or director.

2. In calculating payments for property and services the following may be excluded:

A. Payments where the rates or charges involved in the transaction are determined by competitive bids, or the transaction involves the rendering of services as a common contract carrier, or public utility, at rates or charges fixed in conformity with law or governmental authority;

B. Payments that arise solely from the ownership of securities of the registrant and no extra or special benefit not shared on a pro rata basis by all holders of the class of securities is received; or

C. Payments made or received by subsidiaries other than significant subsidiaries as defined in Rule 1–02(v) of Regulation S–X, provided that all such subsidiaries making or receiving payments, when considered in the aggregate as a single subsidiary, would not constitute a significant subsidiary as defined in Rule 1–02(v).

3. In calculating indebtedness the following may be excluded:

A. Debt securities that have been publicly offered, admitted to trading on a national securities exchange, or quoted on the automated quotation system of a registered securities association;

B. Amounts due for purchases subject to the usual trade terms; or

C. Indebtedness incurred by subsidiaries other than significant subsidiaries as defined in Rule 1–02(v) of Regulation S–X, provided that all such subsidiaries incurring indebtedness, when considered in the aggregate as a single subsidiary, would not constitute a significant subsidiary as defined in Rule 1–02(v).

4. No information called for by paragraph (b) need be given respecting any director who is no longer a director at the time of filing the registration statement or report containing such disclosure. If such information is being presented in a proxy or information statement, no information need be given respecting any director whose term of office as a director will not continue after the meeting to which the statement relates.

(c) *Indebtedness of management.* If any of the following persons has been indebted to the registrant or its subsidiaries at any time since the beginning of the registrant's last fiscal year in an amount in excess of $60,000, indicate the name of such person, the nature of the person's relationship by reason of which such person's indebtedness is required to be described, the largest aggregate amount of indebtedness outstanding at any time during such period, the nature of the indebtedness and of the transaction in which it was incurred, the amount thereof outstanding as of the latest practicable date and the rate of interest paid or charged thereon:

(1) Any director or executive officer of the registrant;

(2) Any nominee for election as a director;

(3) Any member of the immediate family of the persons specified in paragraph (c)(1) or (2);

(4) Any corporation or organization (other than the registrant or a majority-owned subsidiary of the registrant) of which any of the persons specified in paragraphs (c)(1) or (2) is an executive officer or partner or is, directly or indirectly, the beneficial owner of ten percent or more of any class of equity securities; and

(5) Any trust or other estate in which any of the persons specified in paragraph (c)(1) or (2) has a substantial beneficial interest or as to which such person serves as a trustee or in a similar capacity.

Instructions to Paragraph (c) of Item 404. 1. For purposes of paragraph (c), the members of a person's immediate family are those persons specified in Instruction 2 to Item 404(a).

2. Exclude from the determination of the amount of indebtedness all amounts due from the particular person for purchases subject to usual trade terms, for ordinary travel and expense payments and for other transactions in the ordinary course of business.

3. If the lender is a bank, savings and loan association, or broker-dealer extending credit under Federal Reserve Regulation T and the loans are not disclosed as nonaccrual, past due, restructured or potential problems (see Item III.C.1. and 2. of Industry Guide 3, Statistical Disclosure by Bank Holding Companies), disclosure may consist of a statement, if such is the case, that the loans to such persons (A) were made in the ordinary course of business, (B) were made on substantially the same terms, including interest rates and collateral, as those prevailing at the time for comparable transactions with other persons, and (C) did not involve more than the normal risk of collectibility or present other unfavorable features.

4. If any indebtedness required to be described arose under Section 16(b) of the Exchange Act and has not been discharged by payment, state the amount of any profit realized, that such profit will inure to the benefit of the registrant or its subsidiaries and whether suit will be brought or other steps taken to recover such profit. If, in the opinion of counsel, a question reasonably exists as to the recoverability of such profit, it will suffice to state all facts necessary to describe the transactions, including the prices and number of shares involved.

(d) *Transactions with promoters.* Registrants that have been organized within the past five years and that are filing a registration statement on Form S–1 under the Securities Act or on Form 10 under the Exchange Act shall:

(1) State the names of the promoters, the nature and amount of anything of value (including money, property, contracts, options or rights of any kind) received or to be received by each

promoter, directly or indirectly, from the registrant and the nature and amount of any assets, services or other consideration therefor received or to be received by the registrant; and

(2) As to any assets acquired or to be acquired by the registrant from a promoter, state the amount at which the assets were acquired or are to be acquired and the principal followed or to be followed in determining such amount and identify the persons making the determination and their relationship, if any, with the registrant or any promoter. If the assets were acquired by the promoter within two years prior to their transfer to the registrant, also state the cost thereof to the promoter.

Instructions to Item 404. 1. No information need be given in response to any paragraph of Item 404 as to any compensation or other transaction reported in response to any other paragraph of Item 404 or to Item 402 of Regulation S–K (§ 229.402 of this chapter) or as to any compensation or transaction with respect to which information may be omitted pursuant to any other paragraph of Item 404 or Item 402.

2. If the information called for by Item 404 is being presented in a registration statement filed pursuant to the Securities Act or the Exchange Act, information shall be given for the periods specified in this Item and, in addition, for the two fiscal years preceding the registrant's last fiscal year.

3. A non-Canadian foreign private issuer eligible to use Form 20–F may respond to Item 404 only to the extent that the registrant discloses to its security holders or otherwise makes public the information specified in that Item.

Subpart 500—Registration Statement and Prospectus Provisions

Item 501. Forepart of Registration Statement and Outside Front Cover Page of Prospectus

(a) *Facing page.* The facing page of every registration statement shall set forth the approximate date of proposed sale to the public and, where appropriate, the delaying amendment legend as set forth in Regulation C.

(b) *Cross-reference sheet.* Immediately following such facing page, there shall be included a cross reference sheet showing the location in the prospectus of the information required to be included in the prospectus in response to the items of the form. If any such item is inapplicable, or the answer thereto is in the negative and is omitted from the prospectus, a statement to that effect shall be made in the cross reference sheet. The cross reference sheet need not be included in the prospectus.

(c) *Outside front cover page of prospectus.* The following information (to the extent appropriate) shall appear on the outside front cover page of the prospectus with appropriate cross references to more detailed discussion elsewhere in the prospectus:

(1) Name of the registrant and, in the case of a foreign private registrant, an English translation of such name. Where the name of the registrant is the same as that of another well-known company and it appears likely that the registrant may be confused with the other company, or where the name indicates a line of business in which the registrant is not engaged or is engaged to only a limited extent, a statement may be necessary to prevent the confusion of the two companies or to remove a misleading inference that may be drawn from the name as to the nature of the registrant's business. In some circumstances, however, disclosure may not be sufficient, and a change of name may be the only way to preclude confusion of the companies or misleading inferences from registrant's name. Such disclosure or name change is not necessary in the case of an established registrant that over a period of years has changed the general character of its business and the investing public is aware generally of the change and the character of the registrant's present business;

(2) Title and amount of securities offered and a brief description of such securities (unless not necessary to indicate the material terms of the securities, as in the case of an issue of common stock with full voting rights and the dividend and liquidation rights usually associated with common stock);

(3) Where any of the securities to be registered are to be offered for the account of security holders, a statement to that effect;

(4) Cross reference, where applicable to the discussion in the prospectus prescribed by Item 503 of Regulation S–K, of material risks in connection with the purchase of the securities, printed in bold-face

roman type at least as high as ten-point modern type and at least two points leaded.

(5) The following statement in capital letters printed in bold-face roman type at least as high as ten-point modern type and at least two points leaded: THESE SECURITIES HAVE NOT BEEN APPROVED OR DISAPPROVED BY THE SECURITIES AND EXCHANGE COMMISSION NOR HAS THE COMMISSION PASSED UPON THE ACCURACY OR ADEQUACY OF THIS PROSPECTUS. ANY REPRESENTATION TO THE CONTRARY IS A CRIMINAL OFFENSE.

(6) In the case of any preliminary prospectus that is circulated by registrants not subject to the reporting provisions of section 13(a) or 15(d) of the Exchange Act immediately prior to the filing of the registration statement, a bona fide estimate of the range of the maximum offering price and maximum number of shares or other units of securities to be offered, or a bona fide estimate of the principal amount of debt securities to be offered;

(7) Where securities are to be offered for cash, other than on a registration statement on Form S–8; the information called for by the following table, in substantially the tabular form indicated, as to all securities to be registered (estimated, if necessary):

	Price to public	Underwriting discounts and commissions	Proceeds to issuer or other persons
Per unit....	....	....	....
Total	....	....	....

(8) In the case of any prospectus to be used prior to the effective date of the registration statement, in red ink, the caption "Preliminary Prospectus," the date of its issuance, and the following statement printed in type as large as that generally in the body of such prospectus:

A registration statement relating to these securities has been filed with the Securities and Exchange Commission but has not yet become effective. Information contained herein is subject to completion or amendment. These securities may not be sold nor may offers to buy be accepted prior to the time the registration statement becomes effective. This prospectus shall not constitute an offer to sell or the solicitation of an offer to buy nor shall there be any sale of these securities in any State in which such offer, solicitation or sale would be unlawful prior to registration or qualification under the securities laws of any such State;

(9) Any legend or information required by the law of any State in which the securities are to be offered; and

(10) The date of the prospectus.

Instructions to Item 501. 1. The term "commissions" is defined in paragraph (17) of Schedule A of the Securities Act. Only commissions paid by the registrant or selling security holders in cash are to be included in the table. Commissions paid by other persons, and other considerations to the underwriters, shall be set forth in a note to the table with a reference thereto in the second column of the table. Any finder's fee or similar payments shall be disclosed appropriately.

2. If it is impracticable to state the price to the public, the method by which it is to be determined shall be explained. In addition, if the securities are to be offered at the market, or if the offering price is to be determined by a formula related to market prices, indicate the market involved and the market price as of the latest practicable data.

3. If the securities are to be offered on a best efforts basis, set forth the termination date of the offering, any minimum required purchase and any arrangements to place the funds received in an escrow, trust, or similar arrangement. If no such arrangements have been made, so state. The following tabular presentation of the total maximum and minimum securities to be offered shall be combined with the table required above:

	Price to public	Underwriting discounts and commissions	Proceeds to issuer or other persons
Total minimum.	....	....	....
Total maximum.	....	....	....

4. Where an underwriter has received an over-allotment option, maximum-minimum information shall be presented in the price table, or in a note thereto, based on the purchase of all or none of the shares subject to the option. The terms of the option may be described in response to Item 508 of Regulation S--K rather than on the cover page of the prospectus.

5. The total of "other expenses of issuance and distribution" called for by Item 511 of Regulation S–K, stated separately for the registrant and for the selling security holders, if any, shall be set forth in a note to the proceeds column of the distribution table.

Item 502. Inside Front and Outside Back Cover Pages of Prospectus

The following information, to the extent applicable, shall appear on the inside front cover page of the prospectus (except that the information required by paragraphs (e) and (g) of this Item may be set forth on the outside back cover page).

(a) *Available information.* Registrants subject to the reporting requirements of section 13(a) or 15(d) of the Exchange Act immediately prior to the filing of the registration statement shall:

(1) State that the registrant is subject to the informational requirements of the Exchange Act and in accordance therewith files reports and other information with the Securities and Exchange Commission;

(2) State that reports (and where registrant is subject to sections 14(a) and 14(c) of the Exchange Act proxy and information statements) and other information filed by the registrant can be inspected and copied at the public reference facilities maintained by the Commission in Washington, D.C., and at certain of its Regional Offices, and state the current address of each such facility, and that copies of such material can be obtained from the Public Reference Section of the Commission, Washington, D.C. 20549 at prescribed rates; and

(3) Name any national securities exchange on which the registrant's securities are listed and state that reports (and where registrant is subject to sections 14(a) and 14(c) of the Exchange Act proxy and information statements,) and other information concerning the registrant can be inspected at such exchanges.

(b) *Reports to security holders.* Where a registrant may not be required to deliver an annual report to security holders (or holders of American depository receipts) pursuant to section 14 of the Exchange Act or stock exchange requirements, describe briefly the nature and frequency of reports that will be given to such holders in such event, specifying whether or not such reports will contain financial information that has been examined and reported upon, with an opinion expressed by, an independent public or certified public accountant, and, in the case of the reports of a foreign private registrant that will not contain financial information prepared in accordance with United States generally accepted accounting principles, state whether the report will include a reconciliation of such information with such accounting principles.

(c) *Incorporation by reference.* Where any document or part thereof is incorporated by reference in the prospectus but not delivered therewith, include an undertaking to provide without charge to each person to whom a prospectus is delivered, upon written or oral request of such person a copy of any and all of the information that has been incorporated by reference in the registration statement (not including exhibits to the information that is incorporated by reference unless such exhibits are specifically incorporated by reference into the information that the prospectus incorporates), and the address (including title or department) and telephone number to which such a request is to be directed.

(d) *Stabilization.* (1) If the registrant or any of the underwriters knows or has reason to believe that there is an intention to over-allot or that the price of any security may be stabilized to facilitate the offering of the registered securities, set forth a statement in substantially the following form, subject to appropriate modification where circumstances require. Such statement shall be in capital letters, printed in boldface roman type at least as large as ten-point modern type and at least two points leaded: IN CONNECTION WITH THIS OFFERING, THE UNDERWRITERS MAY OVER-ALLOT OR EFFECT TRANSACTIONS WHICH STABILIZE OR MAINTAIN THE MARKET PRICE OF (Identify each class of securities in which such transactions may be effected) AT A

LEVEL ABOVE THAT WHICH MIGHT OTHERWISE PREVAIL IN THE OPEN MARKET. SUCH TRANSACTIONS MAY BE EFFECTED ON (Identify each exchange on which stabilizing transactions may be effected; if none, omit this sentence.) SUCH STABILIZING, IF COMMENCED, MAY BE DISCONTINUED AT ANY TIME.

(2) If the stabilizing began prior to the effective date of the registration statement, set forth the amount of securities bought, the prices at which bought and the period within which they were bought.

(3) If the securities being registered are to be offered to existing security holders pursuant to warrants or rights and any securities not taken by security holders are to be reoffered to the public after the expiration of the rights offering period, there shall be set forth, by supplement or otherwise, in the prospectus used in connection with such reoffering (i) the amount of securities bought in stabilization activities during the rights offering period and the price or range of prices at which such securities were bought, (ii) the amount of the offered securities subscribed for during such period, (iii) the amount of the offered securities subscribed for by the underwriters during such period, (iv) the amount of the offered securities sold during such period by the underwriters and the price, or range of prices, at which such securities were sold, and (v) the amount of the offered securities to be reoffered to the public and the public offering price.

(e) *Delivery of prospectuses by dealers.* The legend below shall be set forth inserting the expiration date of the period prescribed by section 4(3) of the Securities Act and Rule 174 thereunder except that this legend need not be included if, pursuant to Rule 174, dealers are not required to deliver a prospectus, or if the exemption provided by section 4(3) of the Securities Act is not applicable because of the provisions of section 24(d) of the Investment Company Act. If such expiration date is not known on the effective date of the registration statement it shall be included in the prospectus, copies of which are required to be filed pursuant to Rule 424(b) under the Securities Act. The following legend shall be printed in boldface or italic type at least as large as eight-point modern type and at least two points leaded:

Until (insert date) all dealers effecting transactions in the registered securities, whether or not participating in this distribution, may be required to deliver a prospectus. This is in addition to the obligation of dealers to deliver a prospectus when acting as underwriters and with respect to their unsold allotments or subscriptions.

(f) *Enforceability of civil liabilities against foreign persons.* In the case of a foreign private registrant, a statement of how the enforcement by investors of civil liabilities under the Federal securities laws may be affected by the fact that the registrant is located in a foreign country, that certain of its officers and directors are residents of a foreign country, that certain underwriters or experts named in the registration statement are residents of a foreign country, and that all or a substantial portion of the assets of the registrant and of said persons are located outside the United States. Such disclosure need not be included on the inside front cover page of the prospectus, if it is included, under appropriate caption, elsewhere in the forepart of the prospectus.

(1) Such disclosure shall indicate:

(i) Whether investors will be able to effect service of process within the United States upon such persons;

(ii) Whether investors will be able to enforce, in United States courts, judgments against such persons, judgments obtained in such courts predicated upon the civil liability provisions of the Federal securities laws;

(iii) Whether the appropriate foreign courts would enforce judgments of United States courts obtained in actions against such persons predicated upon the civil liability provisions of the Federal securities laws; and

(iv) Whether the appropriate foreign courts would enforce, in original actions, liabilities against such persons predicated solely upon the Federal securities laws.

(2) If any portions of such disclosures are stated to be based upon an opinion of counsel, such counsel shall be named in the prospectus and an appropriate manually signed consent to the use of such name and opinion shall be included as an exhibit to the registration statement.

(g) *Table of contents.* Include a reasonably detailed table of contents showing the subject matter of the various sections or subdivisions of the prospectus and the page number on which each such section or subdivision begins.

Item 503. Summary Information, Risk Factors and Ratio of Earnings to Fixed Charges

(a) *Summary.* Registrants should include a summary of the information contained in the prospectus where the length or complexity of the prospectus makes such a summary appropriate.

(b) *Address and telephone number.* Registrants shall include in the forepart of the prospectus the complete mailing address, including zip code, and the telephone number, including area code of their principal executive offices.

(c) *Risk factors.* Registrants, where appropriate, shall set forth on the page immediately following the cover page of the prospectus (or following the summary, if included) under an appropriate caption, a discussion of the principal factors that make the offering speculative or one of high risk; these factors may be due, among other things, to such matters as an absence of an operating history of the registrant, an absence of profitable operations in recent periods, the financial position of the registrant, the nature of the business in which the registrant is engaged or proposes to engage, or, if common equity or securities convertible into or exercisable for common equity are being offered, the absence of a previous market for the registrant's common equity.

(d) *Ratio of earnings to fixed charges.* The ratio of earnings to fixed charges or the ratio of earnings to combined fixed charges and preferred stock dividends (the "ratio") should be disclosed * *

Item 504. Use of Proceeds

State the principal purposes for which the net proceeds to the registrant from the securities to be offered are intended to be used and the approximate amount intended to be used for each such purpose. Where registrant has no current specific plan for the proceeds, or a significant portion thereof, the registrant shall so state and discuss the principal reasons for the offering.

Instructions to Item 504. 1. Where less than all the securities to be offered may be sold and more than one use is listed for the proceeds, indicate the order of priority of such purposes and discuss the registrant's plans if substantially less than the maximum proceeds are obtained. Such discussion need not be included if underwriting arrangements with respect to such securities are such that, if any securities are sold to the public, it reasonably can be expected that the actual proceeds will not be substantially less than the aggregate proceeds to the registrant shown pursuant to Item 501 of Regulation S–K.

2. Details of proposed expenditures need not be given; for example, there need be furnished only a brief outline of any program of construction or addition of equipment. Consideration should be given as to the need to include a discussion of certain matters addressed in the discussion and analysis of registrant's financial condition and results of operations, such as liquidity and capital expenditures.

3. If any material amounts of other funds are necessary to accomplish the specified purposes for which the proceeds are to be obtained, state the amounts and sources of such other funds needed for each such specified purpose and the sources thereof.

4. If any material part of the proceeds is to be used to discharge indebtedness, set forth the interest rate and maturity of such indebtedness. If the indebtedness to be discharged was incurred within one year, describe the use of the proceeds of such indebtedness other than short-term borrowing used for working capital.

5. If any material amount of the proceeds is to be used to acquire assets, otherwise than in the ordinary course of business, describe briefly and state the cost of the assets and, where such assets are to be acquired from affiliates of the registrant or their associates, give the names of the persons from whom they are to be acquired and set forth the principle followed in determining the cost to the registrant.

6. Where the registrant indicates that the proceeds may, or will, be used to finance acquisitions of other businesses, the identity of such businesses, if known, or, if not known, the nature of the businesses to be sought, the status of any negotiations with respect to the acquisition, and a brief description of

such business shall be included. Where, however, pro forma financial statements reflecting such acquisition are not required by Regulation S–X to be included, in the registration statement, the possible terms of any transaction, the identification of the parties thereto or the nature of the business sought need not be disclosed, to the extent that the registrant reasonably determines that public disclosure of such information would jeopardize the acquisition. Where Regulation S–X would require financial statements of the business to be acquired to be included, the description of the business to be acquired shall be more detailed.

7. The registrant may reserve the right to change the use of proceeds, provided that such reservation is due to certain contingencies that are discussed specifically and the alternatives to such use in that event are indicated.

Item 505. Determination of Offering Price

(a) *Common equity.* Where common equity is being registered for which there is no established public trading market for purposes of paragraph (a) of Item 201 of Regulation S–K or where there is a material disparity between the offering price of the common equity being registered and the market price of outstanding shares of the same class, describe the various factors considered in determining such offering price.

(b) *Warrants, rights and convertible securities.* Where warrants, rights or convertible securities exercisable for common equity for which there is no established public trading market for purposes of paragraph (a) of Item 201 of Regulations S–K are being registered, describe the various factors considered in determining their exercise or conversion price.

Item 506. Dilution

Where common equity securities are being registered and there is substantial disparity between the public offering price and the effective cash cost to officers, directors, promoters and affiliated persons of common equity acquired by them in transactions during the past five years, or which they have the right to acquire, and the registrant is not subject to the reporting requirements of section 13(a) or 15(d) of the Exchange Act immediately prior to filing of the registration statement, there shall be included a comparison of the public contribution under the proposed public offering and the effective cash contribution of such persons. In such cases, and in other instances where common equity securities are being registered by a registrant that has had losses in each of its last three fiscal years and there is a material dilution of the purchasers' equity interest, the following shall be disclosed:

(a) The net tangible book value per share before and after the distribution;

(b) The amount of the increase in such net tangible book value per share attributable to the cash payments made by purchasers of the shares being offered; and

(c) The amount of the immediate dilution from the public offering price which will be absorbed by such purchasers.

Item 507. Selling Security Holders

If any of the securities to be registered are to be offered for the account of security holders, name each such security holder, indicate the nature of any position, office, or other material relationship which the selling security holder has had within the past three years with the registrant or any of its predecessors or affiliates, and state the amount of securities of the class owned by such security holder prior to the offering, the amount to be offered for the security holder's account, the amount and (if one percent or more) the percentage of the class to be owned by such security holder after completion of the offering.

Item 508. Plan of Distribution

(a) *Underwriters and underwriting obligation.* If the securities are to be offered through underwriters, name the principal underwriters, and state the respective amounts underwritten. Identify each such underwriter having a material relationship with the registrant and state the nature of the relationship. State briefly the nature of the obligation of the underwriter(s) to take the securities.

Instruction to Paragraph 508(a). All that is required as to the nature of the underwriters' obligation is whether the underwriters are or will be committed to take and to pay for all of the securities if any are taken, or whether it is merely an agency or the type of "best efforts" arrangement under which the underwriters are required to take and to pay for only such securities as they may sell to the public. Conditions precedent to the underwriters' taking the securities, including "market-outs," need not be described except in the case of an agency or "best efforts" arrangement.

(b) *New underwriters.* Where securities being registered are those of a registrant that has not previously been required to file reports pursuant to section 13(a) or 15(d) of the Exchange Act, or where a prospectus is required to include reference on its cover page to material risks pursuant to Item 501 of Regulation S–K, and any one or more of the managing underwriter(s) (or where there are no managing underwriters, a majority of the principal underwriters) has been organized, reactivated, or first registered as a broker-dealer within the past three years, these facts concerning such underwriter(s) shall be disclosed in the prospectus together with, where applicable, the disclosures that the principal business function of such underwriter(s) will be to sell the securities to be registered, or that the promoters of the registrant have a material relationship with such underwriter(s). Sufficient details shall be given to allow full appreciation of such underwriter(s) experience and its relationship with the registrant, promoters and their controlling persons.

(c) *Other distributions.* Outline briefly the plan of distribution of any securities to be registered that are to be offered otherwise than through underwriters.

(1) If any securities are to be offered pursuant to a dividend or interest reinvestment plan the terms of which provide for the purchase of some securities on the market, state whether the registrant or the participant pays fees, commissions, and expenses incurred in connection with the plan. If the participant will pay such fees, commissions and expenses, state the anticipated cost to participants by transaction or other convenient references.

(2) If the securities are to be offered through the selling efforts of brokers or dealers, describe the plan of distribution and the terms of any agreement, arrangement, or understanding entered into with broker(s) or dealer(s) prior to the effective date of the registration statement, including volume limitations on sales, parties to the agreement and the conditions under which the agreement may be terminated. If known, identify the broker(s) or dealer(s) which will participate in the offering and state the amount to be offered through each.

(3) If any of the securities being registered are to be offered otherwise than for cash, state briefly the general purposes of the distribution, the basis upon which the securities are to be offered, the amount of compensation and other expenses of distribution, and by whom they are to be borne. If the distribution is to be made pursuant to a plan of acquisition, reorganization, readjustment or succession, describe briefly the general effect of the plan and state when it became or is to become operative. As to any material amount of assets to be acquired under the plan, furnish information corresponding to that required by Instruction 5 of Item 504 of Regulation S–K.

(d) *Offerings on exchange.* If the securities are to be offered on an exchange, indicate the exchange. If the registered securities are to be offered in connection with the writing of exchange-traded call options, describe briefly such transactions.

(e) *Underwriters' compensation.* To the extent not set forth on the cover page of the prospectus, describe the discounts and commissions to be allowed or paid to the underwriters, and all other items that would be deemed by the National Association of Securities Dealers to constitute underwriting compensation for purposes of the Association's Rule of Fair Practice.

(f) *Underwriter's representative on board of directors.* Describe any arrangement whereby the underwriter has the right to designate or nominate a member or members of the board of directors of the registrant. The registrant shall disclose the identity of any director so designated or nominated, and indicate whether or not a person so designated or nominated or allowed to be designated or nominated by the underwriter is or may be a director, officer, partner, employee or affiliate of the underwriter.

(g) *Indemnification of underwriters.* If the underwriting agreement provides for indemnification by the registrant of the underwriters or their controlling persons against any liability arising under the Securities Act, furnish a brief description of such indemnification provisions.

(h) *Dealers' compensation.* State briefly the discounts and commissions to be allowed or paid to dealers, including all cash, securities, contracts or other considerations to be received by any dealer in connection with the sale of the securities. If any dealers are to act in the capacity of subunderwriters and are to be allowed or paid any additional discounts or commissions for acting in such capacity, a general statement to that effect will suffice without giving the additional amounts to be sold.

(i) *Finders.* Identify any finder and, if applicable, describe the nature of any material relationship between such finder and the registrant, its officers, directors, principal stockholders, finders or promoters or the principal underwriter(s), or if there is a managing underwriter(s), the managing underwriter(s), (including, in each case, affiliates or associates thereof).

(j) *Discretionary accounts.* If the registrant was not, immediately prior to the filing of the registration statement, subject to the requirements of section 13(a) or 15(d) of the Exchange Act, identify any principal underwriter that intends to sell to any accounts over which it exercises discretionary authority and include an estimate of the amount of securities so intended to be sold. The response to this paragraph shall be contained in a pre-effective amendment which shall be circulated if the information is not available when the registration statement is filed.

Item 509. Interests of Named Experts and Counsel

If (a) any expert named in the registration statement as having prepared or certified any part thereof (or is named as having prepared or certified a report or valuation for use in connection with the registration statement), or (b) counsel for the registrant, underwriters or selling security holders named in the prospectus as having given an opinion upon the validity of the securities being registered or upon other legal matters in connection with the registration or offering of such securities, was employed for such purpose on a contingent basis, or at the time of such preparation, certification or opinion or at any time thereafter through the date of effectiveness of the registration statement or that part of the registration statement to which such preparation, certification or opinion relates, had, or is to receive in connection with the offering, a substantial interest, direct or indirect, in the registrant or any of its parents or subsidiaries or was connected with the registrant or any of its parents or subsidiaries as a promoter, managing underwriter (or any principal underwriter, if there are no managing underwriters) voting trustee, director, officer, or employee, furnish a brief statement of the nature of such contingent basis, interest, or connection.

Instructions to Item 509. 1. The interest of an expert (other than an accountant) or counsel will not be deemed substantial and need not be disclosed if the interest, including the fair market value of all securities of the registrant owned, received and to be received, or subject to options, warrants or rights received or to be received by the expert or counsel does not exceed $50,000. For the purpose of this Instruction, the term "expert" or counsel includes the firm, corporation, partnership or other entity, if any, by which such expert or counsel is employed or of which he is a member or of counsel to and all attorneys in the case of counsel, and all nonclerical personnel in the case of named experts, participating in such matter on behalf of such firm, corporation, partnership or entity.

2. Accountants, providing a report on the financial statements, presented or incorporated by reference in the registration statement, should note § 210.2–01 of Regulation S–X for the Commission's requirements regarding "Qualification of Accountants" which discusses disqualifying interests.

Item 510. Disclosure of Commission Position on Indemnification for Securities Act Liabilities

In addition to the disclosure prescribed by Item 702 of Regulation S–K, if the undertaking required by paragraph (i) of Item 512 of Regulation S–K is not required to be included in the registration statement because acceleration of the effective date of the registration statement is not being requested, and if waivers have not been obtained comparable to those specified in paragraph (i), a brief description of the indemnification provisions relating to directors, officers and controlling persons of the registrant against liability arising under the Securities Act (including any provision of the underwriting agreement which relates to indemnification of the underwriter or its controlling persons by the registrant against such liabilities where a director, officer or controlling person of the registrant is such an underwriter or controlling person thereof or a member of any firm which is such an underwriter) shall be included in the prospectus, together with a statement in substantially the following form:

Insofar as indemnification for liabilities arising under the Securities Act of 1933 may be permitted to directors, officers or persons controlling the registrant pursuant to the foregoing provisions, the registrant has been informed that in the opinion of the Securities and Exchange Commission such indemnification is against public policy as expressed in the Act and is therefore unenforceable.

Item 511. Other Expenses of Issuance and Distribution

Furnish a reasonably itemized statement of all expenses in connection with the issuance and distribution of the securities to be registered, other than underwriting discounts and commissions. If any of the securities to be registered are to be offered for the account of security holders, indicate the portion of such expenses to be borne by such security holder.

Instruction to Item 511. Insofar as practicable, registration fees, Federal taxes, State taxes and fees, trustees' and transfer agents' fees, costs of printing and engraving, and legal, accounting, and engineering fees shall be itemized separately. Include as a separate item any premium paid by the registrant or any selling security holder on any policy obtained in connection with the offering and sale of the securities being registered which insures or indemnifies directors or officers against any liabilities they may incur in connection with the registration, offering, or sale of such securities. The information may be given as subject to future contingencies. If the amounts of any items are not known, estimates, identified as such, shall be given.

Item 512. Undertakings

Include each of the following undertakings that is applicable to the offering being registered.

(a) *Rule 415 offering.* Include the following if the securities are registered pursuant to Rule 415 under the Securities Act:

The undersigned registrant hereby undertakes:

(1) To file, during any period in which offers or sales are being made, a post-effective amendment to this registration statement:

(i) To include any prospectus required by section 10(a)(3) of the Securities Act of 1933;

(ii) To reflect in the prospectus any facts or events arising after the effective date of the registration statement (or the most recent post-effective amendment thereof) which, individually or in the aggregate, represent a fundamental change in the information set forth in the registration statement;

(iii) To include any material information with respect to the plan of distribution not previously disclosed in the registration statement or any material change to such information in the registration statement;

Provided, however, that paragraphs (a)(1)(i) and (a)(1)(ii) do not apply if the registration statement is on Form S–3 or Form S–8, and the information required to be included in a post-effective amendment by those paragraphs is contained in periodic reports filed by the registrant pursuant to section 13 or section 15(d) of the Securities Exchange Act of 1934 that are incorporated by reference in the registration statement.

(2) That, for the purpose of determining any liability under the Securities Act of 1933, each such post-effective amendment shall be deemed to be a new registration statement relating to the securities offered therein, and the offering of such securities at that time shall be deemed to be the initial bona fide offering thereof.

(3) To remove from registration by means of a post-effective amendment any of the securities being registered which remain unsold at the termination of the offering.

(b) *Filings incorporating subsequent Exchange Act documents by reference.* Include the following if the registration statement incorporates by reference any Exchange Act document filed subsequent to the effective date of the registration statement:

The undersigned registrant hereby undertakes that, for purposes of determining any liability under the Securities Act of 1933, each filing of the registrant's annual report pursuant to section 13(a) or section 15(d) of the Securities Exchange Act of 1934 (and, where applicable, each filing of an employee benefit plan's annual report pursuant to section

15(d) of the Securities Exchange Act of 1934) that is incorporated by reference in the registration statement shall be deemed to be a new registration statement relating to the securities offered therein, and the offering of such securities at that time shall be deemed to be the initial bona fide offering thereof.

(c) *Warrants and rights offerings.* Include the following, with appropriate modifications to suit the particular case, if the securities to be registered are to be offered to existing security holders pursuant to warrants or rights and any securities not taken by security holders are to be reoffered to the public:

The undersigned registrant hereby undertakes to supplement the prospectus, after the expiration of the subscription period, to set forth the results of the subscription offer, the transactions by the underwriters during the subscription period, the amount of unsubscribed securities to be purchased by the underwriters, and the terms of any subsequent reoffering thereof. If any public offering by the underwriters is to be made on terms differing from those set forth on the cover page of the prospectus, a post-effective amendment will be filed to set forth the terms of such offering.

(d) *Competitive bids.* Include the following, with appropriate modifications to suit the particular case, if the securities to be registered are to be offered at competitive bidding:

The undersigned registrant hereby undertakes (1) to use its best efforts to distribute prior to the opening of bids, to prospective bidders, underwriters, and dealers, a reasonable number of copies of a prospectus which at that time meets the requirements of section 10(a) of the Act, and relating to the securities offered at competitive bidding, as contained in the registration statement, together with any supplements thereto, and (2) to file an amendment to the registration statement reflecting the results of bidding, the terms of the reoffering and related matters to the extent required by the applicable form, not later than the first use, authorized by the issuer after the opening of bids, of a prospectus relating to the securities offered at competitive bidding, unless no further public offering of such securities by the issuer and no reoffering of such securities by the purchasers is proposed to be made.

(e) *Incorporated annual and quarterly reports.* Include the following if the registration statement specifically incorporates by reference (other than by indirect incorporation by reference through a Form 10–K report) in the prospectus all or any part of the annual report to security holders meeting the requirements of Rule 14a–3 or Rule 14c–3 under the Exchange Act:

The undersigned registrant hereby undertakes to deliver or cause to be delivered with the prospectus, to each person to whom the prospectus is sent or given, the latest annual report to security holders that is incorporated by reference in the prospectus and furnished pursuant to and meeting the requirements of Rule 14a–3 or Rule 14c–3 under the Securities Exchange Act of 1934; and, where interim financial information required to be presented by Article 3 or Regulation S–X are not set forth in the prospectus, to deliver, or cause to be delivered to each person to whom the prospectus is sent or given, the latest quarterly report that is specifically incorporated by reference in the prospectus to provide such interim financial information.

(f) *Employee plans on Form S–8.* Include the following if the registration statement is on a Form S–8:

(1) The undersigned registrant hereby undertakes to deliver or cause to be delivered with the prospectus to each employee to whom the prospectus is sent or given a copy of the registrant's annual report to stockholders for its last fiscal year, unless such employee otherwise has received a copy of such report, in which case the registrant shall state in the prospectus that it will promptly furnish, without charge, a copy of such report on written request of the employee. If the last fiscal year of the registrant has ended within 120 days prior to the use of the prospectus, the annual report of the registrant for the preceding fiscal year may be so delivered, but within such 120 day period the annual report for the last fiscal year will be furnished to each such employee.

(2) The undersigned registrant hereby undertakes to transmit or cause to be transmitted to all employees participating in the plan who do not otherwise receive such material as stockholders of the registrant, at the time and in the manner such material is sent to its stockholders, copies of all reports, proxy statements and other communications distributed to its stockholders generally.

(3) Where interests in a plan are registered herewith, the undersigned registrant and plan hereby undertake to transmit or cause to be transmitted promptly, without charge, to any participant in the plan who makes a written request, a copy of the then latest annual report of the plan filed pursuant to section 15(d) of the Securities Exchange Act of 1934 (Form 11–K). If such report is filed separately on Form 11–K, such form shall be delivered upon written request. If such report is filed as a part of the registrant's annual report on Form 10–K, that entire report (excluding exhibits) shall be delivered upon written request. If such report is filed as a part of the registrant's annual report to stockholders delivered pursuant to paragraph (1) or (2) of this undertaking, additional delivery shall not be required.

* * *

(g) *Equity offerings of nonreporting registrants.* Include the following if equity securities of a registrant that prior to the offering had no obligation to file reports with the Commission pursuant to section 13(a) or 15(d) of the Exchange Act are being registered for sale in an underwritten offering:

The undersigned registrant hereby undertakes to provide to the underwriter at the closing specified in the underwriting agreements certificates in such denominations and registered in such names as required by the underwriter to permit prompt delivery to each purchaser.

(h) *Registration on Form S–14, S–4 or F–4 of securities offered for resale.* Include the following if the securities are being registered on Form S–14, S–4 or F–4 in connection with a transaction specified in paragraph (a) of Rule 145.

(1) The undersigned registrant hereby undertakes as follows: that prior to any public reoffering of the securities registered hereunder through use of a prospectus which is a part of this registration statement, by any person or party who is deemed to be an underwriter within the meaning of Rule 145(c), the issuer undertakes that such reoffering prospectus will contain the information called for by the applicable registration form with respect to reofferings by persons who may be deemed underwriters, in addition to the information called for by the other Items of the applicable form.

(2) The registrant undertakes that every prospectus (i) that is filed pursuant to paragraph (i) immediately preceding, or (ii) that purports to meet the requirements of section 10(a)(3) of the Act and is used in connection with an offering of securities subject to Rule 415, will be filed as a part of an amendment to the registration statement and will not be used until such amendment is effective, and that, for purposes of determining any liability under the Securities Act of 1933, each such post-effective amendment shall be deemed to be a new registration statement relating to the securities offered therein, and the offering of such securities at that time shall be deemed to be the initial bona fide offering thereof.

(i) *Acceleration of effectiveness.* Include the following if any acceleration is requested of the effective date of the registration statement pursuant to Rule 461 under the Securities Act, and (1) any provision or arrangement exists whereby the registrant may indemnify a director, officer or controlling person of the registrant against liabilities arising under the Securities Act, or (2) the underwriting agreement contains a provision whereby the registrant indemnifies the underwriter or controlling persons of the underwriter against such liabilities and a director, officer or controlling person of the registrant is such an underwriter or controlling person thereof or a member of any firm which is such an underwriter, and (3) the benefits of such indemnification are not waived by such persons.

Insofar as indemnification for liabilities arising under the Securities Act of 1933 may be permitted to directors, officers and controlling persons of the registrant pursuant to the foregoing provisions, or otherwise, the registrant has been advised that in the opinion of the Securities and Exchange Commission such indemnification is against public policy as expressed in the Act and is, therefore, unenforceable. In the event that a claim for indemnification against such liabilities (other that the payment by the registrant of expenses incurred or paid by a director, officer or controlling person of the registrant in the successful defense of any action, suit or proceeding) is asserted by such director, officer or controlling person in connection with the securities being registered, the registrant will, unless in the opinion of its counsel the matter has been settled by controlling precedent, submit to a court of appropriate jurisdiction the question whether such indemnification by it is against public policy as expressed in the Act and will be governed by the final adjudication of such issue.

Subpart 600—Exhibits

Item 601. Exhibits

(a) *Exhibits and index required.* (1) Subject to Rule 411(c) under the Securities Act and Rule 12b–32 under the Exchange Act regarding incorporation of exhibits by reference the exhibits required by in the exhibit table shall be filed as indicated, as part of the registration statement or report. * * *

* * *

Exhibit Table

Instructions to the Exhibit Table. 1. The exhibit table indicates those documents that must be filed as exhibits to the respective forms listed.

2. The "X" designation indicates the documents which are required to be filed with each form even if filed previously with another document. Provided, However, that such previously filed documents may be incorporated by reference to satisfy the filing requirements.

3. The number used in the far left column of the table refers to the appropriate subsection in paragraph (b) where a description of the exhibit can be found. Whenever necessary, alphabetical or numerical subparts may be used.

* * *

Exhibit Table

	Securities Act forms											Exchange Act forms			
	S–1	*S–2*	*S–3*	*S–4* [3]	*S–8*	*S–11*	*S–18*	*F–1*	*F–2*	*F–3*	*F–4* [3]	*10*	*8–K*	*10–Q*	*10–K*
(1) Underwriting agreement	×	×	×	×	..	×	×	×	×	×	×	..	×	..	..
(2) Plan of acquisition, reorganization, arrangement, liquidation or succession	×	×	×	×	..	×	..	×	×	×	×	×	×	×	..
(3) Articles of Incorporation and by-laws	×	..	..	×	..	×	×	×	..	..	×	×	..	..	×
(4) Instruments defining the rights of security holders, including indentures	×	×	×	×	×	×	×	×	×	×	×	×	×	×	×
(5) Opinion re legality	×	×	×	×	×	×	×	×	×	×	×	..	..	..	..
(6) Opinion re discount on capital shares	×	×	..	×	..	×	×	×	×	..	×	×	..	..	..
(7) Opinion re liquidation preference	×	×	..	×	..	×	×	×	×	..	×	×	..	..	..
(8) Opinion re tax matters	×	×	×	×	..	×	×	×	×	×	×	..	..	..	..
(9) Voting trust agreement	×	..	..	×	..	×	×	×	..	..	×	×	..	..	×
(10) Material contracts	×	×	..	×	..	×	×	×	×	..	×	×	..	..	×
(11) Statement re computation of per share earnings	×	×	..	×	..	×	..	×	×	..	×	×	..	×	×
(12) Statements re computation of ratios	×	×	×	×	..	×	..	×	×	..	×	×	..	..	×
(13) Annual report to security holders, Form 10–Q or quarterly report to security holders [1]	..	×	..	×	..	..	..	..	..	..	..	..	..	..	×
(14) Material foreign patents	×	..	..	×	..	..	×	×	..	..	×	×	..	..	..
(15) Letter re unaudited interim financial information	×	×	×	×	×	×	×	×	×	×	×	..	..	×	..
(16) Letter re change in certifying accountant	× [4]	× [4]	..	× [4]	..	× [4]	× [4]	..	..	..		× [4]	×	..	× [4]
(17) Letter re director resignation	..	..	..	..	..	..	..	..	..	..	..	..	×	..	..
(18) Letter re change in accounting principles	..	..	..	..	..	..	..	..	..	..	..	..	..	×	×
(19) Previously unfiled documents	..	..	..	..	..	..	..	..	..	..	..	..	..	×	×
(20) Report furnished to security holders	..	..	..	..	..	..	..	..	..	..	..	..	..	×	..
(21) Other documents or statements to security holders	..	..	..	..	..	..	..	..	..	..	..	..	×	..	..
(22) Subsidiaries of the registrant	×	..	..	×	..	×	..	×	..	..	×	×	..	..	×
(23) Published report regarding matters submitted to vote of security holders	..	..	..	..	..	..	..	..	..	..	..	..	..	×	×
(24) Consents of experts and counsel	×	×	×	×	×	×	×	×	×	×	×	..	× [2]	× [2]	× [2]
(25) Power of attorney	×	×	×	×	×	×	×	×	×	×	×	×	×	×	×
(26) Statement of eligibility of trustee	×	×	×	×	..	×	×	×	×	×	×	..	..	..	..
(27) Invitations for competitive bids	×	×	×	×	..	..	×	×	×	×	×	..	..	..	..
(28) Additional exhibits	×	×	×	×	×	×	×	×	×	×	×	×	×	×	×
(29) Information from reports furnished to state insurance regulatory authorities	×	×	×	×	×	..	..	..	..	..	..	×	..	..	×

[1] Where incorporated by reference into the text of the prospectus and delivered to security holders along with the prospectus as permitted by the registration statement; or, in the case of the Form 10–K, where the annual report to security holders is incorporated by reference into the text of the Form 10–K.

[2] Where the opinion of the expert or counsel has been incorporated by reference into a previously filed Securities Act registration statement.

[3] An exhibit need not be provided about a company if (1) with respect to such company an election has been made under Forms S–4 or F–4 to provide information about such company at a level prescribed by Forms S–2, S–3, F–2 or F–3 and (2) the form, the level of which has been elected under Forms S–4 or F–4, would not require such company to provide such exhibit if it were registering a primary offering.

[4] If required pursuant to Item 304 of Regulation S–K.

[E1121]

Subpart 700—Miscellaneous

Item 701. Recent Sales of Unregistered Securities

Securities. Furnish the following information as to all securities of the registrant sold by the registrant within the past three years which were not registered under the Securities Act. Include sales of reacquired securities, as well as new issues, securities issued in exchange for property, services, or other securities, and new securities resulting from the modification of outstanding securities.

(a) *Securities sold.* Give the date of sale and the title and amount of securities sold.

(b) *Underwriters and other purchasers.* Give the names of the principal underwriters, if any. As to any such securities not publicly offered, name the persons or identify the class of persons to whom the securities were sold.

(c) *Consideration.* As to securities sold for cash, state the aggregate offering price and the aggregate underwriting discounts or commissions. As to any securities sold otherwise than for cash, state the nature of the transaction and the nature and aggregate amount of consideration received by the registrant.

(d) *Exemption from registration claimed.* Indicate the section of the Securities Act or the rule of the Commission under which exemption from registration was claimed and state briefly the facts relied upon to make the exemption available.

Instructions: 1. Information required by this Item 701 need not be set forth as to notes, drafts, bills of exchange, or bankers' acceptances which mature not later than one year from the date of issuance.

2. If the sales were made in a series of transactions, the information may be given by such totals and periods as will reasonably convey the information required.

Item 702. Indemnification of Directors and Officers

State the general effect of any statute, charter provisions, by-laws, contract or other arrangements under which any controlling persons, director or officer of the registrant is insured or indemnified in any manner against liability which he may incur in his capacity as such.

Subpart 800—List of Industry Guides

Item 801. Securities Act Industry Guides

(a) Guide 1. Disclosure of principal sources of electric and gas revenues.

(b) Guide 2. Disclosure of oil and gas operations.

(c) Guide 3. Statistical disclosure by bank holding companies.

(d) Guide 4. Prospectuses relating to interests in oil and gas programs.

(e) Guide 5. Preparation of registration statements relating to interests in real estate limited partnerships.

Item 802. Exchange Act Industry Guides

(a) Guide 1. Disclosure of principal sources of electric and gas revenues.

(b) Guide 2. Disclosure of oil and gas operations.

(c) Guide 3. Statistical disclosure by bank holding companies.

CORPORATION LAW

A. DELAWARE GENERAL CORPORATION LAW

As amended through the First Session (1987) of the 134th General Assembly

[Edited]

Table of Sections

* Also includes 1987 amendments received prior to publication of this pamphlet.

§ 101. Incorporators; How Corporation Formed; Purposes

(a) Any person, partnership, association or corporation, singly or jointly with others, and without regard to his or their residence, domicile or state of incorporation, may incorporate or organize a corporation under this chapter by filing with the Secretary of State a certificate of incorporation which shall be executed, acknowledged, filed and recorded in accordance with section 103 of this title.

(b) A corporation may be incorporated or organized under this chapter to conduct or promote any lawful business or purposes, except as may otherwise be provided by the constitution or other law of this State.

(c) Corporations for constructing, maintaining and operating public utilities, whether in or outside of this State, may be organized under this chapter, but corporations for constructing, maintaining and operating public utilities within this State shall be subject to, in addition to the provisions of this chapter, the special provisions and requirements of Title 26 applicable to such corporations.

§ 102. Contents of Certificate of Incorporation

(a) The certificate of incorporation shall set forth:

(1) The name of the corporation which shall contain one of the words "association", "company", "corporation", "club", "foundation", "fund", "incorporated", "institute", "society", "union", "syndicate", or "limited", or one of the abbreviations ["co.", "corp.", "inc.", "ltd."], or words or abbreviations of like import in other languages (provided they are written in Roman characters or letters), and which shall be such as to distinguish it upon the records in the office of the Secretary of State from the names of other corporations organized, reserved or registered as a foreign corporation under the laws of this State;

(2) The address (which shall include the street, number, city and county) of the corporation's registered office in this State, and the name of its registered agent at such address;

(3) The nature of the business or purposes to be conducted or promoted. It shall be sufficient to state, either alone or with other businesses or purposes, that the purpose of the corporation is to engage in any lawful act or activity for which corporations may be organized under the General Corporation Law of Delaware, and by such statement all lawful acts and activities shall be within the purposes of the corporation, except for express limitations, if any.

(4) If the corporation is to be authorized to issue only 1 class of stock, the total number of shares of stock which the corporation shall have authority to issue and the par value of each of such shares, or a statement that all such shares are to be without par value. If the corporation is to be authorized to issue more than one class of stock, the certificate of incorporation shall set forth the total number of shares of all classes of stock which the corporation shall have authority to issue and the number of shares of each class, and shall specify each class the shares of which are to be without par value and each class the shares of which are to have par value and the par value of the shares of each such class. The certificate of incorporation shall also set forth a statement of the designations and the powers, preferences and rights, and the qualifications, limitations or restrictions thereof, which are permitted by § 151 of this title in respect of any class or classes of stock or any series of any class of stock of the corporation and the fixing of which by the certificate of incorporation is desired, and an express grant of such authority as it may then be desired to grant to the board of directors to fix by resolution or resolutions any thereof that may be desired but which shall not be fixed by the certificate of incorporation. The foregoing provisions of this paragraph shall not apply to corporations which are not organized for profit and which are not to have authority to issue capital stock. In the case of such corporations, the fact that they are not to have authority to issue capital stock shall be stated in the certificate of incorporation. The conditions of membership of such corporations shall likewise be stated in the certificate of incorporation or the certificate may provide that the conditions of membership shall be stated in the bylaws;

(5) The name and mailing address of the incorporator or incorporators;

(6) If the powers of the incorporator or incorporators are to terminate upon the filing of the certificate of incorporation, the names and mailing addresses of the persons who are to serve as directors until the first annual meeting of stockholders or until their successors are elected and qualify.

(b) In addition to the matters required to be set forth in the certificate of incorporation by subsection (a) of this section, the certificate of incorporation may also contain any or all of the following matters:

(1) Any provision for the management of the business and for the conduct of the affairs of the corporation, and any provision creating, defining, limiting and regulating the powers of the corporation, the directors, and the stockholders, or any class of the stockholders, or the members of a non-stock corporation; if such provisions are not contrary to the laws of this State. Any provision which is required or permitted by any section of this chapter to be stated in the by-laws may instead be stated in the certificate of incorporation;

(2) The following provisions, in haec verba, viz.—

"Whenever a compromise or arrangement is proposed between this corporation and its creditors or any class of them and/or between this corporation and its stockholders or any class of them, any court of equitable jurisdiction within the State of Delaware may, on the application in a summary way of this corporation or of any creditor or stockholder thereof or on the application of any receiver or receivers appointed for this corporation under the provisions of section 291 of Title 8 of the Delaware Code or on the application of trustees in dissolution or of any receiver or receivers appointed for this corporation under the provisions of section 279 of Title 8 of the Delaware Code order a meeting of the creditors or class of creditors, and/or of the stockholders or class of stockholders of this corporation, as the case may be, to be summoned in such manner as the said court directs. If a majority in number representing three-fourths in value of the creditors or class of creditors, and/or of the stockholders or class of stockholders of this corporation, as the case may be, agree to any compromise or arrangement and to any reorganization of this corporation as consequence of such compromise or arrangement, the said compromise or arrangement and the said reorganization shall, if sanctioned by the court to which the said application has been made, be binding on all the creditors or class of creditors, and/or on all the stockholders or class of stockholders, of this corporation, as the case may be, and also on this corporation;"

(3) Such provisions as may be desired granting to the holders of the stock of the corporation, or the holders of any class or series of a class thereof, the preemptive right to subscribe to any or all additional issues of stock of the corporation of any or all classes or series thereof, or to any securities of the corporation convertible into such stock. No stockholder shall have any preemptive right to subscribe to an additional issue of stock or to any security convertible into such stock unless, and except to the extent that, such right is expressly granted to him in the certificate of incorporation. All such rights in existence on July 3, 1967, shall remain in existence unaffected by this paragraph (3) unless and

until changed or terminated by appropriate action which expressly provides for such change or termination;

(4) Provisions requiring for any corporate action, the vote of a larger portion of the stock or of any class or series thereof, or of any other securities having voting power, or a larger number of the directors, than is required by this chapter;

(5) A provision limiting the duration of the corporation's existence to a specified date; otherwise, the corporation shall have perpetual existence;

(6) A provision imposing personal liability for the debts of the corporation on its stockholders or members to a specified extent and upon specified conditions; otherwise, the stockholders or members of a corporation shall not be personally liable for the payment of the corporation's debts except as they may be liable by reason of their own conduct or acts;

(7) A provision eliminating or limiting the personal liability of a director to the corporation or its stockholders for monetary damages for breach of fiduciary duty as a director, provided that such provision shall not eliminate or limit the liability of a director: (i) For any breach of the director's duty of loyalty to the corporation or its stockholders; (ii) for acts or omissions not in good faith or which involve intentional misconduct or a knowing violation of law; (iii) under § 174 of this title; or (iv) for any transaction from which the director derived an improper personal benefit. No such provision shall eliminate or limit the liability of a director for any act or omission occurring prior to the date when such provision becomes effective. All references in this paragraph to a director shall also be deemed to refer to a member of the governing body of a corporation which is not authorized to issue capital stock.

(c) It shall not be necessary to set forth in the certificate of incorporation any of the powers conferred on corporations by this chapter.

§ 103. Execution, Acknowledgment, Filing, Recording and Effective Date of Original Certificate of Incorporation and Other Instruments; Exceptions

(a) Whenever any provision of this chapter requires any instrument to be filed with the Secretary of State or in accordance with this section or chapter, such instrument shall be executed as follows:

(1) The certificate of incorporation, and any other instrument to be filed before the election of the initial board of directors if the initial directors were not named in the certificate of incorporation, shall be signed by the incorporator or incorporators.

(2) All other instruments shall be signed—

(i) By the chairman or vice-chairman of the board of directors, or by the president, or by a vice president, and attested by the secretary or an assistant secretary (or by such officers as may be duly authorized to exercise the duties, respectively, ordinarily exercised by the president or vice president and by the secretary or assistant secretary of a corporation); or

(ii) If it shall appear from the instrument that there are no such officers, then by a majority of the directors or by such directors as may be designated by the board; or

(iii) If it shall appear from the instrument that there are no such officers or directors, then by the holders of record, or such of them as may be designated by the holders of record, of a majority of all outstanding shares of stock; or

(iv) By the holders of record of all outstanding shares of stock.

(b) Whenever any provision of this chapter requires any instrument to be acknowledged, such requirement is satisfied by either:

(1) The formal acknowledgement by the person or one of the persons signing the instrument that it is his act and deed or the act and deed of the corporation, as the case may be, and that the facts stated therein are true. Such acknowledgement shall be made before a person who is authorized by the law of the place of execution to take acknowledgements of deeds and who, if he has a seal of office, shall affix it to the instrument.

(2) The signature, without more, of the person or persons signing the instrument, in which case such signature or signatures shall constitute the affirmation or acknowledgement of the signatory, under penalties of perjury, that the instrument is his act and deed or the act and deed of the corporation, as the case may be, and that the facts stated therein are true.

(c) Whenever any provision of this chapter requires any instrument to be filed with the Secretary of State or in accordance with this section or chapter, such requirement means that:

(1) The original signed instrument, together with a duplicate copy which may be either a signed or conformed copy, shall be delivered to the office of the Secretary of State.

(2) All taxes and fees authorized by law to be collected by the Secretary of State in connection with the filing of the instrument shall be tendered to the Secretary of State.

(3) Upon delivery of the instrument, and upon tender of the required taxes and fees, the Secretary of State shall certify that the instrument has been filed in his office by endorsing upon the original signed instrument the word "Filed", and the date and hour of its filing. This endorsement is the "filing date" of the instrument, and is conclusive of the date and time of its filing in the absence of actual fraud. The

Secretary of State shall thereupon file and index the endorsed instrument.

(4) The Secretary of State shall compare the duplicate copy with the original signed instrument, and if he finds that they are identical, he shall certify the duplicate copy by making upon it the same endorsement which is required to appear upon the original, together with a further endorsement that the duplicate copy is a true copy of the original signed instrument.

(5) The duplicate copy of the instrument so certified by the Secretary of State shall be recorded in the office of the Recorder of the county in which the corporation's registered office in this State is, or is to be, located.

(6) The Recorder of the county shall, upon receipt of the certified copy of the instrument, record and index it in a book kept for that purpose.

(d) Any instrument filed in accordance with subsection (c) of this section shall be effective upon its filing date. However, if the instrument is not recorded in accordance with paragraph (5) of subsection (c) of this section within 20 days after its filing date, the recording fee to be collected by the recorder shall be increased by 25 percent. Any instrument may provide that it is not to become effective until a specified time subsequent to the time it is filed, but such time shall not be later than a time on the 90th day after the date of its filing.

(e) If another section of this chapter specifically prescribes a manner of executing, acknowledging, filing or recording a specified instrument or a time when such instrument shall become effective which differs from the corresponding provisions of this section, then the provisions of such other section shall govern.

(f) Whenever any instrument authorized to be filed with the Secretary of State under any provision of this title has been so filed and is an inaccurate record of the corporate action therein referred to, or was defectively or erroneously executed, sealed or acknowledged, such instrument may be corrected by filing with the Secretary of State a certificate of correction of such instrument which shall be executed, acknowledged, filed and recorded in accordance with this section. The certificate of correction shall specify the inaccuracy or defect to be corrected and shall set forth the portion of the instrument in corrected form. The corrected instrument shall be effective as of the date the original instrument was filed, except as to those persons who are substantially and adversely affected by the correction and as to those persons the corrected instrument shall be effective from the filing date.

§ 104. Certificate of Incorporation; Definition

The term "certificate of incorporation", as used in this chapter, unless the context requires otherwise, includes not only the original certificate of incorporation filed to create a corporation but also all other certificates, agreements of merger or consolidation, plans of reorganization, or other instruments, howsoever designated, which are filed pursuant to sections 102, 133–136, 151, 241–245, 251–258, 303, or any other section of this title, and which have the effect of amending or supplementing in some respect a corporation's original certificate of incorporation.

§ 105. Certificate of Incorporation and Other Certificates; Evidence

A copy of a certificate of incorporation, or of a composite or restated certificate of incorporation, or of any other certificate which has been filed in the office of the Secretary of State as required by any provision of this title shall, when duly certified by the Secretary of State and accompanied by the certificate of the recorder of the county in which it has been recorded under his hand and the seal of his office stating the fact and record of its recording in his office, be received in all courts, public offices, and official bodies as prima facie evidence of:

(a) due execution, acknowledgment, filing and recording of the instrument;

(b) observance and performance of all acts and conditions necessary to have been observed and performed precedent to the instrument becoming effective; and of

(c) any other facts required or permitted by law to be stated in the instrument

§ 106. Commencement of Corporate Existence

Upon the filing with the Secretary of State of the certificate of incorporation, executed and acknowledged in accordance with section 103, the incorporator or incorporators who signed the certificate, and his or their successors and assigns, shall, from the date of such filing, be and constitute a body corporate, by the name set forth in the certificate, subject to the provisions of section 103(d) of this title and subject to dissolution or other termination of its existence as provided in this chapter.

§ 107. Powers of Incorporators

If the persons who are to serve as directors until the first annual meeting of stockholders have not been named in the certificate of incorporation, the incorporator or incorporators, until the directors are elected, shall manage the affairs of the corporation and may do whatever is necessary and proper to perfect the organization of the corporation, including the adoption of the original by-laws of the corporation and the election of directors.

§ 108. Organization Meeting of Incorporators or Directors Named in Certificate of Incorporation

(a) After the filing of the certificate of incorporation an organization meeting of the incorporator or incorporators, or of the board of directors if the initial directors were named in the certificate of incorporation, shall be held, either within or without this State, at the call of a majority of the incorporators or directors, as the case may be, for the purposes of adopting by-laws, electing directors (if the meeting is of the incorporators) to serve or hold office until the first annual meeting of stockholders or until their successors are elected and qualify, electing officers if the meeting is of the directors, doing any other or further acts to perfect the organization of the corporation, and transacting such other business as may come before the meeting.

(b) The persons calling the meeting shall give to each other incorporator or director, as the case may be, at least 2 days written notice thereof by any usual means of communication, which notice shall state the time, place and purposes of the meeting as fixed by the persons calling it. Notice of the meeting need not be given to anyone who attends the meeting or who signs a waiver of notice either before or after the meeting.

(c) Any action permitted to be taken at the organization meeting of the incorporators or directors, as the case may be, may be taken without a meeting if each incorporator or director, where there is more than one, or sole incorporator or director where there is only one, signs an instrument which states the action so taken.

§ 109. By-Laws

(a) The original or other by-laws of a corporation may be adopted, amended, or repealed by the incorporators, by the initial directors if they were named in the certificate of incorporation, or, before a corporation has received any payment for any of its stock, by its board of directors. After a corporation has received any payment for any of its stock, the power to adopt, amend or repeal by-laws shall be in the stockholders entitled to vote, or, in the case of a nonstock corporation, in its members entitled to vote; provided, however, any corporation may, in its certificate of incorporation, confer the power to adopt, amend, or repeal by-laws upon the directors or, in the case of a non-stock corporation, upon its governing body by whatever name designated. The fact that such power has been so conferred upon the directors or governing body, as the case may be, shall not divest the stockholders or members of the power, nor limit their power to adopt, amend or repeal by-laws.

(b) The by-laws may contain any provision, not inconsistent with law or with the certificate of incorporation, relating to the business of the corporation, the conduct of its affairs, and its rights or powers or the rights or powers of its stockholders, directors, officers or employees.

§ 110. Emergency By-Laws and Other Powers in Emergency

(a) The board of directors of any corporation may adopt emergency by-laws, subject to repeal or change by action of the stockholders, which shall notwithstanding any different provision elsewhere in this chapter or in Chapters 3 and 5 of Title 26, or in Chapter 7 of Title 5, or in the certificate of incorporation or by-laws, be operative during any emergency resulting from an attack on the United States or on a locality in which the corporation conducts its business or customarily holds meetings of its board of directors or its stockholders, or during any nuclear or atomic disaster, or during the existence of any catastrophe, or other similar emergency condition, as a result of which a quorum of the board of directors or a standing committee thereof cannot readily be convened for action. The emergency by-laws may make any provision that may be practical and necessary for the circumstances of the emergency, including provisions that:

(1) A meeting of the board of directors or a committee thereof may be called by any officer or director in such manner and under such conditions as shall be prescribed in the emergency by-laws;

(2) The director or directors in attendance at the meeting, or any greater number fixed by the emergency by-laws, shall constitute a quorum; and

(3) The officers or other persons designated on a list approved by the board of directors before the emergency, all in such order of priority and subject to such conditions and for such period of time (not longer than reasonably necessary after the termination of the emergency) as may be provided in the emergency by-laws or in the resolution approving the list, shall, to the extent required to provide a quorum at any meeting of the board of directors, be deemed directors for such meeting.

(b) The board of directors, either before or during any such emergency, may provide, and from time to time modify, lines of succession in the event that during such emergency any or all officers or agents of the corporation shall for any reason be rendered incapable of discharging their duties.

(c) The board of directors, either before or during any such emergency, may, effective in the emergency, change the head office or designate several alternative head offices or regional offices, or authorize the officers so to do.

(d) No officer, director or employee acting in accordance with any emergency by-laws shall be liable except for willful misconduct.

(e) To the extent not inconsistent with any emergency by-laws so adopted, the by-laws of the corporation shall remain in effect during any emergency and upon its termination the emergency by-laws shall cease to be operative.

(f) Unless otherwise provided in emergency by-laws, notice of any meeting of the board of directors during such an emergency may be given only to such of the directors as it may be feasible to reach at the time and by such means as may be feasible at the time, including publication or radio.

(g) To the extent required to constitute a quorum at any meeting of the board of directors during such an emergency, the officers of the corporation who are present shall, unless otherwise provided in emergency by-laws, be deemed, in order of rank and within the same rank in order of seniority, directors for such meeting.

(h) Nothing contained in this section shall be deemed exclusive of any other provisions for emergency powers consistent with other sections of this title which have been or may be adopted by corporations created under the provisions of this chapter.

§ 121. General Powers

(a) In addition to the powers enumerated in Section 122 of this title, every corporation, its officers, directors, and stockholders shall possess and may exercise all the powers and privileges granted by this chapter or by any other law or by its certificate of incorporation, together with any powers incidental thereto, so far as such powers and privileges are necessary or convenient to the conduct, promotion or attainment of the business or purposes set forth in its certificate of incorporation.

(b) Every corporation shall be governed by the provisions and be subject to the restrictions and liabilities contained in this chapter.

§ 122. Specific Powers

Every corporation created under this chapter shall have power to:

(1) Have perpetual succession by its corporate name, unless a limited period of duration is stated in its certificate of incorporation;

(2) Sue and be sued in all courts and participate, as a party or otherwise, in any judicial, administrative, arbitrative or other proceeding, in its corporate name;

(3) Have a corporate seal, which may be altered at pleasure, and use the same by causing it or a facsimile thereof, to be impressed or affixed or in any other manner reproduced;

(4) Purchase, receive, take by grant, gift, devise, bequest or otherwise lease, or otherwise acquire, own, hold, improve, employ, use and otherwise deal in and with real or personal property, or any interest therein, wherever situated, and to sell, convey, lease, exchange, transfer or otherwise dispose of, or mortgage or pledge, all or any of its property and assets, or any interest therein, wherever situated;

(5) Appoint such officers and agents as the business of the corporation requires and to pay or otherwise provide for them suitable compensation;

(6) Adopt, amend and repeal by-laws;

(7) Wind up and dissolve itself in the manner provided in this chapter;

(8) Conduct its business, carry on its operations, and have offices and exercise its powers within or without this State;

(9) Make donations for the public welfare or for charitable, scientific or educational purposes, and in time of war or other national emergency in aid thereof;

(10) Be an incorporator, promoter, or manager of other corporations of any type or kind;

(11) Participate with others in any corporation, partnership, limited partnership, joint venture, or other association of any kind, or in any transaction, undertaking or arrangement which the participating corporation would have power to conduct by itself, whether or not such participation involves sharing or delegation of control with or to others;

(12) Transact any lawful business which the corporation's board of directors shall find to be in aid of governmental authority;

(13) Make contracts, including contracts of guaranty and suretyship, incur liabilities, borrow money at such rates of interest as the corporation may determine, issue its notes, bonds and other obligations, and secure any of its obligations by mortgage, pledge or other encumbrance of all or any of its property, franchises and income, and make contracts of guaranty and suretyship which are necessary or convenient to the conduct, promotion or attainment of the business of (a) a corporation all of the outstanding stock of which is owned, directly or indirectly, by the contracting corporation, or (b) a corporation which owns, directly or indirectly, all of the outstanding stock of the contracting corporation, or (c) a corporation all of the outstanding stock of which is owned, directly or indirectly, by a corporation which owns, directly or indirectly, all of the outstanding stock of the contracting corporation, which contracts of guaranty and suretyship shall be deemed to be necessary or convenient to the conduct, promotion or attainment of the business of the contracting corporation, and make other contracts of guaranty and suretyship which are necessary or convenient to the conduct, promotion or attainment of the business of the contracting corporation;

(14) Lend money for its corporate purposes, invest and reinvest its funds, and take, hold and deal with real and personal property as security for the payment of funds so loaned or invested;

(15) Pay pensions and establish and carry out pension, profit sharing, stock option, stock purchase, stock bonus, retirement, benefit, incentive and compensation plans, trusts and provisions for any or all of its

directors, officers, and employees, and for any or all of the directors, officers, and employees of its subsidiaries;

(16) Provide insurance for its benefit on the life of any of its directors, officers, or employees, or on the life of any stockholder for the purpose of acquiring at his death shares of its stock owned by such stockholder.

§ 123. Powers Respecting Securities of Other Corporations or Entities

Any corporation organized under the laws of this State may guarantee, purchase, take, receive, subscribe for or otherwise acquire; own, hold, use or otherwise employ; sell, lease, exchange, transfer, or otherwise dispose of; mortgage, lend, pledge or otherwise deal in and with, bonds and other obligations of, or shares or other securities or interests in, or issued by, any other domestic or foreign corporation, partnership, association, or individual, or by any government or agency or instrumentality thereof. A corporation while owner of any such securities may exercise all the rights, powers and privileges of ownership, including the right to vote.

§ 124. Lack of Corporate Capacity or Power; Effect; Ultra Vires

No act of a corporation and no conveyance or transfer of real or personal property to or by a corporation shall be invalid by reason of the fact that the corporation was without capacity or power to do such act or to make or receive such conveyance or transfer, but such lack of capacity or power may be asserted:

(1) In a proceeding by a stockholder against the corporation to enjoin the doing of any act or acts or the transfer of real or personal property by or to the corporation. If the unauthorized acts or transfer sought to be enjoined are being, or are to be, performed or made pursuant to any contract to which the corporation is a party, the court may, if all of the parties to the contract are parties to the proceeding and if it deems the same to be equitable, set aside and enjoin the performance of such contract, and in so doing may allow to the corporation or to the other parties to the contract, as the case may be, such compensation as may be equitable for the loss or damage sustained by any of them which may result from the action of the court in setting aside and enjoining the performance of such contract, but anticipated profits to be derived from the performance of the contract shall not be awarded by the court as a loss or damage sustained.

(2) In a proceeding by the corporation, whether acting directly or through a receiver, trustee, or other legal representative, or through stockholders in a representative suit, against an incumbent or former officer or director of the corporation, for loss or damage due to his unauthorized act.

(3) In a proceeding by the Attorney General to dissolve the corporation, or to enjoin the corporation from the transaction of unauthorized business.

* * *

§ 131. Registered Office in State; Principal Office or Place of Business in State

(a) Every corporation shall have and maintain in this State a registered office which may, but need not be, the same as its place of business.

(b) Whenever the term "corporation's principal office or place of business in this State" or "principal office or place of business of the corporation in this State", or other term of like import, is or has been used in a corporation's certificate of incorporation, or in any other document, or in any statute, it shall be deemed to mean and refer to, unless the context indicates otherwise, the corporation's registered office required by this section; and it shall not be necessary for any corporation to amend its certificate of incorporation or any other document to comply with this section.

§ 132. Registered Agent in State; Resident Agent

(a) Every corporation shall have and maintain in this State a registered agent, which agent may be either an individual resident in this State whose business office is identical with the corporation's registered office, or a domestic corporation (which may be itself), or a foreign corporation authorized to transact business in this State, having a business office identical with such registered office.

(b) Whenever the term "resident agent" or "resident agent in charge of a corporation's principal office or place of business in this State", or other term of like import which refers to a corporation's agent required by statute to be located in this State, is or has been used in a corporation's certificate of incorporation, or in any other document, or in any statute, it shall be deemed to mean and refer to, unless the context indicates otherwise, the corporation's registered agent required by this section; and it shall not be necessary for any corporation to amend its certificate of incorporation or any other document to comply with this section.

§ 133. Change of Location of Registered Office; Change of Registered Agent

Any corporation may, by resolution of its board of directors, change the location of its registered office in this State to any other place in this State. By like resolution, the registered agent of a corporation may be changed to any other person or corporation including itself. In either such case, the resolution shall be as detailed in its statement as is required by section 102(a)(2) of this title. Upon the adoption of such a resolution, a certificate certifying the change shall be executed, acknowledged, and filed in accordance with section 103 of this title; and a certified copy shall be recorded in the office of the Recorder for the county in which the new office is located; and, if such new office is located in a county other than that in which the former office was located, a certified copy of such certificate shall also be recorded in the office of the Recorder for the county in which such former office was located.

§ 134. Change of Address of Registered Agent

(a) A registered agent may change the address of the registered office of the corporation or corporations for which he is registered agent to another address in this State by filing with the Secretary of State a certificate, executed and acknowledged by such registered agent, setting forth the names of all the corporations represented by such registered agent, and the address at which such registered agent has maintained the registered office for each of such corporations, and further certifying to the new address to which each such registered office will be changed on a given day, and at which new address such registered agent will thereafter maintain the registered office for each of the corporations recited in the certificate. Upon the filing of such certificate, the Secretary of State shall furnish a certified copy of the same under his hand and seal of office, and the certified copy shall be recorded in the office of the Recorder of the county where the registered office of the corporation is located in this State, and thereafter, or until further change of address, as authorized by law, the registered office in this State of each of the corporations recited in the certificate shall be located at the new address of the registered agent thereof as given in the certificate. If the location of such office shall be changed from one county to another county, a certified copy of such certificate shall also be recorded in the office of the Recorder for the county in which such office was formerly located.

(b) In the event of a change of name of any person or corporation acting as registered agent in this State, such registered agent shall file with the Secretary of State a certificate, executed and acknowledged by such registered agent, setting forth the new name of such registered agent, the name of such registered agent before it was changed, the names of all the corporations represented by such registered agent, and the address at which such registered agent has maintained the registered office for each of such corporations. Upon the filing of such certificate, the Secretary of State shall furnish a certified copy of the same under his hand and seal of office, and the certified copy shall be recorded in the office of the recorder of the county where the registered office of each of the corporations recited in the certificate is located in this State.

§ 135. Resignation of Registered Agent Coupled With Appointment of Successor

The registered agent of one or more corporations may resign and appoint a successor registered agent by filing a certificate with the Secretary of State, stating the name and address of the successor agent, in accordance with section 102(a)(2) of this title. There shall be attached to such certificate a statement of each affected corporation ratifying and approving such change of registered agent. Each such statement shall be executed and acknowledged in accordance with section 103 of this title. Upon such filing, the successor registered agent shall become the registered agent of such corporations as have ratified and approved such substitution and the successor registered agent's address, as stated in such certificate, shall become the address of each such corporation's registered office in this State. The Secretary of State shall then issue his certificate that the successor registered agent has become the registered agent of the corporations so ratifying and approving such change, and setting out the names of such corporations. The certificate of the Secretary of State shall be recorded in accordance with section 103 of this title, and the Recorder shall forthwith make a note of the change of registered office and registered agent on the margin of the record of the certificates of incorporation of those corporations which have ratified and approved such change. If the location of such office shall be changed from one county to another county, a certified copy of such certificate shall also be recorded in the office of the Recorder for the county in which such office will thereafter be located.

§ 136. Resignation of Registered Agent Not Coupled With Appointment of Successor

(a) The registered agent of one or more corporations may resign without appointing a successor by filing a certificate with the Secretary of State; but such resignation shall not become effective until 60 days after the certificate is filed. There shall be attached to such certificate an affidavit of such registered agent, if an individual, or of the president, a vice president or the secretary thereof, if a corporation, that at least 30 days prior to the date of the filing of said certificate, due notice was sent by certified or registered mail to the corporation for which such registered agent was acting, at the principal office thereof outside the State, if known to such registered agent or, if not, to the last known address of the attorney or other individual at whose request such registered agent was appointed for such corporation, of the resignation of such registered agent.

(b) Upon the filing of such certificate of resignation with the Secretary of State, the Secretary of State shall then notify the Recorder for the county in which the certificate of incorporation of such corporation is recorded of the resignation of its registered agent as set forth in such certificate and the Recorder shall forthwith make a note of the resignation of such registered agent on the margin of the record of the certificate of incorporation of such corporation.

(c) After receipt of the notice of the resignation of its registered agent, provided for in subsection (a) of this section, the corporation for which such registered agent was acting shall obtain and designate a new registered agent to take the place of the registered agent so resigning in the same manner as provided in section 133 of this title for change of registered agent. If such corporation being a corporation of this State, fails to obtain and designate a new registered agent as aforesaid prior to the expiration of the period of 60 days after the filing by the registered agent of the certificate of resignation, the Secretary of State shall declare the charter of such corporation forfeited. If such corporation, being a foreign corporation, fails to obtain and designate a new registered agent as aforesaid prior to the expiration of the period of 60 days after the filing by the registered agent of the certificate of resignation, the Secretary of State shall forfeit its authority to do business in this State.

(d) After the resignation of the registered agent shall have become effective as provided in this section and if no new registered agent shall have been obtained and designated in the time and manner aforesaid, service of legal process against the corporation for which the resigned registered agent had been acting shall thereafter be upon the Secretary of State in accordance with section 321 of this title.

§ 141. Board of Directors; Powers; Number, Qualifications, Terms and Quorum; Committees; Classes of Directors; Non-profit Corporations; Reliance Upon Books; Action Without Meeting; Removal

(a) The business and affairs of every corporation organized under this chapter shall be managed by or under the direction of a board of directors, except as may be otherwise provided in this chapter or in its certificate of incorporation. If any such provision is made in the certificate of incorporation, the powers and duties conferred or imposed upon the board of directors by this chapter shall be exercised or performed to such extent and by such person or persons as shall be provided in the certificate of incorporation.

(b) The board of directors of a corporation shall consist of one or more members. The number of directors shall be fixed by, or in the manner provided in, the by-laws, unless the certificate of incorporation fixes the number of directors, in which case a change in the number of directors shall be made only by amendment of the certificate. Directors need not be stockholders unless so required by the certificate of incorporation or the by-laws. The certificate of incorporation or by-laws may prescribe other qualifications for directors. Each director shall hold office until his successor is elected and qualified or until his earlier resignation or removal. Any director may resign at any time upon written notice to the corporation. A majority of the total number of directors shall constitute a quorum for the transaction of business unless the certificate of incorporation or the by-laws require a greater number. Unless the certificate of incorporation provides otherwise, the by-laws may provide that a number less than a majority shall constitute a quorum which in no case shall be less than one-third of the total number of directors except that when a board of one director is authorized under the provisions of this section, then one director shall constitute a quorum. The vote of the majority of the directors present at a meeting at which a quorum is present shall be the act of the board of directors unless the certificate of incorporation or the by-laws shall require a vote of a greater number.

(c) The board of directors may, by resolution passed by a majority of the whole board, designate 1 or more committees, each committee to consist of 1 or more of the directors of the corporation. The board may designate 1 or more directors as alternate members of any committee, who may replace any absent or disqualified member at any meeting of the committee. The bylaws may provide that in the absence or disqualification of a member of a committee, the member or members present at any meeting and not disqualified from voting, whether or not he or they constitute a quorum, may unanimously appoint another member of the board of directors to act at the meeting in the place of any such absent or disqualified member. Any such committee, to the extent provided in the resolution of the board of directors, or in the bylaws of the corporation, shall have and may exercise all the powers and authority of the board of directors in the management of the business and affairs of the corporation, and may authorize the seal of the corporation to be affixed to all papers which may require it; but no such committee shall have the power or authority in reference to amending the certificate of incorporation (except that a committee may, to the extent authorized in the resolution or resolutions providing for the issuance of shares of stock adopted by the board of directors as provided in subsection (a) of § 151 of this title, fix the designations and any of the preferences or rights of such shares relating to dividends, redemption, dissolution, any distribution of assets of the corporation or the conversion into, or the exchange of such shares for, shares of any other class or classes or any other series of the same or any other class or classes of stock of the corporation or fix the number of shares of any series of stock or authorize the increase or decrease of the shares of any series), adopting an agreement of merger or consolidation under § 251 or 252 of this title, recommending to the stockholders the sale, lease or exchange of all or substantially all of the corporation's property and assets, recommending to the stockholders a dissolution of the corporation or a revocation of a dissolution, or amending the bylaws of the corporation; and, unless the resolution, bylaws or certificate of incorporation expressly so provides, no such committee shall have the power or authority to declare a dividend, to authorize the issuance of stock or to adopt a certificate of ownership and merger pursuant to § 253 of this title.

(d) The directors of any corporation organized under this chapter may, by the certificate of incorporation or by an initial by-law, or by a by-law adopted by a vote of the stockholders, be divided into 1, 2 or 3 classes; the term of office of those of the first class to expire at the annual meeting next ensuing; of the second class 1 year thereafter; of the third class 2 years thereafter; and at each annual election held after such classification and election, directors shall be chosen for a full term, as the case may be, to succeed those whose terms expire. The certificate of incorporation may confer upon holders of any class or series of stock the right to elect one or more directors who shall serve for such term, and have such voting powers as shall be stated in the certificate of incorporation. The terms of office and voting powers of the directors elected in the manner so provided in the certificate of incorporation may be greater than or less than those of any other director or class of directors. If the certificate of incorporation provides that directors elected by the holders of a class or series of stock shall have more or less than 1 vote per director on any matter, every reference in this chapter to a majority or other proportion of directors shall refer to a majority or other proportion of the votes of such directors.

(e) A member of the board of directors, or a member of any committee designated by the board of directors, shall, in the performance of his duties, be fully protected in relying in good faith upon the records of the corporation and upon such information, opinions, reports or statements presented to the corporation by any of the corporation's officers or employees, or committees of the board of directors, or by any other person as to matters the member reasonably believes are within such other person's professional or expert competence and who has been selected with reasonable care by or on behalf of the corporation.

(f) Unless otherwise restricted by the certificate of incorporation or by-laws, any action required or permitted to be taken at any meeting of the board of directors, or of any committee thereof may be taken without a meeting if all members of the board or committee, as the case may be, consent thereto in writing, and the writing or writings are filed with the minutes of proceedings of the board, or committee.

(g) Unless otherwise restricted by the certificate of incorporation or by-laws, the board of directors of any corporation organized under this chapter may hold its meetings, and have an office or offices, outside of this State.

(h) Unless otherwise restricted by the certificate of incorporation or by-laws, the board of directors shall have the authority to fix the compensation of directors.

(i) Unless otherwise restricted by the certificate of incorporation or by-laws, members of the board of directors of any corporation, or any committee designated by such board, may participate in a meeting of such board, or committee by means of conference telephone or similar communications equipment by means of which all persons participating in the meeting can hear each other, and participation in a meeting pursuant to this subsection shall constitute presence in person at such meeting.

(j) The certificate of incorporation of any corporation organized under this chapter which is not authorized to issue capital stock may provide that less than one-third of the members of the governing body may constitute a quorum thereof and may otherwise provide that the business and affairs of the corporation shall be managed in a manner different from that provided in this section. Except as may be otherwise provided by the certificate of incorporation, the provisions of this section shall apply to such a corporation, and when so applied, all references to the board of directors, to members thereof, and to stockholders shall be deemed to refer to the governing body of the corporation, the members thereof and the members of the corporation, respectively.

(k) Any director or the entire board of directors may be removed, with or without cause, by the holders of a majority of the shares then entitled to vote at an election of directors, except as follows:

(i) Unless the certificate of incorporation otherwise provides, in the case of a corporation whose board is classified as provided in subsection (d) of this section, shareholders may effect such removal only for cause; or

(ii) In the case of a corporation having cumulative voting, if less than the entire board is to be removed, no director may be removed without cause if the votes cast against his removal would be sufficient to elect him if then cumulatively voted at an election of the entire board of directors, or, if there be classes of directors, at an election of the class of directors of which he is a part.

Whenever the holders of any class or series are entitled to elect one or more directors by the provisions of the certificate of incorporation, the provisions of this subsection shall apply, in respect to the removal without cause of a director or directors so elected, to the vote of the holders of the outstanding shares of that class or series and not to the vote of the outstanding shares as a whole.

§ 142. Officers; Titles; Duties; Selection; Term; Failure to Elect; Vacancies

(a) Every corporation organized under this chapter shall have such officers with such titles and duties as shall be stated in the by-laws or in a resolution of the board of directors which is not inconsistent with the by-laws and as may be necessary to enable it to sign instruments and stock certificates which comply with sections 103(a)(2) and 158 of this chapter. One of the officers shall have the duty to record the proceedings of the meetings of the stockholders and directors in a book to be kept for that purpose. Any number of offices may be held by the same person unless the certificate of incorporation or by-laws otherwise provide.

(b) Officers shall be chosen in such manner and shall hold their offices for such terms as are prescribed by the by-laws or determined by the board of directors or other governing body. Each officer shall hold his office until his successor is elected and qualified or until his earlier resignation or removal. Any officer may resign at any time upon written notice to the corporation.

(c) The corporation may secure the fidelity of any or all of its officers or agents by bond or otherwise.

(d) A failure to elect officers shall not dissolve or otherwise affect the corporation.

(e) Any vacancy occurring in any office of the corporation by death, resignation, removal or otherwise, shall be filled as the by-laws provide. In the absence of such provision, the vacancy shall be filled by the board of directors or other governing body.

§ 143. Loans to Employees and Officers; Guaranty of Obligations of Employees and Officers

Any corporation may lend money to, or guarantee any obligation of, or otherwise assist any officer or other employee of the corporation or of its subsidiary, including any officer or employee who is a director of the corporation or its subsidiary, whenever, in the judgment of the directors, such loan, guaranty or assistance may reasonably be expected to benefit the corporation. The loan, guaranty or other assistance may be with or without interest, and may be unsecured, or secured in such manner as the board of directors shall approve, including, without limitation, a pledge of shares of stock of the corporation. Nothing in this section contained shall be deemed to deny, limit or restrict the powers of guaranty or warranty of any corporation at common law or under any statute.

§ 144. Interested Directors; Quorum

(a) No contract or transaction between a corporation and one or more of its directors or officers, or between a corporation and any other corporation, partnership, association, or other organization in which one or more of its directors or officers are directors or officers, or have a financial interest, shall be void or voidable solely for this reason, or solely because the director or officer is present at or participates in the meeting of the board or committee thereof which authorizes the contract or transaction, or solely because his or their votes are counted for such purpose, if;

(1) The material facts as to his relationship or interest and as to the contract or transaction are disclosed or are known to the board of directors or the committee, and the board or committee in good faith authorizes the contract or transaction by the affirmative votes of a majority of the disinterested directors, even though the disinterested directors be less than a quorum; or

(2) The material facts as to his relationship or interest and as to the contract or transaction are disclosed or are known to the shareholders entitled to vote thereon, and the contract or transaction is specifically approved in good faith by vote of the shareholders; or

(3) The contract or transaction is fair as to the corporation as of the time it is authorized, approved or ratified, by the board of directors, a committee thereof, or the shareholders.

(b) Common or interested directors may be counted in determining the presence of a quorum at a meeting of the board of directors or of a committee which authorizes the contract or transaction.

§ 145. Indemnification of Officers, Directors, Employees and Agents; Insurance

(a) A corporation shall have power to indemnify any person who was or is a party or is threatened to be made a party to any threatened, pending or completed action, suit or proceeding, whether civil, criminal, administrative or investigative (other than an action by or in the right of the corporation) by reason of the fact that he is or was a director, officer, employee or agent of the corporation, or is or was serving at the request of the corporation as a director, officer, employee or agent of another corporation, partnership, joint venture, trust or other enterprise, against expenses (including attorneys' fees), judgments, fines and amounts paid in settlement actually and reasonably incurred by him in connection with such action, suit or proceeding if he acted in good faith and in a manner he reasonably believed to be in or not opposed to the best interests of the corporation, and, with respect to any criminal action or proceeding, had no reasonable cause to believe his conduct was unlawful. The termination of any action, suit or proceeding by judgment, order, settlement, conviction, or upon a plea of *nolo contendere* or its equivalent, shall not, of itself, create a presumption that the person did not act in good faith and in a manner which he reasonably believed to be in or not opposed to the best interests of the corporation, and, with respect to any criminal action or proceeding, had reasonable cause to believe that his conduct was unlawful.

(b) A corporation may indemnify any person who was or is a party or is threatened to be made a party to any threatened, pending or completed action or suit by or in the right of the corporation to procure a judgment in its favor by reason of the fact that he is or was a director, officer, employee or agent of the corporation, or is or was serving at the request of the corporation as a director, officer, employee or agent of another corporation, partnership, joint venture, trust or other enterprise against expenses (including attorneys' fees) actually and reasonably incurred by him in connection with the defense or settlement of such action or suit if he acted in good faith and in a manner he reasonably believed to be in or not opposed to the best interests of the corporation and except that no indemnification shall be made in respect of any claim, issue or matter as to which such person shall have been adjudged to be liable to the corporation unless and only to the extent that the Court of Chancery or the court in which such action or suit was brought shall determine upon application that, despite the adjudication of liability but in view of all the circumstances of the case, such person is fairly and reasonably entitled to indemnity for such expenses which the Court of Chancery or such other court shall deem proper.

(c) To the extent that a director, officer, employee or agent of a corporation has been successful on the merits or otherwise in defense of any action, suit or proceeding referred to in subsections (a) and (b), or in defense of any claim, issue or matter therein, he shall be indemnified against expenses (including attorneys' fees) actually and reasonably incurred by him in connection therewith.

(d) Any indemnification under subsections (a) and (b) (unless ordered by a court) shall be made by the corporation only as authorized in the specific case upon a determination that indemnification of the director, officer, employee or agent is proper in the circumstances because he has met the applicable standard of conduct set forth in subsections (a) and (b). Such determination shall be made (1) by the board of directors by a majority vote of a quorum consisting of directors who were not parties to such action, suit or proceeding, or (2) if such a quorum is not obtainable, or, even if obtainable a quorum of disinterested directors so directs, by independent legal counsel in a written opinion, or (3) by the stockholders.

(e) Expenses incurred by an officer or director in defending a civil or criminal action, suit or proceeding may be paid by the corporation in advance of the final disposition of such action, suit or proceeding upon receipt of an undertaking by or on behalf of such director or officer to repay such amount if it shall ultimately be determined that he is not entitled to be indemnified by the corporation as authorized in this section. Such expenses incurred by other employees and agents may be so paid upon such terms and conditions, if any, as the board of directors deems appropriate.

(f) The indemnification and advancement of expenses provided by, or granted pursuant to, the other subsections of this section shall not be deemed exclusive of any other rights to which those seeking indemnification or advancement of expenses may be entitled under any bylaw, agreement, vote of stockholders or disinterested directors or otherwise, both as to action in his official capacity and as to action in another capacity while holding such office.

(g) A corporation shall have power to purchase and maintain insurance on behalf of any person who is or was a director, officer, employee or agent of the corporation, or is or was serving at the request of the corporation as a director, officer, employee or agent of another corporation, partnership, joint venture, trust or other enterprise against any liability asserted against him and incurred by him in any such capacity, or arising out of his status as such, whether or not the corporation would have the power to indemnify him against such liability under the provisions of this section.

(h) For purposes of this section, references to "the corporation" shall include, in addition to the resulting corporation, any constituent corporation (including any constituent of a constituent) absorbed in a consolidation or merger which, if its separate existence had continued, would have had power and authority to indemnify its directors, officers, and employees or agents, so that any person who is or was a director, officer, employee or agent of such constituent corporation, or is or was serving at the request of such constituent corporation as a director, officer, employee or agent of another corporation, partnership, joint venture, trust or other enterprise, shall stand in the same position under the provisions of this section with respect to the resulting or surviving corporation as he would have with respect to such constituent corporation if its separate existence had continued.

(i) For purposes of this section, references to "other enterprises" shall include employee benefit plans; references to "fines" shall include any excise taxes assessed on a person with respect to an employee benefit plan; and references to "serving at the request of the corporation" shall include any service as a director, officer, employee or agent of the corporation which imposes duties on, or involves services by, such director, officer, employee, or agent with respect to an employee benefit plan, its participants, or beneficiaries; and a person who acted in good faith and in a manner he reasonably believed to be in the interest of the participants and beneficiaries of an employee benefit plan shall be deemed to have acted in a manner "not opposed to the best interests of the corporation" as referred to in this section.

(j) The indemnification and advancement of expenses provided by, or granted pursuant to, this section shall, unless otherwise provided when authorized or ratified, continue as to a person who has ceased to be a director, officer, employee or agent and shall inure to the benefit of the heirs, executors and administrators of such a person.

§ 151. Classes and Series of Stock; Rights

(a) Every corporation may issue one or more classes of stock or one or more series of stock within any class thereof, any or all of which classes may be of stock with par value or stock without par value and which classes or series may have such voting powers, full or limited, or no voting powers, and such designations, preferences and relative, participating, optional or other special rights, and qualifications, limitations or restrictions thereof, as shall be stated and expressed in the certificate of incorporation or of any amendment thereto, or in the resolution or resolutions providing for the issue of such stock adopted by the board of directors pursuant to authority expressly vested in it by the provisions of its certificate of incorporation. Any of the voting powers, designations, preferences, rights and qualifications, limitations or restrictions of any such class or series of stock may be made dependent upon facts ascertainable outside the certificate of incorporation or of any amendment thereto, or outside the resolution or resolutions providing for the issue of such stock adopted by the board of directors pursuant to authority expressly vested in it by its certificate of incorporation, provided that the manner in which such facts shall operate upon the voting powers, designations, preferences, rights and qualifications, limitations or restrictions of such class or series of stock is clearly and expressly set forth in the certificate of incorporation or in the resolution or resolutions providing for the issue of such stock adopted by the board of directors. The power to increase or decrease or otherwise adjust the capital stock as provided in this chapter shall apply to all or any such classes of stock.

(b) Any stock which is entitled upon any distribution of the corporation's assets, whether by dividend or by liquidation, to a preference over another class or series of stock may be made subject to redemption by the corporation at its option or at the option of the holders of such stock or upon the happening of a specified event. Any stock of a regulated investment company registered under the Investment Company Act of 1940, as heretofore or hereafter amended, may be given the right to require the corporation to redeem or repurchase the stock at the option of the holder of the stock, provided such redemption or repurchase would not impair or cause a further impairment of the capital of the corporation. Any stock of a corporation which has a license or franchise from a governmental agency to conduct its business or is a member of a national securities exchange, which license, franchise or membership is conditioned upon some or all of the holders of its stock possessing prescribed qualifications, may be made subject to redemption by the corporation to the extent necessary to prevent the loss of such license, franchise or membership or to reinstate it. Any stock which may be made redeemable under this section may be redeemed for cash, property or rights, including securities of the same or another corporation, at such time or times, price or prices, or rate or rates, and with such adjustments, as shall be stated in the certificate of incorporation or in the resolution or resolutions providing for the issue of such stock adopted by the board of directors as hereinabove provided.

(c) The holders of preferred or special stock of any class or of any series thereof shall be entitled to receive dividends at such rates, on such conditions and at such times as shall be stated in the certificate of incorporation or in the resolution or resolutions providing for the issue of such stock adopted by the board of directors as hereinabove provided, payable in preference to, or in such relation to, the dividends payable on any other class or classes or of any other series of stock, and cumulative or non-cumulative as shall be so stated and expressed. When dividends upon the preferred and special stocks, if any, to the extent of the preference to which such stocks are entitled, shall have been paid or declared and set apart for payment, a dividend on the remaining class or classes or series of stock may then be paid out of the remaining assets of the corporation available for dividends as elsewhere in this chapter provided.

(d) The holders of the preferred or special stock of any class or of any series thereof shall be entitled to such rights upon the dissolution of, or upon any distribution of the assets of, the corporation as shall be stated in the certificate of incorporation or in the resolution or resolutions providing for the issue of such stock adopted by the board of directors as hereinabove provided.

(e) Any stock of any class or of any series thereof may be made convertible into, or exchangeable for, at the option of either the holder or the corporation or upon the happening of a specified event, shares of any other class or classes or any other series of the same or any other class or classes of stock of the corporation, at such price or prices or at such rate or rates of exchange and with such adjustments as shall be stated in the certificate of incorporation or in the resolution or resolutions providing for the issue of such stock adopted by the board of directors as hereinabove provided.

(f) If any corporation shall be authorized to issue more than one class of stock or more than one series of any class, the powers, designations, preferences and relative, participating, optional or other special rights of each class of stock or series thereof and the qualifications, limitations or restrictions of such preferences and/or rights shall be set forth in full or summarized on the face or back of the certificate which the corporation shall issue to represent such class or series of stock, provided that, except as otherwise provided in section 202 of this title, in lieu of the foregoing requirements, there may be set forth on the face or back of the certificate which the corporation shall issue to represent such class or series of stock, a statement that the corporation will furnish without charge to each stockholder who so requests the powers, designations, preferences and relative, participating optional or other special rights of each class of stock or series thereof and the qualifications, limitations or restrictions of such preferences and/or rights. Within a reasonable time after the issuance or transfer of uncertificated stock, the corporation shall send to the registered owner thereof a written notice containing the information required to be set forth or stated on certificates pursuant to this section or § 156, 202(a) or 218(a) of this title or with respect to this section a statement that the corporation will furnish without charge to each stockholder who so requests the powers, designations, preferences and relative participating, optional or other special rights of each class of stock or series thereof and the qualifications, limitations or restrictions of such preferences and/or rights. Except as otherwise expressly provided by law, the rights and obligations of the holders of uncertificated stock and the rights and obligations of the holders of certificates representing stock of the same class and series shall be identical.

(g) When any corporation desires to issue any shares of stock of any class or of any series of any class of which the powers, designations, preferences and relative, participating, optional or other rights, if any, or the qualifications, limitations or restrictions thereof, if any, shall not have been set forth in the certificate of incorporation or in any amendment thereto but shall be provided for in a resolution or resolutions adopted by the board of directors pursuant to authority expressly vested in it by the certificate of incorporation or any amendment thereto, a certificate of designations setting forth a copy of such resolution or resolutions and the number of shares of stock of such class or series as to which the resolution or resolutions apply shall be executed, acknowledged, filed, recorded and shall become effective, in accordance with § 103 of this title. Unless otherwise provided in any such resolution or resolutions, the number of shares of stock of any such series to which such resolution or resolutions apply may be increased (but not above the total number of authorized shares of the class) or decreased (but not below the number of shares thereof then outstanding) by a certificate likewise executed, acknowledged, filed and recorded setting forth a statement that a specified increase or decrease therein had been authorized and directed by a resolution or resolutions likewise adopted by the board of directors. In case the number of such shares shall be decreased the number of shares so specified in the certificate shall resume the status which they had prior to the adoption of the first resolution or resolutions. When no shares of any such class or series are outstanding, either because none were issued or because no issued shares of any such class or series remain outstanding, a certificate setting forth a resolution or resolutions adopted by the board of directors that none of the authorized shares of such class or series are outstanding, and that none will be issued subject to the certificate of designations previously filed with respect to such class or series, may be executed, acknowledged, filed and recorded in accordance with § 103 of this title and, when such certificate becomes effective, it shall have the effect of eliminating from the certificate of incorporation all matters set forth in the certificate of designations with respect to such class or series of stock. Unless otherwise provided in the certificate of incorporation, if no shares of stock have been issued of a class or series of stock established by a resolution of the board of directors, the voting powers, designations, preferences and relative, participating, optional or other rights, if any, or the qualifications, limitations or restrictions thereof, may be amended by a resolution or resolutions adopted by the board of directors. A certificate which (1) states that no shares of the class or series have been issued, (2) sets forth a copy of the resolution or resolutions and (3) if the designation of the class or series is being changed, indicates the original designation and the new designation, shall be executed, acknowledged, filed, recorded shall become effective, in accordance with § 103 of this title. When any certificate filed under this subsection becomes effective, it shall have the effect of amending the certificate of incorporation; except that neither the filing of such certificate nor the filing of a restated certificate of incorporation pursuant to § 245 of this title shall prohibit the board of directors from subsequently adopting such resolutions as authorized by this subsection.

§ 152. Issuance of Stock; Lawful Consideration; Fully Paid Stock

The consideration, as determined pursuant to subsections (a) and (b) of Section 153 of this title, for subscriptions to, or the purchase of, the capital stock to be issued by a corporation shall be paid in such form and in such manner as the board of directors shall determine. In the absence of actual fraud in the transaction, the judgment of the directors as to the value of such consideration shall be conclusive. The capital stock so issued shall be deemed to be fully paid and nonassessable stock, if: (1) the entire amount of such consideration has been received by the corporation in the form of cash, services rendered, personal property, real property, leases of real property, or a combination thereof; or (2) not less than the amount of the consideration determined to be capital pursuant to Section 154 of this title has been received by the corporation in such form and the corporation has received a binding obligation of the subscriber or purchaser to pay the balance of the subscription or purchase price; provided, however, nothing contained herein shall prevent the board of directors from issuing partly paid shares under Section 156 of this title.

§ 153. Consideration for Stock

(a) Shares of stock with par value may be issued for such consideration, having a value not less than the par value thereof, as is determined from time to time by the board of directors, or by the stockholders if the certificate of incorporation so provides.

(b) Shares of stock without par value may be issued for such consideration as is determined from time to time by the board of directors, or by the stockholders if the certificate of incorporation so provides.

(c) Treasury shares may be disposed of by the corporation for such consideration as may be determined from time to time by the board of directors, or by the stockholders if the certificate of incorporation so provides.

(d) If the certificate of incorporation reserves to the stockholders the right to determine the consideration for the issue of any shares, the stockholders shall, unless the certificate requires a greater vote, do so by a vote of a majority of the outstanding stock entitled to vote thereon.

§ 154. Determination of Amount of Capital; Capital, Surplus and Net Assets Defined

Any corporation may, by resolution of its board of directors, determine that only a part of the consideration which shall be received by the corporation for any of the shares of its capital stock which it shall issue from time to time shall be capital; but, in case any of the shares issued shall be shares having a par value, the amount of the part of such consideration so determined to be capital shall be in excess of the aggregate par value of the shares issued for such consideration having a par value, unless all the shares issued shall be shares having a par value, in which case the amount of the part of such consideration so determined to be capital need be only equal to the aggregate par value of such shares. In each such case the board of directors shall specify in dollars the part of such consideration which shall be capital. If the board of directors shall not have determined (1) at the time of issue of any shares of the capital stock of the corporation issued for cash or (2) within 60 days after the issue of any shares of the capital stock of the corporation issued for property other than cash what part of the consideration for such shares shall be capital, the capital of the corporation in respect of such shares shall be an amount equal to the aggregate par value of such shares having a par value, plus the amount of the consideration for such shares without par value. The amount of the consideration so determined to be capital in respect of any shares without par value shall be the stated capital of such shares. The capital of the corporation may be increased from time to time by resolution of the board of directors directing that a portion of the net assets of the corporation in excess of the amount so determined to be capital be transferred to the capital account. The board of directors may direct that the portion of such net assets so transferred shall be treated as capital in respect of any shares of the corporation of any designated class or classes. The excess, if any, at any given time, of the net assets of the corporation over the amount so determined to be capital shall be surplus. Net assets means the amount by which total assets exceed total liabilities. Capital and surplus are not liabilities for this purpose.

§ 155. Fractions of Shares

A corporation may, but shall not be required to, issue fractions of a share. If it does not issue fractions of a share, it shall (1) arrange for the disposition of fractional interests by those entitled thereto, (2) pay in cash the fair value of fractions of a share as of the time when those entitled to receive such fractions are determined or (3) issue scrip or warrants in registered form (either represented by a certificate or uncertificated) or in bearer form (represented by a certificate) which shall entitle the holder to receive a full share upon the surrender of such scrip or warrants aggregating a full share. A certificate for a fractional share or an uncertificated fractional share shall, but scrip or warrants shall not unless otherwise provided therein, entitle the holder to exercise voting rights, to receive dividends thereon and to participate in any of the assets of the corporation in the event of liquidation. The board of directors may cause scrip or warrants to be issued subject to the conditions that they shall become void if not exchanged for certificates representing the full shares of uncertificated full shares before a specified date, or subject to the conditions that the shares for which scrip or warrants are exchangeable may be sold by the corporation and the proceeds thereof distributed to the holders of scrip or warrants, or subject to any other conditions which the board of directors may impose.

§ 156. Partly Paid Shares

Any corporation may issue the whole or any part of its shares as partly paid and subject to call for the remainder of the consideration to be paid therefor. Upon the face or back of each stock certificate issued to represent any such partly paid shares, or upon the books and records of the corporation in the case of uncertificated partly paid shares, the total amount of the consideration to be paid therefor and the amount paid thereon shall be stated. Upon the declaration of any dividend on fully paid shares, the corporation shall declare a dividend upon partly paid shares of the same class, but only upon the basis of the percentage of the consideration actually paid thereon.

§ 157. Rights and Options Respecting Stock

Subject to any provisions in the certificate of incorporation, every corporation may create and issue, whether or not in connection with the issue and sale of any shares of stock or other securities of the corporation, rights or options entitling the holders thereof to purchase from the corporation any shares of its capital stock of any class or classes, such rights or options to be evidenced by or in such instrument or instruments as shall be approved by the board of directors. The terms upon which, including the time or times, which may be limited or unlimited in duration, at or within which, and the price or prices at which any such shares may be purchased from the corporation upon the exercise of any such right or option, shall be such as shall be stated in the certificate of incorporation, or in a resolution adopted by the board of directors providing for the creation and issue of such rights or options, and, in every case, shall be set forth or incorporated by reference in the instrument or instruments evidencing such rights or options. In the absence of actual fraud in the transaction, the judgment of the directors as to the consideration for the issuance of such rights or options and the sufficiency thereof shall be conclusive. In case the shares of stock of the corporation to be issued upon the exercise of such rights or options shall be shares having a par value, the price or prices so to be received therefor shall not be less than the par value thereof. In case the shares of stock so to be issued shall be shares of stock without par value, the consideration therefor shall be determined in the manner provided in section 153 of this title.

§ 158. Stock Certificates; Uncertificated Shares

The shares of a corporation shall be represented by certificates, provided that the board of directors of the corporation may provide by resolution or resolutions that some or all of any or all classes or series of its stock shall be uncertificated shares. Any such resolution shall not apply to shares represented by a certificate until such certificate is surrendered to the corporation. Notwithstanding the adoption of such a resolution by the board of directors, every holder of stock represented by certificates and upon request every holder of uncertificated shares shall be entitled to have a certificate signed by, or in the name of the corporation by the chairman or vice-chairman of the board of directors, or the president or vice-president, and by the treasurer or an assistant treasurer, or the secretary or an assistant secretary of such corporation representing the number of shares registered in certificate form. Any or all the signatures on the certificate may be a facsimile. In case any officer, transfer agent or registrar who has signed or whose facsimile signature has been placed upon a certificate shall have ceased to be such officer, transfer agent or registrar before such certificate is issued, it may be issued by the corporation with the same effect as if he were such officer, transfer agent or registrar at the date of issue.

§ 159. Shares of Stock; Personal Property, Transfer and Taxation

The shares of stock in every corporation shall be deemed personal property and transferable as provided in Article 8 of Subtitle I of Title 6. No stock or bonds issued by any corporation organized under this chapter shall be taxed by this State when the same shall be owned by non-residents of this State, or by foreign corporations. Whenever any transfer of shares shall be made for collateral security, and not absolutely, it shall be so expressed in the entry of transfer if, when the certificates are presented to the corporation for transfer or uncertificated shares are requested to be transferred, both the transferor and transferee request the corporation to do so.

§ 160. Corporation's Powers Respecting Ownership, Voting, etc., of Its Own Stock; Rights of Stock Called for Redemption

(a) Every corporation may purchase, redeem, receive, take or otherwise acquire, own and hold, sell, lend, exchange, transfer or otherwise dispose of, pledge, use and otherwise deal in and with its own shares; provided, however, that no corporation shall—

1. Purchase or redeem its own shares of capital stock for cash or other property when the capital of the corporation is impaired or when such purchase or redemption would cause any impairment of the capital of the corporation, except that a corporation may purchase or redeem out of capital any of its own shares which are entitled upon any distribution of its assets, whether by dividend or in liquidation, to a preference over another class or series of its stock if such shares will be retired upon their acquisition and the capital of the corporation reduced in accordance with Sections 243 and 244 of this title. Nothing in this subsection shall invalidate or otherwise affect a note, debenture or other obligation of a corporation given by it as consideration for its acquisition by purchase, redemption or exchange of its shares of stock if at the time such note, debenture or obligation was delivered by the corporation its capital was not then impaired or did not thereby become impaired;

2. Purchase, for more than the price at which they may then be redeemed, any of its shares which are redeemable at the option of the corporation; or,

3. Redeem any of its shares unless their redemption is authorized by Section 151(b) of this title and then only in accordance with such Section and the certificate of incorporation.

(b) Nothing in this section limits or affects a corporation's right to resell any of its shares theretofore purchased or redeemed out of surplus and which have not been retired, for such consideration as shall be fixed by the board of directors.

(c) Shares of its own capital stock belonging to the corporation or to another corporation, if a majority of the shares entitled to vote in the election of directors of such other corporation is held, directly or indirectly, by the corporation, shall neither be entitled to vote nor be counted for quorum purposes. Nothing in this section shall be construed as limiting the right of any corporation to vote stock, including but not limited to its own stock, held by it in a fiduciary capacity.

(d) Shares which have been called for redemption shall not be deemed to be outstanding shares for the purpose of voting or determining the total number of shares entitled to vote on any matter on and after the date on which written notice of redemption has been sent to holders thereof and a sum sufficient to redeem such shares has been irrevocably deposited or set aside to pay the redemption price to the holders of the shares upon surrender of certificates therefor.

§ 161. Issuance of Additional Stock; When and by Whom

The directors may, at any time and from time to time, if all of the shares of capital stock which the corporation is authorized by its certificate of incorporation to issue have not been issued, subscribed for, or otherwise committed to be issued, issue or take subscriptions for additional shares of its capital stock up to the amount authorized in its certificate of incorporation.

§ 162. Liability of Stockholder or Subscriber for Stock Not Paid in Full

(a) When the whole of the consideration payable for shares of a corporation has not been paid in, and the assets shall be insufficient to satisfy the claims of its creditors, each holder of or subscriber for such shares shall be bound to pay on each share held or subscribed for by him the sum necessary to complete the amount of the unpaid balance of the consideration for which such shares were issued or to be issued by the corporation.

(b) The amounts which shall be payable as provided in subsection (a) of this section may be recovered as provided in section 325 of this title, after a writ of execution against the corporation has been returned unsatisfied as provided in that section.

(c) Any person becoming an assignee or transferee of shares or of a subscription for shares in good faith and without knowledge or notice that the full consideration therefor has not been paid shall not be personally liable for any unpaid portion of such consideration, but the transferor shall remain liable therefor.

(d) No person holding shares in any corporation as collateral security shall be personally liable as a stockholder but the person pledging such shares shall be considered the holder thereof and shall be so liable. No executor, administrator, guardian, trustee or other fiduciary shall be personally liable as a stockholder, but the estate or funds held by such executor, administrator, guardian, trustee or other fiduciary in such fiduciary capacity shall be liable.

(e) No liability under this section or under section 325 of this title shall be asserted more than six years after the issuance of the stock or the date of the subscription upon which the assessment is sought.

(f) In any action by a receiver or trustee of an insolvent corporation or by a judgment creditor to obtain an assessment under this section, any stockholder or subscriber for stock of the insolvent corporation may appear and contest the claim or claims of such receiver or trustee.

§ 163. Payment for Stock Not Paid in Full

The capital stock of a corporation shall be paid for in such amounts and at such times as the directors may require. The directors may, from time to time, demand payment, in respect of each share of stock not fully paid, of such sum of money as the necessities of the business may, in the judgment of the board of directors, require, not exceeding in the whole the balance remaining unpaid on said stock, and such sum so demanded shall be paid to the corporation at such times and by such installments as the directors shall direct. The directors shall give written notice of the time and place of such payments, which notice shall be mailed at least 30 days before the time for such payment, to each holder of or subscriber for stock which is not fully paid at his last known postoffice address.

§ 164. Failure to Pay for Stock; Remedies

When any stockholder fails to pay any installment or call upon his stock which may have been properly demanded by the directors, at the time when such payment is due, the directors may collect the amount of any such installment or call or any balance thereof remaining unpaid, from the said stockholder by an action at law, or they shall sell at public sale such part of the shares of such delinquent stockholder as will pay all demands then due from him with interest and all incidental expenses, and shall transfer the shares so sold to the purchaser, who shall be entitled to a certificate therefor. Notice of the time and place of such sale and of the sum due on each share shall be given by advertisement at least one week before the sale, in a newspaper of the county in this State where such corporation's registered office is located, and such notice shall be mailed by the corporation to such delinquent stockholder at his last known postoffice address, at least 20 days before such sale. If no bidder can be had to pay the amount due on the stock, and if the amount is not collected by an action at law, which may be brought within the county where the corporation has its registered office, within one year from the date of the bringing of such action at law, the said stock and the amount previously paid in by the delinquent stockholder on the stock shall be forfeited to the corporation.

§ 165. Revocability of Preincorporation Subscriptions

Unless otherwise provided by the terms of the subscription, a subscription for stock of a corporation to be formed shall be irrevocable, except with the consent of all other subscribers or the corporation, for a period of 6 months from its date.

§ 166. Formalities Required of Stock Subscriptions

A subscription for stock of a corporation, whether made before or after the formation of a corporation, shall not be enforceable against a subscriber, unless in writing and signed by the subscriber or by his agent.

* * *

§ 169. Situs of Ownership of Stock

For all purposes of title, action, attachment, garnishment and jurisdiction of all courts held in this State, but not for the purpose of taxation, the situs of the ownership of the capital stock of all corporations existing under the laws of this State, whether organized under this chapter or otherwise, shall be regarded as in this State.

§ 170. Dividends; Payment; Wasting Asset Corporations

(a) The directors of every corporation, subject to any restrictions contained in its certificate of incorporation, may declare and pay dividends upon the shares of its capital stock either (1) out of its surplus, as defined in and computed in accordance with sections 154 and 244 of this title, or (2) in case there shall be no such surplus, out of its net profits for the fiscal year in which the dividend is declared and/or the preceding fiscal year. If the capital of the corporation, computed in accordance with sections 154 and 244 of this title, shall have been diminished by depreciation in the value of its property, or by losses, or otherwise, to an amount less than the aggregate amount of the capital represented by the issued and outstanding stock of all classes having a preference upon the distribution of assets, the directors of such corporation shall not declare and pay out of such net profits any dividends upon any shares of any classes of its capital stock until the deficiency in the amount of capital represented by the issued and outstanding stock of all classes having a preference upon the distribution of assets shall have been repaired.

(b) Subject to any restrictions contained in its certificate of incorporation, the directors of any corporation engaged in the exploitation of wasting assets (including but not limited to a corporation engaged in the exploitation of natural resources or other wasting assets, including patents, or engaged primarily in the liquidation of specific assets) may determine the net profits derived from the exploitation of such wasting assets or the net proceeds derived from such liquidation without taking into consideration the depletion of such assets resulting from lapse of time, consumption, liquidation or exploitation of such assets.

§ 171. Special Purpose Reserves

The directors of a corporation may set apart out of any of the funds of the corporation available for dividends a reserve or reserves for any proper purpose and may abolish any such reserve.

§ 172. Liability of Directors as to Dividends or Stock Redemption

A member of the board of directors, or a member of any committee designated by the board of directors, shall be fully protected in relying in good faith upon the records of the corporation and upon such information, opinions, reports or statements presented to the corporation by any of its officers or employees, or committees of the board of directors, or by any other person as to matters the director reasonably believes are within such other person's professional or expert competence and who has been selected with reasonable care by or on behalf of the corporation, as to the value and amount of the assets, liabilities and/or net profits of the corporation, or any other facts pertinent to the existence and amount of surplus or other funds from which dividends might properly be declared and paid, or with which the corporation's stock might properly be purchased or redeemed.

§ 173. Declaration and Payment of Dividends

No corporation shall pay dividends except in accordance with this chapter. Dividends may be paid in cash, in property, or in shares of the corporation's capital stock. If the dividend is to be paid in shares of the corporation's theretofore unissued capital stock the board of directors shall, by resolution, direct that there be designated as capital in respect of such shares an amount which is not less than the aggregate par value of par value being declared as a dividend and, in the case of shares without par value shares being declared as a dividend, such amount as shall be determined by the board of directors. No such designation as capital shall be necessary if shares are being distributed by a corporation pursuant to a split-up or division of its stock rather than as payment of a dividend declared payable in stock of the corporation.

§ 174. Liability of Directors for Unlawful Payment of Dividend or Unlawful Stock Purchase or Redemption; Exoneration from Liability; Contribution Among Directors; Subrogation

(a) In case of any willful or negligent violation of the provisions of sections 160 or 173 of this title, the directors under whose administration the same may happen shall be jointly and severally liable, at any time within six years after paying such unlawful dividend or after such unlawful stock purchase or redemption, to the corporation, and to its creditors in the event of its dissolution or insolvency, to the full amount of the dividend unlawfully paid, or to the full amount unlawfully paid for the purchase or redemption of the corporation's stock, with interest from the time such liability accrued. Any director who may have been absent when the same was done, or who may have dissented from the act or resolution by which the same was done, may exonerate himself from such liability by causing his dissent to be entered on the books containing the minutes of the proceedings of the directors at the time the same was done, or immediately after he has notice of the same.

(b) Any director against whom a claim is successfully asserted under this section shall be entitled to contribution from the other directors who voted for or concurred in the unlawful dividend, stock purchase or stock redemption.

(c) Any director against whom a claim is successfully asserted under this section shall be entitled, to the extent of the amount paid by him as a result of such claim, to be subrogated to the rights of the corporation against stockholders who received the dividend on, or assets for the sale or redemption of, their stock with knowledge of facts indicating that such dividend, stock purchase or redemption was unlawful under this chapter, in proportion to the amounts received by such stockholders respectively.

§ 201. Transfer of Stock, Stock Certificate and Uncertificated Stock

Except as otherwise provided in this chapter, the transfer of stock and the certificates of stock which represent the stock or uncertificated stock shall be governed by Article 8 of Subtitle I of Title 6. To the extent that any provision of this chapter is inconsistent with any provision of subtitle I of Title 6, of this chapter shall be controlling.

§ 202. Restriction on Transfer of Securities

(a) A written restriction on the transfer or registration of transfer of a security of a corporation, if permitted by this section and noted conspicuously on the certificate representing the security or, in the case of uncertificated shares, contained in the notice sent pursuant to subsection (f) of § 151 of this title, may be enforced against the holder of the restricted security or any successor or transferee of the holder including an executor, administrator, trustee, guardian or other fiduciary entrusted with like responsibility for the person or estate of the holder. Unless noted conspicuously on the certificate representing the security or, in the case of uncertificated shares, contained in the notice sent pursuant to subsection (f) of § 151 of this title, a restriction, even though permitted by this section, is ineffective except against a person with actual knowledge of the restriction.

(b) A restriction on the transfer or registration of transfer of securities of a corporation may be imposed either by the certificate of incorporation or by the bylaws or by an agreement among any number of security holders or among such holders and the corporation. No restriction so imposed shall be binding with respect to securities issued prior to the adoption of the restriction unless the holders of the securities are parties to an agreement or voted in favor of the restriction.

(c) A restriction on the transfer of securities of a corporation is permitted by this section if it:

(1) Obligates the holder of the restricted securities to offer to the corporation or to any other holders of securities of the corporation or to any other person or to any combination of the foregoing, a prior opportunity, to be exercised within a reasonable time, to acquire the restricted securities; or

(2) Obligates the corporation or any holder of securities of the corporation or any other person or any combination of the foregoing, to purchase the securities which are the subject of an agreement respecting the purchase and sale of the restricted securities; or

(3) Requires the corporation or the holders of any class of securities of the corporation to consent to any proposed transfer of the restricted securities or to approve the proposed transferee of the restricted securities; or

(4) Prohibits the transfer of the restricted securities to designated persons or classes of persons, and such designation is not manifestly unreasonable.

(d) Any restriction on the transfer of the shares of a corporation for the purpose of maintaining its status as an electing small business corporation under subchapter S of the United States Internal Revenue Code or of maintaining any other tax advantage to the corporation is conclusively presumed to be for a reasonable purpose.

(e) Any other lawful restriction on transfer or registration of transfer of securities is permitted by this section.

§ 211. Meetings of Stockholders

(a) Meetings of stockholders may be held at such place, either within or without this State, as may be designated by or in the manner provided in the by-laws or, if not so designated, at the registered office of the corporation in this State.

(b) An annual meeting of stockholders shall be held for the election of directors on a date and at a time designated by or in the manner provided in the by-laws. Any other proper business may be transacted at the annual meeting.

(c) A failure to hold the annual meeting at the designated time or to elect a sufficient number of directors to conduct the business of the corporation shall not affect otherwise valid corporate acts or work a forfeiture or dissolution of the corporation except as may be otherwise specifically provided in this chapter. If the annual meeting for election of directors is not held on the date designated therefor, the directors shall cause the meeting to be held as soon thereafter as convenient. If there be a failure to hold the annual meeting for a period of thirty days after the date designated therefor, or if no date has been designated, for a period of thirteen months after the organization of the corporation or after its last annual meeting, the Court of Chancery may summarily order a meeting to be held upon the application of any stockholder or director. The shares of stock represented at such meeting, either in person or by proxy, and entitled to vote thereat, shall constitute a quorum for the purpose of such meeting, notwithstanding any provision of the certificate of incorporation or by-laws to the contrary. The Court of Chancery may issue such orders as may be appropriate, including, without limitation, orders designating the time and place of such meeting, the record date for determination of stockholders entitled to vote, and the form of notice of such meeting.

(d) Special meetings of the stockholders may be called by the board of directors or by such person or persons as may be authorized by the certificate of incorporation or by the by-laws.

(e) All elections of directors shall be by written ballot, unless otherwise provided in the certificate of incorporation.

§ 212. Voting Rights of Stockholders; Proxies; Limitations

(a) Unless otherwise provided in the certificate of incorporation and subject to the provisions of section 213 of this title, each stockholder shall be entitled to one vote for each share of capital stock held by such stockholder. If the certificate of incorporation provides for more or less than one vote for any share, on any matter, every reference in this chapter to a majority or other proportion of stock shall refer to such majority or other proportion of the votes of such stock.

(b) Each stockholder entitled to vote at a meeting of stockholders or to express consent or dissent to corporate action in writing without a meeting may authorize another person or persons to act for him by proxy, but no such proxy shall be voted or acted upon after three years from its date, unless the proxy provides for a longer period.

(c) A duly executed proxy shall be irrevocable if it states that it is irrevocable and if, and only as long as, it is coupled with an interest sufficient in law to support an irrevocable power. A proxy may be made irrevocable regardless of whether the interest with which it is coupled is an interest in the stock itself or an interest in the corporation generally.

§ 213. Fixing Date for Determination of Stockholders of Record

(a) In order that the corporation may determine the stockholders entitled to notice of or to vote at any meeting of stockholders or any adjournment thereof, the board of directors may fix a record date, which record date shall not precede the date upon which the resolution fixing the record date is adopted by the board of directors, and which record date shall not be more than sixty nor less than ten days before the date of such meeting. If no record date is fixed by the board of directors, the record date for determining stockholders entitled to notice of or to vote at a meeting of stockholders shall be at the close of business on the day next preceding the day on which notice is given, or, if notice is waived, at the close of business on the day next preceding the day on which the meeting is held. A determination of stockholders of record entitled to notice of or to vote at a meeting of stockholders shall apply to any adjournment of the meeting; provided, however, that the board of directors may fix a new record date for the adjourned meeting.

(b) In order that the corporation may determine the stockholders entitled to consent to corporate action in writing without a meeting, the board of directors may fix a record date, which record date shall not precede the date upon which the resolution fixing the record date is adopted by the board of directors, and which date shall not be more than ten days after the date upon which the resolution fixing the record date is adopted by the board of directors. If no record date has been fixed by the board of directors, the record date for determining stockholders entitled to consent to corporate action in writing without a meeting, when no prior action by the board of directors is required by this chapter, shall be the first date on which a signed written consent setting forth the action taken or proposed to be taken is delivered to the corporation by delivery to its registered office in this State, its principal place of business, or an officer or agent of the corporation having custody of the book in which proceedings of meetings of stockholders are recorded. Delivery made to a corporation's registered office shall be by hand or by certified or registered mail, return receipt requested. If no record date has been fixed by the board of directors and prior action by the board of directors is required by this chapter, the record date for determining stockholders entitled to consent to corporate action in writing without a meeting shall be at the close of business on the day on which the board of directors adopts the resolution taking such prior action.

(c) In order that the corporation may determine the stockholders entitled to receive payment of any dividend or other distribution or allotment of any rights or the stockholders entitled to exercise any rights in respect of any change, conversion or exchange of stock, or for the purpose of any other lawful action, the board of directors may fix a record date, which record date shall not precede the date upon which the resolution fixing the record date is adopted, and which record date shall be not more than sixty days prior to such action. If no record date is fixed, the record date for determining stockholders for any such purpose shall be at the close of business on the day on which the board of directors adopts the resolution relating thereto.

§ 214. Cumulative Voting

The certificate of incorporation of any corporation may provide that at all elections of directors of the corporation, or at elections held under specified circumstances, each holder of stock or of any class or classes or of a series or series thereof shall be entitled to as many votes as shall equal the number of votes which (except for such provision as to cumulative voting) he would be entitled to cast for the election of directors with respect to his shares of stock multiplied by the number of directors to be elected by him, and that he may cast all of such votes for a single director or may distribute them among the number to be voted for, or for any two or more of them as he may see fit.

* * *

§ 216. Quorum and Required Vote for Stock Corporations

Subject to this chapter in respect of the vote that shall be required for a specific action, the certificate of incorporation or by-laws of any corporation authorized to issue stock may specify the number of shares and/or amount of other securities having voting power the holders of which shall be present or represented by proxy at any meeting in order to constitute a quorum for, and the votes that shall be necessary for, the transaction of any business, but in no event shall a quorum consist of less than one-third of the shares entitled to vote at the meeting. In the absence of such specification in the certificate of incorporation or by-laws of the corporation:

(1) A majority of the shares entitled to vote, present in person or represented by proxy, shall constitute a quorum at a meeting of stockholders;

(2) In all matters other than the election of directors, the affirmative vote of the majority of shares present in person or represented by proxy at the meeting and entitled to vote on the subject matter shall be the act of the stockholders;

(3) Directors shall be elected by a plurality of the votes of the shares present in person or represented by proxy at the meeting and entitled to vote on the election of directors; and

(4) Where a separate vote by a class or classes is required, a majority of the outstanding shares of such class or classes, present in person or represented by proxy, shall constitute a quorum entitled to take action with respect to that vote on that matter and the affirmative vote of the majority of shares of such class or classes present in person or represented by proxy at the meeting shall be the act of such class.

§ 217. Voting Rights of Fiduciaries, Pledgors and Joint Owners of Stock

(a) Persons holding stock in a fiduciary capacity shall be entitled to vote the shares so held. Persons whose stock is pledged shall be entitled to vote, unless in the transfer by the pledgor on the books of the corporation he has expressly empowered the pledgee to vote thereon, in which case only the pledgee, or his proxy, may represent such stock and vote thereon.

(b) If shares or other securities having voting power stand of record in the names of two or more persons, whether fiduciaries, members of a partnership, joint tenants, tenants in common, tenants by the entirety or otherwise, or if two or more persons have the same fiduciary relationship respecting the same shares, unless the secretary of the corporation is given written notice to the contrary and is furnished with a copy of the instrument or order appointing them or creating the relationship wherein it is so provided, their acts with respect to voting shall have the following effect:

(1) If only one votes, his act binds all;

(2) If more than one vote, the act of the majority so voting binds all;

(3) If more than one vote, but the vote is evenly split on any particular matter, each faction may vote the securities in question

proportionally, or any person voting the shares, or a beneficiary, if any, may apply to the Court of Chancery or such other court as may have jurisdiction to appoint an additional person to act with the persons so voting the shares, which shall then be voted as determined by a majority of such persons and the person appointed by the Court. If the instrument so filed shows that any such tenancy is held in unequal interests, a majority or even-split for the purpose of this subsection shall be a majority or even-split in interest.

§ 218. Voting Trusts and Other Voting Agreements

(a) One or more stockholders may by agreement in writing deposit capital stock of an original issue with or transfer capital stock to any person or persons, or corporation or corporations authorized to act as trustee, for the purpose of vesting in such person or persons, corporation or corporations, who may be designated voting trustee, or voting trustees, the right to vote thereon for any period of time determined by such agreement, not exceeding 10 years, upon the terms and conditions stated in such agreement. The agreement may contain any other lawful provisions not inconsistent with such purpose. After the filing of a copy of the agreement in the registered office of the corporation in this State, which copy shall be open to the inspection of any stockholder of the corporation or any beneficiary of the trust under the agreement daily during business hours, certificates of stock or uncertificated stock shall be issued to the voting trustee or trustees to represent any stock of an original issue so deposited with him or them, and any certificates of stock or uncertificated stock so transferred to the voting trustee or trustees shall be surrendered and cancelled and new certificates or uncertificated stock shall be issued therefore to the voting trustee or trustees. In the certificate so issued, if any, it shall be stated that it is issued pursuant to such agreement, and that fact shall also be stated in the stock ledger of the corporation. The voting trustee or trustees may vote the stock so issued or transferred during the period specified in the agreement. Stock standing in the name of the voting trustee or trustees may be voted either in person or by proxy, and in voting the stock, the voting trustee or trustees shall incur no responsibility as stockholder, trustee or otherwise, except for his or their own individual malfeasance. In any case where 2 or more persons are designated as voting trustees, and the right and method of voting any stock standing in their names at any meeting of the corporation are not fixed by the agreement appointing the trustees, the right to vote the stock and the manner of voting it at the meeting shall be determined by a majority of the trustees, or if they be equally divided as to the right and manner of voting the stock in any particular case, the vote of the stock in such case shall be divided equally among the trustees.

(b) At any time within 2 years prior to the time of expiration of any voting trust agreement as originally fixed or as last extended as provided in this subsection, 1 or more beneficiaries of the trust under the voting trust agreement may, by written agreement and with the written consent of the voting trustee or trustees, extend the duration of the voting trust agreement for an additional period not exceeding 10 years from the expiration date of the trust as originally fixed or as last extended, as provided in this subsection. The voting trustee or trustees shall, prior to the time of expiration of any such voting trust agreement, as originally fixed or as previously extended, as the case may be, file in the registered office of the corporation in this State a copy of such extension agreement and of his or their consent thereto, and thereupon the duration of the voting trust agreement shall be extended for the period fixed in the extension agreement; but no such extension agreement shall affect the rights or obligations of persons not parties thereto.

(c) An agreement between 2 or more stockholders, if in writing and signed by the parties thereto, may provide that in exercising any voting rights, the shares held by them shall be voted as provided by the agreement, or as the parties may agree, or as determined in accordance with a procedure agreed upon by them. No such agreement shall be effective for a term of more than 10 years, but, at any time within 2 years prior to the time of the expiration of such agreement, the parties may extend its duration for as many additional periods, each not to exceed 10 years, as they may desire.

(d) The validity of any such voting trust or other voting agreement, otherwise lawful, shall not be affected during a period of 10 years from the date when it was created or last extended by the fact that under its terms it will or may last beyond the 10-year period.

(e) This section shall not be deemed to invalidate any voting or other agreement among stockholders or any irrevocable proxy which is not otherwise illegal.

§ 219. List of Stockholders Entitled to Vote; Penalty for Refusal to Produce; Stock Ledger

(a) The officer who has charge of the stock ledger of a corporation shall prepare and make, at least ten days before every meeting of stockholders, a complete list of the stockholders entitled to vote at the meeting, arranged in alphabetical order, and showing the address of each stockholder and the number of shares registered in the name of each stockholder. Such list shall be open to the examination of any stockholder, for any purpose germane to the meeting, during ordinary business hours, for a period of at least ten days prior to the meeting, either at a place within the city where the meeting is to be held, which place shall be specified in the notice of the meeting, or, if not so specified, at the place where the meeting is to be held. The list shall also be produced and kept at the time and place of the meeting during the whole time thereof, and may be inspected by any stockholder who is present.

(b) Upon the willful neglect or refusal of the directors to produce such a list at any meeting for the election of directors, they shall be ineligible for election to any office at such meeting.

(c) The stock ledger shall be the only evidence as to who are the stockholders entitled to examine the stock ledger, the list required by this section or the books of the corporation, or to vote in person or by proxy at any meeting of stockholders.

§ 220. Stockholder's Right of Inspection

(a) As used in this section, "stockholder" means a stockholder of record.

(b) Any stockholder, in person or by attorney or other agent, shall, upon written demand under oath stating the purpose thereof, have the right during the usual hours for business to inspect for any proper purpose the corporation's stock ledger, a list of its stockholders, and its other books and records, and to make copies or extracts therefrom. A proper purpose shall mean a purpose reasonably related to such person's interest as a stockholder. In every instance where an attorney or other agent shall be the person who seeks the right to inspection, the demand under oath shall be accompanied by a power of attorney or such other writing which authorizes the attorney or other agent to so act on behalf of the stockholder. The demand under oath shall be directed to the corporation at its registered office in this State or at its principal place of business.

(c) If the corporation, or an officer or agent thereof, refuses to permit an inspection sought by a stockholder or attorney or other agent acting for the stockholder pursuant to sub-section (b) or does not reply to the demand within five business days after the demand has been made, the stockholder may apply to the Court of Chancery for an order to compel such inspection. The Court of Chancery is hereby vested with exclusive jurisdiction to determine whether or not the person seeking inspection is entitled to the inspection sought. The Court may summarily order the corporation to permit the stockholder to inspect the corporation's stock ledger, an existing list of stockholders, and its other books and records, and to make copies or extracts therefrom; or the Court may order the corporation to furnish to the stockholder a list of its stockholders as of a specific date on condition that the stockholder first pay to the corporation the reasonable cost of obtaining and furnishing such list and on such other conditions as the Court deems appropriate. Where the stockholder seeks to inspect the corporation's books and records, other than its stock ledger or list of stockholders, he shall first establish (1) that he has complied with the provisions of this section respecting the form and manner of making demand for inspection of such document; and (2) that the inspection he seeks is for a proper purpose. Where the stockholder seeks to inspect the corporation's stock ledger or list of stockholders and he has complied with the provisions of this section respecting the form and manner of making demand for inspection of such documents, the burden of proof shall be upon the corporation to establish that the inspection he seeks is for an improper purpose. The

Court may, in its discretion, prescribe any limitations or conditions with reference to the inspection, or award such other or further relief as the court may deem just and proper. The Court may order books, documents and records, pertinent extracts therefrom, or duly authenticated copies thereof, to be brought within this State and kept in this State upon such terms and conditions as the order may prescribe.

(d) Any director shall have the right to examine the corporation's stock ledger, a list of its stockholders and its other books and records for a purpose reasonably related to his position as a director. The Court of Chancery is hereby vested with the exclusive jurisdiction to determine whether a director is entitled to the inspection sought. The court may summarily order the corporation to permit the director to inspect any and all books and records, the stock ledger and the stock list and to make copies or extracts therefrom. The Court may, in its discretion, prescribe any limitations or conditions with reference to the inspection, or award such other and further relief as the Court may deem just and proper.

§ 221. Voting, Inspection and Other Rights of Bondholders and Debenture Holders

Every corporation may in its certificate of incorporation confer upon the holders of any bonds, debentures or other obligations issued or to be issued by the corporation the power to vote in respect to the corporate affairs and management of the corporation to the extent and in the manner provided in the certificate of incorporation and may confer upon such holders of bonds, debentures or other obligations the same right of inspection of its books, accounts and other records, and also any other rights, which the stockholders of the corporation have or may have by reason of this chapter or of its certificate of incorporation. If the certificate of incorporation so provides, such holders of bonds, debentures or other obligations shall be deemed to be stockholders, and their bonds, debentures or other obligations shall be deemed to be shares of stock, for the purpose of any provision of this chapter which requires the vote of stockholders as a prerequisite to any corporate action and the certificate of incorporation may divest the holders of capital stock, in whole or in part, of their right to vote on any corporate matter whatsoever, except as set forth in paragraph (2) of subsection (b) of § 242 of this title.

§ 222. Notice of Meetings and Adjourned Meetings

(a) Whenever stockholders are required or permitted to take any action at a meeting, a written notice of the meeting shall be given which shall state the place, date and hour of the meeting, and, in the case of a special meeting, the purpose or purposes for which the meeting is called.

(b) Unless otherwise provided in this chapter, the written notice of any meeting shall be given not less than ten nor more than sixty days before the date of the meeting to each stockholder entitled to vote at such meeting. If mailed, notice is given when deposited in the United States mail, postage prepaid, directed to the stockholder at his address as it appears on the records of the corporation. An affidavit of the secretary or an assistant secretary or of the transfer agent of the corporation that the notice has been given shall, in the absence of fraud, be prima facie evidence of the facts stated therein.

(c) When a meeting is adjourned to another time or place, unless the by-laws otherwise require, notice need not be given of the adjourned meeting if the time and place thereof are announced at the meeting at which the adjournment is taken. At the adjourned meeting the corporation may transact any business which might have been transacted at the original meeting. If the adjournment is for more than thirty days, or if after the adjournment a new record date is fixed for the adjourned meeting, a notice of the adjourned meeting shall be given to each stockholder of record entitled to vote at the meeting.

§ 223. Vacancies and Newly Created Directorships

(a) Unless otherwise provided in the certificate of incorporation or by-laws: (1) Vacancies and newly created directorships resulting from any increase in the authorized number of directors elected by all of the stockholders having the right to vote as a single class may be filled by a majority of the directors then in office, although less than a quorum, or by a sole remaining director; (2) Whenever the holders of any class or classes of stock or series thereof are entitled to elect one or more directors by the provisions of the certificate of incorporation, vacancies and newly created directorships of such class or classes or series may be filled by a majority of the directors elected by such class or classes or series thereof then in office, or by a sole remaining director so elected.

If at any time, by reason of death or resignation or other cause, a corporation should have no directors in office, then any officer or any stockholder or an executor, administrator, trustee or guardian of a stockholder, or other fiduciary entrusted with like responsibility for the person or estate of a stockholder, may call a special meeting of stockholders in accordance with the provisions of the certificate of incorporation or the by-laws, or may apply to the Court of Chancery for a decree summarily ordering an election as provided in section 211 of this title.

(b) In the case of a corporation the directors of which are divided into classes, any directors chosen under subsection (a) of this section shall hold office until the next election of the class for which such directors shall have been chosen, and until their successors shall be elected and qualified.

(c) If, at the time of filling any vacancy or any newly created directorship, the directors then in office shall constitute less than a majority of the whole board (as constituted immediately prior to any such increase), the Court of Chancery may, upon application of any stockholder or stockholders holding at least ten percent of the total number of the shares at the time outstanding having the right to vote for such directors, summarily order an election to be held to fill any such vacancies or newly created directorships, or to replace the directors chosen by the directors then in office as aforesaid, which election shall be governed by the provisions of section 211 of this title as far as applicable.

(d) Unless otherwise provided in the certificate of incorporation or by-laws, when one or more directors shall resign from the board, effective at a future date, a majority of the directors then in office, including those who have so resigned, shall have power to fill such vacancy or vacancies, the vote thereon to take effect when such resignation or resignations shall become effective, and each director so chosen shall hold office as provided in this section in the filling of other vacancies.

§ 224. Form of Records

Any records maintained by a corporation in the regular course of its business, including its stock ledger, books of account, and minute books, may be kept on, or be in the form of, punch cards, magnetic tape, photographs, microphotographs, or any other information storage device, provided that the records so kept can be converted into clearly legible written form within a reasonable time. Any corporation shall so convert any records so kept upon the request of any person entitled to inspect the same. Where records are kept in such manner, a clearly legible written form produced from the cards, tapes, photographs, microphotographs or other information storage device shall be admissible in evidence and shall be accepted for all other purposes, to the same extent as an original written record of the same information would have been, when said written form accurately portrays the record.

§ 225. Contested Election of Directors; Proceedings to Determine Validity

(a) Upon application of any stockholder or director, or any officer whose title to office is contested, or any member of a corporation without capital stock, the Court of Chancery may hear and determine the validity of any election of any director, member of the governing body, or officer of any corporation, and the right of any person to hold such office, and, in case any such office is claimed by more than 1 person, may determine the person entitled thereto; and to that end make such order or decree in any such case as may be just and proper, with power to enforce the production of any books, papers and records of the corporation relating to the issue. In case it should be determined that no valid election has been held, the Court of Chancery may order an election to be held in accordance with § 211 or 215 of this title. In any such application, service of copies of the application upon the registered agent of the corporation shall be deemed to be service upon the corporation and upon the person whose title to office is contested and upon the person, if any, claiming such office; and the registered agent shall forward immediately a copy of the application to the corporation and to the person whose title to office is contested and to the person, if any, claiming such office, in a postpaid, sealed, registered letter addressed to such corporation and such person at their post-office addresses last known to the registered agent or furnished to the registered agent by the applicant stockholder. The Court may make such order respecting further or other notice of such application as it deems proper under the circumstances.

(b) Upon application of any stockholder or any member of a corporation without capital stock, the Court of Chancery may hear and determine the result of any vote of stockholders or members, as the case may be, upon matters other than the election of directors, officers or members of the governing body. Service of the application upon the registered agent of the corporation shall be deemed to be service upon the corporation, and no other party need be joined in order for the Court to adjudicate the result of the vote. The Court may make such order respecting notice of the application as it deems proper under the circumstances.

§ 226. Appointment of Custodian or Receiver of Corporation on Deadlock or for Other Cause

(a) The Court of Chancery, upon application of any stockholder, may appoint one or more persons to be custodians, and, if the corporation is insolvent, to be receivers, of and for any corporation when:

(1) At any meeting held for the election of directors the stockholders are so divided that they have failed to elect successors to directors whose terms have expired or would have expired upon qualification of their successors; or

(2) The business of the corporation is suffering or is threatened with irreparable injury because the directors are so divided respecting the management of the affairs of the corporation that the required vote for action by the board of directors cannot be obtained and the stockholders are unable to terminate this division; or

(3) The corporation has abandoned its business and has failed within a reasonable time to take steps to dissolve, liquidate or distribute its assets.

(b) A custodian appointed under this section shall have all the powers and title of a receiver appointed under section 291 of this title, but the authority of the custodian is to continue the business of the corporation and not to liquidate its affairs and distribute its assets, except when the Court shall otherwise order and except in cases arising under subparagraph (a)(3) of this section or section 352(a)(2) of this title.

§ 227. Powers of Court in Elections of Directors

(a) The Court of Chancery, in any proceeding instituted under sections 211, 215 or 225 of this title may determine the right and power of persons claiming to own stock, or in the case of a corporation without capital stock, of the persons claiming to be members, to vote at any meeting of the stockholders or members.

(b) The Court of Chancery may appoint a master to hold any election provided for in sections 211, 215 or 225 of this title under such orders and powers as it deems proper; and it may punish any officer or director for contempt in case of disobedience of any order made by the Court; and, in case of disobedience by a corporation of any order made by the Court, may enter a decree against such corporation for a penalty of not more than $5,000.

§ 228. Consent of Stockholders in Lieu of Meeting

(a) Unless otherwise provided in the certificate of incorporation, any action required by this chapter to be taken at any annual or special meeting of stockholders of a corporation, or any action which may be taken at any annual or special meeting of such stockholders, may be taken without a meeting, without prior notice and without a vote, if a consent or consents in writing, setting forth the action so taken, shall be signed by the holders of outstanding stock having not less than the minimum number of votes that would be necessary to authorize or take such action at a meeting at which all shares entitled to vote thereon were present and voted and shall be delivered to the corporation by delivery to its registered office in this State, its principal place of business, or an officer or agent of the corporation having custody of the book in which proceedings of meetings of stockholders are recorded. Delivery made to a corporation's registered office shall be by hand or by certified or registered mail, return receipt requested.

(b) Unless otherwise provided in the certificate of incorporation, any action required by this chapter to be taken at a meeting of the members of a non-stock corporation, or any action which may be taken at any meeting of the members of a non-stock corporation, may be taken without a meeting, without prior notice and without a vote, if a consent or consents in writing, setting forth the action so taken, shall be signed by members having not less than the minimum number of votes that would be necessary to authorize or take such action at a meeting at which all members having a right to vote thereon were present and voted and shall be delivered to the corporation by delivery to its registered office in this State, its principal place of business, or an officer or agent of the corporation having custody of the book in which proceedings of meetings of stockholders are recorded. Delivery made to a corporation's registered office shall be by hand or by certified or registered mail, return receipt requested.

(c) Every written consent shall bear the date of signature of each stockholder or member who signs the consent and no written consent shall be effective to take the corporate action referred to therein unless, within sixty days of the earliest dated consent delivered in the manner required by this Section to the corporation, written consents signed by a sufficient number of holders or members to take action are delivered to the corporation by delivery to its registered office in this State, its principal place of business or an officer or agent of the corporation having custody of the book in which proceedings of meetings of stockholders are recorded. Delivery made to a corporation's registered office shall be by hand or by certified or registered mail, return receipt requested.

(d) Prompt notice of the taking of the corporate action without a meeting by less than unanimous written consent shall be given to those stockholders or members, as the case may be, who have not consented in writing. In the event that the action which is consented to is such as would have required the filing of a certificate under any other section of this title, if such action had been voted on by stockholders or by members at a meeting thereof, the certificate filed under such other section shall state, in lieu of any statement required by such section concerning any vote of stockholders or members, that written consent has been given in accordance with the provisions of this section, and that written notice has been given as provided in this section.

§ 229. Waiver of Notice

Whenever notice is required to be given under any provision of this chapter or of the certificate of incorporation or by-laws, a written waiver thereof, signed by the person entitled to notice, whether before or after the time stated therein, shall be deemed equivalent to notice. Attendance of a person at a meeting shall constitute a waiver of notice of such meeting, except when the person attends a meeting for the express purpose of objecting, at the beginning of the meeting, to the transaction of any business because the meeting is not lawfully called or convened. Neither the business to be transacted at, nor the purpose of, any regular or special meeting of the stockholders, directors, or members of a committee of directors need be specified in any written waiver of notice unless so required by the certificate of incorporation or the by-laws.

§ 230. Exception to Requirements of Notice

(a) Whenever notice is required to be given, under any provision of this chapter or of the certificate of incorporation or bylaws of any corporation, to any person with whom communication is unlawful, the giving of such notice to such person shall not be required and there shall be no duty to apply to any governmental authority or agency for a license or permit to give such notice to such person. Any action or meeting which shall be taken or held without notice to any such person with whom communication is unlawful shall have the same force and effect as if such notice had been duly given. In the event that the action taken by the corporation is such as to require the filing of a certificate under any of the other sections of this title, the certificate shall state, if such is the fact and if notice is required, that notice was given to all persons entitled to receive notice except such persons with whom communication is unlawful.

(b) Whenever notice is required to be given, under any provision of this title or the certificate of incorporation or bylaws of any corporation, to any stockholder or, if the corporation is a nonstock corporation, to any member, to whom (1) notice of 2 consecutive annual meetings, and all notices of meetings or of the taking of action by written consent without a meeting to such person during the period between such 2 consecutive annual meetings, or (2) all, and at least 2, payments (if sent by first-class mail) of dividends or interest on securities during a 12-month period, have been mailed addressed to such person at his address as shown on the records of the corporation and have been returned undeliverable, the giving of such notice to such person shall not be required. Any action or meeting which shall be taken or held without notice to such person shall have the same force and effect as if such notice had been duly given. If any such person shall deliver to the corporation a written notice setting forth his then current address, the requirement that notice be given to such person shall be reinstated. In the event that the action taken by the corporation is such as to require the filing of a certificate under any of the other sections of this title, the certificate need not state that notice was not given to persons to whom notice was not required to be given pursuant to this subsection.

§ 241. Amendment of Certificate of Incorporation Before Receipt of Payment for Stock

(a) Before a corporation has received any payment for any of its stock, it may amend its certificate of incorporation at any time or times, in any and as many respects as may be desired, so long as its certificate of incorporation as amended would contain only such provisions as it would be lawful and proper to insert in an original certificate of incorporation filed at the time of filing the amendment.

(b) The amendment of a certificate of incorporation authorized by this section shall be adopted by a majority of the incorporators, if directors were not named in the original certificate of incorporation or have not yet been elected, or, if directors were named in the original certificate of incorporation or have been elected and have qualified, by a majority of the directors. A certificate setting forth the amendment and certifying that the corporation has not received any payment for any of its stock and that the amendment has been duly adopted in accordance with the provisions of this section shall be executed, acknowledged, filed and recorded in accordance with section 103 of this title. Upon such filing, the corporation's certificate of incorporation shall be deemed to be amended accordingly as of the date on which the original certificate of incorporation became effective except as to those persons who are substantially and adversely affected by the amendment and as to those persons the amendment shall be effective from the filing date.

§ 242. Amendment of Certificate of Incorporation After Receipt of Payment for Stock; Non-stock Corporations

(a) After a corporation has received payment for any of its capital stock, it may amend its certificate of incorporation, from time to time, in any and as many respects as may be desired, so long as its certificate of incorporation as amended would contain only such provisions as it would be lawful and proper to insert in an original certificate of incorporation filed at the time of the filing of the amendment; and, if a change in stock or the rights of stockholders, or an exchange, reclassification or cancellation of stock or rights of stockholders is to be made, such provisions as may be necessary to effect such change, exchange, reclassification or cancellation. In particular, and without limitation upon such general power of amendment, a corporation may amend its certificate of incorporation, from time to time, so as:

(1) To change its corporate name; or

(2) To change, substitute, enlarge or diminish the nature of its business or its corporate powers and purposes; or

(3) To increase or decrease its authorized capital stock or to reclassify the same, by changing the number, par value, designations, preferences, or relative, participating, optional, or other special rights of the shares, or the qualifications, limitations or restrictions of such rights, or by changing shares with par value into shares without par value, or shares without par value into shares with par value either with or without increasing or decreasing the number of shares; or

(4) To cancel or otherwise affect the right of the holders of the shares of any class to receive dividends which have accrued but have not been declared; or

(5) To create new classes of stock having rights and preferences either prior and superior or subordinate and inferior to the stock of any class then authorized, whether issued or unissued; or

(6) To change the period of its duration.

Any or all such changes or alterations may be effected by one certificate of amendment.

(b) Every amendment authorized by subsection (a) of this section shall be made and effected in the following manner—

(1) If the corporation has capital stock, its board of directors shall adopt a resolution setting forth the amendment proposed, declaring its advisability, and either calling a special meeting of the stockholders entitled to vote in respect thereof for the consideration of such amendment or directing that the amendment proposed be considered at the next annual meeting of the stockholders. Such special or annual meeting shall be called and held upon notice in accordance with section 222 of this title. The notice shall set forth such amendment in full or a brief

summary of the changes to be effected thereby, as the directors shall deem advisable. At the meeting a vote of the stockholders entitled to vote thereon shall be taken for and against the proposed amendment. If a majority of the outstanding stock entitled to vote thereon, and a majority of the outstanding stock of each class entitled to vote thereon as a class has been voted in favor of the amendment, a certificate setting forth the amendment and certifying that such amendment has been duly adopted in accordance with the provisions of this section shall be executed, acknowledged, filed, and recorded, and shall become effective in accordance with section 103 of this title.

(2) The holders of the outstanding shares of a class shall be entitled to vote as a class upon a proposed amendment, whether or not entitled to vote thereon by the provisions of the certificate of incorporation, if the amendment would increase or decrease the aggregate number of authorized shares of such class, increase or decrease the par value of the shares of such class, or alter or change the powers, preferences or special rights of the shares of such class so as to affect them adversely. If any proposed amendment would alter or change the powers, preferences, or special rights of one or more series of any class so as to affect them adversely, but shall not so affect the entire class, then only the shares of the series so affected by the amendment shall be considered a separate class for the purposes of this paragraph. The number of authorized shares of any such class or classes of stock may be increased or decreased (but not below the number of shares thereof then outstanding) by the affirmative vote of the holders of a majority of the stock of the corporation entitled to vote irrespective of the provision of this paragraph (c)(2), if so provided in the original certificate of incorporation, in any amendment thereto which created such class or classes of stock or which was adopted prior to the issuance of any shares of such class or classes of stock, or in any amendment thereto which was authorized by a resolution or resolutions adopted by the affirmative vote of the holders of a majority of such class or classes of stock.

(3) If the corporation has no capital stock, then the governing body thereof shall adopt a resolution setting forth the amendment proposed and declaring its advisability. If at a subsequent meeting, held, on notice stating the purpose thereof, not earlier than 15 days and not later than 60 days from the meeting at which such resolution has been passed, a majority of all the members of the governing body, shall vote in favor of such amendment, a certificate thereof shall be executed, acknowledged, filed, recorded, and shall become effective in accordance with section 103 of this title. The certificate of incorporation of any such corporation without capital stock may contain a provision requiring any amendment thereto to be approved by a specified number or percentage of the members or of any specified class of members of such corporation in which event only one meeting of the governing body thereof shall be necessary, and such proposed amendment shall be submitted to the

members or to any specified class of members of such corporation without capital stock in the same manner, so far as applicable, as is provided in this section for an amendment to the certificate of incorporation of a stock corporation; and in the event of the adoption thereof, a certificate evidencing such amendment shall be executed, filed, acknowledged, recorded and shall become effective in accordance with section 103 of this title.

(4) Whenever the certificate of incorporation shall require for action by the board of directors, by the holders of any class or series of shares or by the holders of any other securities having voting power the vote of a greater number or proportion than is required by any section of this title, the provision of the certificate of incorporation requiring such greater vote shall not be altered, amended or repealed except by such greater vote.

§ 243. Retirement of Stock

(a) A corporation, by resolution of its board of directors, may retire any shares of its capital stock that are issued but are not outstanding.

(b) Whenever any shares of the capital stock of a corporation are retired, they shall resume the status of authorized and unissued shares of the class or series to which they belong unless the certificate of incorporation otherwise provides. If the certificate of incorporation prohibits the reissuance of such shares, or prohibits the reissuance of such shares as a part of a specific series only, a certificate stating that reissuance of the shares (as part of the class or series) is prohibited identifying the shares and reciting their retirement shall be executed, acknowledged and filed and shall become effective in accordance with § 103 of this Title. When such certificate becomes effective, it shall have the effect of amending the certificate of incorporation so as to reduce accordingly the number of authorized shares of the class or series to with such shares belong or, if such retired shares constitute all of the authorized shares of the class or series to which they belong, of eliminating from the certificate of incorporation all reference to such class or series of stock.

(c) If the capital of the corporation will be reduced by or in connection with the retirement of shares, the reduction of capital shall be effected pursuant to Section 244 of this Title.

§ 244. Reduction of Capital

(a) A corporation, by resolution of its board of directors, may reduce its capital in any of the following ways:

1. By reducing or eliminating the capital represented by shares of capital stock which have been retired;

2. By applying to an otherwise authorized purchase or redemption of outstanding shares of its capital stock some or all of the capital represented by the shares being purchased or redeemed, or any capital that has not been allocated to any particular class of its capital stock;

3. By applying to an otherwise authorized conversion or exchange of outstanding shares of its capital stock some or all of the capital represented by the shares being converted or exchanged, or some or all of any capital that has not been allocated to any particular class of its capital stock, or both, to the extent that such capital in the aggregate exceeds the total aggregate par value or the stated capital of any previously unissued shares issuable upon such conversion or exchange; or,

4. By transferring to surplus (i) some or all of the capital not represented by any particular class of its capital stock; (ii) some or all of the capital represented by issued shares of its par value capital stock, which capital is in excess of the aggregate par value of such shares; or (iii) some of the capital represented by issued shares of its capital stock without par value.

(b) Notwithstanding the other provisions of this section, no reduction of capital shall be made or effected unless the assets of the corporation remaining after such reduction shall be sufficient to pay any debts of the corporation for which payment has not been otherwise provided. No reduction of capital shall release any liability of any stockholder whose shares have not been fully paid.

§ 245. Restated Certificate of Incorporation

(a) A corporation may, whenever desired, integrate into a single instrument all of the provisions of its certificate of incorporation which are then in effect and operative as a result of there having theretofore been filed with the Secretary of State one or more certificates or other instruments pursuant to any of the sections referred to in § 104 of this title, and it may at the same time also further amend its certificate of incorporation by adopting a restated certificate of incorporation.

(b) If the restated certificate of incorporation merely restates and integrates but does not further amend the certificate of incorporation, as theretofore amended or supplemented by any instrument that was filed pursuant to any of the sections mentioned in § 104 of this title, it may be adopted by the board of directors without a vote of the stockholders, or it may be proposed by the directors and submitted by them to the stockholders for adoption, in which case the procedure and vote required by § 242 of this title for amendment of the certificate of incorporation shall be applicable. If the restated certificate of incorporation restates and integrates and also further amends in any respect the certificate of incorporation, as theretofore amended or supplemented, it shall be proposed by the directors and adopted by the stockholders in the manner and by the vote prescribed by § 242 of this title "or, if the corporation has not received any payment for any of its stock, in the manner and by the vote prescribed by § 241 of this title."

(c) A restated certificate of incorporation shall be specifically designated as such in its heading. It shall state, either in its heading or in an introductory paragraph, the corporation's present name, and, if it has been changed, the name under which it was originally incorporated, and the date of filing of its original certificate of incorporation with the Secretary of State. A restated certificate shall also state that it was duly adopted in accordance with the provisions of this section. If it was adopted by the board of directors without a vote of the stockholders (unless it was adopted pursuant to the provisions of section 241 of this title), it shall state that it only restates and integrates and does not further amend the provisions of the corporation's certificate of incorporation as theretofore amended or supplemented, and that there is no discrepancy between those provisions and the provisions of the restated certificate. A restated certificate of incorporation may omit (a) such provisions of the original certificate of incorporation which named the incorporator or incorporators, the initial board of directors and the original subscribers for shares, and (b) such provisions contained in any amendment to the certificate of incorporation as were necessary to effect a change, exchange, reclassification or cancellation of stock, if such change, exchange, reclassification or cancellation has become effective. Any such omissions shall not be deemed a further amendment.

(d) A restated certificate of incorporation shall be executed, acknowledged, filed and recorded in accordance with § 103 of this title. Upon its filing with the Secretary of State, the original certificate of incorporation, as theretofore amended or supplemented, shall be superseded; thenceforth, the restated certificate of incorporation, including any further amendments or changes made thereby, shall be the certificate of incorporation of the corporation, but the original date of incorporation shall remain unchanged.

(e) Any amendment or change effected in connection with the restatement and integration of the certificate of incorporation shall be subject to any other provision of this chapter, not inconsistent with this section, which would apply if a separate certificate of amendment were filed to effect such amendment or change.

§ 246. Composite Certificate of Incorporation

The Secretary of State shall prepare and furnish upon request a certified composite certificate of incorporation which shall contain only such provisions of a corporation's certificate of incorporation which are then in effect and operative as a result of there having theretofore been filed with the Secretary of State one or more certificates or other instruments pursuant to any of the sections referred to in section 104 of this title. The Secretary of State shall make in each case such reasonable charge therefor as he deems proper. A composite certificate of incorporation shall not be filed by the Secretary of State as a corporate instrument, nor shall it be recorded in the office of any recorder in this State, unless it is accompanied by a certificate of the corporation, executed and acknowledged in accordance with section 103 of this title, stating that the filing and recording of the composite certificate have been duly authorized by the corporation's board of directors. The filing by a corporation of a composite certificate of incorporation shall not have the effect of superseding its original certificate of incorporation, as theretofore amended or supplemented.

§ 251. Merger or Consolidation of Domestic Corporations

(a) Any two or more corporations existing under the laws of this State may merge into a single corporation, which may be any one of the constituent corporations or may consolidate into a new corporation formed by the consolidation, pursuant to an agreement of merger or consolidation, as the case may be, complying and approved in accordance with this section.

(b) The board of directors of each corporation which desires to merge or consolidate shall adopt a resolution approving an agreement of merger or consolidation. The agreement shall state: (1) the terms and conditions of the merger or consolidation; (2) the mode of carrying the same into effect; (3) in the case of a merger, such amendments or changes in the certificate of incorporation of the surviving corporation as are desired to be effected by the merger, or, if no such amendments or changes are desired, a statement that the certificate of incorporation of the surviving corporation shall be its certificate of incorporation; (4) in the case of a consolidation, that the certificate of incorporation of the resulting corporation shall be as is set forth in an attachment to the agreement; (5) the manner of converting the shares of each of the constituent corporations into shares or other securities of the corporation surviving or resulting from the merger or consolidation, and, if any shares of any of the constituent corporations are not to be converted solely into shares or other securities of the surviving or resulting corporation, the cash, property, rights or securities of any other corporation which the holders of such shares are to receive in exchange for, or upon conversion of such shares and the surrender of any certificates evidencing them, which cash, property, rights or securities of any other corporation may be in addition to or in lieu of shares or other securities of the surviving or resulting corporation; and (6) such other details or provisions as are deemed desirable, including, without limiting the generality of the foregoing, a provision for the payment of cash in lieu of the issuance or recognition of fractional shares, interests or rights, or for any other arrangement with respect thereto, consistent with the provisions of § 155 of this title. The agreement so adopted shall be executed and acknowledged in accordance with § 103 of this title. Any of the terms of the agreement of merger or consolidation may be made dependent upon facts ascertainable outside of such agreement, provided that the manner in which such facts shall operate upon the terms of the agreement is clearly and expressly set forth in the agreement of merger or consolidation.

(c) The agreement required by subsection (b) of this section shall be submitted to the stockholders of each constituent corporation at an annual or special meeting for the purpose of acting on the agreement. Due notice of the time, place and purpose of the meeting shall be mailed to each holder of stock, whether voting or nonvoting, of the corporation at his address as it appears on the records of the corporation, at least 20 days prior to the date of the meeting. The notice shall contain a copy of the agreement or a brief summary thereof, as the directors shall deem advisable. At the meeting, the agreement shall be considered and a vote taken for its adoption or rejection. If a majority of the outstanding stock of the corporation entitled to vote thereon shall be voted for the adoption of the agreement, that fact shall be certified on the agreement by the secretary or assistant secretary of the corporation. If the agreement shall be so adopted and certified by each constituent corporation, it shall then be filed and shall become effective, in accordance with § 103 of this title. It shall be recorded in the office of the recorder of the county of this State in which the registered office of each such constituent corporation is located; or if any of the constituent corporations shall have been specially created by a public act of the General Assembly, then the agreement shall be recorded in the county where such corporation had its principal place of business in this State. In lieu of filing and recording the agreement of merger or consolidation required by this Section, the surviving or resulting corporation may file a certificate of merger or consolidation, executed in accordance with § 103 of this title, which states:

(1) The name and state of incorporation of each of the constituent corporations; (2) That an agreement of merger or consolidation has been approved, adopted, certified, executed and acknowledged by each of the constituent corporations in accordance with this Section; (3) The name of the surviving or resulting corporation; (4) in the case of a merger, such amendments or changes in the certificate of incorporation of the surviving corporation as are desired to be effected by the merger, or, if no such amendments or changes are desired, a statement that the certificate of incorporation of the surviving corporation shall be its certificate of incorporation; (5) in the case of a consolidation, that the certificate of incorporation of the resulting corporation shall be as is set forth in an attachment to the certificate; (6) That the executed agreement of consolidation or merger is on file at the principal place of business of the surviving corporation, stating the address thereof; and (7) That a copy of the agreement of consolidation or merger will be furnished by the

surviving corporation, on request and without cost, to any stockholder of any constituent corporation.

(d) Any agreement of merger or consolidation may contain a provision that at any time prior to the filing of the agreement with the Secretary of State, the agreement may be terminated by the board of directors of any constituent corporation notwithstanding approval of the agreement by the stockholders of all or any of the constituent corporations. Any agreement of merger or consolidation may contain a provision that the boards of directors of the constituent corporations may amend the agreement at any time prior to the filing of the agreement (or a certificate in lieu thereof) with the Secretary of State, provided that an amendment made subsequent to the adoption of the agreement by the stockholders of any constituent corporation shall not (1) alter or change the amount or kind of shares, securities, cash, property and/or rights to be received in exchange for or on conversion of all or any of the shares of any class or series thereof of such constituent corporation, (2) alter or change any term of the certificate of incorporation of the surviving corporation to be effected by the merger or consolidation, or (3) alter or change any of the terms and conditions of the agreement if such alteration or change would adversely affect the holders of any class or series thereof of such constituent corporation.

(e) In the case of a merger, the certificate of incorporation of the surviving corporation shall automatically be amended to the extent, if any, that changes in the certificate of incorporation are set forth in the agreement of merger.

(f) Notwithstanding the requirements of subsection (c), unless required by its certificate of incorporation, no vote of stockholders of a constituent corporation surviving a merger shall be necessary to authorize a merger if (1) the agreement of merger does not amend in any respect the certificate of incorporation of such constituent corporation, (2) each share of stock of such constituent corporation outstanding immediately prior to the effective date of the merger is to be an identical outstanding or treasury share of the surviving corporation after the effective date of the merger, and (3) either no shares of common stock of the surviving corporation and no shares, securities or obligations convertible into such stock are to be issued or delivered under the plan of merger, or the authorized unissued shares or the treasury shares of common stock of the surviving corporation to be issued or delivered under the plan of merger plus those initially issuable upon conversion of any other shares, securities or obligations to be issued or delivered under such plan do not exceed 20 percent of the shares of common stock of such constituent corporation outstanding immediately prior to the effective date of the merger. No vote of stockholders of a constituent corporation shall be necessary to authorize a merger or consolidation if no shares of the stock of such corporation shall have been issued prior to the adoption by the board of directors of the resolution approving the agreement of merger or consolidation. If an agreement of merger is adopted by the constituent corporation surviving the merger, by action of its board of directors and without any vote of its stockholders pursuant to this subsection, the secretary or assistant secretary of that corporation shall certify on the agreement, that the agreement has been adopted pursuant to this subsection and that, as of the date of such certificate, the outstanding shares of the corporation were such as to render this subsection applicable. The agreement so adopted and certified shall then be filed and shall become effective, in accordance with section 103 of this title. Such filing shall constitute a representation by the person who executes the agreement that the facts stated in the certificate remain true immediately prior to such filing.

§ 252. Merger or Consolidation of Domestic and Foreign Corporations; Service of Process Upon Surviving or Resulting Corporation

(a) Any one or more corporations of this State may merge or consolidate with one or more other corporations of any other state or states of the United States, or of the District of Columbia if the laws of such other state or states or of the District permit a corporation of such jurisdiction to merge or consolidate with a corporation of another jurisdiction. The constituent corporations may merge into a single corporation, which may be any one of the constituent corporations, or they may consolidate into a new corporation formed by the consolidation, which may be a corporation of the state of incorporation of any one of the constituent corporations, pursuant to an agreement of merger or consolidation, as the case may be, complying and approved in accordance with this section. In addition, any one or more corporations organized under the laws of any jurisdiction other than one of the United States may merge or consolidate with one or more corporations existing under the laws of this State if the surviving or resulting corporation will be a corporation of this State, and if the laws under which the other corporation or corporations are formed permit a corporation of such jurisdiction to merge or consolidate with a corporation of another jurisdiction.

(b) All the constituent corporations shall enter into an agreement of merger or consolidation. The agreement shall state: (1) The terms and conditions of the merger or consolidation; (2) the mode of carrying the same into effect; (3) the manner of converting the shares of each of the constituent corporations into shares or other securities of the corporation surviving or resulting from the merger or consolidation and, if any shares of any of the constituent corporations are not to be converted solely into shares or other securities of the surviving or resulting corporation, the cash, property, rights or securities of any other corporation which the holders of such shares are to receive in exchange for, or upon conversion of, such shares and the surrender of any certificates evidencing them, which cash, property, rights or securities of any other corporation may be in addition to or in lieu of the shares or other securities of the surviving or resulting corporation; (4) such other details or provisions as are deemed desirable, including, without limiting the generality of the foregoing, a provision for the payment of cash in lieu of the issuance or recognition of fractional shares of the surviving or resulting corporation or of any other corporation the securities of which are to be received in the merger or consolidation, or for some other arrangement with respect thereto consistent with § 155 of this title; and (5) such other provisions or facts as shall be required to be set forth in certificates of incorporation by the laws of the state which are stated in the agreement to be the laws that shall govern the surviving or resulting corporation and that can be stated in the case of a merger or consolidation. Any of the terms of the agreement of merger or consolidation may be made dependent upon facts ascertainable outside of such agreement, provided that the manner in which such facts shall operate upon the terms of the agreement is clearly and expressly set forth in the agreement of merger or consolidation.

(c) The agreement shall be adopted, approved, certified, executed and acknowledged by each of the constituent corporations in accordance with the laws under which it is formed, and, in the case of a Delaware corporation, in the same manner as is provided in § 251 of this title. The agreement shall be filed and recorded and shall become effective for all purposes of the laws of this State when and as provided in § 251 of this title with respect to the merger or consolidation of corporations of this State. In lieu of filing and recording the agreement of merger or consolidation, the surviving or resulting corporation may file a certificate of merger or consolidation, executed in accordance with § 103 of this title, which states: (1) The name and state of incorporation of each of the constituent corporations; (2) That an agreement of merger or consolidation has been approved, adopted, certified, executed and acknowledged by each of the constituent corporations in accordance with this subsection; (3) The name of the surviving or resulting corporation; (4) in the case of a merger, such amendments or changes in the certificate of incorporation of the surviving corporation as are desired to be effected by the merger, or, if no such amendments or changes are desired, a statement that the certificate of incorporation of the surviving corporation shall be its certificate of incorporation; (5) in the case of a consolidation, that the certificate of incorporation of the resulting corporation shall be as is set forth in an attachment to the certificate; (6) That the executed agreement of consolidation or merger is on file at the principal place of business of the surviving corporation and the address thereof; (7) That a copy of the agreement of consolidation or merger will be furnished by the surviving corporation, on request and without cost, to any stockholder of any constituent corporation; (8) If the corporation surviving or resulting from the merger or consolidation is to be a corporation of this State, the authorized capital stock of each constituent corporation which is not a corporation of this State; and (9) The agreement, if any, required by subsection (d) of this section.

(d) If the corporation surviving or resulting from the merger or consolidation is to be governed by the laws of the District of Columbia or any state other than this State, it shall agree that it may be served with process in this State in any proceeding for enforcement of any obligation of any constituent corporation of this State, as well as for enforcement of any obligation of the surviving or resulting corporation arising from the merger or consolidation, including any suit or other proceeding to enforce the right of any stockholders as determined in appraisal proceedings pursuant to the provisions of § 262 of this title, and shall irrevocably appoint the Secretary of State as its agent to accept service of process in any such suit or other proceedings and shall specify the address to which a copy of such process shall be mailed by the Secretary of State. In the event of such service upon the Secretary of State in accordance with this subsection, the Secretary of State shall forthwith notify such surviving or resulting corporation thereof by letter, certified mail, return receipt requested, directed to such surviving or resulting corporation at its address so specified, unless such surviving or resulting corporation shall have designated in writing to the Secretary of State a different address for such purpose, in which case it shall be mailed to the last address so designated. Such letter shall enclose a copy of the process and any other papers served on the Secretary of State pursuant to this subsection. It shall be the duty of the plaintiff in the event of such service to serve process and any other papers in duplicate, to notify the Secretary of State that service is being effected pursuant to this subsection and to pay the Secretary of State the sum of $25 for the use of the State, which sum shall be taxed as part of the costs in the proceeding, if the plaintiff shall prevail therein. The Secretary of State shall maintain an alphabetical record of any such service setting forth the name of the plaintiff and the defendant, the title, docket number and nature of the proceeding in which process has been served upon him, the fact that service has been effected pursuant to this subsection, the return date thereof, and the day and hour service was made. The Secretary of State shall not be required to retain such information longer than five years from his receipt of the service of process.

(e) The provisions of subsection (d) of section 251 of this title shall apply to any merger or consolidation under this section; the provisions of subsection (e) of section 251 shall apply to a merger under this section in which the surviving corporation is a corporation of this State; the provisions of subsection (f) of section 251 shall apply to any merger under this section.

§ 253. Merger of Parent Corporation and Subsidiary or Subsidiaries

(a) In any case in which at least 90 percent of the outstanding shares of each class of the stock of a corporation or corporations is owned by another corporation and one of such corporations is a corporation of this State and the other or others are corporations of this State or of any other state or states or of the District of Columbia and the laws of such other state or states or of the District permit a corporation of such jurisdiction to merge with a corporation of another jurisdiction, the corporation having such stock ownership may either merge such other corporation or corporations into itself and assume all of its or their obligations, or merge itself, or itself and one or more of such other corporations, into one of such other corporations by executing, acknowledging and filing, in accordance with section 103 of this title, a certificate of such ownership and merger setting forth a copy of the resolution of its board of directors to so merge and the date of the adoption thereof; provided, however, that in case the parent corporation shall not own all the outstanding stock of all the subsidiary corporations, parties to a merger as aforesaid, the resolution of the board of directors of the parent corporation shall state the terms and conditions of the merger, including the securities, cash, property, or rights to be issued, paid, delivered or granted by the surviving corporation upon surrender of each share of the subsidiary corporation or corporations not owned by the parent corporation. If the parent corporation be not the surviving corporation, the resolution shall include provision for the pro rata issuance of stock of the surviving corporation to the holders of the stock of the parent corporation on surrender of the certificates therefor, and the certificate of ownership and merger shall state that the proposed merger has been approved by a majority of the outstanding stock of the parent corporation entitled to vote thereon at a meeting thereof duly called and held after 20 days' notice of the purpose of the meeting mailed to each such stockholder at his address as it appears on the records of the corporation if the parent corporation is a corporation of this State or state that the proposed merger has been adopted, approved, certified, executed and acknowledged by the parent corporation in accordance with the laws under which it is organized if the parent corporation is not a corporation of this State. A certified copy of the certificate shall be recorded in the office of the Recorder of the County in this State in which the registered office of each constituent corporation which is a corporation of this State is located. If the surviving corporation exists under the laws of the District of Columbia or any state other than this State, the provisions of section 252(d) of this title shall also apply to a merger under this section.

(b) If the surviving corporation is a Delaware corporation, it may change its corporate name by the inclusion of a provision to that effect in the resolution of merger adopted by the directors of the parent corporation and set forth in the certificate of ownership and merger, and upon the effective date of the merger, the name of the corporation shall be so changed.

(c) Subsection (d) of § 251 of this title shall apply to a merger under this section, and subsection (e) of § 251 of this title shall apply to a merger under this section in which the surviving corporation is the subsidiary corporation and is a corporation of this State. References to "agreement of merger" in subsections (d) and (e) of § 251 of this title shall mean for purposes of this subsection the resolution of merger adopted by the board of directors of the parent corporation. Any merger which effects any changes other than those authorized by this section or made applicable by this subsection shall be accomplished under § 251 or § 252 of this title. Section 262 of this title shall not apply to any merger effected under this section, except as provided in subsection (d) of this section.

(d) In the event all of the stock of a subsidiary Delaware corporation party to a merger effected under this section is not owned by the parent corporation immediately prior to the merger, the stockholders of the subsidiary Delaware corporation party to the merger shall have appraisal rights as set forth in § 262 of this title.

(e) A merger may be effected under this section although one or more of the corporations parties to the merger is a corporation organized under the laws of a jurisdiction other than one of the United States; provided that the laws of such jurisdiction permit a corporation of such jurisdiction to merge with a corporation of another jurisdiction; and provided further that the surviving or resulting corporation shall be a corporation of this State.

* * *

§ 259. Status, Rights, Liabilities, etc., of Constituent and Surviving or Resulting Corporations Following Merger or Consolidation

(a) When any merger or consolidation shall have become effective under this chapter, for all purposes of the laws of this State the separate existence of all the constituent corporations, or of all such constituent corporations except the one into which the other or others of such constituent corporations have been merged, as the case may be, shall cease and the constituent corporations shall become a new corporation, or be merged into one of such corporations, as the case may be, possessing all the rights, privileges, powers and franchises as well of a public as of a private nature, and being subject to all the restrictions, disabilities and duties of each of such corporations so merged or consolidated; and all and singular, the rights, privileges, powers and franchises of each of said corporations, and all property, real, personal and mixed, and all debts due to any of said constituent corporations on whatever account, as well for stock subscriptions as all other things in action or belonging to each of such corporations shall be vested in the corporation surviving or resulting from such merger or consolidation; and all property, rights, privileges, powers and franchises, and all and every other interest shall be thereafter as effectually the property of the surviving or resulting corporation as they were of the several and respective constituent corporations, and the title to any real estate vested by deed or otherwise, under the laws of this State, in any of such constituent corporations, shall not revert or be in any way impaired by reason of this chapter; but all rights of creditors and all liens upon any property of any of said constituent corporations shall be preserved unimpaired, and all debts, liabilities and duties of the respective constituent corporations shall thenceforth attach to said surviving or resulting corporation, and may be enforced against it to the same extent as if said debts, liabilities and duties had been incurred or contracted by it.

(b) In the case of a merger of banks or trust companies, without any order or action on the part of any court or otherwise, all appointments, designations, and nominations, and all other rights and interests as trustee, executor, administrator, registrar of stocks and bonds, guardian of estates, assignee, receiver, trustee of estates of persons mentally ill and in every other fiduciary capacity, shall be automatically vested in the corporation resulting from or surviving such merger; provided, however, that any party in interest shall have the right to apply to an appropriate court or tribunal for a determination as to whether the surviving corporation shall continue to serve in the same fiduciary capacity as the merged corporation, or whether a new and different fiduciary should be appointed.

§ 260. Powers of Corporation Surviving or Resulting From Merger or Consolidation; Issuance of Stock, Bonds or Other Indebtedness

When two or more corporations are merged or consolidated, the corporation surviving or resulting from the merger may issue bonds or other obligations, negotiable or otherwise, and with or without coupons or interest certificates thereto attached, to an amount sufficient with its capital stock to provide for all the payment it will be required to make, or obligations it will be required to assume, in order to effect the merger or consolidation. For the purpose of securing the payment of any such bonds and obligations, it shall be lawful for the surviving or resulting corporation to mortgage its corporate franchise, rights, privileges and property, real, personal or mixed. The surviving or resulting corporation may issue certificates of its capital stock or uncertificated stock if authorized to do so and other securities to the stockholders of the constituent corporations in exchange or payment for the original shares, in such amount as shall be necessary in accordance with the terms of the agreement of merger or consolidation in order to effect such merger or consolidation in the manner and on the terms specified in the agreement.

§ 261. Effect of Merger Upon Pending Actions

Any action or proceeding, whether civil, criminal or administrative, pending by or against any corporation which is a party to a merger or consolidation shall be prosecuted as if such merger or consolidation had not taken place, or the corporation surviving or resulting from such merger or consolidation may be substituted in such action or proceeding.

§ 262. Appraisal Rights

(a) Any stockholder of a corporation of this State who holds shares of stock on the date of the making of a demand pursuant to the provisions of subsection (d) of this section with respect to such shares, who continuously holds such shares through the effective date of the merger or consolidation, who has otherwise complied with the provisions of subsection (d) of this Section and who has neither voted in favor of the merger or consolidation nor consented thereto in writing pursuant to § 228 of this Chapter shall be entitled to an appraisal by the Court of Chancery of the fair value of his shares of stock under the circumstances described in subsections (b) and (c) of this Section. As used in this section, the word "stockholder" means a holder of record of stock in a stock corporation and also a member of record of a nonstock corporation; the words "stock" and "share" mean and include what is ordinarily meant by those words and also membership or membership interest of a member of a nonstock corporation.

(b) Appraisal rights shall be available for the shares of any class or series of stock of a constituent corporation in a merger or consolidation to be effected pursuant to §§ 251, 252, 254, 257 or 258 of this title:

(1) Provided, however, that no appraisal rights under this section shall be available for the shares of any class or series of stock which, at the record date fixed to determine the stockholders entitled to receive notice of and to vote at the meeting of stockholders to act upon the agreement of merger or consolidation, were either (i) listed on a national securities exchange or (ii) held of record by more than 2,000 stockholders; and further provided that no appraisal rights shall be available for any shares of stock of the constituent corporation surviving a merger if the merger did not require for its approval the vote of the stockholders of the surviving corporation as provided in subsection (f) of § 251 of this title.

(2) Notwithstanding paragraph (1) of this subsection, appraisal rights under this section shall be available for the shares of any class or series of stock of a constituent corporation if the holders thereof are required by the terms of an agreement of merger or consolidation pursuant to §§ 251, 252, 254, 257 and 258 of this title to accept for such stock anything except: (i) Shares of stock of the corporation surviving or resulting from such merger or consolidation; (ii) Shares of stock of any other corporation which at the effective date of the merger or consolida-

tion will be either listed on a national securities exchange or held of record by more than 2,000 stockholders; (iii) Cash in lieu of fractional shares of the corporations described in the foregoing subparagraphs a. and b. of this paragraph; or (iv) Any combination of the shares of stock and cash in lieu of fractional shares described in the foregoing subparagraphs a., and b. and c. of this paragraph.

(3) In the event all of the stock of a subsidiary Delaware corporation party to a merger effected under § 253 of this title is not owned by the parent corporation immediately prior to the merger, appraisal rights shall be available for the shares of the subsidiary Delaware corporation.

(c) Any corporation may provide in its certificate of incorporation that appraisal rights under this section shall be available for the shares of any class or series of its stock as a result of an amendment to its certificate of incorporation, any merger or consolidation in which the corporation is a constituent corporation or the sale of all or substantially all of the assets of the corporation. If the certificate of incorporation contains such a provision, the procedures of this section, including those set forth in subsections (d) and (e) of this section, shall apply as nearly as is practicable.

(d) Appraisal rights shall be perfected as follows:

(1) If a proposed merger or consolidation for which appraisal rights are provided under this section is to be submitted for approval at a meeting of stockholders, the corporation, not less than 20 days prior to the meeting, shall notify each of its stockholders entitled to such appraisal rights that appraisal rights are available for any or all of the shares of the constituent corporations, and shall include in such notice a copy of this section. Each stockholder electing to demand the appraisal of his shares shall deliver to the corporation, before the taking of the vote on the merger or consolidation, a written demand for appraisal of his shares. Such demand will be sufficient if it reasonably informs the corporation of the identity of the stockholder and that the stockholder intends thereby to demand the appraisal of his shares. A proxy or vote against the merger or consolidation shall not constitute such a demand. A stockholder electing to take such action must do so by a separate written demand as herein provided. Within 10 days after the effective date of such merger or consolidation, the surviving or resulting corporation shall notify each stockholder of each constituent corporation who has complied with this subsection and has not voted in favor of or consented to the merger or consolidation of the date that the merger or consolidation has become effective; or

(2) If the merger or consolidation was approved pursuant to § 228 or § 253 of this title, the surviving or resulting corporation, either before the effective date of the merger or consolidation or within 10 days thereafter, shall notify each of the stockholders entitled to appraisal rights of the effective date of the merger or consolidation and that

appraisal rights are available for any or all of the shares of the constituent corporation, and shall include in such notice a copy of this section. The notice shall be sent by certified or registered mail, return receipt requested, addressed to the stockholder at his address as it appears on the records of the corporation. Any stockholder entitled to appraisal rights may, within 20 days after the date of mailing of the notice, demand in writing from the surviving or resulting corporation the appraisal of his shares. Such demand will be sufficient if it reasonably informs the corporation of the identity of the stockholder and that the stockholder intends to demand the appraisal of his shares.

(e) Within 120 days after the effective date of the merger or consolidation, the surviving or resulting corporation or any stockholder who has complied with subsections (a) and (d) hereof and who is otherwise entitled to appraisal rights, may file a petition in the Court of Chancery demanding a determination of the value of the stock of all such stockholders. Notwithstanding the foregoing, at any time within 60 days after the effective date of the merger or consolidation, any stockholder shall have the right to withdraw his demand for appraisal and to accept the terms offered upon the merger or consolidation. Within 120 days after the effective date of the merger or consolidation, any stockholder who has complied with the requirements of subsections (a) and (d) hereof, upon written request, shall be entitled to receive from the corporation surviving the merger or resulting from the consolidation a statement setting forth the aggregate number of shares not voted in favor of the merger or consolidation and with respect to which demands for appraisal have been received and the aggregate number of holders of such shares. Such written statement shall be mailed to the stockholder within 10 days after his written request for such a statement is received by the surviving or resulting corporation or within 10 days after expiration of the period for delivery of demands for appraisal under subsection (d) hereof, whichever is later.

(f) Upon the filing of any such petition by a stockholder, service of a copy thereof shall be made upon the surviving or resulting corporation, which shall within 20 days after such service file in the office of the Register in Chancery in which the petition was filed a duly verified list containing the names and addresses of all stockholders who have demanded payment for their shares and with whom agreements as to the value of their shares have not been reached by the surviving or resulting corporation. If the petition shall be filed by the surviving or resulting corporation, the petition shall be accompanied by such a duly verified list. The Register in Chancery, if so ordered by the Court, shall give notice of the time and place fixed for the hearing of such petition by registered or certified mail to the surviving or resulting corporation and to the stockholders shown on the list at the addresses therein stated. Such notice shall also be given by one or more publications at least one week before the day of the hearing, in a newspaper of general circulation published in the City of Wilmington, Delaware or such publication as the Court deems advisable. The forms of the notices by mail and by publication shall be approved by the Court, and the costs thereof shall be borne by the surviving or resulting corporation.

(g) At the hearing on such petition, the Court shall determine the stockholders who have complied with this section and who have become entitled to appraisal rights. The Court may require the stockholders who have demanded an appraisal for their shares and who hold stock represented by certificates to submit their certificates of stock to the Register in Chancery for notation thereon of the pendency of the appraisal proceedings; and if any stockholder fails to comply with such direction, the Court may dismiss the proceedings as to such stockholder.

(h) After determining the stockholders entitled to an appraisal, the Court shall appraise the shares, determining their fair value exclusive of any element of value arising from the accomplishment or expectation of the merger or consolidation, together with a fair rate of interest, if any, to be paid upon the amount determined to be the fair value. In determining such fair value, the Court shall take into account all relevant factors. In determining the fair rate of interest, the Court may consider all relevant factors, including the rate of interest which the surviving or resulting corporation would have had to pay to borrow money during the pendency of the proceeding. Upon application by the surviving or resulting corporation or by any stockholder entitled to participate in the appraisal proceeding, the Court may, in its discretion, permit discovery or other pretrial proceedings and may proceed to trial upon the appraisal prior to the final determination of the stockholder entitled to an appraisal. Any stockholder whose name appears on the list filed by the surviving or resulting corporation pursuant to subsection (f) of this section and who has submitted his certificates of stock to the Register in Chancery, if such is required, may participate fully in all proceedings until it is finally determined that he is not entitled to appraisal rights under this Section.

(i) The Court shall direct the payment of the fair value of the shares, together with interest, if any, by the surviving or resulting corporation to the stockholders entitled thereto. Interest may be simple or compound, as the Court may direct. Payment shall be so made to each such stockholder, in the case of holders of uncertificated stock forthwith, and in the case of holders of shares represented by certificates upon the surrender to the corporation of the certificates representing such stock. The Court's decree may be enforced as other decrees in the Court of Chancery may be enforced, whether such surviving or resulting corporation be a corporation of this State or of any state.

(j) The costs of the proceeding may be determined by the Court and taxed upon the parties as the Court deems equitable in the circumstances. Upon application of a stockholder, the Court may order all or a portion of the expenses incurred by any stockholder in connection with the appraisal proceeding, including, without limitation, reasonable attorney's fees and the fees and expenses of experts, to be charged pro rata against the value of all of the shares entitled to an appraisal.

(k) From and after the effective date of the merger or consolidation, no stockholder who has demanded his appraisal rights as provided in subsection (d) of this section shall be entitled to vote such stock for any purpose or to receive payment of dividends or other distributions on the stock (except dividends or other distributions payable to stockholders of record at a date which is prior to the effective date of the merger or consolidation); provided, however, that if no petition for an appraisal shall be filed within the time provided in subsection (e) of this section, or if such stockholder shall deliver to the surviving or resulting corporation a written withdrawal of his demand for an appraisal and an acceptance of the merger or consolidation, either within 60 days after the effective date of the merger or consolidation as provided in subsection (e) of this section or thereafter with the written approval of the corporation, then the right of such stockholder to an appraisal shall cease. Notwithstanding the foregoing, no appraisal proceeding in the Court of Chancery shall be dismissed as to any stockholder without the approval of the Court, and such approval may be conditioned upon such terms as the Court deems just.

(l) The shares of the surviving or resulting corporation to which the shares of such objecting stockholders would have been converted had they assented to the merger or consolidation shall have the status of authorized and unissued shares of the surviving or resulting corporation.

§ 271. Sale, Lease or Exchange of Assets; Consideration; Procedure

(a) Every corporation may at any meeting of its board of directors or governing body sell, lease or exchange all or substantially all of its property and assets, including its goodwill and its corporate franchises, upon such terms and conditions and for such consideration, which may consist in whole or in part of money or other property, including shares of stock in, and/or other securities of, any other corporation or corporations, as its board of directors or governing body deems expedient and for the best interests of the corporation, when and as authorized by a resolution adopted by the holders of a majority of the outstanding stock of the corporation entitled to vote thereon or, if the corporation is a nonstock corporation, by a majority of the members having the right to vote for the election of the members of the governing body, at a meeting duly called upon at least 20 days' notice. The notice of the meeting shall state that such a resolution will be considered.

(b) Notwithstanding authorization or consent to a proposed sale, lease or exchange of a corporation's property and assets by the stockholders or members, the board of directors or governing body may abandon such proposed sale, lease or exchange without further action by the stockholders or members, subject to the rights, if any, of third parties under any contract relating thereto.

§ 272. Mortgage or Pledge of Assets

The authorization or consent of stockholders to the mortgage or pledge of a corporation's property and assets shall not be necessary, except to the extent that the certificate of incorporation otherwise provides.

§ 273. Dissolution of Joint Venture Corporation Having Two Stockholders

(a) If the stockholders of a corporation of this State, having only two stockholders each of which own 50% of the stock therein, shall be engaged in the prosecution of a joint venture and if such stockholders shall be unable to agree upon the desirability of discontinuing such joint venture and disposing of the assets used in such venture, either stockholder may file with the Court of Chancery a petition stating that it desires to discontinue such joint venture and to dispose of the assets used in such venture in accordance with a plan to be agreed upon by both stockholders or that, if no such plan shall be agreed upon by both stockholders, the corporation be dissolved. Such petition shall have attached thereto a copy of the proposed plan of discontinuance and distribution and a certificate stating that copies of such petition and plan have been transmitted in writing to the other stockholder and to the directors and officers of such corporation. The petition and certificate shall be executed and acknowledged in accordance with section 103 of this title.

(b) Unless both stockholders file with the Court of Chancery (i) within three months of the date of the filing of such petition, a certificate similarly executed and acknowledged stating that they have agreed on such plan, or a modification thereof, and (ii) within one year from the date of the filing of such petition, a certificate similarly executed and acknowledged stating that the distribution provided by such plan has been completed, the Court of Chancery may dissolve such corporation and may by appointment of one or more trustees or receivers with all the powers and title of a trustee or receiver appointed under section 279 of this title, administer and wind up its affairs. Either or both of the above periods may be extended by agreement of the stockholders, evidenced by a certificate similarly executed, acknowledged and filed with the Court of Chancery prior to the expiration of such period.

§ 274. Dissolution Before the Issuance of Shares or Beginning of Business; Procedure

If a corporation has not issued shares or has not commenced the business for which the corporation was organized, a majority of the incorporators, or, if directors were named in the certificate of incorporation or have been elected, a majority of the directors, may surrender all of the corporation's rights and franchises by filing in the office of the Secretary of State a certificate, executed and acknowledged by a majority of the incorporators or directors, stating that no shares of stock have been issued or that the business or activity for which the corporation was organized has not been begun; that no part of the capital of the corporation has been paid, or, if some capital has been paid, that the amount actually paid in for the corporation's shares, less any part thereof disbursed for necessary expenses, has been returned to those entitled thereto; that if the corporation has begun business but it has not issued shares all debts of the corporation have been paid; that if the corporation has not begun business but has issued stock certificates all issued stock certificates, if any, have been surrendered and cancelled; and that all rights and franchises of the corporation are surrendered. Upon such certificate becoming effective in accordance with section 103 of this title, the corporation shall be dissolved.

§ 275. Dissolution; Procedure

(a) If it should be deemed advisable in the judgment of the board of directors of any corporation that it should be dissolved, the board, after the adoption of a resolution to that effect by a majority of the whole board at any meeting called for that purpose, shall cause notice to be mailed to each stockholder entitled to vote thereon of the adoption of the resolution and of a meeting of stockholders to take action upon the resolution.

(b) At the meeting a vote shall be taken upon the proposed dissolution. If a majority of the outstanding stock of the corporation entitled to vote thereon shall vote for the proposed dissolution, a certification of dissolution shall be filed with the Secretary of State pursuant to subsection (d) of this Section.

(c) Dissolution of a corporation may also be authorized without action of the directors if all the stockholders entitled to vote thereon shall consent in writing and a certificate of dissolution shall be filed with the Secretary of State pursuant to subsection (d) of this Section.

(d) If dissolution is authorized in accordance with this Section, a certificate of dissolution shall be executed, acknowledged and filed, and shall become effective, in accordance with § 103 of this Title. Such certificate of dissolution shall set forth:

(i) the name of the corporation;

(ii) the date dissolution was authorized;

(iii) that the dissolution has been authorized by the board of directors and stockholders of the corporation, in accordance with subsections (a) and (b) of this Section, or that the dissolution has been authorized by all of the stockholders of the corporation entitled to vote on a dissolution, in accordance with subsection (c) of this section; and

(iv) the names and addresses of the directors and officers of the corporation.

(e) The resolution authorizing a proposed dissolution may provide that notwithstanding authorization or consent to the proposed dissolution by the stockholders, or the members of a nonstock corporation pursuant to § 276 of this title, the board of directors or governing body may abandon such proposed dissolution without further action by the stockholders or members.

(f) Upon a certificate of dissolution becoming effective in accordance with § 103 of this title, the corporation shall be dissolved.

* * *

§ 277. Payment of Franchise Taxes Before Dissolution

No corporation shall be dissolved under this chapter until all franchise taxes due to or assessable by the State have been paid by the corporation.

§ 278. Continuation of Corporation After Dissolution for Purposes of Suit and Winding Up Affairs

All corporations, whether they expire by their own limitation or are otherwise dissolved, shall nevertheless be continued, for the term of three years from such expiration or dissolution or for such longer period as the Court of Chancery shall in its discretion direct, bodies corporate for the purpose of prosecuting and defending suits, whether civil, criminal or administrative, by or against them, and of enabling them gradually to settle and close their business, to dispose of and convey their property, to discharge their liabilities, and to distribute to their stockholders any remaining assets, but not for the purpose of continuing the business for which the corporation was organized. With respect to any action, suit or proceeding begun by or against the corporation either prior to or within 3 years after the date of its expiration or dissolution the action shall not abate by reason of the dissolution of the corporation; the corporation shall, solely for the purpose of such action, suit or proceeding, be continued as a body corporate beyond the 3-year period and until any judgments, orders or decrees therein shall be fully executed, without the necessity for any special direction to that effect by the Court of Chancery.

§ 279. Trustees or Receivers for Dissolved Corporations; Appointment; Powers; Duties

When any corporation organized under this chapter shall be dissolved in any manner whatever, the Court of Chancery, on application of any creditor, stockholder or director of the corporation, or any other person who shows good cause therefor, at any time, may either appoint one or more of the directors of the corporation to be trustees, or appoint one or more persons to be receivers, of and for the corporation, to take charge of the corporation's property, and to collect the debts and property due and belonging to the corporation, with power to prosecute and defend, in the name of the corporation, or otherwise, all such suits as may be necessary or proper for the purposes aforesaid, and to appoint an agent or agents under them, and to do all other acts which might be done by the corporation, if in being, that may be necessary for the final settlement of the unfinished business of the corporation. The powers of the trustees or receivers may be continued as long as the Court of Chancery shall think necessary for the purposes aforesaid.

§ 280. Notice to Claimants; Filing of Claims

(a)(1) After a corporation has been dissolved in accordance with the procedures set forth in this chapter, the corporation or any successor entity may give notice of the dissolution requesting all persons having a claim against the corporation to present their claims against the corporation in accordance with such notice. Such notice shall state:

(i) that all claims must be presented in writing and must contain sufficient information reasonably to inform the corporation or successor entity of the identity of the claimant and the substance of the claim;

(ii) the mailing address to which a claim must be sent;

(iii) the date by which a claim must be received by the corporation or successor entity, which date shall be no earlier than 60 days from the date thereof; and

(iv) that the corporation or a successor entity may make distributions to other claimants and the corporation's stockholders or persons interested as having been such without further notice to the claimant.

Such notice shall also be published at least once a week for two consecutive weeks in a newspaper of general circulation in the county in which the office of the corporation's last registered agent in this State is located and in the corporation's principal place of business and, in the case of a corporation having $10 million or more in total assets at the time of its dissolution, at least once in all editions of a daily newspaper with a national circulation. On or before the date of the first publication of such notice, the corporation or successor entity shall mail a copy of such notice by certified or registered mail return receipt requested to each known claimant of the corporation.

(2) A corporation or successor entity may reject, in whole or in part, any claim made by a claimant pursuant to this subsection by mailing notice of such rejection by certified mail return receipt requested to the

claimant within 90 days after receipt of such claim and, in all events, at least 150 days before the expiration of the period described in § 278 of this title. A notice sent by a corporation or successor entity pursuant to this subsection shall be accompanied by a copy of §§ 278–283 of this title.

(b)(1) A corporation or successor entity electing to follow the procedures described in subsection (a) of this section shall also give notice of the dissolution of the corporation to persons with claims contingent upon the occurrence or nonoccurrence of future events or otherwise conditional or unmatured, and request that such persons present such claims in accordance with the terms of such notice. Such notice shall be in substantially the form, and sent and published in the same manner, as described in subsection (a)(1) of this section.

(2) The corporation or successor entity shall offer any claimant whose claim is contingent, conditional or unmatured, such security as the corporation or successor entity determines is sufficient to provide compensation to the claimant if the claim matures. The corporation or successor entity shall mail such offer to the claimant by certified mail return receipt requested, within 90 days of receipt of such claim and, in all events, at least 150 days before the expiration of the period described in § 278 of this title. If the claimant offered such security does not deliver in writing to the corporation or successor entity a notice rejecting the offer within 120 days after receipt of such offer for security, the claimant shall be deemed to have accepted such security as the sole source from which to satisfy his claim against the corporation.

(c)(1) A corporation or successor entity which has given notice in accordance with subsections (a) and (b) of this section shall petition the Court of Chancery to determine the amount and form of security that will be sufficient to provide compensation to any claimant who has rejected the offer for security made pursuant to subsection (b)(2) of this section.

(2) A corporation or successor entity which has given notice in accordance with subsection (a) of this section shall petition the Court of Chancery to determine the amount and form of security which will be sufficient to provide compensation to claimants whose claims are known to the corporation or successor entity but whose identities are unknown. The Court of Chancery shall appoint a guardian ad litem to represent all claimants whose identities are unknown in any proceeding brought under this subsection. The reasonable fees and expenses of such guardian, including all reasonable expert witness fees, shall be paid by the petitioner in such proceeding.

(d) The giving of any notice or making of any offer pursuant to the provisions of this section shall not revive any claim then barred or constitute acknowledgment by the corporation or successor entity that any person to whom such notice is sent is a proper claimant and shall not operate as a waiver of any defense or counterclaim in respect of any claim asserted by any person to whom such notice is sent.

(e) As used in this section, the term "successor entity" shall include any trust, receivership or other legal entity governed by the laws of this State to which the remaining assets and liabilities of a dissolved corporation are transferred and which exists solely for the purposes of prosecuting and defending suits, by or against the dissolved corporation, enabling the dissolved corporation to settle and close the business of the dissolved corporation, to dispose of and convey the property of the dissolved corporation, to discharge the liabilities of the dissolved corporation, and to distribute to the dissolved corporation's stockholders any remaining assets, but not for the purpose of continuing the business for which the dissolved corporation was organized.

§ 281. Payment and Distribution to Claimants and Stockholders

(a) A dissolved corporation or successor entity which has followed the procedures described in § 280 of this title (i) shall pay the claims made and not rejected in accordance with § 280(a) of this title, (ii) shall post the security offered and not rejected pursuant to § 280(b)(2) of this title, (iii) shall post any security ordered by the Court of Chancery in any proceeding under § 280(c) of this title and (iv) shall pay or make provision for all other obligations of the corporation or such successor entity. Such claims or obligations shall be paid in full and any such provision for payment shall be made in full if there are sufficient funds. If there are insufficient funds, such claims and obligations shall be paid or provided for according to their priority, and, among claims of equal priority, ratably to the extent of funds legally available therefor. Any remaining funds shall be distributed to the stockholders of the dissolved corporation; provided, however, that such distribution shall not be made before the expiration of 150 days from the date of the last notice of rejections given pursuant to § 280(a)(2) of this title. In the absence of actual fraud, the judgment of the directors of the dissolved corporation or the governing persons of such successor entity as to the provision made for the payment of all obligations under (iv) above shall be conclusive.

(b) A dissolved corporation or successor entity which has not followed the procedures described in Section 280 of this title shall pay or make reasonable provision to pay all claims and obligations, including all contingent, conditional, or unmatured claims known to the corporation or such successor entity and all claims which are known to the dissolved corporation or such successor entity but for which the identity of the claimant is unknown. Such claims shall be paid in full and any such provision for payment made shall be made in full if there are sufficient funds. If there are insufficient funds, such claims and obligations shall be paid or provided for according to their priority and, among claims of equal priority, ratably to the extent of funds legally available therefor.

Any remaining funds shall be distributed to the stockholders of the dissolved corporation.

(c) Directors of a dissolved corporation or governing persons of a successor entity which has complied with subsections (a) or (b) of this section shall not be personally liable to the claimants of the dissolved corporation.

(d) As used in this section, the term "successor entity" has the meaning set forth in § 280(e) of this title.

§ 282. Liability of Stockholders of Dissolved Corporations

(a) A stockholder of a dissolved corporation the assets of which were distributed pursuant to § 281(a) or (b) of this title shall not be liable for any claim against the corporation in an amount in excess of such stockholder's pro rata share of the claim or the amount so distributed to him, whichever is less.

(b) A stockholder of a dissolved corporation the assets of which were distributed pursuant to § 281(a) of this title shall not be liable for any claim against the corporation on which an action, suit or proceeding is not begun prior to the expiration of the period described in § 278 of this title.

(c) The aggregate liability of any stockholder of a dissolved corporation for claims against the dissolved corporation shall not exceed the amount distributed to him in dissolution.

§ 283. Jurisdiction of the Court

The Court of the Chancery shall have jurisdiction of any application prescribed in this subchapter and of all questions arising in the proceedings thereon, and may make such orders and decrees and issue injunctions therein as justice and equity shall require.

§ 284. Revocation or Forfeiture of Charter; Proceedings

(a) The Court of Chancery shall have jurisdiction to revoke or forfeit the charter of any corporation for abuse, mis-use or non-use of its corporate powers, privileges or franchises. The Attorney General shall, upon his own motion or upon the relation of a proper party, proceed for this purpose by complaint in the County in which the registered office of the corporation is located.

(b) The Court of Chancery shall have power, by appointment of receivers or otherwise, to administer and wind up the affairs of any corporation whose charter shall be revoked or forfeited by any court under any section of this title or otherwise, and to make such orders and decrees with respect thereto as shall be just and equitable respecting its affairs and assets and the rights of its stockholders and creditors.

(c) No proceeding shall be instituted under this section for non-use of any corporation's powers, privileges or franchises during the first two years after its incorporation.

§ 285. Dissolution or Forfeiture of Charter by Decree of Court; Filing

Whenever any corporation is dissolved or its charter forfeited by decree or judgment of the Court of Chancery, the decree or judgment shall be forthwith filed by the Register in Chancery of the county in which the decree or judgment was entered, in the office of the Secretary of State, and a note thereof shall be made by the Secretary of State on the corporation's charter or certificate of incorporation and on the index thereof.

§ 291. Receivers for Insolvent Corporations; Appointment and Powers

Whenever a corporation shall be insolvent, the Court of Chancery, on the application of any creditor or stockholder thereof, may, at any time, appoint one or more persons to be receivers of and for the corporation, to take charge of its assets, estate, effects, business and affairs, and to collect the outstanding debts, claims, and property due and belonging to the corporation, with power to prosecute and defend, in the name of the corporation or otherwise, all claims or suits, to appoint an agent or agents under them, and to do all other acts which might be done by the corporation and which may be necessary or proper. The powers of the receivers shall be such and shall continue so long as the court shall deem necessary.

§ 292. Title to Property; Filing Order of Appointment; Exception

(a) Trustees or receivers appointed by the Court of Chancery of and for any corporation, and their respective survivors and successors, shall, upon their appointment and qualification or upon the death, resignation or discharge of any co-trustee or co-receiver, be vested by operation of law and without any act or deed, with the title of the corporation to all of its property, real, personal or mixed of whatsoever nature, kind, class or description, and wheresoever situate, except real estate situate outside this State.

(b) Trustees or receivers appointed by the Court of Chancery shall, within 20 days from the date of their qualification, file in the office of the Recorder in each county in this State, in which any real estate belonging to the corporation may be situated, a certified copy of the order of their appointment and evidence of their qualification.

(c) This section shall not apply to receivers appointed pendente lite.

§ 293. Notices to Stockholders and Creditors

All notices required to be given to stockholders and creditors in any action in which a receiver or trustee for a corporation was appointed shall be given by the Register in Chancery, unless otherwise ordered by the Court of Chancery.

§ 294. Receivers or Trustees; Inventory; List of Debts and Report

Trustees or receivers shall, as soon as convenient, file in the office of the Register in Chancery of the county in which the proceeding is pending, a full and complete itemized inventory of all the assets of the corporation which shall show their nature and probable value, and an account of all debts due from and to it, as nearly as the same can be ascertained. They shall make a report to the Court of their proceedings, whenever and as often as the Court shall direct.

§ 295. Creditors' Proofs of Claims; When Barred; Notice

All creditors shall make proof under oath of their respective claims against the corporation, and cause the same to be filed in the office of the Register in Chancery of the county in which the proceeding is pending within the time fixed by and in accordance with the procedure established by the Rules of the Court of Chancery. All creditors and claimants failing to do so, within the time limited by this section, or the time prescribed by the order of the Court, may, by direction of the Court, be barred from participating in the distribution of the assets of the corporation. The Court may also prescribe what notice, by publication or otherwise, shall be given to the creditors of the time fixed for the filing and making proof of claims.

§ 296. Adjudication of Claims; Appeal

(a) The Register in Chancery, immediately upon the expiration of the time fixed for the filing of claims, in compliance with the provisions of section 295 of this title, shall notify the trustee or receiver of the filing of the claims, and the trustee or receiver, within 30 days after receiving the notice, shall inspect the claims, and if the trustee or receiver or any creditor shall not be satisfied with the validity or correctness of the same, or any of them, the trustee or receiver shall forthwith notify the creditors whose claims are disputed of his decision. The trustee or receiver shall require all creditors whose claims are disputed to submit themselves to such examination in relation to their claims as the trustee or receiver shall direct, and the creditors shall produce such books and papers relating to their claims as shall be required. The trustee or receiver shall have power to examine, under oath or affirmation, all witnesses produced before him touching the claims, and shall pass upon and allow or disallow the claims, or any part thereof, and notify the claimants of his determination.

(b) Every creditor or claimant who shall have received notice from the receiver or trustee that his claim has been disallowed in whole or in part may appeal to the Court of Chancery within 30 days thereafter. The Court, after hearing, shall determine the rights of the parties.

* * *

§ 327. Stockholder's Derivative Action; Allegation of Stock Ownership

In any derivative suit instituted by a stockholder of a corporation, it shall be averred in the complaint that the plaintiff was a stockholder of the corporation at the time of the transaction of which he complains or that his stock thereafter devolved upon him by operation of law.

§ 328. Liability of Corporation, etc., Impairment by Certain Transactions

The liability of a corporation of this State, or the stockholders, directors or officers thereof, or the rights or remedies of the creditors thereof, or of persons doing or transacting business with the corporation, shall not in any way be lessened or impaired by the sale of its assets, or by the increase or decrease in the capital stock of the corporation, or by its merger or consolidation with one or more corporations or by any change or amendment in its certificate of incorporation.

§ 329. Defective Organization of Corporation as Defense

(a) No corporation of this State and no person sued by any such corporation shall be permitted to assert the want of legal organization as a defense to any claim.

(b) This section shall not be construed to prevent judicial inquiry into the regularity or validity of the organization of a corporation, or its lawful possession of any corporate power it may assert in any other suit or proceeding where its corporate existence or the power to exercise the corporate rights it asserts is challenged, and evidence tending to sustain the challenge shall be admissible in any such suit or proceeding.

§ 330. Usury; Pleading by Corporation

No corporation shall plead any statute against usury in any court of law or equity in any suit instituted to enforce the payment of any bond, note or other evidence of indebtedness issued or assumed by it.

§ 341. Law Applicable to Close Corporation

(a) This subchapter applies to all close corporations, as defined in section 342 of this title. Unless a corporation elects to become a close corporation under this subchapter in the manner prescribed in this subchapter, it shall be subject in all respects to the provisions of this chapter, except the provisions of this subchapter.

(b) All provisions of this chapter shall be applicable to all close corporations, as defined in section 342 of this title, except insofar as this subchapter otherwise provides.

§ 342. Close Corporation Defined; Contents of Certificate of Incorporation

(a) A close corporation is a corporation organized under this chapter whose certificate of incorporation contains the provisions required by section 102 of this title and, in addition, provides that:

(1) All of the corporation's issued stock of all classes, exclusive of treasury shares, shall be represented by certificates and shall be held of record by not more than a specified number of persons, not exceeding thirty; and

(2) All of the issued stock of all classes shall be subject to one or more of the restrictions on transfer permitted by section 202 of this title; and

(3) The corporation shall make no offering of any of its stock of any class which would constitute a "public offering" within the meaning of the United States Securities Act of 1933, as it may be amended from time to time.

(b) The certificate of incorporation of a close corporation may set forth the qualifications of stockholders, either by specifying classes of persons who shall be entitled to be holders of record of stock of any class, or by specifying classes of persons who shall not be entitled to be holders of stock of any class or both.

(c) For purposes of determining the number of holders of record of the stock of a close corporation, stock which is held in joint or common tenancy or by the entireties shall be treated as held by one stockholder.

§ 343. Formation of a Close Corporation

A close corporation shall be formed in accordance with sections 101, 102 and 103 of this title, except that:

(a) Its certificate of incorporation shall contain a heading stating the name of the corporation and that it is a close corporation, and

(b) Its certificate of incorporation shall contain the provisions required by section 342 of this title.

§ 344. Election of Existing Corporation to Become a Close Corporation

Any corporation organized under this chapter may become a close corporation under this subchapter by executing, acknowledging, filing and recording, in accordance with section 103 of this title, a certificate of amendment of its certificate of incorporation which shall contain a statement that it elects to become a close corporation, the provisions required by section 342 of this title to appear in the certificate of incorporation of a close corporation, and a heading stating the name of the corporation and that it is a close corporation. Such amendment shall be adopted in accordance with the requirements of section 241 or 242 of this title, except that it must be approved by a vote of the holders of record of at least two-thirds of the shares of each class of stock of the corporation which are outstanding.

§ 345. Limitations on Continuation of Close Corporation Status

A close corporation continues to be such and to be subject to this subchapter until:

(a) It files with the Secretary of State a certificate of amendment deleting from its certificate of incorporation the provisions required or permitted by section 342 of this title to be stated in the certificate of incorporation to qualify it as a close corporation, or

(b) Any one of the provisions or conditions required or permitted by section 342 of this title to be stated in a certificate of incorporation to qualify a corporation as a close corporation has in fact been breached and neither the corporation nor any of its stockholders takes the steps required by section 348 of this title to prevent such loss of status or to remedy such breach.

§ 346. Voluntary Termination of Close Corporation Status by Amendment of Certificate of Incorporation; Vote Required

(a) A corporation may voluntarily terminate its status as a close corporation and cease to be subject to this subchapter by amending its certificate of incorporation to delete therefrom the additional provisions required or permitted by section 342 of this title to be stated in the certificate of incorporation of a close corporation. Any such amendment shall be adopted and shall become effective in accordance with section 242 of this title, except that it must be approved by a vote of the holders of record of at least two-thirds of the shares of each class of stock of the corporation which are outstanding.

(b) The certificate of incorporation of a close corporation may provide that on any amendment to terminate its status as a close corporation, a vote greater than two-thirds or a vote of all shares of any class shall be required; and if the certificate of incorporation contains such a provision, that provision shall not be amended, repealed or modified by any vote less than that required to terminate the corporation's status as a close corporation.

§ 347. Issuance or Transfer of Stock of a Close Corporation in Breach of Qualifying Conditions

(a) If stock of a close corporation is issued or transferred to any person who is not entitled under any provision of the certificate of incorporation permitted by section 342(b) of this title to be a holder of record of stock of such corporation, and if the certificate for such stock conspicuously notes the qualifications of the persons entitled to be holders of record thereof, such person is conclusively presumed to have notice of the fact of his ineligibility to be a stockholder.

(b) If the certificate of incorporation of a close corporation states the number of persons, not in excess of thirty, who are entitled to be holders of record of its stock, and if the certificate for such stock conspicuously states such number, and if the issuance or transfer of stock to any person would cause the stock to be held by more than such number of persons, the person to whom such stock is issued or transferred is conclusively presumed to have notice of this fact.

(c) If a stock certificate of any close corporation conspicuously notes the fact of a restriction on transfer of stock of the corporation, and the restriction is one which is permitted by section 202 of this title, the transferee of the stock is conclusively presumed to have notice of the fact that he has acquired stock in violation of the restriction, if such acquisition violates the restriction.

(d) Whenever any person to whom stock of a close corporation has been issued or transferred has, or is conclusively presumed under this section to have, notice either (i) that he is a person not eligible to be a holder of stock of the corporation, or (ii) that transfer of stock to him would cause the stock of the corporation to be held by more than the number of persons permitted by its certificate of incorporation to hold stock of the corporation, or (iii) that the transfer of stock is in violation of a restriction on transfer of stock, the corporation may, at its option, refuse to register transfer of the stock into the name of the transferee.

(e) The provisions of subsection (d) shall not be applicable if the transfer of stock, even though otherwise contrary to subsections (a), (b) or (c), has been consented to by all the stockholders of the close corporation, or if the close corporation has amended its certificate of incorporation in accordance with section 346 of this title.

(f) The term "transfer," as used in this section, is not limited to a transfer for value.

(g) The provisions of this section do not in any way impair any rights of a transferee regarding any right to rescind the transaction or to recover under any applicable warranty express or implied.

§ 348. Involuntary Termination of Close Corporation Status; Proceeding to Prevent Loss of Status

(a) If any event occurs as a result of which one or more of the provisions or conditions included in a close corporation's certificate of incorporation pursuant to section 342 of this title to qualify it as a close corporation has been breached, the corporation's status as a close corporation under this subchapter shall terminate unless

(1) within thirty days after the occurrence of the event, or within thirty days after the event has been discovered, whichever is later, the corporation files with the Secretary of State a certificate, executed and acknowledged in accordance with section 103 of this title, stating that a specified provision or condition included in its certificate of incorporation pursuant to section 342 of this title to qualify it as a close corporation has ceased to be applicable, and furnishes a copy of such certificate to each stockholder, and

(2) the corporation concurrently with the filing of such certificate takes such steps as are necessary to correct the situation which threatens its status as a close corporation, including, without limitation, the refusal to register the transfer of stock which has been wrongfully transferred as provided by section 347 of this title, or a proceeding under subsection (b) of this section.

(b) The Court of Chancery, upon the suit of the corporation or any stockholder, shall have jurisdiction to issue all orders necessary to prevent the corporation from losing its status as a close corporation, or to restore its status as a close corporation by enjoining or setting aside any act or threatened act on the part of the corporation or a stockholder which would be inconsistent with any of the provisions or conditions required or permitted by section 342 of this title to be stated in the certificate of incorporation of a close corporation, unless it is an act approved in accordance with section 346 of this title. The Court of Chancery may enjoin or set aside any transfer or threatened transfer of stock of a close corporation which is contrary to the terms of its certificate of incorporation or of any transfer restriction permitted by section 202 of this title, and may enjoin any public offering, as defined in section 342 of this title, or threatened public offering of stock of the close corporation.

§ 349. Corporate Option Where a Restriction on Transfer of a Security is Held Invalid

If a restriction on transfer of a security of a close corporation is held not to be authorized by § 202 of this title, the corporation shall nevertheless have an option, for a period of 30 days after the judgment setting aside the restriction becomes final, to acquire the restricted security at a price which is agreed upon by the parties, or if no agreement is reached as to price, then at the fair value as determined by the Court of Chancery. In order to determine fair value, the Court may appoint an appraiser to receive evidence and report to the Court his findings and recommendation as to fair value.

§ 350. Agreements Restricting Discretion of Directors

A written agreement among the stockholders of a close corporation holding a majority of the outstanding stock entitled to vote, whether solely among themselves or with a party not a stockholder, is not invalid, as between the parties to the agreement, on the ground that it so relates to the conduct of the business and affairs of the corporation as to restrict or interfere with the discretion or powers of the board of directors. The effect of any such agreement shall be to relieve the directors and impose upon the stockholders who are parties to the agreement the liability for managerial acts or omissions which is imposed on directors to the extent and so long as the discretion or powers of the board in its management of corporate affairs is controlled by such agreement.

§ 351. Management by Stockholders

The certificate of incorporation of a close corporation may provide that the business of the corporation shall be managed by the stockholders of the corporation rather than by a board of directors. So long as this provision continues in effect,

(1) No meeting of stockholders need be called to elect directors;

(2) Unless the context clearly requires otherwise, the stockholders of the corporation shall be deemed to be directors for purposes of applying provisions of this chapter; and

(3) The stockholders of the corporation shall be subject to all liabilities of directors.

Such a provision may be inserted in the certificate of incorporation by amendment if all incorporators and subscribers or all holders of record of all of the outstanding stock, whether or not having voting power, authorize such a provision. An amendment to the certificate of incorporation to delete such a provision shall be adopted by a vote of the holders of a majority of all outstanding stock of the corporation, whether or not otherwise entitled to vote. If the certificate of incorporation contains a provision authorized by this section, the existence of such provision shall be noted conspicuously on the face or back of every stock certificate issued by such corporation.

§ 352. Appointment of Custodian for Close Corporation

(a) In addition to the provisions of section 226 of this title respecting the appointment of a custodian for any corporation, the Court of Chancery, upon application of any stockholder, may appoint one or more persons to be custodians, and, if the corporation is insolvent, to be receivers, of any close corporation when:

(1) Pursuant to section 351 of this title the business and affairs of the corporation are managed by the stockholders and they are so divided

that the business of the corporation is suffering or is threatened with irreparable injury and any remedy with respect to such deadlock provided in the certificate of incorporation or by-laws or in any written agreement of the stockholders has failed; or

(2) The petitioning stockholder has the right to the dissolution of the corporation under a provision of the certificate of incorporation permitted by section 355 of this title.

(b) In lieu of appointing a custodian for a close corporation under this section or section 226 of this title the Court of Chancery may appoint a provisional director, whose powers and status shall be as provided in section 353 of this title if the Court determines that it would be in the best interest of the corporation. Such appointment shall not preclude any subsequent order of the Court appointing a custodian for such corporation.

§ 353. Appointment of a Provisional Director in Certain Cases

(a) Notwithstanding any contrary provision of the certificate of incorporation or the by-laws or agreement of the stockholders, the Court of Chancery may appoint a provisional director for a close corporation if the directors are so divided respecting the management of the corporation's business and affairs that the votes required for action by the board of directors cannot be obtained with the consequence that the business and affairs of the corporation can no longer be conducted to the advantage of the stockholders generally.

(b) An application for relief under this section must be filed (1) by at least one-half of the number of directors then in office, (2) by the holders of at least one-third of all stock then entitled to elect directors, or, (3) if there be more than one class of stock then entitled to elect one or more directors, by the holders of two-thirds of the stock of any such class; but the certificate of incorporation of a close corporation may provide that a lesser proportion of the directors or of the stockholders or of a class of stockholders may apply for relief under this section.

(c) A provisional director shall be an impartial person who is neither a stockholder nor a creditor of the corporation or of any subsidiary or affiliate of the corporation, and whose further qualifications, if any, may be determined by the Court of Chancery. A provisional director is not a receiver of the corporation and does not have the title and powers of a custodian or receiver appointed under sections 226 and 291 of this title. A provisional director shall have all the rights and powers of a duly elected director of the corporation, including the right to notice of and to vote at meetings of directors, until such time as he shall be removed by order of the Court of Chancery or by the holders of a majority of all shares then entitled to vote to elect directors or by the holders of two-thirds of the shares of that class of voting shares which filed the application for appointment of a provisional director. His compensation shall be determined by agreement between him and the corporation subject to approval of the Court of Chancery, which may fix his compensation in the absence of agreement or in the event of disagreement between the provisional director and the corporation.

(d) Even though the requirements of subsection (b) of this section relating to the number of directors or stockholders who may petition for appointment of a provisional director are not satisfied, the Court of Chancery may nevertheless appoint a provisional director if permitted by subsection (b) of section 352 of this title.

§ 354. Operating Corporation as Partnership

No written agreement among stockholders of a close corporation, nor any provision of the certificate of incorporation or of the by-laws of the corporation, which agreement or provision relates to any phase of the affairs of such corporation, including but not limited to the management of its business or declaration and payment of dividends or other division of profits or the election of directors or officers or the employment of stockholders by the corporation or the arbitration of disputes, shall be invalid on the ground that it is an attempt by the parties to the agreement or by the stockholders of the corporation to treat the corporation as if it were a partnership or to arrange relations among the stockholders or between the stockholders and the corporation in a manner that would be appropriate only among partners.

§ 355. Stockholders' Option to Dissolve Corporation

(a) The certificate of incorporation of any close corporation may include a provision granting to any stockholder, or to the holders of any specified number or percentage of shares of any class of stock, an option to have the corporation dissolved at will or upon the occurrence of any specified event or contingency. Whenever any such option to dissolve is exercised, the stockholders exercising such option shall give written notice thereof to all other stockholders. After the expiration of 30 days following the sending of such notice, the dissolution of the corporation shall proceed as if the required number of stockholders having voting power had consented in writing to dissolution of the corporation as provided by section 228 of this title.

(b) If the certificate of incorporation as originally filed does not contain a provision authorized by subsection (a), the certificate may be amended to include such provision if adopted by the affirmative vote of the holders of all the outstanding stock, whether or not entitled to vote, unless the certificate of incorporation specifically authorizes such an amendment by a vote which shall be not less than two-thirds of all the outstanding stock whether or not entitled to vote.

(c) Each stock certificate in any corporation whose certificate of incorporation authorizes dissolution as permitted by this section shall conspicuously note on the face thereof the existence of the provision. Unless noted conspicuously on the face of the stock certificate, the provision is ineffective.

§ 356. Effect of This Subchapter on Other Laws

The provisions of this subchapter shall not be deemed to repeal any statute or rule of law which is or would be applicable to any corporation which is organized under the provisions of this chapter but is not a close corporation.

B. REVISED MODEL BUSINESS CORPORATION ACT

Reproduced with kind permission of the American Bar Foundation.

Table of Sections

CHAPTER 1. GENERAL PROVISIONS

SUBCHAPTER A. SHORT TITLE AND RESERVATION OF POWER

SUBCHAPTER B. FILING DOCUMENTS

SUBCHAPTER C. SECRETARY OF STATE

SUBCHAPTER D. DEFINITIONS

CHAPTER 2. INCORPORATION

CHAPTER 3. PURPOSES AND POWERS

CHAPTER 4. NAME

CHAPTER 5. OFFICE AND AGENT

CHAPTER 6. SHARES AND DISTRIBUTIONS

SUBCHAPTER A. SHARES

SUBCHAPTER B. ISSUANCE OF SHARES

SUBCHAPTER C. SUBSEQUENT ACQUISITION OF SHARES BY SHAREHOLDERS AND CORPORATION

SUBCHAPTER D. DISTRIBUTIONS

CHAPTER 7. SHAREHOLDERS

SUBCHAPTER A. MEETINGS

SUBCHAPTER B. VOTING

SUBCHAPTER C. VOTING TRUSTS AND AGREEMENTS

SUBCHAPTER D. DERIVATIVE PROCEEDINGS

CHAPTER 8. DIRECTORS AND OFFICERS

SUBCHAPTER A. BOARD OF DIRECTORS

SUBCHAPTER B. MEETINGS AND ACTION OF BOARD OF DIRECTORS

SUBCHAPTER C. STANDARDS OF CONDUCT

SUBCHAPTER D. OFFICERS

CHAPTER 13. DISSENTERS' RIGHTS

SUBCHAPTER A. RIGHT TO DISSENT AND OBTAIN PAYMENT FOR SHARES

SUBCHAPTER B. PROCEDURE FOR EXERCISE OF DISSENTERS' RIGHTS

SUBCHAPTER C. JUDICIAL APPRAISAL OF SHARES

CHAPTER 14. DISSOLUTION

SUBCHAPTER A. VOLUNTARY DISSOLUTION

SUBCHAPTER B. ADMINISTRATIVE DISSOLUTION

SUBCHAPTER C. JUDICIAL DISSOLUTION

SUBCHAPTER D. MISCELLANEOUS

[CHAPTER 15. FOREIGN CORPORATIONS—OMITTED]

CHAPTER 16. RECORDS AND REPORTS

SUBCHAPTER A. RECORDS

SUBCHAPTER B. REPORTS

CHAPTER 17. TRANSITION PROVISIONS

CHAPTER 1. GENERAL PROVISIONS

SUBCHAPTER A. SHORT TITLE AND RESERVATION OF POWER

§ 1.01 Short Title

This Act shall be known and may be cited as the "[name of state] Business Corporation Act."

§ 1.02 Reservation of power to amend or repeal

The [name of state legislature] has power to amend or repeal all or part of this Act at any time and all domestic and foreign corporations subject to this Act are governed by the amendment or repeal.

SUBCHAPTER B. FILING DOCUMENTS

§ 1.20 Filing Requirements

(a) A document must satisfy the requirements of this section, and of any other section that adds to or varies these requirements, to be entitled to filing by the secretary of state.

(b) This Act must require or permit filing the document in the office of the secretary of state.

(c) The document must contain the information required by this Act. It may contain other information as well.

(d) The document must be typewritten or printed.

(e) The document must be in the English language. A corporate name need not be in English if written in English letters or Arabic or Roman numerals, and the certificate of existence required of foreign corporations need not be in English if accompanied by a reasonably authenticated English translation.

(f) The document must be executed:

(1) by the chairman of the board of directors of a domestic or foreign corporation, by its president, or by another of its officers;

(2) if directors have not been selected or the corporation has not been formed, by an incorporator; or

(3) if the corporation is in the hands of a receiver, trustee, or other court-appointed fiduciary, by that fiduciary.

(g) The person executing the document shall sign it and state beneath or opposite his signature his name and the capacity in which he signs. The document may but need not contain: (1) the corporate seal, (2) an attestation by the secretary or an assistant secretary, (3) an acknowledgement, verification, or proof.

(h) If the secretary of state has prescribed a mandatory form for the document under section 1.21, the document must be in or on the prescribed form.

(i) The document must be delivered to the office of the secretary of state for filing and must be accompanied by one exact or conformed copy (except as provided in sections 5.03 and 15.09), the correct filing fee, and any franchise tax, license fee, or penalty required by this Act or other law.

§ 1.21 Forms

(a) The secretary of state may prescribe and furnish on request forms for: (1) an application for a certificate of existence, (2) a foreign corporation's application for a certificate of authority to transact business in this state, (3) a foreign corporation's application for a certificate of withdrawal, and (4) the annual report. If the secretary of state so requires, use of these forms is mandatory.

(b) The secretary of state may prescribe and furnish on request forms for other documents required or permitted to be filed by this Act but their use is not mandatory.

§ 1.22 Filing, Service and Copying Fees

(a) The secretary of state shall collect the following fees when the documents described in this subsection are delivered to him for filing:

Document	Fee
(1) Articles of incorporation	$______.
(2) Application for use of indistinguishable name	$______.
(3) Application for reserved name	$______.
(4) Notice of transfer of reserved name	$______.
(5) Application for registered name	$______.
(6) Application for renewal of registered name	$______.
(7) Corporation's statement of change of registered agent or registered office or both	$______.
(8) Agent's statement of change of registered office for each affected corporation	$______.
not to exceed a total of	$______.
(9) Agent's statement of resignation	No fee.
(10) Amendment of articles of incorporation	$______.
(11) Restatement of articles of incorporation	$______.
with amendment of articles	$______.
(12) Articles of merger or share exchange	$______.
(13) Articles of dissolution	$______.
(14) Articles of revocation of dissolution	$______.
(15) Certificate of administrative dissolution	No fee.
(16) Application for reinstatement following administrative dissolution	$______.
(17) Certificate of reinstatement	No fee.
(18) Certificate of judicial dissolution	No fee.
(19) Application for certificate of authority	$______.
(20) Application for amended certificate of authority	$______.

Document	Fee
(21) Application for certificate of withdrawal	$_____.
(22) Certificate of revocation of authority to transact business	No fee.
(23) Annual report	$_____.
(24) Articles of correction	$_____.
(25) Application for certificate of existence or authorization	$_____.
(26) Any other document required or permitted to be filed by this Act.	$_____.

(b) The secretary of state shall collect a fee of $_____ each time process is served on him under this Act. The party to a proceeding causing service of process is entitled to recover this fee as costs if he prevails in the proceeding.

(c) The secretary of state shall collect the following fees for copying and certifying the copy of any filed document relating to a domestic or foreign corporation:

(1) $_____ a page for copying; and

(2) $_____ for the certificate.

§ 1.23 Effective Time and Date of Document

(a) Except as provided in subsection (b) and section 1.24(c), a document accepted for filing is effective:

(1) at the time of filing on the date it is filed, as evidenced by the secretary of state's date and time endorsement on the original document; or

(2) at the time specified in the document as its effective time on the date it is filed.

(b) A document may specify a delayed effective time and date, and if it does so the document becomes effective at the time and date specified. If a delayed effective date but no time is specified, the document is effective at the close of business on that date. A delayed effective date for a document may not be later than the 90th day after the date it is filed.

§ 1.24 Correcting Filed Document

(a) A domestic or foreign corporation may correct a document filed by the secretary of state if the document (1) contains an incorrect statement or (2) was defectively executed, attested, sealed, verified, or acknowledged.

(b) A document is corrected:

(1) by preparing articles of correction that (i) describe the document (including its filing date) or attach a copy of it to the articles, (ii) specify the incorrect statement and the reason it is incorrect or the manner in which the execution was defective, and (iii) correct the incorrect statement or defective execution; and

(2) by delivering the articles to the secretary of state for filing.

(c) Articles of correction are effective on the effective date of the document they correct except as to persons relying on the uncorrected document and adversely affected by the correction. As to those persons, articles of correction are effective when filed.

§ 1.25 Filing Duty of Secretary of State

(a) If a document delivered to the office of the secretary of state for filing satisfies the requirements of section 1.20, the secretary of state shall file it.

(b) The secretary of state files a document by stamping or otherwise endorsing "Filed," together with his name and official title and the date and time of receipt, on both the original and the document copy and on the receipt for the filing fee. After filing a document, except as provided in sections 5.03 and 15.10, the secretary of state shall deliver the document copy, with the filing fee receipt (or acknowledgement of receipt if no fee is required) attached, to the domestic or foreign corporation or its representative.

(c) If the secretary of state refuses to file a document, he shall return it to the domestic or foreign corporation or its representative within five days after the document was delivered, together with a brief, written explanation of the reason for his refusal.

(d) The secretary of state's duty to file documents under this section is ministerial. His filing or refusing to file a document does not:

(1) affect the validity or invalidity of the document in whole or part;

(2) relate to the correctness or incorrectness of information contained in the document;

(3) create a presumption that the document is valid or invalid or that information contained in the document is correct or incorrect.

§ 1.26 Appeal From Secretary of State's Refusal to File Document

(a) If the secretary of state refuses to file a document delivered to his office for filing, the domestic or foreign corporation may appeal the refusal to the [name or describe] court [of the county where the corporations's principal office (or, if none in this state, its registered office) is or will be located] [of $______ county]. The appeal is commenced by petitioning the court to compel filing the document and by attaching to the petition the document and the secretary of state's explanation of his refusal to file.

(b) The court may summarily order the secretary of state to file the document or take other action the court considers appropriate.

(c) The court's final decision may be appealed as in other civil proceedings.

§ 1.27 Evidentiary Effect of Copy of Filed Document

A certificate attached to a copy of the document filed by the secretary of state, bearing his signature (which may be in facsimile) and the seal of this state, is conclusive evidence that the original document is on file with the secretary of state.

§ 1.28 Certificate of Existence

(a) Anyone may apply to the secretary of state to furnish a certificate of existence for a domestic corporation or a certificate of authorization for a foreign corporation.

(b) A certificate of existence or authorization sets forth:

(1) the domestic corporation's corporate name or the foreign corporation's corporate name used in this state;

(2) that (i) the domestic corporation is duly incorporated under the law of this state, the date of its incorporation, and the period of its duration if less than perpetual; or (ii) that the foreign corporation is authorized to transact business in this state;

(3) that all fees, taxes, and penalties owed to this state have been paid, if (i) payment is reflected in the records of the secretary of state and (ii) nonpayment affects the existence or authorization of the domestic or foreign corporation;

(4) that its most recent annual report required by section 16.22 has been delivered to the secretary of state;

(5) that articles of dissolution have not been filed; and

(6) other facts of record in the office of the secretary of state that may be requested by the applicant.

(c) Subject to any qualification stated in the certificate, a certificate of existence or authorization issued by the secretary of state may be relied upon as conclusive evidence that the domestic or foreign corporation is in existence or is authorized to transact business in this state.

§ 1.29 Penalty for Signing False Document

(a) A person commits an offense if he signs a document he knows is false in any material respect with intent that the document be delivered to the secretary of state for filing.

(b) An offense under this section is a [ ] misdemeanor [punishable by a fine of not to exceed $______].

SUBCHAPTER C. SECRETARY OF STATE

§ 1.30 Powers

The secretary of state has the power reasonably necessary to perform the duties required of him by this Act.

SUBCHAPTER D. DEFINITIONS

§ 1.40 Act Definitions

In this Act:

(1) "Articles of incorporation" include amended and restated articles of incorporation and articles of merger.

(2) "Authorized shares" means the shares of all classes a domestic or foreign corporation is authorized to issue.

(3) "Conspicuous" means so written that a reasonable person against whom the writing is to operate should have noticed it. For example, printing in italics or boldface or contrasting color, or typing in capitals or underlined, is conspicuous.

(4) "Corporation" or "domestic corporation" means a corporation for profit, which is not a foreign corporation, incorporated under or subject to the provisions of this Act.

(5) "Deliver" includes mail.

(6) "Distribution" means a direct or indirect transfer of money or other property (except its own shares) or incurrence of indebtedness by a corporation to or for the benefit of its shareholders in respect of any of its shares. A distribution may be in the form of a declaration or payment of a dividend; a purchase, redemption, or other acquisition of shares; a distribution of indebtedness; or otherwise.

(7) "Effective date of notice" is defined in section 1.41.

(8) "Employee" includes an officer but not a director. A director may accept duties that make him also an employee.

(9) "Entity" includes corporation and foreign corporation; not-for-profit corporation; profit and not-for-profit unincorporated association; business trust, estate, partnership, trust, and two or more

persons having a joint or common economic interest; and state, United States, and foreign government.

(10) "Foreign corporation" means a corporation for profit incorporated under a law other than the law of this state.

(11) "Governmental subdivision" includes authority, county, district, and municipality.

(12) "Includes" denotes a partial definition.

(13) "Individual" includes the estate of an incompetent or deceased individual.

(14) "Means" denotes an exhaustive definition.

(15) "Notice" is defined in section 1.41.

(16) "Person" includes individual and entity.

(17) "Principal office" means the office (in or out of this state) so designated in the annual report where the principal executive offices of a domestic or foreign corporation are located.

(18) "Proceeding" includes civil suit and criminal, administrative, and investigatory action.

(19) "Record date" means the date established under chapter 6 or 7 on which a corporation determines the identity of its shareholders and their shareholdings for purposes of this Act. The determination shall be made as of the close of business on the record date unless another time for doing so is specified when the record date is fixed.

(20) "Secretary" means the corporate officer to whom the board of directors has delegated responsibility under section 8.40(c) for custody of the minutes of the meetings of the board of directors and of the shareholders and for authenticating records of the corporation.

(21) "Share" means the unit into which the proprietary interests in a corporation are divided.

(22) "Shareholder" means the person in whose name shares are registered in the records of a corporation or the beneficial owner of shares to the extent of the rights granted by a nominee certificate on file with a corporation.

(23) "State," when referring to a part of the United States, includes a state and commonwealth (and their agencies and governmental subdivisions) and a territory, and insular possession (and their agencies and governmental subdivisions) of the United States.

(24) "Subscriber" means a person who subscribes for shares in a corporation, whether before or after incorporation.

(25) "United States" includes district, authority, bureau, commission, department, and any other agency of the United States.

(26) "Voting group" means all shares of one or more classes or series that under the articles of incorporation or this Act are entitled

to vote and be counted together collectively on a matter at a meeting of shareholders. All shares entitled by the articles of incorporation or this Act to vote generally on the matter are for that purpose a single voting group.

§ 1.41 Notice

(a) Notice under this Act shall be in writing unless oral notice is reasonable under the circumstances.

(b) Notice may be communicated in person; by telephone, telegraph, teletype, or other form of wire or wireless communication; or by mail or private carrier. If these forms of personal notice are impracticable, notice may be communicated by a newspaper of general circulation in the area where published; or by radio, television, or other form of public broadcast communication.

(c) Written notice by a domestic or foreign corporation to its shareholder, if in a comprehensible form, is effective when mailed, if mailed postpaid and correctly addressed to the shareholder's address shown in the corporation's current record of shareholders.

(d) Written notice to a domestic or foreign corporation (authorized to transact business in this state) may be addressed to its registered agent at its registered office or to the corporation or its secretary at its principal office shown in its most recent annual report or, in the case of a foreign corporation that has not yet delivered an annual report, in its application for a certificate of authority.

(e) Except as provided in subsections (c) and (d), written notice, if in a comprehensible form, is effective at the earliest of the following:

(1) when received;

(2) five days after its deposit in the United States Mail, as evidenced by the postmark, if mailed postpaid and correctly addressed;

(3) on the date shown on the return receipt, if sent by registered or certified mail, return receipt requested, and the receipt is signed by or on behalf of the addressee.

(f) Oral notice is effective when communicated if communicated in a comprehensible manner.

(g) If this Act prescribes notice requirements for particular circumstances, those requirements govern. If articles of incorporation or bylaws prescribe notice requirements, not inconsistent with this section or other provisions of this Act, those requirements govern.

§ 1.42 Number of Shareholders

(a) For purposes of this Act, the following identified as a shareholder in a corporation's current record of shareholders constitutes one shareholder:

(1) three or fewer co-owners;

(2) a corporation, partnership, trust, estate, or other entity;

(3) the trustees, guardians, custodians, or other fiduciaries of a single trust, estate, or account.

(b) For purposes of this Act, shareholdings registered in substantially similar names constitute one shareholder if it is reasonable to believe that the names represent the same person.

CHAPTER 2. INCORPORATION

§ 2.01 Incorporators

One or more persons may act as the incorporator or incorporators of a corporation by delivering articles of incorporation to the secretary of state for filing.

§ 2.02 Articles of Incorporation

(a) The articles of incorporation must set forth:

(1) a corporate name for the corporation that satisfies the requirements of section 4.01;

(2) the number of shares the corporation is authorized to issue;

(3) the street address of the corporation's initial registered office and the name of its initial registered agent at that office; and

(4) the name and address of each incorporator.

(b) The articles of incorporation may set forth:

(1) the names and addresses of the individuals who are to serve as the initial directors;

(2) provisions not inconsistent with law regarding:

(i) the purpose or purposes for which the corporation is organized;

(ii) managing the business and regulating the affairs of the corporation;

(iii) defining, limiting, and regulating the powers of the corporation, its board of directors, and shareholders;

(iv) a par value for authorized shares or classes of shares;

(v) the imposition of personal liability on shareholders for the debts of the corporation to a specified extent and upon specified conditions; and

(3) any provision that under this Act is required or permitted to be set forth in the bylaws.

(c) The articles of incorporation need not set forth any of the corporate powers enumerated in this Act.

§ 2.03 Incorporation

(a) Unless a delayed effective date is specified, the corporate existence begins when the articles of incorporation are filed.

(b) The secretary of state's filing of the articles of incorporation is conclusive proof that the incorporators satisfied all conditions precedent to incorporation except in a proceeding by the state to cancel or revoke the incorporation or involuntarily dissolve the corporation.

§ 2.04 Liability for Preincorporation Transactions

All persons purporting to act as or on behalf of a corporation, knowing there was no incorporation under this Act, are jointly and severally liable for all liabilities created while so acting.

§ 2.05 Organization of Corporation

(a) After incorporation:

(1) if initial directors are named in the articles of incorporation, the initial directors shall hold an organizational meeting, at the call of a majority of the directors, to complete the organization of the corporation by appointing officers, adopting bylaws, and carrying on any other business brought before the meeting;

(2) if initial directors are not named in the articles, the incorporator or incorporators shall hold an organizational meeting at the call of a majority of the incorporators:

(i) to elect directors and complete the organization of the corporation; or

(ii) to elect a board of directors who shall complete the organization of the corporation.

(b) Action required or permitted by this Act to be taken by incorporators at an organizational meeting may be taken without a meeting if the action taken is evidenced by one or more written consents describing the action taken and signed by each incorporator.

(c) An organizational meeting may be held in or out of this state.

§ 2.06 Bylaws

(a) The incorporators or board of directors of a corporation shall adopt initial bylaws for the corporation.

(b) The bylaws of a corporation may contain any provision for managing the business and regulating the affairs of the corporation that is not inconsistent with law or the articles of incorporation.

§ 2.07 Emergency Bylaws

(a) Unless the articles of incorporation provide otherwise, the board of directors of a corporation may adopt bylaws to be effective only in an emergency defined in subsection (d). The emergency bylaws, which are subject to amendment or repeal by the shareholders, may make all provisions necessary for managing the corporation during the emergency, including:

(1) procedures for calling a meeting of the board of directors;

(2) quorum requirements for the meeting; and

(3) designation of additional or substitute directors.

(b) All provisions of the regular bylaws consistent with the emergency bylaws remain effective during the emergency. The emergency bylaws are not effective after the emergency ends.

(c) Corporate action taken in good faith in accordance with the emergency bylaws:

(1) binds the corporation; and

(2) may not be used to impose liability on a corporate director, officer, employee, or agent.

(d) An emergency exists for purposes of this section if a quorum of the corporation's directors cannot readily be assembled because of some catastrophic event.

CHAPTER 3. PURPOSES AND POWERS

§ 3.01 Purposes

(a) Every corporation incorporated under this Act has the purpose of engaging in any lawful business unless a more limited purpose is set forth in the articles of incorporation.

(b) A corporation engaging in a business that is subject to regulation under another statute of this state may incorporate under this Act only if permitted by, and subject to all limitations of, the other statute.

§ 3.02 General Powers

Unless its articles of incorporation provide otherwise, every corporation has perpetual duration and succession in its corporate name and has the same powers as an individual to do all things necessary or convenient to carry out its business and affairs, including without limitation power:

(1) to sue and be sued, complain and defend in its corporate name;

(2) to have a corporate seal, which may be altered at will, and to use it, or a facsimile of it, by impressing or affixing it or in any other manner reproducing it;

(3) to make and amend bylaws, not inconsistent with its articles of incorporation or with the laws of this state, for managing the business and regulating the affairs of the corporation;

(4) to purchase, receive, lease, or otherwise acquire, and own, hold, improve, use, and otherwise deal with, real or personal property, or any legal or equitable interest in property, wherever located;

(5) to sell, convey, mortgage, pledge, lease, exchange, and otherwise dispose of all or any part of its property;

(6) to purchase, receive, subscribe for, or otherwise acquire; own, hold, vote, use, sell, mortgage, lend, pledge, or otherwise dispose of; and deal in and with shares or other interests in, or obligations of, any other entity;

(7) to make contracts and guarantees, incur liabilities, borrow money, issue its notes, bonds, and other obligations, (which may be convertible into or include the option to purchase other securities of the corporation), and secure any of its obligations by mortgage or pledge of any of its property, franchises, or income;

(8) to lend money, invest and reinvest its funds, and receive and hold real and personal property as security for repayment;

(9) to be a promoter, partner, member, associate, or manager of any partnership, joint venture, trust, or other entity;

(10) to conduct its business, locate offices, and exercise the powers granted by this Act within or without this state;

(11) to elect directors and appoint officers, employees, and agents of the corporation, define their duties, fix their compensation, and lend them money and credit;

(12) to pay pensions and establish pension plans, pension trusts, profit sharing plans, share bonus plans, share option plans, and benefit or incentive plans for any or all of its current or former directors, officers, employees, and agents;

(13) to make donations for the public welfare or for charitable, scientific, or educational purposes;

(14) to transact any lawful business that will aid governmental policy;

(15) to make payments or donations, or do any other act, not inconsistent with law, that furthers the business and affairs of the corporation.

§ 3.03 Emergency Powers

(a) In anticipation of or during an emergency defined in subsection (d), the board of directors of a corporation may:

(1) modify lines of succession to accommodate the incapacity of any director, officer, employee, or agent; and

(2) relocate the principal office, designate alternative principal offices or regional offices, or authorize the officers to do so.

(b) During an emergency defined in subsection (d), unless emergency bylaws provide otherwise:

(1) notice of a meeting of the board of directors need be given only to those directors whom it is practicable to reach and may be given in any practicable manner, including by publication and radio; and

(2) one or more officers of the corporation present at a meeting of the board of directors may be deemed to be directors for the meeting, in order of rank and within the same rank in order of seniority, as necessary to achieve a quorum.

(c) Corporate action taken in good faith during an emergency under this section to further the ordinary business affairs of the corporation:

(1) binds the corporation; and

(2) may not be used to impose liability on a corporate director, officer, employee, or agent.

(d) An emergency exists for purposes of this section if a quorum of the corporation's directors cannot readily be assembled because of some catastrophic event.

§ 3.04 Ultra Vires

(a) Except as provided in subsection (b), the validity of corporate action may not be challenged on the ground that the corporation lacks or lacked power to act.

(b) A corporation's power to act may be challenged:

(1) in a proceeding by a shareholder against the corporation to enjoin the act;

(2) in a proceeding by the corporation, directly, derivatively, or through a receiver, trustee, or other legal representative, against an incumbent or former director, officer, employee, or agent of the corporation; or

(3) in a proceeding by the Attorney General under section 14.30.

(c) In a shareholder's proceeding under subsection (b)(1) to enjoin an unauthorized corporate act, the court may enjoin or set aside the act, if equitable and if all affected persons are parties to the proceeding, and may award damages for loss (other than anticipated profits) suffered by the corporation or another party because of enjoining the unauthorized act.

CHAPTER 4. NAME

§ 4.01 Corporate Name

(a) A corporate name:

(1) must contain the word "corporation," "incorporated," "company," or "limited," or the abbreviation "corp.," "inc.," "co.," or "ltd.", or words or abbreviations of like import in another language; and

(2) may not contain language stating or implying that the corporation is organized for a purpose other than that permitted by section 3.01 and its articles of incorporation.

(b) Except as authorized by subsections (c) and (d), a corporate name must be distinguishable upon the records of the secretary of state from:

(1) the corporate name of a corporation incorporated or authorized to transact business in this state;

(2) a corporate name reserved or registered under section 4.02 or 4.03;

(3) the fictitious name adopted by a foreign corporation authorized to transact business in this state because its real name is unavailable; and

(4) the corporate name of a not-for-profit corporation incorporated or authorized to transact business in this state.

(c) A corporation may apply to the secretary of state for authorization to use a name that is not distinguishable upon his records from one or more of the names described in subsection (b). The secretary of state shall authorize use of the name applied for if:

(1) the other corporation consents to the use in writing and submits an undertaking in form satisfactory to the secretary of state to change its name to a name that is distinguishable upon the records of the secretary of state from the name of the applying corporation; or

(2) the applicant delivers to the secretary of state a certified copy of the final judgment of a court of competent jurisdiction establishing the applicant's right to use the name applied for in this state.

(d) A corporation may use the name (including the fictitious name) of another domestic or foreign corporation that is used in this state if the other corporation is incorporated or authorized to transact business in this state and the proposed user corporation:

(1) has merged with the other corporation;

(2) has been formed by reorganization of the other corporation; or

(3) has acquired all or substantially all of the assets, including the corporate name, of the other corporation.

(e) This Act does not control the use of fictitious names.

§ 4.02 Reserved Name

(a) A person may reserve the exclusive use of a corporate name, including a fictitious name for a foreign corporation whose corporate name is not available, by delivering an application to the secretary of state for filing. The application must set forth the name and address of the applicant and the name proposed to be reserved. If the secretary of state finds that the corporate name applied for is available, he shall reserve the name for the applicant's exclusive use for a nonrenewable 120-day period.

(b) The owner of a reserved corporate name may transfer the reservation to another person by delivering to the secretary of state a signed notice of the transfer that states the name and address of the transferee.

§ 4.03 Registered Name

(a) A foreign corporation may register its corporate name, or its corporate name with any addition required by section 15.06, if the name is distinguishable upon the records of the secretary of state from the corporate names that are not available under section 4.01(b)(3).

(b) A foreign corporation registers its corporate name, or its corporate name with any addition required by section 15.06, by delivering to the secretary of state for filing an application:

(1) setting forth its corporate name, or its corporate name with any addition required by section 15.06, the state or country and date of its incorporation, and a brief description of the nature of the business in which it is engaged; and

(2) accompanied by a certificate of existence (or a document of similar import) from the state or country of incorporation.

(c) The name is registered for the applicant's exclusive use upon the effective date of the application.

(d) A foreign corporation whose registration is effective may renew it for successive years by delivering to the secretary of state for filing a renewal application, which complies with the requirements of subsection (b), between October 1 and December 31 of the preceding year. The renewal application renews the registration for the following calendar year.

(e) A foreign corporation whose registration is effective may thereafter qualify as a foreign corporation under that name or consent in writing to the use of that name by a corporation thereafter incorporated under this Act or by another foreign corporation thereafter authorized to transact business in this state. The registration terminates when the domestic corporation is incorporated or the foreign corporation qualifies or consents to the qualification of another foreign corporation under the registered name.

CHAPTER 5. OFFICE AND AGENT

§ 5.01 Registered Office and Registered Agent

Each corporation must continuously maintain in this state:

(1) a registered office that may be the same as any of its places of business; and

(2) a registered agent, who may be:

(i) an individual who resides in this state and whose business office is identical with the registered office;

(ii) a domestic corporation or not-for-profit domestic corporation whose business office is identical with the registered office; or

(iii) a foreign corporation or not-for-profit foreign corporation authorized to transact business in this state whose business office is identical with the registered office.

§ 5.02 Change of Registered Office or Registered Agent

(a) A corporation may change its registered office or registered agent by delivering to the secretary of state for filing a statement of change that sets forth:

(1) the name of the corporation,

(2) the street address of its current registered office;

(3) if the current registered office is to be changed, the street address of the new registered office;

(4) the name of its current registered agent;

(5) if the current registered agent is to be changed, the name of the new registered agent and the new agent's written consent (either on the statement or attached to it) to the appointment; and

(6) that after the change or changes are made, the street addresses of its registered office and the business office of its registered agent will be identical.

(b) If a registered agent changes the street address of his business office, he may change the street address of the registered office of any corporation for which he is the registered agent by notifying the corporation in writing of the change and signing (either manually or in facsimile) and delivering to the secretary of state for filing a statement that complies with the requirements of subsection (a) and recites that the corporation has been notified of the change.

§ 5.03 Resignation of Registered Agent

(a) A registered agent may resign his agency appointment by signing and delivering to the secretary of state for filing the signed original and two exact or conformed copies of a statement of resignation. The statement may include a statement that the registered office is also discontinued.

(b) After filing the statement the secretary of state shall mail one copy to the registered office (if not discontinued) and the other copy to the corporation at its principal office.

(c) The agency appointment is terminated, and the registered office discontinued if so provided, on the 31st day after the date on which the statement was filed.

§ 5.04 Service on Corporation

(a) A corporation's registered agent is the corporation's agent for service of process, notice, or demand required or permitted by law to be served on the corporation.

(b) If a corporation has no registered agent, or the agent cannot with reasonable diligence be served, the corporation may be served by registered or certified mail, return receipt requested, addressed to the secretary of the corporation at its principal office. Service is perfected under this subsection at the earliest of:

(1) the date the corporation receives the mail;

(2) the date shown on the return receipt, if signed on behalf of the corporation; or

(3) five days after its deposit in the United States Mail, if mailed postpaid and correctly addressed.

(c) This section does not prescribe the only means, or necessarily the required means, of serving a corporation.

CHAPTER 6. SHARES AND DISTRIBUTIONS

SUBCHAPTER A. SHARES

§ 6.01 Authorized Shares

(a) The articles of incorporation must prescribe the classes of shares and the number of shares of each class that the corporation is authorized to issue. If more than one class of shares is authorized, the articles of incorporation must prescribe a distinguishing designation for each class, and prior to the issuance of shares of a class the preferences, limitations, and relative rights of that class must be described in the articles of incorporation. All shares of a class must have preferences, limitations, and relative rights identical with those of other shares of the same class except to the extent otherwise permitted by section 6.02.

(b) The articles of incorporation must authorize (1) one or more classes of shares that together have unlimited voting rights, and (2) one or more classes of shares (which may be the same class or classes as those with voting rights) that together are entitled to receive the net assets of the corporation upon dissolution.

(c) The articles of incorporation may authorize one or more classes of shares that:

(1) have special, conditional, or limited voting rights, or no right to vote, except to the extent prohibited by this Act;

(2) are redeemable or convertible as specified in the articles of incorporation (i) at the option of the corporation, the shareholder, or another person or upon the occurrence of a designated event; (ii) for cash, indebtedness, securities, or other property; (iii) in a designated amount or in an amount determined in accordance with a designated formula or by reference to extrinsic data or events;

(3) entitle the holders to distributions calculated in any manner, including dividends that may be cumulative, noncumulative, or partially cumulative;

(4) have preference over any other class of shares with respect to distributions, including dividends and distributions upon the dissolution of the corporation.

(d) The description of the designations, preferences, limitations, and relative rights of share classes in subsection (c) is not exhaustive.

§ 6.02 Terms of Class or Series Determined by Board of Directors

(a) If the articles of incorporation so provide, the board of directors may determine, in whole or part, the preferences, limitations, and relative rights (within the limits set forth in section 6.01) of (1) any class of shares before the issuance of any shares of that class or (2) one or more series within a class before the issuance of any shares of that series.

(b) Each series of a class must be given a distinguishing designation.

(c) All shares of a series must have preferences, limitations, and relative rights identical with those of other shares of the same series and, except to the extent otherwise provided in the description of the series, of those of other series of the same class.

(d) Before issuing any shares of a class or series created under this section, the corporation must deliver to the secretary of state for filing articles of amendment, which are effective without shareholder action, that set forth:

(1) the name of the corporation;

(2) the text of the amendment determining the terms of the class or series of shares;

(3) the date it was adopted; and

(4) a statement that the amendment was duly adopted by the board of directors.

§ 6.03 Issued and Outstanding Shares

(a) A corporation may issue the number of shares of each class or series authorized by the articles of incorporation. Shares that are issued are outstanding shares until they are reacquired, redeemed, converted, or cancelled.

(b) The reacquisition, redemption, or conversion of outstanding shares is subject to the limitations of subsection (c) of this section and to section 6.40.

(c) At all times that shares of the corporation are outstanding, one or more shares that together have unlimited voting rights and one or more shares that together are entitled to receive the net assets of the corporation upon dissolution must be outstanding.

§ 6.04 Fractional Shares

(a) A corporation may:

(1) issue fractions of a share or pay in money the value of fractions of a share;

(2) arrange for disposition of fractional shares by the shareholders;

(3) issue scrip in registered or bearer form entitling the holder to receive a full share upon surrendering enough scrip to equal a full share.

(b) Each certificate representing scrip must be conspicuously labeled "scrip" and must contain the information required by section 6.25(b).

(c) The holder of a fractional share is entitled to exercise the rights of a shareholder, including the right to vote, to receive dividends, and to participate in the assets of the corporation upon liquidation. The holder of scrip is not entitled to any of these rights unless the scrip provides for them.

(d) The board of directors may authorize the issuance of scrip subject to any condition considered desirable, including:

(1) that the scrip will become void if not exchanged for full shares before a specified date; and

(2) that the shares for which the scrip is exchangeable may be sold and the proceeds paid to the scripholders.

SUBCHAPTER B. ISSUANCE OF SHARES

§ 6.20 Subscription for Shares Before Incorporation

(a) A subscription for shares entered into before incorporation is irrevocable for six months unless the subscription agreement provides a longer or shorter period or all the subscribers agree to revocation.

(b) The board of directors may determine the payment terms of subscriptions for shares that were entered into before incorporation, unless the subscription agreement specifies them. A call for payment by the board of directors must be uniform so far as practicable as to all shares of the same class or series, unless the subscription agreement specifies otherwise.

(c) Shares issued pursuant to subscriptions entered into before incorporation are fully paid and nonassessable when the corporation receives the consideration specified in the subscription agreement.

(d) If a subscriber defaults in payment of money or property under a subscription agreement entered into before incorporation, the corporation may collect the amount owed as any other debt. Alternatively, unless the subscription agreement provides otherwise, the corporation may rescind the agreement and may sell the shares if the debt remains unpaid more than 20 days after the corporation sends written demand for payment to the subscriber.

(e) A subscription agreement entered into after incorporation is a contract between the subscriber and the corporation subject to section 6.21.

§ 6.21 Issuance of Shares

(a) The powers granted in this section to the board of directors may be reserved to the shareholders by the articles of incorporation.

(b) The board of directors may authorize shares to be issued for consideration consisting of any tangible or intangible property or benefit to the corporation, including cash, promissory notes, services performed, contracts for services to be performed, or other securities of the corporation.

(c) Before the corporation issues shares, the board of directors must determine that the consideration received or to be received for shares to be issued is adequate. That determination by the board of directors is conclusive insofar as the adequacy of consideration for the issuance of shares relates to whether the shares are validly issued, fully paid, and nonassessable.

(d) When the corporation receives the consideration for which the board of directors authorized the issuance of shares, the shares issued therefor are fully paid and nonassessable.

(e) The corporation may place in escrow shares issued for a contract for future services or benefits or a promissory note, or make other arrangements to restrict the transfer of the shares, and may credit distributions in respect of the shares against their purchase price, until the services are performed, the note is paid, or the benefits received. If the services are not performed, the note is not paid, or the benefits are not received, the shares escrowed or restricted and the distributions credited may be cancelled in whole or part.

§ 6.22 Liability of Shareholders

(a) A purchaser from a corporation of its own shares is not liable to the corporation or its creditors with respect to the shares except to pay the consideration for which the shares were authorized to be issued (section 6.21) or specified in the subscription agreement (section 6.20).

(b) Unless otherwise provided in the articles of incorporation, a shareholder of a corporation is not personally liable for the acts or debts of the corporation except that he may become personally liable by reason of his own acts or conduct.

§ 6.23 Share Dividends

(a) Unless the articles of incorporation provide otherwise, shares may be issued pro rata and without consideration to the corporation's shareholders or to the shareholders of one or more classes or series. An issuance of shares under this subsection is a share dividend.

(b) Shares of one class or series may not be issued as a share dividend in respect of shares of another class or series unless (1) the articles of incorporation so authorize, (2) a majority of the votes entitled to be cast by the class or series to be issued approve the issue, or (3) there are no outstanding shares of the class or series to be issued.

(c) If the board of directors does not fix the record date for determining shareholders entitled to a share dividend, it is the date the board of directors authorizes the share dividend.

§ 6.24 Share Options

A corporation may issue rights, options, or warrants for the purchase of shares of the corporation. The board of directors shall determine the terms upon which the rights, options, or warrants are issued, their form and content, and the consideration for which the shares are to be issued.

§ 6.25 Form and Content of Certificates

(a) Shares may but need not be represented by certificates. Unless this Act or another statute expressly provides otherwise, the rights and obligations of shareholders are identical whether or not their shares are represented by certificates.

(b) At a minimum each share certificate must state on its face:

(1) the name of the issuing corporation and that it is organized under the law of this state;

(2) the name of the person to whom issued; and

(3) the number and class of shares and the designation of the series, if any, the certificate represents.

(c) If the issuing corporation is authorized to issue different classes of shares or different series within a class, the designations, relative rights, preferences, and limitations applicable to each class and the variations in rights, preferences, and limitations determined for each series (and the authority of the board of directors to determine variations for future series) must be summarized on the front or back of each certificate. Alternatively, each certificate may state conspicuously on its front or back that the corporation will furnish the shareholder this information on request in writing and without charge.

(d) Each share certificate (1) must be signed (either manually or in facsimile) by two officers designated in the bylaws or by the board of directors and (2) may bear the corporate seal or its facsimile.

(e) If the person who signed (either manually or in facsimile) a share certificate no longer holds office when the certificate is issued, the certificate is nevertheless valid.

§ 6.26 Shares Without Certificates

(a) Unless the articles of incorporation or bylaws provide otherwise, the board of directors of a corporation may authorize the issue of some or all of the shares of any or all of its classes or series without certificates. The authorization does not affect shares already represented by certificates until they are surrendered to the corporation.

(b) Within a reasonable time after the issue or transfer of shares without certificates, the corporation shall send the shareholder a written statement of the information required on certificates by section 6.25(b) and (c), and, if applicable, section 6.27.

§ 6.27 Restriction on Transfer or Registration of Shares and Other Securities

(a) The articles of incorporation, bylaws, an agreement among shareholders, or an agreement between shareholders and the corporation may impose restrictions on the transfer or registration of transfer of shares of the corporation. A restriction does not affect shares issued before the restriction was adopted unless the holders of the shares are parties to the restriction agreement or voted in favor of the restriction.

(b) A restriction on the transfer or registration of transfer of shares is valid and enforceable against the holder or a transferee of the holder if the restriction is authorized by this section and its existence is noted conspicuously on the front or back of the certificate or is contained in the information statement required by section 6.26(b). Unless so noted, a restriction is not enforceable against a person without knowledge of the restriction.

(c) A restriction on the transfer or registration of transfer of shares is authorized:

(1) to maintain the corporation's status when it is dependent on the number or identity of its shareholders;

(2) to preserve exemptions under federal or state securities law;

(3) for any other reasonable purpose.

(d) A restriction on the transfer or registration of transfer of shares may:

(1) obligate the shareholder first to offer the corporation or other persons (separately, consecutively, or simultaneously) an opportunity to acquire the restricted shares;

(2) obligate the corporation or other persons (separately, consecutively, or simultaneously) to acquire the restricted shares;

(3) require the corporation, the holders of any class of its shares, or another person to approve the transfer of the restricted shares, if the requirement is not manifestly unreasonable;

(4) prohibit the transfer of the restricted shares to designated persons or classes of persons, if the prohibition is not manifestly unreasonable.

(e) For purposes of this section, "shares" includes a security convertible into or carrying a right to subscribe for or acquire shares.

§ 6.28 Expense of Issue

A corporation may pay the expenses of selling or underwriting its shares, and of organizing or reorganizing the corporation, from the consideration received for shares.

SUBCHAPTER C. SUBSEQUENT ACQUISITION OF SHARES BY SHAREHOLDERS AND CORPORATION

§ 6.30 Shareholders' Preemptive Rights

(a) The shareholders of a corporation do not have a preemptive right to acquire the corporation's unissued shares except to the extent the articles of incorporation so provide.

(b) A statement included in the articles of incorporation that "the corporation elects to have preemptive rights" (or words of similar import) means that the following principles apply except to the extent the articles of incorporation expressly provide otherwise:

(1) The shareholders of the corporation have a preemptive right, granted on uniform terms and conditions prescribed by the board of directors to provide a fair and reasonable opportunity to exercise the right, to acquire proportional amounts of the corporation's unissued shares upon the decision of the board of directors to issue them.

(2) A shareholder may waive his preemptive right. A waiver evidenced by a writing is irrevocable even though it is not supported by consideration.

(3) There is no preemptive right with respect to:

(i) shares issued as compensation to directors, officers, agents, or employees of the corporation, its subsidiaries or affiliates;

(ii) shares issued to satisfy conversion or option rights created to provide compensation to directors, officers, agents, or employees of the corporation, its subsidiaries or affiliates;

(iii) shares authorized in articles of incorporation that are issued within six months from the effective date of incorporation;

(iv) shares sold otherwise than for money.

(4) Holders of shares of any class without general voting rights but with preferential rights to distributions or assets have no preemptive rights with respect to shares of any class.

(5) Holders of shares of any class with general voting rights but without preferential rights to distributions or assets have no preemptive rights with respect to shares of any class with preferential rights to distributions or assets unless the shares with preferential rights are convertible into or carry a right to subscribe for or acquire shares without preferential rights.

(6) Shares subject to preemptive rights that are not acquired by shareholders may be issued to any person for a period of one year after being offered to shareholders at a consideration set by the board of directors that is not lower than the consideration set for the exercise of preemptive rights. An offer at a lower consideration or after the expiration of one year is subject to the shareholders' preemptive rights.

(c) For purposes of this section, "shares" includes a security convertible into or carrying a right to subscribe for or acquire shares.

§ 6.31 Corporation's Acquisition of Its Own Shares

(a) A corporation may acquire its own shares and shares so acquired constitute authorized but unissued shares.

(b) If the articles of incorporation prohibit the reissue of acquired shares, the number of authorized shares is reduced by the number of shares acquired, effective upon amendment of the articles of incorporation.

(c) Articles of amendment may be adopted by the board of directors without shareholder action, shall be delivered to the secretary of state for filing, and shall set forth:

(1) the name of the corporation;

(2) the reduction in the number of authorized shares, itemized by class and series; and

(3) the total number of authorized shares, itemized by class and series, remaining after reduction of the shares.

SUBCHAPTER D. DISTRIBUTIONS

§ 6.40 Distributions to Shareholders

(a) A board of directors may authorize and the corporation may make distributions to its shareholders subject to restriction by the articles of incorporation and the limitation in subsection (c).

(b) If the board of directors does not fix the record date for determining shareholders entitled to a distribution (other than one involving a repurchase or reacquisition of shares), it is the date the board of directors authorizes the distribution.

(c) No distribution may be made if, after giving it effect:

(1) the corporation would not be able to pay its debts as they become due in the usual course of business; or

(2) the corporation's total assets would be less than the sum of its total liabilities plus (unless the articles of incorporation permit otherwise) the amount that would be needed, if the corporation were to be dissolved at the time of the distribution, to satisfy the preferential rights upon dissolution of shareholders whose preferential rights are superior to those receiving the distribution.

(d) The board of directors may base a determination that a distribution is not prohibited under subsection (c) either on financial statements prepared on the basis of accounting practices and principles that are reasonable in the circumstances or on a fair valuation or other method that is reasonable in the circumstances.

(e) The effect of a distribution under subsection (c) is measured:

(1) in the case of distribution by purchase, redemption, or other acquisition of the corporation's shares, as of the earlier of (i) the date money or other property is transferred or debt incurred by the corporation or (ii) the date the shareholder ceases to be a shareholder with respect to the acquired shares;

(2) in the case of any other distribution of indebtedness, as of the date the indebtedness is distributed;

(3) in all other cases, as of (i) the date the distribution is authorized if the payment occurs within 120 days after the date of authorization or (ii) the date the payment is made if it occurs more than 120 days after the date of authorization.

(f) A corporation's indebtedness to a shareholder incurred by reason of a distribution made in accordance with this section is at parity with the corporation's indebtedness to its general, unsecured creditors except to the extent subordinated by agreement.

CHAPTER 7. SHAREHOLDERS

SUBCHAPTER A. MEETINGS

§ 7.01 Annual Meeting

(a) A corporation shall hold annually at a time stated in or fixed in accordance with the bylaws a meeting of shareholders.

(b) Annual shareholders' meetings may be held in or out of this state at the place stated in or fixed in accordance with the bylaws. If no place is stated in or fixed in accordance with the bylaws, annual meetings shall be held at the corporation's principal office.

(c) The failure to hold an annual meeting at the time stated in or fixed in accordance with a corporation's bylaws does not affect the validity of any corporate action.

§ 7.02 Special Meeting

(a) A corporation shall hold a special meeting of shareholders:

(1) on call of its board of directors or the person or persons authorized to do so by the articles of incorporation or bylaws; or

(2) if the holders of at least 10 percent of all the votes entitled to be cast on any issue proposed to be considered at the proposed special meeting sign, date, and deliver to the corporation's secretary one or more written demands for the meeting describing the purpose or purposes for which it is to be held.

(b) If not otherwise fixed under sections 7.03 or 7.07, the record date for determining shareholders entitled to demand a special meeting is the date the first shareholder signs the demand.

(c) Special shareholders' meetings may be held in or out of this state at the place stated in or fixed in accordance with the bylaws. If no place is stated or fixed in accordance with the bylaws, special meetings shall be held at the corporation's principal office.

(d) Only business within the purpose or purposes described in the meeting notice required by section 7.05(c) may be conducted at a special shareholders' meeting.

§ 7.03 Court-Ordered Meeting

(a) The [name or describe] court of the county where a corporation's principal office (or, if none in this state, its registered office) is located may summarily order a meeting to be held:

(1) on application of any shareholder of the corporation entitled to participate in an annual meeting if an annual meeting was not held within the earlier of 6 months after the end of the corporation's fiscal year or 15 months after its last annual meeting; or

(2) on application of a shareholder who signed a demand for a special meeting valid under section 7.02 if:

(i) notice of the special meeting was not given within 30 days after the date the demand was delivered to the corporation's secretary; or

(ii) the special meeting was not held in accordance with the notice.

(b) The court may fix the time and place of the meeting, determine the shares entitled to participate in the meeting, specify a record date for determining shareholders entitled to notice of and to vote at the meeting, prescribe the form and content of the meeting notice, fix the quorum required for specific matters to be considered at the meeting (or direct that the votes represented at the meeting constitute a quorum for action on those matters), and enter other orders necessary to accomplish the purpose or purposes of the meeting.

§ 7.04 Action Without Meeting

(a) Action required or permitted by this Act to be taken at a shareholders' meeting may be taken without a meeting if the action is taken by all the shareholders entitled to vote on the action. The action must be evidenced by one or more written consents describing the action taken, signed by all the shareholders entitled to vote on the action, and delivered to the corporation for inclusion in the minutes or filing with the corporate records.

(b) If not otherwise determined under sections 7.03 or 7.07, the record date for determining shareholders entitled to take action without a meeting is the date the first shareholder signs the consent under subsection (a).

(c) A consent signed under this section has the effect of a meeting vote and may be described as such in any document.

(d) If this Act requires that notice of proposed action be given to nonvoting shareholders and the action is to be taken by unanimous consent of the voting shareholders, the corporation must give its nonvoting shareholders written notice of the proposed action at least 10 days before the action is taken. The notice must contain or be accompanied by the same material that, under this Act, would have been required to be sent to nonvoting shareholders in a notice of meeting at which the proposed action would have been submitted to the shareholders for action.

§ 7.05 Notice of Meeting

(a) A corporation shall notify shareholders of the date, time, and place of each annual and special shareholders' meeting no fewer than 10 nor more than 60 days before the meeting date. Unless this Act or the articles of incorporation require otherwise, the corporation is required to give notice only to shareholders entitled to vote at the meeting.

(b) Unless this Act or the articles of incorporation require otherwise, notice of an annual meeting need not include a description of the purpose or purposes for which the meeting is called.

(c) Notice of a special meeting must include a description of the purpose or purposes for which the meeting is called.

(d) If not otherwise fixed under sections 7.03 or 7.07, the record date for determining shareholders entitled to notice of and to vote at an annual or special shareholders' meeting is the day before the first notice is delivered to shareholders.

(e) Unless the bylaws require otherwise, if an annual or special shareholders' meeting is adjourned to a different date, time, or place, notice need not be given of the new date, time, or place if the new date, time, or place is announced at the meeting before adjournment. If a new record date for the adjourned meeting is or must be fixed under section 7.07, however, notice of the adjourned meeting must be given under this section to persons who are shareholders as of the new record date.

§ 7.06 Waiver of Notice

(a) A shareholder may waive any notice required by this Act, the articles of incorporation, or bylaws before or after the date and time stated in the notice. The waiver must be in writing, be signed by the shareholder entitled to the notice, and be delivered to the corporation for inclusion in the minutes or filing with the corporate records.

(b) A shareholder's attendance at a meeting:

(1) waives objection to lack of notice or defective notice of the meeting, unless the shareholder at the beginning of the meeting objects to holding the meeting or transacting business at the meeting;

(2) waives objection to consideration of a particular matter at the meeting that is not within the purpose or purposes described in the meeting notice, unless the shareholder objects to considering the matter when it is presented.

§ 7.07 Record Date

(a) The bylaws may fix or provide the manner of fixing the record date for one or more voting groups in order to determine the shareholders entitled to notice of a shareholders' meeting, to demand a special meeting, to vote, or to take any other action. If the bylaws do not fix or provide for fixing a record date, the board of directors of the corporation may fix a future date as the record date.

(b) A record date fixed under this section may not be more than 70 days before the meeting or action requiring a determination of shareholders.

(c) A determination of shareholders entitled to notice of or to vote at a shareholders' meeting is effective for any adjournment of the meeting unless the board of directors fixes a new record date, which it must do if the meeting is adjourned to a date more than 120 days after the date fixed for the original meeting.

(d) If a court orders a meeting adjourned to a date more than 120 days after the date fixed for the original meeting, it may provide that the original record date continues in effect or it may fix a new record date.

SUBCHAPTER B. VOTING

§ 7.20 Shareholders' List for Meeting

(a) After fixing a record date for a meeting, a corporation shall prepare an alphabetical list of the names of all its shareholders who are entitled to notice of a shareholders' meeting. The list must be arranged by voting group (and within each voting group by class or series of shares) and show the address of and number of shares held by each shareholder.

(b) The shareholders' list must be available for inspection by any shareholder, beginning two business days after notice of the meeting is given for which the list was prepared and continuing through the meeting, at the corporation's principal office or at a place identified in the meeting notice in the city where the meeting will be held. A shareholder, his agent, or attorney is entitled on written demand to inspect and, subject to the requirements of section 16.02(c), to copy the list, during regular business hours and at his expense, during the period it is available for inspection.

(c) The corporation shall make the shareholders' list available at the meeting, and any shareholder, his agent, or attorney is entitled to inspect the list at any time during the meeting or any adjournment.

(d) If the corporation refuses to allow a shareholder, his agent, or attorney to inspect the shareholders' list before or at the meeting (or copy the list as permitted by subsection (b)), the [name or describe] court of the county where a corporation's principal office (or, if none in this state, its registered office) is located, on application of the shareholder, may summarily order the inspection or copying at the corporation's expense and may postpone the meeting for which the list was prepared until the inspection or copying is complete.

(e) Refusal or failure to prepare or make available the shareholders' list does not affect the validity of action taken at the meeting.

§ 7.21 Voting Entitlement of Shares

(a) Except as provided in subsections (b) and (c) or unless the articles of incorporation provide otherwise, each outstanding share, regardless of class, is entitled to one vote on each matter voted on at a shareholders' meeting. Only shares are entitled to vote.

(b) Absent special circumstances, the shares of a corporation are not entitled to vote if they are owned, directly or indirectly, by a second corporation, domestic or foreign, and the first corporation owns, directly or indirectly, a majority of the shares entitled to vote for directors of the second corporation.

(c) Subsection (b) does not limit the power of a corporation to vote any shares, including its own shares, held by it in a fiduciary capacity.

(d) Redeemable shares are not entitled to vote after notice of redemption is mailed to the holders and a sum sufficient to redeem the shares has been deposited with a bank, trust company, or other financial institution under an irrevocable obligation to pay the holders the redemption price on surrender of the shares.

§ 7.22 Proxies

(a) A shareholder may vote his shares in person or by proxy.

(b) A shareholder may appoint a proxy to vote or otherwise act for him by signing an appointment form, either personally or by his attorney-in-fact.

(c) An appointment of a proxy is effective when received by the secretary or other officer or agent authorized to tabulate votes. An appointment is valid for 11 months unless a longer period is expressly provided in the appointment form.

(d) An appointment of a proxy is revocable by the shareholder unless the appointment form conspicuously states that it is irrevocable and the appointment is coupled with an interest. Appointments coupled with an interest include the appointment of:

(1) a pledgee;

(2) a person who purchased or agreed to purchase the shares;

(3) a creditor of the corporation who extended it credit under terms requiring the appointment;

(4) an employee of the corporation whose employment contract requires the appointment; or

(5) a party to a voting agreement created under section 7.31.

(e) The death or incapacity of the shareholder appointing a proxy does not affect the right of the corporation to accept the proxy's authority unless notice of the death or incapacity is received by the secretary or other officer or agent authorized to tabulate votes before the proxy exercises his authority under the appointment.

(f) An appointment made irrevocable under subsection (d) is revoked when the interest with which it is coupled is extinguished.

(g) A transferee for value of shares subject to an irrevocable appointment may revoke the appointment if he did not know of its existence when he acquired the shares and the existence of the irrevocable appointment was not noted conspicuously on the certificate representing the shares or on the information statement for shares without certificates.

(h) Subject to section 7.24 and to any express limitation on the proxy's authority appearing on the face of the appointment form, a corporation is entitled to accept the proxy's vote or other action as that of the shareholder making the appointment.

§ 7.23 Shares Held by Nominees

(a) A corporation may establish a procedure by which the beneficial owner of shares that are registered in the name of a nominee is recognized by the corporation as the shareholder. The extent of this recognition may be determined in the procedure.

(b) The procedure may set forth:

(1) the types of nominees to which it applies;

(2) the rights or privileges that the corporation recognizes in a beneficial owner;

(3) the manner in which the procedure is selected by the nominee;

(4) the information that must be provided when the procedure is selected;

(5) the period for which selection of the procedure is effective; and

(6) other aspects of the rights and duties created.

§ 7.24 Corporation's Acceptance of Votes

(a) If the name signed on a vote, consent, waiver, or proxy appointment corresponds to the name of a shareholder, the corporation if acting in good faith is entitled to accept the vote, consent, waiver, or proxy appointment and give it effect as the act of the shareholder.

(b) If the name signed on a vote, consent, waiver, or proxy appointment does not correspond to the name of its shareholder, the corporation if acting in good faith is nevertheless entitled to accept the vote, consent, waiver, or proxy appointment and give it effect as the act of the shareholder if:

(1) the shareholder is an entity and the name signed purports to be that of an officer or agent of the entity;

(2) the name signed purports to be that of an administrator, executor, guardian, or conservator representing the shareholder and, if the corporation requests, evidence of fiduciary status acceptable to the corporation has been presented with respect to the vote, consent, waiver, or proxy appointment;

(3) the name signed purports to be that of a receiver or trustee in bankruptcy of the shareholder and, if the corporation requests, evidence of this status acceptable to the corporation has been presented with respect to the vote, consent, waiver, or proxy appointment;

(4) the name signed purports to be that of a pledgee, beneficial owner, or attorney-in-fact of the shareholder and, if the corporation requests, evidence acceptable to the corporation of the signatory's authority to sign for the shareholder has been presented with respect to the vote, consent, waiver, or proxy appointment;

(5) two or more persons are the shareholder as cotenants or fiduciaries and the name signed purports to be the name of at least one of the coowners and the person signing appears to be acting on behalf of all the coowners.

(c) The corporation is entitled to reject a vote, consent, waiver, or proxy appointment if the secretary or other officer or agent authorized to tabulate votes, acting in good faith, has reasonable basis for doubt about the validity of the signature on it or about the signatory's authority to sign for the shareholder.

(d) The corporation and its officer or agent who accepts or rejects a vote, consent, waiver, or proxy appointment in good faith and in accordance with the standards of this section are not liable in damages to the shareholder for the consequences of the acceptance or rejection.

(e) Corporate action based on the acceptance or rejection of a vote, consent, waiver, or proxy appointment under this section is valid unless a court of competent jurisdiction determines otherwise.

§ 7.25 Quorum and Voting Requirements for Voting Groups

(a) Shares entitled to vote as a separate voting group may take action on a matter at a meeting only if a quorum of those shares exists with respect to that matter. Unless the articles of incorporation or this Act provide otherwise, a majority of the votes entitled to be cast on the matter by the voting group constitutes a quorum of that voting group for action on that matter.

(b) Once a share is represented for any purpose at a meeting, it is deemed present for quorum purposes for the remainder of the meeting and for any adjournment of that meeting unless a new record date is or must be set for that adjourned meeting.

(c) If a quorum exists, action on a matter (other than the election of directors) by a voting group is approved if the votes cast within the voting group favoring the action exceed the votes cast opposing the action, unless the articles of incorporation or this Act require a greater number of affirmative votes.

(d) An amendment of articles of incorporation adding, changing, or deleting a quorum or voting requirement for a voting group greater than specified in subsection (b) or (c) is governed by section 7.27.

(e) The election of directors is governed by section 7.28.

§ 7.26 Action by Single and Multiple Voting Groups

(a) If the articles of incorporation or this Act provide for voting by a single voting group on a matter, action on that matter is taken when voted upon by that voting group as provided in section 7.25.

(b) If the articles of incorporation or this Act provide for voting by two or more voting groups on a matter, action on that matter is taken only when voted upon by each of those voting groups counted separately as provided in section 7.25. Action may be taken by one voting group on a matter even though no action is taken by another voting group entitled to vote on the matter.

§ 7.27 Greater Quorum or Voting Requirements

(a) The articles of incorporation may provide for a greater quorum or voting requirement for shareholders (or voting groups of shareholders) than is provided for by this Act.

(b) An amendment to the articles of incorporation that adds, changes, or deletes a greater quorum or voting requirement must meet the same quorum requirement and be adopted by the same vote and voting groups required to take action under the quorum and voting requirements then in effect or proposed to be adopted, whichever is greater.

§ 7.28 Voting for Directors; Cumulative Voting

(a) Unless otherwise provided in the articles of incorporation, directors are elected by a plurality of the votes cast by the shares entitled to vote in the election at a meeting at which a quorum is present.

(b) Shareholders do not have a right to cumulate their votes for directors unless the articles of incorporation so provide.

(c) A statement included in the articles of incorporation that "[all] [a designated voting group of] shareholders are entitled to cumulate their votes for directors" (or words of similar import) means that the shareholders designated are entitled to multiply the number of votes they are entitled to cast by the number of directors for whom they are entitled to vote and cast the product for a single candidate or distribute the product among two or more candidates.

(d) Shares otherwise entitled to vote cumulatively may not be voted cumulatively at a particular meeting unless:

(1) the meeting notice or proxy statement accompanying the notice states conspicuously that cumulative voting is authorized; or

(2) a shareholder who has the right to cumulate his votes gives notice to the corporation not less than 48 hours before the time set for the meeting of his intent to cumulate his votes during the meeting, and if one shareholder gives this notice all other shareholders in the same voting group participating in the election are entitled to cumulate their votes without giving further notice.

SUBCHAPTER C. VOTING TRUSTS AND AGREEMENTS

§ 7.30 Voting Trusts

(a) One or more shareholders may create a voting trust, conferring on a trustee the right to vote or otherwise act for them, by signing an agreement setting out the provisions of the trust (which may include anything consistent with its purpose) and transferring their shares to the trustee. When a voting trust agreement is signed, the trustee shall prepare a list of the names and addresses of all owners of beneficial interests in the trust, together with the number and class of shares each transferred to the trust, and deliver copies of the list and agreement to the corporation's principal office.

(b) A voting trust becomes effective on the date the first shares subject to the trust are registered in the trustee's name. A voting trust is valid for not more than 10 years after its effective date unless extended under subsection (c).

(c) All or some of the parties to a voting trust may extend it for additional terms of not more than 10 years each by signing an extension agreement and obtaining the voting trustee's written consent to the extension. An extension is valid for 10 years from the date the first shareholder signs the extension agreement. The voting trustee must deliver copies of the extension agreement and list of beneficial owners to the corporation's principal office. An extension agreement binds only those parties signing it.

§ 7.31 Voting Agreements

(a) Two or more shareholders may provide for the manner in which they will vote their shares by signing an agreement for that purpose. A voting agreement created under this section is not subject to the provisions of section 7.30.

(b) A voting agreement created under this section is specifically enforceable.

SUBCHAPTER D. DERIVATIVE PROCEEDINGS

§ 7.40 Procedure in Derivative Proceedings

(a) A person may not commence a proceeding in the right of a domestic or foreign corporation unless he was a shareholder of the corporation when the transaction complained of occurred or unless he became a shareholder through transfer by operation of law from one who was a shareholder at that time.

(b) A complaint in a proceeding brought in the right of a corporation must be verified and allege with particularity the demand made, if any, to obtain action by the board of directors and either that the demand was refused or ignored or why he did not make the demand. Whether or not a demand for action was made, if the corporation commences an investigation of the changes made in the demand or complaint, the court may stay any proceeding until the investigation is completed.

(c) A proceeding commenced under this section may not be discontinued or settled without the court's approval. If the court determines that a proposed discontinuance or settlement will substantially affect the interest of the corporation's shareholders or a class of shareholders, the court shall direct that notice be given the shareholders affected.

(d) On termination of the proceeding the court may require the plaintiff to pay any defendant's reasonable expenses (including counsel fees) incurred in defending the proceeding if it finds that the proceeding was commenced without reasonable cause.

(e) For purposes of this section, "shareholder" includes a beneficial owner whose shares are held in a voting trust or held by a nominee on his behalf.

CHAPTER 8. DIRECTORS AND OFFICERS

SUBCHAPTER A. BOARD OF DIRECTORS

§ 8.01 Requirement for and Duties of Board of Directors

(a) Except as provided in subsection (c), each corporation must have a board of directors.

(b) All corporate powers shall be exercised by or under the authority of, and the business and affairs of the corporation managed under the direction of, its board of directors, subject to any limitation set forth in the articles of incorporation.

(c) A corporation having 50 or fewer shareholders may dispense with or limit the authority of a board of directors by describing in its articles of incorporation who will perform some or all of the duties of a board of directors.

§ 8.02 Qualifications of Directors

The articles of incorporation or bylaws may prescribe qualifications for directors. A director need not be a resident of this state or a shareholder of the corporation unless the articles of incorporation or bylaws so prescribe.

§ 8.03 Number and Election of Directors

(a) A board of directors must consist of one or more individuals, with the number specified in or fixed in accordance with the articles of incorporation or bylaws.

(b) If a board of directors has power to fix or change the number of directors, the board may increase or decrease by 30 percent or less the number of directors last approved by the shareholders, but only the shareholders may increase or decrease by more than 30 percent the number of directors last approved by the shareholders.

(c) The articles of incorporation or bylaws may establish a variable range for the size of the board of directors by fixing a minimum and maximum number of directors. If a variable range is established, the number of directors may be fixed or changed from time to time, within the minimum and maximum, by the shareholders or the board of directors. After shares are issued, only the shareholders may change the range for the size of the board or change from a fixed to a variable-range size board or vice versa.

(d) Directors are elected at the first annual shareholders' meeting and at each annual meeting thereafter unless their terms are staggered under section 8.06.

§ 8.04 Election of Directors by Certain Classes of Shareholders

If the articles of incorporation authorize dividing the shares into classes, the articles may also authorize the election of all or a specified number of directors by the holders of one or more authorized classes of shares. Each class (or classes) of shares entitled to elect one or more directors is a separate voting group for purposes of the election of directors.

§ 8.05 Terms of Directors Generally

(a) The terms of the initial directors of a corporation expire at the first shareholders' meeting at which directors are elected.

(b) The terms of all other directors expire at the next annual shareholders' meeting following their election unless their terms are staggered under section 8.06.

(c) A decrease in the number of directors does not shorten an incumbent director's term.

(d) The term of a director elected to fill a vacancy expires at the next shareholders' meeting at which directors are elected.

(e) Despite the expiration of a director's term, he continues to serve until his successor is elected and qualifies or until there is a decrease in the number of directors.

§ 8.06 Staggered Terms for Directors

If there are nine or more directors, the articles of incorporation may provide for staggering their terms by dividing the total number of directors into two or three groups, with each group containing one-half or one-third of the total, as near as may be. In that event, the terms of directors in the first group expire at the first annual shareholders' meeting after their election, the terms of the second group expire at the second annual shareholders' meeting after their election, and the terms of the third group, if any, expire at the third annual shareholders' meeting after their election. At each annual shareholders' meeting held thereafter, directors shall be chosen for a term of two years or three years, as the case may be, to succeed those whose terms expire.

§ 8.07 Resignation of Directors

(a) A director may resign at any time by delivering written notice to the board of directors, its chairman, or to the corporation.

(b) A resignation is effective when the notice is delivered unless the notice specifies a later effective date.

§ 8.08 Removal of Directors by Shareholders

(a) The shareholders may remove one or more directors with or without cause unless the articles of incorporation provide that directors may be removed only for cause.

(b) If a director is elected by a voting group of shareholders, only the shareholders of that voting group may participate in the vote to remove him.

(c) If cumulative voting is authorized, a director may not be removed if the number of votes sufficient to elect him under cumulative voting is voted against his removal. If cumulative voting is not authorized, a director may be removed only if the number of votes cast to remove him exceeds the number of votes cast not to remove him.

(d) A director may be removed by the shareholders only at a meeting called for the purpose of removing him and the meeting notice must state that the purpose, or one of the purposes, of the meeting is removal of the director.

§ 8.09 Removal of Directors by Judicial Proceeding

(a) The [name or describe] court of the county where a corporation's principal office (or, if none in this state, its registered office) is located may remove a director of the corporation from office in a proceeding commenced either by the corporation or by its shareholders holding at least 10 percent of the outstanding shares of any class if the court finds that (1) the director engaged in fraudulent or dishonest conduct, or gross abuse of authority or discretion, with respect to the corporation and (2) removal is in the best interest of the corporation.

(b) The court that removes a director may bar the director from reelection for a period prescribed by the court.

(c) If shareholders commence a proceeding under subsection (a), they shall make the corporation a party defendant.

§ 8.10 Vacancy on Board

(a) Unless the articles of incorporation provide otherwise, if a vacancy occurs on a board of directors, including a vacancy resulting from an increase in the number of directors:

(1) the shareholders may fill the vacancy;

(2) the board of directors may fill the vacancy; or

(3) if the directors remaining in office constitute fewer than a quorum of the board, they may fill the vacancy by the affirmative vote of a majority of all the directors remaining in office.

(b) If the vacant office was held by a director elected by a voting group of shareholders, only the holders of shares of that voting group are entitled to vote to fill the vacancy if it is filled by the shareholders.

(c) A vacancy that will occur at a specific later date (by reason of a resignation effective at a later date under section 8.07(b) or otherwise) may be filled before the vacancy occurs but the new director may not take office until the vacancy occurs.

§ 8.11 Compensation of Directors

Unless the articles of incorporation or bylaws provide otherwise, the board of directors may fix the compensation of directors.

SUBCHAPTER B. MEETINGS AND ACTION OF THE BOARD

§ 8.20 Meetings

(a) The board of directors may hold regular or special meetings in or out of this state.

(b) Unless the articles of incorporation or bylaws provide otherwise, the board of directors may permit any or all directors to participate in a regular or special meeting by, or conduct the meeting through the use of, any means of communication by which all directors participating may simultaneously hear each other during the meeting. A director participating in a meeting by this means is deemed to be present in person at the meeting.

§ 8.21 Action Without Meeting

(a) Unless the articles of incorporation or bylaws provide otherwise, action required or permitted by this Act to be taken at a board of directors' meeting may be taken without a meeting if the action is taken by all members of the board. The action must be evidenced by one or more written consents describing the action taken, signed by each director, and included in the minutes or filed with the corporate records reflecting the action taken.

(b) Action taken under this section is effective when the last director signs the consent, unless the consent specifies a different effective date.

(c) A consent signed under this section has the effect of a meeting vote and may be described as such in any document.

§ 8.22 Notice of Meeting

(a) Unless the articles of incorporation or bylaws provide otherwise, regular meetings of the board of directors may be held without notice of the date, time, place, or purpose of the meeting.

(b) Unless the articles of incorporation or bylaws provide for a longer or shorter period, special meetings of the board of directors must be preceded by at least two days' notice of the date, time, and place of the meeting. The notice need not describe the purpose of the special meeting unless required by the articles of incorporation or bylaws.

§ 8.23 Waiver of Notice

(a) A director may waive any notice required by this Act, the articles of incorporation, or bylaws before or after the date and time stated in the notice. Except as provided by subsection (b), the waiver must be in writing, signed by the director entitled to the notice, and filed with the minutes or corporate records.

(b) A director's attendance at or participation in a meeting waives any required notice to him of the meeting unless the director at the beginning of the meeting (or promptly upon his arrival) objects to holding the meeting or transacting business at the meeting and does not thereafter vote for or assent to action taken at the meeting.

§ 8.24 Quorum and Voting

(a) Unless the articles of incorporation or bylaws require a greater number, a quorum of a board of directors consists of:

(1) a majority of the fixed number of directors if the corporation has a fixed board size; or

(2) a majority of the number of directors prescribed, or if no number is prescribed the number in office immediately before the meeting begins, if the corporation has a variable-range size board.

(b) The articles of incorporation or bylaws may authorize a quorum of a board of directors to consist of no fewer than one-third of the fixed or prescribed number of directors determined under subsection (a).

(c) If a quorum is present when a vote is taken, the affirmative vote of a majority of directors present is the act of the board of directors unless the articles of incorporation or bylaws require the vote of a greater number of directors.

(d) A director who is present at a meeting of the board of directors or a committee of the board of directors when corporate action is taken is deemed to have assented to the action taken unless: (1) he objects at the beginning of the meeting (or promptly upon his arrival) to holding it or transacting business at the meeting; (2) his dissent or abstention from the action taken is entered in the minutes of the meeting; or (3) he delivers written notice of his dissent or abstention to the presiding officer of the meeting before its adjournment or to the corporation immediately after adjournment of the meeting. The right of dissent or abstention is not available to a director who votes in favor of the action taken.

§ 8.25 Committees

(a) Unless the articles of incorporation or bylaws provide otherwise, a board of directors may create one or more committees and appoint members of the board of directors to serve on them. Each committee may have two or more members, who serve at the pleasure of the board of directors.

(b) The creation of a committee and appointment of members to it must be approved by the greater of (1) a majority of all the directors in office when the action is taken or (2) the number of directors required by the articles of incorporation or bylaws to take action under section 8.24.

(c) Sections 8.20 through 8.24, which govern meetings, action without meetings, notice and waiver of notice, and quorum and voting requirements of the board of directors, apply to committees and their members as well.

(d) To the extent specified by the board of directors or in the articles of incorporation or bylaws, each committee may exercise the authority of the board of directors under section 8.01.

(e) A committee may not, however:

(1) authorize distributions;

(2) approve or propose to shareholders action that this Act requires to be approved by shareholders;

(3) fill vacancies on the board of directors or on any of its committees;

(4) amend articles of incorporation pursuant to section 10.02;

(5) adopt, amend, or repeal bylaws;

(6) approve a plan of merger not requiring shareholder approval;

(7) authorize or approve reacquisition of shares, except according to a formula or method prescribed by the board of directors; or

(8) authorize or approve the issuance or sale or contract for sale of shares, or determine the designation and relative rights, preferences, and limitations of a class or series of shares, except that the board of directors may authorize a committee (or a senior executive officer of the corporation) to do so within limits specifically prescribed by the board of directors.

(f) The creation of, delegation of authority to, or action by a committee does not alone constitute compliance by a director with the standards of conduct described in section 8.30.

SUBCHAPTER C. STANDARDS OF CONDUCT

§ 8.30 General Standards for Directors

(a) A director shall discharge his duties as a director, including his duties as a member of a committee:

(1) in good faith;

(2) with the care an ordinarily prudent person in a like position would exercise under similar circumstances; and

(3) in a manner he reasonably believes to be in the best interests of the corporation.

(b) In discharging his duties a director is entitled to rely on information, opinions, reports, or statements, including financial statements and other financial data, if prepared or presented by:

(1) one or more officers or employees of the corporation whom the director reasonably believes to be reliable and competent in the matters presented;

(2) legal counsel, public accountants, or other persons as to matters the director reasonably believes are within the person's professional or expert competence; or

(3) a committee of the board of directors of which he is not a member if the director reasonably believes the committee merits confidence.

(c) A director is not acting in good faith if he has knowledge concerning the matter in question that makes reliance otherwise permitted by subsection (b) unwarranted.

(d) A director is not liable for any action taken as a director, or any failure to take any action, if he performed the duties of his office in compliance with this section.

§ 8.31 Director Conflict of Interest

(a) A conflict of interest transaction is a transaction with the corporation in which a director of the corporation has a direct or indirect interest. A conflict of interest transaction is not voidable by the corporation solely because of the director's interest in the transaction if any one of the following is true:

(1) the material facts of the transaction and the director's interest were disclosed or known to the board of directors or a committee of the board of directors and the board of directors or committee authorized, approved, or ratified the transaction;

(2) the material facts of the transaction and the director's interest were disclosed or known to the shareholders entitled to vote and they authorized, approved, or ratified the transaction; or

(3) the transaction was fair to the corporation.

(b) For purposes of this section, a director of the corporation has an indirect interest in a transaction if (1) another entity in which he has a material financial interest or in which he is a general partner is a party to the transaction or (2) another entity of which he is a director, officer, or trustee is a party to the transaction and the transaction is or should be considered by the board of directors of the corporation.

(c) For purposes of subsection (a)(1), a conflict of interest transaction is authorized, approved, or ratified if it receives the affirmative vote of a majority of the directors on the board of directors (or on the committee) who have no direct or indirect interest in the transaction, but a transaction may not be authorized, approved, or ratified under this section by a single director. If a majority of the directors who have no direct or indirect interest in the transaction vote to authorize, approve, or ratify the transaction, a quorum is present for the purpose of taking action under this section. The presence of, or a vote cast by, a director with a direct or indirect interest in the transaction does not affect the validity of any action taken under subsection (a)(1) if the transaction is otherwise authorized, approved, or ratified as provided in that subsection.

(d) For purposes of subsection (a)(2), a conflict of interest transaction is authorized, approved, or ratified if it receives the vote of a majority of the shares entitled to be counted under this subsection. Shares owned by or voted under the control of a director who has a direct or indirect interest in the transaction, and shares owned by or voted under the control of an entity described in subsection (b)(1), may not be counted in a vote of shareholders to determine whether to authorize, approve, or ratify a conflict of interest transaction under subsection (a)(2). The vote of those shares, however, shall be counted in determining whether the transaction is approved under other sections of this Act. A majority of the shares, whether or not present, that are entitled to be counted in a vote on the transaction under this subsection constitutes a quorum for the purpose of taking action under this section.

§ 8.32 Loans to Directors

(a) Except as provided by subsection (c), a corporation may not lend money to or guarantee the obligation of a director of the corporation unless:

(1) the particular loan or guarantee is approved by a majority of the votes represented by the outstanding voting shares of all classes, voting as a single voting group, except the votes of shares owned by or voted under the control of the benefited director; or

(2) the corporation's board of directors determines that the loan or guarantee benefits the corporation and either approves the specific loan or guarantee or a general plan authorizing loans and guarantees.

(b) The fact that a loan or guarantee is made in violation of this section does not affect the borrower's liability on the loan.

(c) This section does not apply to loans and guarantees authorized by statute regulating any special class of corporations.

§ 8.33 Liability for Unlawful Distributions

(a) Unless he complies with the applicable standards of conduct described in section 8.30, a director who votes for or assents to a distribution made in violation of this Act or the articles of incorporation is personally liable to the corporation for the amount of the distribution that exceeds what could have been distributed without violating this Act or the articles of incorporation.

(b) A director held liable for an unlawful distribution under subsection (a) is entitled to contribution:

(1) from every other director who voted for or assented to the distribution without complying with the applicable standards of conduct described in section 8.30; and

(2) from each shareholder for the amount the shareholder accepted knowing the distribution was made in violation of this Act or the articles of incorporation.

SUBCHAPTER D. OFFICERS

§ 8.40 Required Officers

(a) A corporation has the officers described in its bylaws or appointed by the board of directors in accordance with the bylaws.

(b) A duly appointed officer may appoint one or more officers or assistant officers if authorized by the bylaws or the board of directors.

(c) The bylaws or the board of directors shall delegate to one of the officers responsibility for preparing minutes of the directors' and shareholders' meetings and for authenticating records of the corporation.

(d) The same individual may simultaneously hold more than one office in a corporation.

§ 8.41 Duties of Officers

Each officer has the authority and shall perform the duties set forth in the bylaws or, to the extent consistent with the bylaws, the duties prescribed by the board of directors or by direction of an officer authorized by the board of directors to prescribe the duties of other officers.

§ 8.42 Standards of Conduct for Officers

(a) An officer with discretionary authority shall discharge his duties under that authority:

(1) in good faith;

(2) with the care an ordinarily prudent person in a like position would exercise under similar circumstances; and

(3) in a manner he reasonably believes to be in the best interests of the corporation.

(b) In discharging his duties an officer is entitled to rely on information, opinions, reports, or statements, including financial statements and other financial data, if prepared or presented by:

(1) one or more officers or employees of the corporation whom the officer reasonably believes to be reliable and competent in the matters presented; or

(2) legal counsel, public accountants, or other persons as to matters the officer reasonably believes are within the person's professional or expert competence.

(c) An officer is not acting in good faith if he has knowledge concerning the matter in question that makes reliance otherwise permitted by subsection (b) unwarranted.

(d) An officer is not liable for any action taken as an officer, or any failure to take any action, if he performed the duties of his office in compliance with this section.

§ 8.43 Resignation and Removal of Officers

(a) An officer may resign at any time by delivering notice to the corporation. A resignation is effective when the notice is delivered unless the notice specifies a later effective date. If a resignation is made effective at a later date and the corporation accepts the future effective date, its board of directors may fill the pending vacancy before the effective date if the board of directors provides that the successor does not take office until the effective date.

(b) A board of directors may remove any officer at any time with or without cause.

§ 8.44 Contract Rights of Officers

(a) The appointment of an officer does not itself create contract rights.

(b) An officer's removal does not affect the officer's contract rights, if any, with the corporation. An officer's resignation does not affect the corporation's contract rights, if any, with the officer.

SUBCHAPTER E. INDEMNIFICATION

§ 8.50 Subchapter Definitions

In this subchapter:

(1) "Corporation" includes any domestic or foreign predecessor entity of a corporation in a merger or other transaction in which the predecessor's existence ceased upon consummation of the transaction.

(2) "Director" means an individual who is or was a director of a corporation or an individual who, while a director of a corporation, is or was serving at the corporation's request as a director, officer, partner, trustee, employee, or agent of another foreign or domestic corporation, partnership, joint venture, trust, employee benefit plan, or other enterprise. A director is considered to be serving an employee benefit plan at the corporation's request if his duties to the corporation also impose duties on, or otherwise involve services by,

him to the plan or to participants in or beneficiaries of the plan. "Director" includes, unless the context requires otherwise, the estate or personal representative of a director.

(3) "Expenses" include counsel fees.

(4) "Liability" means the obligation to pay a judgment, settlement, penalty, fine (including an excise tax assessed with respect to an employee benefit plan), or reasonable expenses incurred with respect to a proceeding.

(5) "Official capacity" means: (i) when used with respect to a director, the office of director in a corporation; and (ii) when used with respect to an individual other than a director, as contemplated in section 8.56, the office in a corporation held by the officer or the employment or agency relationship undertaken by the employee or agent on behalf of the corporation. "Official capacity" does not include service for any other foreign or domestic corporation or any partnership, joint venture, trust, employee benefit plan, or other enterprise.

(6) "Party" includes an individual who was, is, or is threatened to be made a named defendant or respondent in a proceeding.

(7) "Proceeding" means any threatened, pending, or completed action, suit, or proceeding, whether civil, criminal, administrative, or investigative and whether formal or informal.

§ 8.51 Authority to Indemnify

(a) Except as provided in subsection (d), a corporation may indemnify an individual made a party to a proceeding because he is or was a director against liability incurred in the proceeding if:

(1) he conducted himself in good faith; and

(2) he reasonably believed:

(i) in the case of conduct in his official capacity with the corporation, that his conduct was in its best interests; and

(ii) in all other cases, that his conduct was at least not opposed to its best interests; and

(3) in the case of any criminal proceeding, he had no reasonable cause to believe his conduct was unlawful.

(b) A director's conduct with respect to an employee benefit plan for a purpose he reasonably believed to be in the interests of the participants in and beneficiaries of the plan is conduct that satisfies the requirement of subsection (a)(2)(ii).

(c) The termination of a proceeding by judgment, order, settlement, conviction, or upon a plea of nolo contendere or its equivalent is not, of itself, determinative that the director did not meet the standard of conduct described in this section.

(d) A corporation may not indemnify a director under this section:

(1) in connection with a proceeding by or in the right of the corporation in which the director was adjudged liable to the corporation; or

(2) in connection with any other proceeding charging improper personal benefit to him, whether or not involving action in his official capacity, in which he was adjudged liable on the basis that personal benefit was improperly received by him.

(e) Indemnification permitted under this section in connection with a proceeding by or in the right of the corporation is limited to reasonable expenses incurred in connection with the proceeding.

§ 8.52 Mandatory Indemnification

Unless limited by its articles of incorporation, a corporation shall indemnify a director who was wholly successful, on the merits or otherwise, in the defense of any proceeding to which he was a party because he is or was a director of the corporation against reasonable expenses incurred by him in connection with the proceeding.

§ 8.53 Advance for Expenses

(a) A corporation may pay for or reimburse the reasonable expenses incurred by a director who is a party to a proceeding in advance of final disposition of the proceeding if:

(1) the director furnishes the corporation a written affirmation of his good faith belief that he has met the standard of conduct described in section 8.51;

(2) the director furnishes the corporation a written undertaking, executed personally or on his behalf, to repay the advance if it is ultimately determined that he did not meet the standard of conduct; and

(3) a determination is made that the facts then known to those making the determination would not preclude indemnification under this subchapter.

(b) The undertaking required by subsection (a)(2) must be an unlimited general obligation of the director but need not be secured and may be accepted without reference to financial ability to make repayment.

(c) Determinations and authorizations of payments under this section shall be made in the manner specified in section 8.55.

§ 8.54 Court-Ordered Indemnification

Unless a corporation's articles of incorporation provide otherwise, a director of the corporation who is a party to a proceeding may apply for indemnification to the court conducting the proceeding or to another court of competent jurisdiction. On receipt of an application, the court after giving any notice the court considers necessary may order indemnification if it determines:

(1) the director is entitled to mandatory indemnification under section 8.52, in which case the court shall also order the corporation to pay the director's reasonable expenses incurred to obtain court-ordered indemnification; or

(2) the director is fairly and reasonably entitled to indemnification in view of all the relevant circumstances, whether or not he met the standard of conduct set forth in section 8.51 or was adjudged liable as described in section 8.51(d), but if he was adjudged so liable his indemnification is limited to reasonable expenses incurred.

§ 8.55 Determination and Authorization of Indemnification

(a) A corporation may not indemnify a director under section 8.51 unless authorized in the specific case after a determination has been made that indemnification of the director is permissible in the circumstances because he has met the standard of conduct set forth in section 8.51.

(b) The determination shall be made:

(1) by the board of directors by majority vote of a quorum consisting of directors not at the time parties to the proceeding;

(2) if a quorum cannot be obtained under subdivision (1), by majority vote of a committee duly designated by the board of directors (in which designation directors who are parties may participate), consisting solely of two or more directors not at the time parties to the proceeding;

(3) by special legal counsel:

(i) selected by the board of directors or its committee in the manner prescribed in subdivision (1) or (2); or

(ii) if a quorum of the board of directors cannot be obtained under subdivision (1) and a committee cannot be designated under subdivision (2), selected by majority vote of the full board of directors (in which selection directors who are parties may participate); or

(4) by the shareholders, but shares owned by or voted under the control of directors who are at the time parties to the proceeding may not be voted on the determination.

(c) Authorization of indemnification and evaluation as to reasonableness of expenses shall be made in the same manner as the determination that indemnification is permissible, except that if the determination is made by special legal counsel, authorization of indemnification and evaluation as to reasonableness of expenses shall be made by those entitled under subsection (b)(3) to select counsel.

§ 8.56 Indemnification of Officers, Employees, and Agents

Unless a corporation's articles of incorporation provide otherwise:

(1) an officer of the corporation who is not a director is entitled to mandatory indemnification under section 8.52, and is entitled to apply for court-ordered indemnification under section 8.54, in each case to the same extent as a director;

(2) the corporation may indemnify and advance expenses under this subchapter to an officer, employee, or agent of the corporation who is not a director to the same extent as to a director; and

(3) a corporation may also indemnify and advance expenses to an officer, employee, or agent who is not a director to the extent, consistent with public policy, that may be provided by its articles of incorporation, bylaws, general or specific action of its board of directors, or contract.

§ 8.57 Insurance

A corporation may purchase and maintain insurance on behalf of an individual who is or was a director, officer, employee, or agent of the corporation, or who, while a director, officer, employee, or agent of the corporation, is or was serving at the request of the corporation as a director, officer, partner, trustee, employee, or agent of another foreign or domestic corporation, partnership, joint venture, trust, employee benefit plan, or other enterprise, against liability asserted against or incurred by him in that capacity or arising from his status as a director, officer, employee, or agent, whether or not the corporation would have power to indemnify him against the same liability under section 8.51 or 8.52.

§ 8.58 Application of Subchapter

(a) A provision treating a corporation's indemnification of or advance for expenses to directors that is contained in its articles of incorporation, bylaws, a resolution of its shareholders or board of directors, or in a contract or otherwise, is valid only if and to the extent the provision is consistent with this subchapter. If articles of incorporation limit indemnification or advance for expenses, indemnification and advance for expenses are valid only to the extent consistent with the articles.

(b) This subchapter does not limit a corporation's power to pay or reimburse expenses incurred by a director in connection with his appearance as a witness in a proceeding at a time when he has not been made a named defendant or respondent to the proceeding.

CHAPTER 9. [RESERVED]

CHAPTER 10. AMENDMENT OF ARTICLES OF INCORPORATION AND BYLAWS

SUBCHAPTER A. AMENDMENT OF ARTICLES OF INCORPORATION

§ 10.01 Authority to Amend

(a) A corporation may amend its articles of incorporation at any time to add or change a provision that is required or permitted in the articles of incorporation or to delete a provision not required in the articles of incorporation. Whether a provision is required or permitted in the articles of incorporation is determined as of the effective date of the amendment.

(b) A shareholder of the corporation does not have a vested property right resulting from any provision in the articles of incorporation, including provisions relating to management, control, capital structure, dividend entitlement, or purpose or duration of the corporation.

§ 10.02 Amendment by Board of Directors

Unless the articles of incorporation provide otherwise, a corporation's board of directors may adopt one or more amendments to the corporation's articles of incorporation without shareholder action:

(1) to extend the duration of the corporation if it was incorporated at a time when limited duration was required by law;

(2) to delete the names and addresses of the initial directors;

(3) to delete the name and address of the initial registered agent or registered office, if a statement of change is on file with the secretary of state;

(4) to change each issued and unissued authorized share of an outstanding class into a greater number of whole shares if the corporation has only shares of that class outstanding;

(5) to change the corporate name by substituting the word "corporation," "incorporated," "company," "limited," or the abbreviation "corp.," "inc.," "co.," or "ltd.," for a similar word or abbreviation in the name, or by adding, deleting, or changing a geographical attribution for the name; or

(6) to make any other change expressly permitted by this Act to be made without shareholder action.

§ 10.03 Amendment by Board of Directors and Shareholders

(a) A corporation's board of directors may propose one or more amendments to the articles of incorporation for submission to the shareholders.

(b) For the amendment to be adopted:

(1) the board of directors must recommend the amendment to the shareholders unless the board of directors determines that because of conflict of interest or other special circumstances it should make no recommendation and communicates the basis for its determination to the shareholders with the amendment; and

(2) the shareholders entitled to vote on the amendment must approve the amendment as provided in subsection (e).

(c) The board of directors may condition its submission of the proposed amendment on any basis.

(d) The corporation shall notify each shareholder, whether or not entitled to vote, of the proposed shareholders' meeting in accordance with section 7.05. The notice of meeting must also state that the purpose, or one of the purposes, of the meeting is to consider the proposed amendment and contain or be accompanied by a copy or summary of the amendment.

(e) Unless this Act, the articles of incorporation, or the board of directors (acting pursuant to subsection (c)) require a greater vote or a vote by voting groups, the amendment to be adopted must be approved by:

(1) a majority of the votes entitled to be cast on the amendment by any voting group with respect to which the amendment would create dissenters' rights; and

(2) the votes required by sections 7.25 and 7.26 by every other voting group entitled to vote on the amendment.

§ 10.04 Voting on Amendments by Voting Groups

(a) The holders of the outstanding shares of a class are entitled to vote as a separate voting group (if shareholder voting is otherwise required by this Act) on a proposed amendment if the amendment would:

(1) increase or decrease the aggregate number of authorized shares of the class;

(2) effect an exchange or reclassification of all or part of the shares of the class into shares of another class;

(3) effect an exchange or reclassification, or create the right of exchange, of all or part of the shares of another class into shares of the class;

(4) change the designation, rights, preferences, or limitations of all or part of the shares of the class;

(5) change the shares of all or part of the class into a different number of shares of the same class;

(6) create a new class of shares having rights or preferences with respect to distributions or to dissolution that are prior, superior, or substantially equal to the shares of the class;

(7) increase the rights, preferences, or number of authorized shares of any class that, after giving effect to the amendment, have rights or preferences with respect to distributions or to dissolution that are prior, superior, or substantially equal to the shares of the class;

(8) limit or deny an existing preemptive right of all or part of the shares of the class; or

(9) cancel or otherwise affect rights to distributions or dividends that have accumulated but not yet been declared on all or part of the shares of the class.

(b) If a proposed amendment would affect a series of a class of shares in one or more of the ways described in subsection (a), the shares of that series are entitled to vote as a separate voting group on the proposed amendment.

(c) If a proposed amendment that entitles two or more series of shares to vote as separate voting groups under this section would affect those two or more series in the same or a substantially similar way, the shares of all the series so affected must vote together as a single voting group on the proposed amendment.

(d) A class or series of shares is entitled to the voting rights granted by this section although the articles of incorporation provide that the shares are nonvoting shares.

§ 10.05 Amendment Before Issuance of Shares

If a corporation has not yet issued shares, its incorporators or board of directors may adopt one or more amendments to the corporation's articles of incorporation.

§ 10.06 Articles of Amendment

A corporation amending its articles of incorporation shall deliver to the secretary of state for filing articles of amendment setting forth:

(1) the name of the corporation;

(2) the text of each amendment adopted;

(3) if an amendment provides for an exchange, reclassification, or cancellation of issued shares, provisions for implementing the amendment if not contained in the amendment itself;

(4) the date of each amendment's adoption;

(5) if an amendment was adopted by the incorporators or board of directors without shareholder action, a statement to that effect and that shareholder action was not required;

(6) if an amendment was approved by the shareholders:

(i) the designation, number of outstanding shares, number of votes entitled to be cast by each voting group entitled to vote separately on the amendment, and number of votes of each voting group indisputably represented at the meeting;

(ii) either the total number of votes cast for and against the amendment by each voting group entitled to vote separately on the amendment or the total number of undisputed votes cast for the amendment by each voting group and a statement that the number cast for the amendment by each voting group was sufficient for approval by that voting group.

§ 10.07 Restated Articles of Incorporation

(a) A corporation's board of directors may restate its articles of incorporation at any time with or without shareholder action.

(b) The restatement may include one or more amendments to the articles. If the restatement includes an amendment requiring shareholder approval, it must be adopted as provided in section 10.03.

(c) If the board of directors submits a restatement for shareholder action, the corporation shall notify each shareholder, whether or not entitled to vote, of the proposed shareholders' meeting in accordance with section 7.05. The notice must also state that the purpose, or one of the purposes, of the meeting is to consider the proposed restatement and contain or be accompanied by a copy of the restatement that identifies any amendment or other change it would make in the articles.

(d) A corporation restating its articles of incorporation shall deliver to the secretary of state for filing articles of restatement setting forth the name of the corporation and the text of the restated articles of incorporation together with a certificate setting forth:

(1) whether the restatement contains an amendment to the articles requiring shareholder approval and, if it does not, that the board of directors adopted the restatement; or

(2) if the restatement contains an amendment to the articles requiring shareholder approval, the information required by section 10.06.

(e) Duly adopted restated articles of incorporation supersede the original articles of incorporation and all amendments to them.

(f) The secretary of state may certify restated articles of incorporation, as the articles of incorporation currently in effect, without including the certificate information required by subsection (d).

§ 10.08 Amendment Pursuant to Reorganization

(a) A corporation's articles of incorporation may be amended without action by the board of directors or shareholders to carry out a plan of reorganization ordered or decreed by a court of competent jurisdiction under federal statute if the articles of incorporation after amendment contain only provisions required or permitted by section 2.02.

(b) The individual or individuals designated by the court shall deliver to the secretary of state for filing articles of amendment setting forth:

(1) the name of the corporation;

(2) the text of each amendment approved by the court;

(3) the date of the court's order or decree approving the articles of amendment;

(4) the title of the reorganization proceeding in which the order or decree was entered; and

(5) a statement that the court had jurisdiction of the proceeding under federal statute.

(c) Shareholders of a corporation undergoing reorganization do not have dissenters' rights except as and to the extent provided in the reorganization plan.

(d) This section does not apply after entry of a final decree in the reorganization proceeding even though the court retains jurisdiction of the proceeding for limited purposes unrelated to consummation of the reorganization plan.

§ 10.09 Effect of Amendment

An amendment to articles of incorporation does not affect a cause of action existing against or in favor of the corporation, a proceeding to which the corporation is a party, or the existing rights of persons other than shareholders of the corporation. An amendment changing a corporation's name does not abate a proceeding brought by or against the corporation in its former name.

SUBCHAPTER B. AMENDMENT OF BYLAWS

§ 10.20 Amendment by Board of Directors or Shareholders

(a) A corporation's board of directors may amend or repeal the corporation's bylaws unless:

(1) the articles of incorporation or this Act reserve this power exclusively to the shareholders in whole or part; or

(2) the shareholders in amending or repealing a particular bylaw provide expressly that the board of directors may not amend or repeal that bylaw.

(b) A corporation's shareholders may amend or repeal the corporation's bylaws even though the bylaws may also be amended or repealed by its board of directors.

§ 10.21 Bylaw Increasing Quorum or Voting Requirement for Shareholders

(a) If expressly authorized by the articles of incorporation, the shareholders may adopt or amend a bylaw that fixes a greater quorum or voting requirement for shareholders (or voting groups of shareholders) than is required by this Act. The adoption or amendment of a bylaw that adds, changes, or deletes a greater quorum or voting requirement for shareholders must meet the same quorum requirement and be adopted by the same vote and voting groups required to take action under the quorum and voting requirement then in effect or proposed to be adopted, whichever is greater.

(b) A bylaw that fixes a greater quorum or voting requirement for shareholders under subsection (a) may not be adopted, amended, or repealed by the board of directors.

§ 10.22 Bylaw Increasing Quorum or Voting Requirement for Directors

(a) A bylaw that fixes a greater quorum or voting requirement for the board of directors may be amended or repealed:

(1) if originally adopted by the shareholders, only by the shareholders;

(2) if originally adopted by the board of directors, either by the shareholders or by the board of directors.

(b) A bylaw adopted or amended by the shareholders that fixes a greater quorum or voting requirement for the board of directors may provide that it may be amended or repealed only by a specified vote of either the shareholders or the board of directors.

(c) Action by the board of directors under subsection (a)(2) to adopt or amend a bylaw that changes the quorum or voting requirement for the board of directors must meet the same quorum requirement and be adopted by the same vote required to take action under the quorum and voting requirement then in effect or proposed to be adopted, whichever is greater.

CHAPTER 11. MERGER AND SHARE EXCHANGE

§ 11.01 Merger

(a) One or more corporations may merge into another corporation if the board of directors of each corporation adopts and its shareholders (if required by section 11.03) approve a plan of merger.

(b) The plan of merger must set forth:

(1) the name of each corporation planning to merge and the name of the surviving corporation into which each other corporation plans to merge;

(2) the terms and conditions of the merger; and

(3) the manner and basis of converting the shares of each corporation into shares, obligations, or other securities of the surviving or any other corporation or into cash or other property in whole or part.

(c) The plan of merger may set forth:

(1) amendments to the articles of incorporation of the surviving corporation; and

(2) other provisions relating to the merger.

§ 11.02 Share Exchange

(a) A corporation may acquire all of the outstanding shares of one or more classes or series of another corporation if the board of directors of each corporation adopts and its shareholders (if required by section 11.03) approve the exchange.

(b) The plan of exchange must set forth:

(1) the name of the corporation whose shares will be acquired and the name of the acquiring corporation;

(2) the terms and conditions of the exchange;

(3) the manner and basis of exchanging the shares to be acquired for shares, obligations, or other securities of the acquiring or any other corporation or for cash or other property in whole or part.

(c) The plan of exchange may set forth other provisions relating to the exchange.

(d) This section does not limit the power of a corporation to acquire all or part of the shares of one or more classes or series of another corporation through a voluntary exchange or otherwise.

§ 11.03 Action on Plan

(a) After adopting a plan of merger or share exchange, the board of directors of each corporation party to the merger, and the board of directors of the corporation whose shares will be acquired in the share exchange, shall submit the plan of merger (except as provided in subsection (g)) or share exchange for approval by its shareholders.

(b) For a plan of merger or share exchange to be approved:

(1) the board of directors must recommend the plan of merger or share exchange to the shareholders, unless the board of directors determines that because of conflict of interest or other special circumstances it should make no recommendation and communicates the basis for its determination to the shareholders with the plan; and

(2) the shareholders entitled to vote must approve the plan.

(c) The board of directors may condition its submission of the proposed merger or share exchange on any basis.

(d) The corporation shall notify each shareholder, whether or not entitled to vote, of the proposed shareholders' meeting in accordance with section 7.05. The notice must also state that the purpose, or one of the purposes, of the meeting is to consider the plan of merger or share exchange and contain or be accompanied by a copy or summary of the plan.

(e) Unless this Act, the articles of incorporation, or the board of directors (acting pursuant to subsection (c)) require a greater vote or a vote by voting groups, the plan of merger or share exchange to be authorized must be approved by each voting group entitled to vote separately on the plan by a majority of all the votes entitled to be cast on the plan by that voting group.

(f) Separate voting by voting groups is required:

(1) on a plan of merger if the plan contains a provision that, if contained in a proposed amendment to articles of incorporation, would require action by one or more separate voting groups on the proposed amendment under section 10.04;

(2) on a plan of share exchange by each class or series of shares included in the exchange, with each class or series constituting a separate voting group.

(g) Action by the shareholders of the surviving corporation on a plan of merger is not required if:

(1) the articles of incorporation of the surviving corporation will not differ (except for amendments enumerated in section 10.02) from its articles before the merger;

(2) each shareholder of the surviving corporation whose shares were outstanding immediately before the effective date of the merger will hold the same number of shares, with identical designations, preferences, limitations, and relative rights, immediately after;

(3) the number of voting shares outstanding immediately after the merger, plus the number of voting shares issuable as a result of the merger (either by the conversion of securities issued pursuant to the merger or the exercise of rights and warrants issued pursuant to the merger), will not exceed by more than 20 percent the total number of voting shares of the surviving corporation outstanding immediately before the merger; and

(4) the number of participating shares outstanding immediately after the merger, plus the number of participating shares issuable as a result of the merger (either by the conversion of securities issued pursuant to the merger or the exercise of rights and warrants issued pursuant to the merger), will not exceed by more than 20 percent the total number of participating shares outstanding immediately before the merger.

(h) As used in subsection (g):

(1) "Participating shares" means shares that entitle their holders to participate without limitation in distributions.

(2) "Voting shares" means shares that entitle their holders to vote unconditionally in elections of directors.

(i) After a merger or share exchange is authorized, and at any time before articles of merger or share exchange are filed, the planned merger or share exchange may be abandoned (subject to any contractual rights), without further shareholder action, in accordance with the procedure set forth in the plan of merger or share exchange or, if none is set forth, in the manner determined by the board of directors.

§ 11.04 Merger of Subsidiary

(a) A parent corporation owning at least 90 percent of the outstanding shares of each class of a subsidiary corporation may merge the subsidiary into itself without approval of the shareholders of the parent or subsidiary.

(b) The board of directors of the parent shall adopt a plan of merger that sets forth:

(1) the names of the parent and subsidiary; and

(2) the manner and basis of converting the shares of the subsidiary into shares, obligations, or other securities of the parent or any other corporation or into cash or other property in whole or part.

(c) The parent shall mail a copy or summary of the plan of merger to each shareholder of the subsidiary who does not waive the mailing requirement in writing.

(d) The parent may not deliver articles of merger to the secretary of state for filing until at least 30 days after the date it mailed a copy of the plan of merger to each shareholder of the subsidiary who did not waive the mailing requirement.

(e) Articles of merger under this section may not contain amendments to the articles of incorporation of the parent corporation (except for amendments enumerated in section 10.02).

§ 11.05 Articles of Merger or Share Exchange

(a) After a plan of merger or share exchange is approved by the shareholders, or adopted by the board of directors if shareholder approval is not required, the surviving or acquiring corporation shall deliver to the secretary of state for filing articles of merger or share exchange setting forth:

(1) the plan of merger or share exchange;

(2) if shareholder approval was not required, a statement to that effect;

(3) if approval of the shareholders of one or more corporations party to the merger or share exchange was required:

(i) the designation, number of outstanding shares, and number of votes entitled to be cast by each voting group entitled to vote separately on the plan as to each corporation; and

(ii) either the total number of votes cast for and against the plan by each voting group entitled to vote separately on the plan or the total number of undisputed votes cast for the plan separately by each voting group and a statement that the number cast for the plan by each voting group was sufficient for approval by that voting group.

(b) Unless a delayed effective date is specified, a merger or share exchange takes effect when the articles of merger or share exchange are filed.

§ 11.06 Effect of Merger or Share Exchange

(a) When a merger takes effect:

(1) every other corporation party to the merger merges into the surviving corporation and the separate existence of every corporation except the surviving corporation ceases;

(2) the title to all real estate and other property owned by each corporation party to the merger is vested in the surviving corporation without reversion or impairment;

(3) the surviving corporation has all liabilities of each corporation party to the merger;

(4) a proceeding pending against any corporation party to the merger may be continued as if the merger did not occur or the

surviving corporation may be substituted in the proceeding for the corporation whose existence ceased;

(5) the articles of incorporation of the surviving corporation are amended to the extent provided in the plan of merger; and

(6) the shares of each corporation party to the merger that are to be converted into shares, obligations, or other securities of the surviving or any other corporation or into cash or other property are converted and the former holders of the shares are entitled only to the rights provided in the articles of merger or to their rights under chapter 13.

(b) When a share exchange takes effect, the shares of each acquired corporation are exchanged as provided in the plan, and the former holders of the shares are entitled only to the exchange rights provided in the articles of share exchange or to their rights under chapter 13.

§ 11.07 Merger of Share Exchange With Foreign Corporation

(a) One or more foreign corporations may merge or enter into a share exchange with one or more domestic corporations if:

(1) in a merger, the merger is permitted by the law of the state or country under whose law each foreign corporation is incorporated and each foreign corporation complies with that law in effecting the merger;

(2) in a share exchange, the corporation whose shares will be acquired is a domestic corporation, whether or not a share exchange is permitted by the law of the state or country under whose law the acquiring corporation is incorporated;

(3) the foreign corporation complies with section 11.05 if it is the surviving corporation of the merger or acquiring corporation of the share exchange; and

(4) each domestic corporation complies with the applicable provisions of sections 11.01 through 11.04 and, if it is the surviving corporation of the merger or acquiring corporation of the share exchange, with section 11.05.

(b) Upon the merger or share exchange taking effect, the surviving foreign corporation of a merger and the acquiring foreign corporation of a share exchange is deemed:

(1) to appoint the secretary of state as its agent for service of process in a proceeding to enforce any obligation or the rights of dissenting shareholders of each domestic corporation party to the merger or share exchange; and

(2) to agree that it will promptly pay to the dissenting shareholders of each domestic corporation party to the merger or share

exchange the amount, if any, to which they are entitled under chapter 13.

(c) This section does not limit the power of a foreign corporation to acquire all or part of the shares of one or more classes or series of a domestic corporation through a voluntary exchange or otherwise.

CHAPTER 12. SALE OF ASSETS

§ 12.01 Sale of Assets in Regular Course of Business and Mortgage of Assets

(a) A corporation may, on the terms and conditions and for the consideration determined by the board of directors:

(1) sell, lease, exchange, or otherwise dispose of all, or substantially all, of its property in the usual and regular course of business,

(2) mortgage, pledge, dedicate to the repayment of indebtedness (whether with or without recourse), or otherwise encumber any or all of its property whether or not in the usual and regular course of business, or

(3) transfer any or all of its property to a corporation all the shares of which are owned by the corporation.

(b) Unless the articles of incorporation require it, approval by the shareholders of a transaction described in subsection (a) is not required.

§ 12.02 Sale of Assets Other Than in Regular Course of Business

(a) A corporation may sell, lease, exchange, or otherwise dispose of all, or substantially all, of its property (with or without the good will), otherwise than in the usual and regular course of business, on the terms and conditions and for the consideration determined by the corporation's board of directors, if the board of directors proposes and its shareholders approve the proposed transaction.

(b) For a transaction to be authorized:

(1) the board of directors must recommend the proposed transaction to the shareholders unless the board of directors determines that because of conflict of interest or other special circumstances it should make no recommendation and communicates the basis for its determination to the shareholders with the submission of the proposed transaction; and

(2) the shareholders entitled to vote must approve the transaction.

(c) The board of directors may condition its submission of the proposed transaction on any basis.

(d) The corporation shall notify each shareholder, whether or not entitled to vote, of the proposed shareholders' meeting in accordance with section 7.05. The notice must also state that the purpose, or one of the purposes, of the meeting is to consider the sale, lease, exchange, or other disposition of all, or substantially all, the property of the corporation and contain or be accompanied by a description of the transaction.

(e) Unless the articles of incorporation or the board of directors (acting pursuant to subsection (c)) require a greater vote or a vote by voting groups, the transaction to be authorized must be approved by a majority of all the votes entitled to be cast on the transaction.

(f) After a sale, lease, exchange, or other disposition of property is authorized, the transaction may be abandoned (subject to any contractual rights) without further shareholder action.

(g) A transaction that constitutes a distribution is governed by section 6.40 and not by this section.

CHAPTER 13. DISSENTERS' RIGHTS

SUBCHAPTER A. RIGHT TO DISSENT AND OBTAIN PAYMENT FOR SHARES

§ 13.01 Definitions

In this chapter:

(1) "Corporation" means the issuer of the shares held by a dissenter before the corporate action, or the surviving or acquiring corporation by merger or share exchange of that issuer.

(2) "Dissenter" means a shareholder who is entitled to dissent from corporate action under section 13.02 and who exercises that right when and in the manner required by sections 13.20 through 13.28.

(3) "Fair value," with respect to a dissenter's shares, means the value of the shares immediately before the effectuation of the corporate action to which the dissenter objects, excluding any appreciation or depreciation in anticipation of the corporate action unless exclusion would be inequitable.

(4) "Interest" means interest from the effective date of the corporate action until the date of payment, at the average rate currently paid by the corporation on its principal bank loans or, if none, at a rate that is fair and equitable under all the circumstances.

(5) "Record shareholder" means the person in whose name shares are registered in the records of a corporation or the beneficial owner of shares to the extent of the rights granted by a nominee certificate on file with a corporation.

(6) "Beneficial shareholder" means the person who is a beneficial owner of shares held in a voting trust or by a nominee as the record shareholder.

(7) "Shareholder" means the record shareholder or the beneficial shareholder.

§ 13.02 Right to Dissent

(a) A shareholder is entitled to dissent from, and obtain payment of the fair value of his shares in the event of, any of the following corporate actions:

(1) consummation of a plan of merger to which the corporation is a party (i) if shareholder approval is required for the merger by section 11.03 or the articles of incorporation and the shareholder is entitled to vote on the merger or (ii) if the corporation is a subsidiary that is merged with its parent under section 11.04;

(2) consummation of a plan of share exchange to which the corporation is a party as the corporation whose shares will be acquired, if the shareholder is entitled to vote on the plan;

(3) consummation of a sale or exchange of all, or substantially all, of the property of the corporation other than in the usual and regular course of business, if the shareholder is entitled to vote on the sale or exchange, including a sale in dissolution, but not including a sale pursuant to court order or a sale for cash pursuant to a plan by which all or substantially all of the net proceeds of the sale will be distributed to the shareholders within one year after the date of sale;

(4) an amendment of the articles of incorporation that materially and adversely affects rights in respect of a dissenter's shares because it:

(i) alters or abolishes a preferential right of the shares;

(ii) creates, alters, or abolishes a right in respect of redemption, including a provision respecting a sinking fund for the redemption or repurchase, of the shares;

(iii) alters or abolishes a preemptive right of the holder of the shares to acquire shares or other securities;

(iv) excludes or limits the right of the shares to vote on any matter, or to cumulate votes, other than a limitation by dilution through issuance of shares or other securities with similar voting rights; or

(v) reduces the number of shares owned by the shareholder to a fraction of a share if the fractional share so created is to be acquired for cash under section 6.04; or

(5) any corporate action taken pursuant to a shareholder vote to the extent the articles of incorporation, bylaws, or a resolution of the board of directors provides that voting or nonvoting shareholders are entitled to dissent and obtain payment for their shares.

(b) A shareholder entitled to dissent and obtain payment for his shares under this chapter may not challenge the corporate action creating his entitlement unless the action is unlawful or fraudulent with respect to the shareholder or the corporation.

§ 13.03 Dissent by Nominees and Beneficial Owners

(a) A record shareholder may assert dissenters' rights as to fewer than all the shares registered in his name only if he dissents with respect to all shares beneficially owned by any one person and notifies the corporation in writing of the name and address of each person on whose behalf he asserts dissenters' rights. The rights of a partial dissenter under this subsection are determined as if the shares as to which he dissents and his other shares were registered in the names of different shareholders.

(b) A beneficial shareholder may assert dissenters' rights as to shares held on his behalf only if:

(1) he submits to the corporation the record shareholder's written consent to the dissent not later than the time the beneficial shareholder asserts dissenters' rights; and

(2) he does so with respect to all shares of which he is the beneficial shareholder or over which he has power to direct the vote.

SUBCHAPTER B. PROCEDURE FOR EXERCISE OF DISSENTERS' RIGHTS

§ 13.20 Notice of Dissenters' Rights

(a) If proposed corporate action creating dissenters' rights under section 13.02 is submitted to a vote at a shareholders' meeting, the meeting notice must state that shareholders are or may be entitled to assert dissenters' rights under this chapter and be accompanied by a copy of this chapter.

(b) If corporate action creating dissenters' rights under section 13.02 is taken without a vote of shareholders, the corporation shall notify in writing all shareholders entitled to assert dissenters' rights that the action was taken and send them the dissenters' notice described in section 13.22.

§ 13.21 Notice of Intent to Demand Payment

(a) If proposed corporate action creating dissenters' rights under section 13.02 is submitted to a vote at a shareholders' meeting, a shareholder who wishes to assert dissenters' rights (1) must deliver to the corporation before the vote is taken written notice of his intent to demand payment for his shares if the proposed action is effectuated and (2) must not vote his shares in favor of the proposed action.

(b) A shareholder who does not satisfy the requirements of subsection (a) is not entitled to payment for his shares under this chapter.

§ 13.22 Dissenters' Notice

(a) If proposed corporate action creating dissenters' rights under section 13.02 is authorized at a shareholders' meeting, the corporation shall deliver a written dissenters' notice to all shareholders who satisfied the requirements of section 13.21.

(b) The dissenters' notice must be sent no later than 10 days after the corporate action was taken, and must:

(1) state where the payment demand must be sent and where and when certificates for certificated shares must be deposited;

(2) inform holders of uncertificated shares to what extent transfer of the shares will be restricted after the payment demand is received;

(3) supply a form for demanding payment that includes the date of the first announcement to news media or to shareholders of the terms of the proposed corporate action and requires that the person asserting dissenters' rights certify whether or not he acquired beneficial ownership of the shares before that date;

(4) set a date by which the corporation must receive the payment demand, which date may not be fewer than 30 nor more than 60 days after the date the subsection (a) notice is delivered; and

(5) be accompanied by a copy of this chapter.

§ 13.23 Duty to Demand Payment

(a) A shareholder sent a dissenters' notice described in section 13.22 must demand payment, certify whether he acquired beneficial ownership of the shares before the date required to be set forth in the dissenter's notice pursuant to section 13.22(b)(3), and deposit his certificates in accordance with the terms of the notice.

(b) The shareholder who demands payment and deposits his shares under section (a) retains all other rights of a shareholder until these rights are cancelled or modified by the taking of the proposed corporate action.

(c) A shareholder who does not demand payment or deposit his share certificates where required, each by the date set in the dissenters' notice, is not entitled to payment for his shares under this chapter.

§ 13.24 Share Restrictions

(a) The corporation may restrict the transfer of uncertificated shares from the date the demand for their payment is received until the proposed corporate action is taken or the restrictions released under section 13.26.

(b) The person for whom dissenters' rights are asserted as to uncertificated shares retains all other rights of a shareholder until these rights are cancelled or modified by the taking of the proposed corporate action.

§ 13.25 Payment

(a) Except as provided in section 13.27, as soon as the proposed corporate action is taken, or upon receipt of a payment demand, the corporation shall pay each dissenter who complied with section 13.23 the amount the corporation estimates to be the fair value of his shares, plus accrued interest.

(b) The payment must be accompanied by:

(1) the corporation's balance sheet as of the end of a fiscal year ending not more than 16 months before the date of payment, an income statement for that year, a statement of changes in shareholders' equity for that year, and the latest available interim financial statements, if any;

(2) a statement of the corporation's estimate of the fair value of the shares;

(3) an explanation of how the interest was calculated;

(4) a statement of the dissenter's right to demand payment under section 13.28; and

(5) a copy of this chapter.

§ 13.26 Failure to Take Action

(a) If the corporation does not take the proposed action within 60 days after the date set for demanding payment and depositing share certificates, the corporation shall return the deposited certificates and release the transfer restrictions imposed on uncertificated shares.

(b) If after returning deposited certificates and releasing transfer restrictions, the corporation takes the proposed action, it must send a new dissenters' notice under section 13.22 and repeat the payment demand procedure.

§ 13.27 After-Acquired Shares

(a) A corporation may elect to withhold payment required by section 13.25 from a dissenter unless he was the beneficial owner of the shares before the date set forth in the dissenters' notice as the date of the first announcement to news media or to shareholders of the terms of the proposed corporate action.

(b) To the extent the corporation elects to withhold payment under subsection (a), after taking the proposed corporate action, it shall estimate the fair value of the shares, plus accrued interest, and shall pay this amount to each dissenter who agrees to accept it in full satisfaction of his demand. The corporation shall send with its offer a statement of its estimate of the fair value of the shares, an explanation of how the interest was calculated, and a statement of the dissenter's right to demand payment under section 13.28.

§ 13.28 Procedure if Shareholder Dissatisfied With Payment or Offer

(a) A dissenter may notify the corporation in writing of his own estimate of the fair value of his shares and amount of interest due, and demand payment of his estimate (less any payment under section 13.25), or reject the corporation's offer under section 13.27 and demand payment of the fair value of his shares and interest due, if:

(1) the dissenter believes that the amount paid under section 13.25 or offered under section 13.27 is less than the fair value of his shares or that the interest due is incorrectly calculated;

(2) the corporation fails to make payment under section 13.25 within 60 days after the date set for demanding payment; or

(3) the corporation, having failed to take the proposed action, does not return the deposited certificates or release the transfer restrictions imposed on uncertificated shares within 60 days after the date set for demanding payment.

(b) A dissenter waives his right to demand payment under this section unless he notifies the corporation of his demand in writing under subsection (a) within 30 days after the corporation made or offered payment for his shares.

SUBCHAPTER C. JUDICIAL APPRAISAL OF SHARES

§ 13.30 Court Action

(a) If a demand for payment under section 13.28 remains unsettled, the corporation shall commence a proceeding within 60 days after receiving the payment demand and petition the court to determine the fair value of the shares and accrued interest. If the corporation does not commence the proceeding within the 60-day period, it shall pay each dissenter whose demand remains unsettled the amount demanded.

(b) The corporation shall commence the proceeding in the [name or describe] court of the county where a corporation's principal office (or, if none in this state, its registered office) is located. If the corporation is a foreign corporation without a registered office in this state, it shall commence the proceeding in the county in this state where the registered office of the domestic corporation merged with or whose shares were acquired by the foreign corporation was located.

(c) The corporation shall make all dissenters (whether or not residents of this state) whose demands remain unsettled parties to the proceeding as in an action against their shares and all parties must be served with a copy of the petition. Nonresidents may be served by registered or certified mail or by publication as provided by law.

(d) The jurisdiction of the court in which the proceeding is commenced under subsection (b) is plenary and exclusive. The court may appoint one or more persons as appraisers to receive evidence and recommend decision on the question of fair value. The appraisers have the powers described in the order appointing them, or in any amendment to it. The dissenters are entitled to the same discovery rights as parties in other civil proceedings.

(e) Each dissenter made a party to the proceeding is entitled to judgment (1) for the amount, if any, by which the court finds the fair value of his shares, plus interest, exceeds the amount paid by the corporation or (2) for the fair value, plus accrued interest, of his after-acquired shares for which the corporation elected to withhold payment under section 13.27.

§ 13.31 Court Costs and Counsel Fees

(a) The court in an appraisal proceeding commenced under section 13.30 shall determine all costs of the proceeding, including the reasonable compensation and expenses of appraisers appointed by the court. The court shall assess the costs against the corporation, except that the court may assess costs against all or some of the dissenters, in amounts the court finds equitable, to the extent the court finds dissenters acted arbitrarily, vexatiously, or not in good faith in demanding payment under section 13.28.

(b) The court may also assess the fees and expenses of counsel and experts for the respective parties, in amounts the court finds equitable:

(1) against the corporation and in favor of any or all dissenters if the court finds the corporation did not substantially comply with the requirements of sections 13.20 through 13.28; or

(2) against either the corporation or a dissenter, in favor of any other party, if the court finds that the party against whom the fees and expenses are assessed acted arbitrarily, vexatiously, or not in good faith with respect to the rights provided by this chapter.

(c) If the court finds that the services of counsel for any dissenter were of substantial benefit to other dissenters similarly situated, and that the fees for those services should not be assessed against the corporation, the court may award to these counsel reasonable fees to be paid out of the amounts awarded the dissenters who were benefited.

CHAPTER 14. DISSOLUTION

SUBCHAPTER A. VOLUNTARY DISSOLUTION

§ 14.01 Dissolution by Incorporators or Initial Directors

A majority of the incorporators or initial directors of a corporation that has not issued shares or has not commenced business may dissolve the corporation by delivering to the secretary of state for filing articles of dissolution that set forth:

(1) the name of the corporation;

(2) the date of its incorporation;

(3) either (i) that none of the corporation's shares has been issued or (ii) that the corporation has not commenced business;

(4) that no debt of the corporation remains unpaid;

(5) that the net assets of the corporation remaining after winding up have been distributed to the shareholders, if shares were issued; and

(6) that a majority of the incorporators or initial directors authorized the dissolution.

§ 14.02 Dissolution by Board of Directors and Shareholders

(a) A corporation's board of directors may propose dissolution for submission to the shareholders.

(b) For a proposal to dissolve to be adopted:

(1) the board of directors must recommend dissolution to the shareholders unless the board of directors determines that because of conflict of interest or other special circumstances it should make no recommendation and communicates the basis for its determination to the shareholders; and

(2) the shareholders entitled to vote must approve the proposal to dissolve as provided in subsection (e).

(c) The board of directors may condition its submission of the proposal for dissolution on any basis.

(d) The corporation shall notify each shareholder, whether or not entitled to vote, of the proposed shareholders' meeting in accordance with section 7.05. The notice must also state that the purpose, or one of the purposes, of the meeting is to consider dissolving the corporation.

(e) Unless the articles of incorporation or the board of directors (acting pursuant to subsection (c)) require a greater vote or a vote by voting groups, the proposal to dissolve to be adopted must be approved by a majority of all the votes entitled to be cast on that proposal.

§ 14.03 Articles of Dissolution

(a) At any time after dissolution is authorized, the corporation may dissolve by delivering to the secretary of state for filing articles of dissolution setting forth:

(1) the name of the corporation;

(2) the date dissolution was authorized;

(3) if dissolution was approved by the shareholders:

(i) the number of votes entitled to be cast on the proposal to dissolve; and

(ii) either the total number of votes cast for and against dissolution or the total number of undisputed votes cast for dissolution and a statement that the number cast for dissolution was sufficient for approval.

(4) If voting by voting groups is required, the information required by subparagraph (3) shall be separately provided for each voting group entitled to vote separately on the plan to dissolve.

(b) A corporation is dissolved upon the effective date of its articles of dissolution.

§ 14.04 Revocation of Dissolution

(a) A corporation may revoke its dissolution within 120 days of its effective date.

(b) Revocation of dissolution must be authorized in the same manner as the dissolution was authorized unless that authorization permitted revocation by action by the board of directors alone, in which event the board of directors may revoke the dissolution without shareholder action.

(c) After the revocation of dissolution is authorized, the corporation may revoke the dissolution by delivering to the secretary of state for filing articles of revocation of dissolution, together with a copy of its articles of dissolution, that set forth:

(1) the name of the corporation;

(2) the effective date of the dissolution that was revoked;

(3) the date that the revocation of dissolution was authorized;

(4) if the corporation's board of directors (or incorporators) revoked the dissolution, a statement to that effect;

(5) if the corporation's board of directors revoked a dissolution authorized by the shareholders, a statement that revocation was permitted by action by the board of directors alone pursuant to that authorization; and

(6) if shareholder action was required to revoke the dissolution, the information required by section 14.03(3) or (4).

(d) Unless a delayed effective date is specified, revocation of dissolution is effective when articles of revocation of dissolution are filed.

(e) When the revocation of dissolution is effective, it relates back to and takes effect as of the effective date of the dissolution and the corporation resumes carrying on its business as if dissolution had never occurred.

§ 14.05 Effect of Dissolution

(a) A dissolved corporation continues its corporate existence but may not carry on any business except that appropriate to wind up and liquidate its business and affairs, including:

(1) collecting its assets;

(2) disposing of its properties that will not be distributed in kind to its shareholders;

(3) discharging or making provision for discharging its liabilities;

(4) distributing its remaining property among its shareholders according to their interests; and

(5) doing every other act necessary to wind up and liquidate its business and affairs.

(b) Dissolution of a corporation does not:

(1) transfer title to the corporation's property;

(2) prevent transfer of its shares or securities, although the authorization to dissolve may provide for closing the corporation's share transfer records;

(3) subject its directors or officers to standards of conduct different from those prescribed in chapter 8;

(4) change quorum or voting requirements for its board of directors or shareholders; change provisions for selection, resignation, or removal of its directors or officers or both; or change provisions for amending its bylaws;

(5) prevent commencement of a proceeding by or against the corporation in its corporate name;

(6) abate or suspend a proceeding pending by or against the corporation on the effective date of dissolution; or

(7) terminate the authority of the registered agent of the corporation.

§ 14.06 Known Claims Against Dissolved Corporation

(a) A dissolved corporation may dispose of the known claims against it by following the procedure described in this section.

(b) The dissolved corporation shall notify its known claimants in writing of the dissolution at any time after its effective date. The written notice must:

(1) describe information that must be included in a claim;

(2) provide a mailing address where a claim may be sent;

(3) state the deadline, which may not be fewer than 120 days from the effective date of the written notice, by which the dissolved corporation must receive the claim; and

(4) state that the claim will be barred if not received by the deadline.

(c) A claim against the dissolved corporation is barred:

(1) if a claimant who was given written notice under subsection (b) does not deliver the claim to the dissolved corporation by the deadline;

(2) if a claimant whose claim was rejected by the dissolved corporation does not commence a proceeding to enforce the claim within 90 days from the effective date of the rejection notice.

(d) For purposes of this section, "claim" does not include a contingent liability or a claim based on an event occurring after the effective date of dissolution.

§ 14.07 Unknown Claims Against Dissolved Corporation

(a) A dissolved corporation may also publish notice of its dissolution and request that persons with claims against the corporation present them in accordance with the notice.

(b) The notice must:

(1) be published one time in a newspaper of general circulation in the county where the dissolved corporation's principal office (or, if none in this state, its registered office) is or was last located;

(2) describe the information that must be included in a claim and provide a mailing address where the claim may be sent; and

(3) state that a claim against the corporation will be barred unless a proceeding to enforce the claim is commenced within five years after the publication of the notice.

(c) If the dissolved corporation publishes a newspaper notice in accordance with subsection (b), the claim of each of the following claimants is barred unless the claimant commences a proceeding to enforce the claim against the dissolved corporation within five years after the publication date of the newspaper notice:

(1) a claimant who did not receive written notice under section 14.06;

(2) a claimant whose claim was timely sent to the dissolved corporation but not acted on;

(3) a claimant whose claim is contingent or based on an event occurring after the effective date of dissolution.

(d) A claim may be enforced under this section:

(1) against the dissolved corporation, to the extent of its undistributed assets; or

(2) if the assets have been distributed in liquidation, against a shareholder of the dissolved corporation to the extent of his pro rata share of the claim or the corporate assets distributed to him in liquidation, whichever is less, but a shareholder's total liability for all claims under this section may not exceed the total amount of assets distributed to him.

SUBCHAPTER B. ADMINISTRATIVE DISSOLUTION

§ 14.20 Grounds for Administrative Dissolution

The secretary of state may commence a proceeding under section 14.21 to administratively dissolve a corporation if:

(1) the corporation does not pay within 60 days after they are due any franchise taxes or penalties imposed by this Act or other law;

(2) the corporation does not deliver its annual report to the secretary of state within 60 days after it is due;

(3) the corporation is without a registered agent or registered office in this state for 60 days or more;

(4) the corporation does not notify the secretary of state within 60 days that its registered agent or registered office has been changed, that its registered agent has resigned, or that its registered office has been discontinued; or

(5) the corporation's period of duration stated in its articles of incorporation expires.

§ 14.21 Procedure for and Effect of Administrative Dissolution

(a) If the secretary of state determines that one or more grounds exist under section 14.20 for dissolving a corporation, he shall serve the corporation with written notice of his determination under section 5.04.

(b) If the corporation does not correct each ground for dissolution or demonstrate to the reasonable satisfaction of the secretary of state that each ground determined by the secretary of state does not exist within 60 days after service of the notice is perfected under section 5.04, the secretary of state shall administratively dissolve the corporation by signing a certificate of dissolution that recites the ground or grounds for dissolution and its effective date. The secretary of state shall file the original of the certificate and serve a copy on the corporation under section 5.04.

(c) A corporation administratively dissolved continues its corporate existence but may not carry on any business except that necessary to wind up and liquidate its business and affairs under section 14.05 and notify claimants under sections 14.06 and 14.07.

(d) The administrative dissolution of a corporation does not terminate the authority of its registered agent.

§ 14.22 Reinstatement Following Administrative Dissolution

(a) A corporation administratively dissolved under section 14.21 may apply to the secretary of state for reinstatement within two years after the effective date of dissolution. The application must:

(1) recite the name of the corporation and the effective date of its administrative dissolution;

(2) state that the ground or grounds for dissolution either did not exist or have been eliminated;

(3) state that the corporation's name satisfies the requirements of section 4.01; and

(4) contain a certificate from the [taxing authority] reciting that all taxes owed by the corporation have been paid.

(b) If the secretary of state determines that the application contains the information required by subsection (a) and that the information is correct, he shall cancel the certificate of dissolution and prepare a certificate of reinstatement that recites his determination and the effective date of reinstatement, file the original of the certificate, and serve a copy on the corporation under section 5.04.

(c) When the reinstatement is effective, it relates back to and takes effect as of the effective date of the administrative dissolution and the corporation resumes carrying on its business as if the administrative dissolution had never occurred.

§ 14.23 Appeal From Denial of Reinstatement

(a) If the secretary of state denies a corporation's application for reinstatement following administrative dissolution, he shall serve the corporation under section 5.04 with a written notice that explains the reason or reasons for denial.

(b) The corporation may appeal the denial of reinstatement to the [name or describe] court within 30 days after service of the notice of denial is perfected. The corporation appeals by petitioning the court to set aside the dissolution and attaching to the petition copies of the secretary of state's certificate of dissolution, the corporation's application for reinstatement, and the secretary of state's notice of denial.

(c) The court may summarily order the secretary of state to reinstate the dissolved corporation or may take other action the court considers appropriate.

(d) The court's final decision may be appealed as in other civil proceedings.

SUBCHAPTER C. JUDICIAL DISSOLUTION

§ 14.30 Grounds for Judicial Dissolution

The [name or describe court or courts] may dissolve a corporation:

(1) in a proceeding by the attorney general if it is established that:

(i) the corporation obtained its articles of incorporation through fraud; or

(ii) the corporation has continued to exceed or abuse the authority conferred upon it by law;

(2) in a proceeding by a shareholder if it is established that:

(i) the directors are deadlocked in the management of the corporate affairs, the shareholders are unable to break the deadlock, and irreparable injury to the corporation is threatened or being suffered, or the business and affairs of the corporation can no longer be conducted to the advantage of the shareholders generally, because of the deadlock;

(ii) the directors or those in control of the corporation have acted, are acting, or will act in a manner that is illegal, oppressive, or fraudulent;

(iii) the shareholders are deadlocked in voting power and have failed, for a period that includes at least two consecutive annual meeting dates, to elect successors to directors whose terms have expired; or

(iv) the corporate assets are being misapplied or wasted;

(3) in a proceeding by a creditor if it is established that:

(i) the creditor's claim has been reduced to judgment, the execution on the judgment returned unsatisfied, and the corporation is insolvent; or

(ii) the corporation has admitted in writing that the creditor's claim is due and owing and the corporation is insolvent; or

(4) in a proceeding by the corporation to have its voluntary dissolution continued under court supervision.

§ 14.31 Procedure for Judicial Dissolution

(a) Venue for a proceeding by the attorney general to dissolve a corporation lies in [name the county or counties]. Venue for a proceeding brought by any other party named in section 14.30 lies in the county where a corporation's principal office (or, if none in this state, its registered office) is or was last located.

(b) It is not necessary to make shareholders parties to a proceeding to dissolve a corporation unless relief is sought against them individually.

(c) A court in a proceeding brought to dissolve a corporation may issue injunctions, appoint a receiver or custodian pendente lite with all powers and duties the court directs, take other action required to preserve the corporate assets wherever located, and carry on the business of the corporation until a full hearing can be held.

§ 14.32 Receivership or Custodianship

(a) A court in a judicial proceeding brought to dissolve a corporation may appoint one or more receivers to wind up and liquidate, or one or more custodians to manage, the business and affairs of the corporation. The court shall hold a hearing, after notifying all parties to the proceeding and any interested persons designated by the court, before appointing a receiver or custodian. The court appointing a receiver or custodian has exclusive jurisdiction over the corporation and all its property wherever located.

(b) The court may appoint an individual or a domestic or foreign corporation (authorized to transact business in this state) as a receiver or custodian. The court may require the receiver or custodian to post bond, with or without sureties, in an amount the court directs.

(c) The court shall describe the powers and duties of the receiver or custodian in its appointing order, which may be amended from time to time. Among other powers:

(1) the receiver (i) may dispose of all or any part of the assets of the corporation wherever located, at a public or private sale, if authorized by the court; and (ii) may sue and defend in his own name as receiver of the corporation in all courts of this state;

(2) the custodian may exercise all of the powers of the corporation, through or in place of its board of directors or officers, to the extent necessary to manage the affairs of the corporation in the best interests of its shareholders and creditors.

(d) The court during a receivership may redesignate the receiver a custodian, and during a custodianship may redesignate the custodian a receiver, if doing so is in the best interests of the corporation, its shareholders, and creditors.

(e) The court from time to time during the receivership or custodianship may order compensation paid and expense disbursements or reimbursements made to the receiver or custodian and his counsel from the assets of the corporation or proceeds from the sale of the assets.

§ 14.33 Decree of Dissolution

(a) If after a hearing the court determines that one or more grounds for judicial dissolution described in section 14.30 exist, it may enter a decree dissolving the corporation and specifying the effective date of the dissolution, and the clerk of the court shall deliver a certified copy of the decree to the secretary of state, who shall file it.

(b) After entering the decree of dissolution, the court shall direct the winding up and liquidation of the corporation's business and affairs in accordance with section 14.05 and the notification of claimants in accordance with sections 14.06 and 14.07.

SUBCHAPTER D. MISCELLANEOUS

§ 14.40 Deposit With State Treasurer

Assets of a dissolved corporation that should be transferred to a creditor, claimant, or shareholder of the corporation who cannot be found or who is not competent to receive them shall be reduced to cash and deposited with the state treasurer or other appropriate state official for safekeeping. When the creditor, claimant, or shareholder furnishes satisfactory proof of entitlement to the amount deposited, the state treasurer or other appropriate state official shall pay him or his representative that amount.

[CHAPTER 15. FOREIGN CORPORATIONS. OMITTED.]

CHAPTER 16. RECORDS AND REPORTS

SUBCHAPTER A. RECORDS

§ 16.01 Corporate Records

(a) A corporation shall keep as permanent records minutes of all meetings of its shareholders and board of directors, a record of all actions taken by the shareholders or board of directors without a meeting, and a record of all actions taken by a committee of the board of directors in place of the board of directors on behalf of the corporation.

(b) A corporation shall maintain appropriate accounting records.

(c) A corporation or its agent shall maintain a record of its shareholders, in a form that permits preparation of a list of the names and addresses of all shareholders, in alphabetical order by class of shares showing the number and class of shares held by each.

(d) A corporation shall maintain its records in written form or in another form capable of conversion into written form within a reasonable time.

(e) A corporation shall keep a copy of the following records at its principal office:

(1) its articles or restated articles of incorporation and all amendments to them currently in effect;

(2) its bylaws or restated bylaws and all amendments to them currently in effect;

(3) resolutions adopted by its board of directors creating one or more classes or series of shares, and fixing their relative rights, preferences, and limitations, if shares issued pursuant to those resolutions are outstanding;

(4) the minutes of all shareholders' meetings, and records of all action taken by shareholders without a meeting, for the past three years;

(5) all written communications to shareholders generally within the past three years, including the financial statements furnished for the past three years under section 16.20;

(6) a list of the names and business addresses of its current directors and officers; and

(7) its most recent annual report delivered to the secretary of state under section 16.22.

§ 16.02 Inspection of Records by Shareholders

(a) Subject to section 16.03(c), a shareholder of a corporation is entitled to inspect and copy, during regular business hours at the corporation's principal office, any of the records of the corporation described in section 16.01(e) if he gives the corporation written notice of his demand at least five business days before the date on which he wishes to inspect and copy.

(b) A shareholder of a corporation is entitled to inspect and copy, during regular business hours at a reasonable location specified by the corporation, any of the following records of the corporation if the shareholder meets the requirements of subsection (c) and gives the corporation written notice of his demand at least five business days before the date on which he wishes to inspect and copy:

(1) excerpts from minutes of any meeting of the board of directors, records of any action of a committee of the board of directors while acting in place of the board of directors on behalf of the corporation, minutes of any meeting of the shareholders, and records of action taken by the shareholders or board of directors without a meeting, to the extent not subject to inspection under section 16.02(a);

(2) accounting records of the corporation; and

(3) the record of shareholders.

(c) A shareholder may inspect and copy the records identified in subsection (b) only if:

(1) his demand is made in good faith and for a proper purpose;

(2) he describes with reasonable particularity his purpose and the records he desires to inspect; and

(3) the records are directly connected with his purpose.

(d) The right of inspection granted by this section may not be abolished or limited by a corporation's articles of incorporation or bylaws.

(e) This section does not affect:

(1) the right of a shareholder to inspect records under section 7.20 or, if the shareholder is in litigation with the corporation, to the same extent as any other litigant;

(2) the power of a court, independently of this Act, to compel the production of corporate records for examination.

(f) For purposes of this section, "shareholder" includes a beneficial owner whose shares are held in a voting trust or by a nominee on his behalf.

§ 16.03 Scope of Inspection Right

(a) A shareholder's agent or attorney has the same inspection and copying rights as the shareholder he represents.

(b) The right to copy records under section 16.02 includes, if reasonable, the right to receive copies made by photographic, xerographic, or other means.

(c) The corporation may impose a reasonable charge, covering the costs of labor and material, for copies of any documents provided to the shareholder. The charge may not exceed the estimated cost of production or reproduction of the records.

(d) The corporation may comply with a shareholder's demand to inspect the record of shareholders under section 16.02(b)(3) by providing him with a list of its shareholders that was compiled no earlier than the date of the shareholder's demand.

§ 16.04 Court-Ordered Inspection

(a) If a corporation does not allow a shareholder who complies with section 16.02(a) to inspect and copy any records required by that subsection to be available for inspection, the [name or describe court] of the county where the corporation's principal office (or, if none in this state, its registered office) is located may summarily order inspection and copying of the records demanded at the corporation's expense upon application of the shareholder.

(b) If a corporation does not within a reasonable time allow a shareholder to inspect and copy any other record, the shareholder who complies with section 16.02(b) and (c) may apply to the [name or describe court] in the county where the corporation's principal office (or, if none in this state, its registered office) is located for an order to permit inspection and copying of the records demanded. The court shall dispose of an application under this subsection on an expedited basis.

(c) If the court orders inspection and copying of the records demanded, it shall also order the corporation to pay the shareholder's costs (including reasonable counsel fees) incurred to obtain the order unless the corporation proves that it refused inspection in good faith because it had a reasonable basis for doubt about the right of the shareholder to inspect the records demanded.

(d) If the court orders inspection and copying of the records demanded, it may impose reasonable restrictions on the use or distribution of the records by the demanding shareholder.

SUBCHAPTER B. REPORTS

§ 16.20 Financial Statements for Shareholders

(a) A corporation shall furnish its shareholders annual financial statements, which may be consolidated or combined statements of the corporation and one or more of its subsidiaries, as appropriate, that include a balance sheet as of the end of the fiscal year, an income statement for that year, and a statement of changes in shareholders' equity for the year unless that information appears elsewhere in the financial statements. If financial statements are prepared for the corporation on the basis of generally accepted accounting principles, the annual financial statements must also be prepared on that basis.

(b) If the annual financial statements are reported upon by a public accountant, his report must accompany them. If not, the statements must be accompanied by a statement of the president or the person responsible for the corporation's accounting records:

(1) stating his reasonable belief whether the statements were prepared on the basis of generally accepted accounting principles and, if not, describing the basis of preparation; and

(2) describing any respects in which the statements were not prepared on a basis of accounting consistent with the statements prepared for the preceding year.

(c) A corporation shall mail the annual financial statements to each shareholder within 120 days after the close of each fiscal year. Thereafter, on written request from a shareholder who was not mailed the statements, the corporation shall mail him the latest financial statements.

§ 16.21 Other Reports to Shareholders

(a) If a corporation indemnifies or advances expenses to a director under section 8.51, 8.52, 8.53, or 8.54 in connection with a proceeding by or in the right of the corporation, the corporation shall report the indemnification or advance in writing to the shareholders with or before the notice of the next shareholders' meeting.

(b) If a corporation issues or authorizes the issuance of shares for promissory notes or for promises to render services in the future, the corporation shall report in writing to the shareholders the number of shares authorized or issued, and the consideration received by the corporation, with or before the notice of the next shareholders' meeting.

§ 16.22 Annual Report for Secretary of State

(a) Each domestic corporation, and each foreign corporation authorized to transact business in this state, shall deliver to the secretary of state for filing an annual report that sets forth:

(1) the name of the corporation and the state or country under whose law it is incorporated;

(2) the address of its registered office and the name of its registered agent at that office in this state;

(3) the address of its principal office;

(4) the names and business addresses of its directors and principal officers;

(5) a brief description of the nature of its business;

(6) the total number of authorized shares, itemized by class and series, if any, within each class; and

(7) the total number of issued and outstanding shares, itemized by class and series, if any, within each class.

(b) Information in the annual report must be current as of the date the annual report is executed on behalf of the corporation.

(c) The first annual report must be delivered to the secretary of state between January 1 and April 1 of the year following the calendar year in which a domestic corporation was incorporated or a foreign corporation was authorized to transact business. Subsequent annual reports must be delivered to the secretary of state between January 1 and April 1 of the following calendar years.

(d) If an annual report does not contain the information required by this section, the secretary of state shall promptly notify the reporting domestic or foreign corporation in writing and return the report to it for correction. If the report is corrected to contain the information required by this section and delivered to the secretary of state within 30 days after the effective date of notice, it is deemed to be timely filed.

CHAPTER 17. TRANSITION PROVISIONS

§ 17.01 Application to Existing Domestic Corporations

This Act applies to all domestic corporations in existence on its effective date that were incorporated under any general statute of this state providing for incorporation of corporations for profit if power to amend or repeal the statute under which the corporation was incorporated was reserved.

§ 17.02 Application to Qualified Foreign Corporations

A foreign corporation authorized to transact business in this state on the effective date of this Act is subject to this Act but is not required to obtain a new certificate of authority to transact business under this Act.

§ 17.03 Saving Provisions

(a) Except as provided in subsection (b), the repeal of a statute by this Act does not affect:

(1) the operation of the statute or any action taken under it before its repeal;

(2) any ratification, right, remedy, privilege, obligation, or liability acquired, accrued, or incurred under the statute before its repeal;

(3) any violation of the statute, or any penalty, forfeiture, or punishment incurred because of the violation, before its repeal;

(4) any proceeding, reorganization, or dissolution commenced under the statute before its repeal, and the proceeding, reorganization, or dissolution may be completed in accordance with the statute as if it had not been repealed.

(b) If a penalty or punishment imposed for violation of a statute repealed by this Act is reduced by this Act, the penalty or punishment if not already imposed shall be imposed in accordance with this Act.

§ 17.04 Severability

If any provision of this Act or its application to any person or circumstance is held invalid by a court of competent jurisdiction, the invalidity does not affect other provisions or applications of the Act that can be given effect without the invalid provision or application, and to this end the provisions of the Act are severable.

§ 17.05 Repeal

The following laws and parts of laws are repealed: [to be inserted].

§ 17.06 Effective Date

This Act takes effect ______________________________.

CROSS–REFERENCE TABLE

1969 Model Act to 1984 Revised Model Act *

1969 Model Act, as amended	1984 Revised Model Act
Sec. 1	§ 1.01
2	1.40
3	3.01
4	3.02
5	8.50–8.58
6	6.31
7	3.04
8	4.01
9	4.02
10	4.03
11	4.03
12	5.01
13	5.02, 5.03
14	5.04
15	6.01, 6.02
16	6.02
17	6.20
18	6.21
19	6.21
20	6.24
21	Repealed
22	6.28
23	6.25, 6.26
24	6.04
25	6.22
26	6.30
26A	6.30
27	2.06, 10.20–10.22
27A	2.07, 3.03
28	7.01, 7.02
29	7.05
30	7.07
31	7.20
32	7.25
33	7.21, 7.24

* As adapted from 1983 Revised Model Business Corporation Act (Exposure Draft, March 1983) with permission of The American Bar Foundation and of the Reporter for the Model Business Corporation Act Revision Project.

1969 Model Act, as amended		1984 Revised Model Act
Sec.	34	§ 7.30, 7.31
	35	8.01, 8.11, 8.30
	36	8.03, 8.05
	37	8.06
	38	8.05, 8.10
	39	8.08
	40	8.24
	41	8.31
	42	8.25
	43	8.20, 8.22, 8.23
	44	8.21
	45	6.40
	46	Deleted
	47	8.32
	48	8.33
	49	7.40
	50	8.40, 8.41
	51	8.43, 8.44
	52	16.01–16.04
	53	2.01
	54	2.02
	55	2.03
	56	2.03
	57	2.05
	58	10.01
	59	10.02, 10.03, 10.05
	60	10.04
	61	10.06
	62	10.06
	63	10.09
	64	10.07
	65	10.08
	66	Deleted
	67	Repealed
	68	Repealed
	69	Repealed
	70	Repealed
	71	11.01
	72	Deleted
	72–A	11.02
	73	11.03
	74	11.05
	75	11.04
	76	11.06
	77	11.07
	78	12.01
	79	12.02

1969 Model Act, as amended	1984 Revised Model Act
Sec. 80	§ 13.02, 13.03
81	13.02, 13.20–13.28
82	14.01
83	14.03
84	14.02, 14.03
85	Deleted
86	Deleted
87	14.05, 14.06
88	14.04
89	14.04
90	14.04
91	14.04
92	14.03
93	14.03
94	14.30, 14.31
95	14.20
96	14.31
97	14.30, 14.31
98	14.30, 14.31
99	14.31, 14.32
100	14.33
101	14.32
102	14.33
103	14.33
104	14.40
105	14.07

* * *

125	16.22
126	16.22
127	Deleted
128	1.22
129	1.22
130	Deleted
131	Deleted
132	Deleted
133	Deleted
134	Deleted
135	Deleted
136	1.29
137	Deleted
138	Deleted
139	1.30
140	1.26
141	1.27

1969 Model Act, as amended	1984 Revised Model Act
Sec. 142	§ 1.21
143	7.27
144	7.06, 8.23
145	7.04
146	2.04
147	17.01
148	Deleted
149	1.02
150	17.03
151	17.04
152	17.05

†